FROMMER'S

BUDGET TRAVEL GUIDE

NEW ZEALAND '93-'94 ON $45 A DAY

by Susan Poole

PRENTICE HALL TRAVEL

NEW YORK • LONDON • TORONTO • SYDNEY • TOKYO • SINGAPORE

FROMMER BOOKS

Published by Prentice Hall General Reference
A division of Simon & Schuster Inc.
15 Columbus Circle
New York, NY 10023

ISBN 0-13-333618-2
ISSN 1045-9111

Design by Robert Bull Design
Maps by Geografix Inc.

FROMMER'S NEW ZEALAND ON $45 A DAY '93-'94

Editor-in-Chief: Marilyn Wood
Senior Editors: Alice Fellows, Lisa Renaud, Judith de Rubini
Editors: Thomas F. Hirsch, Paige Hughes, Peter Katucki, Sara Hinsey Raveret, Theodore
    Stavrou
Assistant Editors: Margaret Bowen, Ian Wilker
Managing Editor: Leanne Coupe

SPECIAL SALES

Bulk purchases of Frommer's Travel Guides are available at special discounts. The publishers are
happy to custom-make publications for corporate clients who wish to use them as premiums or
sales promotions. We can excerpt the contents, provide covers with corporate imprints, or create
books to meet specific needs. For more information write to Special Sales, Prentice Hall Travel,
Paramount Communications Building, 15th floor, 15 Columbus Circle, New York, NY 10023.

CONTENTS

LIST OF MAPS

INVITATION TO THE READERS

In researching this book, I have come across many wonderful establishments, the best of which I have included here. I am sure that many of you will also come across appealing hotels, inns, restaurants, guest houses, shops, and attractions. Please don't keep them to yourself. Share your experiences, especially if you want to comment on places that have been included in this edition that have changed for the worse. You can address your letters to:

Susan Poole
Frommer's New Zealand on $45 a Day '93–'94
c/o Prentice Hall Travel
15 Columbus Circle
New York, NY 10023

A DISCLAIMER

Readers are advised that prices fluctuate in the course of time and travel information changes under the impact of the varied and volatile factors that affect the travel industry. Neither the author nor the publisher can be held responsible for the experiences of readers while traveling. Readers are invited to write to the publisher with ideas, comments, and suggestions for future editions.

SAFETY ADVISORY

Whenever you're traveling in an unfamiliar city or country, stay alert. Be aware of your immediate surroundings. Wear a moneybelt and keep a close eye on your possessions. Be particularly careful with cameras, purses, and wallets, all favorite targets of thieves and pickpockets.

TELEPHONE NUMBERS

As we go to press, the New Zealand Number Update is in the process of changing all telephone numbers to seven digits. Those numbers in this book that have not been changed at press time are marked with an asterisk, and you can call the Helpline (0155) for the new number. For directory assistance throughout New Zealand, when you don't know a telephone number, you can call 018.

CHAPTER 1

GETTING TO KNOW NEW ZEALAND

There are probably as many misconceptions about New Zealand as there are people who have never been there, and one that is particularly popular with Americans is the notion that it is virtually a suburb of Australia. Don't you believe it! True, they are both in the southern hemisphere, and on any map they appear to be close South Pacific neighbors. But that's *1,600 miles* of Tasman Sea separating them, and their separations are by no means limited to those of a watery nature.

One of the most basic differences between the two countries is also one of the most visible—the land itself. While Australia presents a dramatic, hot landscape of brilliant reds and oranges ringed by splendid white beaches shading out to the deep blue of its oceans, New Zealand offers the striking contrast of lush, semitropical rain-forest greenery, cascading waterfalls, playful geysers, wondrous thermal grounds sporting halos of live steam, and more than 5,700 miles of glorious coastline winding in and out of island-studded bays and harbors. In fact, there is such a wealth of nature's blessings that even the most hidebound urbanite cannot escape their inner stirrings—New Zealand is, above all else, the perfect setting for getting back in touch with the harmony that should (and so seldom does) exist between humans and their environment.

1. GEOGRAPHY, HISTORY & POLITICS

GEOGRAPHY

Surely one of the world's most beautiful countries, New Zealand is composed of two major islands plus little Stewart Island pointing off toward Antarctica. It is bounded on the north and east by the South Pacific, on the west by the Tasman Sea, and on the south by the Southern Ocean. And it's a mere speck on the map—a small country,

? DID YOU KNOW . . . ?

- New Zealand's 3,500,000 population takes a numerical back seat to its 72,000,000 sheep and 9,000,000 cattle.
- If you're invited to a North Islander's *bach* (pronounced batch), don't look for a bachelor party—you'll be visiting a weekend or holiday cottage on the shore, a lake, or in the mountains.
- Down on the South Island, a *crib* is the same as a *bach* up north.
- Look carefully when you pull the plug in a washbasin or bathtub—chances are (though not always), the water will drain out in a counterclockwise direction rather than the clockwise drainage we're accustomed to in the northern hemisphere.
- When a Kiwi tells you he's "in the big bickies now," he's letting you know he's moved up into the upper-income bracket.
- Its South Pacific location between latitudes 34° south and 47° south sets New Zealand about 6,800 miles from Los Angeles, 5,600 miles from Japan, 4,600 miles from Honolulu, and 1,600 miles from Australia.
- If you're asked to "call in," don't reach for the telephone—it means you should come in person. To call someone on the phone, you "ring" them.
- In the New Zealand educational system, high schools are called colleges, and component parts of a university are called faculties.
- Public school teachers in New Zealand under the age of 30 must serve 3 years teaching in rural schools before they can be considered for salary raises.
- Small, owner-run neighborhood shops that sell canned (tinned) goods, fresh vegetables, and magazines and newspapers, as well as ice cream and other dairy products are called "dairies."
- A "hooker" in New Zealand has nothing to do with those ladies of the street—it's a front-row rugby player.

right? Well, not all *that* small. From tip to tip, it measures a long 1,000 miles, although at its widest it's no more than 280 miles across.

New Zealand's land area is comparable to that of Colorado, 104,000 square miles. Its population totals 3.5 million, with 818,000 concentrated in Auckland, 342,000 in the capital city of Wellington, and 321,000 in the South Island's largest city, Christchurch. New Zealand lies across the international date line and below the Tropic of Cancer, some 6,800 miles southwest of Los Angeles and 5,600 miles southeast of Tokyo. Its nearest neighbor, Australia, is some 1,600 miles to the west across the Tasman Sea.

Within those perimeters there is such an astounding array of natural beauty, sporting activities, and sightseeing "musts" that you can banish any thought of "doing" it in a few days or just 1 week—you couldn't even scratch the surface in that short a time!

Allow at least 10 days just to sample the highlights—and I should issue the warning that once there, you'll want to spend months to see it all. Since most of us don't really have that kind of time, you'll find some suggested itineraries in Chapter 2 to help you use whatever time you have to get around to the highlights that most interest you. No matter what your itinerary, one promise I can make unconditionally: You're going to fall head-over-heels in love with New Zealand's scenery.

THE REGIONS IN BRIEF

On the North Island, you surely won't want to miss the very special Bay of Islands, rich in history and a rare haven of tranquillity. Or a day or so along the eastern "Sunrise Coast," where New Zealand's first light of day illuminates breathtakingly beautiful headlands. Or Rotorua's steamy thermal hotpot. Or Auckland's surprisingly sophisticated urban scene. Or Waitomo's glowworms. Or Wellington's spectacular harbor and steep hills. All that takes time—and that's just a *taste* of the North Island!

Then there's that marvelous ferry ride across the Cook Strait to the South Island, where golden sunsets and exotic coastal drives lure you the length of the West Coast, where the Southern Alps cover more territory than the entire country of Switzerland, where glaciers beckon you to their mountaintop source,

IMPRESSIONS

Lo! Here where each league hath its fountains
In isles of deep fern and tall pine,
And breezes snow-cooled on the mountains,
Or keen from the limitless brine,
See men to the battlefield pressing
To conquer one foe—the stern soil,
Their kingship in labor expressing
Their lordship in toil.
—WILLIAM PEMBER REEVES, 1893

where Stewart Island dares you to come as close as possible to the South Pole without shipping out for Cape Horn, where every day's drive is an education in the definition of "sheep station," where Dunedin unfolds its Scottish charms, and where Christchurch is waiting to show you its mirror image of England. More time.

HISTORY

MAORI SETTLEMENT

When it comes to New Zealand's first inhabitants, there is more than one theory as to how they settled here. From the mists of prehistory comes the Maori legend of Kupe, who sailed from the traditional homeland of the Polynesians, Hawaiki, around A.D. 950. Even legend doesn't tell us exactly where Hawaiki was located in the vast South Pacific, but present-day authorities believe it was one of the Society Islands group that includes Tahiti. One version of Kupe's adventures has it that he murdered the carver Hoturapa, and with the murdered man's wife and canoe set off on a long, wandering voyage, which eventually brought the pair to the place he named Aotearoa, which means "land of the long white cloud." Another says that he was in pursuit of a mammoth octopus when he happened onto New Zealand. Both versions agree that he returned to Hawaiki, taking with him sailing instructions for reaching the uninhabited "Fish of Maui." From some historians comes another explanation—that the first Maori canoes to reach New Zealand came by accident, after having been blown off course at sea.

In the 12th century, two more Maori canoes are said to have touched the shores of Aotearoa. A young Polynesian, Whatonga, was swept out to sea during canoe races, and his grandfather, Toi, went in search of him. When the two were reunited somewhere in the Whakatane region in the Bay of Plenty, they found people already living there and the newcomers intermarried with those we know simply as moa-hunters because they hunted a meaty, wingless bird by that name, which reached heights of up to 13 feet. Nothing more is known about them, and they are sometimes referred to as the Archaic Maori. Descendants of the two Polynesian canoers and moa-hunters now form the basis of two of today's Maori tribes.

DATELINE

- **950** Estimated date of first New Zealand landfall by Maori.
- **Mid-1300s** First great influx of Maori settlers.
- **1642** Abel Tasman first European to discover South Island.
- **1769** Capt. James Cook begins 6-month mapping of North and South Islands.
- **1773** Cook's second visit to New Zealand.
- **1777** Cook's third and final visit to New Zealand.
- **1792** First sealers and whalers arrive in New Zealand waters.
- **1814** First Christian missionary, Rev. Samuel Marsden, arrives in Bay of Islands.
- **1831** James Busby named as "British Resident"

(continues)

NORTH ISLAND

South Pacific Ocean

Tasman Sea

Spirits Bay
North Cape
Cape Reinga
Awanui
Kaitaia
Mangonui
10
Cape Karikuri
Keri Keri
Waitangi
The Bay of Islands
12 14
Whangarei
Hen & Chicken Islands
Dargaville
Maungaturoto
Coromandel Peninsula
Warkworth
Waiwera 16
Orewa
Kaipara Harbour
Hauraki Gulf
Whitianga
Whangaparaoa
Auckland
Thames
25
Bay of Plenty
Te Aruroa
Te Puia
Gisborne
Whakatane
Kawenau
Opotiki
36
Tauranga
Matamata
Cambridge
Lake Rotorua
Rotorua
38
5
Lake Taupo
Taupo
Huiarau Mts
Hawke's Bay
Napier
Hastings
Ngaruawahia
Hamilton
Huntly
Wairoa
Waitomo
Turangi
Mangakino
Tongariro National Park
Chateau
Tokoroa
Ruahine Mts
Kaimai
50
Taihape
Mangaweka
Cape Turnagain
Tokaanu
Kaitaanu
4
Feilding
Woodville
Palmerston North
Pahiatua
52
Masterton
New Plymouth
43
Hawera
Patea
Wanganui
Foxton
Levin 58
53
Upper Hutt
Tararua Mts
Waikanae
Lower Hutt
Wellington
Cape Egmont
45
30
Tasman Bay
Cook's
Motueka
Tasman
Picton
Karamea

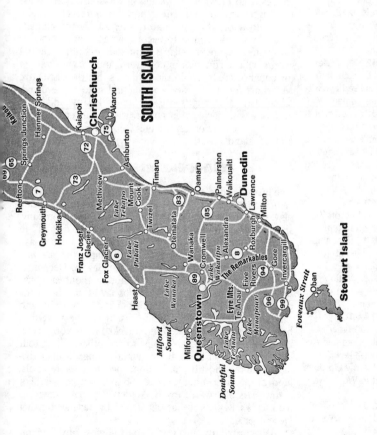

NEW ZEALAND

SOUTH ISLAND

Stewart Island

Christchurch
Kaiapoi
Akarou
Hanmer Springs
Springs Junction
Reefton
Wairou
Ashburton
Timaru
Oamaru
Palmerston
Waikouaiti
Dunedin
Lawrence
Milton
Roxburgh
Alexandra
Gore
Invercargill
Oban
Foveaux Strait
Greymouth
Hokitika
Franz Josef Glacier
Fox Glacier
Methview
Mount Cook
Lake Tekapo
Twizel
Otematata
Lake Pukaki
Wanaka
Cromwell
Lake Wakatipu
The Remarkables
Five Rivers
Eyre Mts.
Te Anau
Lake Te Anau
Lake Manapouri
Haast
Lake Wanaka
Milford Sound
Milford
Queenstown
Doubtful Sound

69
65
7
73
72
75
83
85
6
89
8
94
96
99

DATELINE

under jurisdiction of New South Wales.

- **1839–43** New Zealand Company sends out 57 ships carrying 19,000 settlers.
- **1840** Treaty of Waitangi with Maori chiefs signed in Bay of Islands.
- **1844** Maori Chief Hone Heke chops down British flagpole in Bay of Islands, beginning a 20-year revolt centered around land rights.
- **1852** New Zealand Constitution Act passed by British Parliament.
- **1860s** Discovery of gold on South Island's west coast and North Island's east coast, creating several boomtowns.
- **1860–81** Second Maori War over land rights.
- **1882** First shipment of lamb to England.
- **1893** Voting rights extended to women.
- **1914–18** 100,000 New Zealanders join Australia–New Zealand Army Corps to fight in World War I.
- **1939** New Zealand enters World War II.
- **1947** Statute of Westminster

(continues)

It was not until the mid-14th century that Maori arrived in great numbers. They came from Hawaiki because of devastating tribal wars, which had erupted in the wake of overpopulation and severe food shortages. If we are to believe Maori tradition, seven oceangoing canoes sailed in a group, which has come to be known as "the fleet." Others sailed in groups of one or two; some came singly. On making landfall, canoe groups kept together, settling in various parts of the country, and it is from these first canoes that most modern-day Maori trace their roots.

By the time "the fleet" arrived, the moa had been hunted to extinction, along with other bird species, such as giant rails, swans, and geese. There were, however, bounteous supplies of fish and seafood to be had for the taking, as well as berries and a few other edible plants, which were supplemented by tropical plants such as taro, yams, and kumara (a kind of sweet potato) that had come in the canoes from Hawaiki. Dogs and rats had also been canoe passengers and became an important source of protein. The cultivation of these imported vegetables and animals gradually led the Maori to become an agricultural society living in permanent villages centered around a central *marae* (village common or courtyard) and *whare runanga* (meetinghouse). It was in these villages that the distinctive Maori art forms of wood carving and tattooing evolved, along with a strong sense of family loyalty and total harmony with their environment. It was this culture that thrived at the time of Capt. James Cook's first contact with New Zealand's Maori.

EUROPEAN DISCOVERY

The first recorded sighting of New Zealand by Europeans came on December 13, 1642, when Abel Tasman, scouting new trade territory for the Dutch East India Company, spied what he described as "a great high, bold land" in the Hokitika region of the South Island's west coast. Sailing north in his two tall-masted ships, the *Heemskirk* and *Zeehaen,* he entered Golden Bay on December 18, where he encountered the Maori without ever setting foot on land. As the two ships lay at anchor in the peaceful bay, several war canoes put out from shore and shouted challenges from a safe distance. The next day, however, they were bolder and attacked a cockboat rowing from one of Tasman's ships to the other, killing four sailors in the brief battle before withdrawing. Tasman, dismayed at this hostility and disinclined to seek reprisals, fired at the retreating canoes and put out to sea. For many years afterward, lovely Golden Bay was known as Murderer's Bay, as it was christened by Tasman on that December day.

As it turned out, this was his only glimpse of the Maori since bad weather prevented his entering Cook Strait, so he proceeded up the west coast of the North Island, failed to find a suitable landing spot, and left what he charted as a vast southern continent to sail on to Tonga and Fiji. But for that bad weather and the hostile Maori, the first European exploration of New Zealand would almost certainly have been Dutch. But that distinction was left for an Englishman more than a century later.

THE COMING OF CAPTAIN COOK

When Capt. James Cook left England in 1768 on the 368-ton bark *Endeavour,* he was under orders from King George III to sail to Tahiti to observe the transit of the planet Venus across the sun, a once-a-century happening. But the Yorkshireman carried "secret additional orders," which he opened only when his initial duty was accomplished. King George had directed him to sail southwest in search of the "continent" reported by Tasman. If he found it uninhabited, he was to plant the English flag and claim it for the king; if not, his instructions were to take possession of "convenient situations" but only with the consent of the indigenous people. In addition, he was to study the nature of the soil, its flora and fauna, and to make charts of its coastal waters.

It was on October 7, 1769, that New Zealand was first sighted by the surgeon's boy, Nicholas Young, from his perch in the mast. Naming the headland (in the Gisborne area) Young Nick's Head, Captain Cook sailed into a crescent-shaped bay and put down anchor. A rather kindly man, Captain Cook made every effort to cultivate Maori friendship, communicating by way of a young Tahitian chief named Tupea who had come along as guide and interpreter. The Maori, although they understood and could converse with Tupea, remained hostile even in the face of gifts the captain offered. Nor would they permit him to put aboard the food and water his men so badly needed. Disappointed and bitter, Cook weighed anchor after claiming the country for King George and naming the beautiful bay Poverty Bay because, as he noted in his journal, "it afforded us no one thing we wanted."

Sailing north, Captain Cook rounded the tip of the North Island and went on to circumnavigate both islands during the next 6 months, charting them with amazing accuracy, missing only such details as the entrance to Milford Sound (which is quite invisible from the open sea) and the fact that Stewart Island was not a part of the mainland (he mistakenly believed Foveaux Strait to be a bay). In addition, he recorded the flora and fauna as instructed and brought back sketches of the indigenous people, who grew more friendly as word of the gift-bearing Pakeha (fair-skinned men) spread. He also recorded details of Maori customs and described the "Indians" as "a brave, open, warlike people." Even today, the journal he kept so meticulously makes fascinating reading.

Captain Cook returned to New Zealand for a month in 1773 and again in 1777. Until his death at the hands of indigenous people in Hawaii on February 14, 1779, he ranged the length and breadth of the South Pacific, sailing as far north as the Arctic

DATELINE

adopted by government, achieving full independence from Britain.

- **1951** New Zealand ratifies Australia–New Zealand–United States (Anzus) mutual security pact.

- **1960s** New Zealand begins monitoring radioactivity in region as France accelerates nuclear testing in its Polynesian possessions.

- **1973** Britain joins European Economic Community (Common Market) with subsequent disastrous reduction in imports from New Zealand.

- **1983** As a move against deep economic recession, New Zealand signs Closer Economic Relations (CER) agreement with Australia.

- **1984** All nuclear-armed and nuclear-powered vessels banned from New Zealand ports.

- **1985** Greenpeace *Rainbow Warrior* sunk by French terrorists in Auckland harbor.

Circle and as far south as Antarctica. He and the *Endeavour* have in fact become as much a part of New Zealand legend as those early Maori chiefs and their mighty canoes.

EUROPEAN SETTLEMENT

Organized European settlement in New Zealand did not get underway with any success until 1840, and the unorganized settlement that preceded it was, for the most part, a disaster.

Sealers began arriving in 1792 and virtually denuded South Island waters of what had been flourishing colonies of seals through their policies of killing cows and pups and allowing no closed seasons or limit on skins (some ships carried off as many as 60,000 per year). By 1820 they moved on to more profitable waters.

Whalers, too, discovered rich hunting grounds in New Zealand waters and arrived in droves. Oil vats soon dotted the Bay of Islands, where safe anchorage was an added attraction. Their unscrupulous methods were much like those of the sealers, and New Zealand's coastal waters were no longer a natural haven for the mammoth animals. Unlike the sealers, however, the whalers brought in their wake a multitude of land-based evils in the form of an attendant population, which Charles Darwin described after his 1835 visit as "the very refuse of Society." Consisting of escapees from Australia's penal colonies, ex-convicts, runaway sailors, and a motley collection of "beachcombers," and concentrated in the Kororareka settlement (now known as Russell)—their groceries (drinking spots), brothels, and lawlessness earned it the nickname "hellhole of the Pacific." Ships that would have normally called in at the port stayed away in fear of the widespread practice of shanghaiing sailors for whaling vessels that were shorthanded.

Legitimate traders and merchants, attracted by the wealth of flax and trees such as the kauri—which were ideal for shipbuilding—as well as the lucrative trade in muskets and other European goods with the Maori, while law-abiding (that is, observing such law as there was), were little better than the sealers and whalers in respecting the country's natural resources. Great forests were felled with no eye to replanting; luxuriant bushlands disappeared in flames to clear hills and valleys for man's encroachment; and when a commercial value was placed on the tattooed and preserved heads that were a part of Maori culture, even the native population was threatened for a time as chiefs eager to purchase muskets lopped off more and more heads, both friend and foe. The latter was a short-lived trade, but quite lively while it lasted.

The immigration of Europeans had a devastating impact on Maori culture. Most destructive were the introduction of liquor, muskets, and European diseases against which the Maori had no immunity. Muskets in particular set off decimation of Maori on a grand scale, for they intensified the fierce intertribal warfare, which for centuries had been a part of the Maori lifestyle—tens of thousands were killed off by the fire-spouting sticks until the availability of muskets became so general that no one tribe had superiority in firepower and by about 1830 chiefs began to realize that the weapon was literally destroying all tribes.

Missionaries were the one benign group to arrive during this period, spearheaded by the Rev. Samuel Marsden, who arrived in the Bay of Islands in 1814 and preached

IMPRESSIONS

There is nothing soft about New Zealand, the country. It is very hard and sinewy, and will outlast many of those who try to alter it.
—JOHN MULGAN, 1947

his first sermon to the Maori on Christmas Day with the help of a young chief he had befriended. His was a practical brand of Christianity; and when his duties as chaplain to the convict settlement in Sydney demanded his return, he left behind a carpenter, a shoemaker, and a schoolteacher to instruct the Maori. Most of those men of the cloth who followed were of the same persuasion, and they were responsible for setting down the Maori language in writing (largely for the purpose of translating and printing the Bible), establishing mission schools (by the 1840s large numbers of Maori could both read and write), and upgrading agricultural methods through the use of plows and windmills, for instance.

On the religious front, their progress was slow—to their credit, they were determined not to baptize any Maori until he had a full understanding of the Christian faith—and it was some 11 years before they made the first Maori convert. That the missionaries went about their conversions in much too puritanical a manner is illustrated by the fate of one who admonished a chief for fishing on Sunday: "You are a wicked, bad man . . . You have broken the Sabbath . . . you and your people will all go to hell and be burnt with fire for ever and ever." As the chief's great-grandson reported many years later, "To have put up with insult without avenging it according to its nature would have been fatal to a chief occupying a leading position and injurious to the tribe, as it would render it contemptible to its neighbors." Accordingly, "in less time than it takes to remove the feathers from a fat pigeon, the man of incantation was in an oven and prevented from creating further mischief."

By the late 1830s, however, Maori were ready to accept the concept of a god of peace, undoubtedly influenced greatly by the vastly changed nature of warfare since the coming of the musket. They were also a literal-minded, practical people, much impressed by the missionaries' ability to cure diseases that resisted all efforts by their own healers, as well as the white man's imperviousness to Maori witchcraft. Christianity was in fact the beginning of the end of many aspects of Maori tribal society as it had existed for centuries.

As the number of British in New Zealand grew, so, too, did lawlessness, with many atrocities committed against both Maori and settlers. The missionaries were foremost among those who complained to the British government, which was by no means anxious to recognize the faraway country as a full-fledged colony, having already experienced difficulties with America and Canada, and struggled through the Napoleonic Wars and revolts on various other fronts. As a substitute, in 1831 the Crown placed New Zealand under the jurisdiction of New South Wales and sent James Busby as "British Resident," with full responsibilities for enforcing law and order, but with such laughable means of meeting those responsibilities that he was nicknamed "the man-of-war without guns." Needless to say, he was completely ineffectual.

Back in Britain, the newly formed New Zealand Company began sending out ships to buy land from the Maori and establish permanent settlements. Their methods were questionable to say the least, and caused increasing alarm in London. It must be noted, however, that between 1839 and 1843 the New Zealand Company sent out 57 ships carrying 19,000 settlers, the nucleus of a stable British population. In 1839 Capt. William Hobson was sent out by the government to sort things out, and by catering to the Maori sense of ceremony (and some mild arm-twisting), he arranged an assembly of chiefs at the Busby residence in the Bay of Islands. There, on February 6, 1840, the famous Treaty of Waitangi, after lengthy debate, was signed with much pomp.

The treaty guaranteed the Maori "all the Rights and Privileges of British Subjects" in exchange for their acknowledgment of British sovereignty, while granting the Crown exclusive rights to buy land from the Maori. The fact that many of the chiefs had no idea of the treaty's meaning is clear from one chief's later explanation that he had merely signed a receipt for a blanket sent by the queen as a gift! Nevertheless, 45 of the Maori chiefs at the assembly did sign, and when it was circulated around the country, another 500 also signed. Instead of easing things, however, the Treaty of Waitangi ushered in one of the bloodiest periods in New Zealand's history.

The British were eager to exercise that exclusive right to purchase Maori land, and while some chiefs were just as eager to sell, others wanted only to hold on to their native soil. As pressures were brought to bear to force them to sell, revolt quickly surfaced, and when Chief Hone Heke (ironically, the first to sign the treaty) hacked down the British flagpole at Kororareka (Russell) in 1844, it signaled the beginning of some 20 years of fierce fighting.

The Maori, always outnumbered and outarmed, won the unqualified respect and admiration of the British as brave and masterful warriors. The British, on the other hand, were regarded with the same degree of respect by the chiefs, who had not expected that the Pakeha could put up any sort of real fight. At last the British emerged as victors, but out of the bloody confrontations came the basis of a relationship, which to this day is based on that same mutual respect as well as on many of those same tensions.

Today there is a population base of 3.5 million people (most of similar backgrounds) that today supports 72 million sheep and more than 9 million cattle!

POLITICS

In 1852 the British Parliament passed the New Zealand Constitution Act, and self-government was administered through a governor appointed in London, a Legislative Council appointed by the governor, and an elected House of Representatives. Elected, that is, by Pakeha landowners who argued that the Maori communal land ownership disfranchised them, as the vote was only extended to "individual landowners." That situation was corrected in 1867, and women were granted the vote in 1893, a full quarter of a century before it happened in Britain or America.

The government also pioneered such social reforms as minimum-wage laws, old-age pensions, paid vacations, labor arbitration, and child-welfare programs. Thus New Zealand became in many respects a "welfare state," its economy based on exports of lamb, mutton, butter, and eggs to England. Throughout the ups and downs of economic developments since, it has retained its humanitarian approach to government.

The parliamentary form of government recognizes the queen of England as head of state, and she's represented by a governor-general, with a locally elected prime minister and members of Parliament.

2. FLORA & FAUNA

New Zealand has been, in a sense, one huge botanical garden during its relatively short life. Undisturbed for the most part by the destructive influence of mankind, its forests and plant life flourished, regulated by no forces save those of Mother Nature. Luxuriant ground covering, ferns ranging in size from tiny plants attached to mossy tree trunks all the way to tree-size pongas, more than 100 species of trees, and garlands of starry white clematis and blossoms of other flowering vines created hundreds of miles of cool, dim, tree-vaulted "cathedrals."

The first humans to arrive, themselves closely attuned to nature, accorded the forests due reverence, with just the proper mix of awe and fear. As Peter Hooper, one of New Zealand's best writers and a leading conservationist, says in his excellent book *Our Forests, Ourselves* (published by John McIndoe, Ltd.), "Landscape possesses *mauri*—soul or mind—and it is the outward and visible form of an inward invisible power." And an acute awareness of that quality is inescapable when one walks the present-day forests of New Zealand. Its effect can be profound. As Mr. Hooper goes on to say, "The tonic wildness of natural spaces is essential to the physical/mental/spiritual wholeness of the individual." You have my personal promise of just such a restorative experience upon entering any one of the forests, which will never be too far away throughout your visit.

As if to reinforce the above, the Department of Conservation (DOC), P.O. Box 10-420, Wellington, stressed low-impact tourism and has issued a 10-point *Environmental Car Code* to support environmentally sensitive recreation in the outdoors, as well as information on health and safety for visitors to back country areas.

In the northern quarter of the North Island, you'll find the surviving stands of tall, stately kauri trees, whose hardwood trunks—unblemished by knots or other imperfections—were so prized for shipbuilding by early settlers. Replacement planting is now underway to bring back these magnificent trees for future generations.

During December and January, North Island cliffs and lakeshores are a mass of scarlet when the *pohutukawa* (or Christmas tree) bursts into bloom, while its kinsman, the *rata*, is doing likewise down in the South Island. In early spring, the *kowhai*, which makes no distinction between north and south but grows almost everywhere, is a profusion of large golden blossoms. The *totara* has always been much loved by the Maori, who find its light, durable timber just right for making canoes, as well as for their magnificent carvings. Then there are the pines, including the *rimu* (red), *matai* (black), *kahikatea* (white), and *Dacrydium laxifolium* (pigmy). And the beeches—red, black, and silver. Almost all are evergreen, and seasonal color changes are subtle.

New Zealand also has an astounding array of flowering plants, a full 80% of which are not to be found anywhere else in the world. Undisputed queen of blossoms has to be the world's largest buttercup, the Mount Cook lily. There are almost 60 varieties of mountain daisies, and a curious "vegetable sheep," which grows in mountainous terrain and has large, cushiony blooms that look like sheep even when you take a close-up look. Bright orange-and-yellow "red hot pokers" look like just that. Up to a dozen white, fringed, saucer-shaped blooms adorn a single flower stalk of the *hinau,* and the golden *kumarahou* bloom has been used over the years in medicinal herb mixtures.

An added joy in tramping the forests is the fact that you never have to be afraid to put your foot down—there's not one snake in the entire country! Nor are there any predatory animals. In fact there's only one poisonous spider, and it's rarely found anywhere except on a few scattered sand dunes.

Most of New Zealand's animals did not originate there but were imported by various settler groups. The Maori brought over dogs (and rats, though I can't say if *that* was intentional!). Captain Cook released a pig, whose wild descendants are still about. Other importees include the red deer, opossum, hedgehog, weasel, and rabbit (which were brought over for skins and meat but became so numerous and destructive that another animal, the stoat, had to be brought in to control the rabbit population).

As for birds, the more species you see, the curiouser and curiouser they get. The kiwi, whose name New Zealanders have adopted as their own, is one of the most

IMPRESSIONS

The day was the perfection of New Zealand weather, which is the perfection of all climates—hot, but rarely sultry; bright but not glaring, from the vivid green with which the earth is generally clothed.
—BISHOP GEORGE AUGUSTUS SELWYN, 1843

curious. Wingless and about the size of a chicken, it lives in hollow trunks or holes in the ground; emerges only at night to forage for insects and worms with a long, curved beak, which has nostrils at its tip; and emits a shrill, penetrating whistle. The female lays one gigantic egg and then leaves the hatching to the male! These days it's rare to see the kiwi in the wild, but you'll find them in special kiwi houses around the country, which simulate nocturnal lighting so you and I can see them during "normal" hours.

Down in the mountains of the South Island there's a comical mountain parrot that is as bold as the kiwi is shy. The kea nests among the rocks, but keeps an eye on the main roads and is quick to investigate any newcomers. It's not unusual, for instance, to see as many as three (as I once did) camped alongside the Milford Sound road—and if you stop, their antics will have you grinning in no time. But it's just as well you keep a sharp eye on them, for those cunning cut-ups are quick to steal jewelry or other shiny objects and to attack such formidable targets as automobile parts with their strong, curved beaks. Campers and trampers in the know are careful to keep their gear well beyond the reach of the mischievous little kea.

If you hear a series of pure, bell-like sounds pouring through the forest air, it's likely to be the song of the lovely bellbird. Only slightly different in sound is the handsome tui. Around swampy areas, those ear-piercing screams you hear in the night will be coming from the pukeko. And the forest-dwelling morepork's call (often heard at dusk or after dark) may give you a start—it sounds just like its name. The graceful gannet is found only on offshore islands, with one exception, Cape Kidnappers near Napier; there are white herons at Okarito, a unique albatross colony out from Dunedin, and penguins in many spots around the country.

As curious as are some New Zealand birds, however, none of them holds a candle to the tuatara, a reptilian "living fossil" whose prehistoric ancestors became extinct 100 million years ago. It is completely harmless—that is, if its looks don't scare you to death. Shaped like a miniature dinosaur, complete with a spiny ridge down the back and a thick tail, it's protected by law and confined to offshore islets.

Prominent among marine animals who call New Zealand waters home are whales, dolphins, and seals.

The richness of New Zealand flora and fauna will be within easy reach wherever you find yourself around the country, and if you should miss some particular species, there are excellent zoos as well.

3. NEW ZEALAND'S FAMOUS PEOPLE

Jane [Jean] Gardner Batten (1909–82) Internationally known native of Rotorua, Batten is still honored for her record-setting solo flights. From her early twenties, this intrepid aviatrix conquered the skies in aircraft quite crude by today's standards. In 1933, she flew solo from England to India; in 1934 from England to Australia, returning to England in 1935 to become the first woman to fly both ways; in 1935 from England to Brazil; and in 1936, from England to New Zealand, the first ever solo flight, establishing a new solo record on her return in 1937. In *Alone in the Sky*, she paints a vivid picture of her solo flight around the world. A recluse in later life, she was interred in a pauper's grave.

Peter James Blake (1949–) Well known among international sailors, Blake is one of the few blue-water sailors to have participated in all Whitbread round-the-world races, racking up an impressive quarter-of-a-million ocean miles. In the 1985–86 race, he skippered the New Zealand designed, sponsored, and crewed *Lion New Zealand*.

Walter Godfrey Bowen (1922–) Familiarly known as Godfrey to New Zealanders and sheepshearers around the world, Bowen began his career at the age of 16. His first world record came in 1953 for shearing 456 sheep in 9 hours, bettered in 1960, when he sheared 559 sheep in Wales. In New Zealand, he was one of the driving spirits behind the founding of the Agrodome agricultural exhibition center near Rotorua.

Neil Mullane Finn (1958–) Winner of several impressive awards, Finn embarked on a solo career in 1964 after 7 years with the musical group Split Enz. Since then, he has garnered the International Artist of the Year award in New Zealand; Best Songwriter of the Year (2 years in succession) and Song of the Year in Australia. In 1988, his highly successful album *Tim Finn* was launched.

Janet Paterson Frame (1924–) Born in Dunedin, Frame is one of New Zealand's most brilliant writers. Her first international success was *Owls Do Cry*, in 1957, and she has produced a steady stream of novels since then. Emerging from a youth spent largely in mental hospitals after being wrongly diagnosed as schizophrenic, she has enjoyed literary accolades both at home and around the world. *An Angel at My Table,* part of her three-volume autobiography, has been televised and aired in the U.K. as well as New Zealand, and her awards include two New Zealand Book Awards, the Hubert Church Award, the New Zealand Scholarship in Letters award, and the Robert Burns Fellowship.

Charles Frederick Goldie (1870–1947) An Aucklander, Goldie studied painting in Paris for 6 years, and upon returning to New Zealand embarked on a series of Maori portraits for which he is best known. *The Arrival of the Maori in New Zealand,* painted in collaboration with L. J. Steele, is one of the most widely reproduced paintings in the country. His moving depictions of Maori subjects are the result of much time spent photographing and sketching in Rotorua over a 10-year period.

Sir Edmund Percival Hillary (1919–) Revered in his native country, Sir Edmund Hillary was the first to conquer the heights of Mount Everest, the world's highest mountain. Born in Auckland, he undertook two sessions of climbing in the area before reaching the summit in 1953, on the eve of Queen Elizabeth's coronation. He was promptly knighted for his achievement. Another "first" was his trans-Antarctic dash that made his the first vehicle party to reach the South Pole overland. He has been involved in building hospitals and schools for the Sherpa people of the Himalayan region, and in 1975 wrote the compelling *Nothing Venture, Nothing Win.*

Keri Hulme (1947–) Born in Christchurch of Maori, English, and Orkney ancestry, Hulme is one of her country's finest novelists and poets. Her 1983 novel, *The Bone People,* won the New Zealand Book Award for Fiction and the Pegasus Prize for Maori writing in 1984, as well as Britain's prestigious Booker Prize for Fiction in 1985. Settling into the remote southern West Coast village of Okarito, she continues to produce sensitive novels of the highest literary standards.

Katherine Mansfield (1888–1923) Widely regarded as one of the finest short-story writers in English, Mansfield is probably the best known and most respected internationally of New Zealand writers. Born in Wellington, she began writing for publication at the age of 9. After living a rather bohemian life in London for several years, she returned to New Zealand, drawing on that country and its people for some of her finest and most mature work. Outstanding short stories include "Prelude," "At the Bay," and "The Garden Party," and several collections have been published, as well as omnibus collections of her works and letters. She died at the age of 34 of tuberculosis in France, where she had lived for some years.

Dame Kiri Te Kanawa (1944–) One of the world's leading operatic sopranos, Dame Kiri was born in Gisborne and educated in Auckland. In 1966 she was awarded a bursary for study in London, and in 1971 made her debut at Covent Garden in *The Marriage of Figaro,* the first of many performances that have won her international acclaim. In addition to featuring in many operatic recordings, she sang at the royal wedding of Prince Charles and Lady Diana. She is currently based in London.

4. ART, ARCHITECTURE & LITERATURE

ART

MAORI ART   Much of New Zealand's most distinctive art originates with Maori traditions, dating back to the Archaic Maori (or moa-hunters), whose bone carvings and stone work are essentially superb sculpture. The Classic Maori who came later glorified the valor of their warriors in the ornamentation of bone, wood, and stone weapons, as well as war canoes and artistic tattoos and garments.

Dating from the Historic Maori period, communal meetinghouses (*whare runanga*) hold some of the finest Maori art, with *tikis* (human forms of wood, bone, or greenstone representing ancestors or gods); *manaia* (beaked-headed "birdman" figures with human forms, whose meaning and origins remain a mystery); *pakake* (stylized whales and other creatures of the deep); and symbols of religious or powerful supernatural beings (often represented by trees and other natural objects they were believed to inhabit).

The Modern Maori period actually dates from the mid-19th century, and during the 20th century has featured more abstract and stylized applications of traditional Maori art from all periods, thanks in large part to Sir Apirana Ngata and Sir Peter Buck (Te Rangi Hiroa), who spearheaded the revival and modernization of ancient art forms.

Many outstanding examples of Maori art are found in the Auckland War Memorial Museum's Maori Court and in the Bay of Plenty and Rotorua areas of the North Island.

PAKEHA ART   Since the earliest arrival of Europeans, painters have worked to capture New Zealand's magnificent light and landscape on canvas. One of the most popular of today's traditional landscape painters is Peter McIntyre, while Gordon Walters concentrates on abstractions of ancient symbols such as the *koru* (whose stylized interpretation has been adopted by Air New Zealand) in a style reminiscent of Mondrian or Klee.

Works of these leading New Zealand painters command substantial prices, but there are many fine—unknown—painters working away in virtually every region of the country, and some of my most prized New Zealand souvenirs are paintings picked up around the country for very low prices. I also make it a practice to keep an eye out for pottery and ceramics—many such items are works of art as well as functional.

ARCHITECTURE

Although Auckland, Wellington, Christchurch, and Dunedin are dotted with more giant cranes and building sites for ultramodern, glass-and-steel skyscrapers on every visit, for the most part Americans are likely to experience a rush of recognition—even in the cities—at the sight of colonial-style homes, shop fronts, and roofed sidewalks that could have been imported intact from our Wild West movies. And, indeed, the style (still adhered to in many contemporary residences) arrived here in the 1800s, at the same time settlers were building similar structures as the western United States opened up. However, along with those modern high-rise office buildings, you will find a smattering of Mediterranean and ultramodern residences, most located along waterfront drives or in resort areas. Dunedin, on the other hand, is a treasure trove of Victorian, Edwardian, and Flemish Renaissance architecture, with public buildings awash in towers and turrets, spires and gables.

LITERATURE

Katherine Mansfield and Janet Frame lead New Zealand's literary giants. Both have written from the perspective of a love-hate relationship with their native country, as did poet A. R. D. Fairburn, while the poetry of James K. Baxter (whose work was cut short by early death) concerns itself with religion and social injustices. On the contemporary poetry scene is the prolific Sam Hunt, self-styled Bard of Bottle Creek, who is a familiar figure around the country giving his poetic recitations in bars, restaurants, and other public forums.

Novelist and naturalist Peter Hooper celebrates the South Island's West Coast, where he lives and teaches, interweaving legend and myth with historical fact. He has also produced quite brilliant booklets on New Zealand's trees and forests.

In recent years, more and more writing of high literary quality has emerged from the Maori community. Writing in English, writers such as Keri Hulme, Rowley Habib, Witi Thumaera, and Patricia Grace have brought to vivid life Maori life in New Zealand.

5. RELIGION, MYTH & FOLKLORE

RELIGION

Missionary efforts in New Zealand were spearheaded by the Rev. Samuel Marsden, who arrived in 1814. It took the missionaries years to make their first Maori convert. Nor is it surprising that it took so long, for deeply imbedded in the indigenous culture were such practices as cannibalism, infanticide, and the worship of gods of war. In embracing the doctrines of Christianity they relinquished much of the sensual beauty embodied in their own complex, age-old religious traditions. Naked bodies must now be covered; symbolic carvings of the gods of fertility must be destroyed; the reverence and fear once accorded a tribe's chief must now be transferred to this new god.

These days, only artistic vestiges of the ancient pagan gods remain. Most New Zealanders—Maori and Pakeha—practice the Protestant religions, with most denominations represented and the Church of England first numerically. Catholic congregations may also be found around the country.

MYTH & FOLKLORE

You have your choice of two theories on just how New Zealand came about. Geologists will tell you that its islands are the relatively young remnants of a continental mass separated by violent shifts in the earth's crust. Its location on a major

IMPRESSIONS

The longer I live the more I turn to New Zealand, I thank God I was born in New Zealand. A young country is a real heritage, though it takes time to recognize it. But New Zealand is in my very bones.
—KATHERINE MANSFIELD, 1922

fault line accounts for frequent earthquake activity, volcanic mountains, the drowned glacial valleys of Fiordland, and the string of mountain ranges that stretches, with a few interruptions, from the alpine peaks of the South Island up to the blunted headland at Cape Reinga.

But ask any Maori and you'll get a far different story. Now, maybe this theory won't be as authentic, but it's a lot more fun.

According to Maori legend, in the days of the gods and demigods, the frail fifth son of a woman named Taranga was thrown into the sea by his mother, who felt the infant was too weak to survive. He was rescued, however, by Rangi, the Sky Father, who raised him through childhood, then returned him to his amazed mother, complete with a full set of magical abilities and the enchanted jawbone of his grandmother. The overjoyed mother doted on Maui, her restored offspring, to such an extent that his brothers quickly developed an oversize case of sibling jealousy, which really wasn't eased much when Maui pulled off such astonishing feats as snaring the sun in the pit from which it rose each morning, then smashing its face with that all-powerful jawbone until it was too weak to do anything but creep across the sky, thus giving all the people longer days in which to fish and eliciting buckets of gratitude and respect for Maui.

Needless to say, when Maui set out to fish, his was always the record catch, while his nonmagical brothers barely brought home enough to feed their families—much to the consternation of their wives, who duly complained to Maui. With a condescending (and irritating) wave of his hand, Maui promptly promised his sisters-in-law one load of fish so large it would go bad before they could eat it all. They were delighted; but their husbands were frustrated, angry, and determined to beat Maui to the punch with one last fishing expedition, which they launched at dawn.

The clever (and probably obnoxious) Maui, however, had hidden under the flooring mats of his brothers' canoe, armed with a special fishhook whose point was fashioned from a chip of the precious jawbone. It wasn't until they were well out to sea that he made his appearance, which sent the brothers into a rage. But their luck was running true to form, and when Maui assured them that it would turn in their favor if they'd only sail out of sight of any land, they grumpily agreed, and sure enough, they soon filled the canoe with fish. It was so full, in fact, that they began to take on water, and the brothers were all for turning back for home. To their consternation, the arrogant Maui insisted they sail still farther into the unknown waters and calmly produced his magic hook. Their protests fell on deaf ears, so—bailing and complaining—they sailed on until at last Maui struck his nose until it bled, smeared his blood on the hook as bait, and threw his line overboard while chanting an incantation for "the drawing up of the world."

Well, what he hooked turned out to be a gigantic fish, as large as the gable of a whare runanga (meetinghouse), whose very size rendered it tapu (sacred). With it came a large wedge of land, which we know today as New Zealand's North Island. Maui, respectful of the tapu, quickly departed for home for a priest, leaving his brothers behind with strict orders not to cut up the fish until his return. He was no sooner out of sight than the brothers disobeyed that order, scaling and cutting the huge fish. Now, the gods were much angered at such flagrant disregard for tapu, and they set that great fish to lashing about, throwing cut-up chunks in every direction—which is a perfect explanation for the North Island's mountains and offshore islands! And while we may call it the North Island, any Maori knows it is really Te Ika a Maui, "the Fish of Maui."

The South Island is actually Maui's canoe, with Stewart Island as its anchor stone. And up in Hawke's Bay, that famous fishhook has been transformed into Cape Kidnappers.

So take your pick—geological fault line or magical Maori. And, as you travel around the country, inquire about local natural attractions (mountains, lakes, etc.) as

IMPRESSIONS

One superstition seems general with all the tribes respecting the formation of the world; or, rather, of their own island. . . . They say a man, or a god, or some great spirit was fishing in his war-canoe, and pulled up a large fish, which instantly turned into an island; and a lizard came upon that, and brought up a man out of the water by his long hair; and he was the father of all the New Zealanders.
—AUGUSTUS EARLE, 1832

---

you go—chances are there's a Maori explanation for their existence that beats scientific theory six ways to Sunday!

6. CULTURAL & SOCIAL LIFE

New Zealanders are so . . . well, civilized. They have good manners (they don't push or utter rude remarks on the street, or mark public buildings with graffiti). They have an innate sense of decency that sends them rushing to the aid of strangers and keeps them on cordial terms with the original New Zealanders. Above all, a strong respect for order pervades their daily lives. Things work as they're supposed to work—and if they don't, somebody fixes them. In short, all the human virtues we remember (or remember hearing about) are in abundant supply in New Zealand. Now I'll wager you'll hear at least once the remark from another traveler that the country is so charming because "it's 20 years behind the times." Well, for my money, all the "progress" in all the rest of the world is miles behind the sort of human progress New Zealand has managed to achieve!

You're going to bring back many things from your New Zealand visit—memories, souvenirs, friendships—and unless I miss my guess, among them will be some irresistible expressions, which will have beguiled their way into your vocabulary. Just try not to adopt the lovable "Spot on!" Or the complimentary "Good as gold." And when tempers flare back home, what better way to cool them than with a smiling "Just don't get your knickers in a knot, mate"?

MAORI & PAKEHA

In modern New Zealand, it is to the credit of both Maori and Pakeha that their widely differing cultures and a history encompassing long years of cruel warfare have been overcome to generate an environment that is peaceful even though not entirely trouble-free. The difficult journey has required a great deal of restraint on both sides and a willingness to put aside the past. Yet today their goodwill is being tested as Maori and Pakeha debate the provisions of the 150-year-old Treaty of Waitangi, which functions as a Bill of Rights for Maori New Zealanders. In asserting those rights, Maori are regaining confiscated land and fishing rights, as well as making significant gains in placing more emphasis on their culture and language in the country's educational system.

Maori have seen their numbers increase from a low of 42,000 at the turn of the century to more than 400,000 today, about 13% of the population. From a people suffering from the imported alcoholism and diseases that produced a depression afflicting the race as a whole with a debilitating lethargy, they have become a largely urban people, participating in the middle-class benefits of their Pakeha brethren while holding fast to as much of their traditional culture as survived those early years of European settlement.

They have demonstrated a surprising adaptability to the ways of democracy, and the skills acquired through mission schools have been improved and honed to expertise, with more and more additions as industrial development moved across the country.

The political arena has afforded them access to power acquired through the oratorical prowess and widespread popularity of such leaders as Apirana Ngata, Te Rangi Hiroa, and Maui Pomare—all of whom were knighted and served as cabinet members—and their Young Maori Party. Because of their political, educational, and professional achievements, Maori candidates often are elected by substantially Pakeha constituencies. They have been quick to take advantage of educational opportunities, with a high percentage of college graduates among the current Maori population. And they have managed to imbue the Pakeha population with a marvelous appreciation for their ancient culture.

To experience that culture in its purest form, the visitor these days must travel to Rotorua (a Maori center) or stumble upon a communal village. It is here that you'll find wood-carvers and mat weavers demonstrating the arts that adorn their great meetinghouses with such stylized masterpieces and their bodies with such colorful garb.

Yet even deep in the heart of New Zealand's largest cities (which are home for some 76% of the Maori population), it's easy to observe the traditional lifestyle rhythm that supersedes the white man's alarm clock. When a Maori loved one dies, respect must be shown with attendance at the *tangi*, or funeral, no matter how far away it is. Ancient tribal celebrations also demand time off work, and one's family always comes first. And while the old war *hakas* (complete with foot stomping and protruding tongues) and graceful *poi* dance are mainly performed in shows staged for visitors, most Maori city dwellers have a large repertoire of such melodies as the world-famous "Now Is the Hour" (or, Maori Farewell), which was actually written by an Englishman before World War I. And in national elections, they are free to vote in the Pakeha district in which they reside or in one of the four official Maori electorates.

One sad by-product of the Maoris' move from rural to urban areas, however, has been a gradual weakening of those tribal and family ties that have always been at the very heart of their culture. When there is no *marae* in which to gather at the end of the day, youngsters tend to lose contact with their elders, and even the elders are less closely bound together. In some of the North Island cities (where the Maori concentration is heaviest), social problems are beginning to crop up that can be traced directly to the feeling of isolation that has developed among a younger generation adrift without strong identity support systems. To counteract that trend, the Maori people are establishing urban *marae,* which are used daily by numerous groups. The ancient ties are gaining strength, as are the ancient teachings, which are passed down to the young from their elders.

You'll also find most of New Zealand's whites living in the cities. Or at least working in cities. More and more, as centers such as Auckland grow larger and larger, the people who work there go home at night to the same sort of small suburban satellite communities popular in the United States. Those miles of dual-lane express motorways leading into Auckland, and the sprawling shopping malls in the dozen or so communities that surround it, will have a surprising familiarity!

For most of us, though, there will be a fascinating unfamiliarity about the lifestyle of other Pakeha who live and work on New Zealand's farmlands (which bring in a whopping 60% of the country's export income from meat, dairy products, and wool). From high-country "stations," which concentrate on wool production, to lower pastures, which fatten up lamb and mutton on the hoof, most certainly we'll click our cameras at lovable sheep that seem to have been born with a one-track mind—a fun game when you're traveling is to try to find the sheep that's not eating!

For the farmer, it's a hardworking life of comparative isolation, with socializing more or less relegated to the occasional drop-in at the local tavern. Some of your own best socializing may very well come from just such a drop-in if your timing is good enough to coincide with one or two of the farmers. Or better yet, if you're in the tavern when a gaggle of shearers come in at the end of a busy day.

In the North Island, the cattle that supply all that rich, yummy cream and butter and milk—as well as the 10 extra pounds you'll probably carry home—spend winters and summers in the pastures, for grass grows year round in this perfect growing climate. The New Zealand dairyman is more likely to be found in city or small-town watering holes, since his grazing lands are not so spread out and towns are more plentiful up north.

Actually, about three-quarters of all those people in the cities depend on the output of these country folk for prosperity, involved as they are in the processing and marketing of farm products.

City dweller or farmer, the average Pakeha is more likely to be found messing around in boats or out tramping in the bush than in dancing and singing in the manner of the Maori neighbor.

And how do they get on with those neighbors? Very well, most of the time, thank you. Pakeha don't really participate in Maori cultural activities very much, but you can be sure they're proud of that culture. You can virtually count on being dragged off to a Maori concert, *hangi* (feast), or some other event by every other Pakeha with whom you spend any time. And you'll be very welcome—as I said before, New Zealanders live together with only an occasional flareup of racial tensions.

THE MAORI LANGUAGE

As for their language, with its colorful and vivid imagery, well, the Maori came very close to losing it. Living in a predominantly European culture, they were forced by circumstance and education to use the English language. However, the growth of *kohanga heo,* or language nests, has resulted in thousands of Maori preschoolers and their parents learning the beautiful Maori language from tribal elders, and it's being heard increasingly in homes, schools, and universities. It also is often heard on the radio and is sometimes used to begin the evening's TV newscast with the traditional Maori greeting, *Haere Mai.*

You will be surrounded by words and phrases, both in place-names and names of objects always identified by their Maori names. It's a lot more fun to travel around New Zealand if you know, for example, that *roto* is the Maori word for "lake" and *rua* for "two"; hence, Rotorua.

Bear in mind, also, that in the Maori language some words may be both singular and plural, thus words such as Maori, Pakeha, and Kea never have an "s" even to denote plural (like the English deer and fish).

The following are a few of the most commonly used prefixes and suffixes for place names:

Ao Cloud
Ika Fish
Nui Big, or plenty of
Roto Lake
Rua Cave, or hollow, or two
  (Rotorua's two lakes)

Tahi One, single
Te The
Wai Water
Whanga Bay, inlet, or stretch of water

Other frequently used words:

Ariki Chief or priest
Atua Supernatural being, such as a
  god or demon

Haka Dance (war, funeral, etc.)

Hangi An oven made by filling a hole with heated stones; and the feast roasted in it

Karakia Prayer or spell

Kereru Wood pigeon

Kumara Sweet potato

Mana Authority, prestige, psychic force

Marae Courtyard, village common

Mere War club made of greenstone (jade)

Pa Stockade or fortified place

Pakeha White-skinned person; primarily used to refer to Europeans

Poi Bulrush ball with string attached twirled in action song

Tangi Funeral mourning or lamentation

Tapu Under religious or superstitious restriction ("taboo")

Tiki Grotesque human image, sometimes carved of greenstone

Whare House

7. PERFORMING ARTS & EVENING ENTERTAINMENT

Except in larger cities, nightlife is quiet, quiet, quiet. Quiet, that is, when it isn't totally nonexistent. New Zealand will have little appeal for travelers who require a swinging nightlife that goes on into the wee hours. In Auckland and Wellington, supper clubs and a few nightspots offer revues or other entertainment. And of course there are the Maori concerts in Rotorua and nighttime visits to Waitomo's glowworm grotto.

In a more cultural vein, there is quite good theater around the country, often featuring plays with local playwrights. Check out the Mercury Theatre in Auckland, Downstage and Circa in Wellington, and the Court in Christchurch. Musically, The new Aotea Centre in Auckland is a major venue for concerts, opera, and ballet. Also, look for performances in large cities of the New Zealand Symphony, Auckland's Philharmonia, and the New Zealand String Quartet. Similarly, the Royal New Zealand Ballet performs in large cities.

Lucky you if you're in Wellington in early spring in a year of that city's biennial International Festival of the Arts, featuring internationally known overseas and local artists. Usually held in March, it is next scheduled for 1994.

My very best advice, however, is to do as the Kiwis do—enjoy full, bracing days of outdoor activity followed by a satisfying evening meal followed by quiet visits with friends or a little time in front of the telly followed by an early bedtime. It makes a refreshing change from our frenetic pace at home, and you may be surprised to find how ready you are for those early evenings after a day or so of heavy sightseeing.

8. SPORTS & RECREATION

SPECTATOR SPORTS

RUGBY On the sports scene rugby dominates from Easter through September, with Saturday matches featuring Kiwi males from schoolboys to businessmen to members of the national team (the All Blacks, who are elevated to a status in national esteem approaching reverence), to senior citizens. International matches are held in Auckland's Eden Park, Wellington's Athletic Park, Dunedin's Carisbrook Park, and Lancaster Park in Christchurch. If you're a football nut at home and think our players are pretty tough hombres, be sure to take in at least one match and watch the lads rough-and-tumble around the pitch in knee pants—with nary a padded shoulder to be seen!

HORSE RACING After rugby, it's horse racing that claims national affection in New Zealand. There are 271 days of licensed racing (133 of trotting) during the year, and race meets take place in informal beach settings or open fields with the same degree of enthusiasm as those at the larger tracks around the country. In January there's the New Zealand Cup, a highlight of the racing year—if you're there and are overcome by gambling fever, go ahead and indulge: Betting is perfectly legal, both on and off the track.

RECREATION

WATER SPORTS New Zealanders are water bugs! Anytime they're not slaving away in an office or some other workplace, you'll find them in the water, on the water, or fishing the waters. As a visitor, you can participate in all sorts of water sports. There are pleasant beaches in the Bay of Islands, the Gisborne area, the Marlborough Sound area, and around Nelson. Surfing is especially good around the Bay of Plenty, with Tauranga offering what a Kiwi friend assures me is "the best surf of any New Zealand beach." Sailing is available to visitors in the Bay of Island, where you can indulge in deep-sea fishing jaunts as well.

FISHING Angling for rainbow and brown trout can put dinner on the table as well as provide a day in the open. Rotorua and Taupo are trout-fishing centers, but it's hard to fish any river or lake in the country without coming up with a good catch. In Rotorua, look up Barry Jaeger in the Hunting and Fishing Office; he can point you to especially good fishing spots in the area. In Taupo, Brian Leverell at Taupo River Guides is one of the North Island's best fishing guides and will practically guarantee you at least one trout on a half- or full-day fishing trip. Down south, Tony Busch of Sportsgoods Nelson Ltd. will do the same. The season is a long one—from the first Saturday in October to the end of April (year round at Rotorua and Taupo), and you can buy a special 1-month Tourist Fishing License from most fishing tackle or sporting goods stores and NZTP Travel Offices.

In the North Island, deep-sea fishing comes into its own along some 300 miles of coastline. Waters less than an hour from shore hold such trophies as marlin, mako shark, thresher shark, hammerhead shark, tiger shark, five species of tuna, broadbill, and yellowtail. The season runs from mid-January through April, and you'll find good, well-equipped bases at the Bay of Islands, Whitianga in Mercury Bay, Tauranga, and Whakatane. No license required.

HIKING Trekking, or tramping is another popular sport, and as you move around the country good tracks are almost always right at hand. The 10 national parks, which cover more than five million acres, all have well-defined trails, and many provide bunkhouses or huts for overnight stops. Even when you're based in a city, there will be scenic walks in the vicinity; I'll tell you about some in the chapters to come, and tourist offices can furnish brochures for their area. In fact, it's possible to hike most of the 1,000-mile length of New Zealand, and if that's your inclination, contact the Department of Conservation, P.O. Box 10-420, Wellington, for details of connecting regional and local walks. Hostel wardens are also very knowledgeable about trails in their particular area. The most famous—and one of the most splendid—is the guided 4-day Milford Track walk in Fiordland National Park, which draws trekkers from around the world. You can book the guided walk through tourist offices, or contact

Conservation Officers if you'd like to strike out on your own. Tramping is best in New Zealand from late November through April, when temperatures are their most moderate.

READERS RECOMMEND: HIKING

"Visitors who enjoy tramping should bring along good gear (boots, fleecy clothing). Also, in addition to the wealth of material available from the Department of Lands & Survey, there's a very good book on sale in New Zealand [and in the U.S.], Tramping in New Zealand, by Jim DuFresne (published by Lonely Planet Publications). [Author's note: Another excellent reference book is Top Ten Tracks, by Mark Pickering, published by Heinemann Reed in 1990.] Also, it cannot be stressed enough that the Milford Track must be booked well in advance, and the Routeburn Track is very overcrowded over Easter and the summer holiday break, so it should be avoided at those times if at all possible."—L. Best, Queenstown, New Zealand

SKIING New Zealand has some of the best ski terrain in the world, which, for North Americans, makes year-round skiing possible, since the season runs from mid-July through September—just in time to take up when our season leaves off and ends just prior to the beginning of ours. Major ski fields in the South Island are at Queenstown, Tekapo, Wanaka, Mount Hutt, and—for advanced skiers—famed Mount Cook, where you fly by skiplane to the 8,000-foot-high head of the Tasman Glacier and ski down the 12-mile run. In the north, there's good skiing at Tongariro and Turoa.

GOLF There are over 300 registered golf clubs in New Zealand, and members of overseas clubs are granted guest privileges in most private clubs. Clubs and a "trundler" (don't expect motorized carts) can be rented, and greens fees are low. One of the most outstanding courses is 50 miles south of Rotorua at Wairakei. You may find courses a bit crowded on weekends, much less so during the week. New Zealand Tourism publishes a helpful, detailed booklet *Golf* **New Zealand**, which should be required advance reading if you're planning a golf holiday.

9. FOOD & DRINK

FOOD

Mention New Zealand and food to almost anyone and the response is "lamb." Well, I'm told by my Kiwi friends, with a groan, that the best lamb gets shipped out to the likes of you and me on our home turf. That may well be so, but I've had very good lamb in New Zealand—as well as some that wasn't so very good. No matter what the quality, however, it's served as a roast more often than not, and a well-done roast at that. Quite frankly, I've become very fond of roast hogget (that's sheep a little older than lamb and a little younger than mutton), and I rather suspect that's what comes to table many times under the "lamb" label. What's not so well known outside New Zealand is their beef, and it's superb. Steaks and roast beef are plentiful and inexpensive. In the last year or two, venison has also appeared in more and more restaurants.

The star of Kiwi cuisine, as far as I'm concerned, however, is seafood, always fresh and of a wide variety. Bluff oysters are a treat on which I shamelessly gorge myself every trip—they're large and tangy, with a strong taste of the sea. Then there are the tiny whitebait, usually served in fritters, sometimes crisply fried. And the crayfish (you'll recognize the taste as that of the New Zealand rock lobster we buy frozen in the States), which is more expensive than other seafood, but worth every penny. And a fish with which I'm on a first-name basis—the John Dory—is as sweet and succulent as any I've ever tasted. Up in the north of the North Island, you can sometimes find toheroa soup, a delicacy made from a small shellfish much like a cockle, which is served in a rich chowder. Trout, of course, abound in the rivers and lakes of New Zealand, but they are not sold commercially (seems Kiwis adhere to the theory that for such a sporting fish, it would be a deep indignity to be eaten by anyone who didn't land him in a fair fight!). Nevertheless, it does occasionally appear on a menu (maybe when the chef is a fisherman?).

Dairy products, too, play a starring role in the New Zealand diet, and you'll know why after your first taste of rich, creamy milk and butter that reminds you of what it used to taste like in this country. Both are served in generous portions in restaurants and guesthouses, so enjoy. Government subsidies keep prices low, so you can afford to indulge even for those meals you cook in motel flats. Cheeses are also delicious and inexpensive. A loaf of vogel bread (rich, whole-grain bread, which you'll find in almost any health-food store and many supermarkets), a selection of cheeses, and a bottle of good wine or beer make the perfect picnic lunch on long drives.

You'll find meat pies everywhere, from lunch counters in rail and bus stations to pubs to take-away shops. They're thick-crusted little pies filled with chunks of meat and gravy, and can be quite delicious. That's if they're the homemade variety, with light, flaky crusts and just the right combination of mild spices and herbs. Keep an eye out for the "homemade" sign, which is more prevalent than you might imagine, and avoid whenever you can the tasteless factory-mades.

I've been told that the traditional New Zealand dessert is called pavlova because it's "as light and airy as the great dancer for whom it is named," and I don't doubt that for one moment. It consists of a large meringue made of stiffly beaten egg whites, which has been baked slowly at a low temperature to form a crusty outside and soft inside. Shaped like a large cake, its top is usually filled with whipped cream and fruit (kiwifruit when it's available)—great!

DRINK

Beer is the closest thing to a national drink (though wine is gaining in popularity), and you'll have to do a bit of sampling to find your own favorite brew among the many brands—friends of mine spend a lot of time debating the merits of DB (Dominion Breweries), Lion, Steinlager, and a few others. Be cautious, however, when testing those labeled "Export"—they're more than twice as potent as American beer! If you're a dedicated beer drinker or have a large party, you'll save money by ordering a "jug of draft," which holds about five 8-ounce glasses.

In recent years New Zealand's vineyards have been producing better and better wines. Labels like McWilliams, Montana, Mission, Corbans, and Penfolds are surprisingly inexpensive and varied in their offerings. Prices are even lower when you buy half-gallon flagons. Spirits have risen in price somewhat when purchased by the bottle, but are quite cheap (by U.S. standards) by the drink. You may want to stock up in Dunedin, where the bottle shop at the Robbie Burns Hotel has some of the lowest prices in the country.

Alcohol is only sold in licensed premises, bottle shops, and wholesale bottle stores (the best bargains are in the latter). Wholesale does not mean they won't sell individual bottles (although some have minimum-purchase requirements), so look for that name, usually in city-center shopping areas. Licensed hotels serve drinks from 11am to 10pm (11pm on Saturday, never on Sunday) in their bars and lounges, but anytime with a meal. Registered guests may be served anytime, regardless of the hour. Hotels with a Tourist House License are allowed to serve alcohol only to residents. Licensed restaurants serve drinks only with meals, and many unlicensed restaurants invite you to bring your own wine (most post a BYO notice—some don't, so it pays to inquire).

10. RECOMMENDED BOOKS, FILMS & RECORDINGS

BOOKS

MAORI WRITINGS   If Maori legend and language catch your imagination, you may want to look for *The Caltex Book of Maori Lore* (published by A. H. & A. W. Reed Ltd.), by James Cowan, who spent much time among the Maori; and *A Dictionary of the Maori Language,* by H. W. Williams, grandson of Bishop William Williams, who compiled the first dictionary at Pahia in 1844. *The Coming of the Maori* (Whitcombe and Tombs, 1974) by Sir P. Buck, a distinguished Maori and Pacific authority, is an account of the first Polynesian migration, and *The Maori of New Zealand* (Rutledge, London, 1976) by J. Metge is one of the best introductions to Maori life before and after European settlement. An excellent collection of Maori writings is *Into the World of Light: An Anthology of Maori Writing* (Heinemann, 1982), edited by Witi Ihimaera and D. S. Long. *No Ordinary Sun* (McIndoe, 1977) is a collection of New Zealand's leading Maori poet.

NONFICTION   One of my own most treasured reference books is the *New Zealand Encyclopedia* (David Bateman Ltd., 1984) edited by Gordon Mcuchlan, which covers every aspect of the country from A to Z. For insight into social concerns, look for *Social Policy and the Welfare State in New Zealand* (Allen and Unwin, 1980), by B. Easton. The most popular history, written by a professor of history at the University of Auckland, is *History of New Zealand* (Allen Lane, London, 1980; in paperback by Penguin), by Keith Sinclair.

FICTION & POETRY   *New Zealand Short Stories* (Oxford University Press, 1984) is a good collection selected by Lydia Wevers; *Owls Do Cry* (W. H. Allen, 1961), *A State of Siege* (Pegasus Press, 1967), and *Living in the Maniototo* (Braziller, New York, 1979) are three representative novels by New Zealand's most distinguished living novelist, Janet Frame. Collections of Katherine Mansfield's short stories include: *Prelude, Bliss and Other Stories,* and *The Garden Party and Other Stories.* One of my favorite New Zealand novels is *Song of the Forest,* by Peter Hooper (McIndoe).

Two excellent collections of contemporary poetry, both published by Oxford University Press, are *Anthology of Twentieth Century New Zealand Poetry* and *Oxford Book of Contemporary New Zealand Poetry.*

FILMS

Outstanding films produced in New Zealand are *Sleeping Dogs,* featuring outstanding actor Sam Neill (made in 1977—look for a video); *Smash Palace,* a compelling look at marital relations in New Zealand, featuring Roger Donaldson; *Utu,* a look at Maori and Pakeha relations in the last century; and *Goodbye Pork Pie,* about a mini-car that takes over the two male and one female passengers. *A word of warning:* If you find videos of these films, be *sure* to check that they will play on U.S. equipment.

RECORDINGS

Look for the *Tim Finn* tape by one of New Zealand's best rock musicians, and any recording by Split Enz, a group with which he played for several years. Opera lovers should seek out recordings of Dame Kiri Janette Te Kanawa, both solo performances and singing leading roles that include Mozart's *Vespers*, as well as *Exultate Jubilate* and *Don Giovanni*. The many Maori musical recordings are too numerous to list here, but the very special melodic sweetness and unique voice quality of most make this a souvenir that should be in every homeward-bound visitor's luggage. At many Maori concerts, it is possible to buy a tape made by the evening's performers.

CHAPTER 2

PLANNING A TRIP TO NEW ZEALAND

While certainly not the most exciting words between the covers of this book, this chapter may well be some of the most important reading you'll do before setting off on your New Zealand trip. It deals with the preplanning and "homework," which can make the difference between returning with pleasant, happy memories or with a feeling of frustration and bewilderment.

What I'll be talking about here are the details that will help you plan a trip as carefree as possible. You'll *need* to know about such things as currency, the rate of exchange, and travel documents. You'll *want* to know when to go, how long your trip should be, what sort of clothes to pack, and what you may expect in terms of accommodations, restaurants, shopping, and things to see and do.

1. INFORMATION, ENTRY REQUIREMENTS & MONEY

SOURCES OF INFORMATION

One of the most useful things you can do in planning a visit to New Zealand is to contact the **New Zealand Tourism Office** nearest you in North America for their comprehensive publication, *The New Zealand Book.* It will be your constant traveling companion, and even before leaving home it's a perfect complement to your advance reading (like this book!). They'll also include helpful brochures on virtually any specific sport, sightseeing highlights, and other special interests. Travel consultants in each office will be happy to help with any specific queries you may have.

When you arrive in New Zealand, there are friendly staffs in the more than 40 local **Visitor Information Network** offices around the country who are experts in all aspects of your holiday and are eager to help you in any way possible. Look for the identifying green **"i"** that make Visitor Information offices easy to spot.

You'll find New Zealand addresses for New Zealand Tourism regional offices and Visitor Information offices listed in each destination section. They are also listed in *The New Zealand Book* mentioned above. You can also contact them directly at their head office: New Zealand Tourism, 256 Lambton Quay, Wellington (tel. *04/728-860; fax *04/735-311).

In North America, locations are: New Zealand Tourism, 501 Santa Monica Blvd., Suite 300, Santa Monica, CA 90401 (tel. 310/395-7480, or toll free 800/388-5494; fax 301/395-5453); New Zealand Tourism, Suite 1260, IBM Tower, 701 W. Georgia St., Vancouver, Canada BC V7Y 1B6 (tel. 604/684-2117). Other locations include: New Zealand Tourism, Prudential Finance House, 84 Pitt St., Sydney, NSW 2000, Australia (tel. 2/231-1322); and New Zealand House, Haymarket, SW1Y 4TQ, London, England (tel. 071/973-0363).

Before your trip, you might also want to look at one or two **travel videos** about New Zealand. They really make the country, its diversity, and its people come alive and help you decide on the places you most want to visit. Several good ones—and hopefully one or more of them will be available in the travel section of your local video store—include *New Zealand: A World on Its Own* (25 minutes), *New Zealand on My Mind* (produced by the New Zealand Tourism Office, 25 minutes), and *Utterly New Zealand* with Leeza Gibbons (40 minutes).

ENTRY REQUIREMENTS

DOCUMENTS   You'll need a passport for entry to New Zealand, and it must be valid for no less than 3 months beyond the date you plan to depart. A travel tip about passports: It's a good idea to make two photocopies of the identification page of your passport (the one with your photo), as well as any other travel documents, then leave one copy at home and carry the other with you. You'll save yourself a lot of hassle in case you and those vital papers part company and you have to have them replaced! The photocopies will not serve as valid documents, but they'll furnish the information necessary to cut through miles of red tape to get new ones.

For a stay of less than 3 months, you won't need a visa (providing you don't intend to work, study, or undergo medical treatment) if you're a citizen of the United States, Canada, Great Britain (allowed a 6 months' stay), Australia, Austria, Belgium, Denmark, Finland, Federal Republic of Germany, Greece, Iceland, Ireland, Italy, Japan, Liechtenstein, Luxembourg, Malta, Monaco, the Netherlands, Norway, Portugal, Spain, Sweden, Switzerland, and Singapore. The same applies to French nationals.

Visas   If you wish to stay beyond the limits stated above, or if your nationality is not listed, consult your nearest New Zealand Embassy, High Commission, or consulate for information on obtaining the appropriate visa. Americans who want to stay longer than 3 months may obtain a visa application from the consular office nearest their home. The **New Zealand Embassy** is located at 37 Observatory Circle NW, Washington, DC 20008 (tel. 202/328-4880), and there are consular offices in Los Angeles and New York. Still other consulates may be found at the New Zealand Tourism Office addresses shown above. No fee, but you'll need a photograph. For information on working-holiday visas, inquire at one of the consulates for current regulations. Count on about 2 weeks for processing by mail.

Vaccinations   No certificate of vaccination is currently required of any traveler arriving in New Zealand. However, officials are quick to point out that should you develop an illness or skin rash, you should see a doctor and say you've recently arrived in the country.

CUSTOMS   Three things visitors must show before entry permission is granted: a confirmed onward or round-trip ticket; enough money for their New Zealand stay—figure NZ$1,000 ($571) per person per month, or NZ$400 ($229) with accommodation already paid (credit cards are acceptable as evidence of funds)—and the necessary documents to enter the next country on their itinerary or to reenter the country from which they came.

There is no Customs duty on any personal effects you bring into the country and intend to take away with you. Also duty-free are 200 cigarettes or half a pound of tobacco or 50 cigars, as well as 4.5 liters of wine or beer, one bottle of spirits or liqueur (up to 1.125 liters), and goods up to a total combined value of NZ$500 ($286) for your own use or that you are bringing as a gift. If you plan to take in anything beyond those limits, best contact the New Zealand Customs Department, Head Office, Wellington, New Zealand, or the nearest embassy or consulate office, *before* you arrive. Ask for their publication *Customs Guide for Travelers*.

MONEY

CURRENCY   You won't have any trouble at all with New Zealand currency. It's based on the decimal system and has coins in denominations of 1, 2, 5, 10, 20, and 50 cents, and notes in $1, $2, $5, $10, $20, and $100 amounts. From 1975 until 1982 the New Zealand dollar was at near parity with the U.S. dollar, but things have changed drastically in the past years. As a result, your U.S. money is worth (as we go to press) a little more than half again as much over there as it is at home.

What this means, of course, is that you'll be able to do more, see more, buy more, upgrade accommodations, and still stay within your $45 U.S. per day allowance for room and board. In terms of New Zealand money $45 U.S. is now worth NZ$79. Far be it from me to predict that this exchange rate is going to stay in effect for the entire life of this book, so my very first financial advice is to *check for the current rate* at the outset, before you do any concrete planning. Then make any necessary adjustments to the rates shown in these pages.

The exchange rate in effect as this book is written is $1 U.S. is equal to NZ$1.75 (NZ$1 = U.S. 57¢), and all conversions listed are at that rate. The following table will serve as a general guide, but a small investment in one of the small currency-converter-calculators will pay big dividends in accuracy and time saved.

THE NEW ZEALAND DOLLAR AND THE U.S. DOLLAR

NZ$	$U.S.	NZ$	$U.S.
.50	.28	20.00	11.43
1.00	.57	25.00	14.29
2.00	1.14	27.50	15.71
2.50	1.43	30.00	17.14
3.00	1.71	35.00	20.00
5.00	2.86	40.00	22.86
8.00	4.57	50.00	28.57
10.00	5.71	75.00	42.86
15.00	8.57	100.00	57.14

You may be asked upon arrival to show that you have sufficient funds to cover your expected stay without having to get a job (they're pretty picky about things like that, although I must say I've personally never been questioned). Also, when leaving you will not be allowed to carry more than $100 in New Zealand currency out of the country. It would be best to convert funds into the currency of your next destination before departure time.

There's no need, I'm sure, to say that most of your money should be in traveler's checks, not in cash. But because exchange rates of foreign currencies against the U.S. dollar have fluctuated more radically recently than in years past, the best advice is to start watching daily exchange rates as soon as you know you'll be going to New

Zealand. A variation of only a few cents can sometimes net you considerably more buying power. Of course, for safety's sake, you won't want to convert all your precious travel dollars, no matter what the rate, and even if the rate is exceptionally favorable before you leave home, you should convert no more than half your funds into the foreign currency, and take the balance in traveler's checks.

TRAVELER'S CHECKS   I should also remind you that it's a good idea to keep the record of your traveler's checks separate from the checks themselves, and to be sure to record each one you cash. If the worst should happen and you lose checks, replacement will depend on your having those uncashed numbers. Banks, of course, offer the best exchange rates, *not* hotels, department stores, or restaurants.

Check to see if there is a bank fee for cashing the checks; both American Express and Thomas Cook do not charge for cashing their own checks.

CREDIT CARDS   American Express, MasterCard, Diners Club, and VISA credit cards are widely accepted, even in remote areas.

READERS RECOMMEND: BANKING

"Visitors intending to stay for more than a brief period might consider opening an account at a bank that offers access to automatic teller machines. With a card, there is no need to worry about traveler's checks, and cash can be obtained until 11pm. I found that the Bank of New Zealand offered very good service."—S. Scott, Victoria, B.C., Canada

WHAT THINGS COST IN WELLINGTON (CAPITAL CITY)	U.S. $
Taxi from airport to city center	$7.70
Airport bus to city center	3.15
Double at Harbour City Motor Inn (moderate)	79.00
Double at Tinakori Lodge (budget)	44.00
Lunch for one at Greta Point Tavern (moderate)	8.00
Lunch for one at Mangiare (budget)	5.70
Dinner for one, without wine, at Whitby's Brasserie (moderate)	15.00
Dinner for one, without wine, at Glossops (budget)	6.00
Bottle of beer	1.70
Cup of coffee	.90
Roll of ASA 100 Kodacolor film, 36 exposures	4.45
Admission to National Museum	Free
Movie ticket	4.60
Concert and/or theater ticket	15.00–20.00

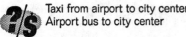

WHAT THINGS COST IN DUNEDIN (PROVINCIAL TOWN)	U.S. $
Taxi from airport to city center	$26.00
Airport bus to city center	5.70

	U.S. $
Double at Southern Cross Hotel (deluxe)	70.00
Double at Aberdeen Motel (moderate)	46.00
Double at Sahara Guesthouse (budget)	31.00
Lunch for one at The Best Cafe (moderate)	7.50
Lunch for one at Stewart's Coffee House (budget)	3.45
Dinner for one, without wine, at 95 Filleul Restaurant (deluxe)	35.00
Dinner for one, without wine, at Palms Café (moderate)	15.00
Dinner for one, without wine, at Heffe's (budget)	5.70
Bottle of beer	1.45
Cup of coffee	1.75
Roll of ASA 100 Kodacolor film, 36 exposures	4.45
Admission to Otago Museum	Free
Movie ticket	2.90
Concert and/or theater ticket	5.70

2. WHEN TO GO — CLIMATE, HOLIDAYS & EVENTS

CLIMATE

Weatherwise, you're safe to visit New Zealand any time of the year. Temperatures are never extreme, although I've experienced days warmer than those midsummer averages and a degree or two below the midwinter averages quoted. One thing to keep in mind, however, is that on a visit that takes you to both islands, you'll be going from a subtropical climate in the north of the North Island to the coolness (sometimes coldness) of the South Island.

Nor is there a specific rainy season, although the west coast of the South Island can experience up to 100 inches or more of rain a year on its side of the Southern Alps, while just over those mountains to the east rainfall will be a moderate 20 to 30 inches. Rain is heavier in the west on the North Island as well, with precipitation on the whole ranging from 40 to 70 inches annually. Milford Sound holds the record as the wettest spot in the country (and also perhaps the most beautiful—a personal bias!) with an annual downpour of 365 inches; fortunately, it doesn't rain every day or all day long.

As for sunshine, you'll find more in the north and east of both islands, with the Bay of Islands and the Nelson/Marlborough Sound area leading sun spots. Frost and snow in the North Island are mainly confined to high country such as Mount Egmont and the peaks in Tongariro National Park, so if it's snow or snow-related sports you're after, look for them in the South Island. Even there, skiing is not a year-round activity, so a little research on specific destinations is in order before you set your dates. One of my visits to Queenstown, for example, was in mid-June, and local headlines announced "One More Dump and We Ski." I'll get into that in more detail later in this chapter (see "Ski Holidays" below).

SEASONS In New Zealand, seasons are those of the southern hemisphere, thus the exact opposite of ours. There just isn't a bad season to travel, so your own schedule and interests will set your timing priorities. A fundamental guideline, however, is that during Kiwi holiday times, accommodations can be very tight. So if you plan to come between mid-December and January 30, when New Zealand families are traveling about their country on annual "hols," or during the Easter, May, or August school holidays (see below), prebooking is an absolute must.

Spring September, October, November. This is one of the best times to visit, since Kiwis are going about their business activities, schools are in full session, innkeepers will greet you with delight—with or without a booking—and the countryside is bright with blossoming fruit trees and brand-new baby lambs.

Summer December, January, February. Beaches and boats are primary preoccupations of the natives during these months, and resorts are booked to capacity. Advance planning will let you share these sun-filled days, although you should be prepared for slightly higher accommodation rates. It's a fun time to visit if you get your bookings underway early enough.

Fall March, April, May. In my personal opinion, this is a great time to visit New Zealand. The weather is pleasant and just cool enough in southern parts to remind you that winter is on its way, while in the Bay of Islands region midday and early afternoons are still shirt-sleeve warm. Poplars are a brilliant gold, and more subtle foliage changes can be seen in the forests. Just remember those Easter and May (2 weeks) school holidays, when bookings may be tight.

Winter June, July, August. Okay, you ski buffs—this is the time when your ski calendar goes on a year-round basis. From about mid-June on, the slopes are a skier's dream. Booking ahead at major ski resorts is certainly advisable, but you can nearly always count on finding accommodations within an easy drive even if you arrive with nothing confirmed. Around the rest of the country, this is another season you can pretty much amble around without booking ahead—except, of course, for that aforementioned 2-week school holiday in August.

HOLIDAYS

Statutory holidays are: January 1 (New Year's Day), January 2 (New Year Holiday), February 6 (Waitangi Day), Good Friday, Easter Monday, April 25 (Anzac Day), June 3 (Queen's Birthday), October 28 (Labor Day), December 25 (Christmas Day), and December 26 (Boxing Day).

Holidays celebrated locally are: January 22 (Wellington), January 29 (Auckland), January 29 (Northland, that is, Bay of Islands), February 1 (Nelson), March 23 (Otago and Southland, that is, Dunedin, Queenstown, Invercargill), March 31 (Taranaki), November 1 (Hawke Bay and Marlborough), December 1 (Westland), and December 16 (Canterbury).

School holidays last for 2½ to 3 weeks and fall in May, August, and December—and I repeat, that's when Kiwi families are on the move holidaying it up, so be sure of your bookings during those months.

NEW ZEALAND CALENDAR OF EVENTS

JANUARY

☐ **Summer City Festival, Wellington.** Daily cultural, entertainment, and recreational events in the capital city. January and February.

☐ **Wellington Cup, Wellington.** Leading horse-racing event (galloping). Late January.

☐ **National Yearling Sales, Wellington.** Held in conjunction with Wellington Cup.

☐ ✪ **Fiordland Festival Week, Te Anau.** Arts and crafts, food stalls, and street entertainment. Mid-January.

FEBRUARY

☐ ✪ **Waitangi Day Celebrations, Bay of Islands.** New Zealand's national day, celebrating signing of treaty with Maori. February 6.

☐ **Martinborough Country Fairs, Martinborough.** Popular gathering of crafts artisans from around the country. First Saturday in February and March.

☐ **Floral Festival, Christchurch.** Garden visits, floating gardens, floral carpets in the "Garden City" of the South Island. First 2 weeks in February.

MARCH

☐ **Festival of Arts (even-numbered years only), Wellington.** Important festival of the performing arts, by both internationally known artists and street entertainers. First 3 weeks of March.

☐ **Martinborough Country Fairs.** First Saturday in February and March. See February, above.

☐ ✪ **International Shearing Contest, Masterton.** Three-day contests for wool handling, lamb and goat shearing. Early March.

☐ **Dukes International Billfish Tournament, Bay of Islands.** Draws the fishing crowd from around the world. Early March.

☐ **Summer Festival Week, Dunedin.** Street entertainment, cultural and sporting events. Mid-March.

☐ ✪ **Ngaruawahia River Regatta, Turangawoewoe Marae, Ngaruawahia.** Canoe races, Maori songs and dances performed by cultural groups. Mid-March.

☐ ✪ **New Zealand National Highland Games, Tauranga Domain.** Two-day celebration of Scottish heritage, with Highland games, military tattoo, and wood-chopping contest. Late March.

☐ **Hokitika Wild Foods Festival, Hokitika.** Wild pig, venison, possum pâté, goat, all sorts of wild herbs, honey, and fish from local waters star in this 1-day West Coast celebration. Great fun. Third or fourth week in March.

APRIL–SEPTEMBER

☐ **Rugby Season, Countrywide.**

APRIL

☐ **Arrowtown Autumn Festival, Arrowtown.** Week of market days, miners' band, and street entertainment celebrating the gold-mining era. Early April.

☐ ✪ **Bluff Oyster Festival, Bluff Township.** Celebrating opening of oyster season, with shucking and eating contests. Early April.

☐ **Highland Games, Hastings.** Contestants from all over the country and Australia vie for championships in tossing the caber, sheaf throwing, and other field games. Mid-April.

☐ **Mackenzie Highland Show, Fairlie.** One of New Zealand's largest agricultural and produce shows, featuring horses, sheep, cattle, dog trials, wood chopping, and Highland dancing. Easter Saturday.

☐ ✪ **National Jazz Festival, Tauranga.** Youth bands and overseas acts join with local professionals. Easter weekend.

MAY

☐ **Fletcher Challenge Marathon, Rotorua.** Grueling footrace. Early May.
☐ **Hot Air Balloon Fiesta, Hamilton.** Three-day competitions in New Zealand's ballooning capital. First weekend in May.

JUNE

☐ **DB Draught Marathon, Christchurch.** Hotly contested by runners from around the country. Early June.
☐ ✪ **National Agricultural Field Days, Hamilton.** Largest field day in Australasia, covering every type of rural activity, as well as stock sales that reach astronomical prices. Mid-June.

JULY

☐ ✪ ✪ **Queenstown Winter Festival, Queenstown.** Boisterous, fun-filled celebration of winter season, with ski events and street entertainment. Early July.

AUGUST

☐ **Wanaka Snowfest, Wanaka and Treble Cone Ski Field.** Lots of skiing events in this winter festival. Late August.

SEPTEMBER

☐ **Alexandra Blossom Festival, Alexandra.** Floral parade, displays of local arts and crafts, garden tours, and entertainment. Late September, early October.

OCTOBER

☐ ✪ **Rhododendron Week, Dunedin.** Fun-filled days highlighted by garden tours and cultural events to celebrate this city's magnificent displays of rhododendron blooms. Mid-October.
☐ **Lifespan Mountains to Sea Multi-Sports Event, Tongariro and Whanganui National Park.** Labor Weekend, late October.
☐ **Maritime Mardigras, Stewart Island.** A lively festival of the sea. Late October.

NOVEMBER

☐ **Whangamomona Republic Day, Whangamomono.** Passports are issued and entry visas sold to visitors when borders are closed around this self-styled republic formed after boundary changes moved Whangamomona from the Tarankai region to that of Wanganui-Manawatu. All sorts of street entertainment and food stalls, with proceeds going to charity. Nearest Saturday to November 1.
☐ **International Trout Fishing Competition, Rotorua.** International anglers gather to compete with the locals, fishing 14 lakes in 4 days. Mid-November.

DECEMBER

☐ **BP National Tennis Championships, Wellington.** International-class men's tournament. Late December, early January.

AUCKLAND
CALENDAR OF EVENTS

JANUARY

☐ ✪ **Auckland Cup Horse Racing.** One of the country's richest horse races. January 1.
☐ ✪ **Anniversary Day Regatta.** Colorful sailing event, with local and international entrants. January 27.
☐ **Men's International Tennis Tournament.** Late January, early February.
☐ **Women's International Tennis Tournament.** Late January, early February.

FEBRUARY

☐ **Polo.** Check locally for dates throughout the month.
☐ **Cricket.** Various dates throughout the month.

MARCH

☐ **World Carnival of Harness Racing.** A 2-week schedule of races and related events. First 2 weeks in March.
☐ ✪ **Savile Polo Cup, Auckland Pologround, Clevedon.** One of New Zealand's oldest sporting trophies, the Savile pits domestic teams against international contenders. Mid-March.
☐ **Round the Bays Run.** Great fun, with runners from around the South Pacific participating, ending with a barbecue in one of the city's parks. Late March.

APRIL

☐ **Auckland Racing Club Easter Festival.** Annually attracts more than 1,000 competitors, and incorporates elements of an Agricultural and Pastoral Show. Mid-April.

MAY

☐ ✪ **New Zealand Brass Band Championships.** Soloists, small groups, and large bands compete in marching events as well as other performances. Mid-May.

JUNE

☐ ✪ **Great Northern Steeplechase.** The country's leading steeplechase event, run over Auckland's Ellerslie Racecourse's famous "Hill." Early June.

AUGUST

☐ **Bledisloe Rugby Cup.** Fiercely competitive rugby series between New Zealand and Australia. Late August.

SEPTEMBER

☐ **World's Trampoline Championships.** Competitors from more than 30 countries gather in Auckland's ASB Stadium. Early September.

DECEMBER

☐ **Nissan Mobil 500 Series, Pukekohe Raceway.** Two touring car events, with teams from all over the world. Early December.

☐ **Horse Racing (✪ NZ Derby, Queen Elizabeth Auckland Handicap, and others).** Check locally for specific dates of individual events during the month.

3. HEALTH & INSURANCE

BEFORE YOU GO

Health Preparations   If you take any form of medication, it's a good idea to bring along prescriptions from your doctor in case you need refills. This also applies to prescriptions for eyeglasses or contact lenses.

Insurance   Before leaving home, check to be sure that your property insurance is in good order, with premium payments up to date and full coverage for fire, theft, etc. It's a good idea, also, to have health and accident insurance when traveling. If your present policy does not provide coverage when you're out of the country, check with your insurance carrier about temporary medical coverage for the duration of your trip. Most travel agents can arrange this, along with travel-delay or cancellation, and lost-luggage insurance.

IN NEW ZEALAND

Accident Compensation   As a visitor to New Zealand, you are automatically covered, from the time you arrive until you leave, by the same no-fault **accident compensation** plan as Kiwis. And it doesn't cost you one red cent! Benefits include compensation for reasonable expenses (by New Zealand standards) directly resulting from the accident, such as medical and hospital expenses, as well as lump-sum payments for permanent incapacity. No matter if the accident was your fault or not, you'll be covered. Be sure to note, however, that this compensation plan does not cover sickness, trip cancellation, etc. For more information, contact your nearest New Zealand Tourism office. Benefits are determined by the Accident Compensation Corporation. Their head office is at Renouf House, 154 Featherston St., Wellington (tel. *04/724-434), and you should contact them immediately if you should—God forbid!—have an accident.

Medical Attention   This is *not* free like accident compensation, but medical care is so inexpensive by comparison to costs elsewhere that it would almost pay to get sick while in New Zealand! Medical facilities are excellent and health care is of a very high standard.

4. WHAT TO PACK

When planning your New Zealand wardrobe, there is one basic tenet you can hang on to, no matter when you plan to go or what you plan to do: Dress in Kiwiland, for the most part, is informal. Men will want to take along a jacket and tie; women, at least one dress or skirt for those restaurants or hotels that have a dress code at dinner. Otherwise, casual is the keynote.

When you plan to come will of, course, play a big part in your dress decisions, so study the next section carefully and remember that the seasons will be those of the southern hemisphere. There are, however, few temperature extremes either in the subtropical tip of the North Island or in the cooler South Island. Auckland, for example, has an average midsummer temperature of 73°F, with 57°F the midwinter average. Queenstown's summer average is 72°F, with 46°F about the lowest in winter. Generally, you can look for balmy days in the Bay of Islands, cool-to-cold down in the Southern Alps. That translates into layering: a warm sweater, long-sleeved blouses to be worn over short sleeves, sleeveless knit vests—that sort of thing. One item I've found useful is a pair of cotton knit or polypropylene "longjohns" to wear under lightweight trousers when I get down to the cooler climes. Combined with a zip-in-lining jacket, they've seen me through several fall-to-winter stays.

What you plan to do will also determine what clothes you pack. New Zealand offers some of the best tramping in the world, and if that's what you plan to do, bring along suitable clothing, sturdy boots, backpack, and the necessary utensils if you'll be camping overnight. I might add here that you needn't bring along boots and heavy coats if the extent of your tramping will be an organized trek on the glaciers—both will be provided by your guide. If you travel like most people, you'll simply be moving from place to place and sightseeing, and for that just be sure the clothes you take along are comfortable, easy to pack, and washable. Incidentally, most of those great motels I'll be telling you about later in this chapter have washing and drying facilities. One item no one should omit is comfortable shoes—no place on earth is appealing when your feet hurt!

Now for one bit of advice that stems from my own experience of returning with an overstuffed suitcase that was nice and light when I left home: There's no way you're going to be able to resist those terrific natural-wool sweaters (especially the hand-knits), and you'll save yourself oodles of packing troubles if you leave the ones you now own at home, then pick up one (I *dare* you to buy just one!) and wear it during your trip. Men will no doubt be tempted in warm weather to adopt the universal New Zealand male dress of walking shorts, high socks, and short-sleeve shirts. In other words, leave some packing room—you'll be wearing some of your nicest souvenirs.

Besides clothing, there are a few other carry-alongs: a washcloth in a plastic bag, since they're seldom furnished in New Zealand accommodations; a travel alarm clock; prescriptions for any medication or glasses that are essential to your comfort and well-being; a small calculator or currency converter, a flashlight if you'll be driving after dark; a pen for all those postcards; and any small personal items you're just not comfortable without.

Sports enthusiasts may want to bring along favorite fishing rods, golf clubs, or skis, all of which are allowed through Customs, but these items are readily available in New Zealand. Many fishing guides furnish equipment, and clubs can be rented at most golf courses. If the hostels will be your home away from home, bring along a sleeping bag or sheets and a pillowcase. Blankets and linens can be rented.

5. TIPS FOR SPECIAL TRAVELERS

FOR THE DISABLED Recognizing that all too often the wheelchair traveler, as well as his or her traveling companions, are excluded from guesthouse and other accommodations because of narrow doors, steps, and inaccessibility to toilets, the

New Zealand accommodations industry has encouraged accommodation design to circumvent these problems. Since 1975, in fact, every new public building and every major reconstruction in the country is required to provide reasonable and adequate access for the disabled. Accommodations with nine or more units must also provide one or more accessible facilities for the disabled.

Driving in New Zealand for the handicapped is an easy matter, since **Budget Rent a Car** has become the first to offer rentals especially adapted to meet the needs of handicapped drivers. You can get advance information on booking through **New Zealand Tourism Office,** 501 Santa Monica Blvd., Suite 300, Santa Monica, CA 90401 (tel. toll free 800/388-5494), or through travel agents. Travel agents can also book.

An essential part of every disabled visitor's before-travel plans should be the comprehensive guide *Access: A Guide for the Less Mobile Traveler,* available from NZ Tourism offices. Included are an up-to-date list of hotels, motels, and guesthouses that do provide accommodations designed for the comfort and convenience of the disabled; sightseeing attractions that provide such facilities; and even a listing of New Zealand thermal pools equipped for easy access. Thermal pools, which New Zealand has in abundance, have long been known to bring relief to many of the disabled; however, recent years have seen the growth of those devoted solely to recreational purposes, a fact that makes this booklet extremely valuable when selecting those to visit.

FOR SENIORS   Accommodation discounts for those over 65 are becoming more and more frequent in New Zealand, although most apply almost exclusively to off- or low-season rates at the moment. However, as I said, senior citizen discounts are the coming thing, so *be sure to inquire when booking,* and if you're booking through an agent, stress that the discount should be requested, since it may not be offered voluntarily.

Some sightseeing attractions have senior citizen prices, and again, it pays to inquire when you pay your admission fee.

FOR SINGLES   Almost all of my traveling in New Zealand has been done alone, and I can tell you from firsthand experience that being a single traveler has never been a problem. On the social scene, there just aren't any places I hesitate to go on my own, and restaurants have yet to stick me next to the kitchen door or at the most undesirable table in the place. As for motel and guesthouse hosts, they unfailingly go out of their way to make me feel at home, often taking great pains to see that I know as much as they themselves know about the location and what's on at the moment.

Having said all that, I must add a cautionary note about hitchhiking or wandering around city streets in the wee hours on your own—although New Zealand still enjoys a relatively low crime rate, you are well advised to team up with someone else if you plan to do either.

It is also true that in New Zealand, as in most of the rest of the world, I frequently (but I hasten to say, not *always*) pay a slightly higher per-person rate for accommodations than if I were one half of a couple—one of the realities of travel. The only tip I can offer in this regard is to look about for another single traveler and team up as roommates.

FOR FAMILIES   Go ahead, bring the kids! New Zealand is especially well suited for memorable family holidays. Even in these turbulent times, the family unit is still very much the core of Kiwi life, and visiting families are welcomed with open arms. And, contrary to many other cultures, New Zealanders don't frown on children in restaurants.

An increasingly popular family holiday with our readers is that spent in New Zealand farmhouses—children and parents alike are utterly delighted to walk the fields with the farmer and, more often than not, lend a helping hand with farm chores. For the city-bred American, that's a lovely treat. New Zealand Tourism offices can furnish two useful brochures: *New Zealand Farm Holidays,* and *New Zealand Association Farm & Home Hosts,* which lists farm hosts in both islands.

On the budgetary front, motel units usually come complete with kitchen facilities, and easily prepared meals are a money-saving device when you have so many mouths to feed. If the thought of all that cooking and washing up brings groans from the distaff side of the family, there is the consoling counterthought that marketing in New Zealand—be it in small neighborhood "dairies" or supermarkets much like those at home—is loads of fun. You'll see many familiar products, and a host of unfamiliar brands, cuts of meat, and canned products. Any shopkeeper or grocery clerk, however, will delight in telling you all about them and how they should be used or cooked.

You might also consider using New Zealand's excellent YHA hostel accommodations (see p. 55). There is no membership requirement for children under 15 traveling with families of adult memberships. Since all hostels do not have suitable rooms—and since those that do, have them in limited number—you should write for their handbook (see below) and book as far in advance as possible.

When it comes to keeping the children amused, what child wouldn't be happy exploring sheep farms, glowworm caves, wide beaches with weird rock formations, forests alive with exotic birds, and small towns that smack of their image of our own "Wild West." Sports, music, dancing, and a host of other activities are also geared for the young and available wherever you go in the country. White-water rafting, glacier walking, and the like will not only delight youngsters, but will provide lifelong memories of unique experiences. Parents will be happy to know that virtually every sightseeing attraction admits children at half-price, and many have family prices as well.

After dark, older children will enjoy entertainments such as Maori dinner shows (don't be surprised if you hear your offsprings' rendition of the fierce war *haka* for months after your return home!). Most guesthouses, motels, and hotels have babysitters on hand for the small fry when it's an adult night out that's called for.

FOR STUDENTS The **International Student Identity Card** opens doors to marvelous events and activities aimed only at students, and also offers substantial discounts on almost every facet of travel. You must, however, arm yourself with this valuable document before you leave home. The cost in 1992 was $10, and you can obtain your card through CIEE (Council on International Educational Exchange), 205 E. 42nd St., New York, NY 10017 (tel. 212/661-1414), or at any of the 30 Council Travel offices or 440 campus issuing offices across the country.

For economical accommodations, as well as a great way to meet other traveling students, join **American Youth Hostels,** Box 37613, Washington, DC 20013-7613 (tel. 202/783-6161). Membership will entitle you to an International Guest Card from YHA of New Zealand, as well as many travel and sightseeing discounts. Should you arrive in New Zealand without a membership card, you will be issued an International Guest Card, which costs NZ$4 ($2.30) per night, or NZ$24 ($13.75) for your entire stay. Membership issuing agencies are known as **YHA Travel Centres,** with locations in Auckland (Customs and Gore Streets) in Wellington (in Port Nicholson Hostel), and Christchurch (Gloucester and Manchester Streets). Apply by mail to **YHA National Office,** P.O. Box 436, Christchurch (tel. *03/799-970).

Intercity also offers the **Backpacker's Pass** and **Kiwi Experience Pass,** both of which may be purchased in segments, with savings of up to 30%.

One of the leading student travel **tour operators** is **Contiki Holidays,** 1432 E. Katella Ave., Anaheim, CA 92805 (tel. toll free 800/626-0611), for ages 18 through 35. **Arista Student Travel Association, Inc.,** 11 E. 44th St., New York, NY 10017 (tel. 212/687-5121, or toll free 800/356-8861), caters for ages 15 to 20.

Student unions at universities can also often be helpful to traveling students, and remember, too, to *always* ask about **student discount tickets to attractions.**

6. ALTERNATIVE/ADVENTURE TRAVEL

FARM HOLIDAYS In a country where agriculture reigns supreme, I can't think of a better place to feel the pulse of the people than on a working farm. A firsthand knowledge of just what it takes to raise all those sheep and cattle and kiwifruit will give you more insight into New Zealand life than you could gain in any other way. And what a joy to wake in the mornings to pastoral beauty and a charming country home in the midst of a host family who are delighted to have you as a guest and eager to show you around the farm!

There are rugged South Island sheep stations, dairy farms, farms with glowworm caves, Maori burial sites, hot springs, trout fishing, and scenery that includes magnificent mountains and coastlines. And if you want to jump in and help muster sheep on that station or groom one of the thoroughbred horses, well, you have only to let your wishes be known. On the other hand, if a day or so of quiet rusticating suits you better, that's okay too. You will have your own bedroom (sometimes with a private bath, but more often it's on a share-with-the-family basis), plus two hearty farm meals each day (dinner and breakfast), which you'll take around the family dining table.

Air New Zealand also offers a **fly/drive farm holiday** plan with the option of staying in the family home or in self-catering cottages on the premises. Other options include an InterCity Railways Travelpass instead of a car, and a "Go as You Please" plan that lets you arrange your own itinerary rather than prebook the entire stay. Prices vary according to your choice of options and are quite reasonable. Bookings must be made through travel agents. With such a widespread network of host farms, you'll be able to stay on a farm in virtually every location you want to visit. Daily charges for bed, breakfast, and dinner, per person, average NZ$80 to NZ$175 ($46 to $100).

Any New Zealand Tourism office can put you in touch with several organizations that offer close-up experience on farms throughout the country. Farmhouses are listed in their own *Where to Stay* guide, and you can locate some wonderful farm-stay possibilities on the North and South Islands through **New Zealand Farm Holidays,** P.O. Box 256, Silverdale, Auckland (tel. 09/307-2024; fax 0942/68-474); or **Farmhouse and Country Home Holidays,** 31250, Auckland (tel. 09/410-8280). Farm holidays may also be booked through travel agents.

HOME STAYS Kiwi hospitality is, of course, by no means restricted to farms and rural areas—there are warm, friendly homes in cities and towns just as eager to welcome you as are the farm families. You'll find them in beachfront and lake locations as well as in city suburbs, and all are invaluable "data banks" of local attractions, sightseeing, and history.

In most, you will be the only guest, becoming an instant member of the family. Some offer private baths; at others you'll share with the family. All serve a full cooked breakfast, and your evening meal is optional. (*Note:* Comparing notes and reporting on the day's activities over the dinner table is a decided plus when you're staying with a local family.) There are smoking and nonsmoking hosts, those with and those without pets, retired couples with no live-in children, and others with lively youngsters a vital part of the family scene.

A wide variety of home-stay packages lets you choose a prebooked holiday or a freewheeling itinerary (whether you're driving, biking, or using public transport). Expect to pay about NZ$125 ($71) per person per night, including meals.

New Zealand Home Hospitality Ltd., P.O. Box 309, Nelson (tel. 03/548-2424), can put you up with host families whose only interest is in seeing that you enjoy your time in their locality. All packages may be booked through travel agents or any New Zealand Tourism office. Or write direct for their helpful brochure describing all options in detail.

READERS RECOMMEND

*Home Hosting-Rural Tours, P.O. Box 228, Cambridge. Tel. Helen Hicks at *071/278-055. "We found Home Hosting-Rural Tours, in Cambridge, to be small, personal, and great value. This was definitely a highlight of our brief stay in a beautiful country. Dinner and breakfast are included, lunch is always possible, and the selection of homes in the Cambridge area is superb!"—J. Smith, Kelowna, B.C., Canada*

Hospitality Haere Mai, P.O. Box 56-175, Auckland. Tel. 09/309-3869. "We found one home-stay organization absolutely wonderful. They put you with families throughout New Zealand, and have a choice of Budget, Medium, and Deluxe price ranges. We stayed Budget and Medium, and found the food and hosts wonderful in every case. But the best thing is that it was very inexpensive. Contact: Graeme and Judy McLean or partners Pat and Leslie Fallon."—C. Feldmann, Bonners Ferry, Idaho

HISTORIC SITES TOUR   New Zealand's varied history can form the basis of an interesting itinerary. You might begin at the top of the North Island, with the oldest surviving building in all of New Zealand, Kemp House (1821–22) in the Kerikeri Basin, the reconstructed Maori village of Keri Park near Kerikeri, Russell's Pompallier House, and the Treaty House in Waitangi. Auckland, of course, bristles with historic sites, as does Wellington. That's just a small sample of historic sightseeing. There are a host of other North and South Island historic sites that will leave you with a deeper, more vivid, impression of this country's background and the elements that have shaped its people. For help in planning an itinerary to suit your particular historical interests, contact: The Director, **New Zealand Historic Places Trust,** P.O. Box 2629, Wellington.

SKI HOLIDAYS   New Zealand attracts dedicated skiers like a magnet—not surprising when its upside-down ski season allows those from the northern hemisphere to hit the slopes year round. In the North Island, the two commercial ski fields are Whakapapa and Turoa, both in the Tongariro National Park on the slopes of Mount Ruapehu, an active volcano that soars some 2,796 meters (9,200 ft.) high. Whakapapa is the largest ski field, and it offers facilities for beginners to the most advanced. Turoa, on Mount Ruapehu's south side, is beloved for its long spring season that lasts into early November.

Down south, the Southern Lakes Ski Region includes the internationally respected Remarkables, Cardrona, Treble Cone, and Coronet Peak. There's also a new Nordic ski area and several heliski operations. From early June right through October, the area around Queenstown and Wanaka offers some of the world's best skiing. In central South Island, Mount Hutt, near Christchurch, dominates the skiing scene. That is not to discount the attractions of Mount Cook, with its famous—and *very* challenging—Tasman Glacier ski trip and the newer heliskiing.

Lift prices range from $30 to $41; skis, boots, and poles rentals, $19 to $22; and lessons are about $22 for group classes, $50 for individual instruction.

Arm yourself with the New Zealand Tourism publications **New Zealand Outdoor Holidays** and **New Zealand Ski Area Guide** before planning your itinerary. There are a number of good, value-for-money, ski-holiday packages available that merit a good look before you book. Mount Cook Line has a popular range of Ski Holiday packages that include accommodation, skiing, transport to and from Queenstown and the ski areas, and the services of special ski hosts. Details are available through travel agents or the airline's head office: **Mount Cook Line,** Head Office, 47 Riccarton Rd. (P.O. Box 4544), Christchurch (tel. 03/314-8099; fax 03/314-8099; or toll free 800/262-0248 in the U.S., 800/468-2665 in California, 800/999-9306 in Canada). (If the skiing bug should bite *after* you arrive in New Zealand, head for one of Mount Cook Line's extensive network of Travel Centres in all major cities and tourist centers.) **Ski Season Tours,** 150 Powell St., Suite 407, San Francisco, CA 94102 (tel. 415/421-3171), are also skilled in setting up ski holidays.

BOATING HOLIDAYS Join the Kiwis in their favorite pastime, messing about in boats. The long coastline offers hundreds of possibilities, from exploring the thousands of secluded inlets and tranquil bays, sailing to uninhabited islands, or even heading out to the high seas.

Boat-charter possibilities abound, for both experienced sailors who may want to captain their own vessel to just plain lovers of the sea who want to relax and let an experienced boatman take the helm. And to cut expenses, you can join a group for one or more of the "adventure sails" on offer. "Adventure" can translate, among other things, into sailing to Great Barrier Island (east of Auckland) and north to Kawau Island; a 5-day jet-boat journey on the Wanganui River, or even a tranquil self-drive houseboat on Lake Rotorangi near Wanganui deep into native bush.

Costs will, of course, depend on just what type of boat charter you choose and when you plan to sail. The most popular—and most expensive—season runs from November to February, and you should book several months in advance if that is your preference. Prices drop considerably from mid-February to October, and there is a wider choice of boats. On average, per-day costs will run from $80 to $600, depending on the size of the boat, and adventure cruises can range from $340 to $1,000 all inclusive. In most cases, all equipment is supplied with the boat, although groceries will be your own responsibility.

Rainbow Yacht Charters, Opua Wharf, Opua, Bay of Islands (tel. *0885/27-821; fax *0885/27-546), offers an extensive range of charters, and their Auckland branch (P.O. Box 8327, Symonds St., Auckland; tel. 09/308-9419; fax 09/790-457), books Hauraki Gulf cruises for six to eight people. Other reliable operators are: **Marlborough Sounds Charters Ltd.,** P.O. Box 284, Picton (tel. 057/573-7726); **Charter Link,** P.O. Box 82111, Highland Park, Auckland (tel. 09/535-8710; fax 09/537-0196); and **Naturally New Zealand Holidays,** New Zealand Central Reservations Office, Los Angeles, CA 90045 (tel. 213/388-1538, or toll free 800/351-2317 in California, 800/351-2323 elsewhere in the U.S.).

NEW ZEALAND ON FOOT Whether you're a tramper (or "freedom walker" as the Kiwis will label you) or a trekker who walks with organized groups, you'll be in your element in New Zealand. The country is cobwebbed with a network of tracks and walkways, from city walks to mountain tracks to national park walks. Take it in short doses of 1-day hikes, or opt for 2- to 6-day treks on the country's internationally famed Milford, Routeburn, Greenstone Valley Hollyford, Kepler, Abel Tasman, and Heaphy tracks for which you must book in advance, whether on your own or in a group. No worries about snakes or dangerous denizens of the wild, only an abundance of benign wildlife (deer and the like) and rivers and streams teeming with trout and other species of fish for which the country is well known. The only precaution you really need take to protect yourself in the wilderness areas is plenty of insect repellent to combat the ever-present sand fly, so vicious it attacks without so much as the warning buzz of a mosquito.

New Zealand Walkabout hiking and camping safaris in scenic national parks and wilderness areas are conducted by **Pacific Exploration Co.,** Box 3042-G, Santa Barbara, CA 93130 (tel. 805/687-7282). The **Department of Conservation,** P.O. Box 10-420, Wellington, can furnish details of walks and tracks the length and breadth of New Zealand, including Conservation campsites (with the most basic of facilities) and backcountry huts. Any New Zealand Tourism office can furnish details of walks around the country. It is also a good idea to contact them for copies of their **New Zealand Outdoor Holidays, Walk New Zealand,** and **See New Zealand** (detailing forest, national, and maritime parks) for advance reading. (See also Section 8 of Chapter 1.)

7. GETTING THERE

In this section we'll be dealing with the single largest item in any budget for New Zealand travel—the cost of getting there. While not nearly as costly as it once was, transportation across the South Pacific is the first financial hurdle in your planning. Once you arrive, you'll have a number of options as to how much or how little to spend on transport around New Zealand.

BY PLANE

You *could* go by ship, of course—one of the luxury liners that sails maybe twice a year, or a freighter making stops all across the Pacific—but for most of us, the only practical way to go is by jet plane. And although airfare cannot be called cheap, it can be called a travel bargain if you utilize the options wisely. More about that later.

The most important part of your holiday planning begins with predeparture research on airfares. There are differences in the types of fares and seasonal charges, and there are differences in airlines. Your first task should be to study these differences, decide on the one best suited to your needs, then telephone or visit a qualified travel agent or the individual airline offices. Be forearmed with a list of the specific information you need so that answers to your questions can be as direct as possible.

THE AIRLINES

All other things being equal (fares, schedules, etc.), there is much to be said for choosing any country's national airline, since flying with the locals enables you to encounter en route the people you'll be visiting. In the case of **Air New Zealand,** there was an added inducement for me—the praises sung long and loud by everyone who had ever traveled with them. Those praises, I must now admit, gave rise to my natural skepticism about the delights of almost *any* airline, a skepticism based on more than a few disappointments.

Well, that skepticism began to vanish before we even left the ground. The Air New Zealand crew introduced me from the very first to the unique brand of Kiwi friendliness that typifies their native land. Once we were airborne, the intercom crackled and the captain's welcome was surprising: "Welcome aboard, ladies and gentlemen, girls and boys. We're going to do everything we can to see that you have a good flight. In the meantime, get comfortable, look around, and maybe introduce yourself to that fellow or girl sitting next to you—who knows, you may make a friend for life." Friendlier than that, it's hard to get.

From a pampered standpoint, I love the food, which features New Zealand specialties such as lamb with a genuine "home-cooked" flavor, fresh vegetables, hot rolls, a great dessert, cheese, and fruit. Breakfasts were every bit as good, and when I commented on the fresh, sweet taste of both milk and butter, my host informed me that Air New Zealand flies these supplies to departure points so that only good, native dairy products are served on all planes. Now, that's attention to detail!

The combination of all these factors undoubtedly accounts for Air New Zealand topping international airline passenger polls year after year. Those who sing its praises know whereof they sing—and, as I said, it's a great way to begin to experience New Zealand before you reach New Zealand!

Incidentally, if you're curious about the symbol that adorns the tail of every Air New Zealand plane, it's called the koru, and it's an ancient Maori motif that was first seen on the prows of those mighty canoes that navigated the Pacific many centuries ago.

All direct flights to New Zealand from the United States depart from Los Angeles or Honolulu, with Canadian service departing Toronto and Vancouver. All fly to Auckland International Airport (flights between Australia and New Zealand also fly into Wellington). Air New Zealand is the only airline flying from North America directly to Christchurch in the South Island. Principal airlines offering service are:

- Air New Zealand (tel. toll free 800/262-1234)
- American (tel. toll free 800/433-7300)
- British Airways (tel. toll free 800/247-9297)
- Continental (tel. toll free 800/231-0856)
- Canadian Airlines (tel. toll free 800/426-7000)
- Qantas (tel. toll free 800/227-4500)
- UTA French Airlines (tel. 800/282-4484)

AIRLINE FARES

Set out below are the various types of fares available and their costs as this book is written. Remember, however, that these figures are far from cast in stone—nor are the fare types, for that matter. Fares can change in a matter of days as airlines rush to introduce new and more competitive fare structures. Use these as a guide, then shop around carefully.

Airport Departure Tax On *all* fares, there is a departure tax of NZ$16 ($9.15) at Auckland and Christchurch airports, and NZ$20 ($11.45) at Wellington.

Seasonal Savings When you travel can have real impact on your airline costs. The basic season runs from May through August; shoulder season includes March and April and September through November; peak season is December through February.

Best-For-The-Budget Fares

Well, as I said at the beginning, getting to New Zealand can hardly be called cheap. However, if you choose one of the fare classifications that permits en-route stopovers, you will be purchasing transportation to as many as four destinations for the same fare you would pay just to get to New Zealand—four travel experiences for the price of one, with the option of adding still others for less than $100 for each additional airfare. And a little beforehand research will reveal further savings in package deals that include reduced land costs. So instead of just a New Zealand vacation, you could include stopovers in Australia, Fiji, and Hawaii before returning home.

All fares listed below have reductions for children.

Promotional Fares Every airline comes up each year with special bargain fares for limited time periods. Savings can be considerable, although many times there are restrictions you must meet to qualify for the fare. Before you book, be sure to check for any on offer when you plan to travel.

Super APEX Restrictions on this category include a 21-day advance-purchase requirement, cancellation and/or changes penalty, and children's fares of 67% (infants, 10%). Minimum stay 10 days; maximum stay 1 month; two stopovers permitted. Round-trip fare in 1992 was $1,150 basic; $1,325 shoulder; $1,576 peak.

Special APEX Must be booked and paid 21 days in advance, cancellation and changes penalties; two stopovers permitted, one of which must be Honolulu;

minimum stay 7 days, maximum 2 months. Round-trip fares in 1992 were $1,300 basic; $1,550 shoulder; $1,800 peak.

APEX Fare   Advance booking and payment 14 days before departure; cancellation and changes penalties; three stopovers permitted; minimum stay 5 days; maximum stay 3 months. Fares in 1992 were $1,500 basic; $1,750 shoulder; $2,010 peak.

Excursion   No advance purchase required; small charge for changes and limited refund for cancellation; four stopovers permitted; minimum stay 5 days, maximum stay 1 year.

Regular Fares

We budget travelers should probably disregard this section entirely—except, of course, for comparison to the savings realized by booking one of the special fares.

First Class   This is the costliest way to travel, of course, but the fare carries with it many extras, such as no advance-purchase requirement, virtually unlimited stopovers en route, no penalty for changes or cancellations, a maximum stay of 1 year, and many in-flight comfort and service perks. In 1992 the round-trip fare was $7,522.

Business Class   Called Pacific Class on Air New Zealand flights, this classification differs from first class chiefly in in-flight comfort and service (seats are not as wide, menu choices not as varied). Other conditions are the same as for first class. Round-trip fare in 1992 was $4,860.

Economy Class   Regular economy class is the next rung down on the comfort and service ladder, but includes the same no advance purchase, stopovers en route, and other provisions as the two classes above. Round-trip fare in 1992 was $3,600.

A TRAVEL FANTASY: AROUND THE WORLD

Well, why not! After all, you'll have come virtually halfway around the world by the time you travel from North America to New Zealand. Instead of backtracking across the Pacific, this is the perfect time to circle the globe. I must admit this fantasy has nagged at me on each trip to New Zealand, and while I've not yet managed the free time, it's definitely in my future. Air New Zealand makes this dream trip available on an individual basis (interlining with other airlines), with some restrictions, for around $3,500. Other carriers such as TWA and British Airways also give flight to around-the-world fantasies. It's certainly worth thinking about.

TRAVEL TIPS

No matter which airline you choose, if you fly direct, it's going to be a long 13-hour flight during which you cross the international date line and lose one whole calendar day (which you gain, of course, on the return trip), go through four time zones, and turn the seasons upside down. There's no way your body is not going to suffer the pangs of jet lag!

There are as many ways to minimize that malady of long-distance travel as there are long-distance travelers, but here are two strategies that work for me: First, I make it a point to get up from my seat at least once an hour when not sleeping and walk around the plane to keep my legs and feet from swelling, and I try very hard to stick to nonalcoholic beverages (very hard to do when faced with those New Zealand wines!); and second, I plan a stopover of at least 24 hours (48 hours or more when I can manage it) en route both ways—gradually, I'm getting to know those South Pacific islands, and my body gets to make the time adjustment in easy stages. You, of course, no doubt have your own, time-tested jet-lag remedies. If they really work, drop me a line.

FROMMER'S SMART TRAVELER: AIRFARES

1. Shop all airlines that fly to your destination.
2. Always ask for the *lowest* fare, not just discounts.
3. Keep calling the airline—availability of cheap seats changes daily, and airlines would rather sell a discounted seat than fly with that seat empty. As departure date approaches, additional low-cost seats sometimes open up.
4. Ask about air/land packages—hotels and rental cars are often cheaper when booked in conjunction with airfares.
5. Look for special, limited-time promotions offered by major carriers that may fall within your travel period.

READERS RECOMMEND

"I followed the 'Overcoming Jet Lag' program by Ehert and Scanlon that combines diet and avoidance of caffeine, depending on direction of travel and time zones crossed. While I was tired, I had no real jet lag going or coming"—E. Angeletti, Greenville, S.C.

PACKAGE TOURS

There are several excellent package plans on the market that offer good value to the budget traveler. In addition to airfare, they include ground transportation, lodging, and some sightseeing discounts. New Zealand Tourism publishes an excellent booklet, **New Zealand Best Value Book,** that highlights well-priced vacations and travel services. **Air New Zealand,** for example, often offers a hotel accommodation package for a mere pittance above its promotional fares. That's hard to beat, as are other money-saving packages including "Hotpac" and "Lodgepass" accommodation vouchers in good-quality motels and lodges at reduced rates. There's a good range of fly/drive, farm- and home-stay, and ski packages—for details contact Air New Zealand (tel. 213/615-1111, or toll free 800/262-1234) or your travel agent.

For those in the 18-to-35 age bracket, **Contiki Holidays** has offered great South Pacific holidays for more than a quarter century. While travel is with a group, these trips could hardly be called "group tours"—schedules are such that ample freewheeling time is allowed, and for virtually every planned activity there is at least one option. Transportation and accommodations are top-notch (Contiki is presently building its own accommodations in many New Zealand locations), and activities include such unusual events as beachside barbecues, white-water rafting, and ballooning. In short, these are fun tours and appeal to those lively souls who are young at heart as well as in years. Best of all, they offer one of the best value-for-dollar bargains in the business. On some tours, there's a free stopover in one of several South Pacific islands. For details of their current offerings, contact your travel agent or Contiki Holidays, 1432 E. Katella Ave., Anaheim, CA 92805 (tel. toll free 800/626-0611, 800/624-0611 in California).

Jetset Tours has been getting people around Australia since the early 1960s and now covers New Zealand and most of the South Pacific as well. There are well-organized group tours, fly/drive tours, and a 300-page Australia/New Zealand "Silver Book" offering hundreds of hotels, sightseeing activities, and tours. The booking desk can arrange flights on Air New Zealand. Details may be obtained through travel agents or direct from Jetset Tours, 8383 Wilshire Blvd., Suite 450, Beverly Hills, CA 90211 (tel. toll free 800/453-8738).

Two other long-established operators in the South Pacific who have built solid reputations for reliability and good prices are Ted Cook's **Islands in the Sun,** P.O.

Box 1398, Newport Beach, CA 92663 (tel. 714/645-8300, or toll free 800/854-3413 in the U.S. and Canada); and **Globus-Gateway,** 95-25 Queens Blvd., Rego Park, NY 11374 (tel. 718/268-1700, or toll free 800/221-0090 in the eastern U.S.), and 150 S. Los Robles Ave., Suite 860, Pasadena, CA 91101 (tel. 818/449-0919, or toll free 800/556-5454 in the western U.S. outside California). Both are also represented by travel agents.

8. GETTING AROUND

When it comes to getting around New Zealand, you can pick and choose, mix and match, modes of transport. As I said earlier in this book, things *work* in this country. Bus and rail transportation are reliable, car-rental firms are dependable, and airlines furnishing domestic service cover longer stretches with ease. Driving, of course, affords the most flexibility, as you are tied to no one's schedule except your own. However, public transportation is an economical, pleasant way to go, and in one form or another will reach any destination within the country.

BY AIR

Air New Zealand (Head Office, Private Bag, Auckland; tel. *09/797-515), **Mount Cook Line** (Head Office, P.O. Box 4644, Christchurch; tel. *03/482-099), and **Ansett New Zealand** (Head Office, P.O. Box 4168, Auckland; tel. 09/309-6235) fly internal routes in New Zealand. All have offices in major cities as well as those listed above. Schedules are frequent and convenient, and equipment is modern and comfortable on all three.

DISCOUNT FARES

For those whose time is limited (or those who simply want to vary their modes of travel), Air New Zealand's **Explore New Zealand** program (tel. 800/262-1234) is a godsend. For NZ$399 ($217) you purchase 3 coupons good for any 3 of their 200 daily flights; 6 coupons cost NZ$756 ($414); children's fares (ages 4 to 14) are NZ$267 ($146) for 3 coupons and NZ$507 ($277) for 6 coupons. The coupons (which are good for 60 days from the date of your first flight) must be purchased *before you reach New Zealand* and must be bought in conjunction with international travel. You don't have to book individual flights, however, until you actually reach New Zealand, and unused coupons may be turned in for a refund before you leave New Zealand.

Mount Cook Line links New Zealand's major tourist areas to each other and to Auckland and Christchurch. Schedules are designed to connect with Air New Zealand's domestic service, as well as international flights.

Mount Cook also provides some of the most spectacular flightseeing tours in the world. If you splurge (as you most certainly should) on a glacier flight, you'll be flying Mount Cook Line. And if you're on one of those short-stay itineraries, it's Mount Cook Line that can get you around to the sightseeing points that top your list. In that case, you should definitely consider the **Kiwi Air Pass,** which must be purchased before you arrive in New Zealand. For NZ$799 ($457) you can take a circle trip around New Zealand, with stops at any point. Travel must be within 30 consecutive days, and must be in one direction—no backtracking. The pass is also valid on Mount Cook Line's coach service if it's substituted for air travel. You can purchase it through qualified travel agents in the U.S. or by calling toll free 800/468-2665 (in the Los Angeles area, 213/649-6185).

Ansett New Zealand is an offshoot of an Australian airline, now operating throughout New Zealand. They offer several **Good Buy Special Fares** and **See New Zealand** fares with discounts up to 30%. They are available at their offices or through travel agents within New Zealand.

BY BUS & TRAIN

Most rail and bus services are provided by **InterCity,** which operates all railways, most provincial buses, some suburban buses, ferry service between the North and South Islands, and many of the better sightseeing tours. For the budget traveler, they offer what is probably the least expensive way of getting around the country.

A personal word here: As a veteran of several seven-week-long jaunts around New Zealand by train and bus, I can tell you that—aside from a few early-morning departures, which are a bit hard on my late-rising psyche—this method of travel has much to offer.

Consider: You travel with New Zealanders who are not touring, but simply going about their own business—a chance to rub elbows in the most elementary way.
Consider: On many of the buses (particularly in the South Island), drivers give an excellent commentary on the countryside—not for tourists, mind you, but for Kiwis who may travel the route frequently but who seem as interested as those of us who are traveling through for the first time.
Consider: Trains run along coastlines and mountain gorges with fantastic views, which are completely hidden from highways that run farther inland or on higher ground.
Consider: When you leave the driving to someone else, there's no need to worry about driving on the left, keeping one eye glued to the map, or looking for road signs rather than all those scenic splendors. I admit it—I'm positively addicted to InterCity.

Discounts   Aside from all the above, a very good reason to travel this way is the money-saving **Travelpass.** You get unlimited travel by rail, coach, and ferry for 8 days of travel in a 14-day period for NZ$344 ($197), 15 days of travel in a 22-day period for NZ$447 ($255), or 22 days within a 31-day period for NZ$551 ($315). Children 4 to 15 travel for half price; under-4s, free. The pass may be purchased through travel agents in the United States or in New Zealand at an InterCity travel center, NZ Tourism office, or travel agency. Pass holders also receive discounts on designated motels, hotels, and tours.

Mount Cook Line offers the **Kiwi Coach Pass,** which is good for coach service on Mount Cook Landline and some routes of InterCity, and Newmans. The cost for 7 days (within an 11-day period) is NZ$285 ($163); for 10 days (within 16 days), NZ$329 ($188); for 15 days (within 23 days) NZ$375 ($214); for 25 days (within 35 days) NZ$570 ($326); 35 days (within 45 days) NZ$640 ($367). It may be purchased in the U.S. from travel agents or NZ Tourism offices; you'll be given a certificate that you trade in for the pass when you reach New Zealand.

You should know that all bus and rail journeys must be *booked in advance*—this is particularly important during peak travel periods. Bookings may be made at any InterCity station or through NZ Tourism offices as much as 6 months in advance. I must add that I've never once seen anyone just show up without a booking and be *refused* a seat, but I wouldn't recommend chancing that. Sometimes there is only one bus a day.

To preplan your entire trip before leaving home, write to the Passenger Manager, InterCity, Private Bag, Wellington, and tell them where you'd like to go and your time limit—they'll respond with an itinerary planned to your requirements and provide you with a complete set of timetables covering rail, bus, and ferry services.

BUSES

The **InterCity** service network is extensive, and there are good connections with **Newmans** or **Mount Cook Landline** to those few points they don't reach. For example, if you cross Cook Strait from Wellington to Picton en route to the South Island's west coast, you'll travel by Newmans as far as Greymouth. Your vouchers or Travelpass will not apply on those portions of your travel.

All buses are comfortable; some are carpeted and most have individual reading lights. Frequent stops for tea or refreshments are scheduled, and as I mentioned above, on many runs you'll hear an interesting, informative narrative about the country through which you're traveling. In rural areas, buses often pull up in front of T-bars alongside the road and drivers lean out to collect mail sacks to be dropped off at the next post office. All sorts of other freight travels along with you as well—a close-up look at Kiwi life outside the cities!

In addition to regularly scheduled services, New Zealand bus lines run excellent **sightseeing and excursion day-trips.** Details are in the appropriate chapters.

TRAINS

All trains in the country are operated by **InterCity,** and all are quite comfortable, although the equipment can be anything from older suburban cars to very good overnight sleepers to sleek, modern rail cruisers. The major rail services and fares are:

Auckland-Wellington: The Northerner, an overnight nonsleeper, has twinette sleeper cars and normal seated carriages, plus a licensed buffet car where drinks and buffet food are served. One-way fare is NZ$74 ($42).

The day trip is via the **Silver Fern,** and there's an informative commentary as you pass through fern forests, sacred Maori burial grounds, and volcanic peaks. Free morning and afternoon tea is served by uniformed hostesses and stewards, who also provide newspapers and magazines and will take drink orders to be served at your seat. There's a lunch stop at Taihape Station. One-way fare, NZ$98 ($56).

Christchurch-Dunedin-Invercargill: Daily except Sunday, the **Southerner,** an overnight nonsleeper, makes this run, one train in each direction. There's a buffet car that serves drinks and buffet food, and drinks may also be ordered from the service staff in your carriage. You're given an illustrated map of the route, which passes some quite spectacular coastal scenery as well as pastoral scenes of grazing sheep and wheat fields. One-way fare, NZ$68 ($39).

The Northerner, Silver Fern, and Southerner express trains are the showpieces of the system. They're carpeted, attractive in decor, and well heated, air-conditioned, or ventilated. Other comfortable trains include the daylight **Bay Express,** between Wellington and Napier (NZ$44, $25); the daylight **Trans-Alpine Express** between Christchurch and Greymouth (NZ$74, $42); and the **Coastal Pacific,** between Christchurch and Picton that connects with the Picton-Wellington ferry (NZ$48, U.S. $27). Although there are no service staff or buffet cars on these trains, refreshment stops are made en route.

BY CAR

New Zealand is a driver's paradise. You can wander at will over roads that (outside the larger cities) carry light traffic. Better yet, you can stop at will to take a closer look at an inviting seascape or lush fern forest. When lunchtime arrives, you can picnic at whichever scenic spot takes your fancy. Bus and train rider that I am, I usually plan to drive at least one segment of the trip just for the joy of all that freedom. And if you can possibly afford it, I highly recommend the experience. One caution, however: New Zealand distances can be deceiving—check the mileage charts and driving times shown on most maps. Also, pick up a copy of *The New Zealand Motoring Book* from NZ Tourism—it's full of useful information.

New Zealand roads are exceptionally well maintained, except for a few mountainous stretches in the South Island, where you sometimes wonder how they managed to carve out a road in the first place. And speaking of mountains, let me say—as one who has driven for donkey's years in all sorts of terrain—that if you're not accustomed to mountain driving, you should consider using public transportation from Hokitika to the glaciers, Queenstown, Te Anau, and Milford Sound, then resuming your journey by car from Te Anau. I've been assured by my Kiwi friends in this area that such a plan is entirely unnecessary and that driving is not that difficult in this part of the South Island. All I can say is that I feel much more secure when someone else is navigating along those mountain roads.

Rentals Nearly all New Zealand car-rental firms offer unlimited-mileage rates, a decided plus for budgeteers. One of the best bargains I've been able to unearth is through **Maui Econocar Rentals** (tel. toll free 800/351-2323 in the U.S., 800/351-2317 in California), which provides late-model cars at low daily rates ranging from NZ$55 to NZ$105 ($31 to $60), plus GST, depending on the size car you rent (capacity ranges from 2- to 10-passenger vehicles). That's with unlimited mileage—insurance is about NZ$15 ($9) per day. With offices in Auckland and Christchurch, they don't even charge for pickup in one island and dropoff in the other. They also have terrific rates for caravans (more about that later). You can book through NZ Tourism offices in North America, or contact them directly at: Maui Econocar Rentals, Richard Pearse Drive, Mangere, Auckland (tel. 09/275-3013; fax 09/275-9690); or 430-544 Memorial Ave., Christchurch (tel. 03/358-4159 or *0800/651-080), both open daily from 8:30am to 5pm. (*Note:* One reader has complained that the company limits the last day's rental to 5pm that day for the return of the car, rather than a full 24 hours; check before you sign the contract.)

Avis, Hertz, Budget (prebook through U.S. offices), and **Letz** (prebook and prepay through Letz Rent a Car, Suite 105, 1448 15th St., Santa Monica, CA 90404; tel. 213/393-8262, or toll free 800/551-2012 in California), have branches in all major cities and airports, with daily costs averaging from about NZ$100 ($57) for economy models up to NZ$150 ($86) for larger models. All offer reductions for longer rental periods.

Driving Rules and Maps You must be at least 21 to rent a car in New Zealand, and must possess a current driver's license that you have held for at least 1 year from the United States, Australia, Canada, the United Kingdom, and a few other countries, or an International Driving Permit. You drive on the left and must—by law—buckle that seatbelt when the car is moving. Speed limit on the open road is 60 m.p.h. (100 kmph), and in congested areas, towns and cities, 30 m.p.h. (50 kmph). Drive with extreme caution when an area is signposted "LSZ" (Limited Speed Zone). Signposting, incidentally, is very good all through the country—there's little chance of losing your way.

You'll be given a set of maps when you pick up your rental car, and if you're a member of the Automobile Association in the States, Australia, Britain, or some European countries, you'll have reciprocal privileges with the New Zealand AA, which includes their very good maps, plus "strip maps" of your itinerary and comprehensive guidebooks of accommodations (some of which give discounts to AA members). You can contact the **New Zealand Automobile Association,** 99 Albert St., Auckland; 343 Lambton Quay, Wellington; 210 Hereford St., Christchurch. **Wises Mapping,** 368 Dominion Rd., Mt. Eden, Auckland (tel. *09/685-095), produces one of the best maps of New Zealand, available from newsagents and bookshops.

BY TAXI

Taxi ranks are located at all terminals and on major shopping streets, and you may not hail one on the street within a quarter mile of a rank. They're on call 24 hours a day, and telephone numbers are in local directories, but there's an additional charge if you phone for one. Rates vary from place to place, but all city taxis are metered (in smaller localities, there's often a local driver who will quote a flat fee). Drivers don't expect a tip just to transport you, but if they handle a lot of luggage or perform any other special service, it's very much in order.

READERS RECOMMEND

Renny Rent a Car, 113 Tuam St., Christchurch. Tel. *03/666-790. "The cheapest rental-car agency we found was a small agency in Christchurch called Renny Rent a Car. They were very nice people, as well, and we were able to see the South Island in one of their cars for a reasonable price."—L. Breihan, Austin, Texas [Author's note: This company only operates in Christchurch, but offers a 10% discount to readers who show this book when reserving.]

Southern Cross Car Rental 105-107 Victoria St., Christchurch. Tel. *03/794-547. "This firm gave us the best deal by far, and superior service. They were extremely helpful and courteous and supply so many extras at a truly budget price."—M. L. Thie, Coupeville, Wash. [Author's note: Pickups and drop-offs may be made in Picton, Christchurch, Dunedin, Queenstown, Wellington, and Auckland.]

BY RV   If you want to take advantage of New Zealand's budget motor camps—or if you're simply a caravaner at heart—**Maui Rentals** (tel. toll free 800/351-2323 in the U.S., 800/351-2317 in California), **Mount Cook Line** (tel. toll free 800/262-0248 in the U.S., 800/468-2665 in California, 800/999-9306 in Canada), and **Newmans** (tel. 09/302-1582 in Auckland) offer motor homes at seasonal prices that range from NZ$80 to NZ$135 ($46 to $77) for two berths; NZ$107 to NZ$189 ($61 to $108) for four berths; and NZ$120 to NZ$205 ($69 to $117). Advance booking through New Zealand Tourism offices or telephone numbers in North America listed above. In New Zealand, caravans may be booked at any local office of these firms.

BY INTER-ISLAND FERRY   Even if you fly the better part of your trip, try to plan a crossing of Cook Strait on the Wellington-Picton ferry in at least one direction. You'll get a look at both islands from the water, as well as the near-mystical Marlborough Sound, just as those early Maoris and Europeans did. The crossing is one of New Zealand's very best travel experiences. *If you plan to bring a car by ferry, you need a confirmed reservation.* Buy your ticket ahead to avoid a potential delay of a day or more. The rate for taking the car or caravan with you in 1992 was NZ$106 to NZ$140 ($61 to $80), depending on size. For more information, check the details in Section 11, Chapter 7.

BY HITCHHIKING   Hitchhiking is relatively safe in New Zealand, and many friendly Kiwis are quick to give you a lift. However, general safety rules apply, and you should avoid hitching alone.

9. SUGGESTED ITINERARIES

Deciding how long to stay can be a problem, for New Zealand has so much to see and do you'll have a hard time fitting in everything. But it is possible to plan itineraries that will hit the high spots. Travel counselors at NZ Tourism offices are most helpful in this respect. Here are a few sample itineraries as well. You'll note that you'll have to cover some of the longer stretches by flying. Those flights, however, will be on rather small, low-flying planes, with breathtaking views of the countryside below and awesome mountain peaks that ring the landscape.

All these itineraries are possible, but I strongly recommend that, if there's any way you can manage it, you plan a minimum of 3 weeks to see both islands at something like a leisurely pace. Some of New Zealand's beauty spots simply invite (almost demand) lingering, and there are several you will have to omit on a shorter visit. A month would be even better. Failing that, I personally would stick to one island per visit for the shorter time periods and take in such memorable extras as the Bay of Islands and the Coromandel Peninsula on the North Island and the Banks Peninsula and Stewart Island in the south. You will have come a long way to see New Zealand, and it would be a shame to get around at too fast a trot.

CITY HIGHLIGHTS On the North Island, **Auckland, Rotorua,** and **Wellington** are absolute "must sees," and if it is in any way possible, include **Coromandel Peninsula, Bay of Islands, Napier,** and **Whanganui.**
Any South Island itinerary should include **Christchurch (and nearby Mount Cook), Dunedin, Queenstown (with a trip to Milford Sound),** and **Nelson.** With any extra time, get down to **Stewart Island** and over on the West Coast to **Hokitika.**

IF YOU HAVE 1 WEEK

Touring the North Island Only

Day 1: Arrive Auckland in early morning; sightseeing in afternoon.
Day 2: Drive from Auckland (or take tour bus, which allows time for sightseeing) to Waitomo, tour caves and glowworm grotto, then on through wooded hills and pastureland dotted with sheep and cattle to Rotorua (221 miles).
Day 3: Full day of sightseeing; Maori concert or hangi in evening.
Day 4: Early-morning flight to Bay of Islands; launch cruise in afternoon.
Day 5: Entire day of sightseeing, or take the day-long bus excursion to Cape Reinga and the Ninety-Mile Beach.
Day 6: Drive from Bay of Islands to Auckland (234 miles, about 7½ hours), with sightseeing stops at Waipoua Kauri Forest, Dargaville.
Day 7: Sightseeing most of day; early-evening departure for overseas destination.

Touring the South Island Only

Day 1: Arrive Auckland early morning; fly to Christchurch; sightseeing in afternoon.
Day 2: Drive along the East Coast from Christchurch to Dunedin (225 miles, about 5½ hours), across part of the Canterbury Plains and through the seaside resort of Timaru and the "White Stone City" of Oamaru.
Day 3: Entire day sightseeing in Dunedin, with drive or tour-bus excursion to Otago Peninsula to see Larnach Castle, Penguin Place, and the royal albatross colony (get your visitor's permit in Dunedin).
Day 4: Early start for drive from Dunedin to Queenstown (176 miles, about 5 hours), through pleasant farmland; sightseeing in late afternoon.
Day 5: Day-long excursion to Milford Sound (bus in, fly out), including launch cruise to Tasman Sea. (If you're pressed for time, fly in and out; the cruise is included in the price.)
Day 6: Allow about 10 hours for the drive from Queenstown to Christchurch (302 miles), which passes through beautiful Kawarau Gorge, then north past breathtaking views of Mount Cook at Lake Pukaki and on across the Canterbury Plains. (*Note:* An option is an early-morning flight to Mount Cook, with flightseeing in the afternoon, flying on to Christchurch and Auckland on Day 7.)
Day 7: Sightseeing in the morning; midafternoon flight to Auckland, arriving in time for evening overseas departure.

IF YOU HAVE 10 DAYS

Day 1: Arrive in Auckland in early morning; sightseeing in afternoon.

Day 2: Drive or take tour bus to Rotorua via Waitomo caves and glowworm grotto.

Day 3: Full day of sightseeing in Rotorua; Maori concert or hangi in evening.

Day 4: Early-morning flight from Rotorua to Christchurch, sightseeing in afternoon.

Day 5: Early-morning flight to Mount Cook; flightseeing over glaciers, icefields, and mountains in afternoon.

Day 6: Early-morning flight to Queenstown; sightseeing in afternoon.

Day 7: Day-long trip to Milford Sound (by tour bus and/or plane) for launch cruise to Tasman Sea.

Day 8: Early-afternoon flight to Dunedin; sightseeing in late afternoon.

Day 9: Drive or take tour-bus excursion to Otago Peninsula to see Larnach Castle, Penguin Place, and the royal albatross colony.

Day 10: Sightseeing in morning; early-afternoon flight to Auckland (with plane change in Christchurch), arriving in time for evening overseas departure.

IF YOU HAVE 2 WEEKS

Day 1: Arrive Auckland early morning; fly to Christchurch; spend afternoon sightseeing.

Day 2: Early-morning flight over Canterbury Plains to Mount Cook, in the heart of the Southern Alps; flightseeing in afternoon.

Day 3: Early-morning flight to Queenstown; sightseeing in afternoon.

Day 4: Day-long tour-bus excursion to Milford Sound for launch cruise to Tasman Sea.

Day 5: Drive from Queenstown to Dunedin (176 miles, about 5 hours), through pleasant farming country.

Day 6: Drive or take tour-bus excursion to Otago Peninsula to visit Larnach Castle, Penguin Place, and the royal albatross colony.

Day 7: Scenic early-morning flight from Dunedin to Wellington, following the east coastline and crossing Cook Strait; sightseeing in afternoon.

Day 8: Sightseeing in Wellington.

Day 9: Drive or take InterCity coach from Wellington to Napier (203 miles) through rugged—and scenic—Manawatu Gorge.

Day 10: Sightseeing in the Hawke Bay area around Napier; then drive to Taupo (96 miles) and on to Rotorua (55 miles).

Day 11: Full day of sightseeing in Rotorua; Maori concert or hangi in evening.

Day 12: Drive or take tour bus to Waitomo to tour caves and glowworm grotto; then on to Auckland (221 miles).

Day 13: Full day of sightseeing in Auckland.

Day 14: Depart Auckland for overseas destination.

IF YOU HAVE 3 WEEKS

Day 1: Arrive Auckland early morning; fly to Christchurch; spend afternoon sightseeing.

Day 2: Early-morning flight over Canterbury Plains to Mount Cook, in the heart of the Southern Alps; flightseeing in afternoon, returning to Christchurch.

Day 3–7: Train to Picton, pick up car and drive to Nelson and down the West Coast to Greymouth and Hokitika; drive to Fox and Franz Josef Glaciers; drive to Wanaka and Queenstown.

Day 8: Sightseeing and lake cruise.

Day 9: Day-long tour-bus excursion to Milford Sound for launch cruise to Tasman Sea.

Day 10: Drive from Queenstown to Dunedin (176 miles, about 5 hours), through pleasant farming country.

Day 11: Drive or take tour-bus excursion to Otago Peninsula to visit Larnach Castle, Penguin Place, and the royal albatross colony.

Day 12: Scenic early-morning flight from Dunedin to Wellington, following the east coastline and crossing Cook Strait; sightseeing in afternoon.

Day 13: Sightseeing in Wellington.

Day 14: Drive or take InterCity coach from Wellington to Napier (203 miles) through rugged—and scenic—Manawatu Gorge.

Day 15: Sightseeing in the Hawke Bay area around Napier; then drive to Taupo (96 miles) and on to Rotorua (55 miles).

Day 16: Full-day sightseeing in Rotorua; Maori concert or hangi in evening.

Days 17 and 18: Drive or take tour bus to Waitomo to tour caves and glowworm grotto; over night in Waitomo; then on to Auckland (221 miles).

Day 19: Full day of sightseeing in Auckland.

Day 20: Drive to Thames, on Coromandel Peninsula.

Day 21: Depart Auckland for overseas destination.

IF YOU HAVE A MONTH

To the 3-week itinerary above, add 2 days to Day 20, for a full exploration of the Coromandel Peninsula; another 4 days, the first to drive to Bay of Islands, with 1 full day of sightseeing and a second for cruising the bay, and another for the return drive to Auckland.

10. ENJOYING NEW ZEALAND ON A BUDGET

You have undoubtedly bought *New Zealand on $45 a Day* with finances uppermost in your mind. Well, they have been my foremost consideration too, but far more than currency has played a part in the preparation of this book. What you'll find in its pages is a guide to the total New Zealand travel experience—a sort of love letter to that country's inordinate sense of decency and order, its gorgeous landscape, and its endearing people. Having made the decision to visit Kiwiland, you're in for one of the travel treats of your life, dear reader—enjoy every minute!

THE $45-A-DAY BUDGET

In a world of fast disappearing budget-travel destinations, New Zealand continues to offer exceptional value. Still, the scoffers will say that New Zealand on $45 a Day is a fantasy. Not so. Consider the following.

First of all, as with all Frommer budget guides, the cover price quoted is meant to take care of only your basic daily travel expenses: That is, a roof over your head and three square meals a day. Transportation, entertainment, sightseeing, shopping, and any other expenses are in addition to that $45 a day. Of these, your getting-there transportation will be the single largest expense item, and I have included some money-saving tips to help you trim that as much as possible. This book will, however, point out best buys in each of these categories to help you hold down all costs.

As to specifics, that $45 U.S. translates into NZ$79 at the exchange rate used throughout this edition of NZ$1.75 for $1 U.S.! Thus, in many cases what would be "moderate" in New Zealand currency becomes "budget" in U.S. dollars. Throughout this guide, I'll give you both New Zealand prices and their U.S. dollar equivalents so you can make your own comparisons.

Two other factors must also be taken into consideration: The first is a 12.5% Goods and Services Tax (GST) that applies across the board to both accommodations and meals; and the second is a fluctuating economy with a very high current inflation rate. While the GST is likely to be around for the foreseeable future, stringent steps are being taken by the current government to reduce the inflation rate quickly, which should at the very least halt the upward climb of prices and quite possibly bring about some reduction. With political and economic conditions so uncertain, it is impossible to predict the exact course of prices over the life of this book, but what can be stated with some degree of certainty is that value for dollar will continue to be high for the traveler to New Zealand.

Let's look at those basic expenses in detail. You'll find good accommodations listed that average about NZ$55 ($31) single, NZ$65 ($37) double ($18.50 per person). Since each accommodation may elect to include or exclude GST in its rates, you'll need to take particular notice of this when reading those listed in this book and make the necessary 12.5% adjustment. On a per-person basis, unfortunately it is as true in New Zealand as it is in other parts of the globe that two people traveling together will travel more cheaply than those on their own.

Sticking with budget meals—breakfasts averaging NZ$6 ($3.45), lunch NZ$10 ($5.75), and dinner NZ$20 ($11.45)—a couple will come in well under the U.S. $45-per-person figure. But one of the joys (in terms of the pocketbook) of traveling in New Zealand is that almost all the "best-buy" accommodations come in the form of motel flats with complete kitchens, which means you can save as much or as little as you choose on the cost of meals. The bed-and-breakfast accommodations that are the mainstay of budget travelers in Europe have been relatively scarce in New Zealand in past years but are now beginning to appear in more and more locales. You'll find many recommended in these pages, and a stay in any one will, of course, eliminate the breakfast cost from that $45 budget.

SAVING MONEY ON ACCOMMODATIONS

New Zealand presents a vast supermarket of accommodation choices even in our budget range. The sheer number and variety of places to lay your weary head will add spice to your trip, and although there is no national system for inspection or grading, it is rare to come across a single one that isn't spotlessly clean, an accomplishment I rarely find in my travels around other countries.

We'll examine the variety in detail below, but first, there are some elements they all share. Check-in time is usually around 2pm; checkout, 10am. There's no tipping (unless you feel especially grateful for some special service). Some hotels and motels charge an extra NZ$1 (60¢) for 1-night stays, and in some resort areas, such as the Bay of Islands and Queenstown, rates go up during peak seasons. Almost all have discount rates for children. Even the most "budget" of budget accommodations will have an electric kettle (which goes by the name of "jug" in New Zealand), tea and coffee, sugar and milk, either in your room or in a centrally located public room—at no charge (they know it's too much to ask of guests to send them out for such necessities). All have telephones either in-room or in a public room, hall, or office available to guests, except in the case of some hostels. Almost all have laundry facilities, which means electric washing machines and either a dryer or drying rooms—and there's only a small charge for their use. With the exception of some hostels and cabins, all have good winter heating, either central or individual room heaters. There's not much air conditioning, but not much need for it either.

To the above, I'd like to add one little message from my New Zealand accommodations friends: It seems that we Americans are highly valued as guests for many reasons, including the fact that they say we always leave the premises in such good order (for once, we're the "pretty Americans"). Our one failing has to do with that "jug," and I think it's because we're so accustomed to appliances being turned on and off by thermostatic controls. Well, where the jugs are concerned, in most cases it's up to you to unplug it or flip the control switch on the wall socket when the water comes to a boil; otherwise, it keeps boiling away, the jug's heating element burns out, and our "highly valued" status becomes a little less so. So keep an eye on it and be sure it's turned off when you've made your tea or coffee.

I know I've told you this before, but it bears repeating: During peak travel months, you must book ahead. "Peak" means mid-December through January, Easter, and the two (2-week) school holidays in May and August. New Zealanders are on the road in droves during those periods—most spend their holidays within their own country, and most are as budget-conscious as we are. They do their booking months in advance, and so should you to avoid disappointment. When you have selected the accommodations you prefer, simply write as early as possible enclosing a money order or bank draft to cover the first night's lodging and an International Reply Coupon for confirmation to be mailed back to you. If you should have to cancel and you do it within a reasonable time, you'll usually receive a prompt refund, although occasionally there will be a small service charge.

The accommodations listed in this book, I rather immodestly believe, are a pretty select group, but for a complete listing of all accommodations available around the country, the NZ Tourism Travel Department publishes an excellent *Where to Stay* guide, which you can obtain from all their offices in North America. It lists hotel, motel, bed-and-breakfast, and farm accommodations, as well as private-home-host organizations. All price ranges are included. Also, the **Automobile Association** covers the subject very comprehensively in a series of accommodation guidebooks: hotels and motels in the North Island, motor camps and campgrounds in the North Island, and a "South Island Handbook." If you're an AAA member at home, you'll have reciprocal privileges in New Zealand and will have no difficulty picking up all three guides. Or contact them in advance at P.O. Box 5, Auckland.

See also "Alternative/Adventure Travel" earlier in this chapter for information on farm and home stays.

Booking Services The more than 40 **Visitor Information offices** throughout the country operate a "Book-a-Bed-Ahead" system of accommodation bookings. You'll find addresses in appropriate chapters of this book. In addition, many of the motel chains such as Best Western (see below) will book ahead to their member properties at little or no charge.

YOUTH HOSTELS

You'll be way below our $45-a-day cost if you utilize New Zealand's excellent network of hostels. And aside from saving all that money, you'll be mingling with hostelers from all over the world as well as a fair few friendly natives. It's a great way to travel, and you'll find Kiwi hostels—both private and members of the Youth Hostels Association—way above average in quality.

There are more than 52 **YHA hostels** throughout New Zealand, many in choice scenic locations—you'll be paying hostel rates for a beachfront, lakefront, or mountainside room just down the way from a luxury hotel whose guests are paying an arm and a leg for the same view! The hostels vary both in size and style, and their architecture ranges from comfortable old farmhouses to slick, modern edifices.

To qualify, you must be a Youth Hostel member (and, if you're age 5 or over, "youth" has no age limitations) with a valid membership card. In the United States, you can join through **American Youth Hostels, Inc.,** P.O. Box 37613, Washington, DC 20013-7613, by sending $10 if you're under 18 (youth membership), $25 if you're 18 to 54 (adult), or $15 if you're 55 or older (senior). Should you arrive in New Zealand without a membership card, you will be issued an **International Guest Card**, which costs NZ$4 ($2.30) per night, or NZ$24 ($13.75) for your entire stay. Pick up a copy of the invaluable **New Zealand YHA Handbook**, which describes each hostel in detail, with transportation, food shops, and other useful information for each location. It also sets out all hostel rules and regulations (leave things tidy, no drugs, liquor, gambling, or animals). Membership issuing agencies are known as **YHA Travel Centres,** with locations in Auckland (Customs and Gore Streets), Wellington (in Port Nicholson Hostel), and Christchurch (Gloucester and Manchester Streets). Apply by mail to **YHA National Office,** P.O. Box 436, Christchurch (tel. *03/799-970).

You'll need to bring a sleeping bag or rent linens for a nominal fee; blankets are provided. Also, if you plan to use the fully equipped kitchens, bring your own cup, plate, and cutlery, as well as a tea towel. Managers are called wardens, and most reside in the hostel itself, and those who don't live nearby—the warden is the person to whom you show your card and pay your fee. Bookings are usually held only until 7pm, so when you cross the Cook Strait by ferry in either direction, be sure it's the afternoon crossing, since the evening ferry will arrive too late for you to stay in a YHA hostel. (Private hostels may have space and be open later.) While most hostels used to be closed several hours each day, all are now open all day.

New Zealanders are great hostelers within their own country—there are some 31,000 native members—which makes advance booking every bit as important at hostels during peak months as in any other type of accommodation. In fact, you'll be well advised to book ahead in all major resort areas or large cities at any time of the year. You can do so by sending, *at least 14 days prior to your first requested booking,* a money order, bank draft, or information (card number, expiration date, and your name as it appears on the card) for American Express, Diners Club, VISA, or MasterCard to pay for your entire stay, along with an International Reply Coupon, directly to the warden of each hostel, or to the **YHA National Reservations Centre,** P.O. Box 68-149, Auckland. Bookings are usually limited to 3 consecutive nights in any one hostel, and overnight fees range from NZ$7 to NZ$16 ($4 to $9).

There are a number of benefits that come along with your YHA membership, such as travel insurance, discounts on rail and ferry transportation, sightseeing attractions and activities, and clothing. There's also a helpful Travel Section which actually offers hostel package tours. Planned with a great deal of flexibility, they're based on public transportation and the use of hostels throughout. The Travel Section issues several informative touring booklets, which outline services and tours; they are available (along with any specific information you'd like) by writing YHANZ Travel Section, P.O. Box 436, Christchurch.

National headquarters for the **Youth Hostel Association of New Zealand (YHANZ)** is in Christchurch, Corner of Gloucester and Manchester Streets (tel. *03/799-970), with hours Monday to Friday of 8:30am to 5pm.

There are also some good privately run hostels, and you will find many listed in this book. Ask NZ Tourism offices for *The Good Bed Guide* and *New Zealand Backpackers Accommodation* (which lists accommodations in the $10 to $15 range).

MOTOR CAMPS, CABINS & CAMPING

New Zealand is a camper's delight, whether you're toting a tent to pitch, backpacking and looking for a cabin at night, or hauling along a motor caravan. There are facilities to suit all needs, and they're all over the place. The nice thing is that you'll many times find the whole array available in a single motor camp!

On grounds that are sometimes quite extensive—and many times in prime mountain, lakeside, or beachfront locations—there are campsites that can cost as little as NZ$8 ($4.60) per person per night. Caravan sites with power connections run about NZ$10 ($5.70) per person per night.

Then, there are rustic cabins or huts that contain beds or bunks, pillows, a table, and chairs. Many times, linen and blankets can be rented; otherwise, you bring your own. You must also supply your own crockery and cutlery in most cases. Cabins come with two, four, or six beds, and on average the cost for a basic cabin is NZ$30 ($17.15) for two people. A "Tourist" cabin, which has hot and cold water and cooking facilities, will run about NZ$32 ($18) per night for two. Both cabins and campsite occupants have full use of centrally located shower and laundry facilties. There is also a centrally located modern kitchen, with hot- and cold-water sink units, fridge, and hotplates—a great place to meet fellow travelers. Needless to say, the "leave it tidy" doctrine applies.

Rubbing elbows with those "bare essentials" accommodations, almost all motor camps will have at least one block of tourist flats. They are rustic in decor, and you still must bring the bedding, but they have one or two separate bedrooms, cooking facilities (all have running water), and private showers. Prices run about NZ$50 ($29) for double occupancy.

In the chapters that follow, you'll find several motor camps listed, which I believe are outstanding, and for a complete directory and their free official publication, just contact the Executive Director, **Camp & Cabin Association of New Zealand,** Paraparaumu, North Island, New Zealand (tel. and fax *058/83-283).

Trampers will find basic, rustic **bunkhouses or huts** in all national parks, with water and outdoor cooking areas provided. Maps of their locations are furnished by park rangers, who also collect the small fee, or the **Department of Conservation,** P.O. Box 10-420, Wellington.

THE YS

Unlike other New Zealand accommodations, both the YWCA and YMCA hostels are booked to capacity from February through November, when students fill the available space. This can be a real boon, however, especially in city areas, if you have trouble finding a room during those peak months of December through February when students are on holiday.

Most Y rooms are, as you might expect, very basic, and in a few cases have a rather grubby aspect, while others are as light and cheerful as you could wish. Beds are narrow, floors are rugless, and showers and baths are down the hall, with no water basins in rooms. There are, however, laundry rooms, TV lounges, and the usual Y facilities. Some provide full board, and all serve breakfast. You'll find Ys in Auckland, Wanganui, Christchurch, and Dunedin (see the individual chapter listings). Each has its own rate structure, but you can expect them to be in the neighborhood of NZ$17 ($9.75) or slightly higher.

Especially for the young traveler, the Ys are a pleasant travel base, since the majority of other guests are likely to be in the same age group (although that should by no means deter those in upper-age brackets). For more information, write to the **YWCA of New Zealand,** P.O. Box 1780, Wellington.

BED & BREAKFASTS

I have always favored B&B accommodations when traveling, both because that terrific cooked breakfast will very often see me through until dinnertime (saving the cost of lunch) and because when I'm tired of my own company, there are always other guests to get to know in the lounge (I've made some enduring friendships in just this way over the years).

Unfortunately, New Zealand is not blessed with a plentiful supply of the bed-and-breakfast establishments that so many travelers consider the only way to travel. They are on the increase, however, and I have managed to ferret out a number that are real gems. You'll find them described in detail in the following chapters.

When doing your scouting, you should know that B&Bs go by two names in New Zealand: **guesthouses and private hotels.** Both provide comfortable, homey (New Zealanders say "homely") rooms with hot and cold running water, bath and shower down the hall, and a huge cooked breakfast. And both are unlicensed (serve no liquor). Guesthouses, however, are limited to bed and breakfast, with dinners sometimes served guests by special arrangement, but never to nonguests. Private hotels (which are usually much larger), on the other hand, serve all meals to both residents and nonresidents. Rates in both will run about NZ$70 ($40) double.

One of the most reliable of several organizations that specialize in bed-and-breakfast bookings throughout New Zealand is **New Zealand Home Hospitality Limited.** Details are available through travel agents and New Zealand Tourism offices; in New Zealand, contact the Visitor Information offices.

There is also an excellent directory, published by Moonshine Press, 27 Marine Dr., Mahina Bay, Eastbourne, Wellington, called *The New Zealand Bed and Breakfast Book,* and available in most New Zealand bookshops. Descriptions are written by the hosts themselves in such surprisingly revealing style that you get a sense of their personality from their own words.

If you have chosen **Air New Zealand** as your international carrier, an added bonus is that you're eligible for **Hotpac** discounts on accommodations, as well as a wide range of sightseeing attractions and activities. Ask for **"The Go as You Please Book"** and the **"Good Night Book"** from your travel agent or any Air New Zealand travel center in New Zealand, or call toll free in the United States 800/223-9494.

READERS RECOMMEND

*N.Z. Travel Hotels/Motels Federation, Inc., 52 Armagh St., Christchurch. Tel. *03/661-503. "I especially want to inform you of an excellent group of B&Bs that have joined together to form this group. I stayed in nine of the Federation group and found them all to be very comfortable, offering full English-style breakfasts (and sometimes dinners) and maintaining a consistently high standard of excellence."*—G. Grenfell, Hollister, Calif.

MOTEL FLATS

I once wrote in a travel guide, "A motel is a motel is a motel." Well, while that was certainly true for the location under discussion, it is definitely *not* true for New Zealand! If you think you've seen enough motels to know all variations, just wait until you see them in this country—they give a new definition to the word. Get set for a rave about the best budget-travel value you're likely to run across anywhere.

You'll note that the heading for this section is "Motel Flats," not simply "Motels." And therein lies the difference between New Zealand's offerings and those we're accustomed to under that latter label. Most—if not all—have been built in recent years, since tourism as a full-fledged industry has been a late bloomer in New Zealand. What this means is that all modern conveniences have been incorporated in their designs. And the last few years have seen the addition of spa pools (we know those as Jacuzzis) in most properties. All of which is a bonus, but not the biggest bonus. That comes in the form of a "flat," a fully developed, fully equipped apartment as opposed to the room (no matter how spacious, a room is not a flat!) and bath that comprise our motel units.

In Kiwi motel flats, you'll find a lounge, usually with sofas that open into beds; one or two separate bedrooms (except in the case of "bed-sitters," when the lounge becomes your bedroom at night); a kitchen or kitchenette (and here's where "fully equipped" takes on special meaning, for they come with everything from pots and pans to dishes and silverware to potato peelers to the obligatory electric jug to coffee, tea, sugar, and milk in the fridge, right down to the tea towel); and a bathroom. If you're a taker of baths, I should warn you that most bathrooms have showers rather than a bathtub, although more and more places are installing both, and in some the shower rim is built up and there's a stopper for the drain, so you can fill the "shower" and proceed to bathe in a square "tub." The units are so well planned that where there are two bedrooms, the bathroom is usually accessible to each separately, thus providing privacy for two couples or a family traveling together. There's a TV and radio in virtually every unit, telephones in most, and personal touches such as plants, paintings, and tablecloths in all. Heating is usually by means of individual heaters, and beds come with electric blankets or (most often) electric underblankets. You can count on a laundry room with automatic washer and dryer (or a drying room with a clothesline), many times with soap powder for guests' use, and most are available at a minimal charge. There are few motels (or motor inns) without an outdoor swimming pool.

It should be noted that, just like home, you'll be expected to do such elementary household chores as make beds and wash dishes. Motel flats are not serviced. But everything you'll need to take care of those basic jobs will be right there—dishwashing detergent, fresh linen twice a week, clean tea towels daily. Now, that's entirely to my own tastes, for I must confess to being a slow mover in the early morning, and it's a relief to loiter leisurely, secure in the knowledge that "housekeeping" won't be pounding on the door.

A continental or cooked breakfast can be ordered the night before, with the makings brought to your room that evening so you can please yourself as to breakfast time if you're going continental, or the hot meal delivered to your unit at a prearranged time in the morning. Few motels have restaurants, but if you don't choose to eat in, a good restaurant will be close by.

In addition to all this, there is a bonus that goes beyond monetary values. Almost all motels are owner-operated, which means there's no possibility of your running into impersonal, uncaring attitudes. To the contrary, you're very likely to leave each establishment on a first-name basis with the owners and all their family. In fact, it's one of the best ways I know to get to meet and know New Zealanders.

That, dear reader, is the description of budget accommodations in New Zealand! The average cost for a double in these homelike dwellings is NZ$65 ($37.15) or $18.60 U.S. per person. Singles, as I said earlier, don't fare quite as well, with an average price of NZ$55 ($31.45). And, of course, the per-person cost goes down as the number of occupants goes up: You'll pay about NZ$12 ($6.90) per extra adult, bringing the individual cost for a party of four way down.

As you can see, all New Zealand motel flats are a bargain, but the **Best Western** chain takes things a little further and offers a bargain on top of a bargain with their **Gold Crown Club.** After a once-only fee of NZ$25 ($14.30), you'll receive a 10% discount on all rates by presenting your card on arrival. You'll be given priority bookings through their computerized booking system that will either book ahead as you go or book the entire trip in advance if you prefer.

I've found that without exception Best Westerns are tops in this type of accommodation in New Zealand, with many extras such as a higher percentage of in-house restaurants and locations that are choice for the region. In some cases their rates will be slightly higher than others in the same locality, but generally that difference is equalized by the discount program. Incidentally, Best Western motels are individually owned and operated, not franchised. The "chain" aspect only means that each property is rigidly inspected on a regular basis to be sure that the high standards are being maintained (those copper-bottomed pots must have shiny copper bottoms!).

For a directory of all Best Western motels in New Zealand and your arrival accommodations booking, contact **Best Western USA,** P.O. Box 10203, Phoenix, AZ 85064 (tel. toll free 800/528-1234; fax 802/957-5696). Information on the Gold

Crown Club should be obtained directly from Best Western in New Zealand. Write in advance, call, or drop by their friendly office as soon as you set foot in the country: **Best Western New Zealand,** 19 Great South Rd., P.O. Box 74346, Auckland 5 (tel. 09/520-5418; telex 60689; fax 09/520-5413). Your first Best Western host will also be able to give you full details and sign you up for the discount program.

SERVICED MOTELS

This term refers to motels just like those at home—one room and private bath—with one (very important to this tea and coffee drinker) difference: the ever-present electric jug plus tea bags and instant coffee. You'll find some listings of serviced motels, scattered through the following pages, but because those in our price range tend to be small and sparsely furnished and not nearly as good value as motel flats, their numbers are few. Still, if you have a thing about not making the bed in the morning or you'd rather someone else flicked a dustcloth around, you may find them to your liking. I must say that the ones recommended here are quite on a par with their counterparts in the U.S.

LICENSED HOTELS

Most of the licensed hotels in New Zealand are luxury establishments and in a price range beyond our budget. And many of those that we could budget for, we wouldn't want to—they're relics of the days when sleeping accommodations had to be offered in order for drink to be served, and bedrooms invariably came off second (or third, fourth, or fifth) to the public drinking rooms. I've found a few whose rooms are clean, comfortable, and inexpensive. If, however, you are tempted by a budget listing in any of the accommodations guidebooks mentioned above, I strongly recommend that you insist on a personal inspection before plunking down a night's rent.

There is one important exception to all the above, and that is the THC hotels. **The Tourist Hotel Corporation of New Zealand** has long operated about a dozen semi-luxury hotels in some of the country's remote beauty spots where commercially owned hotels would have a hard time making a go of it. The avowed purpose of the corporation was to "provide suitable accommodation in vital but remote areas." That's an admirable goal, and one that was realized in admirable style: Some of the hotels have gained international recognition, such as the Château, a white-gabled, country mansion in Tongariro National Park, and the window-walled Hermitage, facing Mount Cook's majestic peak. Others of special note are at Milford Sound, Waitomo, and Franz Josef. (There are others in not-so-remote spots, such as Queenstown and Rotorua.) At this writing, the THC is in the process of divesting themselves of hotel ownership, and many are now under private ownership, with the high standards maintained and in some cases enhanced.

You may well choose one of these as your "Worth the Extra Money" indulgence spot, since budget accommodations in off-the-beaten-track areas are sparse. Whether or not you book in, you're likely to spend some time at a THC facility somewhere along the line, for they're the very center of tourist activity in their areas—that's where you'll book many sightseeing tours, find the most pleasant public bar (and often inexpensive pub grub, as well), and go for nighttime entertainment. Pricewise, they fall into the moderately expensive category, with rates ranging from NZ$75 to NZ$150 ($43 to $86) double. Just as is the case with much pricier luxury hotels, however, THCs in virtually every location often offer weekend or off-season specials that bring a sparkle to bargain hunters' eyes—how about NZ$99 ($62), plus GST per person, double occupancy, for two nights, two breakfasts, and one lunch. It pays, then, to inquire about any specials offered during your visit so your itinerary can be planned to take advantage of them.

You'll find the following THCs in the North Island: THC Waitangi, Paihia; THC Auckland Airport; THC Waitomo; THC Rotorua; THC Tokaanu, Lake Taupo; THC

Wairakei (near Lake Taupo); THC Château, Tongariro National Park; THC James Cook, Wellington. In the South Island: THC Franz Josef; THC The Hermitage, Mount Cook; THC Wanaka; THC Queenstown; THC Milford Sound; THC Te Anau.

SPORTING LODGES

A relatively new development in New Zealand is deluxe lodges set in idyllic country surroundings. Definitely "upmarket" properties, these small retreats are—if I may coin a phrase—rustically luxurious. Well worth considering for a big splurge or two, they offer the very best in facilities, personal service, activity specials such as on-site professional guides and helipads so you can be whisked away on a moment's whim, and gourmet meals accompanied by vintage wines.

There are lodges in prime fishing country, lodges that concentrate on skiing nearby slopes, lodges that feature tramping and/or horseback riding, lodges where white-water rafting is a part of every day's activity, and . . . well, if you have a special interest, more than likely there's a host lurking somewhere in one of these lodges who'd love to cater to that and in the process pamper you within an inch of your life. If, on the other hand, your idea of perfect pampering is doing absolutely nothing but relaxing and enjoying the good life, that particular special interest is catered to in every one of the lodges.

If all that sounds like a fantasy, just take my word for it that in some of these establishments you'd have to be quite a fantasizer to dream up the extras on hand. Splurges they are—but if you're going to spend big bucks, you'll not get better value for every dollar spent than in one of these lodges. Prices in these dream spots average between NZ$250 and NZ$300 ($143 to $171), plus GST, per person per day for accommodation and meals. But, as I said, if you decide to go for it, you'll know it's money well spent.

In the United States, **Ambassador Travel,** 1035 Redondo Ave., Long Beach, CA 90804, or 3030 S. College Ave., Fort Collins, CO 80525 (tel. toll free 800/234-8040), can furnish details and help you find those that best fit your dreams and your "splurge" pocketbook, as can other travel agents and any NZ Tourism office—in the States or in New Zealand.

SAVING MONEY ON MEALS

The budget-wise thing to do is to breakfast at your lodging place, have pub grub at lunch (look for the "bistro" signs for pubs that serve food), and take your main meal in the evening in one of the many inexpensive and quite acceptable restaurants. A bistro lunch (which usually offers a choice of hot dishes such as pot roast, steak-and-kidney pie, and stew, served with potatoes and vegetables; or cold platters) will run around NZ$8 ($5), but an even better buy are the buffet lunches where you can eat your fill for no more than NZ$5 ($3).

Of course, the *most* economical way to eat your way around New Zealand is to utilize those marvelous motel flat kitchens to prepare the bulk of your meals at "home." And if you're near one of the ubiquitous "dairies" (delis), it's a simple matter to take home a quite good dinner that only needs warming up. When you *do* opt for a meal out, those BYO (bring your own) restaurants are a real budget bonus—you'll pay only a small corkage fee (about NZ 50¢, 30¢).

New Zealand has in the last few years seen the birth of some truly fine restaurants, with elegant decor, polished service, and superb international cuisine. They're too pricey for budget travel, true, but—holding firmly to the belief that there comes a time in every trip when you just can't stand to pinch one more penny—I've listed some of the more outstanding for those "big splurge" dinners. Expect to pay NZ$40 ($23) or slightly more (without wine) at these establishments, and if you should unearth others you feel warrant that kind of expenditure, do let me know about them.

One thing that will take some getting used to is the use of "entrée" to mean not the main course (which they call the "main course"), but a small serving of a hot dish immediately before the main course. Most New Zealanders eat an entrée, main course, and dessert (or two entrées and dessert) and I usually do the same. I've never been able to manage five courses at one sitting, and unless the set dinner price covers all five, I save my money. You may want to do the same.

READERS RECOMMEND

New Zealand Ice Cream. "*New Zealand makes the very best ice cream in the world—it's so rich and creamy, made with the incredible dairy products here! Hokey Pokey is a butterscotch flavor with pieces of candy in it—too good to be true!*"—D. Smith, Portland, Ore. [*Author's note: Amen!*]

"Taste of New Zealand." "*We highly recommend the NZTP's Taste of New Zealand* booklet for an evening restaurant guide.—M. Luciano, Norwich, N.Y.

SAVING MONEY ON SIGHTSEEING & ENTERTAINMENT

No matter how you budget your sightseeing, you'll be treated to some of this world's most magnificent scenery at absolutely no cost—Mount Cook, Milford, Doubtful, and Marlborough Sounds, the Coromandel Peninsula, the Bay of Islands, the Southern Alps, glaciers, rushing rivers, moonlike thermal-crater scapes, sheep and kiwifruit farms, and caves and dells filled with glowworms.

Pubs often provide an inexpensive evening's socializing, but what with those early closing hours (10pm Monday to Thursday, 11pm Friday and Saturday), after that, you're on your own. My only suggestion is, as I said earlier in Chapter 1, best head home for an early bedtime so you'll be fit for all that outdoorsy stuff the next day.

SAVING MONEY ON SHOPPING

Before we get into specifics, let me say that shopping is fun in New Zealand, with craft, hand-knit woolens, and souvenir shops cropping up in the most unexpected places. Prices are sometimes better in these out-of-the-way shops than in tourist centers—they're best at the duty-free shops in Auckland, Wellington, and Christchurch, but selections can be very limited in both. My own credo has been to buy something that appeals wherever I find it—price variations aren't that wide, and there's always the possibility of not finding it again.

Best Buys   New Zealand wools, leathers, and knits are sold all over both islands, as are sheepskin rugs. Really bulky purchases can be mailed home, but I've found that half the fun of buying a suede coat or woolen sweater is using it there. And look for the hand-knits rather than machine-made sweaters—one of my most prized sweaters was handmade by a lovely little lady in the Bay of Islands, another by a talented knitter in Hokitika on the South Island. Both served me well as I traveled the country.

Souvenirs feature Maori carvings or designs, and there's a wide selection, from greenstone tiki figures on neck chains to carved wooden key chains to coasters, place mats, and small replicas of beautifully carved war canoes. Items made from paua shell are also very popular. You'll surely want to bring home at least one Maori concert record or tape, probably more—a marvelous way to trigger instant memories once you're back home. Pottery and ceramics will tempt you, especially in places like Nelson and Taupo, where many are made by fine craftspeople, and prices are inexpensive to moderate.

Paintings of the gorgeous scenery by New Zealand artists are on sale almost everywhere. Some are quite good, and a small oil can sometimes be found for an amazingly low price. You're almost certain to find one depicting that bit of Kiwiland you fell in love with, and, like the Maori music, a painting is instant mental transport back to a lovely experience.

Duty Free and GST   You'll pay no Goods and Services Tax on purchases in duty-free shops; however, even if you shop in duty-free shops in downtown locations, your purchases cannot be claimed until you reach the departure area. GST on those goods you've bought elsewhere may *not* be claimed back.

SAVING MONEY ON TRANSPORTATION   See the "Getting Around" section earlier in this chapter for money-saving tips and information on discount passes.

SAVING MONEY ON SERVICES & OTHER TRANSACTIONS

A blessing that has not changed over the years is New Zealand's **tipping** policy. You'll seldom find a service charge added to your hotel or restaurant bill—it's strictly on a "when and if you want to" basis, with never any obligation. That's a big budget bonus, but I'll confess that when a taxi driver or porter shifts heavy baggage with a smile or restaurant service has been especially good, my American training takes over and I reach for a 15% tip. Feel free to let your conscience be your guide—no Kiwi is going to give you less than top-notch service whether you tip or not!

Most banks charge a commission for **cashing traveler's checks;** in 1992, that was generally NZ5¢ (3¢) per check, but Countrywide Bank charged nothing at all.

Hairdressing prices are reasonable—NZ$35 ($20) for women and NZ$20 ($11) for men—and neither barbers nor hairdressers will be looking for a tip.

There is no inexpensive time to make **overseas telephone calls**—it's a flat rate. Within New Zealand, economy rates are from 7 to 8am and 6 to 10pm weekdays and 7am to 10pm weekends; no matter the day, 10pm to 7am is the most economical calling time. If you call during the day, choose the afternoon over the morning; it's somewhat less expensive.

WORTH THE EXTRA MONEY

As a confirmed budget traveler, I have always loved staying in the sort of small, homey places we've been talking about thus far. It takes a lot to induce me to "bust the budget" and spring for lodgings in large, luxury establishments. But there comes a time when I've pinched my pennies to the "nth" degree and something in my soul rebels. One short, really big splurge usually puts me back in touch with both my budget and my love for the personal touch so often found only in moderately priced places. It's happened to me wherever I've traveled, and New Zealand is no exception. With the thought that this affliction is not mine alone, I've listed in the chapters to come establishments that are "Worth the Extra Money" in major destinations that do the most for my budget-battered psyche and offer the best value for my carefully hoarded "bust out" dollars.

 FAST FACTS   *NEW ZEALAND*

American Express   The American Express Travel Service office is at 95 Queen St., Auckland (tel. *09/798-243). Other agencies (mostly travel-agent offices) around the country are located in Christchurch, Dunedin, Lower Hutt (near Wellington), Napier, Nelson, Queenstown, Rotorua, Wellington, and Whangarei. They accept mail for clients (you're a client if you have an American Express credit card or traveler's checks), forward mail for a small fee, issue and change traveler's checks, and replace lost or stolen traveler's checks and American Express credit cards.

Business Hours Banks in international airports are open for all incoming and outgoing flights; others are open from 9am to 4:30pm Monday through Friday. Shops are usually open from 9am (sometimes 8am) to 5:30pm Monday through Thursday, until 9pm on either Thursday or Friday. Increasingly, shops are open on Saturday morning, from 9:30 or 10am until noon; most shops are closed on Sunday. Shops connected to hotels sell alcoholic beverages during pub hours, 11am to 10pm, but never on Sunday. Pub hours are 11am to 10pm Monday through Thursday, to 11pm on Friday and Saturday; closed Sunday.

Camera and Film Film is expensive in New Zealand, so bring as much as you can with you. You're not limited by Customs regulations, just by baggage space. Most brands are available in larger cities. There is also same-day developing service in most cities.

Cigarettes You can bring in 200 cigarettes per person, as allowed by Customs regulations. Most brands for sale in New Zealand are English or European, although more and more American brands are appearing on the market.

Climate See "When to Go" earlier in this chapter.

Crime See "Safety," below.

Currency See "Information, Entry Requirements, and Money" in this chapter.

Customs See "Information, Entry Requirements, and Money" earlier in this chapter.

Documents Required See "Information, Entry Requirements, and Money" earlier in this chapter.

Driving Rules See "Getting Around" earlier in this chapter.

Drug Laws Because of its long, indented coastline, New Zealand has been easy prey for drug traffickers. As a result, laws are not only among the world's most strict, they're also stringently enforced. Don't even be tempted!

Drugstores Pharmacies observe regular local shop hours, but each locality usually will have an Urgent Pharmacy, which remains open until about 11pm every day except Sunday, when there will be two periods during the day when it's open. You'll find them listed in local telephone directories. There's a minimal extra charge for prescriptions filled during nonshop hours.

Electricity New Zealand's voltage is 230 volts, and plugs are the three-pin flat type. If your hairdryer or other small appliances are different, you'll need a converter/adapter. Most motels and better hotels have built-in wall converters for 110-volt, two-prong razors, but if you're going to be staying in hostels, cabins, or guesthouses, better bring a converter/adapter.

Embassies and Consulates The Embassy of the United States of America is at 29 Fitzherbert Terrace (Thorndon), Wellington (tel. 04/472-2068). Hours are Monday to Friday from 8:15am to 5pm.

Emergencies Dial 111 anyplace in New Zealand for police, ambulance, or to report a fire. Should you need a doctor, either consult the New Zealand Tourist and Publicity (NZTP) office or prevail on your motel or guesthouse host to direct you to one. Even most small towns have medical centers.

Etiquette Mind your manners! They're highly valued in New Zealand, and the Kiwis are among the most mannerly people on the face of the earth. If you're uncertain what to do in a social situation, just hold on to the rudiments of common courtesy and you'll be fine. More than that, I cannot say.

Hitchhiking See "Getting Around" earlier in this chapter.

Holidays See "When to Go" earlier in this chapter.

Information See "Information, Entry Requirements, and Money" earlier in this chapter.

Language English is spoken by all New Zealanders—Maori and Pakeha.

You'll hear Maori spoken on some TV and radio programs and in some Maori settlements, but it's seldom used in conversation in the presence of overseas visitors.

Laundry   No matter whether you'll be staying in hostels or motels, there will usually be a well-equipped laundry on the premises for your use. Cities have commercial laundries, but most visitors have little need for them.

Liquor Laws   The minimum drinking age is 20 in pubs, 18 in licensed restaurants or with parent or guardian. Children are allowed in pubs with their parents.

Mail   New Zealand post offices will receive mail for you and hold it for a month. Just have it addressed to you c/o Chief Post Office of the city or town you'll be visiting. American Express will receive and forward mail for its clients. Allow 10 days for delivery from the United States. It costs NZ$1.50 (85¢) to send an airmail letter or postcard to the United States, NZ$1 (60¢) to Australia, and NZ$1.80 ($1.05) to the United Kingdom or Europe. Fast Post mail within New Zealand costs NZ80¢ (45¢) per card or letter.

Maps   Wises Mapping, 368 Dominion Rd., Mt. Eden, Auckland (tel. *09/685-095), produces one of the best maps of New Zealand, available from newsagents and bookshops. Rental-car firms furnish a map with every car booked.

Newspapers and Magazines   New Zealand has no national newspapers, although most large city newspapers carry national and international, as well as local, news. Leading newspapers are *New Zealand Herald* (Auckland) and *Dominion* (Wellington).

Passports   See "Information, Entry Requirements, and Money" earlier in this chapter.

Pets   Because of its dependence on a disease-free agricultural environment, New Zealand has restrictions on the importation of most animals. If you must bring a pet, check first with the Ministry of Agriculture and Fisheries, P.O. Box 2526, Wellington, or any New Zealand embassy or consulate.

Radio and TV   The BCNZ (Broadcasting Council of New Zealand) is the major broadcaster in New Zealand, operating TV Channel 1 and TV Channel 2, both color since 1974, and Radio New Zealand. The majority of TV productions come from Britain and America. You'll be surprised and pleased to know that commercials are never shown on Sunday, when some of the best shows are on. Television transmission hours are 10am to about midnight. News junkies may go into withdrawal in New Zealand: Channel 1 broadcasts a half hour of news at 9:30pm (on weekends, make that 10 to 15 minutes of news at 9:15pm), and Channel 2 provides 20 minutes of news weekdays at 5:40pm. For current scheduling, check the listings in daily newspapers. And to hear the country's beautiful national anthem, "God Defend New Zealand," sung in both English and Maori, tune in to Channel 1 at sign-off time.

There's a "Traveller's Rundown" every morning on the radio, which gives a roundup of weather in all tourist areas. Weather reports are also given at the end of the 5:40pm TV newscast.

Restrooms   There are "public conveniences" strategically located and well signposted in all cities and many small towns. You'll find public restrooms at most service stations.

Local Plunket Rooms are a real boon to mothers traveling with small children, for they come with a "Mother's Room," where you can change diapers and do any necessary tidying up. The Plunket Society is a state-subsidized organization, which provides free baby care to all New Zealand families, and their volunteers are on duty in the Plunket Rooms—no charge, but they'll welcome a donation.

Safety   Whenever you're traveling in an unfamiliar city or country, stay alert. Be aware of your immediate surroundings. Wear a moneybelt and don't sling your camera or purse over your shoulder. This will minimize the possibility of your becoming a victim of crime. Every society has its criminals. It's your responsibility to be aware and alert even in the most heavily touristed areas.

Taxes Be sure to save enough New Zealand currency to pay the departure charge of NZ$16 ($9.15) in Auckland, NZ$20 ($11.45) in Wellington. A Goods and Services Tax (GST) was instituted in 1986—the amount is 12.5%.

Telephone, Telegram, and Fax As we go to press, the New Zealand Number Update is in the process of *changing all telephone numbers to 7 digits.* Those numbers in this book that have not been changed at press time are marked with an asterisk, and you should call the Helpline 0155 for the new number.

The telephone area code in New Zealand is known as the STD (subscriber toll dialing); if a given number has no STD, you must go through the operator. For operator assistance within New Zealand, dial 018. For an international operator, call 0170; if you need directory assistance for an international call, dial 0172.

The most economical way to make an international telephone call from New Zealand is to charge it to an international calling card (they are free, so get one before you go) or to dial direct. To call the United States from New Zealand, first dial the international access code, 001, then the area code and local number. Most calls, even the international ones, may be made from a pay-phone booth. When you make a long-distance call from your motel, hotel, or at Telecom, expect to pay a NZ$2 ($1.15) surcharge.

All telegrams are sent through the post office, either by telephone or in person. The cheapest rate is "Letter Rate," which takes about 24 hours for delivery; rates for telegrams sent after regular post office hours can be as much as double.

Fax facilities are offered at many hotels and motels, as well as some local post offices.

Time New Zealand is located just west of the international date line, and its standard time is 11 hours and 30 minutes ahead of Greenwich mean time. A 30-minute daylight saving is permanently observed, which puts New Zealand exactly 12 hours ahead of GMT. Thus at noon in New Zealand, standard time in Sydney is 10am; London, midnight of the previous day; San Francisco, 4pm the previous day; New York, 7pm the previous day; Singapore, 7:30am the same day; and Tokyo, 9am the same day.

Tipping See "Saving Money on Services and Other Transactions" earlier in this chapter.

Tourist Offices See "Information, Entry Requirements, and Money" earlier in this chapter.

Visas See "Information, Entry Requirements, and Money" earlier in this chapter.

Water Drink away—New Zealand waters are pollution free and safe to drink anywhere you develop a thirst.

CHAPTER 3

AUCKLAND

New Zealand's largest city was its capital until 1864, and now holds a full 24% of the entire country's population; adds many thousands each year, making it the country's fastest-growing city; has the largest Polynesian population of any city in the world; and its international airport is most often the oversea visitor's introduction to this delightful land and its people.

Straddling a narrow, pinched-in isthmus that was created by the activity of some 60 volcanoes over a period of more than 50,000 years, Auckland is said by Maori legend to have been inhabited by giants in the days before the moa-hunters. Its present-day giants are commerce and industry, but the attraction for both ancient and latter-day Goliaths was probably the same—its excellent twin harbors. Europeans arrived in Auckland in 1839, and when the Waitangi treaty was signed in 1840, negotiations with the Maoris transferred the isthmus to British ownership. The flag was hoisted on September 18, 1840, an event marked annually by the Anniversary Day Regatta (celebrated in January because of better sailing conditions). The thriving town served as New Zealand's first capital until 1864, when the seat of government was transferred to Wellington because of its central location.

Today's Auckland is nestled among volcanic peaks that have settled into gently rounded hills, minor mountains, and sloping craters. North Head and Bastion Point stand like sentinels on either side of Waitemata Harbour's entrance, and Rangitoto, the largest and more recently active volcano (it erupted in the 13th century), sits in majestic splendor just offshore. Mount Eden's eastern slopes are marked by Maori earthworks, and One Tree Hill has become an archeological field monument because of the large Maori *pa* (fort) that once existed there.

What is possibly the world's finest collection of Maori artifacts can be seen in the Auckland War Memorial Museum, along with a display of the moa, that giant bird that stood 10 feet from beak to toe and that has been extinct for centuries. Colonial-style homes and an astonishing array of towering skyscrapers in the city center are monuments to its Pakeha development. Side by side with reminders of its history are modern Auckland's diversions—outstanding restaurants, more entertain-

WHAT'S SPECIAL ABOUT AUCKLAND

Beaches
☐ Devonport, on Auckland's North Shore, boasts no fewer than five excellent beaches.

Museums
☐ Auckland War Memorial Museum, with perhaps the best collection of Maori and South Pacific artifacts in the world.

Harbor Spectacles
☐ The Devonport Ferry, a short ferry ride to the Devonport suburb, with splendid views of the city from the water.

☐ Harbor cruises that range from trips to outlying islands to dinner harbor cruises.

☐ Anniversary Day Regatta, January 27, when the harbor is alive with colorful sailing craft of all sizes and shapes both local and international.

City Spectacles
☐ One Tree Hill, site of an ancient Maori fort, with marvelous views over the city and harbor.

☐ Waterfront Promenade, from Princes Wharf around the harbor to Kelly Tarlton's Underwater World.

☐ Kelly Tarlton's Underwater World, a world-class aquarium that features New Zealand sea creatures.

Historic Buildings
☐ Ewelme Cottage, a kauri cottage from the 1860s.

☐ Kinderhouse, built in 1862 of volcanic stone from Rangitoto Island in the harbor for one of Auckland's early painters and photographers.

☐ Massey Homestead, in Mangere East, built in the 1850s of home-made bricks and native timber.

Markets
☐ Victoria Park Market, with over 50 stalls and several cafés and restaurants.

☐ China Oriental Markets, on the Quay, with over 140 stalls, permanent Chinese lantern exhibit, and food stalls featuring ethnic cuisines from around the world.

☐ Parnell Village, a collection of colonial-style boutiques, craft shops, and restaurants.

Great Neighborhoods
☐ Devonport, a colonial-style suburb with a great waterfront promenade, Mount Victoria, and an excellent colony of craftspeople.

Parks/Gardens
☐ Winter Garden, tropical hothouse in the Auckland Domain, with some 10,000 varieties, including New Zealand's exotic ferns.

☐ Auckland Zoological Gardens, with a fine collection of animals housed in natural habitats.

☐ Parnell Rose Garden, with magnificent rose displays and terrific views of the city and harbor.

☐ Eden Gardens, beautifully landscaped, on the eastern side of Mount Eden on an old quarry site.

ment than you'll find in other parts of the country, and an ambience that grows more cosmopolitan every year. The city warrants a few days of your time, with much to offer that will enhance the remainder of your New Zealand visit.

1. FROM A BUDGET TRAVELER'S POINT OF VIEW

BUDGET BESTS & DISCOUNTS Otto and Joan Spinka have operated **Touristop** since 1978, located in Auckland's Downtown Airline Terminal, 86-94 Quay St. (tel. *09/775-783; fax *09/776-325). This knowledgeable couple specializes in offering value-for-dollar services such as bookings for accommodations, tours, rental cars, sightseeing tours, harbor cruises, and just about anything else associated with New Zealand–wide travel at the best possible price. They are also agents for Newmans coachlines nationwide network, with coaches departing just outside. They issue 1- and multiday coach passes, as well as all backpacker coach passes. There's never any booking fee! They're open daily from 7:30am to 6pm (until 9pm on Friday), and you'll also find magazines, maps, film, candies, coins, and a nice selection of New Zealand souvenirs at Touristop—but most of all, you'll find a warm, friendly helping hand.

2. ORIENTATION

ARRIVING

BY PLANE The **Auckland International Airport** lies 13 miles south of the city just behind Manukau Harbour. You'll find the **Downtown Airline Terminal** (tel. *796-056) at 86-94 Quay St. at the corner of Albert Street next to the Travelodge Motel.

Coach fare between the airport and bus station is NZ$9 ($5.15). If you're staying at a city hotel on the direct bus route, the driver will drop you off upon request. A **shuttle bus** connects the International Terminal to the Domestic Terminal, about a mile away, for NZ$3 ($1.75). **Taxi** fares between the airport and the city center run about NZ$35 ($20) on weekdays, a little higher on weekends and at night. A budget bonus is the **Taxi Share** fare of Auckland Co-op Taxi (tel. *792-792). Three people sharing a taxi to or from the airport pay NZ$10 ($5.75) each—may take a little longer if you're the last dropoff, but well worth it for such a saving.

Minibus transport between the airport and downtown hotels and motels is supplied by Super Shuttle and the Airporter Express for NZ$14 ($8) per person one-way (ask about discounts for two people traveling together). If you plan to take the Airporter Express (tel. 256-0333) to or from the airport, book at least 2 hours before you want to travel. The Super Shuttle (tel. 307-5210) performs a similar and equally reliable service.

Drivers will find spacious car parks in front of both terminals, and **rental-car desks** are on the ground floors of both terminals.

At the International Terminal, there's a **Visitor Information Centre,** coffee shop, licensed restaurant, bar, bank, post office, rental-car desk, and rental showers. The attractive terminal building's decor is designed to showcase New Zealand's character through the use of murals, timber, stone finishes, and wool carpets.

BY TRAIN OR BUS InterCity trains and buses arrive and depart from the **Auckland Railway Station** just east of the city center and Queen Street on Beach Road (tel. *792-500).

N

GREATER
AUCKLAND

ATTRACTIONS:
Alexandra Park Raceway **1**
Auckland Zoo **2**
Avondale Racecourse **3**
Devonport ferry ride **4**
Ellerslie Racecourse **5**
Howick Colonial Village,
  Pakuranga **6**
Kelly Tarlton's Underwater
  World **7**
Parnell Rose Gardens **8**
Rainbow's End Adventure Park **9**

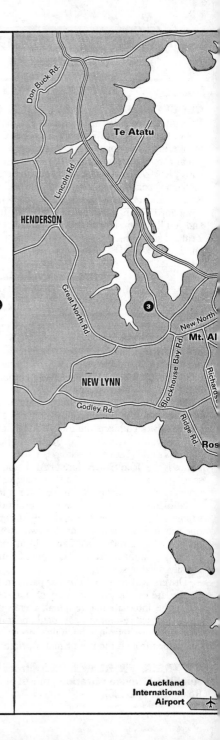

GREATER AUCKLAND

TOURIST INFORMATION

The **Auckland Visitors Centre,** 299 Queen St., at Aotea Square (tel. 09/366-6888; fax *09/6893), is open from 8:30am to 5:30pm Monday through Friday and 9am to 4pm weekends and public holidays. Go by to pick up free brochures, any specific help you may need with accommodations, sightseeing attractions, or ongoing transport. Look for a copy of *Auckland A–Z* and the *Auckland Tourist Times* (which are also distributed free by many hotels) for a listing of current daytime and nighttime happenings. **The North Shore Visitors Centre,** Shop 9, Takapuna Village, Northcroft Street, Takapuna (tel. *09/460-060), is open Monday through Friday from 10am to 3pm; and the Visitor Information Centre at **Auckland Airport International Terminal** (tel. 09/275-7467 or 276-7467) is open 24 hours daily.

Other useful information services are: **Department of Conservation Centre,** corner of Karangahape Road and Liverpool Street (tel. 09/307-9279), with details of walks, camping grounds, Gulf islands, and national parks, open 1 to 4:30pm Monday through Friday; and **Regional Parks Central Office,** Corner Office, corner of Hopetoun and Pitt Streets (tel. 09/366-2166 or *794-420), open Monday through Friday from 8:15am to 4:30pm.

CITY LAYOUT

You can credit the Kiwi's inborn desire for a home and garden to the fact that central Auckland is surrounded by districts that have become cities in their own right—people may *work* in the inner city, but when evening comes, they're off to wider spaces. And the homeward journey will take them over at least one of the many bridges (they cross the harbor, rivers, creeks, and bays) and possibly onto the speeding motorway that runs north-south through the city. That motorway can be a blessing for the visitor unfamiliar with the territory and driving on the left, for it virtually eliminates the possibility of losing your way when you set out for the Bay of Islands, Rotorua, or other major points.

MAIN ARTERIES   The city itself is also fairly straightforward. The main street is **Queen Street,** which ends in Queen Elizabeth's Square at **Quay Street.** Quay Street runs along the Waitemata harborfront. At the other end of Queen Street is **Karangahape Road** (pronounce it "Ka-ranga-happy," or simply call it "K" Street as Aucklanders do), a mere 1¼ miles from Quay Street. Within that area you'll find most of the city's shops, restaurants, nightspots, and hotels, as well as bus, rail, and air terminals.

3. GETTING AROUND

BY BUS   The city's bus system is quite good, reaching all districts with convenient and rather frequent schedules. You can pick up route maps and timetables from most newsagents or the **Downtown Bus Terminal,** Commerce Street and Britomart Place (behind the Chief Post Office). Airport and sightseeing buses depart from the Downtown Airline Terminal, Quay Street. For schedule and fare information, call Buz-a-Bus, *797-119.

Fares are by zone, running from NZ40¢ to NZ$1.20 (25¢ to 70¢). Children under 15 pay half fare; under 4, free. You must have the exact change. If you're going to be using the buses a lot, you can purchase a 1-day **Busabout Pass** for unlimited bus travel for NZ$8 ($4.60) adults, NZ$4 ($2.30) children. There's also a **Family Pass** for NZ$12 ($6.90). Buy them on the buses or at the Downtown Bus Centre.

An **Inner City Shuttle** bus (it's the one painted yellow, with a red band and the destination "000" (yes, that's how it's marked!) runs every 10 minutes from the Railway Station along Customs Street, up Queen Street to Karangahape Road, then back to the station by way of Mayoral Drive and Queen Street for a fare of NZ50¢ (30¢), no matter how far you ride.

The **Explorer Bus** is a double-decker tourist bus departing from the Downtown Airline Terminal, Quay Street, on the hour from 10am to 4pm daily. There are dropoffs and pickups at five major Auckland attractions and in general it's a convenient way to get around for a set fare of NZ$7 ($4).

One word of caution when you're planning evening activities: Auckland buses stop running around 11:30pm on weekdays and Saturday (10pm on Sunday), so if your evening is going to be a late one, plan on taking a taxi home.

BY TAXI Taxi ranks are at all terminals and on the corner of Customs Street West at Queen Street, or you can phone for a taxi (tel. *792-792 or *392-000). At flag fall, the fare is NZ$2 ($1.15), with the meter rising NZ$1.28 (75¢) per kilometer. Waiting time costs 38¢ per minute.

BY BICYCLE Well, I suppose you *could*. Still, what with Auckland's up-and-down terrain, it might be pretty tiring. Bikes are, of course, wonderful for harborfront rides and a few other level stretches, but all in all, you're better off on foot or using the bus.

BY CAR Auckland has a high percentage of drivers per capita, and driving in the city can be a real hassle. My best advice is to park the car and use that excellent bus system as much as possible. If you must drive into the city, you can park the car for the day in parking lots (called car parks hereabouts) operated by the City Council. They're on Beresford Street, just off Karangahape Road; near the waterfront on Albert Street, west of Queen; on Victoria Street, just east of Queen; Britomart, off Customs Street to the east of Queen Street; downtown to the east of Queen Street; downtown to the west of Queen Street with an entrance from Customs Street West; Civic Underground on Mayoral Drive; and Victoria Street East. All are open 7 days a week, 24 hours a day, and rates are quite reasonable.

BY FERRY The Devonport ferry departs regularly from the Queen's Wharf Terminal on Quay Street (tel. 303-3319). One-way fare is NZ$6 ($3.45).

FAST AUCKLAND

Airlines Air New Zealand flights can be booked at Air New Zealand House, Quay Street (tel. *09/793-510). For flight arrival information, dial *09/294-910; for departure information, *09/793-595).

American Express American Express Travel Services, 95 Queen St., P.O. Box 2412, Auckland (tel. *09/798-243).

Area Code Auckland's telephone prefix is 09.

Babysitters Most hotels and motels can furnish babysitters. The following Child Care Centres can also provide daytime child care and help in arranging babysitters for the evening: Auckland City Creche, Freyberg Place (tel. *735-251); Community Childcare Centre, Princes Street (tel. 302-2629); and Freemans Bay Child Care, Pratt Street (tel. *767-282).

Currency Exchange Cash traveler's checks and exchange any other currency at city-center banks and some neighborhood branches. Hotels and restaurants will usually cash traveler's checks in another currency, but you'll get a much better rate at banks.

Dentist   For urgent and/or after-hours dental service, call 09/520-6609.

Disabled Services   For information on ramps, toilets, car parks, telephones, etc., contact the Disability Resource Centre, 14 Epson Ave., Royal Oak (tel. *09/658-069), or write P.O. Box 24-042, Royal Oak, Auckland.

Doctor   For emergency medical care, ring 09/524-5943; for emergency ambulance service, ring 111.

Embassies and Consulates   The United States Consulate is at the corner of Shortland and O'Connell Streets (tel. 09/303-2724); United Kingdom Consulate, 151 Queen St. (tel. 09/303-2971); Canadian Consulate, Princes Court, 2 Princes St. (tel. 09/309/8516); Irish Consulate, Dingwall Bldg., 87 Queen St. (tel. 09/302-2867).

Emergencies   Dial 111.

Hospitals   Auckland Hospital, Park Road, Grafton City (tel. *09/797-440); Greenland Hospital, Greenlane Road, Greenlane (tel. *09/689-909); National Women's Hospital, Claude Road, Epson (tel. *09/689-919); North Shore Hospital, Shakespeare Road, Takapuna (tel. 09/486-1491).

Hotlines   Citizens Advice Bureau (tel. *09/773-313); Drug Dependency (tel. *09/765-272); Emergency Accommodation (tel. *09/773-313); Life Line (tel. *09/607-706); Salvation Army (tel. *09/773-102).

Libraries   Auckland Public Library, Lorne Street (tel. *09/770-209), open 9:30am to 8pm Monday through Thursday, to 9pm Friday, 10am to 1:30pm Saturday, 1 to 5pm Sunday.

Lost Property   Contact the Central Police Station (tel. *09/794-240) or any local police station.

Luggage Storage and Lockers   There are Left Luggage facilities at the Visitors Information Centre in the International Terminal of Auckland airport, open 24 hours; and at the Downtown Airline Terminal, Quay Street, open 7am to 8:30pm daily.

Newspapers/Magazines   The morning *New Zealand Herald* and afternoon *Auckland Star* are published Monday through Friday; *Sunday Star, Sunday Times,* and *Sunday News* are Sunday-morning publications.

Police   See "Emergencies," above.

Post Office   The Chief Post Office (CPO) is between Quay and Customs Streets on Queen Street, and is open Monday through Thursday from 8am to 5pm, until 7pm on Friday.

Religious Services   *Protestant:* Holy Trinity Cathedral, Parnell Road, Parnell (Anglican); Tabernacle, 429 Queen St. (Baptist); Central Mission, opposite Hotwn Hall (Methodist); St. Andrews, 2 Symonds St. (Presbyterian); Meeting House, 113 Mt. Eden Rd., Mt. Eden (Quaker). *Catholic:* St. Patrick's Cathedral, 43 Wyndham St.

Restrooms   Public restrooms are situated in handy locations throughout the city, some in multistory car parks. Those in the Downtown Bus Terminal and Albert Park are open 24 hours, 7 days.

Taxes   A 12.5% Goods and Services Tax (GST) applies across the board.

Telegrams, Telex, and Fax   All telegrams are sent through the post office, either by telephone or in person. The cheapest rate is "Letter Rate," which takes about 24 hours for delivery; rates for telegrams sent after regular post office hours can be as much as double. Fax and telex facilities are available through leading hotels and motels, as well as the main post office.

Telephone   As we go to press, the New Zealand Number Update is in the process of changing all telephone numbers to 7 digits. Those numbers in this book that have not been changed at press time are marked with an asterisk, and you should call the Helpline 0155 for the new number. For directory assistance within the country (when you don't know the number), call 018; for international directory assistance, call 0172. Local calls from public booths cost NZ20¢ (11¢) per minute, and many public phones accept only Phone Cards, which may be purchased from newsagents and some retail outlets in denominations of NZ$5 ($2.90), NZ$10 ($5.75), NZ$20 ($11.45), and NZ$50 ($28.60).

Weather Information   For Auckland regional forecasts, call *09/999-09; 24-hour service.

4. WHERE TO STAY

The most important thing to remember about accommodations in Auckland is that you should book your first night accommodation *before you leave home*—I can think of few things worse than arriving *anywhere* after a 13-hour flight and having to look for a room! A room reservation is especially important on weekends, when Auckland can be very tightly booked. If you should arrive without a room already reserved, however, turn immediately to the nearest Visitor Information Centre (there's one in the International Arrivals Building at the airport). Just keep in mind that you'll be in no position to do much shopping around for budget accommodations.

Except where noted, rates quoted below include GST.

A SERVICED MOTEL

AUCKLAND AIRPORT SKYWAY LODGE, 30 Kirkbride Rd., Mangere (P.O. Box 73119), Auckland Airport. Tel. 09/275-4443 or 275-5012. 27 beds in single, twin, or family rms, (2 motel units with private bath). TV

Transportation: Courtesy van, airport and city center.

$ Rates (including GST): NZ$28 ($16) bunk in dorm; NZ$41 ($23.45) single; NZ$51 ($29) double; NZ$77 ($44) motel-flat double. Extra adult NZ$11 ($6.30). MC, V.

Offering a whole range of accommodation choices, the Skyway Lodge is far from the city center, but has a courtesy van as well as convenient bus transportation. It's an attractive modern building, with a TV lounge, pool table, sauna, spa pool, swimming pool, tea and coffee facilities, and ample guest parking. To begin at the lower end of the accommodation scale, although this is in no way a hostel, there are dormitories of four bunks each, with budget rates, then there are single, twin, and family serviced rooms. At the top of the scale are the two motel-flat units that accommodate from two to seven, in two bedrooms with double and single beds. These come with fully equipped kitchens, private baths, and color TV.

MOTEL FLATS

BEACH COURT MOTEL, 5 The Esplanade, Eastern Beach, Auckland. Tel. 09/534-5159. Fax 09/534-5159. 17 flats (all with bath). TV TEL

$ Rates: NZ$75 ($43) single or double. AE, DC, MC, V.

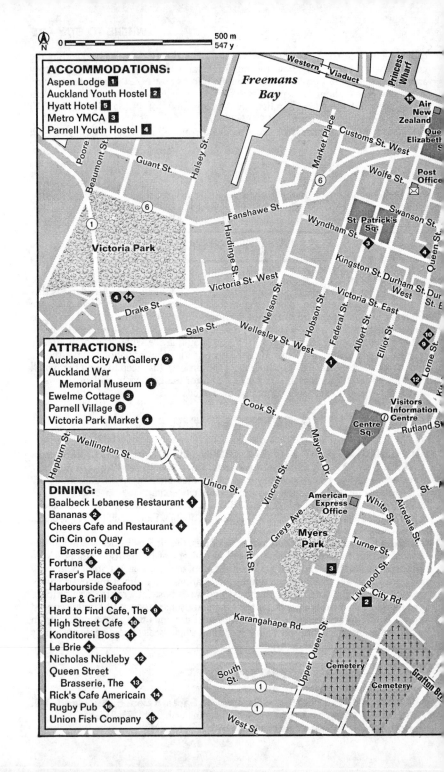

ACCOMMODATIONS:
Aspen Lodge **1**
Auckland Youth Hostel **2**
Hyatt Hotel **5**
Metro YMCA **3**
Parnell Youth Hostel **4**

ATTRACTIONS:
Auckland City Art Gallery **2**
Auckland War
    Memorial Museum **1**
Ewelme Cottage **3**
Parnell Village **5**
Victoria Park Market **4**

DINING:
Baalbeck Lebanese Restaurant **1**
Bananas **2**
Cheers Cafe and Restaurant **4**
Cin Cin on Quay
    Brasserie and Bar **5**
Fortuna **6**
Fraser's Place **7**
Harbourside Seafood
    Bar & Grill **8**
Hard to Find Cafe, The **9**
High Street Cafe **10**
Konditorei Boss **11**
Le Brie **3**
Nicholas Nickleby **12**
Queen Street
    Brasserie, The **13**
Rick's Cafe Americain **14**
Rugby Pub **16**
Union Fish Company **15**

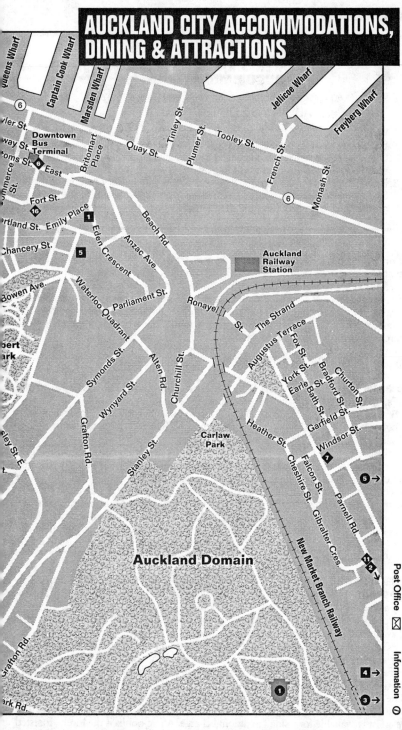

AUCKLAND CITY ACCOMMODATIONS, DINING & ATTRACTIONS

Queens Wharf

Captain Cook Wharf

Marsden Wharf

Jellicoe Wharf

Freyberg Wharf

Tinley St.

Plumer St.

Tooley St.

French St.

Monash St.

⑥ wler St.

way St.

toms St.

Commerce St.

Downtown Bus Terminal

Quay St.

Britomart Place

◆ ⑥ East

Fort St.

⑯

Portland St.

Emily Place

1

Chancery St.

5

Beach Rd.

Anzac Ave.

Eden Crescent

Bowen Ave.

Waterloo Quadrant

Parliament St.

Ronayel St.

Auckland Railway Station

Auckland Railway Station

The Strand

Augustus Terrace

bert ark

Symonds St.

Wynyard St.

Alten Rd.

Churchill St.

Fox St.

York St.

Earle St.

Bradford St.

Bath St.

Churton St.

Garfield St.

Windsor St.

Grafton Rd.

ley St. E.

Stanley St.

Carlaw Park

Heather St.

Falcon St.

Cheshire St.

⑦

⑤→

Auckland Domain

Pannell Rd.

Gibralter Cres.

New Market Branch Railway

⑪→
⑫→

Grafton Rd.

rk Rd.

1

④→

③→

Post Office ⊠ Information ⊕

**FROMMER'S SMART TRAVELER:
ACCOMMODATIONS**

VALUE-CONSCIOUS TRAVELERS SHOULD TAKE
ADVANTAGE OF THE FOLLOWING:

1. Weekend rates—which at some locations cover Friday, Saturday, and Sunday nights—with reductions of 30% to 50%.
2. Off-season rate reductions at coastal and mountain resorts—often as much as 50% to 70% lower than those in season.
3. Rate reductions for seniors, families, and active-duty military personnel.
4. Special-interest package rates, such as golf packages, which may include greens fees, entrance fees, and some meals.

Set on a gorgeous beachfront, this motel may tempt you to loiter a day or two to prepare for strenuous sightseeing ahead or to rest up at the end of your trip. There are marvelous views of Hauraki Gulf with its islands, and a very good swimming beach (safe for children) just across the road. The Beach Court also has a spa pool. All units are exceptionally spacious, with full kitchen, lounge, and one or two bedrooms. Ideal for families—with large public tennis courts immediately behind the motel and a 5-acre municipal playground adjoining—the flats are brightly decorated, will sleep four to six comfortably, and have an ironing board and iron. The motel is 21 kilometers (12½ miles) from the city center, a 25-minute drive.

DOMAIN LODGE, 155 Park Rd., Grafton, Auckland. Tel. 09/303-2509.
Fax 09/358-0677. 14 rms (all with bath). TV TEL
$ Rates (excluding GST): NZ$70 ($40) single bed-sitter, NZ$80 ($46) single with bedroom; NZ$80 ($46) double bed-sitter, NZ$90 ($51) double with 1 or 2 bedrooms. AE, MC, V.
At this nice lodge, a location convenient to the city center comes along with a rare opportunity to do a good deed with your travel dollars. Beautifully situated overlooking the 200-acre Domain Park, it is owned by the Auckland Division of the Cancer Society (patients being treated at Auckland Hospital stay free), and superior accommodations are available to the public on an as-available basis. There are bed-sitter units with tea and coffee facilities, and one- and two-bedroom units with complete cooking facilities. Best of all, your room rent goes directly to help the society's good work. Domain Lodge is adjacent to Domain Park; there is good public bus transportation.

GREEN GLADE MOTEL, 27 Ocean View Rd., Northcote, Auckland. Tel. 09/480-7445. Fax 09/480-7439. 13 units (all with bath). A/C TV TEL **Transportation:** Owners will pick you up from the Downtown Airline Terminal.
$ Rates (including GST): NZ$68.50 ($39) single; NZ$85.50 ($49) double. Best Western discounts available. AE, DC, MC, V.
The Green Glade is run with loving care by owners Gill and Geoff Calvert, who know their country well and maintain a tour desk to assist guests in planning itineraries. There are eight one- and two-bedroom units with complete kitchens, and five with tea and toast facilities. All have modern furnishings and bright, cheerful decor, and all come with radio, central heating, and electric blankets. This Best Western member has a swimming pool, heated spa pool, and a guest laundry. Continental or hot breakfast is available for a small additional charge. A real bonus is the lovely, forested

public reserve with stands of white pine just back of the motel, great for peaceful walks. Nearby are a number of good restaurants, golf course, beaches, and shopping centers. The motel is on the North Shore, across the Harbour Bridge, 5 miles from the city center. There's good public bus transportation to the center of Auckland.

MT. EDEN MOTEL, 47 Balmoral Rd., Mount Eden, Auckland 3. Tel. *09/687-187. Fax 09/609-563. 26 units (all with bath). TV TEL
$ Rates: NZ$67–NZ$75 ($38–$43) single; NZ$74–NZ$82 ($42–$47) double. Extra person NZ$12 ($7). AE, DC, MC, V.

If it's a quiet residential location you're after, this will certainly fill the bill. Only a short, pleasant walk from Mount Eden and Mount Eden Village shops, the motel is set back from the road, eliminating traffic noise. In fact, with off-street parking just outside your unit you can forget driving into the city, since there's good bus service just a few minutes away. There are one-and two-bedroom units, as well as bed-sitters with double and twin beds, all with full kitchens and radios. Facilities include an outdoor swimming pool, indoor Jacuzzi and two saunas, guest laundry, car wash, and barbecue area. Breakfasts are available, and there are restaurants nearby. Robyn and Jim Baker, the owner/operators, are both interested in and knowledgeable about helping with your sightseeing and ongoing itinerary.

OLIVE TREE MOTEL, 24 Glencoe Rd., Browns Bay, Auckland 10. Tel. 09/478-7679. 8 units (all with bath). TV TEL
$ Rates: NZ$72 ($41) single; NZ$78 ($45) double. Extra person NZ$11 ($6).

Out in the delightful Browns Bay section, this attractive small motel is in a peaceful location near good beaches as well as restaurants and shops. Facilities include a pool, spa, and trampoline, and all units have a complete kitchen. There's a honeymoon suite, and one luxurious two-bedroom executive suite. The motel is located 2 kilometers (1 mile) off City Motorway North, 15 minutes from the city center. There is public bus service into the city center.

RACEWAY MOTOR LODGE, 67 St. Vincent Ave., Remuera, Auckland. Tel. 09/520-0880 or 520-0155. Fax 09/520-0155. 10 units (all with bath). TV TEL **Directions:** Take the Greenlane exit on the motorway toward Ellerslie Racecourse, and it's the second turn on the left.
$ Rates: NZ$75 ($43) single or double. AE, MC, V.

Located in a tranquil spot, yet handy to the city center, this motor lodge is near Ellerslie Racecourse and Alexandra Park, only a short walk from a good shopping center and licensed restaurants. All units have complete kitchens, videos, and radios, and there's a guest laundry, as well as covered parking. Cots and highchairs are available, and if you can't face the kitchen in the morning, both continental and cooked breakfasts are available through room service. Public bus transportation is nearby.

RANFURLY COURT MOTEL, 285 Manukau Rd. (near Ranfurly Rd.), Auckland. Tel. *09/689-059. Fax *09/608-374. 12 flats (all with bath). TV TEL
$ Rates: NZ$70 ($40) single or double. Extra adult NZ$12 ($7). Best Western discounts available. AE, MC, V.

This two-story Best Western member has a pleasant setting of manicured lawn, roses, and hedges. There are 12 lovely one-bedroom flats, each accommodating two to four people. Each unit has one full window wall, is nicely decorated, and comes equipped with telephone, radio, color TV, and electric blankets. And unlike most motel flats, these are serviced daily. There is a guest laundry, as well as car-wash facilities, on the premises, and a shopping center is just 100 yards away. Five different breakfasts are available, ranging from NZ$5 ($3) for a continental breakfast to NZ$9 ($5) for a cooked meal. On the direct airport bus route, Ranfurly Court is 5 kilometers (3 miles) from the city center. A public bus stops at the door.

BED & BREAKFASTS

AACHEN HOUSE, 39 Market Rd., Remuera, Auckland. Tel. 09/520-2329. Fax 09/524-2898. 7 rms (none with bath). TV TEL
$ Rates (including breakfast): NZ$45 ($26) single; NZ$68 ($39) double. MC, V.
Aachen House sits on a hill in a charming neighborhood, overlooking Hobson Park. It is one of a pair of two-story residences built back in 1905 that were known as the "Two Old Ladies of Market Road." There's a decided Victorian air about the place, with its rounded turret wing off to one side and lots of gingerbread trim. Jean and Donald Goldschmidt are the friendly, helpful hosts. Rooms all have high ceilings, some have bay windows looking out onto nice views, and all share the three baths at one end of the upstairs hall. A hot English breakfast is served in a quaint old dining room, and there's a TV lounge with tea and coffee makings. On cool evenings, the lounge is warmed by an open fire. On fine evenings, guests often play croquet on the large back lawn. No smoking. Located 4 kilometers (2½ miles) from downtown, with public bus service 1 block away.

ASPEN LODGE, 62 Emily Place, Auckland. Tel. *09/796-698. Fax *09/777-625. 26 rms (all with bath). TV TEL
$ Rates (including breakfast): NZ$42 ($24) single; NZ$60 ($34) double. AE, MC, V.
This small neat establishment is conveniently located a short walk from Queen Street in the city center and also from the main rail and coach station. The rooms are on the small side, but clean and bright, and the hearty breakfasts here are outstanding. Facilities include tea and coffee facilities, a guest laundry, and bikes for hire. They can also arrange car and campervan rentals, as well as sightseeing tours. Aspen Lodge is on the airport shuttle route; there is good city bus service.

BAVARIA BED AND BREAKFAST HOTEL, 83 Valley Rd., Mount Eden, Auckland. Tel. 09/638-9641. Fax 09/638-9665. 11 rms (all with bath). TV TEL
$ Rates (including breakfast): NZ$49 ($28) single; NZ$79 ($45) double. No credit cards.
Situated in a quiet residential area on the western slope of Mount Eden, close to restaurants, shops, and banks, Bavaria is owned and operated by Rudi and Ulrike Stephan, who came to New Zealand as tourists and stayed as permanent residents. The colonial-style house is surrounded by private gardens, and guest rooms—single, double, and family size—are spacious and attractively furnished. The TV lounge

 FROMMER'S COOL FOR KIDS: ACCOMMODATIONS

Beach Court Motel *(see p. 75)* A safe swimming beach, public tennis courts, and a municipal playground nearby will keep the younger set happy.

Green Glade Motel *(see p. 78)* Swimming at nearby beaches and romps through the pine forest just back of the motel are sure to appeal to youngsters.

opens to a sun deck, and the sunny breakfast area overlooks the gardens. Located 2 kilometers (1 mile) from the city center and 15 minutes from the airport. There is a bus stop nearby.

CHALET CHEVRON TOURIST HOTEL, 14 Brighton Rd., Parnell, Auckland. Tel. 09/309-0290. Fax *09/735-754. 15 rms (all with shower). TV TEL
$ Rates (including breakfast): NZ$48 ($27) single; NZ$76 ($43) double. AE, DC, MC, V.

One of our faithful readers gets full credit for leading me to this "small, clean, comfortable, and *happy*" place run by Jane Nilsson, an enthusiastic and informative host with a genuine interest in her guests' enjoyment of Auckland and New Zealand, as well as in their comfort. Guest rooms are pleasant and comfortable, and there are two family units. The hotel is a short walk from Parnell Village. There's good bus service to the city center.

CHELTENHAM-BY THE SEA, 2 Grove Rd., Devonport, Auckland. Tel. 09/445-9437. 2 rms (both with bath). TV TEL
$ Rates (including breakfast; excluding GST): NZ$45 ($26) single; NZ$60 ($35) double. No credit cards.

Joyce and Harry Mossmans' large home is set amid shade trees and a spacious lawn, only a minute from Cheltenham Beach and just a little farther from shops, restaurants, and bus transportation. Joyce and Harry offer two bedrooms, each with twin beds, private entrance, and bath with shower, hot water, and toilet. Complimentary tea and coffee are provided, and they'll prepare an evening meal with advance notice. They will also arrange local and North Shore tours for guests. Their son, Mark, is co-owner of one of Devonport's most popular restaurants, The Low Flying Duck, nearby at 99 Victoria Rd. Located on the North Shore, the property is 20 minutes from the city center via the Harbour Bridge or Devonport ferry. It's served by the airport shuttle bus.

DEVONPORT VILLA, 21 Cheltenham Rd., Devonport, Auckland. Tel. 09/445-2529. Fax 09/445-7623. 4 rms (sharing 2 baths), 1 suite (with bath). TV TEL
$ Rates (including breakfast): NZ$55–NZ$75 ($31–$43) single; NZ$80–NZ$100 ($46–$57) double. AE, MC, V.

This charming colonial-style bungalow is within walking distance of an excellent beach (1 block from Cheltenham Beach) and North Head, which affords a fine view of the harbor and Auckland. There's a lovely living room, dining room featuring lots of light woods, three working fireplaces, verandas, and a super patio and swimming pool out back, overlooked by the dining room and two guest rooms. Owner Jackie Cozby (from Carmel, Calif.) has furnished three guest rooms with queen-size beds plus a single, one room with a double bed; all have feather comforters. The stellar breakfast includes fresh orange juice, homemade muesli, muffins, a choice of egg dishes, and freshly brewed coffee and teas. A delightful Auckland area base, Devonport Villa is located on the North Shore, ½ mile from the ferry, shops, and restaurants.

JANET AND JIM MILLAR, 10 Ngaroma Rd., Epsom, Auckland. Tel. *09/657-336. 4 rms (sharing 2 baths).
$ Rates (including breakfast): NZ$35 ($20) single; NZ$55 ($31) double. Dinner NZ$15 ($9) upon request. No credit cards.

Janet and Jim Millar's three-quarters-of-a-century-old bungalow has four bedrooms, with two baths and two lounges. They are especially adept at working out family accommodations (their grandchildren are frequent and welcomed visitors, so little ones are no problem here). There's a path at one end of the street that leads directly to

Maungakiekie (One Tree Hill Domain). Both experienced travelers, the Millars enjoy talking about travel with their guests. Early arrivals are welcome. There's nearby bus service into the city center.

REMUERA HOUSE, 500 Remuera Rd., Remuera, Auckland. Tel. 09/526-794 or 520-3175. 14 rms (sharing bath). TV TEL **Bus:** No. 635, 645, or 655 stop out front.

$ Rates (including hot breakfast): NZ$38 ($22) single; NZ$56 ($32) double; NZ$67 ($38) triple. AE, MC, V.

"Old-fashioned" best describes Remuera House, which dates from 1901 and has a big bay window—in fact, large windows everywhere—and wisteria growing in the backyard. Pictures of the grandparents of host Ray King, who has an avid interest in genealogy, hang on the dining room wall. The house has comfortable rooms (single guests will love corner Room 5), a sun porch, a TV lounge with tea and coffee facilities, and laundry. It's 10 minutes from downtown Auckland.

READERS RECOMMEND

Karin's Garden Villa, 14 Sinclair St., Devonport. Tel. 09/458-689. "Karin Loesch's delightful old villa has a large lawn and fruit trees at the end of a quiet cul-de-sac, just a few minutes' walk from the beach and golf course. She and her two children are multi-lingual (English, German, Malaysian) and have traveled widely. There is a double room with bath and two singles with a shared bath. Guests are free to use the kitchen and laundry, and Karin will meet you at the ferry. I stayed several days and look forward to a longer stay on my next trip."—Bryce Moore, Col. USAF Ret., Hiwasswe, Ariz. [Author's Note: Col. Moore's sentiments were echoed by reader Caroline Hoffman, of Albany, Calif.]

HOSTELS & A YMCA

AUCKLAND YOUTH HOSTEL, City Rd. and Liverpool St. (P.O. Box 68-441), Auckland. Tel. 09/309-2801. 142 beds (none with bath). **Transportation:** 24-hour airport shuttle service, all Queen St. city buses.

$ Rates: NZ$19 ($11) per person per night. MC, V.

Centrally located off Queen St., this is Auckland's top hostel accommodation. The high-quality, inexpensive rooms include tea and coffee facilities, but no private baths—separate male and female bathrooms are provided on each floor. There are also a limited number of family units. Most rooms have a good view of the harbor; all are attractively decorated, and there's one paraplegic unit. There's a guest lounge and a separate one for TV, as well as a good moderately priced restaurant that serves from 7am to 3pm (they'll also provide picnic boxes with advance notice). Laundry service is available, and if your itinerary calls for it, you can arrange early check-in or late checkout. The friendly, 24-hour staff can also book ongoing travel and accommodations and arrange discounts.

HEKERUA HOUSE, 11 Hekerua Rd., Waiheke Island, Auckland. Tel. *09/728-371. 16 bunks, 6 double rms (none with bath). **Transportation:** Ferry from Auckland's Ferry Terminus to Matiatia Wharf on the island, three times daily (20% ferry discount, ask when booking); local Palm Beach bus to Hekerua Rd.

$ Rates: NZ$13 ($7) dorm bed; NZ$15 ($9) per person double; NZ$10 ($6) tent site. No credit cards.

Just a short ferry ride across Auckland harbor to the island, and you'll find the private hostel set in a Maori reserve close to good swimming beaches and shops. There's a large lounge that opens to the sun deck, a swimming pool, summer barbecues, and the beach is only 5 minutes away. Other island activities include fishing, swimming, horse riding, tramping, and windsurfing.

METRO YMCA, Pitt St. and Greys Ave., Auckland. Tel. 09/303-2068. Fax 09/776-770. 128 rms (none with bath).
$ Rates: NZ$30 ($17) per person per night, NZ$22.50 ($14) per night thereafter. No credit cards.

One of the best in the country, this Y in the city center is a centrally heated, five-story gray-and-white building with small, neat rooms, all singles. All are carpeted, have a window, and are fitted out with reading lamps and desks. The Y has a shower on each floor, an elevator, and a laundry. Parking is available, and there are two TV lounges. Men and women over the age of 17 are welcome, and about half of the rooms are filled with permanent guests, either students or working people. Full board includes breakfast, a cold lunch during the week and hot lunch on weekends, and dinner. Convenient to good city bus service.

ONETANGI YHA HOSTEL, Seaview Rd., Waiheke Island, Auckland. Tel. *09/72-8971. 38 beds. **Transportation:** Ferry from Auckland's Ferry Terminus to Matiatia Wharf on the island, three times daily; local bus to Onetangi.
$ Rates: NZ$14 ($8) per person per night. Discounts for ferry/bus/hostel package. No credit cards.

To really get away from it all, there's no better place than Onetangi. Just a short ferry ride across Auckland harbor to the island, and you'll find the hostel set into a hillside overlooking Onetangi Bay. Bunkrooms are for two, there's a large common room, outdoor eating facilities, and island activities include fishing, swimming, horse riding, tramping, and windsurfing. The hostel's spacious grounds are also dotted with large trees, with ropes for climbing, à la Tarzan.

PARNELL YOUTH HOSTEL, 2 Churton St., Parnell, Auckland. Tel. *09/ 793-731 or *790-258. 81 beds in 11 dorms. **Transportation:** Bus service between airport and city from 7am to 10pm, pickup service from airport after 10pm; city bus service, a 10-minute walk from City Bus Station.
$ Rates: NZ$16 ($9) per person per night. MC, V.

Within walking distance of the city center, this handsome youth hostel near Parnell Village draws rave reviews for the cheerful colors used throughout, the inviting dining room with pine tables and chairs, the yard (three-quarters of an acre) filled with fruit trees and picnic tables, and the view of the harbor from the upstairs rooms. It also has a TV room, a large lounge downstairs, a smaller one upstairs filled with books and games, a laundry, baggage storage, showers and toilets for the disabled, and an enormous number of brochures on New Zealand. One self-contained dorm is available as a family room. Videos about the country are shown throughout the day, and all your ongoing travel bookings can be made right in the hostel. And they'll hold your mail while you're traveling.

CAMPING & CABINS

The **North Shore Caravan Park Cabins & Motels,** 52 Northcote Rd., Takapuna, Auckland (tel. 09/419-13 or 418-2578), a member of the Top 10 Group of Holiday Parks, boasts a first-rate location, the closest to downtown Auckland via the Harbour Bridge. There are 30 tent sites, 130 caravan sites, cabins, bunkrooms, and four motel units, as well as large bathroom and kitchen facilities. Other facilities include a large laundry with dryers, and a TV room. It's handy to frequent bus service, shops, and restaurants. Rates are NZ$14 ($8.50) single, NZ$20 ($11) double for tent sites; NZ$30 ($17) single, NZ$40 ($23) double for most cabins; NZ$40 ($23) single,

NZ$50 ($29) double for luxury cabins, and NZ$60 ($34) single, NZ$72 ($41) double for the motel units, all including GST.

READERS RECOMMEND

Marco Polo Backpackers Inn, *2D Hammond Ave., Hatfields Beach, Orewa. Tel. 09/426-8455. "We found the Marco Polo, just 40km (24 miles) north of Auckland on Hwy. 1, to be a nice alternative to city accommodations. There's good bus service into town. There's a fully equipped kitchen, laundry facilities, and linens for hire (blankets were free). They also stored our luggage at no cost. Jan and Marleen, the owners, organized coastal walks at low tide to Waiwera hotpools, and a snorkeling tour to Goat Island Marine Reserve, at a low price that even included masks, snorkel, and fins."*—S. Caliri, San Francisco, Calif.

WORTH THE EXTRA MONEY

There was a time, not so long ago, when Auckland's luxury or near-luxury accommodations were almost nonexistent. Not so today, however. As New Zealand has become more and more attractive to corporations as well as tourists, upscale hotels, motor inns, and even bed-and-breakfast accommodations have sprung up to meet a growing demand. Those listed below are, I believe, not only posh enough to provide every ounce of pampering your splurge dollars should buy, but offer the best value in every respect for those hard-earned dollars.

ASCOT PARNELL, 36 St. Stephens Ave., Parnell, Auckland 1. Tel. 09/309-9012. Fax 09/309-3729. 9 rms (all with bath). TEL **Transportation:** Airport bus stops in front, city bus service one block away.

$ Rates (including breakfast): NZ$72 ($41) single; NZ$99 ($57) double. Extra adult NZ$24 ($14); children under 12 NZ$12 ($7). AE, MC, V.

This bed and breakfast is one of Auckland's most pleasant and atmospheric lodgings, just a short walk from Parnell Village, the Auckland War Memorial Museum, and the Rose Gardens, and a longish walk (about 1½ miles) from the city center. The grounds feature lovely shrubbery and flowers, many native to New Zealand, with a gigantic, century-old pin oak tree that's registered as a "historic tree." The house itself dates from 1910 and, under the loving care of Alfred and Heidi Hassencamp, it is beautifully maintained to preserve its informal elegance. Guest rooms here are especially spacious, each with a individual decor, and some family rooms will accommodate up to four people. There's a pretty dining room, a TV lounge (where coffee and tea are free), and off-street parking. I've had nothing but good reports from readers, many of whom comment on the Hassencamps's friendly, personalized travel advice. Because it is so popular, book as far in advance as you possibly can. (*Note:* Be sure to ask for an introduction to "George.")

BARRYCOURT MOTOR INN, 10-20 Gladstone Rd., Parnell, Auckland. Tel. toll-free in the U.S.A. 800/528-1234 or 09/303-3789 or 303-3789. Fax 09/773-309. 67 kitchen flats, 40 hotel rms (all with bath). A/C TV TEL **Transportation:** City bus stops right at the door; Explorer Bus stops every hour; Airport bus every half-hour; airport shuttle on request.

$ Rates (excluding GST): All rates single or double: Lodge unit (kitchen facilities) NZ$76–NZ$86 ($43–$49); studio unit with kitchen (for two or three) NZ$90–NZ$156 ($51–$89); 1-bedroom suite with kitchen (for two to five) NZ$126–NZ$172 ($72–$98); 2-bedroom suite with kitchen (for two to six) NZ$160–NZ$186 ($91–$106); hotel room NZ$96–NZ$126 ($55–$72). AE, DC, MC, V.

This Best Western motor inn is a personal favorite not only because of the quality of the units but also because the staff is unfailingly pleasant, friendly, and helpful—a reflection of owner Norm Barry's business philosophy. It's also conveniently located less than a mile from the CPO and within easy walking distance of Parnell Road's quaint shopping district. The original part of the motor inn consists of 22 units in a modern brick building: bed-sitters and one-bedroom and two-bedroom flats sleeping two to five people, with especially well-equipped kitchens and ample closets (both features throughout the Barrycourt). The Executive Block holds 80 units, most with private balconies and harbor views. All units have tea- and coffee-making facilities, radios, and refrigerators; many also have complete kitchens, and two-bedroom suites have their own clothes washer and dryer—worth the splurge just to go home without dirty laundry! All suites and units have sunny aspects, and those with private balconies have marvelous views of Auckland's spectacular harbor. The best bets for budgeteers are five units in a lodge at the bottom of the property. Some rooms have oak paneling, beamed ceilings, stained-glass panels, and leaded-glass windows. TV reception includes U.S. and Australian satellite channels.

Facilities include four spa pools, sunbed solarium, swimming pool, self-service laundry, same-day dry cleaning and laundry; photocopying; rental cars and cycles; foreign currency exchange, and a Victorian building that houses the excellent Brasserie restaurant (see "Where to Eat," below). There's ample parking, and there's a separate building to store any luggage you won't need while exploring the rest of New Zealand.

HYATT HOTEL, 2 Princes St. (P.O. Box 3938), Auckland. Tel. 09/366-1234, 09/309-1818 for reservations, or toll free 800/228-9000 in the U.S., Fax 09/303-2932. Telex NZ2298. 275 rms (all with bath). A/C MINIBAR TV TEL
   Transportation: Good city bus service; airport shuttle available.
$ Rates (excluding GST): NZ$235–NZ$270 ($134–$154) single or double; NZ$300 ($171) Regency Club single or double; NZ$400 ($229) Regency Club Suite; NZ$950 ($543) Presidential Suite. AE, DC, MC, V.
Set on high ground at the edge of the city center off Queen Street, the Hyatt overlooks the greenery of adjacent Albert Park and affords terrific views of the harbor. Until early 1984 this was the Inter-Continental, always a favorite with Kiwis and international visitors. Since the Hyatt management took over, however, the hotel has been given a loving facelift, with everything from lobby and public rooms to guest rooms to restaurants renovated with quiet elegance. All of the rooms have oversize beds, individually controlled heating and air conditioning, two direct-dial telephones, fridge, and complimentary tea and coffee facilities. Each room has either a harbor or park view. If you want to splurge all the way, opt for the Regency Club, a "hotel within a hotel"—three floors that have been set aside to provide the services of a concierge, a private lounge, complimentary continental breakfast, evening canapés, and such extras as cuddly bathrobes and deluxe toiletries. *Note:* There is also an excellent Hyatt hotel in Rotorua.
   Dining/Entertainment: There are two cocktail lounges with music, a café for casual surroundings, and the gourmet Top of the Town restaurant that not only serves up some of the best food and service in town, but throws in a magnificent harbor view as well (see "Where to Eat," below).
   Services: Dry cleaning, babysitting, airport limousine service, currency exchange.
   Facilities: Shops, laundry.

TAKAPUNA BEACH MOTEL, The Promenade, Takapuna Beach, Auckland. Tel. 09/489-7126. Fax 09/489-8563. 20 rms, 20 suites (all with bath). TV TEL
$ Rates: NZ$90 ($51) single or double standard room; NZ$120 ($69) single or double poolside room; NZ$165 ($94) single or double poolside suite. Best Western discounts available. AE, DC, MC, V.
This lovely motel over on the North Shore is set back off the street in beautifully

landscaped grounds. The luxury suites, all with complete kitchens, are grouped around a heated pool and barbecue area, the focal point of convivial guest gatherings virtually every evening. All suites will sleep two to six people, are nicely decorated, and have attractive modern furnishings, and there are a few with water beds. The beach (excellent swimming and windsurfing) is just a few steps away, and village shops and restaurants are quite close by. This is one of the prettiest lodgings in the area, and I highly recommend it. The motel, about 10 minutes north of Devonport, is accessible via the Harbour Bridge or ferry.

Facilities: Spa pool, games room, and guest laundry.

READERS RECOMMEND

Siesta Motel, 70 Great South Rd., Remuera, Auckland. Tel. 09/520-2106. *"We were delighted with the Siesta. The location is right on the bus line to the center of the city and close to the race courses."*—J. and E. Vick, Longmont, Colo.

The Tane Tourist Lodge, 558 Great South Rd., Papatoetoe, Auckland Tel. 09/278-5725. *"This was our "find" of the trip, out toward the airport. We enjoyed a shiny, clean kitchen and the camaraderie of people from South Africa, England, and the U.S."*—I. See, Long Creek, Ore.

5. WHERE TO EAT

Eating out in Auckland can be just about anything you want it to be. There are scads of small, attractive, and inexpensive coffee shop–type eateries, a wide range of cuisine at moderate prices, and an impressive array of posh restaurants serving international dishes. They're scattered all over the city, but there are interesting concentrations along Parnell and Ponsonby Roads (a large percentage along the latter fall into a high price range, which can only have a place in any budget vacation as a "big splurge"). You'll find examples of each in these pages, but you should also pick up a copy of the free *Auckland Dining Guide,* published quarterly and available at many hotels, as well as Visitor Information Centres. Its listings are quite complete and there's a city map included showing restaurant locations. Remember: *GST of 12.5% must be added to all prices listed here.*

BAALBECK LEBANESE RESTAURANT, 58 Wellesley St. (at Federal St.). Tel. *734-693.
Cuisine: LEBANESE. **Reservations:** Recommended.
$ **Prices:** Average dinner NZ$60 ($34). MC, V.
Open: Dinner daily 6pm–late.

For an exotic dining experience in the city center, you'll like the Baalbeck. The food is genuine Lebanese—lamb, beef, chicken, stuffed cabbage leaves, and shish kebab. Belly dancers and Middle East music add zest to your evening. Best book ahead on Friday and Saturday. BYO.

BANANAS, 317 Parnell Rd. Tel. *799-360.
Cuisine: ASIAN. **Reservations:** Recommended.
$ **Prices:** Complete meal NZ$10–NZ$20 ($6–$11). AE, DC, MC, V.
Open: Lunch Tues–Sun noon–2:30pm; dinner daily 6:45pm–late.

For an exciting taste of Asia, climb the stairs to this Parnell Village restaurant, where the atmosphere is intimate and the mix of foods from 10 Asian countries tantalizing. Consider hot-and-sour soup (here they call it "tummy warmer"), Vietnamese spring roll, mien gay (cold Chinese noodles with shredded chicken and sesame dressing), and satay (grilled in the evenings). Try for a balcony seat on a nice day—actually, you'd

FROMMER'S SMART TRAVELER:
RESTAURANTS

1. Plan your main meal at lunch—prices are lower than in the evening, and in many top restaurants the menu is much the same.
2. Take a picnic, with take-outs from fast-food shops or your own fixings from local grocers—a terrific way to meet the locals!
3. Nothing runs up a restaurant bill as fast as wine or other spirits—take advantage of Auckland's many BYO eateries, and take along your own bottle.

best reserve it ahead of time. The wheelchair-bound will find easy access and ample room at table, as well as accessible restrooms.

BRASSERIE, in the Barrycourt Motor Inn, 10-20 Gladstone Rd. (off St. Stephens Ave.), Parnell. Tel. 303-3789 or 303-3789.
  Cuisine: NEW ZEALAND. **Reservations:** Recommended.
$ Prices: Appetizers NZ$4.50–NZ$12 ($3–$7); main courses NZ$11–NZ$20 ($6–$11). AE, DC, MC, V.
  Open: Daily 11:30am–1am.
It's unusual to mention a restaurant that is part of a hotel or motel in this section, but for sophisticated dining and attentive service at a reasonable price, you can't make a better choice than this. The Brasserie is Barrycourt's light and airy eatery set in an extension to a turn-of-the-century home. The wine list is impressive, and the fare—all manner of fish and meat dishes prepared in traditional Kiwi or South Pacific style (I especially like the way they treat lamb)—is excellent. Save room for the great homemade ice cream. Licensed. There's good city bus service to the restaurant's Parnell address.

LE BRIE, St. Patrick's Sq. (off Wyndham St.). Tel. *733-935.
  Cuisine: FRENCH. **Reservations:** Recommended.
$ Prices: Appetizers NZ$10 ($6); main courses NZ$20 ($11). AE, DC, MC, V.
  Open: Lunch Mon–Fri noon–2pm; dinner Mon–Sat 6–10pm.
Lovers of French cuisine will find a home in the city center at this charming little bistro, with its blackboard menu and dark-green walls. Goodies such as rabbit casserole, a variety of terrines, escargots, and other traditional French dishes are served up at surprisingly moderate prices. It's licensed, but you can bring your own wine. Service here is a real delight.

CHEERS CAFE & BAR, 12 Wyndham St. (just off Queen St.). Tel. 309-8779.
  Cuisine: SALADS/PASTA/MEAT/FISH/POULTRY. **Reservations:** Not required.
$ Prices: Appetizers NZ$5.20–NZ$9.50 ($3–$5); main courses NZ$8.95–NZ$14.50 ($5–$8). AE, DC, MC, V.
  Open: Daily 11am–1am.
This licensed café in the city center is a bright, airy place with lots of blond wood, greenery, and a fountain. The tempting and varied menu includes angel-hair pasta with steamed mussels, clams, tomato, chili, and basil; stir-fried lamb with garlic and mint; fresh fish filets or steaks (choose either blackened or baked with beurre blanc); and chicken thighs pan-fried with tomato pesto and fresh chilis. Cheers is well known for its inventive cocktails, large range of beers, and wide selection of local and imported wines. There's also an "On the Wagon" assortment of freshly squeezed juices, teas, and cappuccinos.

CIN CIN ON QUAY BRASSERIE AND BAR, 99 Quay St. Tel. *376-966 or *376-967.

Cuisine: INTERNATIONAL. **Reservations:** Recommended for lunch.
$ Prices: Average meal NZ$10–NZ$16 ($6–$9). AE, DC, MC, V.
Open: Breakfast daily 7:30–11am; lunch and dinner daily 10am–2am; bar open until 3am.

This eclectic, stylish waterfront eatery in the old ferry building is a focal point for ferrygoers, but more than that, for Aucklanders who know the credentials of its chef de cuisine Warwick Brown, winner of some 53 international medals in his 17-year career. This unusual place features a wood-burning pizza oven, wood-fired grill with mesquite wood, and open kitchen. The chef oversees a menu that includes Italian, French, Chinese, and Japanese cuisine. The large bar serves drinks outside all day, specializing in imported beers and wines by the glass. Inside, marble floors add a touch of elegance to the large, casual dining area, and soft colors dominate the decor. Upstairs, there's mezzanine dining with a more formal ambience. Prices are surprisingly moderate. Light meals and snacks of Italian pastries and the like are also served.

THE FISH POT (4 locations, see below); 998 Tamaki Dr., Mission Bay (BYO). Tel. 528-4097.

Cuisine: FISH & CHIPS/SEAFOOD MEALS/TAKE-AWAYS. **Reservations:** Not required weekdays, recommended Fri–Sat for dinner.
$ Prices: Fish-and-chips NZ$15 ($9); full meals NZ$13–NZ$17 ($7–$10); children's menu NZ$5–NZ$8 ($3–$5). AE, DC, MC, V.
Open: Daily noon–late.

All four locations of The Fish Pot chain have rapidly become favorite gathering places for Auckland residents, as well as visitors. You can't beat them for both superb seafood—whether you go for fish-and-chips (better than any you've had before, I'll wager) or a main course that comes with a side salad and crisp fries. The super fish-and-chips use snapper with a light, crisp batter, the secret of which they refuse to divulge, and I am personally partial to the bay combo, filet of flounder with squid and mussels in a light curry cream sauce. Wine lists are extensive and moderately priced. Fun places to eat, and very good value for money.

The other Fish Pot locations are at Drake St., Victoria Park Market (fully licensed; tel. *734-530); Hauraki Corner, Takapuna (BYO, tel. 486-2542); and Queens Rd., Panmure (fully licensed and BYO; tel. 570-1126).

FORTUNA, 55 Customs St. East. Tel. *732-421.

Cuisine: CANTONESE. **Reservations:** Recommended.
$ Prices: Main courses NZ$8–NZ$12 ($5–$7); 20-course buffet lunch NZ$12 ($7); Sun 24-course smörgåsbord dinner NZ$17 ($10); children under age 11 free if accompanied by an adult. AE, DC, MC, V.
Open: Lunch daily noon–2:30pm; dinner Mon–Sat 6–11pm, Sun 6–9:30pm.
Closed: Christmas Day.

The menu in this attractive, family-run restaurant (the first licensed Chinese restaurant in Auckland when it opened in 1975 just up the street) is mostly Cantonese, with choices from Malaysia and Singapore as well. All five chefs trained in top Hong Kong restaurants. Eat your fill at lunch from selections of seafoods, poultry, beef, pork, lamb, and a choice of soups and desserts—terrific value for money. An especially good value is the Saturday and Sunday Yum Char lunch at NZ$12 ($7). The sumptuous Sunday smörgåsbord dinner offers even more choices. A great favorite with locals, it's on the waterfront in the center of the city.

FRASER'S PLACE, 116 Parnell Rd. Tel. *774-080.

Cuisine: DELI/SALADS/INTERNATIONAL. **Reservations:** Not required.
Transportation: Parnell area; good city bus service.

$ Prices: Deli NZ$2 ($1); lunch NZ$6–NZ$12.50 ($3–$7). No credit cards.
Open: Lunch Mon–Sat noon–2:30pm.

This is one of the special little places beloved by local residents and so seldom found by visitors. Ian Fraser left a successful business career to follow his heart into the kitchen of this sparkling deli/restaurant. You enter through the deli, which displays such unexpected treasures as those melt-in-your-mouth Greek spinach-and-cheese pies and mini-quiches, to be eaten at the pine-stool counter just back of the shop or to take home for that late-night snack when you don't want to go out. All sorts of sausages, cheeses, salads, and rolls as well. Upstairs, there are three distinctly different dining rooms: the Graffiti Room (you can leave your mark if you can find a spot on the wall), the Piaf Room, and the Conversation Room. The decor throughout is a treat, but it's the food that makes this place special. Ian was brought up in the East, and you'll find several spicy dishes on the menu like goulash, chili con carne, and mustard veal. Salad platters include smoked salmon, coppa and paw paw, shrimp and avocado, spanakopita Greek salad, and assorted cheese and fruit platters. Pâtés are homemade and out of this world. Be sure to include this stop in any Parnell Road wanderings. No wine license, but there are four special liqueur coffees. BYO.

HARBOURSIDE SEAFOOD BAR AND GRILL, Ferry Building, 94 Quay St.
Tel. *370-486 or *370-556.
Cuisine: SEAFOOD/PASTA/VENISON/POULTRY. **Reservations:** Recommended.
$ Prices: Appetizers NZ$6–NZ$12 ($3–$7); main courses NZ$12–NZ$23 ($7–$13); brunch NZ$20 ($11). AE, DC, MC, V.
Open: Daily 11:30am–10pm. **Closed:** Christmas Day.

This stylish second-floor restaurant on the waterfront in the city center has a terrific view of the harbor—do ask for a window seat. Decor is modern, with paintings, dividing screens, a marbled entrance, and a crayfish tank. Seafood dishes have won their fair share of kudos, and there's a good, extensive wine list. The menu features oysters in several guises, smoked seafood platter, char-grilled snapper, and salmon filet. My personal favorite is orange roughy steamed with prawns, served with a coriander-and-lime vinaigrette. An excellent brunch is served on Saturday, Sunday, and holidays. Licensed.

THE HARD TO FIND CAFE, 47 High St. Tel. *734-681.
Cuisine: MEXICAN. **Reservations:** Not required.
$ Prices: Snacks NZ$2.50–NZ$7.50 ($1–$4); main dishes NZ$5–NZ$14 ($3–$8). No credit cards.
Open: Lunch Mon–Fri noon–2:30pm; dinner daily 5:30–10pm.

The menu and prices make this an Auckland favorite. Owner/chef David Breen serves some of the best Mexican food I've had anywhere in the world (including my favorite New York City spot). His marvelous tacos come with all kinds of fillings, including vegetarian, and the nachos are really crispy. Although the enchilada salad and sour cream alone makes a good lunch, for something even more filling, try the enchilada and taco with rice and salad. There's a daily fish dish, blackboard specials, a nice selection of desserts, and several special coffees. No alcohol is served, but you're welcome to bring your own beer or wine. In the city center.

HIGH ST. CAFE, 51 High St. Tel. *799-067.
Cuisine: GAME/NEW ZEALAND. **Reservations:** Not required.
$ Prices: Appetizers NZ$3–NZ$6 ($2–$3); main courses NZ$6–NZ$18 ($6–$10). MC, V.
Open: Breakfast Mon–Fri 7–10am; lunch Mon–Fri 11:30am–2:30pm; dinner daily 6–11pm; late supper daily 10pm–1am.

This bright, attractive place in the city center serves food at virtually any hour. There's a long menu that includes such delicacies as smoked quail, médaillons of venison, smoked salmon quenelles, and lamb sweetbreads, as well as fish, pork, chicken, fettuccine, calves' liver, and a host of other dishes. Almost every dish can be ordered as an entree (small portion) or a main dish. A great favorite with Aucklanders. Licensed.

KONDITOREI BOSS, 305 Parnell Rd. Tel. *778-953.

Cuisine: QUICHE/SALADS/PASTRIES. **Reservations:** Not required.

$ Prices: Average lunch NZ$3.50–NZ$10 ($2–$6). MC, V.

Open: Daily 8am–5pm.

This Parnell Village place is cafeteria style yet quite stylish. It's a grand place for breakfast—you can sit and read the newspaper or plot the day's activities. The front porch is inviting, and it's handy for those in wheelchairs, who can just wheel right up. You can order everything from danish and coffee (or cappuccino) to fruit cups to meat-filled croissants to cheese pies. Everything is homemade, including good, hearty German-style bread. Pastries are terrific, as is their Black Forest cake.

NICHOLAS NICKLEBY, 9 High St. Tel. *734-604.

Cuisine: SALADS/QUICHES/LIGHT MEALS. **Reservations:** Not required.

$ Prices: Main dishes NZ$4–NZ$10 ($2–$6). MC, V.

Open: Mon–Fri 7:15am–2:30pm.

This is a real find for budgeteers. It's a small, unpretentious, cozy, downstairs eatery in the city center where everything is homemade and of the very freshest ingredients, and it's a great favorite with office workers (which means you'll do well to go earlier or later than regular office hours). The self-service counter always includes a nice variety of salads, small quiches, meat pies, meat rolls, soups, lasagne, and melt-in-your-mouth muffins and other pastries. Desserts, too, are exceptionally good. A cooked breakfast of bacon and eggs is also available in the morning.

THE QUEEN STREET BRASSERIE, Queen and Customs Sts. Tel. *778-920.

Cuisine: SNACKS/SALADS/TRADITIONAL. **Reservations:** Not required.

$ Prices: Snacks NZ$4–NZ$6 ($2–$3); average 3-course meal NZ$10–NZ$14 ($6–$8). AE, MC, V.

Open: Daily 6:30am–11pm.

On the ground floor of the Parkroyal Hotel in the city center, this handy pit stop is conveniently located near shopping and sights. The menu has a wide variety of offerings, from snacks to light lunches to three-course meals, all at moderate prices. It's fully licensed, and also serves counter lunches and take-aways from its delicatessen on the corner. Licensed.

RICK'S CAFE AMERICAIN, Victoria Park Market, Victoria St. West. Tel. *390-854.

Cuisine: BURGERS/PASTA/SALADS/SEAFOOD. **Reservations:** Not required.

$ Prices: Appetizers NZ$7–NZ$10 ($4–$6); main courses NZ$11–NZ$17 ($6–$10). AE, DC, MC, V.

Open: Mon–Fri 10am–12:30am, Sat–Sun 9am–12:30am; breakfast daily 9am–noon.

It doesn't look much like its *Casablanca* counterpart, but it's a terrific drop-in place in the city center for snacks, light lunches, and moderately priced dinners. The food is good and offerings range from potato skins with sour cream to chili to spareribs to fresh fish. Prices are moderate and light meals can be very inexpensive. Licensed, of course, and sometimes there's live music.

TONY'S MISSION BAY RESTAURANT, 71 Tamaki Dr., Mission Bay. Tel. 528-5419 or 528-6398.
Cuisine: STEAKS/SEAFOOD. **Reservations:** Not required.
$ **Prices:** Appetizers NZ$4–NZ$10 ($2–$6); main courses NZ$16–NZ$20 ($9–$11). AE, DC, MC, V.
Open: Lunch Mon–Fri noon–2:30pm; dinner daily 6–11pm.
Right on the waterfront in Mission Bay, Tony's specializes in steak, but the menu also includes very good seafood, as well as chicken dishes. Drivers will find ample parking, and the thoughtful owners have provided access ramps and table room for wheelchairs. There's good city bus service to the restaurant.

TOPO GIGIO ITALIAN RESTAURANT, 278 Dominion Rd., Mount Eden. Tel. *602-296.
Cuisine: ITALIAN. **Reservations:** Recommended.
$ **Prices:** Appetizers NZ$6–NZ$8 ($3–$5); main courses NZ$12–NZ$19 ($7–$11). AE, DC, MC, V.
Open: Lunch Mon–Fri noon–2pm; dinner daily 6–10:30.
This small, intimate restaurant is a perfect setting for its traditional Italian cuisine. Serving everything from homemade pastas and *gelato* (Italian ice cream) to veal scaloppine to a wide selection of pizzas to a large selection of Italian wines, this pleasant eatery offers very good value for dollar. It's a relaxed, friendly place, with good service and background Italian traditional and contemporary music as well as jazz, blues, and progressive folk. Fully licensed. City buses serve the Mount Eden area.

UNION FISH COMPANY, 16 Quay St. Tel. *396-593.
Cuisine: SEAFOOD. **Reservations:** Required.
$ **Prices:** Average meal NZ$23 ($13). AE, DC, MC, V.
Open: Lunch Mon–Fri noon–2:30pm; dinner daily 6–10:30pm.
This one-time marine repair warehouse on the waterfront in the city center has been converted into a nautical dining room that features a bar in the prow of a boat, a ship's figurehead, touches of brass, original maritime memorabilia, old maritime and early Auckland pictures, and a menu that calls itself a "bill of lading." Many Aucklanders consider this the best place in town for seafood Japanese style. Choose your own crayfish (lobster) from the tank, to be prepared any way you like, or select from such specialties as sashimi (raw fish with wasabi mustard), Bluff oysters, Nelson salmon (fresh or smoked), scallops, green-lipped mussels, or a choice of fish from the daily menu. Licensed.

NEARBY DINING IN DEVONPORT

THE LEFT BANK BRASSERIE, 14 Victoria Rd., Devonport. Tel. *452-615.
Cuisine: SNACKS/SALADS/SEAFOOD. **Reservations:** Not required.
$ **Prices:** Snacks NZ$3.50–NZ$8.50 ($2–$5); salads NZ$11–NZ$12 ($6–$7). AE, DC, MC, V.
Open: Daily noon–11pm.
This congenial, crowded café has a menu that includes tapas (everything from guacamole and corn chips to Thai marinated beef); avocado, bacon, and banana salad; fettuccine; fish of the day; and a sinful chocolate cake with chocolate sauce, almonds, and whipped cream. It's an easy walk from the ferry landing; if driving, take the Harbour Bridge. Licensed and BYO.

THE LOW FLYING DUCK CAFE, 99 Victoria Rd., Devonport. Tel. 445-8133.
Cuisine: MODERN NEW ZEALAND. **Reservations:** Recommended.

$ Prices: Appetizers NZ$7–NZ$10 ($4–$6); main courses NZ$19–NZ$23 ($11–$13). AE, DC, MC, V.

Open: Dinner Mon–Sat 6–10:30pm.

Mark and Gayle, the young partners who run The Low Flying Duck Café, use high quality, New Zealand seafood, beef, lamb, and fowl to create innovative dishes, along with a few old favorites such as Tua Tua fritters. All main dishes come with fresh seasonal vegetables, and there's delightful courtyard dining in summer months. This restaurant on the North Shore is accessible via the Harbour Bridge or ferry.

THE MASONIC TAVERN, King Edward Parade at Church St., Devonport.
Cuisine: BISTRO. **Reservations:** Not required.

$ Prices: Bistro lunch NZ$5–NZ$14 ($3–$8); average dinner NZ$17 ($10). MC, V.

Open: Lunch daily 12:30–2pm; dinner Mon–Sat 6–11pm.

If you're at all interested in an authentic, atmospheric working man's pub, which dishes up massive helpings of good grub at inexpensive prices, don't miss the Masonic Tavern near the ferry landing. I first tasted paua fritters there and they were so delicious I still have fritter-craving attacks! Hot meals, as well as light snacks, all go for wee prices. Burgers, salads, sandwiches, and other light meals supplement the fritters at lunch, with more substantial traditional dishes in the evening. A favorite with Devonport residents.

SOMETHING FISHY, 71 Victoria Rd., Devonport. Tel. 445-4263.
Cuisine: SEAFOOD. **Reservations:** Required.

$ Prices: Appetizers NZ$7.50–NZ$12.50 ($4–$7); main courses NZ$13–NZ$23 ($7–$13). AE, DC, MC, V.

Open: Tues–Sun 6–11pm.

There's nothing fishy about this place, except the specialties—mussels, prawns, squid, crayfish, and snapper, prepared simply and tastily. The popular eatery sports a low-key nautical decor and a crayfish tank from which you choose your own. BYO. Something Fishy is on the North Shore, reached by the Harbour Bridge or ferry.

PUB GRUB

RUGBY PUB, 47-51 Fort St. Tel. *770-725.
Cuisine: PUB GRUB. **Reservations:** Not required.

$ Prices: Sandwiches NZ$2 ($1); average meal NZ$7 ($4). No credit cards.

Open: Pub Mon–Wed 10am–11pm, Thurs–Sat 10am–11pm; lunch served Mon–Fri noon–2:30pm.

One of the most economical meals in town is the pub counter lunch at this small club just a few blocks from Queen Street in the city center. The menu includes fish-and-chips or roast beef on rye, oysters, prawns, and lasagne. An assortment of sandwiches and rolls is also available. The unique collection of rugby memorabilia covers the walls. Licensed.

SHAKESPEARE TAVERN & HATHAWAYS BRASSERIE, 61 Albert St. Tel. 735-396.
Cuisine: PUB GRUB. **Reservations:** Not required.

$ Prices: Under NZ$15 ($9). AE, DC, MC, V.

Open: Hathaway's Mon–Wed 11am–7:45pm, Thurs 11am–9:45pm, Fri–Sat 11am–10:45pm, Sun noon–9:45pm. Tavern daily 11am–7pm.

If it's pub grub you savor, visit New Zealand's only in-house brewery, located in the city center. It makes lager, ale, stout, and even ginger beer (if you try them all, you leave with a certificate). The winsome publican, Peter Barraclough, has been here since 1975, and his friendly daughter, Karen, is often on duty in the lounge upstairs. Hathaway's, the restaurant located downstairs, offers moderately priced fare. You'll probably come away with a T-shirt or mug as a souvenir—it's that kind of place. Licensed, of course.

SPECIALTY DINING

Lunch or Dinner Afloat A lunch or dinner cruise is a teriffic way to explore Auckland's spectacular harbor, and city views are impressive, to say the least, especially in the evening, when city lights are reflected along the shoreline. The freshest of seafoods are served on most cruises, along with beef and other nonseafood dishes. A bit pricey—NZ$40 ($23) for lunch, NZ$66 ($38) for dinner—but well worth every NZ cent! Hours for luncheon cruises are 12:30 to 2:30pm, dinner 6 to 9pm. Book with **The Pride of Auckland Company,** Downtown Airline Terminal Building, corner of Quay and Albert Streets.

Breakfast See full writeups above for details of the following restaurants, all of which serve breakfast as early as 7am or 7:30pm. Best get there before 10am, however, when most begin lunch preparations: **Konditorei Boss,** 305 Parnell Rd. (tel. *778-953); **Cin Cin on Quay Brasserie and Bar,** 99 Quay St. (tel. *376-966 or *376-967); **High St. Café,** 51 High St. (tel. *799-067); **Nicholas Nickleby,** 9 High St. (tel. *734-604); and **The Queen Street Brasserie,** Queen and Customs Streets in the Parkroyal Hotel (tel. *778-920).

Late-Night Dining Check writeups above for full details of these late-serving eateries: **Baalbeck Lebanese Restaurant,** 58 Wellesley St. (at Federal Street) (tel. *734-693); **Cheers Café & Bar,** 12 Wyndham St. (just off Queen Street) (tel. 309-8779); **Cin Cin on Quay Brasserie and Bar,** 99 Quay St. (tel. *376-966 or *376-967); **The Fish Pot** (four locations), 998 Tamaki Dr., Mission Bay (BYO; tel. 528-4097); Drake Street, Victoria Park Market (fully licensed; tel. *734-530); Hauraki Corner, Takapuna (BYO; tel. 486-2542); and Queens Road, Panmure (fully licensed and BYO; tel. 570-1126); and **High St. Café,** 51 High St. (tel. *799-067).

Dining Complexes Be sure to pay a visit to the **China Oriental Markets,** 2 Britomart Place (tel. 302-0678). It's down near the waterfront, and you can't miss the lavender, blue, lime, and yellow facade. Inside there are 130 stalls featuring every type of food (and merchandise) imaginable. It was created in late 1989, and is open 7 days a week.

Victoria Park Market, on Victoria Street West, also has an International Food Hall, as well as several fully licensed restaurants and a McDonald's.

Local Budget Bets One of the most inexpensive ways to eat, of course, is to stop by a deli and pick up the makings of a meal in your motel flat—you'll be getting full value then from that lovely fridge, stove, pots and pans, and dishes.

An alternative, especially on those days when you're absolutely pooped from sightseeing and don't want to face any sort of food preparation, is to order a delicious pizza and have it delivered piping hot right to your door. **Dial-A-Dino's Pizza** (tel. *781-103) delivers from 4:30 to 11pm Sunday through Thursday and 4:30pm to 1am on Friday and Saturday. There's a wide variety of pizza toppings from which to choose: ham, salami, pepperoni, diced beef, mushrooms, onions, olives, prawns, smoked oysters, bacon, anchovies, capers . . . well, that's part of their list. They also offer crusty garlic bread and soft drinks, and delivery is usually within 30 minutes. Pizzas come in 6-, 8-, and 12-slice pies at prices of NZ$14.50 to NZ$30 ($8 to $17).

WORTH THE EXTRA MONEY

With Auckland's wealth of fine dining, it almost seems obligatory to indulge in at least one "big splurge" while you're there. The following are among those I consider worthy of that extra expenditure.

SAILS, The Anchorage, Westhaven Marina (off Fanshawe St.). Tel. *789-890.

Cuisine: SEAFOOD/NEW ZEALAND SPECIALTIES. **Reservations:** Required.
$ Prices: Appetizers NZ$7–NZ$14 ($4–$8); main lunch courses NZ$14–NZ$20 ($8–$11); main dinner courses NZ$20–NZ$25 ($11–$14); average 3-course meal with wine NZ$70 ($40). AE, DC, MC, V.
Open: Lunch Mon–Fri noon–2pm; dinner daily 6:30–10:30pm.

For a water-level view of Auckland's beautiful harbor, head for Sails, nestled beside the approaches to the Auckland Harbour Bridge. The large, light, and airy dining room is decorated in cool shades of green, white, and gray, but its most impressive decor is just outside its wall of windows, where hundreds of private sailboats are anchored in the harbor. The most jaded soul is sure to respond to the sight of gently bobbing boats and sunlight sparkling off the harbor waters. The menu features—what else?—seafood, and I could make a meal just from the starters listed (a seafood terrine of scallops and crab, smoked fish with horseradish cream, oysters grilled with spinach and cheese or champagne and cream, fresh pasta with a garlicky tomato sauce, etc.). Main courses include orange roughy, seafood Mornay, fresh crayfish, and nonfishy specialties of lamb, chicken, and pork. Desserts are excellent (I dare you to try the white-chocolate cups filled with boysenberry cream and served with chocolate-dipped strawberries—sinfully delicious!), and there's a good selection of cheeses. Sails is fully licensed. Coffee lovers will like to know that Twinings Grosvenor roast is served here. A delightful place and very popular, so be sure to book ahead.

TOP OF THE TOWN, in the Hyatt Hotel, 14th floor, 2 Princes St. Tel. 366-1234.
Cuisine: NEW ZEALAND SPECIALTIES/CONTINENTAL. **Reservations:** Required.
$ Prices: 3-course lunch NZ$36 ($21); dinner NZ$50–NZ$100 ($29–$57). AE, DC, MC, V.
Open: Lunch Mon–Fri noon–2:30pm; dinner Mon–Sat 7–10:30pm.

For sheer elegance, your dollars couldn't be better spent than at the Top of the Town, winner of the coveted New Zealand Restaurant of the Year Award three times. The magnificent views of Waitemata Harbour and Albert Park would be justification enough for a meal here, but add to that a luxurious decor, polished and friendly service, and a menu that features the best in New Zealand cuisine, and you'll find yourself yearning to indulge a second time. But if you plan just one visit, I urge you to come in the evening, when soft candlelight is a perfect complement to the spectacular panorama of twinkling city lights outside.

The food is superb no matter when you dine. Lunch specialties include smoked salmon, lamb chops with minted red-currant glaze, beef filet in cognac, and a yeast pastry flan of whitebait and leeks. After dark, choose from such exotic dishes as crayfish rolled in nori over brandy with crab-cream sauce, a brace of stuffed quail with foie gras sauce, grilled filet of beef with raisin and cognac-pepper glaze, médaillons of venison in Chartreuse, and . . . well, you get the idea. There's a good wine list, fabulous desserts and cheeses (imported and domestic) wind things up nicely, and special liqueur coffees concocted and flamed at your table add the final, sinfully indulgent touch. In the city center.

READERS RECOMMEND

Angus Steak House, 35 Albert St., Auckland. *"Geoff Uren's restaurant was a great find for delicious steaks. You pick out your steak from a case with a variety of cuts and sizes, and take it to the chef who cooks it on the grill right before your eyes. There is a nice salad bar, and you also get bread and potato, all at a modest set price. A must for steak lovers."*—Glen R. Murray, Glendale, Calif.

Hammerheads Seafood Restaurant & Bar, Tamaki Dr., Mission Bay, Auckland. Tel.
*521-440. "About two blocks west of Kelly Tarlton's Underwater World, we found this excellent
seafood restaurant with a fabulous view of the bay and a marvelous menu with moderate
prices."*—Mari Fagin, Nichols Hills, Okla.

6. ATTRACTIONS

If your time in Auckland is going to be limited and you can't quite figure out how
you'll work in everything you'd like to see, you should consult the Visitor Information
Centre (see "Tourist Information," above). Just call or go by, and tell them what you
want to see and how much time you have. The following is a *suggested* itinerary, and
you should fit your own time to your own special interests.

A SUGGESTED ITINERARY

Day 1: You'll need at least half the day to see and fully appreciate the **Auckland
War Memorial Museum.** The unique **Kelly Tarlton's Underwater World**
will fill the afternoon, and a nice ending for the day is a dinner cruise of the harbor.
Day 2: Make your second day a step back into Auckland's history by visiting its
Ewelme Cottage, Kinderhouse, and **Massey Homestead.**
Day 3: Take the ferry over to **Devonport,** on Auckland's North Shore, and spend
the day exploring its streets lined with colonial-style bungalows, with a stop by at
least one of its fine beaches.
Day 4: Make this into a market day, with visits to **Victoria Park Market,** the
China Oriental Markets, and **Parnell Village.**
Day 5: Visit the ancient Maori fort on **One Tree Hill,** then plan an afternoon at the
Auckland Zoo.

THE TOP ATTRACTIONS

Before you set out to explore Auckland, arm yourself with the money-saving
Explorer Bus pass for traveling between major attractions (see Section 3, above).

AUCKLAND WAR MEMORIAL MUSEUM, Auckland Domain. Tel. 309-0443.

A visit to this museum is a virtual necessity for a full appreciation of the Maori
culture you'll be exposed to in other parts of the country. The imposing, gleaming-
white museum, surrounded by sweeping lawns and flower gardens right in the city
center, houses the world's largest collection of Maori artifacts, providing you with a
rich background from which to understand the Maoris of today. Be sure to pick up a
free guide map as you enter the museum.

In the **Maori Court,** the most impressive exhibit is probably the 82-foot war
canoe chiseled from one enormous totara trunk and covered with intricate, symbolic
carvings. You'll see that same artistic carving in the 85-foot meetinghouse, whose
painted rafters and carved and painted wall panels are a wonder of red, black, and
white scrollwork. The wall panels also feature tribal-motif carvings interspersed with
traditional woven flax patterns. The meetinghouse sits between two storehouses raised
on stilts to protect community goods from predators. Also in the museum are displays
of gorgeous feather cloaks (each feather knotted in by hand) worn by high-ranking
men, as well as a display of jade tikis. From time to time, there's a demonstration on
the making of the *piu piu* (reed skirt) from flax. Look for the greenstone *mere* (war
club), such a lordly weapon that it was reserved for the slaying of only the

?DID YOU KNOW . . . ?

- Auckland and its environs is New Zealand's largest urban area, home to one-third of its population.
- The city has two harbors, sprinkled with more than 20 islands, with over 100 beaches, and 2,000 hours of sunshine annually.

highest-ranking captives (who considered it an honor to meet their end with such a club). Look also for the Maori portraits, the life's work of famed New Zealand artist C. F. Goldie, a Pakeha who captured on canvas not only the ornate tattoos of chieftains and common folk, but their fierce tribal pride as well.

Elsewhere in the museum, there's a **Hall of South Pacific Art, Hall of Asian Art, Pacific Canoe Hall,** native bird displays (including that giant *moa* exhibit), and much, much more. Especially interesting is **"Centennial Street,"** a reconstruction of an Auckland shopping street of 1866—equally interesting is a comparison of prices then and now!

The shop near the entrance of the museum is worth a little browsing time for publications on Maori art and New Zealand flora and fauna, as well as reproductions and replicas of some of the exhibits—a good place to pick up mementos to carry home. There's also a coffee lounge (open from 10am to 3:45pm), which serves sandwiches, salads, desserts, and beverages.

A nice ending to a museum visit is a call at the nearby **Winter Garden,** on the museum grounds, to view the impressive collection of tropical and subtropical plants.

Admission: Free.

Open: Daily 10am–5pm. **Bus:** No. 635 from the Downtown Bus Terminal.

AUCKLAND CITY ART GALLERY, Kitchener and Wellesley St., intersection of Albert Park. Tel. *792-020 for recorded information, or 309-0831.

New Zealand's oldest and largest art gallery, this is one of the most active art museums in the South Pacific. Its permanent collection ranges from European masters to contemporary international art, plus the most comprehensive collection of New Zealand fine art in the country. Works by New Zealand artists date from 1770 to the present and include a display of fine Maori portraits. A coffee shop offers refreshment, and there's good browsing in the bookshop. On Sunday afternoons in winter the gallery features classical and jazz concerts; call for information.

Admission: Free except for periodic special exhibitions.

Open: Daily 10am–4:30pm (until 9pm the last Thurs of each month). **Transportation:** City bus service.

KELLY TARLTON'S UNDERWATER WORLD, Orakei Wharf, 23 Tamaki Dr. Tel. 528-0603.

This is the inspiration and last work of the late Kelly Tarlton, famed diver whose legacy to the country also includes the outstanding Museum of Shipwrecks in the Bay of Islands. His careful planning literally puts you inside an underwater environment by way of a moving walkway that passes through a clear tunnel surrounded by hundreds of native New Zealand fish swimming freely, apparently paying no mind at all to their gaping visitors. The experience is much the same as that of an actual dive—after passing through heavy "surf," you'll move over a sandy ocean bottom, through forests of waving seaweed, into mysterious underwater caves, and along rocky reefs. Look for sea creatures ranging from tiny sea horses to the leggy octopus, and don't miss the magnificent shark tank with its toothy inhabitants and huge stingrays. Subtropical species, such as the hagfish and piranha, inhabit small tanks. There's good wheelchair access from the car park, and Kelly's Café offers snacks at reasonable prices.

Admission: NZ$9 ($5) adults, NZ$4.50 ($3) children 4–12, free for children under 4. Special rates for family groups and senior citizens.

Open: Daily 9am–9pm. **Transportation:** Mission Bay city bus.

AUCKLAND ZOO, Motions Rd., Western Springs. Tel. *787-487.

One of the few places to observe the kiwi, that flightless bird that has become New Zealand's national symbol, is the Nocturnal House here at the zoo. The birds are exhibited daily in natural bush settings, which resemble a moonlit forest floor. You can watch them foraging, their long beaks seeking food in the leaf-covered ground. Don't plan a quick run out to the zoo just to look at the kiwis, however—more than 2,000 other birds, mammals, fish, and reptiles (representing some 200 species) will entice you from one area to another in the beautifully tended park surroundings. For instance, you can also take a look here at the *tuatara,* Earth's oldest reptile (see Chapter 1).

Admission: NZ$9 ($5) adults, NZ$4.50 ($3) children 5–15, free for children under 5. NZ$24 ($14) family ticket admits two adults and up to four children.

Open: Daily 9:30am–5:30pm (last admission 4:15pm). **Bus:** No. 043, 044, or 045, leaving every 10 minutes from Customs St.

MORE ATTRACTIONS

PARNELL ROSE GARDEN, Gladstone Rd. Tel. *775-359.

If it's rose-blooming time when you visit, be sure to stop to see this garden. Thousands of traditional roses are set in color-coordinated beds. Rose Garden Lounge serves lunches on weekdays.

Admission: Free.

Open: Nov–Mar, daily during daylight hours. **Bus:** No. 702 from the Downtown Bus Terminal.

 FROMMER'S FAVORITE
AUCKLAND EXPERIENCES

A Harbor Cruise Anytime of Day   But especially spectacular in the evening, when city lights add a special magic to the sight.

Browsing Through Shops in Parnell Village   Many feature New Zealand and other South Pacific crafts housed in colonial-style bungalows.

The Ferry Ride to Devonport   Another good harbor view, followed by a leisurely stroll through the interesting streets and lunch at the Masonic Tavern.

A Meal at Sails Restaurant   Really super food comes with a great view of the marina, which sparkles in sunlight at lunch, and with riding lights at night.

A Waterfront Trip Along Tamaki Drive   Travel by car or city bus, curving around Hauraki Gulf, past one of the city's most popular beaches, through Mission Bay and St. Helier's Bay, and Kelly Tarlton's Underwater World.

MUSEUM OF TRANSPORT AND TECHNOLOGY, 825 Great North Rd., Western Springs. Tel. *860-199.

There's a fascinating collection of vehicles, trains, trams, aircraft, steam engines, and pioneer artifacts at the MOTAT, as it is best known. There, you'll find New Zealand's only full-time publicly operating tramway, including Auckland's first electric tram, circa 1902. In the Pioneers of Aviation Pavilion, special tribute is paid to Richard Pearse, who on March 31, 1902, flew an aircraft in the South Island. Life in 1840–90 New Zealand is re-created in the Pioneer Village, where the church is still used for weddings and christenings. There are several food facilities on the grounds, but the 119-year-old Colonial Arms Restaurant is rather special, serving Devonshire teas and à la carte meals. The museum is just 5 kilometers (3 miles) from the city center.

Admission: NZ$9 ($5) adults, NZ$4.50 ($3) children, NZ$6.50 ($4) senior citizens. NZ$23 ($13) family ticket admits two adults and up to four children.

Open: Daily 10am–4pm. **Closed:** Christmas Day. **Bus:** No. 145 from Customs St. East.

EWELME COTTAGE, 14 Ayr St. Tel. *790-202.

This cottage was built by the Rev. Vicesimus Lush (somehow, I find humor in that surname for a minister!) and named for Ewelme Village in England. It has been authentically restored, right down to as much of the original wallpaper as could be salvaged and 19th-century furnishings.

Admission: NZ$2.50 ($1) adults, NZ$.50 (30¢) children.

Open: Daily 10:30am–noon and 1–4:30pm. **Closed:** Good Friday and Christmas Day. **Bus:** No. 635, 645, or 655 from Downtown Bus Terminal.

HOWICK COLONIAL VILLAGE, Lloyd Elsmore Park, Bells Rd., Pakuranga. Tel. 576-9506.

More than 20 buildings in a flowering garden setting take you back to village life in colonial New Zealand. Based on the local military, the village faithfully depicts the 1840–80 decades.

Admission: NZ$9 ($5) adults, NZ$4.50 ($3) children.

Open: Daily 10am–4pm. **Transportation/Directions:** 20-minute drive on Pakuranga Hwy.; Howick and Eastern bus to Fortun's Rd.

OTHER AUCKLAND SIGHTS

The historical **Old Auckland Customhouse** on Customs Street West is an outstanding example of 1880s architecture. It's a massive, but rather graceful-looking building whose halls once rang with waterfront commerce. Today it has been beautifully restored and houses craft shops, two bookshops, Brandy's cocktail bar, and restaurants. Well worth a stop, both inside and out.

Parnell Village is actually a row of restored colonial houses along Parnell Road between St. Stephens Avenue and York Street in what is one of Auckland's oldest suburbs. Nowadays, those quaint old homes hold boutiques so fashionable they border on the trendy, art galleries, eateries, and pubs. But despite the bustle of shoppers, you'll get a real feeling of old Auckland just by ambling along the sidewalks and down tiny alleyways.

With or without binoculars, the view is nothing short of spectacular from the summit of **Mount Eden,** Auckland's highest point. An extinct volcano, which was fortified by Maoris, Mount Eden looks down on the city, both harbors, and Hauraki Gulf. The no. 274 bus from Customs Street East will get you there, or it's a lovely drive.

One Tree Hill (Cornwall Park, Mount Eden) is also an extinct volcano and was also the site of a large Maori *pa* (fort). There's an obelisk on the summit as a memorial to that race. The views are terrific, and the adjoining parkland is great for long walks.

A FERRY RIDE TO DEVONPORT

One of the nicest ways I know to see Auckland is from the harbor ferry, which crosses to the North Shore. Usually you'll be aboard the zippy catamaran *Kea,* but from time to time the much-beloved and semiretired steam ferry MV *Kestrel,* makes the journey. As the city recedes, you're treated to a focused look at big-city growth: the old red-brick ferry building with its clock tower stands in marked contrast to streamlined skyscrapers, and the stately white War Memorial looks down on it all with the dignity born of historical perspective. As you pass the naval base, it's perfectly permissible to raise your hand in salute to New Zealand's seafarers. Then, if you plan it right and return in the evening, the sparkling city lights turn big-city sprawl into diamond-studded magic. You catch the ferry (tel. 303-3319) at the Queen's Wharf terminal on Quay Street (its North Shore destination is Devonport), leaving every hour on the hour from 7am to 11pm, 7 days a week. Round-trip fare is NZ$6 ($3.45).

The little suburb of **Devonport** is where the Maoris say their great ancestral canoe *Tainui* first touched land in this area, somewhere around the 14th century. You'll see a stone memorial to that event on the grassy strip along King Edward Parade foreshore—the bronze sculpture is an orb topped by a *korotangi* (weeping dove), one of the birds the Maoris brought with them from their homeland. There are four white-sand beaches in Devonport, as well as Mount Victoria, which sits near the business center and is now topped by a harbor signal station (great views from up there). You can also walk up to North Head and explore the old military fort with its tunnels and gun sites.

Stroll along **King Edward Parade** and look for no. 7, where one of New Zealand's most talented writers—he was also an artist and a poet—Rex Fairburn (1904–57) once lived. A little farther along, you'll come to the Masonic Hotel at the corner of Church Street. It was built in 1866, and this is where you'll find the **Masonic Tavern** (see "Where to Eat," above). Just across the way, **The Works** is one of my favorite places in the country to watch craftspeople at work. In what was once the Duder Brothers' mercantile store, they and a group of artists open their workshops and offer their wares for sale. It's open from 10am to 4pm Tuesday through Sunday (tel. *453-212). Drop in on historian Paul Titchener at his **Book and Stationery Shop** at 9/11 Victoria Rd. (tel. *453-263), for a chat and to browse. Visit the **Devonport Museum and Gardens,** at 31-A Vauxhall Rd. (tel. *452-661), between 2 and 4pm on weekends. Devonport is full of interesting houses that survive from the 1800s and early 1900s—no. 9 Mays St. is a marvel of cast-iron decoration, and virtually every house on Anne Street is a museum piece. The **Esplanade Hotel,** one of the first things you'll see as you debark from the ferry, dates from 1902.

There are an increasing number of good eateries in Devonport (see "Where to Eat," above) if you should decide to stay over for dinner.

COOL FOR KIDS

RAINBOW'S END ADVENTURE PARK, Great South and Wiri Station Rds., Manukau City, Auckland. Tel. 277-9870.

This leisure park boasts all sorts of action rides, video games, mini-golf, a roller coaster, and the Zim Zam Zoo (you'll have to see it!). The kids—of any age—will love it!

Admission: All-day Super Pass (including rides) NZ$20 ($11) adults, NZ$15 ($9) ages 5–15; under 5, free. Fun Pass (including entry to the park only) NZ$3 ($2) and a NZ$3 ($2) charge for each ride.

Open: Summer, Sun–Fri 10am–5pm, Sat 10am–10pm; winter hours vary.

SPECIAL-INTEREST SIGHTSEEING

One of Auckland's (and indeed, New Zealand's) very best attractions is offered by the **Auckland Tourist Hospitality Scheme,** and it doesn't cost a penny. Do this at the beginning of your trip if possible—it will give more meaning to every Kiwi contact you make thereafter. This group of enthusiastic volunteers will arrange for you to spend a morning, afternoon, or evening with an Auckland family for absolutely no other reason than to have an opportunity to talk on a one-to-one basis in the informal, relaxed atmosphere of a private home. It's a terrific chance to learn about New Zealand daily life firsthand and to exchange views from our different parts of the world. They'll try to match you by profession or hobby from among the 80 Auckland families who participate. They do not arrange overnight stays—just friendly visits. You can call them when you arrive, or better yet, write in advance to any of the following: Mrs. Polly Ring, 775 Riddell Rd., Glendowie, Auckland 5 (tel. 575-6655); Mrs. Jean Mahon, 129 Taylors Rd., Mount Albert, Auckland (tel. *860-342); Mrs. Eve Williamson, 170 Cook St., Howick, Auckland (tel. 535-8098); Mr. Trevor Holloway, 126 Puhinui Rd., Papatoetoe (tel. 278-8434); Mrs. Valerie Blackie, Flat 3, 16 Orakau Ave., Epson (tel. *659-373); and Mrs. Meryl Revell, 60 Prince Regent Dr., Half Moon Bay (tel. 535-5314).

ORGANIZED TOURS

From the **Visitors Information Centre,** you can book several **half- and full-day tours** of the city and its environs. Half-day tours, morning or afternoon, cover sightseeing highlights, and an all-day tour includes eastern and western suburbs, the zoo, and a vineyard. Half-day tours run about NZ$35 ($20) for adults, half that for children, while the day-long tour will cost around NZ$80 ($46) for adults, half that for children. Contact the Visitor Information Centre for current schedules and booking. They can also book 1-, 2-, and 3-day tours to destinations like Waitomo, Rotorua, and the Bay of Islands.

There are also several very good **day tours** from Auckland to sightseeing spots like Waitomo, as well as 2- and 3-day tours at very attractive prices to the Bay of Islands and Rotorua. Check current schedules and prices at the Visitor Information Centre. **Fullers Cruise Centre,** Ferry Building, Quay Street (tel. *774-074), has a terrific **cruise and vineyard tour** to Waiheke Island and vineyard tour that includes a wine tasting. It's a full day (10am to 4:30pm), and the price is about NZ$40 ($23), with lunch extra.

Some of New Zealand's finest wineries are just west of Auckland, and **New Zealand Vineyard Tours,** P.O. Box 10-130, Balmoral, Auckland 4 (tel. *09/398-670), has tours of some of the best, operating from 10am to 3pm every day of the week except Sunday. They'll pick you up at your hotel or motel, and the day will include visits to at least three vineyards, wine tastings, and a three-course lunch (with wine, of course). Call for current schedule and price.

Bush & Beach Ltd., P.O. Box 40-047, Auckland 10 (tel. 473-0189), are outdoor specialists offering a range of small-group (one- to eight-passenger) tours around the Auckland region, traveling in a Toyota Landcruiser. Led by experienced guides, the tours are flexible and focus on the unique aspects of each route. Among the offerings:

a half-day (1 to 5pm) **Waitakere Range** tour that visits surf beaches, rocky headlands, and a subtropical rain forest, with time to explore; a full-day (9am to 5pm) **west coast-east coast tour,** passing through farmlands, vineyards, and orchards, with opportunities for walking; a half-day (9am to noon) tour to a **mainland gannet colony** that is one of only two in the world and 22 miles of black iron sand surf beach (September to April only); and a half-day (9am to noon) walk through native bush, combined with a visit to an extinct volcano and a beach (May through September only). Prices range from NZ$50 to NZ$95 ($29 to $54). They also offer 2- to 3-week **camping tours** and a 3-day tour of Northland and Waitomo/Rotorua/ Coromandel, traveling by minibus, at prices in the NZ$400 to $450 ($229 to $257) range.

Backroad Tours, P.O. Box 31-228, Milford, Auckland (tel. 09/*765-631), has unique **backpacker bus,** 3- to 5-day tours to remote areas of the **East Coast (east of Rotorua), Northland,** and the **West Coast of the South Island** for small groups. Don't think this is a "bare bones" bus—it's outfitted with a traveling coffee lounge, more comfort than most backpackers experience. Recognizing that most visitors' only contact with Maori people is restricted to concerts—and occasionally at a local pub—Steve Sol and Gerry Cornelius arrange visits to a Maori *marae,* the community meetinghouse that is the very heart of native culture. They have asked me to pass along, however, their caution that because Maori consider their culture sacred and are cautious about sharing it, all Backpacker Tour passengers are asked to treat them with respect and sensitivity—to meet Maori as *people,* not as curiosities. All in all, these tours are a terrific way to see New Zealand from a new perspective. Prices run from NZ$99 ($57), plus a NZ$11 to $15 ($6 to $9) per night bed-and-breakfast charge, to NZ$200 ($114), all inclusive.

Guided Walks   The City Council's Parks and Recreation Department sponsors several interesting guided walks around the city at no charge, as well as furnishing maps and booklets for do-it-yourselfers. Ask at the Visitor Information Centre for booklets that give days and times of walks that examine **arts and crafts and specialty shops, current art exhibitions, historic places, marketplaces, the Auckland Domain,** and a **Domain nature walk.**

Self-Guided Walks   If you're a real walker, there's a self-guiding map for an interesting **coast-to-coast walk** across the 9-kilometer (5½-mile) isthmus between the Pacific Ocean and the Tasman Sea. Allow about 4 hours, but since many parts of the track pass near bus routes and car parks, you don't have to do it all at once. Although, perforce, you must walk through industrialized sections, there are many wooded spots, archeological sites, parks, gardens, and panoramic views of the city and harbor which are ideal for a picnic. Booklets outlining this and other do-it-yourself tours are also available from the Visitor Information Centre.

Harbor Cruises   If the 20-minute ferry ride to Devonport just isn't enough time on the water for you, **Fuller's Cruises Ltd.,** Quay Street (tel. *774-074 for information; *771-771 to book), offers a wide variety of cruises around the harbor. Sail out to Rangitoto Island or take shorter cruises concentrating on points of interest in the harbor itself. Call for current schedules and prices, then book through your motel or hotel, or buy tickets at the downtown waterfront ticket office in the Ferry Building. They also run longer cruises to **Waiheke Island** and **Great Barrier Island.**

The **Pride of Auckland Co.,** Downtown Airlines Terminal (tel. *734-557), offers a different type of harbor cruise aboard luxury yachts. Departing the Quayside Launch Landing, Quay Street, under full sail, you cruise the harbor for some two hours, relaxing on the large deck area or in the spacious saloon lounge. An informative commentary fills you in on points of interest, and there are even full sailing suits for those who wish to remain out on deck on cool or rainy days. There's also a bar and a full galley aboard. Schedules include a **morning-coffee cruise, lunch cruise, afternoon-coffee cruise,** and a **dinner cruise.** Fares are NZ$30 ($17) for the coffee and lunch cruises, plus NZ$12 ($7) for luncheon; the dinner-cruise fare of NZ$70 ($40) includes dinner. Seafood is the specialty, and all meals must be preordered. Identify yourself as a Frommer reader and get a **15% discount.** Highly recommended.

READERS RECOMMEND

Waiwera Thermal Pools. "How do you spend a cool, rainy day in Auckland? Take the Waiwera no. 895 bus 1 hour north to the Waiwera Thermal Pools, where both indoor and outdoor pools will soothe away the aches, pains, and frustrations."—B. Lushniak, Chicago, Ill.

7. SPORTS & RECREATION

SPECTATOR SPORTS

Both **horse and greyhound racing** are popular Auckland pastimes, and you can check up on race meets during your visit by calling the 24-hour **Recorded Racing Information Service** (tel. 09/520-7507). Punters will be happy to know that you can place a bet, even if you don't make it to the track—armed with a valid credit card, ring **Telebetting** (tel. 09/520-9988).

Check with the Visitor Information Centre for current schedules of New Zealand's famous **All Black rugby team.**

RECREATION

Golf   Golfers will find themselves welcomed at some 30 fine golf courses in the Auckland area. For details, call 522-0491 Monday through Thursday, 9am to 5pm, and ask for the name of the course nearest you and current greens fees.

Swimming   Accessible from Tamaki Drive (frequent bus service from Downtown Bus Terminal), **Judges Bay, Okahu Bay, Mission Bay, Kohimarama,** and **St. Helier's Bay beaches** are popular inner-harbor swimming venues. It's a good idea to check on tidal conditions before heading out.

Tennis   The Stanley Street Tennis Stadium has racquets and balls for hire. For bookings, call *733-623.

8. SAVVY SHOPPING

THE SHOPPING SCENE

Plan to spend at least half a day shopping or just browsing or sightseeing in **Parnell Village.** That's the stretch of Parnell Road between York Street and St. Stephens Avenue. In restored colonial homes and stores, there are boutiques, art galleries, craft shops, antiques stores, restaurants, and pubs. It's great people-watching territory, and a place you just may pick up that one-of-a-kind souvenir. Most shops, restaurants, and pubs are open Monday through Saturday.

Victoria Park Market, Victoria Street West (tel. *396-140), is a lively gathering place for weavers, potters, leather workers, and other craftspeople, as well as a bustling fruit and vegetable market. It's open 7 days a week from 9am to 7pm (restaurants have later hours).

China Oriental Markets, corner of Quay Street and Britomart Place (on the waterfront), has no less than 140 stalls, selling a wide variety of European and Asian goods.

Some of the best craft shops in Auckland are in the beautifully restored old **Customhouse,** 22 Customs St. West, which dates from 1888. You'll find pottery, quilts, hand-woven wall hangings, hand-knit sweaters, glasswear, porcelain, wood works, and a very good bookshop (which mails books home, saving you the GST). Shop hours are 9am to 5pm Monday through Thursday, until 5:30 on Friday and Saturday, and noon to 5:30pm on Sunday.

Out in the Newmarket section, **Two Double Seven Shopping Center,** 277 Broadway, is one of Auckland's newest shopping complexes. Housed in a sprawling, five-story, block-long building, the center houses specialty stores that include sportswear, jewelry, giftware, music, high-fashion shops, and an International Foodcourt. Drivers will find a covered carpark, and others can take any bus number beginning with 30 or 31 and marked "Onehunga" or "Favona," departing from Victoria Street East (just off Queen Street, outside the A.M.P. Insurance Building.)

Duty Free   At **Regency Duty Free Stores,** they stock an amazing variety of duty-free brands, as well as top quality New Zealand handcrafts and souvenirs. All purchases will be held until your departure from the country. They have two locations in Auckland at Auckland International Airport (tel. 09/275-6893), and 25 Victoria St. West (tel. 09/308-9014).

SPECIALTY SHOPPING

China   At **Tanfield Potter,** 287 Queen St. (tel. 309-0935), they have been importing fine china, crystal, glassware, cutlery, and high-quality giftware since 1861. Probably the best selection in Auckland. Open 9am to 5:30pm Monday through Thursday, 9:30am to 12:30pm Saturday.

Crafts   Auckland is fairly broken out with craft shops, and I found **Parnell Elephant House,** 237 Parnell Rd. (tel. 309-8740), to be outstanding among the lot. It's a large shop, set back from Parnell Road—follow the elephant footprints (printed, of course, not the real thing) down a little alleyway. I can't begin to enumerate all the unique and fascinating craft items, both from New Zealand and countries around the world: wood (carved, turned, and sliced); rocking horses, patchwork, weaving, pottery, batik and silk clothing, stained glass, and jewelry are just a very few. This is a very special shop, with excellent value-for-money prices. They accept credit cards and traveler's checks, and are happy to mail overseas. Open daily from 10am to 5pm.

One of the city's most unusual craft shops is **Radical Internation,** 285 Parnell Rd. (tel. *863-923). It carries exquisite hand carvings and other crafts from Thailand at unbelievably low prices. Lovely delicate colors on the carved pieces are created by vegetable dyes, and sizes vary from tiny to quite large. Not to worry, however, if you just can't resist one of the larger items—they will gladly ship overseas. They accept most credit cards, and hours are 9:30am to 5pm Monday through Friday, 10am to 4pm Saturday and Sunday.

Food   You can purchase preselected packs containing a variety of cuts of New Zealand lamb directly from the **Farm Produce Shop** (tel. *770-610), by the United Airlines check-in counter at the airport at the last minute, since these packs are already documented and ready to go. Hellaby's is open Monday through Friday from 8am to 4pm.

Jewelry   If you're looking for upmarket silver items, dress jewelry, or watches, go by **Queens Arcade Jewellers,** 20 Queens Arcade, Queen Street (tel. *735-435). Friendly service and a good selection. They also do watch repairs. Hours are 10am to 5pm Monday through Friday.

Leather   The purveyors at **Leather Fashions Ltd.,** 530 Ellerslie/Panmure Hwy., Panmure, Auckland (tel. 527-3779 or 527-4789), have won accolades from readers over the years—and with good reason. For budget travelers looking for real value for money, Leather Fashions prices represent one of the *best* bargains I have found in all my New Zealand travels. Savings run from $100 to several times that on all sorts of leather and suede apparel and handbags, in classic as well as trendy designs (no sheepskin—see below). "Buttery soft" isn't really adequate to describe the lovely smoothness of fine deerskin or polished suede with a leather finish. If a jacket, coat, skirt, slacks—and even jumpsuits—you fancy from the racks is the wrong size or color, owner Gwen Hewett, together with her experienced, friendly staff, will duplicate it in the leather, size, and color of your choice. And if you're good enough at sketching a design, they'll execute it faithfully, right down to the last little detail. They furnish complimentary taxi service from the city center, accept all major credit cards, and will gladly ship overseas. Hours are 8:30am to 5pm Monday through Friday, 8:30am to 3pm Saturday, and they also have a showroom at 26 Barry's Point Rd., Takapuna (tel. 488-0301).

Among the exquisite items at **Mark West Suede & Leather,** 82 Queen St. (tel. 303-2790), are "buttery soft" jackets for men and women, and skirts and pants for women, as well as handbags and briefcases. They're open weekdays and Saturday mornings.

Sheepskin   At **Breen's Sheepskins,** 8 Quay St. (tel. *732-788), they boast of having the largest range of sheepskins in New Zealand. There is such a wide variety of styles, colors, and prices that I must confess the terrific assortment of coats and jackets, rugs in several sizes, bed underlays (wonderful for a good night's sleep!), car seats, boots, hats, etc., etc., etc. kept me entranced for most of a morning. Grant Barlow and his staff have specialized in New Zealand sheepskin products for some 17 years, and they can offer good advice and guidance for what may well be some of your most valued purchases in the country. Open Monday through Friday from 9am to 5:30pm, Saturday 10am to 12:30pm.

Another value-for-money sheepskin source is **Jason's,** Queen Street (between Customs and Quay Streets; tel. *798-700). Their large stock includes jackets and coats, footwear, car seat covers, and single or double rugs. They also carry novelty toys and souvenirs made of sheepskin. Open Monday through Thursday from 9am to 5:30pm, Friday 9am to 8pm, and Saturday 10am to 2pm. They also have branches in St. Lukes Square, Mot. Albert, Auckland (tel. *863-860); Shore City, Takapuna, Auckland (tel. *498-039); and Otahuhu (tel. 276-8706).

9. EVENING ENTERTAINMENT

For current cultural and entertainment events in Auckland, **Bass Booking Agency,** Aotea Centre (tel. 307-5000), provides easy credit-card booking with next-day courier delivery of tickets. They can also make bookings around the country—a good way to save time and avoid disappointment by leaving it until you reach your ongoing destinations. In addition to the listings here, you'll find current goings-on in the *Tourist Times*.

The Performing Arts   For cultural offerings that include dance, concerts, and theater, check out what's happening at the **Aotea Centre,** at Aotea Square, 299 Queen St. (tel. 307-5050). The **Mercury Theatre,** 9 France St. (tel. 303-3869), has resident companies, including opera, that perform year round in everything from classics to musicals to modern plays, many of them by New Zealand playwrights. Ticket prices are in the NZ$12 to NZ$35 ($7 to $20) range.

The Pub/Club Scene   Live music is on tap Wednesday through Saturday evenings at the **Queen's Head,** 404 Queen St. (tel. 302-0223), an exceptionally pretty pub that serves light, inexpensive meals. It's open from 11am to 10pm Monday through Thursday, until 11pm on Friday and Saturday. The original facade of a hotel dating from 1890 has been retained, a small architectural jewel that escaped the bulldozer.

Café Zira, in the DFC Building at 380 Queen St. (tel. *350-699), is a jazz club. Jazz buffs will also be happy to know there are jazz cruises in summer—book at Fuller's office in the Ferry Building. **Governor Grey's,** in the Sheraton Auckland, 83 Symonds St. (tel. 795-132), is an elegant, sophisticated nightspot that features an Irish night on Monday and jazz on Wednesday, from 7pm. **The Blues Barn,** 510 Queen St., features live bands Wednesday through Sunday nights; **Jimmy Rocket's,** Old Customhouse, Customs and Albert Streets (tel. 308-9137), is Auckland's only '50s-style American café and serves burgers, hot dogs, nachos, and other light eats; and **Shakespeare Tavern,** corner of Albert and Wyndham Streets (tel. *735-396), has country music Monday nights in downstairs Hathaway's Brasserie and live entertainment in the Bard Lounge on Friday.

Dinner Show At **Baalbeck,** corner of Wellesley and Federal Streets (tel. *734-693), they serve up good, à la carte Lebanese cuisine, along with Middle East music and belly dancing. It's open nightly, and best book ahead on Friday and Saturday nights.

CHAPTER 4

SIDE TRIPS FROM AUCKLAND

1. COROMANDEL PENINSULA

2. THE BAY OF ISLANDS

3. WAITOMO

From Auckland, most tourists head south to Waitomo and its glowworms and black-water rafting, then on to Rotorua and its concentration of Maori culture. And rightly so. Nowhere else in the world will you find anything to compare with the mystical, silent glow of Waitomo's grotto. Nowhere else can you duplicate Rotorua's thermal steaminess or lakes, hills, and valleys alive with myth and legend, along with a Polynesian race who revere those tales of long ago and follow an ancient lifestyle while perfectly at home in the modern culture surrounding them. If push comes to shove and it comes down to north or south, then by all means opt for the southern route.

Ah, but if you can work in an extra two days, which will let you go north *then* south, you're in for one of this world's travel treats. Take the long route up and experience the shady "cathedral" created by centuries-old kauri forests; cut across the northern end of the North Island to Waitangi in the Bay of Islands and walk where the British negotiated with Maori chieftains to establish their first official New Zealand foothold; relive this country's history as you visit its first Christian mission, then the splendidly carved Maori meetinghouse; discover private beaches, some on uninhabited islands that account for the naming of this lovely spot; head out to the open sea for some of the finest deep-water fishing in the world, enjoy sunny days and balmy evenings, a friendly and hospitable local populace. You can plan on two days, but chances are you'll alter plans to extend your stay—or leave looking over your shoulder and wishing you had!

Add that extra day or two before or after the journey north, and a short drive east will bring you to one of New Zealand's nooks and crannies that is all too often overlooked by visitors, although much loved by Auckland area residents. The Coromandel Peninsula, where the Coromandel mountain range forms the spiky spine of this clawlike region that juts out between the Hauraki Gulf and the Pacific, is rich in unspoiled terrain and its coastline is incredibly beautiful. If your experience echoes my own, just reading about it will have your feet itching, and your itinerary turned upside down in your determination to *make* that extra day or two in the North Island.

---

1. COROMANDEL PENINSULA

68 miles E of Auckland

GETTING THERE   By Bus   InterCity buses run regular schedules from Auckland to the entry town of Thames. Once a day an InterCity bus makes a round-trip

SIDE TRIPS FROM AUCKLAND

South Pacific Ocean

Tasman Sea

NORTH ISLAND

South Pacific Ocean

COROMANDEL PENINSULA

THE BAY OF ISLANDS

WAITOMO

Bay of Plenty

Hauraki Gulf

Kaipara Harbour

Spirits Bay

North Cape

Cape Reinga

Awanui

Kaitaia

Mangonui

Cape Karikuri

Keri Keri

Waitangi

Whangarei

Hen & Chicken Islands

Maungaturoto

Dargaville

Warkworth

Waiwera

Orewa

Auckland

Te Aruroa

Te Puia

Gisborne

Whakatane

Kawenau

Opotiki

Hawke's Bay

Napier

Huiarau Mts.

Tauranga

Matamata

Cambridge

Rotorua

Turangi

Lake Rotorua

Taupo

Tongariro National Park

Tokoroa

Chateau

Lake Taupo

Mangakino

Tokaanu

New Plymouth

Ngaruawahia

Hamilton

Huntly

Wairoa

Whitianga

Thames

| 1 | 25 | 16 | 14 | 12 | 10 | 2 | 36 | 38 | 5 | 30 | 3 | 43 | 45 |

AUCKLAND AREA

1 Coromandel Peninsula
2 The Bay of Islands
3 Waitomo

around the peninsula, starting in Thames, and stopping 20 minutes at each destination along the way, for a fare of NZ$25 ($14). It's also possible to link up with a courier who makes the journey; inquire at the Brian Boru Hotel, which also operates a tour service for which you'll pay more, but you'll have more flexibility and time to linger.

By Car   Driving time from Thames to Port Jackson at the tip of the peninsula is about 3 hours; to the town of Coromandel, 1 hour; to Whitianga on the Pacific coast, 2 hours. Drive south from Auckland on National State Highway 1 for about 12 miles (20km), then turn east on National State Highway 2. Petrol (gas) pumps are a bit thin on the ground on the peninsula, and I've noted those in strategic spots along the route.

ESSENTIALS   Thames is the first town of any size as you reach the peninsula from Auckland. **Information centers** are on Queen Street, Thames (tel. *07/87-284); Kapanga Road, Coromandel (tel. *07/58-598); Albert Street, Whitianga (tel. *07/65-555); Port Road, Whangamata (tel. 07/865-8340); Belmont Road, Paeroa (tel. 07/962-8636); and Whitaker Street, Te Aroha (tel. 07/884-8052). They can furnish a wealth of information on the area, along with such helpful guides as the "Coromandel Craft Trail" and other special-interest brochures. **Telephone numbers:** Remember that as we go to press, the New Zealand Number Update is in the process of changing all telephone numbers to 7 digits. Those numbers in this book that have not been changed at press time are marked with an asterisk, and you should call the **Helpline 0155** for the new number. For directory assistance within the country (when you don't know the number), call **018.**

The peninsula is one of the most beloved holiday spots for Aucklanders, and that's easy to understand. For city dwellers, it's a haven of natural beauty that is a world apart from urban hassles, and for the visitor, it provides a capsule version of the North Island's history and glorious scenery.

The 1½-hour drive from Auckland is rewarded by dramatic land- and seascapes; wide sandy beaches; wild and rugged mountain peaks; quaint villages hugging both coastlines; relics of logging, gold mining, and gum fields; and studios of scores of talented artisans who have found an idyllic lifestyle on the peninsula.

While it is certainly possible to make a day-trip to Coromandel Peninsula from Auckland, let me urge you to spend at least one overnight in order to do the relaxed rambling your soul will begin to yearn for from the moment you arrive. At the end of your Auckland stay, try to plan two days on the peninsula before pressing on—you'll have explored a very special, little-known-to-outsiders, part of New Zealand, and you'll travel on exhilarated and refreshed by the experience.

GETTING AROUND   This is a rugged, wild region you've come to, and you should know right off that the only easy driving you can count on is the excellent sealed (paved) road that runs some 50 kilometers (30 miles) from Thames to Coromandel. North of Coromandel, and on routes crossing the width of the peninsula, you'll find everything from partially sealed roads to graveled roadbeds that—in the words of one of my Auckland friends—are "little more than treks." That by no means implies that you should miss any of the spectacular forest and mountain scenery, only that you should drive with extreme caution, or that you should consider letting InterCity act as your personal chauffeur for this portion of your holiday.

WHAT TO SEE & DO

"Spectacular" isn't quite glorious enough to describe the peninsula's landscape—there's something so elemental about this old and historic point of land that it can be moving beyond words. Civilization has changed its face virtually not at all, and don't be surprised to find a sudden lump in your throat at vistas of curving beaches or beautiful old pohutukawa trees, New Zealand's famed "Christmas tree," clinging to cliff faces and lining those beaches, especially during December and January when they're a riot of crimson blooms.

In ancient times, Maori tribes recognized the spirituality of the place and declared its Mount Moehau area *tapu,* a sacred place. Modern man has not been untouched by the same spirit and continues to respect and protect those traditions. It isn't an exaggeration to say that you may well emerge from bush walks here feeling you've had something akin to a religious experience.

You'll find good **walks** around Paeroa (near the Karangahake Gorge), Waihi, Whangamata, Tairua, Whitianga, Colville, Coromandel, and Thames. Headquarters for the ✪ **Coromandel State Forest Park** are at Kauaeranga, just southeast of Thames (tel. *07/86-381 in Thames). They can provide walking guides, help for rockhounds (the peninsula is rich in gemstones), and information on camping within the park.

In Thames, you'll find historic **mining areas** well signposted, and there's an excellent **mineralogical museum** on the corner of Brown and Cochrane streets. About halfway between Thames and Coromandel, stop at the little village of Tapu and ask directions to one of nature's oddities, a 2,500-year-old kauri whose trunk is a perfect square (the **"square kauri"** is out the Whitianga road, but it's best to ask before setting out to find it). Te Mata Beach, also at Tapu, is a good hunting ground for specimens of carnelian-agate gemstones.

There are good **coast and bush walks** all along the road from Thames to Coromandel, and a short detour to Te Kouma leads to a Maori **pa site** enclosed by stone walls. Coromandel is where gold was first discovered in New Zealand, in 1852, and the **School of Mines Museum** contains many relics of those early gold-fever days. It's open Monday through Saturday from 9am to 5pm and free to those under 15, with a NZ$2 ($1) admission for those older. Take time to visit the ✪ **True Colors Craft Co-operative** near the Post Office, where Maureen Lorimer, who specializes in hand-woven, hand-dyed garments, is only one of the craftspeople who share this space. Incidentally, the town, peninsula, and mountain range take their names from the timber-trading ship HMS *Coromandel,* which called into this harbor for kauri spars in 1820. There's a gas pump at the Papa Aroha Motor Camp.

If you plan to drive to the northern tip of the peninsula, you'll find the last gasoline ("petrol") pumps at Colville, along with a good collection of arts-and-crafts studios.

On the peninsula's east coast, Whitianga has an excellent ✪ **historical museum,** ✪ many **arts and crafts studios,** and is a major center for ✪ **boating and charter fishing.** Across the inlet at Ferry Landing is the country's oldest stone wharf. At **Hot Water Beach,** ask the time of the next low tide—that's when you can dig a hole in the beach, settle in and soon find yourself immersed in hot sea water, your own private spa pool!

While you're in the neighborhood, stop at the **Celenso Orchard and Herb Garden Tearoom,** between Coroglen and Tairua and a 5-minute drive from the Hot Water Beach. Orchard owners Ruth and Andy Pettit serve Devonshire tea, fresh juice, homemade scones and muffins with cream and jam, or soup and toast. You can eat on the porch or inside, where strains of classical music set just the right scene. The tearoom, which has a tempting gift shop, is open daily from 10am to 6pm (to 5pm in winter).

___

READERS RECOMMEND

Driving Creek Railroad, Coromandel. *"This was the highlight of our two days in Coromandel. It's a don't-miss opportunity, and Barry Brickell is truly a man with a vision"*—K. Reilly and J. Stein, Bayside, N.Y. [*Author's note:* For a NZ$5 ($3) fare, visitors may ride on engineer/conservationist Brickell's 1.8-mile narrow-gauge railway by appointment or daily at 5pm in summer and learn about his native forest restoration program. Native plants and Brickell's pottery are for sale. Inquire at the Brian Boru Hotel in Thames.]

WHERE TO STAY

North Islanders flock to the Coromandels during December and January, so if you're coming then, be sure to book ahead. If you arrive during other months, you'll usually be able to find accommodations through the local information centers.

Unless noted otherwise, rates below include GST.

IN THAMES
A Licensed Hotel

BRIAN BORU HOTEL, Pollen and Richmond Sts., Thames. Tel. *07/86-523. Fax *07/39-760. 31 rms (21 with bath).

$ Rates: NZ$45 ($26) single without bath, NZ$59 ($34) single with shower and toilet; NZ$66 ($38) double without bath, NZ$88 ($50) double with shower and toilet; NZ$65 ($37) single for room with spa bath, shower, tea-making facilities, and fridge. Backpackers pay from NZ$15 ($9) per person (double or more) during off-season. Agatha Christie weekends (see below) NZ$355 ($202). AE, MC, V.

This marvelous two-story kauri building with a veranda dates back to 1874 and is a focal point for locals, who love the bar and the fine dining room (which serves great seafood meals and good pub grub for moderate prices). Incidentally, Barbara Doyle, the managing director here, runs some lively "Agatha Christie–style Weekends" twice a month, and if you're in a sleuthing mood, you might check to see if one is scheduled during your visit—good fun, and good value, since the fee covers accommodation, meals, and sleuthing from Friday night to Sunday lunch. It's located in the center of town.

Motels

BEST WESTERN CRESCENT MOTEL, 100 Fenton St. (P.O. Box 384), Thames. Tel. *0843/86-506. 8 units (all with bath). TV TEL

$ Rates: NZ$58.50 ($33) single; NZ$67.50 ($39) double. AE, DC, MC, V.

If you blink when you drive into Thames, you might miss the special welcome given by Bonnie and Peter Aldridge, who own this small motel on the outskirts. In the summer they host barbecues, and in the winter Bonnie's cheese muffins are a special treat. They'll provide a filling dinner in your room (6 to 7:30pm) for NZ$16 ($9) or homemade toasted sandwiches for NZ$6 ($3), each with only an hour's notice. Their breakfast menu has six different choices, ranging from NZ$6 to NZ$10 ($3 to $6). The units have a kitchen, video, and separate bedroom, and sleep two to six people.

SEASPRAY MOTEL, 613 Coast Rd. (P.O. Box 203), Thames. Tel. *0843/78-863. 8 units (all with bath). TV TEL **Directions:** Go 14km (8½ miles) north of Thames on the coast road.

$ Rates: NZ$50 ($29) single; NZ$60 ($34) double. MC, V.

At Seaspray, Waiomu Bay is so close you feel you're sleeping on an ocean liner. There are one- and two-bedroom flats, a self-service laundry on the premises, and out back a stately Norfolk pine and a picnic area.

TE PURU PARK MOTEL, West Crescent and Main Rd., Puru Bay (P.O. Box 439, Thames). Tel. *0843/78-686. 6 units (all with bath). TV TEL **Directions:** Take the Coromandel Road 11km (6½ miles) north of Thames.

$ Rates: NZ$50 ($29) single; NZ$55–NZ$65 ($31–$37) double. AE, DC, MC, V.

Set in landscaped grounds in Puru Bay, these attractive, recently refurbished motel flats are spacious and comfortably furnished. Each sleeps two to four people. There's a self-service laundry, a children's play area, and tennis courts next door. The beach and a boating ramp are nearby, and there's bus service into Thames and Coromandel.

A Bed and Breakfast

**GLENYS AND RUSSELL RUTHERFORD, 110 Hape Rd., Thames. Tel.
*0843/87-788.** Fax *0843/75-135. 3 rms (1 with bath).
$ Rates (including breakfast): NZ$35 ($20) single; NZ$55 ($31) double. No credit cards.

Glenys and Russell Rutherford's home overlooks the lovely Firth of Thames. They have a double room with private facilities and two single rooms without, and there's a games room and lounge, as well as a swimming pool. They'll provide dinner with advance notice. This engaging couple really know their area and some of the painters and potters who live here, and they're always glad to direct their guests to studios, as well as to historic and scenic points of interest.

IN COROMANDEL

Motels

**ANGLERS LODGE & CARAVAN PARK, Amodeo Bay, Coromandel. Tel.
*0843/58-584.** 7 units (all with bath). TV TEL
$ Rates: NZ$68 ($39) single; NZ$83 ($47) double. MC, V.

Merv and Lois Groucott's pleasant beachfront complex includes one- and two-bedroom units, all with complete cooking facilities, and you can buy provisions from the small store right on the premises. Other amenities include a swimming pool, a spa pool in a glass geodesic dome, tennis court, play area with trampoline, barbecue kiosk, lounge with billiard table, and boats for rent. Good bush and coastal walks are right at hand. The site is located 16 kilometers (9½ miles) north of the town of Coromandel.

**COROMANDEL COLONIAL COTTAGES, Ring Rd., Coromandel. Tel.
*0843/58-857.** 8 units (all with bath). TV TEL
$ Rates: NZ$65 ($37) single; NZ$75 ($43) double. Extra adult NZ$15 ($9.40); extra child NZ$11 ($6.90). AE, MC, V.

All units here have two bedrooms and sleep up to six. Each has its own carport, and the restful rural setting (there's a creek at the back of the property) includes such amenities as a spa pool, children's playground, barbecue area, billiard room, and croquet lawn. Their rental four-wheel-drive bush vehicle is a great way to go exploring, and beaches, golf courses, and shops are close by. A good restaurant is just 2 minutes away, and a courtesy car is provided. Families are preferred. It's located on the outskirts of town.

A Bed and Breakfast

FIRLAWN HOUSE, Kapanga Rd., Coromandel. Tel. *0843/58-947. Fax
*0843/89-760. 3 rms (none with bath).
$ Rates (including light breakfast; excluding GST): NZ$55 ($31) single; NZ$75–NZ$88 ($43–$50) double. No credit cards.

This 1881 house, perfectly framed by magnolia, camellia, orange, rimu, and totara trees, is filled with Oriental appointments and touches. One of its three guest rooms boasts a magnificent Chinese wedding bed, and there's an elegantly furnished TV lounge. There's a BYO restaurant on the premises, and the house has access for the disabled. Smoking is not allowed indoors. Breakfast includes tea and toast only. Firlawn House is located in town, next to the Coromandel Hotel.

Worth the Extra Money

PUKA PARK LODGE, Private Bag, Pauanui Beach, Coromandel Peninsula. Tel. *0843/48-080. Fax *0843/48-112. 32 chalets (all with bath). MINIBAR TV TEL **Transportation:** Chauffeured limousine service available; 25 minutes by fixed-wing aircraft from Auckland to Pauanui Airport; helicopter pad on lodge grounds.

$ Rates: NZ$280 ($160) per person single or double. AE, DC, MC, V.

★ I can imagine no better personal indulgence than a day or two at this terrific lodge tucked away in lush native forest overlooking the white-sand beaches of Pauanui. Each chalet sleeps two and has a tastefully decorated and comfortably furnished sitting area, spacious bedroom, bath, and minibar, as well as a private balcony (for that evening drink from the minibar?). The chalets are set around a central lodge complex, where the lounge features an open fire and a balcony with heavenly panoramic views. Meals can be served in your chalet by room service or in the first-class restaurant, where there's a good wine list, a selection of light meals, or gourmet dishes of seafood and game. This is a "don't miss" if the budget can stand the strain. Puka Park, located 45 kilometers (28 miles) northeast of Thames, is a 2-hour drive from Auckland.

A MOTOR LODGE NEAR BUFFALO BEACH

MERCURY BAY BEACH FRONT RESORT, 111 Buffalo Beach Rd. North (P.O. Box 9), Whitianga. Tel. *0843/65-637. 8 2-rm suites (all with bath). TV TEL

$ Rates (excluding GST): NZ$31.50–NZ$55 ($18–$31) single; NZ$41.50–NZ$65 ($24–$37) double. Discounts available. AE, DC, MC, V.

★ This motor lodge sits right on the edge of Buffalo Beach, with wonderful sea views and fully equipped units, a laundry with dryers, and a car wash. Right on the beachfront, it gives you a delicious sense of having your own private beach

⑤ just outside your door. There's a spa pool, and Windsurfer and sailing catamaran for your use. The folks here, Liz and Tom True, are especially helpful in arranging boat trips, fishing expeditions, and bush walks; she's a Kiwi, and he's a Floridian who gave up a career in the oil business for a more tranquil lifestyle.

A HOSTEL NEAR TE AROHA

There's a delightful small **YHA Hostel** on Miro Street (P.O. Box 72), Te Aroha (tel. 07/884-8739). Nestled in the foothills of Mount Te Aroha, it's only 10 minutes away from the famous hot-spring baths of Te Aroha. Rates are NZ$10 ($6).

CAMPGROUNDS ON THE PENINSULA

Van and caravan sites are available on a first-come, first-served basis in **Conservation Lands and Farm Parks** around the peninsula. Camping fees are NZ$3 ($2) per adult, NZ$2 ($1) for school-age children; free for preschoolers. For details, contact the Department of Conservation, P.O. Box 78, Thames (tel. *0843/89-732).

The **Waiomu Bay Holiday Park,** P.O. Box 556, Thames (tel. 07/868-2777), has tent and caravan sites, bunkrooms, tourist cabins, and tourist flats in a wooded setting on the coast road, 13 kilometers (7¾ miles) from Thames. Amenities include tennis courts, a swimming pool, barbecue area, and games hall. Tent sites are NZ$8 ($5) per adult; caravan sites, NZ$8.50 ($5) per adult; bunkrooms, NZ$12 ($7) per adult, NZ$5 ($3) per child; cabins, NZ$30 ($17) double; and tourist flats, NZ$40 ($23) double—all including GST.

✪ **Buffalo Beach Tourist Park,** Eyre Street (P.O. Box 19), Whitianga (tel.

*0843/65-854), is adjacent to the beachfront, within easy walking distance of six beaches, the wharf, and the shopping center. There are powered caravan sites, as well as tent sites, three on-site caravans, a heated bunkroom, and a lodge for international backpackers. Owners Trudi and Alan Hopping even provide thermal hot pools. Rates run NZ$8.50 ($5) per adult for tent and caravan sites, NZ$14 ($8) per person for backpackers, NZ$15 ($9) for the bunkroom, and NZ$34 ($20) double for on-site caravans. All rates are exclusive of GST.

WHERE TO EAT

You'll find small, local eateries in good supply around the peninsula, and your best bet is to look to the natives for pointers on the right choice. Failing that, look for hotel dining rooms, few though they are in number, to provide good, plain food at moderate prices. And do give a thought to picnicking along the way—even peanut-butter sandwiches would taste elegant in a setting of such natural splendor!

IN THAMES

BRIAN BORU HOTEL, Pollen and Richmond Sts. Tel. *0843/86-523.
   Cuisine: BISTRO/SEAFOOD/NEW ZEALAND. **Reservations:** Not required.
$ **Prices:** Breakfast NZ$14 ($8); bistro lunches NZ$12–NZ$15 ($7–$9); dinner NZ$15–NZ$25 ($9–$14). AE, DC, MC, V.
   Open: Breakfast daily 7:30–10am; lunch daily noon–2:30pm; dinner daily 6–10pm.

This marvelous old hotel in the center of Thames is so evocative of the past that you get a trip back in time thrown in for free. The small bar is one of the most attractive on the peninsula. The breakfast menu is quite varied and features freshly perked coffee. All three meals are served daily, and the à la carte menu features fresh local seafood at modest prices.

IN COROMANDEL

COROMANDEL HOTEL, Kaponga Rd., Coromandel. Tel. *0843/58-760.
   Cuisine: BISTRO/NEW ZEALAND. **Reservations:** Not required.
$ **Prices:** Breakfast NZ$10 ($6); lunch NZ$10–NZ$12 ($6–$7); dinner NZ$15–NZ$20 ($9–$11). AE, MC, V.
   Open: Daily 8am–8:30pm.

In the center of Coromandel, this is a pleasant, understated, old-fashioned kind of a place, well worth a stop for a pint or a simple meal.

FROM AUCKLAND TO THE BAY OF ISLANDS

In your trek north to the Bay of Islands then back south, you're going to have to come back through Auckland—luckily, however, *not* over the same route. There's a long route that wanders through 234 miles of New Zealand scenic splendor and history, and that will take a full day (count on at least 7 or 8 hours for the trip). Then there's the direct, 150-mile State Highway 1, which can take anywhere from 3 to 4 hours. Heed the voice of experience and take the long way up, the short route back. There's the distinct possibility that you'll stay over an extra day up north (that's what happened to me), and even if you don't, time pressures may begin to set in and you'll skip that long drive back, thus missing out on a part of New Zealand you really shouldn't miss.

Most of the longer route is over well-paved roads, but the most interesting part—the part that makes this whole day's drive worthwhile—will be along about 43 miles of gravel-surfaced, winding roads through the majestic **Waiopua Kauri Forest.** It's a good idea to pack picnic provisions, since you could well be miles from an eatery when your lunchtime alarm goes off, and besides, there's an idyllic picnic spot right in the forest. And be sure to get an early start—you'll need the whole day.

The Long Route   Leave Auckland via the Harbour Bridge (no toll) and take the East Coast Bays Road off Route 1 to pass through North Shore residential districts, superb beaches at pleasant seaside resort towns like **Orewa** and **Waipu** (resist the urge to stop for a swim—you can do that on your way back!), and as you turn inland, hills and farmland, which lead you into **Silverdale,** where you'll rejoin Highway 1. (If you strike Warkworth at morning teatime, try the **Dome Valley Tea Rooms,** just north of town.) Just above Kaiwaka, turn into Route 12 toward Dargaville.

From Dargaville, it's only 30 miles north to the kauri forest (see below), the highlight of this drive. On the other side of the forest, you pass through seaside settlements of **Omapere** and **Opononi** before heading inland to **Ohaeawai** and Route 10, which will lead you to **Paihia** on the shore of the Bay of Islands.

WHAT TO SEE & DO EN ROUTE

IN MATAKOHE

OTAMATEA KAURI AND PIONEER MUSEUM, Church Rd., Matakohe, Northland. Tel. 09/431-7417.

This was a thriving timber-and-gum industry area during the late 1800s, and scene of some of the most devastating kauri-forest slaughters in the country. Other trees were felled too—totara, rimu, and kaihikatea—but the kauri was the most sought-after because of its straight, firm trunk, which made it ideal for ship masts, and its beautifully mottled grain, much prized for making furniture. You'll see remains of numerous lumber mills along your way. Kauri gum was the source of many fortunes during those days, as well as the grinding poverty of gum diggers (Maoris and Yugoslav immigrants, mostly) who dug the gum from underneath peat for criminally low wages. The gum was scraped and washed for use as a base in paint and varnish, or polished to rich, clear amber, brown, or black to be used in the making of costume jewelry.

A stop at this interesting museum lets you relive those days of forest and labor exploitation via photographs, gum displays—over 1,700 pieces, the largest collection in the world—and kauri furniture. The implements of the trade will bring it vividly alive: gum washing and digging equipment, a bush dam model and whim model, a bullock wagon and the 1929 tractor that replaced it, large kauri logs, and a bush hut. There's also a kauri house to visit, a tearoom, and a souvenir shop.

Admission: NZ$4 ($2) adults, NZ$1.50 (90¢) children.
Open: Daily 9am–5pm. **Closed:** Christmas.

IN DARGAVILLE

NORTHERN WAIROA MUSEUM, Harding Park, Dargaville. Tel. *0884/7555.

This museum, with its beautiful hilltop setting in Harding Park, has a panoramic view of Dargaville and the Northern Wairoa River as it winds its way down to the Kaipara Harbour, some 58 kilometers (35 miles) away. The museum specializes in the area's maritime history, and features a collection of relics recovered from some of the 110 recorded shipwrecks around the local peninsula. On a contemporary note, this is where you will find the masts from the Greenpeace ship *Rainbow Warrior,* which was sunk in 1985 by the French while moored in Auckland.

Other sections feature local Maori and pioneer history, while the archives section has local newspapers dating back more than a century, as well as Kaipara Harbour logbooks.

Picnic tables, barbecue pits, and toilets are situated on the grounds, and there's a restaurant.

Admission: NZ$2.50 ($1.45) adults, NZ50¢ (30¢) children.
Open: Summer, daily 9am–6pm; winter, Wed–Sun.

READERS RECOMMEND

Awakino Point Lodge, P.O. Box 168, Dargaville. Tel. 09/439-7870. "We found the most wonderful bed-and-breakfast accommodation in Dargaville, only 2 kilometers (1½ miles) from town on Highway 14. The two-room suites with private bath are beautifully and comfortably furnished and very clean. The lodge is on a 10-acre farmlet, attractively landscaped with shrubs, flowers, and fruit trees. The hosts, Wally and June Birch, are warm and hospitable, and June is an excellent cook, who will prepare dinner by prior arrangement. We had dinner, bed, and breakfast at a very reasonable rate. It was a great experience and we loved it."—N. Elias, Floral Park, N.Y.

Solitaire Guest House, Waimamaku St. (P.O. Box 51), Hokianga, Northland. Tel. 09/405-4891. "We found this to be an excellent place to stay when we wanted to explore the kauri forest and coast tracks. The owners were the friendliest people we met in a land of friendly people. Their home is a beautifully restored kauri house, and for a very moderate price we had a room, dinner, and breakfast."—G. Brandenburg, San Diego, Calif.

WAIPOUA KAURI FOREST

Within this 22,500-acre preserve north of Dargaville, ✪ **kauri** stands account for some 9,000 acres! Tall and slender, with straight, firm trunks reaching up to branches that grow at the very top and arch into a dim, cool canopy, the kauri is such a commanding presence that you understand forthwith the Maoris' imparting of deity to the mighty tree. It is *lordly!* I don't even have to caution against rushing through this awesome abode of natural treasures—you won't! Be sure, however, to stop by the **Fire Lookout,** signposted to your left near the entrance—the 1,010-feet-above-sea-level observation post provides a breathtaking panorama of hills, forests, and sea. Forest headquarters is at the next left turn, where you can inspect the **Maxwell Cottage,** which includes kauri wood in its construction and was the 1890s home of the first forest caretaker. A 15-minute walk off the road at the sign reading "Te Matua Ngahere" will bring you to the "Father of the Forest," a 98-foot-tall tree, 58 feet 10 inches around, whose exact age is shrouded in the mists of time. A short distance away stands the unique grouping of four trunks growing from one root, known as the Four Sisters. Farther north, just off the main road, the mundane sign stating "Big Kauri Tree" hardly prepares you for **Tane Mahuta,** "God of the Forest." This immense tree soars to 169 feet, has a girth of 43 feet, and is estimated to be 1,200 years old! This is where you'll find that picnic spot I mentioned, set among tall punga ferns just across the road—a place to sit, absorb the silence and peace of the forest, and ponder the fact that once these giant trees were only a small part of thousands more.

2. THE BAY OF ISLANDS

For New Zealanders, this is where it all began. "Civilization" in the guise of British culture, that is. But long before Capt. James Cook anchored the *Endeavour* off Motuarohia Island in 1769, civilization of the Maori sort existed in perfect harmony with the soft forces of nature, often at considerable *disharmony* with their tribal neighbors. Maori history tells of the arrival of Kupe and Ngahu from Hawaiki, then of Whatonga and Toi, and later of the great chiefs Ruatara, Hongi Hika, and Tamati Waaka Nene. It speaks of the waterfront settlement at Kororareka, already well established when Captain Cook appeared and gave the region its Pakeha name. Be that as it may, New Zealand's modern history also begins here in the Bay of Islands.

British settlers first set foot on New Zealand soil in 1804, and a whole litany of British "firsts" follows that date: 1814, the first Christian sermon (today, you'll find a large Celtic cross memorial planted on that very spot, a stretch of beach on the north side of Rangihoua Bay); 1820, the first plow introduced; 1831, the first European marriage; 1835, the first printing press; 1839, the first bank; and 1840, a whole slew of important "first" events—post office, Customs House, and official treaty between the British and Maori chieftains. After that, the British brand of civilization was in New Zealand to stay.

The Bay of Islands you will encounter today is a happy blend of all that history—pride in those important happenings—and relaxed contentment in the natural attributes, which make this (as any resident is quick to tell you) "the best spot in the country to live—or play." And play they do, for recreation is the chief industry up here. Setting and climate combine to create about as ideal a resort area as you could wish. Imagine a deeply indented coastline whose waters hold some 150 islands, most with sandy stretches of beach. Imagine waters so filled with sporting fish like the kingfish (yellowtail) that every world record for their capture has been set here. Imagine, too, a climate with average temperatures of 85°F (70°F is considered a cooler-than-usual winter day!), maximum humidity of 40%, and cool bay breezes every day of the year. Imagine all that and you'll know what to expect in the Bay of Islands!

However, you won't find a local transportation system in any form other than the delightful little ferry that delivers schoolchildren, businesspeople, tourists, and freight from one shore to the other. Nor will you find any sort of wild nightlife. Toting up the "wills" and "won'ts," I'd have to say you come up with a balance in favor of a perfect place in which to soak up sun and sea and fresh air, and put the frenetic pleasures of big city life on hold.

GETTING THERE   By Air   Mount Cook Airlines has daily flights between Auckland and Kerikeri, with a shuttle bus into Paihia; one-way fare in 1992 was NZ$169 ($97). Book at any Mount Cook office.

By Bus   InterCity has daily bus service between Auckland and Paihia (one-way fare NZ$36, U.S. $21); Newmans has Monday through Friday service to Paihia (one-way fare NZ$35, U.S. $20).

ORIENTATION   There are three distinct resort areas in the Bay of Islands: **Paihia** (throw in adjacent Waitangi—it means "weeping water"), **Russell,** and **Kerikeri.** If you've come for the fishing, you'll want to be based in Russell, on the eastern shore and home of most charter boats; for almost every other activity, Paihia, across on the western shore, is the central location; and Kerikeri is the center of a thriving citrus-growing industry as well as a small, interesting "don't miss" sightseeing side trip.

Essentials   The **area code** for Paihia and Russell is 09.

Information   You'll find the **Bay of Islands Information Centre,** Waterfront, Paihia (tel. 09/402-7426). The friendly staff will arrange accommodations bookings throughout the entire Bay of Islands—bed and breakfast, motel flats, motor camp, or tent site. They also keep up-to-the-minute information on all sightseeing and other activities. The office is staffed daily from 8am to 5pm (to 4:30pm in winter).

Fullers Northland (tel. 402-7421 in Paihia, 403-7866 in Russell), locally known simply as Fullers, operate a **Travel Centre** in the Maritime Building in Paihia that early on will begin to feel like your second Bay of Islands home—they're the ones you'll turn to for any area cruises or coach tours (for details of the wide range of sightseeing cruises and outings run by Fullers, see "Organized Tours," below); all InterCity bookings; passenger and car-ferry bookings; and airline information and bookings (including international flights). All these services, plus all marine activity offices, are in the Maritime Building on the Paihia wharf or from their office on the Strand in Russell.

GETTING AROUND   By Car   Driving is easy and parking seldom a problem in the Bay of Islands. If you arrive via air or bus, **rental cars** are available through Fullers Travel Centre, Maritime Building, Paihia (tel. 402-7421), or the Strand in Russell (tel. 403-7866).

On Foot   Shanks' mare is actually the *best* way to move around each location in the Bay of Islands, since towns are small and distances short between attractions. It's when you move from the Paihia/Russell area to Kerikeri, etc, that you may yearn for wheels.

By Taxi   For taxi service, call either of the Fullers offices shown above. The **Bays Water Taxi** (book at Fullers) offers 24-hour service, and fares depend on the hour and number of passengers.

By Ferry   No matter where you settle, you're going to come to know that neat little ferry intimately—unless you have your own boat, that's the only inexpensive way to get from one shore to another (well, there is a long-way-round drive, but it's much too time-consuming). Personally, I have a real fondness for that 15-minute voyage—for that little space of time, you're in close contact with the daily lives of the locals as you cross with women returning from a supermarket run, school kids as rambunctious on the after-school run as on schoolbuses the world over, and all sorts of daily-living goods being transported. It runs at hourly intervals beginning at 7am (on the hour from Russell, the half-hour from Paihia) and ending at 6:30pm (from Paihia). In summer, crossings are extended to 10:30pm, and on Sunday there's no 8:30am service. Fares are NZ$4.40 ($3) round-trip for adults, NZ$2.20 ($1.25) for children 5 to 15. You'll soon have that schedule firmly fixed in your mind—it's important to be on the same side of the water as your bed when the service shuts down! If you should find yourself stranded, however, all is not lost—just considerably more expensive via water taxi.

Three miles south of Paihia, at **Opua,** there's a flat-bottom car-ferry for drivers that crosses the narrow channel to Okiato Point, 5 miles from Russell. Crossings are every 10 minutes from 9am to 9pm, and the one-way fare for car and driver is NZ$7 ($4) plus NZ$1 (60¢) for each adult passenger.

WHAT TO SEE & DO

The very first thing on your agenda should be to go by the **Bay of Islands Information Centre** or Fullers Travel Centre and pick up brochures outlining the various bay cruises and setting out schedules and prices for each. The information center can furnish specific information on just about any of the other activities listed in this section, although you'll have to make the reservations yourself.

There's a wealth of sightseeing to be done on land in the Bay of Islands, but nothing compares with the bay itself. All those islands are set in a bay so sheltered that it's known to mariners as one of the best hurricane anchorages in the South Pacific. And if you do no other sightseeing during your stay, you should take one of the **bay cruises** that circumnavigate these islands. There's the 3-hour ✪ **Cape Brett cruise,** with its breathtaking passage through the **"Hole in the Rock"** when the weather is right; the price is NZ$42 ($24) for adults, NZ$19 ($11) for children. Then there's the longer (4-hour) ✪ **Cream Trip,** which retraces the route used in years gone by to collect cream for market from the islands and inlets around the bay. Along this route, your knowledgeable skipper will point out Captain Cook's first anchorage in 1769; the spot where Rev. Samuel Marston preached the first Christian sermon on the beach; island locales of violence, murder, and cannibalism; and Otehei Bay, on Urupukapuka Island, which was the site of Zane Grey's camp so well written of in his *The Angler's Eldorado*. The price of the Cream Trip is NZ$45 ($26) for adults, NZ$22 ($13) for children. See "Organized Tours," below.

If time permits (it will take an entire day) I heartily recommend the trip to ✪ **Cape Reinga.** There's something intriguing about being at the very top of New Zealand (and if you visit Stewart Island down south, you'll have seen the country from stem to stern!). And besides, there's a mystical aura about the cape, since the Maoris believed that it was from a gnarled pohutukawa tree in the cliffs here that souls jumped off for the return to their Hawaiki homeland after death. Then there's the drive along hard-packed golden sands of the **Ninety-Mile Beach** (which measures a literal 52 miles!) at low tide. The tour leaves Paihia at 7:30am, returns at 6:30pm, and costs NZ$65 ($37) for adults, NZ$35 ($20) for children.

On land, your sightseeing will be divided between Russell and Waitangi. At the top of your "must see" list should be the **Treaty House** in Waitangi. It's the birthplace of modern New Zealand.

IN WAITANGI

Lucky you if your visit coincides with the February 6 celebration of **Waitangi Day!** It's like being in the United States on the Fourth of July. The center of activity is the **Treaty House** lawn, scene of the Waitangi Treaty signing, with a re-creation of that event, lots of Maori song and dance, and Pakeha officials in abundance, dressed to the nines in resplendent uniforms of yesteryear and today. The Royal New Zealand Navy is there in force, as are crowds of vacationing Kiwis. Book way ahead, then get set to join in the festivities.

TREATY HOUSE, Waitangi National Reserve, Waitangi. Tel. 402-7308.
It was in this Georgian-style house that the British Crown succeeded in having its first treaty ratified by enough chieftains to assure its acceptance by major Maori leaders throughout the country. Set in parklike grounds, this was the home of James Busby from 1832 to 1880, and its broad lawn was the scene of the colorful meeting of Pakeha and Maori during the treaty negotiations over 150 years ago on February 6, 1840. Inside, there's a museum display of a facsimile of the treaty written in Maori, other mementos of those early days, and rooms with period furnishings. An audiovisual presentation of the treaty's history may be seen at the Visitors Centre. On the grounds stands one of the most magnificent *whare runangas* (meetinghouses) in the country, constructed for the 1940 centennial celebration, containing elaborately carved panels from all the Maori tribes in New Zealand. Just below the sweeping lawn, on Hobson's Beach, there's an impressive 117-foot-long ✪ **Maori war canoe,** also made for the centennial, from three giant kauri trees.
   Admission: NZ$5 ($3) adults; children free.
   Open: Daily 9am–5pm. **Transportation/Directions:** You can't miss it!

KELLY TARLTON'S MUSEUM OF SHIPWRECKS. Tel. 402-7108.
✪   As this is written, this wonderful museum ship is awash (you should pardon the pun!) in plans for its future. Look for it in its old location near the Paihia/Waitangi bridge, the Treaty House in Waitangi, or (as present plans project) near the Maritime Building in Paihia. Whatever you do, don't miss it, for if you've an ounce of romance in your soul, you'll treasure a visit to this three-masted bark, the *Tui*. The late Kelly Tarlton, a professional diver, made this the focus of his life's work, excavating treasure from the many ships that have perished in the waters off New Zealand. Beside each display of treasure he brought up from the deep, there's a photograph of the ship from which it was recovered. There's a continuous slide

show depicting Kelly going about his work underwater, and realistic sound effects of storms, the creaking of timbers, and the muffled chant of sea chanteys.

Admission: NZ$5 ($3) adults, NZ$2 ($1) children.

Open (tentative in view of above): Daily 9am–5pm. **Closed:** Christmas Day. **Transportation/Directions:** See above.

IN RUSSELL

Russell is a veritable concentration of historical sites. It was here that the great Maori leader Hone Heke burned everything except mission property at a time when most of what was there *should* have been burned in the interest of morality and environmental beauty, since the town seethed with all sorts of European vices, diseases, and injustices against the indigenous people. The old Anglican church and headstones of sailors buried in its graveyard bear to this day bullet holes from that long-ago battle.

On the highest elevation in Russell stands the **flagstaff** Hone Heke chopped down in defiance of British rule. It is reached by auto or on foot, and the lookout up there affords one of the best views of the bay.

BAY OF ISLANDS MARITIME PARK HEADQUARTERS AND VISITORS CENTRE [RUSSELL MUSEUM], York St., Russell. Tel. 403-7701.

Stop here first and watch the 15-minute audiovisual presentation *The Land Is Enduring* to get a grasp of the Maori and English history of this area. The center has camping information and maps, and sells a variety of books, prints, cards, T-shirts, and sweatshirts. It's located near the waterfront.

Admission: Free.

Open: Daily 10am–4pm (until 4:30pm in winter).

POMPALLIER HOUSE, on the Russell waterfront.

At present closed for renovation, this house was built in 1841 by the French Bishop Pompallier for the Roman Catholic Mission to house a printing press used from 1842 to 1849 to print religious documents in the Maori language. That press is still here today, and there's also a collection of carved whale ivory and various other artifacts of the times. At this writing, only the grounds are open to the public, but the house is expected to reopen sometime in 1993. Check with the Visitors Information Centre in Paihia for opening times and admissions.

IN KERIKERI

You really should take time to make the 20-minute drive to Kerikeri, a small town that figured prominently in the country's early history. It holds the oldest European building in New Zealand, the ✪ **Kemp House,** built between 1832 and 1835 as a mission supply center, which is now a museum and general store. Kerikeri is also an **arts and crafts center,** and you can watch many of the artisans at their work in small shops. A direct descendant of Hone Heke constructed the replica Maori village of **Keri Park** without hammer or nails, as his ancestors built their own dwellings. Another authentic reconstruction of a pre-European Maori settlement is **Rewa's Village.**

ORGANIZED TOURS

Fullers Northland (tel. 402-7421 in Paihia, 403-7866 in Russell) is the largest and most visible tour operator in the Bay of Islands as well the 1990 winner of the New Zealand Tourism Award as the country's best tour operator. Among the half-dozen cruises and outings they offer, the most popular are: the ✪ **Cape Brett Hole-in-the-Rock** cruise aboard the fully licensed catamaran *Tiger Lily III;* the original ✪ **Cream Trip bay cruise** with an island stopover at lunchtime; a day-long coach trip to ✪ **Cape Reinga via Ninety-Mile Beach;** and the **Tu-Tu** (in Maori it means "to play around") Sand Shark Adventure in a 40-seater, six-wheel-drive dune buggy. (For details of the first three, see above).

SPORTS & RECREATION

There are beaches galore for good **swimming** from November through March. They're lined up all along the town waterfronts, and delightful little coves with curving strands are just awaiting your discovery down almost any side road along State Highway 10 headed north—if you pass through privately owned land to reach the water, you may be asked to pay a small fee, something like NZ$1 (60¢).

You can arrange to play **golf** at the beautiful 18-hole waterfront course at Waitangi Golf Course, where clubs are for hire.

Deep-sea fishing is at its best up here. In fact, world records for yellowtail, marlin, shark, and tuna have been set in these waters. There are a couple dozen big-game fishing charter boats operating out of Russell, but I might as well warn you that it can be an expensive proposition unless you can form your own group (or fall in with a group that has a vacancy) to share the NZ$700 to NZ$800 ($400 to $457) cost for 10 hours' fishing. With a party of four (the maximum), the per-person cost becomes more manageable, but is still pretty hefty. If the fact that some 600 striped, blue, and black marlin were landed in these waters makes this an irresistible expense, **Game Fishing Charters,** in the Maritime Building in Paihia, may be able to help you line something up.

Light-line fishing is much more affordable, and the Visitors Information Centre in Paihia can furnish a list of fishing charters available. Most supply rods and bait and run 3- to 5-hour trips.

There's good **scuba diving** in these waters, and **Paihia Dive, Hire and Charters Ltd.,** on Williams Road, can provide all equipment and arrange dives.

The Bay of Islands is rich in excellent ✪ **scenic and historic walks,** and the park rangers at the following addresses can furnish details of all trails, as well as a very good booklet called *Walking in the Bay of Islands Maritime and Historic Park.* Go by Park Headquarters in Russell (P.O. Box 134; tel. *37-685) or the Ranger Station in Kerikeri (P.O. Box 128; tel. *78-474) for their friendly assistance. There are also beautiful camping sites, some of them on uninhabited islands in the bay, with nominal per-night fees. You must reserve with the park rangers at Russell—you might write ahead and ask for their useful booklet *Huts and Camping.* Send $1 U.S. for each booklet.

If the idea of a couple of days of **sailing** aboard a fully equipped yacht appeals to you, get in touch with the people at ✪ **Rainbow Yacht Charters,** on the wharf (P.O. Opua), Paihia (tel. *0885/27-821; fax *0885/27-546). You get to be the skipper, your family or friends the crew. The yachts accommodate six to eight people and may be chartered for a minimum of 2 days, at prices *starting* at NZ$650 ($371) in peak season, NZ$400 ($229) in low season. If you're not ready to venture out on your own, sign up for a Cruise and Learn course that lasts 3 or 4 days; you rent the yacht or launch at the usual rate and pay an additional NZ$320 ($183) for instruction. The boats are a dream, and having been a closet "boatie" all my life, this is another New Zealand treat I'm definitely budgeting time for next trip. For full details, contact the company in the States at Pacific Destination Center, 3471 Via Lido, Suite 206, Newport Beach, CA 92663 (tel. 714/675-5283, or toll free 800/227-0639 outside California; fax 714/675-0639).

SHOPPING

Do take time from all the other activities in the Bay of Islands to browse around the several very good shops in the area. I have lugged home some of my best New Zealand handcrafts from up here, including a gorgeous natural wool, hand-knit sweater from the **House of Gifts,** The Strand, Russell, where Aline and Jim Ryan keep an assortment of good-quality gifts and souvenirs at reasonable prices. Over on the Paihia side, **Classique Souvenirs** is a good bet for good buys; you'll find exceptional craft items at **Katoa Crafts** (pottery, weaving, woodwork, paintings, etc.); and a very good selection is at **Waitangi Crafts and Souvenirs** on Marsden Road. Shop for sweaters at the **THC Waitangi Resort Hotel.** Prices, far from being resort-area-inflated, are competitive with city shops and in many cases lower—and it's fun to shop with the friendly Bay of Islands proprietors, who take a personal interest in seeing that you find what you want. Most are open daily during peak season, and weekdays plus Saturday mornings at other times.

EVENING ENTERTAINMENT

Pub pickings are limited to the **Duke** in the Duke of Marlborough Hotel on the Strand in Russell, where conversation is likely to center around fishing; the **THC Waitangi ☯ pub** and **Anchorage Bar,** where you'll bend an elbow with residents of the Paihia side of the bay, including a Maori or two, and vacationing visitors; and the **Twin Pines Tavern** at the Twin Pines Motor Camp, where campers are joined by neighborhood residents. Other possibilities include the **Lighthouse Tavern,** upstairs in the Selwyn Mall in Paihia; the **Roadrunner Tavern,** 2½ miles south of town; and the **Terrace Nightclub,** on Kawakawa Road in Opua, open nightly from 10pm until late.

WHERE TO STAY

The Bay of Islands is a budget traveler's dream: The area abounds in excellent inexpensive accommodations, and more are being built all the time. Most are of modest size, earning a modest but adequate income for couples or families who seem far more interested in their guests' having a good time than in charging "what the traffic will bear." Rates do fluctuate according to season, however, with a slight increase during holidays and a slightly higher jump during the peak summer months of December through February. Those are also the times it is absolutely essential to book well in advance, since the Bay of Islands is tops on just about every Kiwi family's holiday list, and many book from year to year. If you're planning a visit during any of these seasons, you can either write directly to one of the properties you see listed here, or write to the Visitors Information Centre and put yourself in their capable hands—no risk, I can assure you.

Several readers have suggested that staying on the Paihia side of the bay is more convenient because of late-night crossing difficulties. Having stayed in both Paihia and Russell, I can honestly express no personal preference. However, you may want to consider carefully just where you'll want to be in the wee hours.

Unless otherwise noted, all rates quoted below include GST.

IN RUSSELL

A Licensed Hotel

THE DUKE OF MARLBOROUGH HOTEL, The Strand, Russell. Tel. 09/ 403-7829. Fax 09/403-7760. 29 rms, 1 suite (all with bath). TV TEL
$ Rates: NZ$64–NZ$76 ($37–$43) single; NZ$64–NZ$115 ($37–$66) double; NZ$127 ($73) suite. DC, MC, V.

The Duke of Marlborough has watched the comings and goings of generations of residents and visitors from its waterfront perch since it opened as New Zealand's very first hotel. It has suffered major fires three times and three times been rebuilt. Grand it may be; stuffy it isn't. Just a few steps from the Russell wharf, its covered veranda is the natural gathering place for fishermen at the end of a day on the water in pursuit of those deep-sea fighters. The conversation tends to be lively, attracting locals as well as hotel guests. The Duke, in fact, could be called the social hub of Russell (if Russell could, in fact, be said to have a social hub!). Its public bar, across the street in the back, is also the center of community conviviality.

Regulars come back to the Duke year after year for its old-worldliness, and also for the homey comfort of its rooms. Beds have wicker headboards, floors are carpeted, walls are wood paneled, and tea- and coffee-making facilities are in each room. There's a fine dining room serving all meals (see "Where to Eat," below), a TV lounge, and a charming guest lounge with wicker furniture, a colonial-style bar, and a working fireplace. Prices are a little above budget, but good value for money.

MOTEL FLATS

MOTEL RUSSELL, Matuwhi Bay Rd. (P.O. Box 54), Russell. Tel. and fax 09/403-7854. 13 units (all with bath). TV TEL

$ Rates: NZ$54–NZ$65 ($31–$37) single; NZ$62–NZ$95 ($35–$54) double. Slight decrease during low season. Best Western discounts available. AE, DC, MC, V.

This pretty motel, set in 2 acres of landscaped hillside, is just a 2-minute or so walk from the Russell waterfront. The units have complete kitchens, an attractive decor, and many little extras that add so much to your comfort. For example, there are two units with facilities for the disabled. Six have one bedroom and lounge (will sleep up to four), five with two bedrooms, and two double-bedded units, as well as three very pretty cabin-type units. The location is a wooded hillside, with a swimming pool fed by a picturesque waterfall. There's also a barbecue and a heated spa. So special is this motel that it rates four stars from AA.

WAIRORO PARK, P.O. Box 53, Russell. Tel. 09/403-7255. 5 chalets (all with shower and toilet). TV TEL **Directions:** Go about a mile from the ferry, then turn left up a hilly dirt road (signposted).

$ Rates: NZ$68 ($39) double chalet. Extra adult NZ$12 ($7); extra child NZ$6 ($3). Christmas holiday minimum charge of NZ$133 ($76) per chalet. NZ$45 ($26) cabin. No credit cards.

The hospitality here could probably be labeled Kiwi-Dutch-English, since owner Jan Boerop is Dutch, his wife Beryl is English, and they're both now dyed-in-the-wool Kiwis. They've settled in on the Russell side of the Opua car-ferry in an absolutely idyllic setting of some 160 acres on the shores of a sheltered bay cove. They use a great many of those acres to run cattle and sheep, and in the midst of an orchard just steps away from the beach they have five two-story A-frame chalets. The first level of each holds a large lounge and fully equipped kitchen. There are two bedrooms upstairs, and with the three divans in the lounge, the units accommodate up to eight. There is also a rustic, self-contained cabin that sleeps two. Facilities include a covered carport and decks looking out to gorgeous views. A large three-bedroom chalet is set in its own 18 acres of bushland, with private water access and marvelous seaviews—call for rates and availability. The Boerops thoughtfully provide a dinghy or motorboat and a 12-foot catamaran at no charge for guests who want to fish. Regulars book from one holiday season to the next—which means, of course, that it's a good idea to write as far in advance as possible no matter when you're coming.

A HOSTEL

ARCADIA LODGE, Florence Ave., Russell. Tel. 09/403-7756. 9 backpacker beds, 3 units (all with shared baths).

$ Rates (excluding GST): NZ$14 ($8) dormitory bed; NZ$35–NZ$58 ($20–$33) double. No credit cards.

Linley and Bill Shatwell spent many holidays in the Bay of Islands area before buying this lodge, which includes two attractive, inexpensive units that are spotless and comfortable, and look out onto great views of the bay. Actually they're an extension of the main house. Each is a self-contained unit with kitchen, bath, and toilet, and will sleep four. One large dormitory holds five beds (no bunks), another has four beds. They also have a dinghy and old bikes for guests' use. This is a very popular place with budget travelers, both in New Zealand and among overseas travelers who've heard about it by word of mouth, so it's a good idea to book ahead if you can. It's located on the outskirts of town.

Worth the Extra Money

KIMBERLEY LODGE, P.O. Box 166, Russell. Tel. 09/403-7090. Fax 09/403-7239. 4 suites (all with bath). TV TEL **Transportation:** Transport furnished from ferry landing or Kerikeri Airport upon request.
$ Rates (including breakfast): NZ$195 ($111) single; NZ$250 ($143) double. MC, V.

Set on a wooded hillside among lovely gardens near Pompallier House, Kimberley Lodge looks out to stunning views of the bay. Although it is of recent vintage, there's a decidedly old-world charm in every room and in the verandas that surround both floors. Guest rooms are beautifully appointed and furnished with handcrafted native New Zealand wood furniture. Gourmet dinners are available, and breakfasts are outstanding. Outdoor facilities include a barbecue and a spa-swimming pool.

IN PAIHIA
Motel Flats

BAY OF ISLANDS MOTEL, 6 Tohitapu Rd., Te Haumi Bay (P.O. Box 131), Paihia. Tel. 09/402-7348. Fax 09/402-7348. 10 cottages (all with shower and tub). TV TEL
$ Rates: NZ$59 ($34) single; NZ$68 ($39) double. AE, MC, V.

Set in spacious grounds off Seaview Road, these self-contained colonial-style cottages have a lounge, separate bedroom, bath, and full kitchen. Privacy is assured, since cottages are placed at angles to prevent the windows of one from facing those of another, and the whole effect is that of a charming mini-village. Other facilities include a swimming pool, spa pool, laundry, and a playground for the young fry, who will also enjoy nearby beaches (close enough to hoof it). They can supply cooked or continental breakfasts on request, and are happy to book tours, cruises, and fishing trips right from their office. You'll also enjoy browsing through their shop.

BAYSWATER INN, Marsden Rd., Paihia. Tel. 09/402-7444. 4 flats (all with bath). TV TEL
$ Rates: Summer, NZ$95 ($54) single or double; winter, NZ$65 ($37) double. MC, V.

Chester and Louise Rendell are the proprietors of the four modern, spacious motel flats (each sleeps up to four) located back of an 1884 house set back from the road behind a long, landscaped lawn. The old house in the center of town is now one of Paihia's better restaurants (see "Where to Eat," below), making this a very convenient place to stay. All units are nicely decorated, and each has its own outside deck, complete with chairs for sunning. There's also a hot spa pool.

BEST WESTERN CASA-BELLA MOTEL, McMurray Rd., Paihia. Tel. 09/402-7387. Fax 09/402-7166. 21 units, 1 suite (all with bath). TV TEL

$ Rates (excluding GST): NZ$59 ($34) single; NZ$65 ($37) double; NZ$75 ($43) suite. Best Western discounts. AE, DC, MC, V.

This charming, sparkling-white, red-tile-roofed, Spanish-style complex is close to shops, restaurants, and the beach. There is a variety of nicely furnished units, all with full kitchen facilities, in-house video, and electric blanket. Some have water beds, and one is a very special honeymoon suite. On the premises there's both a heated swimming and a hot spa pool, as well as full laundry facilities. Picnic tables and benches shaded by umbrellas are set about on the landscaped grounds. It's located off Kings Road.

HIDEAWAY BEACH, 3 Bayview Rd. (P.O. Box 106), Paihia. Tel. 09/402-7615. Fax 09/402-7609. 3 units (all with shower). TV

$ Rates (excluding GST): NZ$70–NZ$90 ($40–$51) per person double occupancy. AE, DC, MC, V.

If you're looking for a secluded spot (the kind that travel writers are admonished not to put in their guides so that it stays secluded), try one of these three accommodations. They are located on a hilltop with a 180° view of the Bay of Islands, and a bush walk to the beach. Units include kitchen. There is no phone in the rooms, but there is one on the premises, along with a flower-covered boardwalk and patio and a laundry. It's owned by the nice folks at the Swiss Chalet (see below). The property is located across the street and up the hill from the Paihia cemetery.

Bed & Breakfasts

SWISS CHALET LODGE MOTEL, 3 Bayview Rd. (P.O. Box 106), Paihia. Tel. 09/402-7615. Fax 09/402-7609. 9 rms (8 with bath). TV TEL

$ Rates (including breakfast): NZ$45–NZ$70 ($26–$40) per person double occupancy. Winter packages available. AE, DC, MC, V.

I heard glowing remarks about this place long before I arrived in the Bay of Islands. Inge and Ed Amsler—she's Austrian; he's Swiss—have brought a bit of alpine charm to the South Pacific, and their attention to detail and comfort is scrupulous. The spacious units all have a balcony, conversation area, writing table, video, kitchen, soft duvets on the beds, and a hairdryer in the bathroom. The Swiss-style breakfast includes muesli, fresh or canned fruit, yogurt, croissants, toast, cheese, and boiled eggs. Early-morning tea, cookies, and a newspaper are complimentary, and you'll find a Swiss chocolate on your pillow when you go to bed at night. This pretty property also features a jewelry shop with items from around the world, a barbecue, spa pool, wooden playground equipment handcrafted by Ed (who designed the lodge), and convenient covered parking. Windsurfing and motorboating are available for guests. Inge and Ed also operate The Swiss Café & Grill on the waterfront in Paihia, offering good food at moderate prices.

WAIROA HOME STAYS, c/o MRS. DOROTHY BAYLY, Bayly Rd. (P.O. Box 36), Paihia. Tel. 09/402-7379. 2 rms (with shared bath).

$ Rates: NZ$75 ($43) bed, breakfast, and dinner; NZ$38 ($22) bed and breakfast; NZ$20 ($11) bed only. No credit cards.

Mrs. Bayly extends visitors a warm welcome to her two-story country home, and there's coffee or tea waiting for them anytime during the day. She will also do your washing and take you for a drive around the farm. For a small additional charge, she'll arrange pickup in Paihia. Her three-course dinner includes wine and a before-dinner drink. There's a spa pool and tennis court on the property, with good beach walks and a golf course nearby.

Hostels

CENTABAY BACKPACKERS HOSTEL, Selwyn Rd., Paihia. Tel. 09/402-7466. 18 2- to 7-bed dormitory rms (with shared baths). TV

$ Rates: NZ$13 ($7) per bed; NZ$16 ($9) per person double. Family and group rates available in low season. MC, V.

This is the most centrally located hostel in town and quite appealing. It's run by the ever-helpful Gary and Kay Bathe, who arrange sailing, horseback riding, sea kayaking, fishing, and overnight camping trips to Cape Reinga. In addition to dormitory beds, there are also double rooms. There are no chores, and it is very clean, with dorm accommodations primarily, and some double rooms. Two lounges have a TV, and there are kitchens, a games room, and bike rental. Their booking office can also arrange sightseeing cruises and trips, sometimes with discounted rates.

MAYFAIR LODGE, Puketona Rd., Paihia. Tel. 09/402-7471. 21 dorm beds, 3 rms (all with shared baths). **Transportation:** Pickup provided from town.
$ Rates: NZ$13 ($7) dorm bed; NZ$14 ($8) per person double. No credit cards.
The Mayfair has dormitory accommodation primarily, along with one double room and two twins. There is a games room with table tennis and a pool table, barbecue area, a TV lounge, in-house video, free spa pool, bicycle rental, and a laundry. They supply sheets and blankets, and will pick you up in Paihia. The lodge is located at the Kerikeri turnoff.

Worth the Extra Money

THC WAITANGI RESORT HOTEL, Private Bag, Paihia, Bay of Islands. Tel. 09/402-7411. Fax 09/402-8200. 145 rms (all with bath). MINIBAR TV TEL
$ Rates: NZ$220 ($126) per person single or double. AE, MC, V.

This lovely hotel is actually set in the grounds of the Waitangi National Trust, with superb land and water views. It's a tranquil, relaxing base for sightseeing the entire region. There's 24-hour room service, piano music in the lounge on summer evenings, a good restaurant, and a heated swimming pool. All rooms have tea and coffee facilities, and a small patio. It's a stone's throw from the Treaty House and the Maori war canoe.

IN KERIKERI

A Hostel

YHA KERIKERI YOUTH HOSTEL, P.O. Box 62, Kerikeri. Tel. 09/407-9391. 28 beds.
$ Rates: NZ$13 ($7) seniors; NZ$6.50 ($4) juniors; NZ$17 ($10) for nonmembers. No credit cards.
Set in 2½ shaded acres, this hostel consists of six dormitory rooms, some with six beds, some with four, and a few twin rooms. Other facilities include a communal kitchen and laundry, a lounge and recreation/games room. There is river swimming just a 5-minute walk from the hostel, and many of the area's historic sites are within easy walking distance. The hostel is located on the main road just north of the village.

CABINS & CAMPGROUNDS

Twin Pines Motor Camp, P.O. Box 168, Haruru Falls, Paihia (tel. 09/402-7322), has for 16 years been operated and upgraded by Gordon, John, and Mamie Putt. It's one of the prettiest and best-run camps in these parts, steeped in history and boasting a turn-of-the-century tavern and restaurant on the premises. In a tree-shaded setting, with the falls as a backdrop, it's a restful and convenient location. The Putts, seasoned travelers themselves, provide low-cost accommodations in eight six-berth chalet-style cabins; two four-berth tourist flats; nine on-site caravans with the same rates as cabins; a 25-bed lodge with facilities at the same rates as cabins; and a 12-bed dormitory, with rates ranging from NZ$9 ($5) for tent and power sites to NZ$45 ($26) double for the tourist flat (all rates include GST). There's a communal kitchen, dining room, laundry, car wash, linen rental, color TV, and a barbecue. Fish-smoking facilities are available; river boat cruises and fishing charters can be arranged.

Right next door to the Twin Pines Motor Camp, the ✪ **Falls Motor Inn,** on Puketona Road (P.O. Box 14), Haruru Falls, Paihia (tel. 09/402-7816), has 14 one- and two-bedroom units, tent and caravan sites, a pool with a mesmerizing view of the Waitangi River, a small sandy beach, a dinghy, and an outdoor spa pool. You'll love the point with the flame tree on it (so do those winsome birds, the tuis, and campers); room 10 affords a view of the falls. The activities board will keep you up-to-date on current happenings in the area. The management loves the area and can point out nearby walks and other nature-oriented activities. Room rates are NZ$48 ($27.50) single, NZ$56 ($32) double, plus GST. The minimum fee for a powered site in the motor camp is NZ$16 ($9). The camping fee is NZ$7 ($4) for the first adult and NZ$6 ($3.50) for each additional person. They accept the following credit cards: AE, DC, MC, and V.

The **Bay of Islands Holiday Park,** Lily Pond, Puketona Road, Paihia (tel. 09/402-7646), is midway between Puketona Junction and Paihia, and sits on parklike grounds right at the Waitangi River's edge. There are 250 sites, 100 caravan sites, four on-site caravans, and 11 cabins, all of a quality that has won a four-star grading by the Camp & Cabin Association of New Zealand. You can rent linens, and there's a store on the grounds, a large, modern kitchen for campers, and a separate, fully equipped kitchen for the cabins. Rates are NZ$9 ($5) per person for sites, and NZ$30 ($22) per couple for on-site caravans and cabins.

WHERE TO EAT

As you would expect in such a popular resort area, the Bay of Islands has many good places to eat. Seafood tops the list of menu offerings, with fish coming to your table just hours after they were swimming in the waters offshore.

IN RUSSELL

THE DUKE OF MARLBOROUGH, The Strand, Russell. Tel. 403-7829.
   Cuisine: SEAFOOD/NEW ZEALAND. **Reservations:** Recommended.
$ **Prices:** Appetizers NZ$5–NZ$8 ($3–$5); main courses NZ$16–NZ$35 ($9–$20). Half-price meals for children under 10. AE, DC, MC, V.
   Open: Breakfast daily 7:30–9:30am; lunch daily noon–2:30pm; dinner daily 6:30–9pm.

The Duke serves à la carte meals in its elegant dining room. They've added a salad bar and a dining deck overlooking the bay. Main courses are fresh seafood, roasts of lamb or sirloin, pork, and chicken. The Duke is fully licensed, with an excellent wine cellar.

THE GABLES, The Strand, Russell. Tel. 403-7618.
   Cuisine: SEAFOOD/NEW ZEALAND. **Reservations:** Required.
$ **Prices:** Appetizers NZ$6–NZ$9 ($3–$6); main courses NZ$17–NZ$20 ($10–$12). MC, V.
   Open: Summer, daily 12–2:30pm and 7–11pm. **Closed:** June–July.

This was one of the first buildings on the waterfront, built in 1850, and was a riotous brothel in the days of the whalers. Its construction is pit-sawn kauri on whalebone foundations (in fact, there's a huge piece of whale vertebrae, discovered during the renovation, now on display in the small bar). Decor is early colonial, with a kauri-paneled ceiling in the bar, kauri tables, prints, maps, photographs of early New Zealand, and the cheerful warmth of open fires. The menu changes seasonally, but seafood, beef, lamb, game, and fresh vegetables and fruits are a mainstay. The Gables is fully licensed, with a respectable wine list, or BYO. Bay of Islanders love this place, so book early.

QUARTERDECK, The Strand, Russell. Tel. 403-7761.
Cuisine: SEAFOOD. **Reservations:** Recommended.
$ Prices: Appetizers NZ$7–NZ$9 ($4–$5); main courses NZ$17–NZ$30 ($10–$17). MC, V.
Open: Daily 6–9pm (longer hours in high season). **Closed:** July.

Freshness is something you can count on at the Quarterdeck. In a setting of early Bay of Islands prints and photographs and high-backed booths, there's a terrific seafood platter, as well as snapper or whatever the latest catch has brought in, mixed grill, chicken, and light meals. A free salad bar comes with all meals. In fine weather, there's delightful outdoor dining on the waterfront. BYO.

IN PAIHIA

If you can't muster the energy to go out at the end of the day, in addition to the listings below, there's always **Dial-a-Pizza** (tel. 402-7536).

BISTRO 40 RESTAURANT AND BAR, in the Bayswater Inn, 40 Marsden Rd. Tel. 402-7444.
Cuisine: SEAFOOD/BEEF/GAME. **Reservations:** Required.
$ Prices: Appetizers NZ$9–NZ$11 ($5–$6); main courses NZ$20–NZ$25 ($11–$14). AE, MC, V.
Open: Daily 6–11pm.

This charming house dates back to 1884 and overlooks the bay. Meals are served in a bright sunny front room, and from mid-December through March there's also service on a small terrace shaded by a passionfruit-vine-laden trellis. Specialties are fresh local seafoods, poultry, meat, and game. Go early and enjoy a predinner drink in their garden setting. BYO.

BLUE MARLIN DINER, waterfront, Paihia. Tel. 402-7590.
Cuisine: BREAKFAST/SHORT ORDER. **Reservations:** Not required.
$ Prices: Breakfast under NZ$8 ($5); short orders NZ$7–NZ$19 ($4–$11). No credit cards.
Open: Breakfast daily 7am–3pm; snacks and suppers daily 5:30–8pm.

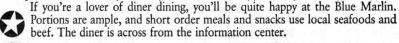 If you're a lover of diner dining, you'll be quite happy at the Blue Marlin. Portions are ample, and short order meals and snacks use local seafoods and beef. The diner is across from the information center.

ESMAE'S, 41 Williams Rd. Tel. 402-8400.
Cuisine: SEAFOOD/LAMB/BEEF/GAME. **Reservations:** Recommended.
$ Prices: Average dinner NZ$30 ($17). AE, DC, MC, V.
Open: Dinner daily 5:30pm–late. **Closed:** Sun in winter.

Named after its consummate hostess, this restaurant features home-style New Zealand cooking and the menu even tells you where the fish or meat comes from. Esmae Dally will meet, greet, and seat you. There are fresh Kerikeri oysters, scallops, local fish, crayfish, and mussels. Non-seafood lovers are catered for, and I am personally fond of marinated lamb steak, grilled and served with emerald sauce. Vegetarians will find at least one offering, such as the vegeroni crêpe, a combination of local vegetables and pasta with a mustard cream sauce. BYO. Esmae's is located in the center of town.

JANE'S RESTAURANT, State Hwy. 10, between Paihia and Kerikeri. Tel. 407-8664.

Cuisine: SEAFOOD/BEEF/CHICKEN. **Reservations:** Required during the season and on weekends.

$ Prices: Average lunch NZ$14 ($8); average dinner NZ$20 ($11). MC, V.

Open: Lunch daily noon–2pm; dinner daily 6:30pm–late.

Jane's looks like a roadhouse on the outside, an Olde English restaurant on the inside. The low-beamed ceiling, fireplaces, ornaments, and paintings make this a cozy, relaxed setting for the superb food that comes to the table. It's a far-ranging menu, with specialties such as lamb loin flamed in Kiwifruit liqueur and mint jelly with a creamy sauce. Fresh seafood is served, and there's a wide selection of steaks. Fully licensed, with a good selection of wines. In summer, there's poolside dining in a picturesque garden setting.

LA SCALA RESTAURANT, Selwyn Road Shopping Center. Tel. 402-7031.

Cuisine: SEAFOOD/STEAKS. **Reservations:** Required.

$ Prices: Main courses NZ$15–NZ$30 ($9–$17). Children's menu NZ$10 ($6). MC, V.

Open: Dinner Tues–Sun 6–10pm.

Located upstairs, La Scala has a pretty garden atmosphere, with window walls, green carpet, light-wood tables, cane-back chairs, and greenery everywhere. Fresh seafood is the specialty, as well as New Zealand steaks. In addition to the fish of the day, scallops, oysters, and crayfish, there are such items as honey prawns (shrimp battered, dipped in honey, and sprinkled with sesame seeds). Fully licensed, it's in the town center.

LEROY'S, 14 Kings Rd. Tel. 402-7783.

Cuisine: SEAFOOD/STEAK/CHICKEN. **Reservations:** Recommended.

$ Prices: Appetizers NZ$2–NZ$7 ($1–$4); main courses NZ$17–NZ$19 ($10–$11). Children's servings half-price. MC, V.

Open: Daily noon–2pm and 5–9pm.

This tiny restaurant is the constant subject of letters from readers, all writing to say how much they've enjoyed the Cape Cod atmosphere of this place, the friendliness of owners and staff, and most of all, the food. Its popularity is well deserved: lightly battered, really fresh seafood comes from the kitchen deep-fried and crisp, accompanied by tartar sauce, fresh vegetables, a salad bowl, and tons of chips, plus bread and butter. But if you're a devotee of the broiler, all you have to do is ask, and yours will arrive broiled to perfection. There are all sorts of seafood offered—the fish of the day, oysters, scallops, shrimp, etc.—and a heaping combination platter. Steaks are on the menu as well. There's also a take-away service for fish-and-chips and full meals. BYO. Leroy's is in the town center, ½ block from the waterfront.

EN ROUTE TO WAITOMO

If you're going from the Bay of Islands directly to Waitomo, count on a long day's drive, shortened considerably if you return to Auckland via the short route, Highway 1 (about a 4-hour drive), and an overnight stay in Waitomo. Along the way, you might stop by the town of **Warkworth,** once the center of extensive sawmilling of kauri spars to furnish masts for the Royal Navy. There are the remains of several Maori *pas* (fortified villages) in the area. About 7 kilometers (4 miles) away, at the coastal town of **Sandspit,** you can take a launch to Kawau Island to visit **Mansion House,** the restored home of Gov. George Grey. Then there are those beautiful beaches nearer Auckland at **Waiwera** and **Orewa.**

From Auckland, the 125-mile drive to Waitomo passes through rich farm country and horse and cattle farms. A good lunch stop is the **Victorian 1870 Restaurant,** Main Highway, at Ngaruawahia (tel. *07124/8121). This is an old clapboard house, built in 1869, which has been in its day a police station, post office, and courthouse, and its atmosphere is still very much of the 19th century, with interesting antiques in the licensed dining room. The fare is simple, good, and moderately priced. Hours vary, so call ahead to check. Closed Monday.

Hamilton is New Zealand's largest inland city and the commercial and industrial center of this agricultural area, as well as the site of the University of Waikato. Several major religions are centered here: it's the see city for the Anglican Diocese of Waikato; the Mormons have their magnificent South Pacific temple headquarters at Temple View, high on a hill at Tuhikaramea southwest of the city center; and there's a Sikh temple on the northern outskirts of town at Horotiu. Throughout the city, you'll see lovely gardens both in city parks and private lawns.

A scant 10 miles before you reach Waitomo and the caves, there's a **Kiwi House** at Otorohanga, as well as an excellent youth hostel, which is open only from December 17 to January 25. The remaining distance to Waitomo runs through more rolling farmland.

A FARM STAY FOR CAMPERVANS EN ROUTE

On State Highway 3, about halfway between Hamilton and Waitomo, the ✪ **Parklands Dairy Farm,** Kio Kio, R.D. 4, Otorohanga (tel. 07/871-1818), is run by Owen Rountree and family, whose hospitality goes far beyond that of most owners. That is undoubtedly because this is their home, and what they're offering—in addition to power points at campervan sites, showers, toilets, and a barbecue—is a real "down home" farm welcome. Guests are invited in for a cuppa in the evening, and when it's farm-chore time, guests often go right along. This really is a motor camp with a difference, and it's a convenient base for Waitomo Caves sightseeing. Rates, which include GST, are NZ$13 ($7) double, NZ$6 ($3) for each additional adult, NZ$4 ($2) for each additional child. The family will provide a cooked farm breakfast for an extra charge, and dinner with advance notice.

---

3. WAITOMO

125 miles SE of Auckland

GETTING THERE   By Bus   There's excellent InterCity transportation from the Bay of Islands to Auckland, and service leaving Auckland at about 9am for Waitomo, which stops for a tour of the caves, then goes on to Rotorua. You can, of course, break the journey with an overnight stay at Waitomo and continue on to Rotorua the next afternoon.

By Car   If you're going from the Bay of Islands directly to Waitomo, count on a long day's drive and plan an overnight stay at Waitomo. There are sightseeing possibilities along the way (see "En Route to Waitomo," above), but on a 1-day drive to Waitomo, you'll have to keep an eye on the clock. If you leave the Bay of Islands around 8am, driving at a steady pace (with a lunch break) will get you to Waitomo not much before about 5pm. An alternative is a leisurely drive back to Auckland or some other intermediate spot for an overnight stop, and an early-morning start to go on to Waitomo the following day.

ESSENTIALS   The **area code** for Waitomo is 0813 at press time, but may well be changed by the time of your visit because the New Zealand Number Update is in the process of changing all telephone numbers to 7 digits. Those numbers in this section that have not been changed at press time are marked with an asterisk, and you should call the **Helpline 0155** for the new number. For directory assistance within the country (when you don't know the number), call **018.**

✪ **The Museum of Caves Information Centre** is on Main Street (P.O. Box 12), Waitomo (tel. *0813/87-640). It's open from 8:30am to 5pm daily, and there's a small admission charge to the museum on the premises.

Should you arrive without wheels of your own, **Otorohanga Taxis,** 63 Hinewai St., Otorohanga (tel. *0813/8279), can get you to and from the caves, and they also offer farm tours and scenic drives.

Waitomo Village owes its existence to the more than 200,000 visitors who come annually to visit three limestone caves, and its main street holds a general store, post office, and tavern (which sells tickets to the caves as well as souvenirs, and has the usual bottle store, public bar, and bistro restaurant). At the top of a gracefully winding driveway stands the THC Waitomo Hotel (with not a budget-priced room under its roof). Across from the general store, a large open field is called The Domain, where cabins may be rented. Waitomo Cave, with its splendid Glowworm Grotto, is some 400 yards beyond the tavern, and about 2½ miles away are Ruakuri and Aranui Caves, both of which rival Waitomo as sightseeing attractions.

WHAT TO SEE & DO

The caves are *the* attraction at Waitomo, chief among them the Waitomo Cave with its Glowworm Grotto. But you should include the Ruakuri and Aranui caves in your sightseeing—each has its own delights, the cost is low, and they're all worth the time.

THE CAVES

Forty-five-minute guided tours are run on regular schedules at all three caves—tickets and tour times are available at the Tavern and at the THC Waitomo Hotel. There's a two-cave combination ticket at NZ$19 ($11) for adults; one cave costs NZ$13 ($7). Children pay half price. Be sure to wear good walking shoes and carry a sweater if the weather is a bit cool—it'll be cooler underground.

For me, the most wonderful time to visit the ✪ **Glowworm Grotto in Waitomo Cave** is in the evening. Crowds are smaller, for one thing, and somehow the experience just seems to be one for after dark. Sheer delight.

About 400 yards from the THC Hotel, a guide greets you at Waitomo's entrance to escort you through large antechambers, pointing out limestone formations with names like "The Organ," 8 feet high with a 24-foot base.

Largest cavern in any of the caves is "The Cathedral," which rises 47 feet and is an acoustically perfect auditorium that has seen performances by such recording artists as the Vienna Boys' Choir and Dame Nellie Melba.

Then it's on to a small grotto festooned with glowworms, where your guide fills you in on the glowworm's life and death cycle. Fascinating! A very short cycle it is, for the adult fly lives exactly 4 days, just long enough to produce the next generation. Having done that, it simply dies and becomes food for the next batch of glowworms.

The whole process begins with a tiny egg, which has a 21-day incubation period, then hatches into an inch-long grub. The grub then cloaks itself in a hollow mucous tubelike nest, which is attached to the grotto roof with a multitude of slender threads, each holding minute drops of acid and suspended like fishing lines down from the roof. The bait for those lines is the hypnotic blue-green light that comes from the larva's light organs (and that, of course, is what you see as you pass through the grotto) to attract a night-flying midge, which is "caught" by the threads, paralyzed by the acid, and reeled up and eaten by the larva. After about 6 months, the larva pupates for about 2 weeks in a hard, brown cocoon about half an inch long and suspended by a circle of those slender threads. The pupa's flirtatious light show attracts several males, which proceed to help the fly escape her cocoon. Four days of egg laying, then it's time to end it all by diving into the lines cast by new larvae as a main course along with the midges.

Now that you understand how and why the glowworms glow, your guide is ready to take you on an unforgettable boat ride down the underground river, which flows through the 100-foot-long, 40-foot-high, 50-foot-wide Glowworm Grotto. As you board the large, flat-bottomed boat, he will caution you that absolute silence is required, since the glowworms will extinguish their lights at the slightest noise. I must say that the warning is probably unnecessary, since the spectacle of more than 10,000 of those tiny pinpricks of light leaves one awed beyond words, and silence seems the only fitting way in which to view them. The boat glides slowly along what is called the "Milky Way," then returns to the dock, where you climb back up through the cave and are given an opportunity to question your guide on any of the things you have seen. It's a unique experience, and one that is sure to live in your memory.

For the adventurous, there's a memorable **Black Water Rafting** experience on an underground river at a cost of NZ$42 ($24).

Ask at the THC Hotel desk if you need transportation to the other two caves, which are some 2½ miles away. Dramatic **Ruakuri,** with its labyrinth of caverns alive with the sound of an underground waterfall and its river, which flashes in and out of sight, is the largest of the three. The smallest is **Aranui,** and many people think it's the loveliest. There's an unusual delicacy about its limestone formations and ivory-colored, translucent stalactites. Light refreshments are available near these two caves.

KIWI HOUSE

While in the area, stop by the ✪ **Otorohanga Nocturnal Kiwi House** on Alex Telfer Drive, off Kakamutu Road (tel. *08133/7391). The Otorohanga Zoological Society always has one pair of the national bird awake and on view, and there's always a knowledgeable person on hand to tell you about them and answer any questions you may have. There's also a large aviary on the grounds, which has an interesting collection of waterfowl. Hours are 10am to 5pm in summer, to 4pm in other months. Admission is NZ$7 ($4) for adults, half that for children; under-7s, free.

WHERE TO STAY

Unless otherwise noted, the rates quoted below include GST.

A LICENSED HOTEL

THE ROYAL HOTEL, Te Kanawa St. (off Maniapoto St.), Otorohanga. Tel. *08133/8129. 15 rms (none with bath), 1 suite (with bath).

$ **Rates:** NZ$40 ($23) single; NZ$55 ($31) double without bath, NZ$75 ($43) suite with bath. MC, V.

Located 10 miles north of the caves, this small hotel has charming, immaculate rooms with flowered carpets and lace curtains. All have hot and cold water, and bath and shower facilities are in the hall. The communal kitchen has tea-making facilities and a laundry. The Rangatira Room restaurant serves good, reasonably priced meals.

A HOSTEL

HAMILTON TOMO GROUP LODGE, on the main road (P.O. Box 11), Waitomo Caves. Tel. *0813/87-442.

$ **Rates** (excluding GST): NZ$8 ($5) bunk.

This is the closest thing Waitomo has to a youth hostel. Backpackers and cavers find it quite adequate. The bunkhouse will sleep 30 (but has been known to accommodate more in a pinch) on wooden bunks that have rubber mattresses. House rules are basic: Guests must tidy up, and lights go out at midnight. The lounge is well equipped with cave games. Reservations? You don't need them—you simply go to the lodge, drop NZ$8 ($5) plus GST, in the Honesty Box, and claim your bunk space. There's not likely to be much space on a weekend, since that's when there's an invasion of great numbers of trampers and cavers who are members of the Hamilton Tomo Group, but you'll be fitted in if possible. Equipment in the lodge includes light, heat, hot water, showers, electric stove (plus all cooking and eating utensils), refrigerator, washing machine, drying room, and radio. There's an interesting caving display, and lots of club photos. You'll need to bring in food from the general store, since there's none closer. The hostel is located ½ mile past the Waitomo Cave on the main road. *Tip:* If you're lucky, you just may be invited to go caving with members of the Hamilton Tomo Group.

A MOTOR CAMP

In Otorohanga, 16 kilometers (10 miles) from Waitomo Caves, the ✪ ⑤ **Otorohanga Motor Camp,** c/o Otorohanga Taxis, Wahanui Crescent, Otorohanga (tel. *08133/8214), is on Domain Drive right next to the Kiwi House and swimming pool. Just help yourself to any unoccupied or unreserved site and the nonresident caretaker calls in the mornings and evenings to collect your fees. There's a kitchen with an electric range, hot- and cold-water sinks, refrigerator, and freezer. Other amenities include toilets, showers, a laundry, a barbecue area, and a play area. Tent sites cost NZ$11 ($6) for two people; an extra person is NZ$6 ($3); children 5 to 16, NZ$4 ($2); and children under 5, free. Caravan sites are NZ$13 ($7) for two people and NZ$6 ($3) for an extra person, and children are charged the same as above. On-site caravans cost NZ$12 ($7) per night, plus camp charges. All prices include GST.

WORTH THE EXTRA MONEY

THC WAITOMO, Waitomo Caves. Tel. *0813/88-227. Fax *0813/88-858. 27 rms (all with bath). TV TEL

$ Rates: NZ$101 ($58) per person single or double. AE, MC, V.

This charming old hotel near the caves was built around the turn of the century and retains much of the character of that period. Guest rooms are quite comfortable, and there's a good restaurant. Sightseeing convenience is also a factor to be considered, since the hotel is the center of bookings for all cave tours.

PUKETAWAI LODGE, R.D. 6, Otorohanga. Tel. *08133/7292. Fax *08133/7272. 4 suites (all with bath). TV TEL

$ Rates: NZ$281 ($161) per person single or double. AE, MC, V.

Set in lush farmland and surrounded by 2 hectares (5 acres) of beautifully maintained lawns and gardens, this luxurious lodge is practically a self-contained resort. In addition to nicely appointed guest rooms, there's a private nine-hole golf course, tennis court, pool, and barbecue. Inside, open fireplaces cozy up the lounge and library, and there's a bar and a games room. Tea and coffee facilities are provided. The lodge is near both the town and the caves.

WHERE TO EAT

Picnics can be a pleasure, either at the outdoor umbrella tables at the general store or the facilities on the Domain. You can also buy hot and cold snacks and light meals at the general store's tearoom.

When it comes to **restaurant meals,** you're pretty much restricted to the licensed restaurant at the THC Waitomo Hotel (see above) or bistro meals at the Tavern; and in Otorohanga, there's a fully licensed restaurant in the ✪ Otorohanga Royal Hotel (see above), and Maniapoto Street has several good, inexpensive restaurants from which to choose.

EN ROUTE TO ROTORUA

It's an easy, 3-hour-or-less drive from Waitomo to Rotorua, through rolling farmland and long stretches of bush. Approaching that steamy thermal town, you'll catch glimpses of its gleaming lakes and volcanic peaks. There's an "other world" aspect (and slight sulfuric odor!) about Rotorua and its environs, which will begin to capture your imagination even before you roll into town.

CHAPTER 5

ROTORUA &
ENVIRONS

- **WHAT'S SPECIAL ABOUT ROTORUA**
1. **ROTORUA**
2. **GISBORNE**
3. **HAWKE'S BAY**

Right in the middle of the North Island, Rotorua is also in the center of the most intense thermal field in New Zealand, the 150-mile-long, 20-mile-wide Taupo Volcanic Plateau. The city and its environs are a veritable wonderland of bubbling mud, incredible silica terraces, and towering geysers. There is also the pervasive, though rather faint, sulfuric odor that comes along with the thermal activity.

This is the very heart of New Zealand's Maori culture, and the city's 50,000 population includes a high percentage of Maori. The city and surrounding area are quite literally soaked with attractions, almost all tied by legend to the Maori.

As to that awesome thermal activity, the Maori are quick to tell you the legend that explains its existence in Maori terms. It seems the great navigator-priest Ngatoroirangi, having reached the summit of Mount Tongariro, suffered greatly from the cold and implored his goddess sisters back in Hawaiki to send along some of their native warmth to this frigid, windswept place. Their response was a generous one—they pitched their gobs of fire across the water, which hopped, skipped, and jumped over the land, touching down at White Island, Rotorua, Wairankei, Taupo, Tokaanu, Ketetahi, finally reaching the freezing Ngatoroirangi at Mount Tongariro. Geologists, on the other hand, simply say that underground lava or superheated rock heats and pressurizes underground water, sending it spouting up via any escape route it can find—natural fissures and porous rock. Personally, I think the Maoris have the better story! Whatever the explanation, today's residents of the area have harnessed that thermal activity to provide heat and hot water for domestic use.

As you can see from all the above, Rotorua should be a focal point of your North Island itinerary. Limited time may well point you from Rotorua to **Taupo,** the **Tongariro National Park,** and **Wanganui.** For those who can spare a few days, however, there is a glorious drive awaiting around what is called New Zealand's **Eastland-Sunrise Coast,** since it is the place where the sun is first seen each morning. Magnificent seascapes (some of the most exciting in the country), secluded coves and bays, deserted beaches, tiny Maori settlements, and finally the Poverty Bay town of **Gisborne** and Hawke's Bay's crowning jewel, **Napier.** It's an area alive with history, both Maori and Pakeha. You'll see where the Arawa canoe made landfall; where Capt. James Cook first saw the New Zealand mainland and where he stopped on his second voyage; where ferocious, decisive battles between Maori and Europeans were fought; and along the way there are some of the finest examples of Maori carvings in New Zealand.

This swing around the Sunrise Coast is an off-the-beaten-track digression that I strongly urge you to take if you can fit it into your timetable. It's a bit of New Zealand far too many visitors miss. But if you just don't have the time, skip this section and proceed to **Taupo.**

WHAT'S SPECIAL ABOUT ROTORUA

Cultural Events/Concerts and Feasts

☐ No visitor should miss one of the authentic Maori concerts and traditional *hangi* feasts offered by Rotorua hotels. Similar in some ways to the Hawaiian luau, the hangi features seafood, succulent meats, and local vegetables cooked in an earthen pit.

Thermal Attractions

☐ The Whakarewarewa Reserve is closest to the city, with a silica terrace pierced by seven active water spouts and Pohutu Geyser, which sends spouts of steam and water some 100 feet into the air.

☐ A short drive from the city, the Waimungu Valley is a glimpse of the classic description of Hell—lakes boil and hiss, and steaming cliff faces are streaked scarlet with baking minerals. Amazingly, in the midst of all this satanic landscape, native New Zealand plants flourish.

Cultural Centers

☐ Adjacent to the Whakarewarewa Reserve is the Maori Arts and Crafts Institute, where you can see fascinating demonstrations of traditional Maori skills such as carving and weaving.

Sporting Activities

☐ On offer in this area are white-water rafting, jet-boat trips, waterskiing, fishing, golf, forest walks, and mountain hikes to see the gigantic cleft of a blown-out crater on Mount Tarawera.

The drive to Taupo is a short 52 miles over excellent roads. Five miles before you reach Taupo, look for the steamy **Wairakei Geothermal Project,** which harnesses all that underground energy to furnish electrical power.

1. ROTORUA

234km (144 miles) SE of Auckland, 150km (93 miles) E of Waitomo Caves

GETTING THERE   By Plane   Mount Cook Lines operates three flights daily between Auckland and Rotorua, with a one-way fare of NZ$147 ($84).

By Bus   InterCity, Mount Cook Lines, and Newmans all have daily bus schedules between Auckland and Rotorua. Average one-way fare is NZ$34 ($19).

By Car   Drive south from Auckland on Highway 1 to Tirau, then east on Highway 5 to Rotorua.

DEPARTING   The Travel Centre (arrival and departure point for all **coaches** and most sightseeing tours) is on Amohau Street (tel. *81-039).

   Air New Zealand has a ticket terminal on Amohau Street, just off Fenton Street (tel. *87-159). **Newmans** office is at 113 Fenton St. (tel. *70-599).

ESSENTIALS   Orientation   Rotorua sits in the curve of Lake Rotorua's southwestern shore, spreading inland in a neat pattern, which will have you oriented in a matter of hours. The center of town is not large: A good ten-minute walk will take you from the southside bus depot **(the Travel Centre)** northward past the **post office** and **Visitors Information Centre** to the lovely **Government Gardens.** Older, downtown hotels are also along this route, while more modern hotels are more or less concentrated along the southern end of Fenton Street, which is the main street, running from the lake for 2 miles south to **Whakarewarewa** (never mind, just call it "Whaka," as the locals do), a thermal reserve owned by the Maori.

Information   The center of tourist information is the **Visitors Information Centre** at 67 Fenton St. on the corner of Haupapa Street (tel. *073/485-179); hours are 8:30am to 5pm daily. It is loaded with tourist information and has a helpful staff who will make bookings. Look for *Thermalair* and *Rotorua Magic,* free publications listing current goings-on, which you'll find in many hotels and in the tourist offices, and check the evening newspaper, the *Daily Post,* for day-to-day events. Tourist information is also available at the **Rotorua Travel Centre,** Amohau Street (tel. *073/481-039), also open daily from 8:30am to 5pm. After hours, ring *481-036.

Telephone   The telephone prefix at press time is 073. Remember, the New Zealand Number Update is in the process of changing all telephone numbers to 7 digits. Those numbers in this chapter that have not been changed at press time are marked with an asterisk, and you should call the Helpline 0155 for the new number. For directory assistance within the country (when you don't know the number), call 018. International telephone service is available from New Zealand Telecom, Pukuatua St.

Mail   The New Zealand Post, Ltd., Hinemoa Street (tel. *477-851), is open from 8:30am to 5pm Monday through Friday.

The first tourists in Rotorua were Maori, members of the Arawa tribe whose seagoing canoe reached the shores of the Bay of Plenty sometime during the 14th century. Pushing inland to Lake Rotorua, they stayed on as settlers. Today's tourist will find some 5,000 of their descendants happily following much of the traditional tribal lifestyle in the largest area in New Zealand that is both preserved and promoted as a showcase for pre-European culture.

Those early arrivals found the area ideally suited to settlement. Nature supplied not only everything they needed for survival, but threw in mysterious volcanic cones, large, deep lakes, and all those steaming thermal pools as natural habitats for innumerable Maori spirit gods who, of course, were unseen passengers in the Arawa canoe as it crossed the Pacific. There's a Maori legend centered on the antics of the gods to be told about almost every one of the natural wonders you'll see in Rotorua.

Because Rotorua sits right in the middle of the most intense activity (that explains the strong smell of sulfur here), overheated water will bubble up all around you in the form of geysers, mud pools, or steam bores. You'll bathe in it, see the locals cooking with it, stay in guesthouses that are heated with it, or simply walk carefully around the boiling mud pools, watching their performance in sheer fascination.

Just as fascinating is the vast gallery of Maori culture through which you will wander. Through song and dance you'll hear some of those legends firsthand; at a hangi feast you'll taste food cooked in a centuries-old manner; in a model Maori village you'll watch the younger generation learning carving and weaving from their elders. In craft shops you'll find a splendid array of "just the right gift" items.

Tours are numerous, well planned, and not too expensive—this is, after all, perhaps the North Island's major tourist town, and you may be sure that whatever you want to do or see, someone will have devised an easy, inexpensive way for you to do it.

GETTING AROUND   There are city and suburban **buses,** but they are infrequent

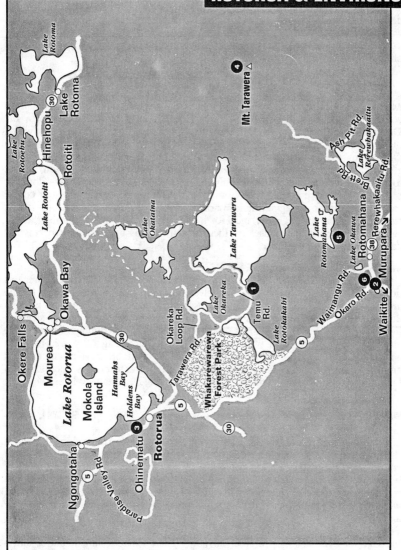

ROTORUA & ENVIRONS

4.83 km / 3 mi

N

Lake Rotoma

Lake Rotoehu

Lake Rotoiti

Hinehopu

Rotoiti

30

Lake Rotoma

Okere Falls

Mourea

Okawa Bay

Lake Rotorua

Mokola Island

Hannahs Bay

Holdens Bay

Ngongotaha

Paradise Valley Rd

Ohinemutu

Rotorua

30

5

5

Lake Okataina

Okareka Loop Rd.

Tarawera Rd.

Whakarewarewa Forest Park

Lake Tarawera

Mt. Tarawera △ 4

Lake Okareka

Temu Rd.

Lake Rotokakahi

Lake Rotomahana

Lake Okawa

Lake Rerewhakaaitu

Ash Pit Rd.

Brett Rd.

Rerewhakaaitu Rd.

Rotomahana

Waimangu Rd.

Okaro Rd.

5

1

5

6

2

38

Waikite

Murupara

5

30

Rotorua

Buried Village of Te Wairoa 1
Lady Knox Geyser 2
Ohinemutu 3
Mount Tarawera 4
Waimangu Geyser 5
Waiotapu Thermal Wonderland 6

(about one an hour) during weekdays and nonexistent on weekends. Unless you're driving, reserve an in-town room and use coach tours to reach those sights out of walking distance.

You'll find **taxi ranks** at the Travel Centre, and on Fenton Street near the Ansett office, or you can call a cab at *485-079.

WHAT TO SEE & DO

Most major attractions are offered on tours, and you can, of course, visit them on your own, especially those in downtown Rotorua such as **Tudor Towers,** the **Government Gardens,** and **Ohinemutu.** Narrowing down your choices of which places to visit is difficult, and it really helps to go to the **Visitors Information Centre** or the **Travel Centre** and look at their short videos of 15 different attractions to get a vivid idea of what each is like. If you just don't have time to get out to the major thermal sites, you can easily view a few on a small scale locally—look for one at the lakeshore behind the Hyatt Hotel; walk around behind the golf course from Tudor Towers, hugging the lakeshore and you should see another on the left; from the parking lot at Geyserland Hotel, you can gaze out over all of the thermal valley. Heavy rainfall increases geothermal activity, so showers won't necessarily dampen your sightseeing here.

THE GOVERNMENT GARDENS.
Stately **Tudor Towers** (one of New Zealand's oldest buildings) reigns over this downtown city park. The gardens themselves are a lovely mix of rose gardens (which are lit at night), croquet and bowling lawns, and steaming thermal pools. They're a delightful in-town resting spot, and the Tudor Towers provides worthwhile sightseeing. Inside, you'll find the **Rotorua Art Gallery,** displaying paintings of both native and international artists as well as the small but interesting **City of Rotorua Museum,** which focuses on a significant collection of Maori carvings and artifacts and the unique history of the volcanic plateau. Admission to both is free. Built as a fashionable bathhouse, the largest in the country, along European spa lines, the Tudor Towers also houses a licensed restaurant.

POLYNESIAN POOLS, in Government Gardens, Minemoa St. Tel. *481-328.
The chief attraction at the gardens is the Polynesian Pools, overlooking the lake in the town center. Here, for a mere pittance, you can experience the mineral pools at your leisure, for as long as you choose, and you can rent a swimsuit and towel, if necessary. There are pools open to the sky, enclosed pools, and private pools. The soft alkaline water in the large pool maintains a constant temperature of about 100°F, while the smaller pools (reached along wooden walkways) contain water high in sulfur and magnesium—very good for sore muscles—at temperatures of 90° to 110°F. Private pools and a sauna are available for NZ$6.50 ($4), as well as gentle water massage for NZ$30 ($17) for half an hour. There's a refreshment parlor and a well-stocked souvenir shop. You can rent a swimsuit and towel for NZ$2 ($1) each, and a locker for NZ$1 (60¢). Just beyond the reception area, be sure to take a look at the excellent mural of the migration of Polynesians from Hawaiki.
  Admission: NZ$5.50 ($3) adults, NZ$2 ($1) children.
  Open: Daily 9am–10pm.

OHINEMUTU, about a half mile north of Rotorua.
This is the suburb where the largest Arawa subtribe, the Ngatiwhakaue, dwells. Although the residences are very much in the Pakeha style—small, everyday bungalows—the lifestyle follows tribal custom. On a *marae* (open courtyard, or clearing) stands the beautifully hand-carved **Tamatekapua meetinghouse.**

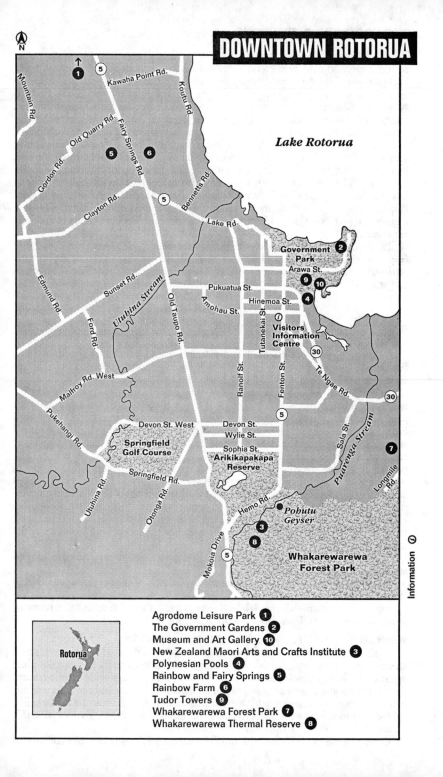

DOWNTOWN ROTORUA

Lake Rotorua

Mountain Rd.

Kawaha Point Rd.

Koutu Rd.

Old Quarry Rd.

Gordon Rd.

Fairy Springs Rd.

Clayton Rd.

Bennetts Rd.

Lake Rd.

Government Park

Arawa St.

Edmund Rd.

Sunset Rd.

Utuhina Stream

Pukuatua St.

Amohau St.

Hinemoa St.

Ford Rd.

Old Taupo Rd.

Tutanekai St.

Fenton St.

Visitors Information Centre

30

Malfroy Rd. West

Ranolf St.

Te Ngae Rd.

30

Pukehangi Rd.

Devon St. West

Devon St.

Wylie St.

Sala St.

Puarenga Stream

Springfield Golf Course

Sophia St.

Arikikapakapa Reserve

Longmile Rd.

Utuhina Rd.

Springfield Rd.

Otonga Rd.

Hemo Rd.

Pohutu Geyser

Mokoia Drive

Whakarewarewa Forest Park

Information

Rotorua

Agrodome Leisure Park ❶
The Government Gardens ❷
Museum and Art Gallery ❿
New Zealand Maori Arts and Crafts Institute ❸
Polynesian Pools ❹
Rainbow and Fairy Springs ❺
Rainbow Farm ❻
Tudor Towers ❾
Whakarewarewa Forest Park ❼
Whakarewarewa Thermal Reserve ❽

This is where most tribal matters are discussed and important decisions made; concerts are also held here every night. Homes are thermally heated, and in every backyard you'll see the steam ovens where much of the family cooking is done.

Perhaps the most outstanding structure you'll see in Ohinemutu is **✪ St. Faith's Anglican Church,** a remarkable representation of the Pakeha Christian faith as interpreted through Maori art. The Tudor-style church building is a revelation of Maori color, intricate carving, exquisite scrollwork, and even an integration of ancient Maori religions, as represented by the figures of mythical demigods and their primitive subjects, which are carved in the base of the pulpit. There's a lovely, truly spiritual, blending of the two cultures in a magnificent plate-glass window looking out to the lake; the window shows a full-size figure of Christ haloed, but clad in a Maori cloak of kiwi feathers, appearing to be walking on the lake. It was sandblasted by a local Pakeha artist, Mr. Mowbray, and in the figure's stance he captured the unmistakable dignity and grace of Maori chieftains. A visit to St. Faith's is a touching, memorable experience.

Tombs of Maori tribal leaders are outside the church, all above ground and safe from the restless rumblings of all that thermal activity. Take time to explore the settlement, as there are other examples of Maori carving and decoration in buildings and statues.

OTHER SIGHTS

RAINBOW AND FAIRY SPRINGS, Fairy Springs Rd., Rotorua. Tel. *479-301.

A sanctuary—that's what you'll find at Rainbow and Fairy Springs north of town. For the world-famous rainbow trout, which grow to gigantic proportions in complete safety from the angler's hook in these protected waters; for birds (several rare species); for trees and plants (some 135 varieties of fern alone); and most of all, perhaps, for mankind. As you follow the map (pick it up at the entrance) around a 350-yard path—meandering through deep bush thick with lush, dark greenery and alive with birdsong from those soaring free or resting in treetops and joined by those in the small aviary; stop to watch the antics of brown and rainbow trout, which push and butt each other in their haste to gobble up food pellets thrown by visitors; gaze at peacefully grazing deer in their paddock—there's an ease of mind that creeps in, bringing with it a sense of the harmony between humanity and nature that has been achieved in this small patch of earth. Along the Fairy Springs walk, Maori myth takes on a little more reality when you see the spring from which more than five million gallons of water per day well up through the black and white sands. It isn't hard at all to credit the Maori belief that here is the home of the legendary Patupaiarehe, the fairy folk.

There's a good souvenir shop, a cafeteria for light snacks, and an attractive licensed restaurant for light, inexpensive meals.

Admission (including Rainbow Farm; see below): NZ$8.50 ($5) adults, NZ$4 ($2) children.

Open: Daily 8am–4:30pm. **Directions:** Hwy. 5 about 2½ miles from Rotorua, north of Ohinemutu. **Bus:** Ngongotaha bus from Travel Centre.

RAINBOW FARM, Fairy Springs Rd. Tel. *478-104.

Rainbow Farm features the entire range of farm animals—horses, cows, goats, sheep, pigs, ducks, and dogs—and genuine gumboot farmers. Shows take place against a backdrop of a 1930s farm scene viewed through stage-wide opening doors. The showmen give a lively commentary of a busy day on a farm and combine working animals with an entertaining, educational, and rather nostalgic view of Kiwi farm life.

Admission: Free with ticket to Rainbow Springs (see above). Shows NZ$6 ($3) adults, NZ$2 ($1) children, NZ$16 ($9) family ticket.

Open: Shows at 10:30am and 1 and 2:30pm, but you're welcome to stroll around the farm anytime before or between shows. **Directions:** Directly across the main Auckland highway from Rainbow and Fairy Springs (see above).

NEW ZEALAND MAORI ARTS AND CRAFTS INSTITUTE, Whakarewarewa Thermal Reserve, Hemo Rd. (P.O. Box 334). Tel. *489-047.

⭐ On Rotorua's southern edge, just at the Whaka Reserve entrance, the institute exists for the sole purpose of keeping alive the ancient skills of Maori tribes. Youngsters are selected from all over the country to come here as apprentices to master artisans. Here, boys study carving for a minimum of three years, after which they may take their newly acquired skills back to their own tribes or stay on to become teachers at the institute. Girls learn to weave traditional cloaks and make distinctive flax skirts and intricately patterned bodices. As a visitor, you are very welcome as an observer, and it's impossible not to respond to this perfect blending of beauty, myth, and spiritual symbolism as one generation passes a living heritage on to the next. Take away a lasting memento in the form of products made here and on sale in the attached shop. The institute is 3 kilometers (about 2 miles) from the city center.

Admission: Institute and Whaka Reserve, NZ$8.80 ($5) for adults, NZ$2.25 ($1) for children.

Open: Daily 8:30am–5pm. **Closed:** Christmas Day.

WHAKAREWAREWA THERMAL RESERVE, Hemo Rd. (P.O. Box 334), Rotorua. Tel. *489-047.

To walk through the Whaka Thermal Reserve (entrance through the Arts and Crafts Institute above) is to view the most dramatic concentration of Rotorua's thermal wonders. There's a free Maori guide to show you through on the hour, every hour from 9am to 4pm. While you're free to wander on your own, I don't advise it for many reasons (you'll miss a lot of information, and you could just miss your footing and land in one of those boiling mud pools). Besides, who but a Maori who knows, understands, and respects this unique landscape could tell you the legends that interpret its many moods? If you must go alone, be sure to stay on the marked paths.

Inside the reserve, there's a model village patterned after Rotowhio, a pre-European village whose layout and construction has been faithfully reproduced. There are eight active geysers, which may perform for you if your timing is right (they don't operate on a fixed schedule, so it's a matter of luck). Adjoining **Prince of Wales, Feathers Geyser,** and **Pohutu Geyser** are particularly impressive and seem to have worked out an act that showcases them all. The Prince gets things started with a jet, which works up to 30 feet, at which time Pohutu goes into action, erupting to as much as 60 feet, with little offshoot eruptions, which sometimes more than double that height. They are, as I said, unpredictable—eruptions have been clocked as little as two and as many as nine in a 24-hour period and lasting sometimes 20 minutes, sometimes only 5. If you're lucky, there'll be a noontime concert (usually Labor Day to Easter, and school holidays). The reserve is 3 kilometers (about 2 miles) from the city center.

Admission: Institute and Whaka Reserve, NZ$8.80 ($5) for adults, NZ$2.25 ($1) for children.

Open: Daily 8:30am–5pm. **Closed:** Christmas Day.

AGRODOME LEISURE PARK, Riverdale Park, Western Rd., Ngongotaha (P.O. Box 634, Rotorua). Tel. *74-350.

⭐ Maybe it's because the shearing of sheep has been a romantic thing for me since I saw Robert Mitchum in *The Sundowners* years ago that I found the Agrodome performance so intriguing I went back for a second show! Whatever the reason, it is a highlight of any Rotorua visit, and I expect to be in the audience any time I'm in the neighborhood. The Agrodome is a huge (1200 sq. ft.) octagonal natural timber building set in 300 acres of farmland, which displays rams of 19 different breeds of sheep in a 60-minute show that packs into an entertaining and delightful commentary more information on the engaging creatures than you probably thought existed. Each ram walks on stage to a live commentary by a professional shearer explaining the origins of the breed, primary uses of its wool or meat, and its importance to New Zealand's sheep industry. When all 19 are on stage, the master shearer explains the tricks and skills of his trade and proceeds to demonstrate his skill on a sheep you'd swear was luxuriating in the whole thing if you hadn't just been told that its relaxation is the result of one of those tricks. The sheep dogs are then whistled in and put through their paces, and the audience is invited to meet the dogs and rams and pose for photos with the stage stars. Then it's everyone outside for a Dog Trial by a Strong-Eye and three stubborn sheep.

Facilities include a farmyard nursery and a dairy display unit. There's a fully licensed restaurant at the complex, and a horse ride or four-wheel farm bike tour through farmland. Incidentally, the sheepskin shop at the Agrodome has been the source of two of my most-prized New Zealand purchases—both the selection and the prices are excellent. The site is 4 miles north of Rotorua.

Admission: NZ$7.50 ($4) adults, NZ$3.75 ($2) children; 10% family discount for adults with school-age children. Horse rides NZ$15 ($9) for 30 minutes; bike tours NZ$12.50 ($7).

Open: Performances daily at 9:15am, 11am, and 2:30pm every day (with additional shows during heavy tourist seasons).

WHAKAREWAREWA FOREST PARK, Long Mile Rd., Rotorua. Tel. *461-155.

This popular forest has an entrance right on the outskirts of town, a refreshing walk into many different types of trees and lush bush. You'll see majestic redwood trees dedicated to the men of New Zealand's Forest Service who gave their lives in both world wars. Look for the network of color-coded walking tracks throughout, all starting from the Visitors Centre on Long Mile Road, just off Tarawera Road. Inside, the Visitors Centre has a helpful staff, interesting displays, refreshments, a film on the history and management of the country's forests, and a variety of woodcrafts for gifts and souvenirs.

Admission: Free.

Open: Visitors Centre, daily 9am–5pm year round.

OTHER ACTIVITIES

For a breathtaking view of Rotorua, the lakes, and the entire steamy landscape that surrounds them, take the **Skyline Skyride,** Fairy Spring Road (tel. *470-027). You ascend some 2,975 feet in a glass-enclosed gondola, and it's well worth the NZ$7.50 ($4) charge for adults, NZ$2 ($1) for children.

If you're intrigued by **mazes,** there's a terrific one about 10 minutes from the city on Highway 30 (tel. *459-565), 3 kilometers (2 miles) past the airport on Te Ngae Road. It's the **Fairbank Maze**—some 1.7 kilometers (about a mile) of pathways, and it's even accessible to wheelchairs. Great fun, and admission is a mere NZ$3 ($2) for adults, NZ$1 (60¢) for children.

Golfers will find a warm welcome at the nine-hole **Government Gardens Golf Course** (tel. 07/348-9126). Located at the Gardens, right on the shores of Lake Rotorua, it's within easy walking distance from the city center, and for real golf buffs, there's a 10-game price concession. Not to worry if you didn't bring clubs, as they're available for rent. There's a snack shop on the premises, and, if you're too far away to walk to the course, they'll arrange transportation. It's open daily, year round, from 8am to dark, with NZ$6 ($3) green fee for 9 holes, NZ$50 ($29) for a 10-game concession.

If you've the urge to do as the black swans do and get out on Lake Rotorua, hop aboard the ✪ **Lakeland Queen,** which offers morning or afternoon tea, lunch, and dinner cruises. The paddlewheeler is fully licensed, and all but the dinner cruise bring you close to Mokoia Island, where legendary lovers Hinemoa and Tutanekai met. The morning tea cruise includes the show at the Agrodome for a fare of NZ$15 ($9) for adults, NZ$5 ($3) for children. The luncheon buffet cruise is NZ$25 ($14); and the dinner buffet cruise includes live entertainment for NZ$38.50 ($22). Book at the office on the lakefront (tel. *486-634).

You can see the lake in other ways too—consider from a **helicopter, float-plane, small airplane,** or **fishing boat.** It's a splurge, for sure, but to find out more, inquire at the visitors center, or at the lakefront.

Fisherfolk who long to try their luck in Rotorua's rich **fishing grounds** should contact **Roger Forrester,** a member of the New Zealand Professional Fishing Guides Association (tel. *479-299). During summer months, Roger can furnish licenses and tackle, and he'll take you out on his cabin cruiser for 3 hours for a charge of about NZ$75 ($43) per person. I can't swear to what kind of catch you'll bring home, but Roger is considered tops by the locals, and if there are fish biting, I'm certain he'll get you to them. Also a member of the association, **Clark Gregor,** 3 Tirita St., Rotorua (tel. 07/347-1730, 24 hours), has gained an international reputation for trout catches and runs 3- and 4-hour fishing charters on Lake Rotorua and other area lakes. His canopied boat is quite comfortable, and tea, coffee, and soft drinks are supplied for adults and children. Prices are similar to the above, and Clark will pick you up and deliver you back to your accommodation.

ORGANIZED TOURS

While "budget" usually translates as "do it yourself," there are two exceptionally good tours in Rotorua that will save you time and inconvenience, which in the long run can mean a dollar savings. One is the ✪ **City Tour,** the other a full-day **Waimangu Round Trip,** which has been one of the area's most popular tours since it began in 1902.

InterCity operates a wide variety of half- and full-day excursions. If you're here for a short stay, I'd say a half-day tour is a must. Coaches depart from the Travel Centre and the Visitors Information Centre. The informative tour of Rainbow and Fairy Springs is only given to bus groups, a decided plus. And at the Whaka Thermal Reserve, bus tours are met by a Maori guide and taken right through, whereas individuals have to wait for a group to form. InterCity tour fares range from NZ$21 to NZ$54 ($12 to $31) for adults and NZ$10 to NZ$26 ($6 to $15) for children. Book through Travel Centre, Visitors Information Centre, or call 07/348-1039.

The full-day ✪ **Waimangu Round Trip** has my wholehearted recommendation. And even though it entails a 3-mile walk through steamy Waimangu Valley, unless you're really infirm it shouldn't be too strenuous. Just be sure to wear comfortable walking shoes. Bus departure is from the **Visitors Information Centre,** 67 Fenton St. (tel. *485-179), at 9am, and you'll return at 4:45pm. There are morning and afternoon tea stops, and you can bring your own lunch or purchase one from the tour operators for NZ$6 ($3). The fare is a hefty NZ$54 ($31) for adults, NZ$26 ($15) for children, but you'll cover 42 miles and the better portion of Rotorua's history. Tours operate daily from December 26 to Easter; on Tuesday, Thursday, Saturday, and Sunday other months.

Heading south past Whaka, you pass **Earthquake Flat** and a crater lake, which changes hue from green to blue every 36 hours, en route to **Waimangu Geyser.** Stilled now, it erupted regularly during the first four years of this century, spewing rocks and earth as far as 1,500 feet and claiming four lives before it fell silent. Its crater gave one gigantic, three-day-long last gasp in 1917, exploding with a violence, which flung debris as far as 1,000 feet. Two weeks later the crater began to fill with water, and in a short time a six-acre boiling lake was formed, which has been aptly named **Frying Pan Lake.** Temperatures of the water from subterranean springs that feed it average 210°F at the surface, 315°F in the depths.

From the lake you strike out on foot for 2½ miles to **Mount Tarawera,** which erupted in 1886 to destroy the famous pink and white silica terraces that had been a popular tourist attraction. Six European visitors lost their lives, and the 800-foot-deep hot Rotomahana Lake was formed. A launch takes you out on the lake, past steaming cliffs, which are stratified with brilliant color—an incredible sight! At the end of the launch cruise, there's another half-mile walk to **Lake Tarawera,** one of the largest in the area and famed for its fishing. After a 7-mile cruise across the lake, with clear views of Mount Tarawera's blasted summit, you're met by coach to travel on to the nearby **Buried Village of Te Wairoa,** which perished in the Mount Tarawera eruption and has been excavated and well preserved. You'll also see the **Wairere Falls,** which descend 150 feet in three stages. The drive back to Rotorua passes both the **Green and Blue Lakes** and the **Redwood Grove Forest.** One suggestion: Those soothing, hot Polynesian pools may be the perfect end to a full and satisfying day!

Not as well known perhaps as Waimangu—and I'm definitely tooting its horn—the **Waiotapu Thermal Wonderland,** 4 kilometers (2½ miles) beyond Waimangu on Highway 5, is the most colorful of all the thermal areas, lavished with hues of yellow, gold, ochre, salmon, orange, and green. It also claims the largest mud pool in the southern hemisphere (you only see about a third of it) and the **Lady Knox Geyser,** which spouts off at 10:15am every day. Some of my favorite spots include the Champagne Pool, complete with bubbles and fizz; the Artist's Palette, which changes constantly; the Opal Pool, which has a vibrant color; the Terraces, where you'll feel as if you're walking on water; and the Maori Sacred Track—all well marked on the map you're given. This thermal preserve has been a family business since 1931 (though not always the same family); the Sewell family is in charge now and runs a top operation, including the souvenir shop, which is large, well stocked, and well priced. There's something spiritual about this place—allow time to enjoy it. You can get a local bus to Waiotapu, but it's a bit of a hike into the thermal park. Hours are 8:30am to 7:30pm (5pm in winter), but the Sewells are flexible "because we live here." Admission is NZ$8 ($5).

SHOPPING

I've already mentioned the excellent shop out at the Agrodome, and you'll find other good shops galore in Rotorua. One, however, is unique—it's the only "straight out" rugby store in New Zealand. It's **Sportsmaker,** 16 Eruera St. (tel. *479-670), where Sel and Elaine Howse have assembled what amounts to a small rugby museum as well as a commercial venture. If you've become a fan, even if only in fantasy, you'll love this place, with its All Black jerseys, T-shirts, pennants, banners, hats, etc. Of course, the All Blacks are not the only rugby team listed—you'll find plenty of souvenirs of other world-famous teams within its walls. Hours are 8:30am to 5pm Monday through Friday and 9am to noon on Saturday.

✪ **Penney's Souvenirs,** corner of Hinemoa and Hinewanu Streets (tel. *485-787), opposite the Hyatt, has a marvelous selection of carvings, greenstone and paua items, sheepskins, and general souvenirs, as well as T-shirts. Owner Reg Durrant will open after hours for a group (call him at *489-717 after hours), a great convenience if you just can't fit shopping into a day of sightseeing. Open daily until 7pm.

You'll have a unique opportunity to watch your New Zealand souvenir in the process of being created if you pay a visit to **Ruihana Carvings,** 35 Lake Rd. (tel. *477-174; after hours, *486-516). Master carver Louis Ruihana Phillips carries on the traditions of his Maori ancestors, and both he and his wife, Mere, will carefully explain the significance of the carvings. They're open seven days a week from 8am to 5:30pm, but they'll open after hours if you call for an appointment. The shop also carries traditional Maori skirts, headbands, and other items, as well as leatherwork.

For general browsing, try the **Tutanekai Mall,** a pedestrian shopping area between Arawa and Pukaki Streets. The most popular **bottle shop** is on Ti Street, off Fenton Street (on the left as you drive out Fenton from downtown).

WHERE TO STAY

Rotorua is replete with accommodations, and they come in all shapes, sizes, and price ranges. In addition to nine major hotels, there are more than 100 motels and 15 motor camps. Those in the budget range are among the best you'll find in this category anywhere in the country. Indeed, don't expect Rotorua to conform to the usual popular resort image of "charging what the traffic will bear for the least service we can get away with"—this is a resort of a different stripe, one where prices are moderate, service friendly and efficient, and accommodation standards exceptionally high.

Unless otherwise noted, prices listed below include GST. Also, remember that the New Zealand Number Update is in the process of changing all telephone numbers to 7 digits. Those numbers in this chapter that have not been changed at press time are marked with an asterisk, and you should call the **Helpline 0155** for the new number. For directory assistance within the country (when you don't know the number), call **018.**

MOTEL FLATS

ACACIA LODGE BEST WESTERN MOTEL, 40 Victoria St., Rotorua. Tel. *073/487-089. Fax *073/461-104. 18 units, 8 suites (all with bath). TV TEL
Transportation: Courtesy-car service to the airport and bus station.
$ Rates (excluding GST): NZ$58 ($33) single; NZ$67 ($38) double; NZ$73 ($42) suite. Best Western discounts available. AE, DC, MC, V.

At this pretty motel, Louise and David McCliskie offer brick units with large picture windows and colorful flower boxes. Each has full kitchen facilities, radio, and central heat. Some have water beds, and there are some family units. Other amenities include a sauna, mineral pools, a nice play area, and laundry facilities. The quiet, peaceful location is near the city center and sightseeing attractions, and the McCliskies are happy to arrange sightseeing tours for their guests.

AMBASSADOR THERMAL MOTEL, corner of Whakaue and Hinemaru Sts. (P.O. Box 1212), Rotorua. Tel. *073/479-581. Fax *073/485-281. 19 flats (all with bath). TV TEL
$ Rates (excluding GST): NZ$60 ($34) single; NZ$70 ($40) double. Best Western discounts available. AE, MC, V.

Just a short walk from the lakefront and town, the Ambassador is an attractive white, three-story building with arched covered balconies and self-contained units, some of which have ceilings with exposed beams. There are two private thermal pools, a swirl pool, outdoor freshwater pool, and a games room with a pool table. Restaurants and a host of attractions are within easy walking distance in this central, but quiet, location where John and Beryl Scott are the friendly hosts. The motel is near Queen Elizabeth Hospital.

BEL AIRE MOTEL, 257 Fenton St., Rotorua. Tel. *073/486-076. 8 flats (all with bath). TV TEL **Transportation:** Owners will pick up and deliver guests to the airport or bus terminal.
$ Rates (excluding GST): NZ$54 ($31) single or double. AE, DC, V.

A reader from Australia wrote to tell me about the Bel Aire, and his recommendation certainly stood the test of close inspection. This small, centrally located motel offers spotless, recently renovated one- and two-bedroom units that sleep two to seven people, each with a full kitchen, geothermal heating, radio, and video. There's a hot mineral pool, as well as a guest laundry, drying room, and the owner/operators, Joan and Mike de Latour, can furnish breakfast on request.

BOULEVARD MOTEL, corner of Fenton and Seddon Sts., Rotorua. Tel. *073/482-074. Fax *073/482-072. 30 rms (all with bath). TV TEL

$ Rates (excluding GST): NZ$42 ($24) single; NZ$62 ($35) double. AE, DC, MC, V.

⭐ The Boulevard is set on 2 acres of landscaped grounds and is family-owned and -operated by the Bradshaws. The white, two-story, balconied motel in the town center also has a restaurant on the premises and is just down the street from a licensed restaurant with entertainment. Flats have a separate lounge, one to three bedrooms, are beautifully furnished, with complete kitchen, and have central heating. There are serviced units (sleeping two), which are smaller and have tea-making facilities, and fridge. Some units have water beds; others have spa pools. Those lovely grounds are set about with garden furniture and hold a multitude of recreational facilities: a putting green, swimming pool, four spa baths, swirl pools, sauna, and games room. There's a laundry, dryer, and steam iron for your use. Units come in sizes that accommodate from three to nine people.

HYLTON MOTEL, 287 Fenton St., Rotorua. Tel. 07/348-5056. 3 units (all with bath). TV TEL **Transportation:** Courtesy car on request.

$ Rates: NZ$70 ($43.75) double; NZ$100 ($62.50) quad. MC, V.

One reader praises the humor and helpfulness of Doreen and Ivan Durr, the owners of this motel, which feels more like a private house. The units have a lounge, two bedrooms, and a kitchen. Facilities include a pool and a laundry, and the Burrs will supply a continental or cooked breakfast on request. They will also conduct personal sightseeing tours. In the town center.

MOTEL SULPHUR CITY, 241 Fenton St., Rotorua. Tel. *073/486-513 or *477-400. 7 units (all with bath). TV TEL **Transportation:** Owners will pick up guests at Travel Centre.

$ Rates (excluding GST): Single or double: NZ$50 ($29) 1 night; NZ$45 ($26) per night for 2 or 3 nights; NZ$40 ($23) per night for 4 or 5 nights; NZ$38 ($22) per night 6 or 7 nights. AE, DC, MC, V.

Owners/operators Tom and Margaret Harrison offer special budget rates for standard units with full kitchen and adjoining lounge, as well as one- and two-bedroom units. There's parking just outside each unit. Light breakfast is available, and the Harrisons provide a good sightseeing map of Rotorua without charge. It's a 5-minute walk from the town center.

STUDIO MOTEL, 315-A Fenton St., Rotorua. Tel. *073/470-360. 3 flats (all with bath). TV TEL

$ Rates (excluding GST): NZ$45 ($26) single or double; NZ$75 ($43) per person for three to five persons. MC, V.

⭐ This economy-priced motel in town has attractive one- and two-bedroom units that can sleep up to five persons, as well as a spa pool. A bonus comes in the form of pottery made by owner Barry Ball, who has had many exhibitions in New Zealand. His studio is on the premises, and his pottery is for sale in the reception room. It's a good idea to reserve ahead.

TOM'S MOTEL, 6 Union St. (P.O. Box 784), Rotorua. Tel. *073/478-062. 10 units (all with bath). TV TEL **Transportation:** Courtesy car.

$ Rates (excluding GST): Single or double, 1–6 nights: NZ$50–NZ$38 ($29–$22) studio; NZ$55–NZ$43 ($31–$25) 1-bedroom unit. Extra person NZ$12 ($7). AE, DC, MC, V.

Tidy, quiet, and economical, Tom's Motel has five studios and five one-bedroom units (for up to five people), which include a kitchen. There's also a heated outdoor pool, an indoor spa pool, a laundry, and car-wash facilities. Breakfast is available on request. This quiet location near the center of town is an ideal sightseeing base for the area, since the longer your stay, the lower the rate.

BED & BREAKFASTS

EATON HALL, 39 Hinemaru St., Rotorua. Tel. 07/347-0366. Fax 07/347-8558. 8 rms (with shared baths).
$ Rates (including breakfast): NZ$38 ($22) single; NZ$60 ($34) double; NZ$80 ($46) triple. No credit cards.

There's a warm, homey air about this two-story house right in the center of town. Grace Dorset has filled it with comfortable furnishings (some antiques), old china, and lots of bric-a-brac. There's a cozy TV lounge. Breakfast is either cooked or continental-style, and evening meals can be booked, with specialties reminiscent of English inns (roast beef and Yorkshire pudding, etc.). A bonus here is the fact that Grace, as a bona-fide ticket agent, can organize and issue tickets for sightseeing attractions, fishing trips, concerts, and sightseeing flights. Corner Room 3 is quiet and cozy.

TRESCO INTERNATIONAL GUEST HOUSE, 3 Toko St., Rotorua. Tel. 07/348-9611. 7 rms (with shared baths). **Transportation:** Courtesy car available.
$ Rates (including breakfast): NZ$38 ($22) single; NZ$60 ($34) double; NZ$75 ($43) triple. No credit cards.

Doreen and Leon Maitland own and operate this guesthouse with attractive, sparkling clean rooms, which include hot and cold running water and tea- and coffee-making facilities. The guesthouse is only one block from the city center, and there's a homey, happy air about this place. In addition to off-street parking, there's a guest laundry, TV lounge with video, and a mineral plunge pool. Breakfast is a four-course cooked meal. The Maitlands are InterCity travel agents and can organize tours and issue tickets not only in this region, but throughout both North and South Islands.

HOSTELS

IVANHOE TOURIST LODGE, 54 Haupapa St. (just off Tutanekai St.), Rotorua. Tel. 07/348-6985. 65 beds (with shared baths).
$ Rates (excluding GST): NZ$14 ($7) small dorm; NZ$21 ($12) double room. No credit cards.

This lodge offers budget, hostel-type accommodations. There are single, twin, and double cabins, all heated, and single, twin, and double rooms. Linen and blankets are available for a small fee. All cabins and rooms are carpeted, and each has mirrors and dressers. Facilities are all communal: a fully equipped, modern kitchen; large dining or common room (with a brilliant mural of the area); hot thermal pool; TV lounge; and games room.

YHA HOSTEL, corner of Eruera and Hinemaru Sts., Rotorua. Tel. 07/347-6810. 68 beds.

$ **Rates:** NZ$16 ($9) per person for members; NZ$20 ($11) for nonmembers. No credit cards.

This hostel is just about the best buy in Rotorua. It's a large, comfortable building, accommodating 68 in 18 rooms, and there are family rooms. There's a well-equipped kitchen as well as steam ovens, a provisions shop, laundry facilities and irons, a recreation room, and bicycles for rent. Situated right in town near the Travel Centre, it's only about two minutes from the bus station.

CABINS & CAMPGROUNDS

Holdens Bay Holiday Park, 21 Robinson Ave., Holdens Bay (P.O. Box 9), Rotorua (tel. and fax 07/345-9925), only 6 kilometers (3½ miles) from Rotorua, has a pretty setting very near Lake Rotorua. On the extensive grounds, there are tent and caravan sites, tourist cabins (bring your own linens and blankets), and modern tourist flats (just bring yourself), as well as a swimming pool, volleyball court, hot spa pools, a store, children's play area, laundry, TVs for rent, a barbecue, car wash, and games room. Rates are NZ$8.80 ($5) per person for tent and caravan sites, NZ$22 ($13) double for standard cabins, NZ$32 ($18) double for tourist cabins, and NZ$48 ($27) double for tourist flats, all including GST.

Besides being secluded, right on the lake and only a little over a mile from downtown Rotorua, **Lakeside Motor Camp,** 54 Whittaker Rd., Rotorua (tel. 07/348-1693), has an abundance of trees, swings and a trampoline, a games and TV room, pool, showers, laundry, communal kitchen, natural steam cooker, car wash, and camp store. Swimming, boating, fishing, and waterskiing are all at your doorstep. All units have full cooking facilities, and you supply linen and blankets. Tent sites are NZ$8 ($5) per person; van sites, NZ$18 ($10) for two people; on-site caravans, NZ$30 ($17) for two; cabins, NZ$33 ($19) double; tourist flats, NZ$44 ($25) double; and chalets, NZ$48 ($27) double. The gate to the property closes at 11pm for security reasons.

A FARM STAY

TE ANA, Pouttakataka Rd., Ngakuru, R.D. 1, Rotorua. Tel. 07/333-2720. 3 rms (with shared bath).

$ **Rates** (including breakfast and dinner): NZ$63 ($36) single; NZ$85 ($49) double. No credit cards.

For more than 10 years, Heather and Brian Oberer have been welcoming guests to their 500-acre dairy, sheep, goat, and deer farm 20 miles south of Rotorua. Guest rooms are beautifully appointed, and Heather's cooking has been described by one reader as "magnificent." Dinners, for example, might feature lamb, beef, venison, chicken, or pork with seasonable vegetables, dessert, and wine—pretty spectacular! There's a canoe to use on Lake Ohakuri, which forms a 1½-mile portion of the farm's boundary, farm walks, and a four-wheel drive tour of the farm. Guests can also go along when it's time to milk the cows.

WORTH THE EXTRA MONEY

Hotels

GEYSERLAND RESORT, Whaka Rd., Rotorua. Tel. 07/348-2039. Fax 07/348-2033. 65 rms (all with bath). A/C MINIBAR TV TEL

$ **Rates:** NZ$120 ($69) single; NZ$130 ($74) double. Children under 12 stay free in parents' room. Inquire about frequent 2-day specials or weekend packages available May–Sept. AE, DC, MC, V.

This listing is—I admit it—a little sneaky. Its prices certainly have no place in a budget travel book. Still, if you're particularly flush when you hit Rotorua (or you're hypnotized by the thermal goings-on hereabouts), you may want to throw the budget out the window and stay at Geyserland Resort. What makes it so special is its panoramic view of the Whaka Thermal Reserve, just outside the windows of most of its rooms. From your room with a window wall facing the reserve, you can watch the Pohutu Geyser shoot up as high as 50 feet in the air, and fascination with those steaming, bubbling mud pools will keep you posted at the window. The hotel itself has the usual luxury hotel trappings, with pretty and comfortable rooms, spa pools, a swimming pool, and a first-class restaurant. If you lean toward luxury hotels, this one is as good as any; but as I said, it's all that steam out there that makes it warrant space in a budget guide, so if you reserve, be sure to specify that you want a room overlooking the thermal reserve, not a poolside room.

HYATT KINGSGATE ROTORUA, Eruera St. (P.O. Box 1044), Rotorua. Tel. 07/347-2234. Fax 07/348-1234. 229 rms (all with bath). A/C MINIBAR TV TEL

$ Rates (excluding GST): From NZ$170 ($97) single or double. Children under 18 stay free in parents' room. Special family package sometimes available. AE, DC, MC, V.

The Hyatt is Rotorua's only luxury hotel right in the heart of town. It holds the country's only retractable glass-domed swimming pool (open to the elements in good weather, protected from them in bad). The lobby features a magnificent Maori carving that depicts Tanemahuta attempting to push his father, Ranginui (Great Sky), and his mother, Papatuanuku (Earth), apart, with symbolic falling rain and rising mist symbolizing the perpetual grief of the parents at their separation. Rooms are top quality, both in furnishings and decor, and two floors are set aside for the deluxe Regency Club rooms for a really big splurge (lots of extra services). All rooms have tea- and coffee-making facilities, fridges, and videos. Of special note, there's wheelchair access to all public areas and guest rooms. In addition to two bars, there are two very good restaurants, six spa rooms, guest laundry, and a fitness center.

THC ROTORUA INTERNATIONAL HOTEL, corner of Tyron and Froude Sts., Rotorua. Tel. 07/348-1189. Fax 07/347-1620. 169 rms (all with bath). MINIBAR TV TEL

$ Rates (excluding GST): NZ$105–NZ$140 ($60–$80) single or double. Special 2-day rates available periodically. AE, DC, MC, V.

This deluxe hotel overlooks the fascinating thermal activity of legendary Whakarewarewa. It is also the setting of Rotorua's most authentic Maori hangi and concert each night, the only one in town that invites guests to witness the actual lifting of the hangi from its earthen oven. Guest rooms have tea- and coffee-making facilities, and fridges. There are two bars, and two excellent restaurants, as well as two heated swimming pools, hot tubs, guest laundry, and a tour desk. Even without a reduction, however, this hotel is a big splurge that offers good value for dollar.

Motels

LEDWICH LODGE, 12–14 Lake Rd. (P.O. Box 769), Rotorua. Tel. 07/349-0049. Fax 07/349-0048. 14 flats (all with bath). TV TEL

$ Rates (excluding GST): NZ$88 ($50) single or double. Extra person NZ$11 ($6). AE, DC, MC, V.

You could walk right by this motel, without giving it a second glance. It's small, with a facade that doesn't draw attention to itself, and it has no grounds. But look again—the lake is its front yard and it's within walking distance of everything in town.

It also has exceptionally pretty units with a bay window, bright tropical-print curtains, a large bath with spa pool, a queen-size bed covered with a feather duvet, a full kitchen, thermal heating (this old-fashioned system that is being phased out in Rotorua), lots of wood trim, and in-house video. In addition, there is a small, thermally heated pool and picnic area, and guests have access to a steam box for hangi-style cooking; breakfast is available. There are larger units, as well as two units for the disabled.

WYLIE COURT MOTOR LODGE, 345 Fenton St., Rotorua. Tel. *073/461-494. Fax *073/477-879. 28 rms, 21 flats (all with bath). A/C MINIBAR TV TEL
  Transportation: Courtesy car to and from the airport.
$ **Rates** (excluding GST): NZ$85 ($49) single; NZ$101 ($58) double; NZ$107 ($61) suite. Best Western discounts available. AE, DC, MC, V.

One of Rotorua's most attractive motels, Wylie Court is set in 2½ landscaped acres on the outskirts of town. The two-story units are decorated in soft colors and have modern, comfortable furnishings. Each unit has a full living room with two convertible sofa beds, full kitchen, and bath on the ground floor; upstairs there's a mezzanine bedroom with a double bed (some have water beds). Each will sleep as many as four in comfort. What wins my heart completely, however, is the pretty roofed and fenced-in patio out back of each unit, with its own private heated plunge pool where you can soak to your heart's content whether or not there's a bathing suit in your luggage—sheer luxury!

Barry and Glen Johnston, their son, Tony, and his wife, Sharon, have provided loads of amenities: a heated swimming pool, children's playground, thermal pool, guest laundry, in-room video, the daily newspaper delivered to your door, and a cooked or continental breakfast at a small additional charge. Highly recommended, both for its facilities and its genial hosts.

READERS RECOMMEND

Budget Accommodation Clusters, Fenton St. *"All one needs to know is that Fenton Street has literally dozens of budget spots side by side for about a mile or so. Just take your pick. I stayed at La Mirage, run by Evelyn and Ross Taylor. Their facilities are excellent: hot tub, full kitchen, clean, tea makings, etc. The Taylors love Yanks and couldn't have been friendlier."*—Donald Y. McCoy, Great Falls, Va.

Morie and Jim Evans, Yankee Rd., R.D. 3 Rerewhakaaitu, Rotorua. Tel. *073/36-804. *"This is a dairy farm 40 kilometers (24 miles) south of Rotorua, and boy, did we ever feel like one of the family! Their enthusiasm about their lifestyle was definitely refreshing and a learning experience. They can accommodate up to four people, and your own private bathroom is down the hall."*—Carol and Harvey Retherford.

WHERE TO EAT

FLOYD'S CAFE, 48 Haupapa St. Tel. 347-0024.
  Cuisine: SEAFOOD/PASTA/VEGETARIAN. **Reservations:** Not required.
$ **Prices:** Average lunch NZ$15 ($9); average dinner NZ$20 ($11). AE, DC, MC, V.
  Open: Mon–Fri 11:30am–2:30pm and 6–9pm, Sat 6–9pm.

This place in the town center is hard to beat for moderately priced food, well prepared and served in a casual atmosphere. The thick, chunky mussel chowder is a standout, as are their seafood crêpe, lasagne, lamb filets, and vegetarian phyllo. BYO.

THE GAZEBO, 45 Pukuatua St. Tel. 348-1911.
  Cuisine: CONTINENTAL. **Reservations:** Not required.
$ **Prices:** Main lunch courses NZ$8–NZ$14 ($5–$8); main dinner courses NZ$12–NZ$27 ($7–$15). AE, DC, MC, V.

Open: Lunch Tues–Fri noon–2pm; dinner Mon–Sat 6–10pm.

This is a casual, cozy spot with a blackboard menu, lots of greenery (as befits its name), and specialties such as terakihi meunière, white veal bratwurst, rigatoni pasta with mushroom sauce, pork loin Continental, and lamb loin devil's style. Attention fisherpeople: If you call in advance, they'll cook the fish you've hooked in local waters. BYO. It's located in the town center.

HYATT KINGSGATE ROTORUA, Eruera St. Tel. 347-7677.
Cuisine: INTERNATIONAL. **Reservations:** Recommended.

$ Prices: All-you-can-eat poolside lunch buffet NZ$10 ($6); Brasserie buffet lunch NZ$18 ($10), buffet dinner NZ$25 ($14). AE, DC, MC, V.
Open: Lunch daily 12–2:30pm; dinner daily 6–10pm.

Surprisingly, one of the best value-for-dollar lunches is found at the posh Hyatt Kingsgate, where an all-you-can-eat theme buffet (Chinese or Italian, for instance) is served poolside for just NZ$7 ($3.30). Don't confuse it with the downstairs Brasserie (also poolside), where light lunches of sandwiches and salads start at under NZ$8 ($5); its lunch and dinner buffets are pricier. Both are fully licensed. In the town center.

LAKE VIEW RESTAURANT, Lake Rd. Tel. *485-585.
Cuisine: SEAFOOD/STEAK/VEGETARIAN **Reservations:** Recommended.

$ Prices: Average meals NZ$8–NZ$16 ($5–$9). MC, V.
Open: Lunch Mon–Sat noon–2pm; dinner Mon–Thurs 6–9pm, Fri–Sat 6–10pm; bar Mon–Thurs 11am–10pm, Fri–Sat 11am–11pm.

This local favorite (likely to become one of yours, as well) is in a century-old building overlooking the lake and Ohinemutu village. In its younger days it served as a leading hotel, but now it's content to meet the eating and imbibing needs of its clientele. The dining room has wood booths with high backs and gold velvet seats, red carpeting and drapes, and impressive Maori portraits in the bar. The large bar and lounge is fitted out with comfortable divans and easy chairs facing large windows looking out onto the lake. Seasonal menus feature steak, chicken, seafood, and vegetarian dishes. Main courses include salad and vegetables. Fully licensed, of course.

LEWISHAM'S, 115 Tutanekai St. Tel. 348-1786.
Cuisine: CONTINENTAL/NEW ZEALAND/AUSTRIAN. **Reservations:** Recommended.

$ Prices: Average lunch NZ$15 ($9); average dinner under NZ$35 ($20). AE, DC, MC, V.
Open: Lunch Mon and Wed–Fri noon–2pm; dinner Wed–Mon 6–10pm.

Set in a colonial cottage that was one of the first houses in Tutanekai Street, this cozy restaurant has an interior of exposed-brick fireplaces and antique furnishings. New Zealand specialties include poached terakihi and South Island baby salmon with béarnaise sauce. Among continental offerings, I favor both the rack of lamb in a herb crust and the sumptuous seafood platter. Very popular with locals as well as visitors.

THC ROTORUA INTERNATIONAL HOTEL, Froude St. Tel. 348-1189.
Cuisine: SEAFOOD. **Reservations:** Required.

$ Prices: Seafood buffet NZ$18 ($10). AE, DC, MC, V.
Open: Lunch daily noon–2:30pm.

Lunch will most assuredly be your main meal of the day if you book for the elaborate seafood buffet here. Be sure to reserve early, for this endless supply of the freshest of seasonal seafoods is a great favorite with locals and other visitors alike. You'll leave knowing you've found real value for your dollars. Licensed. The hotel overlooks Whaka Reserve.

ZANELLI'S ITALIAN CAFE, 23 Amohia St. Tel. 348-4908.
  Cuisine: ITALIAN. **Reservations:** Recommended.
$ **Prices:** Appetizers NZ$8.50 ($5); main courses NZ$15–NZ$18 ($9–$10) AE, DC, MC, V.
  Open: Dinner Mon–Fri 6–9:30pm, Sat–Sun 6–10pm.

Located in town, Zanelli's serves generous portions, and you can easily make do with an entrée and salad. There's a whole blackboard devoted to desserts. The atmosphere is lively, and three-quarters of the tables are no-smoking.

SPECIALTY DINING

TAKE-OUT FOOD For those times when eating in is a good idea either for budget or energy (at the end of a long sightseeing day) reasons, you have two good Rotorua alternatives. If you've a yen for fresh New Zealand specialties like marinated mussels, oysters, clams, or cooked lamb, hie yourself over to **Fenwick's Delicatessen** (tel. 347-0777) next to the Post Office in Hinemoa Centre. It's chock-full of ready-to-eat goodies, as well as a wide selection of cheeses, hot barbecued rôtisserie chicken, salads, sweets, and a host of specialty goods, all at very good prices. Hours are 8am to 5:30pm Monday through Friday, until noon on Saturday; closed Sunday.

You'll have trouble passing the window at **Chez Suzanne Pâtisserie,** 61 Hinemoa St., (tel. 348-6495), next to the *Daily Post* building, without going in. The selection of pastries and sandwiches is excellent, and they are exceedingly fresh. Beverages include cappuccino coffee, espresso coffee, and hot chocolate. This is a small place, with a few booths, a counter, and a few wooden tables with fresh flowers on them. Filled croissants are NZ$2.40 ($1) and sandwiches run NZ$1 (60¢) to NZ$2.50 ($1). It's open Monday to Friday from 9am to 4pm, Saturday 9:30am to 12:30pm; closed some Saturdays.

FAST FOOD On the theory that you can drop in for a Big Mac almost anywhere in the world, I don't normally send readers to ✪ **McDonald's.** In Rotorua, however, I emphatically recommend that you go by the one on the corner of Fenton and Amohau Streets to view the exquisite wall-size carvings done by the Maori Arts and Crafts Institute. Best of all, they give you a free booklet beautifully illustrated with photos and Maori legends. Kudos to McDonald's for this recognition of indigenous culture.

The best burgers in Rotorua, I'm told by someone who's sampled many a one, come from **Chez Bleu,** 160 Fenton St. (tel. 348-1828), and there are 30 to choose from, plus full meals and ice cream. Burger prices range from NZ$2.70 to NZ$9.20 ($1.55 to $5), and you can't beat the hours: 7am to 11:30pm Sunday through Wednesday, until 3am on Thursday, and until 4am on Friday and Saturday. There's delivery service too.

WORTH THE EXTRA MONEY

AORANGI PEAK RESTAURANT, Mountain Rd. Tel. 347-0046.
  Cuisine: NEW ZEALAND **Reservations:** Required. **Transportation:** Mt. Ngongotaha (transport available by cable car or helicopter).
$ **Prices:** Average lunch NZ$20 ($11); average dinner NZ$55 ($31).
  Open: Lunch daily noon–2pm; dinner daily 6–10pm. **Closed:** Christmas Day.

I could recommend this restaurant for the view alone—its mountaintop perch looks down on a dazzling array of lakes and forests and the city—but when you add the elegant octagonal split-level dining room and upstairs lookout lounge and cocktail bar, plus meals of gourmet quality, this is the place to splurge! (If you're into justifying splurges, just count a part of your dinner check as a sightseeing charge.) Personal service and quality are equally important here, so you'll get a bit of pampering. The menu is designed to present the best of New Zealand produce in interesting and innovative ways, complemented by a noteworthy wine list. Among culinary specialties is the rack of lamb with tomato and garlic, with a honey-lemon sauce.

CAESAR'S, 83 Arawa St. Tel. *470-984.

Cuisine: NEW ZEALAND **Reservations:** Recommended.

$ Prices: Appetizers NZ$8.50–NZ$11 ($5–$6); main courses NZ$19–NZ$23 ($11–$13). AE, DC, MC, V.

Open: Dinner daily 6–11pm. **Closed:** Christmas Day.

Your big-splurge dollars will be well spent at Caesar's. The setting is just this side of elegant, the table settings go all the way, and there are innovative dishes of New Zealand foods on the menu. The lamb dishes are award winners, and the smoked chicken and smoked eel with horseradish is outstanding. Service is especially friendly, and your dinner bill will run around NZ$35 ($22). Licensed and BYO. It's located in town.

RUMOURS, 81 Pukuatua St. Tel. *477-277.

Cuisine: CONTINENTAL. **Reservations:** Recommended well in advance.

$ Prices: Average dinner NZ$45 ($26). AE, MC, V.

Open: Dinner Tues–Sat 6–11pm.

Rumours, in the center of town, is a favorite with locals as well as tourists. Decor is modern, and there's a menu featuring seasonal specialties, from seafoods to game dishes, all prepared in sophisticated style. BYO.

EVENING ENTERTAINMENT

Check *Thermalair* for dine-and-dance venues or special events. Or just skip the rest and plan on a Maori concert. You won't be sorry. The **Sheraton Hotel Bar** is a popular gathering spot and a good place to pass a convivial evening.

MAORI CONCERTS & HANGI FEASTS

You'll find some show-stopper Maori concerts in the big hotels (see below), but for authenticity and insight into the Maori musical heritage you can't beat the nightly 8pm concert at the **Tametekapua meetinghouse** in Ohinemutu. The surroundings, for one thing, are authentic in this meetinghouse of the Arawa tribe, which opens to the public only at night. The singing group was founded by the elders of the tribe to help their young people learn to sing and perform the traditional songs. The performers are mostly 13 to 18 years old; the younger ones stand at the back and work their way forward over the years. Tickets are NZ$12 ($7) for adults, NZ$5 ($3) for children, and the money goes for the upkeep of St. Faith's Church and the meetinghouse, and to transport the youth abroad for singing engagements.

Hangi (earth oven) cooking is traditional with the Maoris in preparing their communal meal. A large pit is filled with a wood fire topped by stones; then when the stones are heated through, baskets of food are placed on top and covered with damp cloths. Earth is then shoveled over all to create a natural steam oven. After about three hours, dinner is unveiled, with intermingling flavors of the various foods lightly touched by wood smoke.

There's a **hangi feast** every night of the year at the ❂ **THC International Hotel** on Froude Street, on the edge of the Whaka Reserve (tel. 348-1189). The NZ$36 ($21) tab would put this in the splurge category were it not for the fact that it includes an hour-long **Maori concert** featuring first-class performers. Tickets for the concert only cost NZ$15 ($9). Add GST to both.

Hangi preparations begin long before your scheduled arrival at 6pm. By 3pm the *ngawha* (natural Maori rock steamer) is being filled: Meats like wild pork, lamb, chicken, and venison go in first for longer cooking; vegetables such as pumpkin, kumara, potatoes, and watercress are placed on top. Don't show up any later than 6:15pm or you'll miss the ✪ **opening of the ngawha,** when a costumed Maori maiden lifts the food out with all due ceremony and leads a procession of food-bearing followers into the dining room, where it is spread on a buffet table. Accompaniments like marinated mussels, smoked eel, raw marinated fish, salads, Maori bread, and tamarillos (tree tomatoes) with fresh cream complete the eat-as-much-as-you-can-hold feast. The traditional hangi would never include desserts, but the International provides sweets and Pakeha beverages (tea, coffee, and wine). By 7pm, all is ready for you to dig in. Enjoy!

At 8 o'clock, an outstanding troupe of Maori singers and dancers will begin an hour-long concert of Polynesian dances, action songs, and pois. By any standards, this is a "money's worth" splurge.

A reader wrote to say that of all the hangi and concert offerings in Rotorua, his favorite was at the **Sheraton Rotorua Hotel,** on Fenton Street (tel. 348-7139), and I have to admit that it's polished and fun-filled, with emphasis on audience involvement and enjoyment. The banquet room is warm and inviting, the buffet-style meal elegantly presented, and the tables graced with fresh flowers. The performers have great fun with the music, the dancing, and most of all, the audience. A highlight, especially for children, is singing "Hokey Pokey" using the Maori words for names of body parts. The show ends with audience and performers linking hands and singing together—really quite moving. I asked one of the dancers what the significance of her quivering hands was, and she told me "Life." The meal starts at 7pm, the concert at 8:15pm. The cost of the hangi and concert is NZ$39 ($22); the concert alone, NZ$22 ($13).

EN ROUTE TO GISBORNE

There are two ways of commencing the splendid East Cape drive from Rotorua: Head northeast on Highway 30 for Whakatane in the Bay of Plenty, a 57-mile drive; or take a detour, driving due north for 55 miles to Tauranga, then turning east on Highway 2 for the 62-mile stretch to Whakatane. I'd say that decision rests on where your own interests lie.

LONG ROUTE NORTH VIA TAURANGA & EAST CAPE ROAD

Tauranga, and its adjacent beach resort/port of Mount Maunganui, is now a peaceful center of citrus-fruit farming, but its history is one of fierce battles, both in intertribal Maori wars and between the British and Maoris.

The **Visitors Information Centre,** on The Strand (tel. *075/788-103), can direct you to several interesting historical spots. In summer shopping hours are longer on weekends than most anywhere else in New Zealand: until 4pm on Saturday and, in Mount Maunganui, until 4pm on Sunday as well. A car comes in very handy here, but if you're hoofing it and need a taxi, call *486-086. Fishing trips can be organized easily from the wharf on The Strand.

Tauranga has 45,000 inhabitants; Mount Maunganui, only 14,000. This area is second only to Auckland in popularity among vacationing Kiwis, some 500,000 of whom come here every year, compared to 41,000 international visitors.

The gardens of the **Elms Mission House,** on Mission Street, built by an early missionary and one of the finest examples of colonial architecture of its time (1847), are open to the public Monday through Saturday from 9am to 6pm. The library dates from 1837 and is probably the oldest in the country. On the carefully tended grounds, you'll see kauri, rimu, and orange trees, along with kiwifruit orchards, a special treat if you haven't gotten to see any before now. It's highly recommended, and there's no admission charge.

If you like poking around old cemeteries, as I confess I do, **۞ Otamataha Pa** will be of interest. It was the burial ground for the Church Mission Society from 1835 to 1881, as well as for soldiers and sailors who died in the Land War in 1864–65. It's near the Mission House and just up the hill from **Robbins Park Rose Garden** and picnic area on Cliff Road.

۞ Tauranga Historic Village, on 17th Avenue West (tel. 576-1302), bows to the past with 14 acres of a re-created colonial village, with cobblestone streets, a blacksmith's shop, a military barracks, a Maori village, and much more. Rides by train, double-decker bus, or horse-drawn cart give another perspective. You'll find a tearoom and a licensed restaurant in the village—old-fashioned, of course. It's open daily year round from 10am to 4pm, with a small admission.

Mount Maunganui, a leading port 12½ miles from Tauranga, is best known and loved by thousands of Kiwis for its **Ocean Beach,** a stretch of golden sand along what is called the best surfing beach in New Zealand. (**Papamoa Beach,** on the other hand, is quiet, and there's a take-away restaurant.) The **۞ walking track** around the mountain takes about an hour. You can also climb to the top of the mountain, for which you should allow a couple of hours. At the base of the mountain, on Adams Avenue, are **hot saltwater pools** where, for a small admission fee, you can ease your aches away; there's swimsuit and towel rental for those who arrive unprepared. A fresh water supply fills the pools every 3 hours; open from 8am to 10pm daily year round.

About 19 miles south of Tauranga lies **Te Puke,** the "Kiwifruit Capital of the World," and **Kiwifruit Country,** a popular attraction that you'll recognize by the giant slice of fruit (a camouflaged observation tower) out front. Stop by; there's no admission charge to look around, and you can wander through the grounds and theme orchard, which features 60 different fruits and nuts, from macadamias to feijoas (try this local fruit if you can) to pomegranates. There's also an audiovideo show and children's playground. For a fee, you can take a half-hour tour of the working orchard and listen to a taped commentary; the cost is NZ$8 ($5) for adults, NZ$6 ($3) for senior citizens, and NZ$3 ($2) for children. The fruit is harvested in May and June. Kiwifruit Country also has a children's playground; gift shop featuring kiwifruit products; complimentary tasting of kiwifruit wines, liqueur, and apéritif; and a café featuring kiwi burgers and kiwifruit parfait.

From Highway 2 (a little over 27 miles east of Tauranga) on the drive to Whakatane you can take a short detour to the little settlement of **۞ Maketu** and see the cairn that marks the Arawa canoe landing place, and also the Te Awhi-o-te-rangi meetinghouse, a beautiful example of Maori carvings. Tauranga makes an interesting prelude to the East Cape Drive if time permits.

Where To Stay in Tauranga

AMBASSADOR MOTOR LODGE, 9 15th Ave., Tauranga. Tel. 07/578-5665. Fax 07/578-5226. 8 units (all with bath). TV TEL

$ Rates (excluding GST): NZ$50 ($29) single; NZ$60 ($34) double. Best Western discounts available. AE, DC, MC, V.

You won't get a more pleasant welcome in Tauranga than at this small motel co-owned by a parents/children team, Robert and Janet Wilberfoss and their daughter and her husband, Jane and Alistair Bowden. Facilities include plenty of flowers and gardens, an outdoor pool, a spa pool, trampoline, swings, laundry, and portable barbecue. There are three studios and five larger units, all quite comfortable, with coffee and tea facilities, and nice, hard mattresses. Breakfast is available daily, and dinner during the week, which is nice if you arrive late and don't want to go into town. The Ambassador is two miles south of downtown.

Where To Eat In & Near Tauranga

You can get a quite good, three-course meal in Tauranga at ✪ Ⓢ **Charlie Brown's,** 194 Cameron Rd., in Tauranga (tel. *785-520), for about NZ$16 ($9). There's a children's menu, and the restaurant is licensed. Open daily except Sunday from 5:30pm.

In Katikati, a little north of Morton Estates on the Thames Highway, do as the locals do and drop by the **Katikati Tavern** for fish-and-chips from noon to 2pm.

DRIVING TO GISBORNE VIA WHAKATANE

Stop by the **Visitors Information Centre** on Boon Street (tel. *076/86-058), in Whakatane for details on some of the more interesting sights in the town and nearby. This is the legendary settling place of Toi (see Chapter 1) on his search for his grandson, Whatonga, and the earthworks out on the road to Ohope are traditionally held to be those of his *pa.* It is also the landing place of the great Mataatua canoe, part of the Hawaiki migration fleet. A model of that canoe can be seen next to the imposing rock arch known as ✪ **Pohaturoa Rock** (once part of a sacred Maori cave and now a memorial to those who died in World War I). On Mataatua Street, right in the center of town, you'll see the beautiful **Wairere Waterfall.**

Some 37 miles east of Whakatane, Highway 2 brings you to Opotiki and State Road 35, known as the ✪ **East Cape Road,** which hugs the coastline for most of its 213-mile route up around New Zealand's most easterly point and down to Gisborne on Poverty Bay. The drive—breathtaking in any season—is a heart-stopper during Christmas, when hundreds of pohutukawa trees burst into brilliant scarlet blooms along the cliffs overlooking the sea. All along, you'll find lovely deserted beaches, sea views, and native bush, which combine to make this one of New Zealand's finest scenic drives. This, as you might suspect, is an area with a heavy Maori population, and most of the small villages and towns you'll pass through either still are, or once were, Maori centers. Sadly, some of the most exquisite Maori carvings from the area have been removed: The Auckland War Museum's Te Toki-a-Tapiri war canoe and Wellington's National Museum's Te Hau-ki-Turanga meetinghouse and Nuku te Whatewha storehouse all came from this region. There are, however, still outstanding examples of the art to be seen along the drive.

Many people decide to break the long drive (about 8 hours if you stay behind the wheel) with an overnight stop, and below I'll tell you about accommodations possibilities. Campers will find ample facilities along the way.

Opotiki was once a large Maori settlement, but today is best known for its **Church of St. Stephen the Martyr,** scene of the particularly brutal murder of German Lutheran missionary Carl Sylvius Volkner in 1865. Bloodstained relics of that grim event are on exhibit in the church. At **Te Kaha,** Tu Kaihi meetinghouse in the *marae* has an elaborately carved lintel you'll be welcome to view if you ask permission before entering the marae. A little farther along, **Waihau Bay** has good views across Cape Runaway (so named by Captain Cook as he watched Maori canoes "run away" when shots were fired over their heads), as well as very good beaches. **Whangaparaoa** is where the great migration canoe *Tainui* landed—its captain's wife is credited with bringing the kumara to New Zealand. One of the many turnoffs that will tempt you is that at **Lottin Point** (it's signposted), where a 2½-mile drive through farmland leads to the coast and grasslands growing right to the water's edge.

✪ **Hicks Bay** could well be your overnight stop. It's not quite midway, but has marvelous views, a modern motel, and one of the finest carved meetinghouses on the East Cape. Its name comes from one of Captain Cook's officers, who first sighted it, and it was the site of a tragic Maori massacre in which one European was killed and eaten on his wedding night (after which complaints were registered that he was too tough and stringy to be tasty!). Turn left at the general store to reach the

✪ Tuwhakairiora meetinghouse, whose carvings were done in 1872. It is dedicated to local members of the Ngati Porou tribe who died in overseas wars, and its unique rafter design (found only in this region) is symbolic of the honor of death in battle for the warrior.

A little farther along, the road descends to sea level to follow the narrow bay to where the little town of **Te Araroa** nestles under the cliffs. Thirteen miles east of Te Araroa, along an all-weather road, stands the **East Cape Lighthouse,** in an isolated location. There's been a light here since 1906. The track to the lighthouse must be covered by foot, and it leads up some 600 steps—perhaps a look from afar will suffice. Sunrise is lovely here.

One of New Zealand's most ornate Maori churches is the **✪ Tikitiki Church,** a memorial to Maori soldiers who died in World War I. The carved panels and rafter patterns depict Ngati Porou tribal history, and two war hero brothers are featured in the east window. Closer to Gisborne, you can view another beautifully carved modern meetinghouse near the wharf at **Tokomaru Bay.** This is where a brave band of women, two warriors, and three whalers successfully defended a headland *pa* from attack by a large enemy force. **Anaura Bay,** just 43 miles from Gisborne, was Captain Cook's landing place on his second New Zealand voyage. The *Endeavour* hung around for two days trying to get water casks beyond the surf before heading south for a better watering place. **Whangara,** 17 miles away from Gisborne, is a good spot to fill up the gas tank (petrol stations are few and far between in these parts). And Gisborne, of course, was the place Captain Cook *first* sighted the New Zealand mainland (more about that later).

THE SHORT ROUTE FROM WHAKATANE TO GISBORNE

It must be said that for those who simply wish to reach Gisborne from the Bay of Plenty, there's a shorter, faster way to get there than around the East Cape. Highway 2 is a pleasant, three-hour drive on a winding road through green farmlands, native bush, along rushing mountain rivers, and through **Waioeka Gorge**—not a bad drive, mind you, but nothing to compare with the East Cape.

Where to Stay and Dine en Route

KAWAKAWA HOTEL, P.O. Box 64, Te Araroa. Tel. 06/864-4809. 10 rms (all with bath or shower). TV TEL
$ Rates (excluding GST): NZ$35 ($20) single; NZ$50 ($29) double. AE, MC, V.
At Te Araroa, you will find the country's most easterly hostelry. It is licensed and is known for its restaurant. Rooms are simple, with either baths or showers. The hotel is located 10 kilometers (6 miles) south of Hicks Bay.

WAIHAU BAY LODGE, East Coast Hwy. (Private Bay), Opotiki. Tel. *076/53-804. 9 rms, 6 bunkhouse cabins (with shared baths). TV TEL
$ Rates (excluding GST): Lodge rooms, NZ$35 ($20) single, NZ$55 ($31) double; bunkhouse cabin NZ$20 ($11) single, NZ$35 ($20) double. AE, MC, V.
Tiny Waihau Bay is where you'll find this guesthouse dating to 1914. It has a licensed restaurant, and is close to a fine beach and good fishing. There are one single, four doubles, and three triples. They provide boat hire, charter fishing, and horse riding. The lodge is located 60 kilometers (36 miles) east of Whakatane.

---

2. GISBORNE

287km (177 miles) SE of Rotorua, 298km (184 miles) SE of Tauranga

GETTING THERE   By Bus   There is daily InterCity bus service to Gisborne from Auckland for a one-way fare of NZ$34 ($20), and from Rotorua for NZ$33 ($19) one-way. For bus information, call 868-6196.

By Car Gisborne is reached via State Road 35 (the East Cape Road) from the north, and from Rotorua via Highway 30 to Whakatane, then Highway 2 southeast to Gisborne.

ESSENTIALS Orientation Gisborne is situated on the northern shore of Poverty Bay where the Waimata and Taruheru Rivers come together to form the Turanganui. Riverside park areas abound, and most bridges were built for pedestrian as well as vehicular traffic. The city center is compact, with Gladstone Road a main thoroughfare.

Information The **Eastland Promotion Council Visitors Information Centre** is located at 209 Grey St. (tel. 06/868-6139), where the friendly staff offers enthusiastic assistance to visitors. Summer hours are 8:30am to 9pm Monday through Friday, weekends and holidays 10am to 5pm; in winter Monday through Friday from 8:30am to 5pm, weekends and holidays 10am to 5pm.

Mail The post office is at 74 Grey St. (tel. 867-8869).

Taxis For taxi service, call the Gisborne Taxi Society (tel. 867-8869).

Telephone The telephone prefix is 06. Remember: The New Zealand Number Update is in the process of changing all telephone numbers to 7 digits. Those numbers in this chapter that have not been changed at press time are marked with an asterisk, and you should call the Helpline 0155 for the new number. For directory assistance within the country (when you don't know the number), call **018.**

Because of its closeness to the international date line, Gisborne is judged to be the most easterly city in the world and the first to see the sun's rays each morning. It's also the place where New Zealand's European history began. Capt. James Cook's *Endeavour* entered these waters in early October 1769, and it fell the lot of the 12-year-old surgeon's boy, Nicholas Young, to be the first to sight land—a fact that must have caused some consternation among the rest of the crew, since the good captain had promised a gallon of rum as a reward, two if the sighting should be at night! True to another promise, Captain Cook named the white bluffs the boy had seen at the southern end of the bay's wide entrance "Young Nick's Head." As for Young Nick, he is also celebrated by a statue at the mouth of the Turanganui River at Waikanae Beach. It was two days later, on October 9, 1769, that a party ventured forth from the ship, and after a series of misunderstandings with Maoris over the next two days (during which one Maori was killed when the English thought he was trying to steal a beached longboat, another when he reached toward a sword, and four more when they resisted being taken aboard the *Endeavour* from their canoe), Cook found it impossible to gain Maori cooperation in gathering the fresh water and provisions he needed. Small wonder! At any rate, he left in disgust, writing in his journal that he was sailing "out of the bay, which I have named Poverty Bay because it afforded us not one thing we wanted."

One thing is a virtual certainty: Had Captain Cook gotten off on the right foot with the indigenous people, a name incorporating the word "poverty" would never have occurred to him! Gisborne is in fact the very center of one of New Zealand's most fertile areas, with a balmy climate that sees more than 2,215 hours of bright sunshine annually. It's a gardenland of vegetable farms and orchards bearing citrus fruits, grapes, and kiwifruit. Dairy and sheep farms prosper. That sunny climate, combined with beaches that offer ideal swimming, surfing, and fishing conditions, also make it a holiday resort that is becoming increasingly popular with Kiwis from all over the North Island.

WHAT TO SEE & DO

To get a panoramic view of Poverty Bay, the city, its harbors and rivers, head for ✪ **Kaiti Hill Lookout.** It is signposted at the northern end of Gladstone Bridge, and you can drive most of the way, walking the last little bit to a brick semicircular lookout point at the very edge of the hill. There's a statue of Captain Cook there that looks suspiciously like Napoléon (notice the hand in the jacket, so characteristic of "The Little Emperor") looking out toward Young Nick's Head on the opposite side of the bay.

At the foot of Kaiti Hill, you'll pass one of New Zealand's largest Maori meetinghouses, ✪ **Poho-o-rawiri.** It's so large that the traditional construction of a single ridgepole supported by pillars had to be abandoned in favor of more modern methods. All its carvings (which are splendid) were done in Rotorua. You'll usually find the side door open; if not, look up the caretaker, who lives just next door.

Also at the bottom of Kaiti Hill, on Kaiti Beach Road, there's a memorial on what is thought to be the spot on which Captain Cook landed, as well as a cannon, which may or may not have been salvaged from the wreck of the *Endeavour* (seems there's some dispute because it's made of iron, while Captain Cook's ship supposedly carried brass cannons).

Canadians will want to go by **Alfred Cox Park** on Grey Street to see the giant totem pole, which the Canadian government presented to New Zealand in 1969 to mark the Cook Bicentenary and to acknowledge the debt both countries owe that great explorer. It's adjacent to the Eastland Information Centre.

This area is filled with historic *pa* sites in the hills behind Poverty Bay Flats—ask at the information center if any meetinghouses are open to the public. There are also some excellent walkways in the area, and the information center can furnish detailed trail booklets.

Swimmers will want to take advantage of the superb surf at both **Waikanae** and **Midway Beaches.** Surfers prefer **Wainui and Makarori Beaches.** Small-fry (as well as the young at heart) will enjoy the **Adventure Park** and Young Nick's Playground.

There is excellent **fishing** in these waters, both offshore and in the rivers. You can arrange charter boats and guides through the information center. Anglers will want to ask for the *Guide to Trout Fishing in the Gisborne Area,* compiled by the Gisborne Anglers Club.

The ✪ **Gisborne Museum & Arts Centre,** 18-22 Stout St. (tel. 867-3832), has displays depicting Maori and European history along the East Coast, as well as geological and natural history, colonial technology, decorative arts, and maritime history exhibits. The Art Gallery has an ongoing program of changing art and craft exhibitions (local, national, and international). The Museum Complex, which includes the main museum building, two historic houses and associated outbuildings, and a maritime museum, is open from 10am to 4pm Monday through Friday, and 2 to 4:30pm on Saturday, Sunday, and holidays; longer weekend hours during December and January; closed Christmas Day and Good Friday. Adults pay NZ$2.50 ($1); children and students, NZ$1 (60¢).

Next door to the museum are **Wyllie Cottage,** built in 1872, and the **Star of Canada Maritime Museum.** The ill-fated *Star of Canada* struck rocks at Kaiti Beach in 1912.

There are four 1-hour ✪ **walks** (one is actually 1 to 3 hours) in Gisborne, all easily mapped out in the brochure *Gisborne Walking Tours,* available through the Visitors Information Centre, which can also give you information on four longer walks (2 to 5½ hours) in the Eastland area, in Wharerata, Cook's Cove, Anaura Bay, and Otoko.

The **Eastwoodhill Arboretum,** 35 kilometers (22 miles) due west of Gisborne (tel. *39-800), is the largest collection in the southern hemisphere of trees and plants native to the northern hemisphere. If you're partial to daffodils, you'll find 2½ acres of them in yellow profusion here in spring, and in fall the oaks, maples, and ash put on a show. Open from August through May (call or inquire at Visitors Information Centre for hours); by arrangement other times.

Most of New Zealand's white-wine grapes are grown near Gisborne, so if you are a wine connoisseur, have the Visitors Information Centre direct you to a couple of outstanding **wineries** just outside Gisborne: **Millton Vineyard,** on Papatu Road, Manutuke, Gisborne (tel. 862-8680); or ✪ **Honeywood,** Shelley Road (tel. 867-2708), which produces fruit and honey wines, and has local honey, local pottery, and handmade gift items for sale. Check to make sure they are open to visitors during your visit.

WHERE TO STAY

Unless otherwise noted, rates listed below include GST.

MOTEL FLATS

GISBORNE MOTEL, 509 Gladstone Rd., Gisborne. Tel. 06/868-8899. 12 units (all with bath). TV TEL

$ Rates: NZ$52–NZ$58 ($30–$33) single; NZ$62–NZ$68 ($35–$39) double. AE, DC, MC, V.

My top motel recommendation in town goes to the Gisborne. Its spacious units all have glass window walls to let in that gorgeous sunshine, and all are nicely furnished. There's a guest laundry, heated spa pool, video, and car wash. All units have full kitchens, but cooked and continental breakfasts are also available. Beverley and Alan Staunton have traveled extensively and enjoy meeting their guests with friendly hospitality. They also offer a convenient Dial-a-Meal service for dinner. The location is a short drive (longish walk) into the city center.

TEAL MOTOR LODGE, 479 Gladstone Rd., Gisborne. Tel. 06/868-4019. Fax 06/867-7157. 21 flats, 3 serviced rms (all with bath). TV TEL

$ Rates (excluding GST): NZ$60–NZ$70 ($34–$40) serviced room single or double; NZ$70–NZ$80 ($40–$46) flat single or double. AE, DC, MC, V.

✪ This is something a little different—it's a New Zealand motel with a decidedly Oriental flavor, run by Valmai and John Haynes since 1979. Set on almost 2 acres of shaded and landscaped lawns, only a short walk to the city center, the spacious rooms have an airy look, with exposed beams and stained timber exteriors, and exciting color combinations in decor throughout. There's a restful air about the place, not to mention a saltwater swimming pool and a location that makes walking into town easy. The flats with one or two bedrooms and full kitchens, and three serviced rooms with tea-making facilities. Units sleep two to six.

A BED & BREAKFAST

GREENGABLES TRAVEL HOTEL, 31 Rawiri St., Gisborne. Tel. 06/867-9872. 10 rms (none with bath). TV TEL

$ Rates (including breakfast): NZ$40 ($25) single; NZ$65 ($40.75) double. No credit cards.

✪ My favorite New Zealand bed and breakfast is run by Hilton and Elizabeth
Croskery. Greengables is an old house, set in shaded grounds in town and
approached by a rose-bordered walk, which has been renovated (without losing
$ one bit of its original charm). The rooms are spacious (two of them singles, for
you loners), all with hot and cold running water and nicely furnished. They
share four showers. My own favorite is on the ground floor and has a pretty bay

window. The old-fashioned lounge has a fireplace, and the attractive dining room looks out onto the lawn. This is a friendly, helpful family who provide Kiwi hospitality at its best—and one of the best breakfasts you'll find in Kiwiland.

A HOSTEL

GISBORNE YHA HOSTEL, 32 Harris St., corner of Wainui Rd., Gisborne. Tel. 06/867-3269. 38 beds.
$ Rates (excluding GST): NZ$14 ($8) per person; NZ$7 ($4) under age 18. MC, V.
This hostel is in a relaxed urban setting close to beaches and major sightseeing. There are 38 beds in five rooms, communal showers, full laundry facility, and communal kitchen. Across the street there's a food shop open 7 days a week.

CABINS & CAMPGROUNDS

Gisborne has an excellent motor camp run by the City Council. It's handy to good swimming and surfing beaches, spotless, and provides above-average facilities. During high season (summer months), advance reservations are absolutely necessary, as it is extremely popular with Kiwis.

The ✪ ⑤ **Waikanae Beach Motor Camp,** at the beach end of Grey Street, Gisborne (tel. 06/867-5634), has brown-wood blocks of cabins arranged U-shape around a grassy courtyard with attractive plantings. There are tourist cabins, which sleep four in two twin-bedded rooms and have private toilet and shower, refrigerator, gas range, crockery, cutlery, and cooking utensils; you supply linen and blankets. Charges range from NZ$12 ($7) for two people for tent sites to NZ$14 ($8) for two for power sites to NZ$45 ($26) double for tourist cabins—all plus GST. On the premises is a large laundry, kitchen, showers, children's play area, and tennis courts. The beautiful and safe Waikanae Beach is just across the road, and the city center is an easy walk away. The Olympic Pool complex and mini-golf are nearby.

WHERE TO EAT

For eating on the fly, you have several choices for basic budget fare: **Captain Morgan's,** at 285 Grey St. (tel. 867-7821), a BYO restaurant that also has take-away meals and an ice-cream parlor; **Riverdale Fish Shop,** 279 Stout St. (tel. 867-5429), which offers burgers and toasted sandwiches in addition to the finny specialties; and **Fish 'N Chips,** London Street (tel. 868-8475), with burgers and fish orders.

THE MARINA, Marina Park, Vogel St. Tel. 868-5919.
 Cuisine: SEAFOOD/STEAK/NEW ZEALAND. **Reservations:** Required.
$ Prices: Average dinner NZ$35 ($20). AE, MC, V.
 Open: Daily 6–10pm.
Housed in a white three-story building on the riverbank, the Marina offers quite good fresh local seafoods, veal, chicken, and steak. There's more than a little style in both the setting and food presentation by the friendly, competent staff. It's a favorite with locals, so book early. Fully licensed.

PINEHURST MANOR, 4 Clifford St. Tel. 868-6771.
 Cuisine: CONTINENTAL. **Reservations:** Required.
$ Prices: Average dinner NZ$35 ($20). AE, DC, MC, V.
 Open: Mon–Sat 6:30–11pm.

Easily the most elegant restaurant in Gisborne, Pinehurst Manor is an old-style house with rimu paneling and bay windows in a tranquil residential area close to town. Classic continental dishes include a wide range of specialties utilizing fresh seafoods, chicken, lamb, and beef. It's hard to go wrong here. Book as far ahead as possible.

READERS RECOMMEND

The Mill, *corner of Mill and Gladstone Rds. Tel. 868-3540. "For good home-cooking, go to this family-run restaurant at the southwest end of town. The little diner is immaculate, with moderate prices for eat-in, take-away, or grocery-store goods."*—J. and P. Conrad, San Jose, Calif.

Bread & Roses, *corner of Lowe St. and Reads Quay. Tel. 688-6697. "We warmly recommend this a small restaurant, with a friendly, cozy atmosphere. The service was very good, and the food was excellent."*—G. Speed, Oslo, Norway

EN ROUTE TO NAPIER

The 146-mile drive along Highway 2 from Gisborne to Napier passes through some of the most picturesque natural scenery in the country. Rugged hill-country sheep stations, lush native bush, Lake Tutira, and a breathtaking view of Poverty Bay Flats from the top of the Wharerata Hills some 23 miles outside the city. **Morere Springs Scenic Reserve,** between Poverty and Hawke bays (you'll see the sign along the highway), is a nice stopoff point for forest walks (there are four tracks, from half an hour to three hours, from which to choose), picnicking, or soaking in thermal pools. Incidentally, if you're traveling by public transport, opt for rail on this segment of your trip—the train hugs the coastline for long stretches, giving magnificent sea views not visible from the highway farther inland.

3. HAWKE'S BAY

Hawke's Bay has been called the "Greenhouse of New Zealand" because of its sunny climate and ideal growing conditions for all kinds of vegetables, citrus fruits, and grapes. Indeed, when you see the expanse of vineyards, you may well think of it as the "Winery of New Zealand." Its high-spirited resort center is Napier (pop. 58,000), one of the country's most delightful holiday spots. It is the ideal base for Hawke's Bay exploring.

Just 12 miles from Napier on Highway 2, Hastings is a town of lovely parks and gardens and Spanish Mission–style as well as art deco architecture—most definitely worth a day-trip from Napier. If you're not driving, there is regular bus service between the two towns. Also, the "Getting There" section for Napier below applies to both towns, often called the Twin Cities of Hawke's Bay.

NAPIER

146 miles SW of Gisborne, 423 miles SE of Auckland, 228 miles SE of Rotorua

GETTING THERE   By Plane   Air New Zealand (The Travel Centre, corner of Hastings and Station Streets, Napier; tel. 835-1171), has daily service between the Hawke's Bay Airport and Auckland, Wellington, Dunedin, Nelson, and Christchurch, as well as weekday flights to Hokitika and Invercargill. There's no airport bus into town: taxi fare (Twin City Shuttle Service; tel. 870-0700) is about NZ$15 ($9).

By Train   There is rail service between Hamilton/Napier and Wellington via the *Silver Fern* express train.

By Bus   There is daily coach service between Napier/Hastings and Auckland, Gisborne, Rotorua, Taupo, Tauranga, and Wellington, via Mount Cook Lines and/or InterCity and Newmans coach lines. For schedules and fares, call 835-1063.

By Car   Both Napier and Hastings are on north/south Highway 2; Highway 5 reaches Napier from the northwest, State Road 50 from the southwest.

ESSENTIALS Orientation   The pride—and showplace—of Napier is its **Marine Parade,** a beautiful stretch of waterfront lined with stately Norfolk pines. Many visitor activities center around the Marine Parade, which holds a wide variety of attractions. **Kennedy Road,** the principal thoroughfare, diagonally bisects the town. The best beach in the area is **Westshore Beach,** located in **Westshore Domain,** part of the new-land legacy of the 1931 disaster.

Information   You'll find the **Visitors Information Centre** at the northern end of the Marine Parade (tel. 06/835-7182). Hours are 8:30am to 5pm Monday to Friday, 9am to 5pm Saturday and Sunday and public holidays; closed only on Christmas Day. Racks are filled with helpful brochures, maps (including a scenic drive), and visitor guides. Noreen Young and her staff can help with accommodations and book fishing trips, golf, and sightseeing tours.

Mail   The Chief Post Office (CPO) is on Dickens Street.

Telephone   The **telephone prefix** is 06. Remember: The New Zealand Number Update is in the process of changing all telephone numbers to 7 digits. Those numbers in this chapter that have not been changed at press time are marked with an asterisk, and you should call the **Helpline 0155** for the new number. For directory assistance within the country (when you don't know the number), call **018.**

GETTING AROUND   There is no city bus service. **Taxi** ranks are at Clive Square and at the corner of Emerson and Hastings Streets by the Bank of New Zealand (tel. 835-7777). **Taxis for wheelchairs** are available by calling Dan Stothers at 843-2318.

Spread around the wedge of Bluff Hill (which was virtually an island when Captain Cook described it on his voyage south from Poverty Bay), Napier was founded by whalers in the mid-1800s. You won't find any trace of those early settlers in today's city, however: In 1931 an earthquake of such violence that it was recorded as far away as Cairo and Calcutta demolished the entire city and nearby Hastings, killing hundreds of people. In its aftermath, not only did a completely new city arise, but it arose on new ground, for the quake had lifted the inner harbor floor, creating 10,000 acres of dry land—the site of the present airport, for instance, was under water prior to 1931.

Rebuilt during the depression, the town opted for the art deco and Spanish Mission architecture so popular in the '30s. As a result, Napier claims it probably has the world's largest collection of buildings in these styles (see "Art Deco Walk," below).

WHAT TO SEE & DO

Plan to spend most of your time along the Marine Parade's Golden Mile. In addition to the listings below, as you walk north, you'll come to the **Boating Lake,** with paddleboats for children and adult-size bumper boats, as well as small racing cars, which are open from 10am to 9:30pm every day. Other amusements include children's bumper boats, radio boats, putt-putt golf, and roller-skating. Stop for a while and soak in the beauty of the **Sunken Gardens,** with their waterwheel and floating white lotus sculpture. Then, on past the **information center,** there's the **Sound Shell,** which is used on summer weekends for an arts and crafts market.

THE AQUARIUM, Marine Parade. Tel. 835-7579.

The Aquarium is one of New Zealand's best. Stop for a moment to view the bronze sculpture showing two trawler fishermen hauling a net full of fish. It's so masterfully executed that fishermen have been known to stand and point out each species of fish in the net. The Aquarium's central feature is a huge saltwater oceanarium, which holds over 25 species of ocean-dwelling fish, ranging in size from crayfish to sharks. Feeding time is 3:15pm, which can get pretty exciting. You'll also get to see a crocodile, turtles, vividly colored tropical fish, sea horses, the lethal piranha, and octopi. The Vivarium, on the top floor, holds the tuatara, a living fossil unique to New Zealand, and also aquatic reptiles like water dragons, turtles, and frogs. It's located at the southern end of the Golden Mile.

Admission: NZ$6 ($3) adults, NZ$3 ($2) children.

Open: Daily 9am–5pm (until 9pm Dec 26–Jan). **Closed:** Christmas.

MARINELAND, Marine Parade. Tel. 835-7579.

A 45-minute show puts dolphins, leopard seals, and sea lions through their paces in sports competitions and other antics much like those we see in the States. Also on hand are blue penguins, fur seals, otters, and gannets. Marineland, in the same building as the Aquarium, now houses **Lilliput,** an animated village and model railway with authentic New Zealand rolling stock and locomotives.

Admission: Marineland show and admission to Lilliput NZ$7 ($4) adults, NZ$3.50 ($2) children.

Open: Daily 10am–4:30pm. Show times are 10:30am and 2pm, with an additional 4pm performance Dec 26–Jan.

THE STABLES COLONIAL MUSEUM AND WAXWORKS, Marine Parade. Tel. 835-1937.

This museum re-creates the past with rooms from another era; my favorites depict a man in an outhouse, a doctor taking the blood pressure of a wicker-chair-bound patient, and a prostitute's quarters (this one provokes a bit of speculation about what exactly is going on). But the pièce de résistance of the museum is *Earthquake 31,* a documentary about the infamous earthquake; try to see it at the beginning of your sightseeing to best understand the unique history of this place. The 23-minute film includes actual footage of Napier before and after the earthquake and an interview with older citizens who lived through it, two of them teachers. Outside the movie theater, which has a floor that actually moves during footage of the quake, there is a dramatic replica of the collapse of the local nurses' home and the rescue performed by sailors and firefighters. (If you have to choose one, pick the film.) It's the brainchild of owner Kevin Percy, who runs the place with his wife, Judy. The museum is opposite Marineland.

Admission: Museum only NZ$3.50 ($2); combination museum and film NZ$5 ($3); NZ$3.50 ($2) film only.

Open: Daily 9am–5pm.

HAWKE'S BAY ART GALLERY AND MUSEUM, Marine Parade. Tel. 835-7781.

The museum and gallery on the Golden Mile offer a wide range of exhibits, many of which are related to the art and history of the region. A Tourism Design Award–winning exhibition, "Nga Tukemata" (The Awakening), presents the art of the local Ngati Kahungunu tribe and an audiovisual presentation tells the story of the disastrous Hawke Bay earthquake of 1931. The "Newest City on the Globe" exhibition shows the rebuilding of Napier in the early 1930s in its famed art deco style. Paintings and the decorative arts from this period are also featured.

Admission: NZ$2 ($1).

Open: Tues–Fri 10am–4:30pm, Sat–Sun 1–5pm.

KIWI HOUSE, Marine Parade. Tel. 835-7553.

This is where you are guaranteed to see kiwi birds. Also on view are owls, night herons, sugar gliders, whistling frogs, and many others. There's a live show at 1pm, and the birds are fed at 2pm. There's also a sheepskin shop in the main entrance. Kiwi House is located at the northern end of the Golden Mile.

Admission: NZ$3 ($2) adults, NZ$1 (60¢) children.

Open: Daily 11am–3pm.

Other Sights

The city of Napier itself is virtually an open-air museum of **art deco and Spanish architecture** as a result of massive reconstruction between 1931 and 1933. Half a century later, the buildings are remarkably unchanged and no doubt represent one of the world's most concentrated collections of buildings from this period. (See "Art Deco Walk," below.) Historic **Clive Square,** on Monroe Street between Emerson and Dickens Streets, was the village green from the 1860s to the mid-1880s, when it became a public gardens. After the earthquake, it was the site of "Tin Town," a temporary shopping area.

Westshore Domain is Napier's most popular swimming beach, about a mile and a half of gray sand and pebbles. Surf at the **Marine Parade** beach is a bit too rough for good swimming, but it's a good place to get a little sun. There is, however, a saltwater pool at Marine Parade featuring the "Wild Rampage Ride." **Onekawa Park** at Maadi Road and Flanders Avenue has two Olympic-size pools, one indoor, the other outdoor. Small fee.

ART DECO WALK A map outlining a ✪ **self-guided walk** through the downtown deco area and another showing a more extensive scenic drive are available from the information center for NZ$1 (60¢). **Guided walks** leave the Hawke's Bay Museum every Wednesday at 2pm and include slide and video presentations and refreshments. They are conducted by the Art Deco Trust, which promotes the city's architecture and can be contacted at P.O. Box 429, Napier.

Nearby Attractions

This is the only place in New Zealand where gannets are known to nest on the mainland (they are commonly found on offshore islands). There's a colony of some 6,000 out at ✪ **Cape Kidnappers,** that dramatic line of cliffs that forms Hawke's Bay's southern end some 17 miles south of Napier. The gannet sanctuary is open to the public from late October to June, and the graceful, colorful birds are worth a visit. To reach them, drive 13 miles south to Clifton Domain; then it's a little less than a 2-hour walk along 4 or 5 miles of sandy beach. That walk *must* be made at low tide, since high tides come right up to the base of the steep cliffs, which is why private vehicles may not be taken out to the sanctuary. Be sure to check with the Visitors Information Centre in Napier (tel. 835-7579) or Hastings (tel. 876-0205), or the Department of Conservation in Napier (tel. 835-0415), about the tides or taking a tour there. The best time to view the birds is from early November to late February; migration begins in March.

There are two options to going on your own: ✪ **Burden's Motor Camp** in Te Awanga (tel. 875-0400) runs organized 4-hour trips at moderate prices; and there's a Land Rover half-day trip operated by **Gannet Safaris** (tel. 875-0511) at considerably higher prices. Take along a sweater and some snacks.

There are two important **wineries** you can visit in the Napier vicinity, the Mission Vineyards and Brookfields Winery. Ask at the information center for brochures about tours and directions for reaching them. Also, Napier is where you can see how all those sheep get transformed into car seat covers, rugs, and more. You can take a free 25-minute tour through the ✪ ⑤ **Classic Sheepskin Tannery** at 22 Thames St. off Pandora Road (tel. 835-9662), 7 days a week at 11am and 2pm. The shop there sells sheepskin products at factory prices, and they have a fully insured, worldwide mailing service. There's also a courtesy car available on weekdays.

WHERE TO STAY

Unless otherwise noted, rates listed below include GST.

Motel Flats

In addition to the listings below, some of the area's best motel flats are at **Kennedy Park Motor Camp,** described under "Camping and Cabins," below.

BLUE DOLPHIN MOTEL, 371-373 Kennedy Rd., Napier. Tel. 06/843-9129. Fax 06/843-9227. 9 units (all with bath). TV TEL
$ **Rates** (excluding GST): NZ$56 ($32) single; NZ$66 ($38) double. 10% discount to readers who present this book. AE, DC, MC, V.

✪ ⑤ Paul and Jenny Guest, Napier residents for over 30 years are the friendly owners of the Blue Dolphin. The self-contained units come with full kitchen facilities and separate bedrooms that sleep two to five people. All have radio and video, and are serviced daily. There's a games room, heated outdoor spa pool, and a fully automatic guest laundry. Cooked or continental breakfasts are available.

EDGEWATER MOTOR LODGE, Marine Parade, Napier. Tel. 06/835-1148. Fax 06/835-6600. 19 units (all with bath). TV TEL
$ **Rates:** NZ$79–NZ$99 ($45–$57) studio single or double; NZ$125–NZ$170) one or four people in flat. 10% Motor Lodge discount available. AE, DC, MC, V.

✪ Ideally situated overlooking Hawke Bay, the Edgewater's biggest asset is the fact that every unit has a balcony facing the bay with no buildings obstructing the view—just trees, plants, and a children's playground. The smaller studio units don't have kitchens, but they do have tea and coffee facilities. All units have good lighting (always a plus), in-house videos, and other videos that can be rented out to the room. You'll also find a games room, laundry, saltwater plunge pool, and two spa pools. The units range from studios to two-bedroom, and include a unit for the disabled. Room 20 is especially pretty and features a water bed (if you don't want to slosh when you sleep, choose Room 19).

MAREWA LODGE, 42 Taradale Rd., Napier. Tel. 06/843-5839. Fax 06/843-3232. 30 rms (all with bath). TV TEL
$ **Rates** (excluding GST): NZ$56 ($32) single; NZ$68 ($39) double. AE, DC, MC, V.
Located 2 kilometers (1 mile) from the center of town, these attractive units are arranged in an L-shape around a large lawn and children's playground. All are equipped with radio, electric blanket, and electric heater. Each unit opens up to a terrace furnished with garden chairs for sunbathing. Bed-sitters have rangettes for cooking; other units have full stoves and ovens. There's plenty of parking space, a spa pool, car wash, and laundry facilities. Babysitters are available, and there's a shopping area close by.

REEF MOTEL, 33 Meeanee Quay, Westshore, Napier. Tel. 06/835-4108. 7 units (all with bath). TV TEL **Transportation:** Courtesy car from rail, bus, and air terminals.

$ Rates (excluding GST): NZ$55 ($31) single; NZ$65 ($37) double. AE, DC, MC, V.

Pam and Alex Speers are the friendly, helpful hosts at the Reef. The motel's units each sleep two to six, with separate bedrooms, and a living room that opens into a kitchen. Upstairs units have great views. There's a spa pool and laundry facilities on the premises. Both cooked and continental breakfasts are available.

SNOWGOOSE LODGE MOTEL, 376 Kennedy Rd., Napier. Tel. 06/843-6083. Fax 06/843-6107. 11 units, 3 suites (all with bath). TV TEL
$ Rates: NZ$65 ($37) single; NZ$75 ($43) double; NZ$77–NZ$87 ($44–$50) executive suite. Best Western holiday discounts available. AE, DC, MC, V.

You park outside your own unit at the Snowgoose, where Ray and Pierrine Cooper keep things shining, outside as well as in. The front lawn has even won an award for the best motel garden in Napier. The one- and two-bedroom units are all nicely furnished and have radio and electric blankets. Most also are brightened with one or two of Pierrine's growing plants. There's a newer block of executive suites that have their own spa bath (sheer luxury!). On-premises facilities include a laundry, car wash, children's play area, games room, outdoor swimming pool, and private spa pool—no charge for the use of any. Shops are nearby, and the Coopers can arrange babysitting. All units have full kitchens and the executive units come with spa bath and/or water bed. Highly recommended. The motel is on the main road 3.5 kilometers (2 miles) from the town center.

SPANISH LADY MOTEL, 348 Kennedy Rd., Napier. Tel. 06/843-9188 or 843-9187. Fax 06/843-6064. 11 units (all with bath). TV TEL
$ Rates (excluding GST): NZ$57 ($35.75) single; NZ$67 ($42) double. Best Western discounts available. AE, DC, MC, V.

The unassuming exterior of this small property hides the amenities hard to find in most New Zealand lodgings: washcloths in the bath and a sink with one mixer faucet for both hot and cold water (instead of the inconvenient two). Add to that good lighting and a firm mattress—heaven! There are also jelly beans on the tea tray for the kids, a pool, spa pool, playground, ice machine, and cactus garden. Owners Janice and Don McJorrow have been here since 1979 and their attention to detail shows. There are one- and two-bedroom units, Rooms 4 through 7 have been recently refurbished and are especially comfortable. Ask Don about his golf package. It's on the main road 3.5 kilometers (2 miles) from the center of town.

READERS RECOMMEND

Ormlie Lodge, Omarunui Rd., R.D. 3, Napier. Tel. 06/844-5774. "Ormlie Lodge is a beautiful stately mansion outside Napier. There are rooms in the lodge itself or in brand-new villas, and the food is excellent."—Betty Ann Zimmer, Bloomington, Ill.

A Bed & Breakfast

PINEHAVEN TRAVEL HOTEL, 259 Marine Parade, Napier. Tel. 06/835-5575. 8 rms (with shared bath). TV TEL
$ Rates: NZ$36 ($21) single; NZ$48 ($28) double. MC, V.

The Pinehaven Travel Hotel is down the street from the YHA Hostel and across the road from Marineland. Judith Butt and her family have hosted guests from all over the world off and on for over 10 years. Pinehaven has three family rooms, four twins, and one double, all with hot and cold running water and comfortably furnished. Although the bedrooms are not heated, they all have electric blankets. Downstairs there's a TV lounge with tea- and coffee-making facilities. Continental or cooked breakfast is optional and extra.

A Hostel

YHA HOSTEL, 47 Marine Parade, Napier. Tel. 06/835-7039. 45 beds.
$ Rates: NZ$14 ($8) per person. MC, V.
This hostel couldn't have a better location—it's right on the beachfront, across the street from Marineland. The former guesthouse has 45 beds in 22 rooms. Front rooms overlook the bay, and facilities include a TV and video room, a pleasant kitchen and dining room with a piano, a smoking lounge, laundry facilities, and bike rental.

Camping & Cabins

It's hard to find superlatives strong enough for Napier's **✪ ⑤ Kennedy Park Motor Camp** on Storkey Street, off Kennedy Road, Napier (tel. 06/843-9126; fax 06/843-6113). If you've been impressed with Kiwi motor camps in general, just wait until you see this one! Set in 17 acres of trees, grass, and colorful flowers (including an acre and a half of roses!), with top-grade accommodations, this has to be the "Ritz" of New Zealand camps. Those accommodations run the gamut from tent sites to ungraded cabins to graded (two-star) cabins to tourist flats and motel units. The 110 sites with no power run NZ$14 ($8) single or double, NZ$3 ($2) for a child; those with power, just pennies more. Ungraded cabins come with beds, tables, and chairs, and you supply cooking and eating utensils, linen and blankets, and use the communal toilet and shower facilities. Rates are NZ$29 ($17) single or double. The 16 graded cabins sleep four (plus rollaway bed if needed), have easy chairs, and are furnished with hot- and cold-water sinks, fridge, range, electric jug, toaster, crockery, cutlery, frying pan, pots, and utensils. You supply linen and blanket, and use the communal toilet and shower facilities. Doubles pay NZ$34 ($19). Tourist flats fill that gap between cabins and motel units—they're actually of motel quality, but lack such extras as a TV and telephone, and they're not serviced. You supply linen and blankets (which can be rented from the camp for this type accommodation only). These 20 units cost NZ$54 ($31) single or double. Finally, motel units come in varying sizes: bed-sitters, one- and two-bedrooms. Many have peaked, pine-beamed ceilings, a window wall and stucco and wood-paneled walls. All are of superior quality, and well-chosen furnishings, look out over lawn and gardens, and are NZ$76 ($43) single or double. Add GST to all rates. American Express, Diners Club, MasterCard, and VISA credit cards accepted.

WHERE TO EAT

I'm not really sure this item belongs under "Where to Eat," but because New Zealand budget travel is so closely tied to those wonderful motel flats and their kitchens, I think you should know about **✪ Chantal Wholefoods,** 29 Hastings St. (tel. 835-8036). Even if you're not a strict vegetarian, I think you'll love this store—all sorts of natural foods, dried fruits, nuts, tofu, and in addition, marvelous whole-grain breads to make any sandwich taste its best. Chantal's is very much like an old-fashioned grocery store. The foods are all in open drums and you package them yourself—it's lots of fun, and prices come out cheaper than those in supermarkets.

BEACHES RESTAURANT, Marine Parade. Tel. 835-8180.
   Cuisine: SEAFOOD. **Reservations:** Recommended, especially for window tables.
$ Prices: Main lunch courses from NZ$10 ($6); main dinner courses from NZ$19 ($11). AE, DC, MC, V.
   Open: Lunch Wed–Fri noon–2:30pm; dinner Mon–Sat 6–10pm.
   Located in the War Memorial Building behind the floral clock, this seafood restaurant is at the water's edge, with an expansive view of Hawke's Bay from Mahia Peninsula to Cape Kidnappers. The menu features crayfish, oysters, mussels, paua, calamari, prawns, shrimps, scallops, and fresh fish. Lamb, beef, and

poultry are also available, and vegetarian dishes can be prepared if requested when you make your reservation. There's an extensive all–New Zealand wine list, with selections from most local vineyards.

JUICES & ICES, Emerson St. Tel. 835-9944.

Cuisine: ICE CREAM/SNACKS. **Reservations:** Not required.
$ Prices: Under NZ$10 ($6). No credit cards.
Open: Mon–Fri 8:30am–5pm, Sat 10am–1pm.

This favorite of Napier citizens specializes in homemade ice cream, with a dozen flavors from which to choose. You can also order toasted sandwiches, soup, and fresh fruit juices. Juices & Ices, at Clive Square, has a cheerful ice-cream-parlor ambience.

MABEL'S RESTAURANT, 204 Hastings St. Tel. 835-5655.

Cuisine: BREAKFAST/LIGHT LUNCH. **Reservations:** Not required.
$ Prices: Breakfast under NZ$8 ($5); lunch under NZ$10 ($6). No credit cards.
Open: Mon–Fri 7am–3pm.

⑤ Early risers will appreciate Mabel's, where breakfast is featured weekdays from 6:30am to 9:30am. You can also get a light, reasonably priced meal of soup, quiche, or salad. Just check the blackboard selections. In the center of town.

THE OLD FLAME, Tennyson St. Tel. 835-6829.

Cuisine: NEW ZEALAND SMÖRGÅSBORD. **Reservations:** Recommended, especially on weekends.
$ Prices: Lunch NZ$12 ($7); dinner NZ$15 ($9). No credit cards.
Open: Lunch Mon–Sat noon–2pm; dinner Mon–Sat 6–9pm.

✪ This intimate restaurant occupies a single-story house across from the Municipal Theatre. It's strictly smörgåsbord—tables heaped high with tempt-
⑤ ing New Zealand dishes. The place has a medieval look, rather than deco, for a change. BYO.

READERS RECOMMEND

Buck's Great Wall Restaurant, *Marine Parade. Tel. 835-8800. "Bucks Great Wall has some of the best Chinese food I've had, including Hong Kong and Singapore! On top of that, it's beautiful."*—Betty Ann Zimmer, Bloomington, Ill.

EVENING ENTERTAINMENT After dark, you'll always find folks congregating in the lively **Masonic Hotel** bar and the **Shakespeare Hotel,** Hawke's Bay's major music pub. **Ego's Night Club,** in a small art deco building on Hastings Street (tel. 835-7030), is open Wednesday through Saturday from 8pm until 3am.

Take in a movie at the art deco **State Theatre,** on the corner of Dickens and Dalton Streets; or see a show or concert (very inexpensive) at the **Municipal Theatre** on Tennyson Street (if nothing else, try to see the auditorium).

AN EXCURSION TO HASTINGS

Just 12 miles from Napier on Highway 2, Hastings is a town of lovely parks and gardens and Spanish Mission-style as well as art deco architecture—most definitely worth a visit. If you're not driving, there is regular bus service between the two towns. Stop by the **Visitor Information Centre,** on Russell Street North (mailing address: Private Bag, Hastings; tel. 06/876-0205), for brochures, information, a Spanish Mission Tour map, and a scenic-drive guide. Hours are 8am to 5pm weekdays, to noon on weekends and holidays (extended hours in summer months). Inquire at the information center about tours in a taxi, as well. No matter how you get around, the **scenic drive** is one you really shouldn't miss.

✪ The Hawke's Bay Exhibition Centre, Civic Square, Hastings (tel. 876-2077), is an illuminating stop, with exhibitions of local, national, and international art. There's a shop specializing in local craft souvenirs, and admission is by donation. It's open Monday through Friday from 1pm to 4:30pm. Closed Christmas Day and Good Friday.

Pick up the *Taste Our Tradition* brochure from the information center for directions on visiting the local **wineries.** One of the best is the **✪ Vidal Winery,** 913 St. Aubyn St. East, near Sylvan Road (tel. 876-8105). Vidal has a lot to offer, including the **Vineyard Bar and Barrel Room Restaurant** right on the premises. They have a rustic, wine-cellar setting, with beamed ceiling, old oak casks lining the walls, and candlelight. There's also a barbecue area outside with umbrella trees and a grape arbor. The menu on Saturday night, November through February, includes delicious homemade soup, quiche, baked potato and salad, honeyed chicken, and a variety of steaks. A basket of hot bread and butter accompanies all meals, and need I say you can order wine? Prices are in the NZ$10 to NZ$18 ($6 to $10) range. The Vineyard Bar is open from 10am to 9pm Monday through Saturday; the Barrel Room, from noon to 2pm and 6 to 9pm Monday through Saturday; drinks and light snacks are available in the Vineyard Bar.

Be sure to drive up to **✪ Te Mata Peak,** about seven miles from the Hastings Information Centre. The view is spectacular, and ask locals or the center about the lovely Maori legend from which it took its name. Take Havelock Road to Te Mata Road to Simla Avenue to Te Mata Peak Road and ascend the 1,310-foot-high peak for a stunning 360° panoramic view.

COOL FOR KIDS

Within the 8 acres that make up **✪ Fantasyland,** in Windsor Park, entered via Grove Road (tel. 876-9856), are enough assorted attractions and amusements to delight any child and all but the most hardened of his or her elders. Each time I go there are new additions, all elaborately but tastefully executed. Who wouldn't be intrigued by a pirate ship complete with cannons, a turreted castle, and a spaceship parked on its moon base! The tree house (open to any and all climbers) draws me every time, as does the little village with its firehouse, jail, and stores. A terrific array of playground equipment, go-karts, bumper boats, battery-operated cars and tricycles are available for active youngsters, and for those of us not so active, there's a miniature train ride around the park, along with miniature golf. Canoes and rowboats compete with swans and ducks on the pretty pond, and the shady, landscaped grounds invite an extended spell of just plain loafing—spreading a picnic on the handy tables set about (easily arranged with food from the take-away bar). The tea shop is a refreshment alternative. Admission is NZ$2.50 ($1.45), and children under 15 go in free (some of the rides charge a minimal fare). Open daily from 9am to 5pm.

READERS RECOMMEND

Ebbet Park Lodge, 614 Gordon Rd., Hastings. Tel. 06/876-8086. "*We discovered this reasonably priced, quiet, peaceful, sparkling-clean motel in Hastings that is situated next to Ebbet Park a few blocks from the center of town. The owners [Nola and Rex McLean] personally served us piping-hot bacon, eggs, tomatoes, and toast each morning for breakfast.*"—P. McGilvray, Sacramento, Calif.

The Windsor Park Motor Camp, Windsor Ave., Hastings. Tel. 06/878-6692. "*This lovely motor camp is in a corner of a park and couldn't be a more restful place to lay your head—or sleeping bag. We camped, but there are tourist flats, cabins, and caravan sites too, and the park has a swimming pool and water slide.*"—J. Kelly, Phoenix, Ariz.

EN ROUTE TO TAUPO

Your drive from Napier to Taupo via Highway 5 will take 2 hours, but there was a time when it took two days. That was when stagecoach service was first initiated over a route that had been used by Maoris in pre-European days on forays to collect seafood from Hawke's Bay.

The landscape you'll be passing through changes from lush vineyards to cultivated farm fields to rugged mountain ranges, and it doesn't take much imagination to picture the arduous journey as it was in the early days. About 3½ miles before you reach Taupo, look for the lonely peak of **Mount Tauhara,** an extinct volcanic cone rising from the plains.

CHAPTER 6

LAKE TAUPO & BEYOND

1. TAUPO
- WHAT'S SPECIAL ABOUT LAKE TAUPO
2. TONGARIRO NATIONAL PARK
3. WANGANUI

Whether you come into **Taupo** from Rotorua, past Wairakei's steamy thermal power complex, or from Napier, under the lonely eye of Mount Tauhara, it is the lake on whose shores the town sits that will draw you like a magnet. Lake Taupo, New Zealand's largest (238 sq. miles), opens before you in a broad, shimmering expanse, with its far shores a misty suggestion of cliffs, coves, and wooded hills.

Tongariro National Park was New Zealand's first national park (the world's second, after Yellowstone), and the original 1887 deed from Te Heuheu Tukino IV and other Tu-wharetoa tribal chiefs transferred only some 6,500 acres (all the land within a 1-mile radius of the volcanic peaks), an area that has now been expanded to 30,453 acres.

Wanganui, one of New Zealand's oldest cities, was settled amid much controversy over just how title to the land was obtained by Col. William Wakefield on behalf of the New Zealand Company in 1840. Since those early days, the town has grown and over the years developed into one of the country's most popular holiday spots.

1. TAUPO

173 miles SE of Auckland, 51 miles S of Rotorua, 138 miles NE of Wanganui

GETTING THERE By Bus There is regular bus service via Mount Cook Lines, InterCity, and Newmans between Taupo and Gisborne, Hamilton, Hastings, Napier, New Plymouth, Paihia, Rotorua, Waitomo Caves, Wellington, and Whangarei.

By Car Highways 1 and 5 pass through Taupo.

ESSENTIALS Orientation Taupo is spread along the northeastern tip of the lake, just where the Waikato River, New Zealand's longest, flows out of Lake Taupo's Tapuaeharuru Bay. Its main street is **Tongariro Street,** named after the largest river flowing into the lake. Perpendicular to Tongariro is another important street, named **Heu Heu** (the Maoris pronounce it "hue-hue"; the Pakehas, "who-who"). The small settlements of **Acacia Bay** and **Jerusalem Bay** are just across on the western shore of the bay.

Information The **Visitors Information Centre** is just off the lakefront at 13 Tongariro St. (tel. 07/378-9000; fax 07/378-9002) and can book accommodations, tours, and other activities, as well as provide a wide range of informative brochures on

WHAT'S SPECIAL ABOUT LAKE TAUPO

Recreation Facilities

☐ The lake offers one of the world's best rainbow trout fishing venues.

☐ Pleasure boating and waterskiing are also pursued on the lake by large numbers.

☐ Walks, of the city and its immediate environs, as well as tramping trails, some as far away as Tongariro National Park.

☐ The Wairakei International Golf Course, a challenging course made dramatic by thermal vapors rising in the background.

☐ Lake cruises aboard the steamer *Ernest Kemp* offer tea or buffet lunch as you glide around the lake.

☐ Scenic flights give a bird's-eye view of the lake, Wairakei's steaming valley, Huka Falls, and Tongariro National Park.

☐ Minibus tours cover a wide region around Lake Taupo.

Geothermal Sites

☐ Wairakei Geothermal Project, the first to use wet steam, with some 60 bores and over 12 miles of pipeline.

☐ The eerie Craters of the Moon and nearby Wairakei Thermal Valley are between the Wairakei Geothermal Power Station and Taupo.

Historic Sites

☐ Huka Homestead is a replica of a pioneer village from New Zealand's days of early European settlement.

---

area attractions. Fishing guides may be booked through the Visitors Information Centre, which also provides fishing licenses and information. Hours are 8:30am to 5pm daily.

Mail   The striking purple-and-salmon-colored post office is at the corner of Ruapehu and Horomatangi Streets, and is open weekdays from 8:30am to 4:30pm.

Telephone   The **telephone prefix** at this writing is 07. Remember: The New Zealand Number Update is in the process of changing all telephone numbers to 7 digits. Those numbers in this chapter that have not been changed at press time are marked with an asterisk, and you should call the **Helpline 0155** for the new number. For directory assistance within the country (when you don't know the number), call **018**.

GETTING AROUND   By Bus   There is no local bus service.

By Bike   For getting around Taupo by bicycle, contact Roy's Cycle World, on Ruapehu Street (tel. 378-6117; after hours, 378-4402).

By Car   You won't need one in town.

On Foot   The best way unless you intend to wander the entire region, in which case you should rely on organized tours (see below) or on driving.

By Taxi   Call Taupo Taxis at 378-5100.

There's a bit of magic at work in Taupo—and it's easy to see its immediate attraction to descendants of the *Arawa* canoe. Present-day Maori will tell you that the lake was created by the magic of Ngatoroirangi, the legendary navigator of that migrating canoe. According to the legend, he stood on the summit of Mount Tauhara and flung down a gigantic tree, which landed here, leaving a vast trough as it plowed through the earth. When water welled up to fill the trough, Lake Taupo was born. Its very name is linked to legend—the Maoris called it Taupo-nui-a-Tia, or "the great cloak of Tia," after one of the Arawa chiefs who explored much of this region, naming and claiming choice spots for his tribe. If you don't believe in magic, you'll accept the Pakeha explanation of its origin: that it lies in a series of volcanic craters created in the aftermath of some of the most violent eruptions in the country's history.

Taupo's most appealing aspect to me is the fact that this pleasant, medium-size town of 16,500 people is a *real* place, not just a tourist draw—probably because travelers often rush past it on their way to Rotorua. It certainly welcomes visitors, but you'll also see plenty of people just going about their daily lives, going to work or school, congregating in local cafés, or indulging in an ice-cream cone (half a dozen parlors here encourage just that).

For locals and visitors alike, the lake is as much the central attraction today as it was in those far-off times. The fishing on which the Maori settlers so depended has changed only in the addition of two imported trout species to enhance the native fish population. It was in 1868 that brown trout eggs were introduced from Tasmania, followed by California rainbow trout in 1884. Lake Taupo rainbows are now considered a totally self-supporting wild population. It is the trout that draw anglers here in such numbers that those on shore have been so tightly packed as to be likened to a human picket fence. And there is seldom a time when the lake's surface is not alive with boats trolling lines in their wake.

Pleasure boating is a never-ending diversion in these parts, and waterskiing has gained such popularity that there are now specified ski lanes along the shoreline.

There is also an abundant supply of land-based attractions. Landlubbers have been coming in nearly equal numbers since the late 1870s to visit the thermal pools and view the natural wonders of the lake's environs.

WHAT TO SEE & DO

WATER ACTIVITIES

Well, there's **fishing.** And even if you've never cast a line, this may be the very time to join that "picket fence" and experience the singular thrill of feeling a nibble and pulling in a big one. And they do grow *big* in Lake Taupo—the average trout size is 4½ pounds, with 8 and 10 pounds not unheard of. Just remember that there's a limit of eight rainbow trout and five brook trout per person per day. The visitors center can fix you up with a license (you can get one for just 1 day if you like) and fill you in on rules and regulations, as well as help you find a guide if you'd just rather not be a "picket." Most restaurants are happy to cook up your catch of the day; they aren't allowed to offer it on their menu (which is probably why so many trout live to grow so big).

OTHER SIGHTS & ACTIVITIES

The visitors center puts out an excellent booklet, *Walking Trails,* outlining city and near-city ✪ **walks** as well as tramping trails in the area. There are long walks and short walks, walks close to town and others as far away as Tongariro National Park. What a peaceful interlude to take the 45-minute forest walk, and for sheer scenery excitement there's the contrast of thrilling thermal activity and serene pine plantations along the Craters of the Moon track. The booklet gives clear, concise directions (with maps for most tracks), as well as estimated times and such helpful information as the fact that all of Mount Tauhara is a Maori Reserve and I trust you will treat it with proper respect, leaving only footprints (and perhaps a bit of your heart). A terrific idea is to intersperse sightseeing or other sports activities with a walk into the very soul and being of New Zealand, its forests, mountains, and rivers.

To see firsthand the awesome power of all that steam you've only glimpsed in

Rotorua, take the 5-mile drive out to the ○ **Wairakei Geothermal Project** (tel. *48-216). When work began in 1950 to harness all that power, this was the second-largest such project in the world and the first to use wet steam. Scientists from around the globe came to observe. Using some 60 bores and over 12 miles of pipeline, the project now supplies a great deal of the North Island's electricity requirements. Stop by the Information Centre (on the left as you drive into the valley), which is open from 9am to noon and 1 to 4:30pm every day of the year, including holidays. The display and audiovisual show give a compelling overview of local geothermal activity and furnish answers to all the obvious questions that spring to mind (ask for the sheet titled "Questions Often Asked"). Study the excellent borefield model and drilling-process diagram, then leave the center and follow the marked road, which crosses the borefield itself, to a lookout from which you can view the entire site. You can also visit the power station itself during the hours listed above.

The **Wairakei International Golf Course,** at the THC Wairakei (tel. 374-8152), is challenging, not to mention dramatic, with thermal vapors rising in the background. Visitors are welcome and rental equipment is available; call ahead.

Just in front of the De Brett Thermal Hotel, a short way out of town on Highway 5, a cut has been made through the pumice on the south side of the road and pumice strata has been marked and dated showing ○ **volcanic debris** dating as far back as 1480 B.C. and as "recently" as A.D. 131. It's an eerie feeling to gaze on physical evidence of the earth's history! The De Brett, itself, is worth a short visit, since its grounds incorporate the fabulous **Onekeneke Valley of Hot Pools.**

Be sure to visit ○ **Huka Homestead** (admission NZ$4.50, U.S. $3), a replica pioneer village in which authentic buildings from New Zealand's days of early European settlement have been restored and brought back to life with working exhibits of contemporary village life. One cottage holds a shop stocked with handcrafts. There are **picnic facilities** in this lovely, shaded site, but I strongly recommend that you time your visit to include lunch at the pioneer tea and lunch room (see "Where to Eat," below). The village is out the Huka Falls Road about 1½ miles from the center of town. There is free transportation from the visitors center, but you have to reserve in advance.

Huka Falls themselves aren't huge but are impressive for the speed at which the water moves over the 35-foot drop—62,000 gallons per second. The word "huka" means "foaming" in Maori, and the water does resemble the agitation cycle of a washing machine. If you're in the mood to walk, follow the walkway from town; it should take about an hour. If you feel like walking farther, from here you can walk to **Aratiatia Rapids,** but allow 2 hours to get there. Time your arrival for 10am or 2:30pm, when water is released from the dam, creating quite a difference in water level.

If you find **geothermal areas** compelling—especially if you didn't see any around Rotorua—visit ○ **Craters of the Moon,** on a mile of unpaved road off Highway 1 between the Wairakei Geothermal Power Station and Taupo (watch for the sign). The area looks like the aftermath of a fire, quite eerie, especially with the gurgling sounds the bubbling mud makes. Get out of your car to experience it fully, but be sure to stay on the marked paths. There's no admission charge, whereas you pay NZ$4 ($2.50) at the nearby **Wairakei Thermal Valley.**

SIGHTSEEING CRUISES, FLIGHTS & TOURS

Kurrahe Cruises, Boat Harbour Wharf (tel. 378-3218 or 378-3444), runs marvelous ○ **lake cruises** aboard the steamer *Ernest Kemp* every morning and afternoon, 7 days a week. It's a 2¼-hour sail, well worth the fare of NZ$22 ($13) per adult, NZ$12 ($7) per child (there are special family prices on holidays)—a great way to experience the lake itself and get a very different look at its shoreline. It's essential to book, through the visitors center or at the Boat Harbour Wharf.

The *Taupo Cat* glides all around the lake daily from 9am to 3pm, serving morning tea, a large buffet lunch, and afternoon tea along its route. The inclusive price of this outing is NZ$65 ($37); there is also a sunset cruise. The catamaran departs from Pier 87, an easy walk from the visitors center; make reservations and double-check the schedule at the visitors center, or call *86-052.

Truly thrilling **scenic flights** leave the lakefront by Taupo Boat Harbour, ranging from a 10-minute flight over Wairakei's steaming valley, Huka Falls, and Taupo, to 1-hour forays as far away as Tongariro National Park, to a 2-hour excursion that takes you even farther afield. Prices range from NZ$30 to NZ$99 ($17 to $57)—children pay half. You'll find the **Float Plane Office** (ARK Aviation Limited, P.O. Box 238) at the Boat Harbour (tel. 378-7500 or 378-9441).

Minibus tours of the region around Lake Taupo are given daily by ✪ **Paradise Tours** and led by knowledgeable and affable guide Sue King. Book through the visitors center, or call Sue after hours at 378-9955. The tours, given every morning and afternoon, last 2½ hours.

READERS RECOMMEND: FISHING

"My wife is a wheelchair person, and most of the time when I went fishing, she stayed in the motel alone. However, at Lake Taupo, Roger Jones, of **Taupo Lakeside Services** *(tel. 378-5596), insisted that she always come along, and the fact that she was in a wheelchair made no difference. He lifted her, chair and all, into the boat and she had a glorious time on the water, all because of Roger's thoughtfulness."*—C. Blacharsh, West Hempstead, N.Y.

READERS RECOMMEND: SHOPPING

"I found Taupo to have a small but nice selection of clothing stores with good prices, and **The Pottery,** *at 87 Tongariro St. (tel. 378-3921), had the best prices for pottery I saw in New Zealand. Wayne Porteous's work—everything from cups to tiles to plates—is wonderful."*—S. Craft, Boston, Mass.

WHERE TO STAY

Only during the holiday season should it be necessary to reserve very far in advance, since there are over 3,000 beds available in the immediate vicinity. The efficient, well-run Visitors Information Centre can furnish a list of area accommodations, complete with current prices.

Unless otherwise noted, rates listed below include GST.

MOTEL FLATS

ADELPHI MOTEL, 39-41 Kaimanawa St., P.O. Box 1091, Taupo. Tel. 07/378-7594. 10 units (all with bath). TV TEL

$ Rates (excluding GST): NZ$58 ($33) single; NZ$70 ($40) double. Best Western discounts available. Rates increase during holidays. AE, DC, MC, V.

✪ This attractive in-town motel is presided over by Audrey and Ann Freeman. The only second-floor unit has marvelous views of the lake and mountains. There are one- and two-bedroom units, sleeping two to six, all with fully equipped kitchen, radio, and electric blanket. One is especially designed for the disabled. There are two private spa pools on the premises as well as a laundry, car-washing facilities, and a trampoline. Breakfast is available for a small charge, as is dinner on request. It's at the corner of Kaimanawa and Heu Heu Streets.

CEDAR PARK MOTOR LODGE, Two Mile Bay (P.O. Box 852), Taupo. Tel. 07/378-6325. Fax 07/377-0641. 24 units (all with bath). TV TEL

$ Rates: NZ$66 ($38) single; NZ$80 ($46) double. Rates increase during holidays. DC, MC, V.

Cedar Park is one of the most attractive accommodations in Taupo, with some two-story units that feature peaked ceilings and picture windows looking out over the lake. Each unit has a separate lounge, two bedrooms, complete kitchen, video, radio, and electric blankets. There's a heated swimming pool, hot spa pools, children's play area, barbecue, laundry, and car-wash facilities. Also, a very good BYO restaurant right on the premises (patronized by the locals as well as guests). The property is located across Highway 1 from the lakefront, 4 kilometers (2½ miles) from the center of town.

DUNROVIN MOTEL, 140 Heu Heu St. (P.O. Box 647), Taupo. Tel. 07/378-7384. 8 units (all with bath). TV TEL
$ Rates: NZ$49 ($28) single; NZ$65 ($37) double. AE, DC, MC, V.
The Dunrovin Motel is on a quiet street that is very central to the town. Peter and Jenny Webb offer one- and two-bedroom units, with twin and double beds, sleeping two to eight. All have complete kitchen and radio. A children's play area and a guest laundry are on the premises, and cooked or continental breakfasts are available for an additional charge.

LAKE TERRACE MOTEL, 90 Lake Terrace, Taupo. Tel. 07/378-7842. Fax 07/378-8335. 18 units (all with bath). TV TEL
$ Rates: NZ$60 ($34) single; NZ$70 ($40) double. AE, DC, MC, V.
Located within easy walking distance of downtown, this motel has units that look and feel like cabins; those upstairs feature lake views and balconies, while the ones downstairs have patios with plants, picnic tables, and umbrellas. All have complete kitchen, as well as tea and coffee facilities. The grounds overflow with lush plants. Two-bedroom units accommodate up to six people.

SUNCOURT MOTOR HOTEL, Northcroft St. (P.O. Box 837), Taupo. Tel. 07/378-8265. Fax 07/378-0809. 48 rms (all with bath). MINIBAR TV TEL
$ Rates: NZ$78 ($46) single; NZ$83 ($47) double; NZ$93 ($53) family unit. Children under 12 stay free in parents' room. AE, DC, MC, V.
You can't miss this large property set back from the road on an expansive lawn. The majority of its rooms are singles and doubles, along with 13 family units for up to seven people. The rooms are large, with radio, refrigerator, and bathtub. There's a restaurant with an excellent buffet lunch for just NZ$15 ($9) and an à la carte dinner, a couple of bar/discos, an inviting outdoor pool lined with deck chairs, a spa pool, children's playground, laundry, and plenty of off-street parking. This is a good place for families, and it's an easy walk into town.

TUI OAKS MOTOR INN, Lake Terrace and Tui St. (P.O. Box 31), Taupo. Tel. 07/378-8305. Fax 07/378-8335. 7 studio units, 11 suites (all with bath). TV TEL
$ Rates: NZ$65 ($37) single; NZ$75 ($43) double; NZ$95–NZ$105 ($54–$60) suite. Rates increase during holidays. AE, DC, MC, V.
Just across from the lakefront, this is a convenient place to stay, since on-premises facilities include a house bar, licensed restaurant with lake view open daily, a swimming pool, spa pool, barbecue, laundry room, and a tour desk. Guest units include some serviced motel suites, some of which have complete kitchens, TVs, and radios (there's one water bed). Top-floor units have high ceilings and skylights.

A BED & BREAKFAST

BRADSHAW'S GUEST HOUSE, 130 Heu Heu St., Taupo. Tel. 07/378-8288. 12 rms (7 with bath). TEL TV
$ Rates (including breakfast): NZ$30 ($17) single without bath, NZ$35 ($20) single

with bath; NZ$50 ($29) double without bath, NZ$55 ($31) double with bath. MC, V.

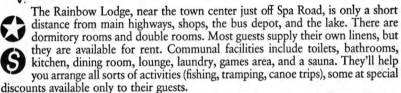

The friendly graciousness of Muriel and Ivan Mapson and their daughter, Helen, who run this B&B has elicited scores of letters from readers, and on one of my research trips for this book I ran into enthusiastic budgeteers singing its praises long before I reached Taupo. Bradshaw's is a homey, white house set on a quiet residential street near the center of town. Rooms are nicely done up, with attractive furnishings and lots of wood paneling. There's a cozy TV lounge (with books for non-tube addicts), a tea and coffee room, laundry, a dining room that faces the lake, and 12 bedrooms, 3 of them singles. A few have private baths (with tub), and three have TV.

A HOSTEL

RAINBOW LODGE BACKPACKERS HOSTEL, 99 Titraupenga St., Taupo. **Tel. 07/378-5754.** 9 rms (none with bath).
$ Rates: NZ$13 ($7) per person for dormitory beds; NZ$30 ($17) double. AE, MC, V.

The Rainbow Lodge, near the town center just off Spa Road, is only a short distance from main highways, shops, the bus depot, and the lake. There are dormitory rooms and double rooms. Most guests supply their own linens, but they are available for rent. Communal facilities include toilets, bathrooms, kitchen, dining room, lounge, laundry, games area, and a sauna. They'll help you arrange all sorts of activities (fishing, tramping, canoe trips), some at special discounts available only to their guests.

CAMPING & CABINS

In a quiet rural setting overlooking the lake, **Acacia Holiday Park,** Acacia Bay Road (P.O. Box 171), Taupo (tel. 07/378-5159), offers tent and caravan sites, cabins, and self-contained tourist flats. On the premises there's a hot spa pool and recreation room with a pool table. Best of all, the friendly owner, Davie Hyland, takes much pleasure in providing visitors with information, maps, and brochures on local attractions. Rates are NZ$8 ($5) per adult, NZ$4 ($2) per child, for tent and caravan sites; NZ$26 ($15) double for cabins, and NZ$46 ($26) double for tourist flats, including GST.

WORTH THE EXTRA MONEY

COTTAGE MEWS, Lake Terrace, Taupo. **Tel. 07/378-3004.** Fax 07/378-3005. 11 units, 5 suites (all with bath). TV TEL
$ Rates (excluding GST): NZ$93 ($53) single or double flat; NZ$87 ($50) single or double suite. AE, DC, MC, V.
The prettiest lodging in town is right beside the lake in a colonial-style motel with gray wood siding and white trim (a bit of New England in the South Pacific). A wheelbarrow filled with bright posies sits at the entrance. Impressive split-level units have a balcony, toilets both upstairs and down, a large spa bath, and striking wood trim throughout. Some units have lake views, private patios, a water bed or a queen-size bed. Breakfast is available at an additional charge. There's a small charge for split-level units, and my favorite is the lakeview accommodation. You couldn't make a lovelier choice. It's located 1 kilometer (½ mile) south of the Napier/Taupo turnoff.

MANUELS BEACH RESORT MOTOR INN, Lake Terrace, Taupo. **Tel. 07/378-5110.** Fax 07/378-5341. 18 rms, 7 suites (all with bath). TV TEL

$ Rates (excluding GST): NZ$113 ($65) single; NZ$146 ($83) double; NZ$175 ($100) suite. AE, DC, MC, V.

For an elegant lakeside stay, try this motor inn that mirrors its owner's love of the Mediterranean. The lobby is welcoming, with a chandelier and giant mirror, and fresh flowers. The standard rooms have either a balcony or patio; all have sofa beds along with a double bed. The suites include a minibar and coffee and tea facilities. A few of the rooms have bathtubs (a favorite feature of mine). The swimming pool is thermally heated, and the grotto spa pool, complete with glowworms, is Disney-inspired. A lounge with overstuffed chairs overlooks the lake, and wrought-iron tables and chairs on the patio at the lakeshore are conducive to sipping the brandy Alexanders or piña coladas available from the bar. The hotel's Edgewater restaurant (see "Where to Eat," below) is one of New Zealand's finest.

THC WAIRAKEI RESORT HOTEL, Private Bag, Taupo. Tel. 07/374-8021.

Fax 07/374-8485. 90 rms, 15 suites (all with bath). MINIBAR TV TEL
$ Rates (excluding GST): NZ$105 ($60) single or double; NZ$195 ($111) suite for one or two. Inquire about special package rates. AE, MC, V.

All guest rooms in this fine hotel have tea and coffee facilities and fridges, and in addition, luxury villa suites are available. Amenities include lighted tennis courts, two heated pools, spa pools, a games room, children's playground, guest laundry, and dry-cleaning service. Golfers will love it here, since there's an 18-hole championship golf course right at hand, and a 9-hole family golf course on the grounds.

The **Graham Room Restaurant** features local fish on its à la carte menu and serves an excellent breakfast buffet every day except Sunday. There's also **Robert's Bistro,** a casual eatery serving lunch and dinner every day.

The hotel is a 15-minute drive from Taupo.

WHERE TO EAT

ECHO CLIFF, 5 Tongariro St. Tel. 378-8539.

Cuisine: INTERNATIONAL. **Reservations:** Recommended.
$ Prices: Appetizers NZ$2–NZ$10 ($1–$6); main courses NZ$12–NZ$20 ($7–$11). AE, DC, MC, V.
Open: Dinner Wed–Mon 5:30–9pm.
You'll find good value at Echo Cliff, right at the lake, upstairs over Sullivan's Sports. The menu includes all the New Zealand standards (seafood, lamb, veal, chicken, beef, etc.), plus Dutch Indonesian and continental dishes. Fully licensed.

THE HOMESTEAD, Historic Huka Village, Huka Falls Rd. Tel. 378-5326.

Cuisine: SNACKS/LIGHT LUNCH/NEW ZEALAND. **Reservations:** Recommended for dinner.
$ Prices: Lunch under NZ$12 ($7); dinner NZ$35 ($20). AE, DC, MC, V.
Open: Lunch daily 11:30am–2:30pm; dinner daily 6:30–11pm.

The Homestead is a special place for lunch at the Historic Village (a sightseeing must), 1½ miles from town. You'll love the farmhouse atmosphere, and the lunch menu offers a wealth of homemade breads, scones, soups, salads, cheeses, meats, and desserts. At dinner, New Zealand fish, meats, and vegetables are served. As for quality, need I add to the fact that the Homestead is a winner of the "Taste New Zealand" award?

MARGARITA'S BAR AND RESTAURANT, 63 Heu Heu St. Tel. 378-9909.

Cuisine: MEXICAN. **Reservations:** Recommended.
$ Prices: Average meal NZ$15–NZ$20 ($9–$11). AE, DC, MC, V.
Open: Dinner daily 5pm–1am.

Located above the Real Estate House in the center of town, Margarita's specializes in Mexican and not-so-Mexican food, creative cocktails, inviting atmosphere, and reasonable prices. Fully licensed, with a complete cocktail bar and live music every night.

POTATO PALACE, corner of Lakeside Terrace and Tongariro St. Tel. 378-1139.
Cuisine: POTATOES—WHAT ELSE!
$ Prices: Under NZ$5 ($3). No credit cards.
Open: Thurs–Tues 11am–7pm (daily in summer).

The Potato Palace serves only two items: filled potatoes and ice cream, and the prices are as low as you'll find. Mind you, those potatoes are *big* potatoes, and come with a huge variety of fillings—easily enough food for a light lunch. Best of all, you can eat them right there or take them away. *Note:* They also rent tandem bikes. A neat place.

WORTH THE EXTRA MONEY

EDGEWATER RESTAURANT, in the Manuels Motor Inn, Lake Terrace. Tel. 378-5110.
Cuisine: NEW ZEALAND. **Reservations:** Required.
$ Prices: Average dinner NZ$60 ($34).
Open: Dinner daily 6:30–11pm.

One of the best and most beautifully prepared meals I've had in New Zealand was at this award-winning restaurant. My avocado appetizer with fresh salsa verde and lamb dish with wild mushrooms and wild-rice crêpe were so beautifully presented I barely had the heart to disturb them with my fork. They were deliciously memorable, as was my window-seat view of the lake and the moon rising above it. The dining room is richly decorated in deep green and mauve.

EVENING ENTERTAINMENT Nightlife is low-key at best in Taupo. There are sometimes disco nights at varying venues around town—your best bet is to check with the Visitors Information Centre to see what's happening when you're there. It must be said, however, that if you've been fishing for trout on Lake Taupo all day, or engaging in any of the wonderful outdoor activities in this area, you'll be more than ready for bed by nightfall anyway.

EN ROUTE TO TONGARIRO

The 58-mile drive from Taupo to Tongariro National Park is an easy one—good roads with changing scenery as you follow Highway 1 along the eastern shore of Lake Taupo through small towns and fishing settlements, around charming bays, always with that vast lake on your right. Look for **Motutaiko Island** (the only one in the lake) as you approach Hatepe. As you near the southern end of the lake, you'll begin to catch glimpses of volcanic cones, which are at the heart of the park. Highway 47 cuts off from Highway 1 to lead you through plateaulike tussocklands across to Highway 48 and the entrance to park headquarters and the elegant Château. It's clearly signposted, and as you leave Lake Taupo behind, the volcanic nature of this terrain begins to dominate the landscape. By the time you reach the Château, you've entered another world from that of the lakeside you've just left.

READERS RECOMMEND: DRIVING

"We felt that the drive up to Turoa ski field on Mount Ruapehu was a prettier drive than the one to the Château and you got much more the feeling of being on a volcano. There are several waterfalls to stop off and walk to."—J. and P. Conrad, San Jose, Calif.

READERS RECOMMEND: SHOPPING

"I highly recommend the Sporting Life Sport Shop, in Turangi at no. 70 Turangi Mall, for accurate, very friendly, and reliable service. The selection of fishing supplies to rent and for sale is excellent, and what the owner, Graham, doesn't know, is not worth knowing!"—S. Martin, Portland, Ore.

WHERE TO STAY & EAT EN ROUTE

BRIDGE FISHING LODGE MOTOR INN, State Hwy. 1 (P.O. Box 42), Turangi. Tel. 07/386-8804. Fax 07/386-8803. 34 rms, 2 suites (all with bath). MINIBAR TV TEL

$ Rates (excluding GST): NZ$85 ($49) single or double; NZ$100 ($57) family suite. Best Western discounts available. AE, DC, MC, V.

The Bridge Fishing Lodge, at the southern end of Lake Taupo, has rooms for single or double occupancy, seven with fully equipped kitchens. Rooms have tea and coffee facilities, fridges, videos, radios, and heaters. There's a licensed restaurant, bar, guest lounge, sauna, barbecue, laundry, and a tour desk at this Motor Lodges member. They'll also rent you fishing tackle and waders if the fish in the lake and river prove too great a temptation. Family units sleep six.

SETTLERS MOTEL, State Hwy. 1 and Arahori St. (P.O. Box 30), Turangi. Tel. 07/386-7745. Fax 07/386-6354. 8 units (all with bath). TV TEL

$ Rates (excluding GST): NZ$62 ($35) studio for one; NZ$75 ($43) studio for two; NZ$81 ($46) 2-bedroom apt for two. AE, MC, V.

At the southern end of Lake Taupo, the Settlers offers eight serviced kitchen units with radios and heaters, and there's a guest laundry. They can provide fishing guides, and they've even included fish-cleaning facilities so you can catch your dinner, then cook it up in your unit. Licensed restaurants and shops are a short walk away. There are also two-bedroom units, and one with a water bed.

2. TONGARIRO NATIONAL PARK

58 miles SW of Taupo, 109 miles SW of Rotorua, 89 miles NE of Wanganui

GETTING THERE **By Train** The Silver Fern express train stops at National Park.

By Bus The nearest bus service is to Taupo (see above).

By Car Highways 1, 4, 47 and 48 reach the national park.

ESSENTIALS The **area code** at the time of writing is 0812. Remember: The New Zealand Number Update is in the process of changing all telephone numbers to 7 digits. Those numbers in this chapter that have not been changed at press time are marked with an asterisk, and you should call the **Helpline 0155** for the new number. For directory assistance within the country (when you don't know the number), call **018.**

Information The THC Château Tongariro and the National Park Headquarters are in the little village of **Whakapapa** at the end of Highway 48. The Château is the center of visitor activities such as booking ski and tour trips, dining, and drinking; the Visitors Centre of the park headquarters is the center of information and assistance in planning tramps through the park. They keep up-to-date weather data, and provide detailed maps, guiding services, camping permission, and hunting permits. The popular ski fields (used by as many as 6,000 visitors per day during season) are 4½ miles above the village.

It's a dramatic landscape, dominated by the three active volcanoes that rise with stark beauty from heathlike plains. Drama-loving Maoris considered the volcanoes sacred (*tapu*) and found mythical explanations for their origins. They even buried their chiefs in caves along the slopes.

Ruapehu, with its 9,175-foot snowcapped summit, is the highest mountain on the North Island and provides its principal skiing facilities while holding in its basin the simmering, ice-ringed Crater Lake. Its most recent eruption was in 1971. **Ngauruhoe,** rising 7,515 feet, smolders constantly and from time to time sends showers of ash and lava spilling from its crater (the last in 1954) to alter its shape once again. **Tongariro,** lowest of the three (6,458 ft.), is also the most northerly and the center of an engaging Maori legend. There were once, so the story goes, many mountains in the North Island's center, all male with the exception of Pihanga, who was wed to Tongariro and was the object of the other mountains' lustful fantasies. According to one version of the legend, Pihanga's heart belonged only to Tongariro, who defeated the other mountains and exiled them from the region. Another version has Pihanga discovered by Tongariro dallying with Taranaki, which resulted in a fierce fight that ended with a swift, hard kick to Taranaki's backside and his hasty retreat to the west coast, where he stands in solitary splendor today as Mount Egmont, an almost perfect replica of Japan's Mount Fuji. You can follow his trail, which became the Wanganui River, and still see the enormous depression under Mount Egmont's Fantham's Peak put there by Tongariro's kick. When mists surround Egmont today, Maoris will tell you he is weeping for his lost love.

For non-legend-believers, there is the nonlegendary fact that the peaks are at the end of a volcanic chain that extends all the way to the islands of Tonga, 1,000 miles away. Their origin is fairly recent, as these things go, dating back only about two million years.

WHAT TO SEE & DO

Skiing is *the* activity during the season, which normally lasts from June 15 to October, with three well-developed fields inside the park. The most popular is **Whakapapa Skifield,** on the northwestern side of Mount Ruapehu just 4½ miles beyond the Château. For **snow and ski information,** call *0658/58-255. The Château can also rent you ski equipment, provide instruction and a current brochure detailing all charges. If you have your own equipment with you, expect to spend about NZ$40 ($25) for lifts and tows for a full day. All facilities operate from 8:30am to 4:30pm unless weather conditions interfere, and there's public transportation via coach to the ski field from the Château, which I heartily recommend that you use, since driving and parking can be a real problem.

In any other season, there are fascinating ✪ **walks** to view more than 500 plant species, the giant rimu trees (some well over 600 years old), and 30 bird species within the park's boundaries. Then there's that hot **Crater Lake** on Mount Ruapehu, the **Ketetahi Hot Springs,** and a pleasant, 20-minute ✪ **Ridge Track.** Ambitious trackers can take a whack at climbing all three volcanoes in 1 day—but believe me, it takes a lot of ambition, with a healthy dose of stamina thrown in! Check with the park headquarters for details on all park possibilities.

WHERE TO STAY

Accommodations are as scarce as the proverbial hen's teeth! If Tongariro National Park is a big stop on your itinerary, you might consider a night or two at the elegant THC Château Tongariro with big-splurge prices. There are also accommodations in our budget range, few though they may be. Need I say that early bookings are absolutely necessary during the skiing season? Actually, it's a good idea to reserve as far in advance as possible in *any* season, with accommodations being so scanty. You might also consider a Turangi base, only a short drive from the park (see "En Route to Tongariro," above).

A MOTEL

BUTTERCUP ALPINE MOTEL, P.O. Box 45, Tongariro National Park. Tel. *0812/22-702.** 4 units, 10 rms (none with bath). TV TEL
$ Rates (including breakfast and dinner): NZ$60 ($34) per person; NZ$40 ($23) children under 13. Babies stay free in their parents' room. MC, V.

Located at the junction of Highways 4 and 47 at National Park township, this friendly place provides a host of planned activities such as white-water rafting, skiing, and hiking expeditions, as well as a nice selection of accommodations. There are eight Red Pool Lodge units sleeping up to four, with private plumbing, tea and coffee facilities, and piped-in music; bathrooms are shared.

The Long Lodge, for singles or couples, has bedrooms with a double bed, and washbasin; again, baths are shared. Both lodges are surrounded by native trees and fern gardens.

The attractive **Butternut Farmhouse Restaurant and Den** has a pot-bellied stove, with musical performances through dinner and sing-alongs around the fire afterward. Hot *Glühwein* is served, and sometimes there are fancy-dress parties. This is a great value, considering rates include two meals.

CAMPING & CABINS

Whakapapa Motor Camp, c/o Department of Conservation, Private Bag, Mount Ruapehu (tel. *0812/22-3897), is down the first right turn after you pass park headquarters. Set on the banks of Whakapapanui Stream, it's surrounded by lush bushland. There are tent and caravan sites (all nicely screened by foliage), four six-berth cabins, and two four-berth cabins. Cabins come with two-tier bunks, table and chairs, and electric heating. On the premises are toilets and showers, electric stoves, a laundry with drying room, and a camp store. Rates: NZ$7 ($4) per adult, NZ$3.50 ($2) for tent sites; NZ$9 ($5) per adult, NZ$4.50 ($3) for caravan sites; and NZ$11 ($6) per person, NZ$33 ($19) minimum, for cabins. Tourist flats are available for NZ$16 ($9) per person, NZ$47 ($27) minimum; and bunkroom accommodation is available from November to the end of June for NZ$12 ($7) per person per night. No credit cards.

Trampers on the mountain slopes can arrange through the park headquarters rangers to use rustic, strategically placed **huts,** which are equipped with bunks and coal stoves, and cost a mere NZ$9 ($5) per person. Tickets are available at the Taupo Visitors Information Centre.

A SKI LODGE

RUAPEHU SKOTEL, c/o Mount Ruapehu Post Office. Tel. *0812/23-719. Fax *0812/23-777. 10 chalets, 14 lodge rms (some with bath). TV TEL
$ Rates: Summer, NZ$46 ($26) single or double without bath, NZ$65 ($37) single or double with bath; NZ$92 ($53) chalet for four. Extra person NZ$7 ($4). Rates higher during ski season. AE, DC, MC, V.

This rustic lodge on the lower slopes of Mount Ruapehu above the Château, offers both self-contained chalets and lodge accommodations. The attractive, paneled, slant-roofed lodge rooms can accommodate two, three, or four; most have hot and cold running water and many have shower and toilet. There's a large, bright guest kitchen with individual food lockers, stoves, and fridge. Also on the premises are a laundry with washers and dryers, a sauna, private spas, a gym, and a large games room. The lounge invites conviviality, and there's a restaurant and bar. Chalets sleep six (four bunks and two single beds); kitchens are completely equipped, and there's a TV. Outside, views of Ngauruhoe's cone are spectacular. All buildings are centrally heated and have piped-in music. This is a lively place, with movies, hikes, fishing, and botany expeditions.

WORTH THE EXTRA MONEY

THC CHATEAU TONGARIRO, Mount Ruapehu, Tongariro National Park. Tel. *0812/23-809. Fax *0812/23-704. 57 rms (all with bath). TV TEL
$ Rates (excluding GST): NZ$213.75 ($122) per person single or double. AE, DC, MC, V.

The Château Tongariro, at the end of Highway 48, is a grand hotel in the manner of years gone by, but with a 1930s deco-style lounge. Rooms and suites are elegant, and there are such additional comforts as a heated pool and sauna. The Château justifies its listing in a budget travel guide on two counts: It's an outstanding hotel, internationally famous; and it's one of the scarce places to stay in this neighborhood!

WHERE TO EAT

THC CHATEAU TONGARIRO, Mount Ruapehu, Tongariro National Park. Tel. *0812/23-809.

You can eat at any price range at the Château. For the truly budget-minded, there's the paneled, no-frills **Cafeteria,** open every day from 8am to 5pm, where you'll find meat pies, sandwiches, salads, and such at low prices. The cozy, publike **Carvery** serves a quite nice NZ$25 ($14) evening meal with a choice of roasts, fish, grills, and salads. For an elegant—and expensive—dinner, it's the high-ceilinged, chandeliered **Ruapehu Room,** from 6:30 to 9pm. The à la carte menu features New Zealand specialties, as well as many exotic dishes, which are prepared or flamed at your table.

The Château can also supply you with **box lunches** for a day on the slopes, and during ski season there are kiosks and snack bars open at the ski fields.

EN ROUTE TO WANGANUI

The 89 miles from Tongariro National Park to Wanganui pass through some of the most scenic countryside in the North Island. Indeed, the 32 miles of winding road between Raetihi and Wanganui pass through what has been labeled the "Valley of a Thousand Hills." These are the **Parapara Hills,** formed from volcanic ash, with shell-rock seams and great walls of "papa" rock (a blue clay), which can, incidentally, be quite slippery when landslides put it across the highway. This entire drive, however, is one to be done at a leisurely pace (with an eye out, especially in winter, for patches of that clay across the road) so as to enjoy the spectacular scenery. Sheep farms line your way, with at least one deer farm visible from the highway. There are numerous rest areas en route, offering delightful panoramic views, and in autumn, silver birches dot the landscape with brilliant golds and oranges.

You'll pass the beautiful **Raukawa Falls,** skirt three small lakes whose waters shade from green into red into black during the course of the year and are held sacred by the Maoris, then cross the Wanganui River over the Dublin Street Bridge to enter Wanganui.

READERS RECOMMEND: DRIVING

"An area that deserves a look is known as Taranaki, the area from Tongariro to New Plymouth, a lovely town with gardens and parks that were the nicest we found on the North Island. The circle drive with three good roads into Mount Egmont are all worth taking. And Mount Egmont itself is superb, just like a volcano cone; it's quite impressive to stand on the beach and look 8,400 feet up the mount. The Whitecliff drive and hike are also super."—J. and P. Conrad, San Jose, Calif.

3. WANGANUI

89 miles SW of Tongariro National Park, 280 miles S of Auckland,
188 miles SW of Rotorua, 138 miles SW of Taupo, 122 miles N of Wellington

GETTING THERE **By Bus** InterCity, Newmans, and Dominion Coachlines provide services between Wanganui and Auckland, Hamilton, and Wellington.

By Car Wanganui can be reached via Highways 3 and 4.

ESSENTIALS **Information** The **Visitors Information Centre** is located at 101 Guyton St. (P.O. Box 637), Wanganui (tel. 06/345-3286; fax 06/345-3355). Pick up a copy of their handy *Wanganui Visitors Guide.* Upholding the city's slogan "Wanganui, the Friendly City," the information center operates a **Host Panel,** a volunteer group of enthusiastic residents, to squire overseas visitors who don't have their own transport around the area. They provide a personal guide who will devote as much time as necessary to seeing that you get to see and do everything there is to see and do in Wanganui. There's never a charge. Your guide will furnish transportation and often steer you to special events you might not have known about otherwise. Every volunteer is knowledgeable about the area, so if you have a special interest (history, archeology, botany), they'll happily take you to spots most likely to appeal to that interest. The information office can also furnish you with useful brochures, book river tours, and provide maps.

Mail The General Post Office is in Ridgeway Street (tel. 345-8349).

Telephone The area code is 06. Remember: The New Zealand Number Update is in the process of changing all telephone numbers to 7 digits. Those numbers in this chapter that have not been changed at press time are marked with an asterisk, and you should call the Helpline 0155 for the new number. For directory assistance within the country (when you don't know the number), call 018.

Wanganui (you'll also see it spelled "Whanganui") was born amid fierce controversy over the way in which Col. William Wakefield, acting for the New Zealand Company in 1840, took title to the land. It seems he came ashore with an assortment of mirrors, blankets, pipes, and other trinkets and piled them on the site of the present-day Moutoa Gardens. With this offering, he "bought" some 40,000 acres of Maori land. The Maoris, however, replaced Wakefield's gifts with 30 pigs and nearly 10 tons of potatoes—their customary "gift for gift"—and had no idea they had transferred title to their lands.

Despite the dispute, settlers began arriving and the town prospered, though constantly caught up in Maori-Pakeha conflicts, some of which were quite violent. It wasn't until 1848 that land problems were laid to rest with the payment of £1,000 for about 80,000 acres clearly defined in a bill of sale from the Maoris, which ended with the words "Now all the land contained within these boundaries . . . we have wept and sighed over, bid farewell to and delivered up forever to the Europeans."

It was the Wanganui River (whose riverbed was carved out by Taranaki in his wild flight from Tongariro's wrath) that made this site such a desirable one for the Europeans. It had long served as an important waterway to the interior, as well as affording an excellent coastal harbor. It was said by the Maoris that the great explorer Kupe sailed the river. Pakehas soon established regular steamer service between the town and Taumarunui, and because of the magnificent scenery along the riverbank, the 3-day journey quickly became an important sightseeing trip for tourists from all over the world. The steamer plied the river until 1934, and it's a pity that fire destroyed the wonderful old hotel and houseboat that provided overnight accommodations to those travelers.

A large portion of the Wanganui River is now part of a national park, with an entrance to its wonderfully wild mix of virgin forest and secondary growth bush at the historic little settlement of Pipiriki. Set right on the river, this was once the terminus for riverboats, and it nestles among wooded hills, with picnic spots and easily accessible bus reserves.

WHAT TO SEE & DO

To put first things first, take a good look at Wanganui and its environs, which will bring everything else you see into perspective—it's the look you get from ✪ **Durie Hill,** at the south end of the Wanganui Bridge at Victoria Avenue. Pick up the souvenir booklet that tells you the history of this place, then go through a 672-foot tunnel to reach a unique elevator, which takes you to the summit, 216 feet up. The round-trip fare is NZ$1 (60¢), and you'll count it money well spent. From the platform at the top, Wanganui is spread before you: The historic river's winding path is clear; to the west stretches the Tasman Sea; and to the north rises Mount Egmont (that unlucky lover, Taranaki). If you're game to walk up 176 steps, the top of the nearby **War Memorial** will give you a view that extends from Mount Ruapehu all the way to the South Island (you'll have to take that on faith—as yet, I haven't summoned up the stamina to make the climb!). Even from the ground, the War Memorial is worth a few minutes of your time. It's constructed of shell rock from the riverbanks, which holds two-million-year-old fossils that prove conclusively Wanganui was once a part of the sea.

There are delightful ✪ **walks** in and around Wanganui. The *Scenic Walks* brochure you can get at the information center guides you around six, which are short and easy and cover most of the things you'll want to visit. Another, the **Atene Skyline Walk,** takes a full day (about 8 hours), but rewards you with stunning views of the area and a "meander" around what was once seabed. Trampers who hanker for a several-days trek through the **Wanganui National Park** should ask for requirements and other details at the Visitors Information Centre.

Children will enjoy the romp, grown-ups the respite, at the **Kowhai Park Playground** on Anzac Parade near the Dublin Street Bridge. The Jaycees of Wanganui built it, and its 4 acres now hold a Tot Town Railway (complete with station, tunnel, and overhead bridge), a huge whale, brontosaurus, clock tower, sea-serpent swings, all sorts of storybook characters, and even a mini-volcano to explore. And speaking of parks, save time for a leisurely stroll through the one at **Virginia Lake** (adjacent to Great North Road and St. John's Hill), whose grounds are a serene haven of trees, flowers, water lilies, ducks, swans, an aviary, and beautiful winter gardens.

The riverside ✪ **Moutoa Gardens** historic reserve is where Maori-Pakeha contact was first made and the first controversial "purchase" of Maori land was transacted. There are memorials to Maori war dead, statues, and the city courthouse there now. It's down at Taupo Quay, off Victoria Quay (beside the huge computer center, a vivid contrast between yesterday and today).

Not quite—but almost—a sightseeing spot is **Victoria Court,** a shopping courtyard off Victoria Avenue near Guyton Street. Interesting crafts and antiques are in the shop, and there's a very good art gallery featuring the works of New Zealand artists. About a mile from the city center, on Tawa Street, **Gonville Cottage Industries** holds a **Craft Market** the first Saturday of each month from March to December, with stalls held by local craftspeople.

OTHER SIGHTS

WANGANUI REGIONAL MUSEUM, Civic Centre, Maria Place. Tel. 345-7443.

You won't want to miss the Wanganui Regional Museum—it's the largest regional museum in the country, and there's a large Maori collection, a gallery showing Maori portraits by Lindauer, a settler's cottage, natural history exhibits, and a 75-foot war canoe built in 1810, which is one of the largest in the country and still has bullets from the Maori wars imbedded in its hull.

Admission: NZ$2 ($1) for adults, NZ60¢ (35¢) for children over 5; free for under 5.

Open: Mon–Fri 10am–4pm, Sat–Sun and public holidays 1–4:30pm. **Closed:** Christmas Day, Good Friday. **Directions:** Walk 1 block east of Victoria Ave. toward the end of Maria Place.

ST. PAUL'S ANGLICAN MEMORIAL CHURCH, in the suburb of Putiki.

St. Paul's was built in 1936 by Maoris and Pakehas working together. The stained-glass Williams Memorial Window features the figure of Christ wearing robes with a Maori-design border, and there is fine carving in the church's interior.

Admission: Free.

Open: Daily 9am–6pm.

PADDLEWHEELER *OTUNUI* AND HOLLY LODGE ESTATE WINERY, Papaiti Rd., Upper Aramoho, Wanganui. Tel. 343-9344.

Plan to spend an hour or two at Holly Lodge Estate Winery. You can drive out Somme Parade to the winery, but the approach by river via the historic paddlewheeler is much more fun. Owners Brian and Erika Schofield will show you around the vineyards and outbuildings where wines are produced, explaining every step of the process as you go. The Wine Shop and Tasting Bar give you a chance to test several of the wines and buy at wholesale prices. Be sure to step into the small craft shop, where most items have been made locally. Another "don't miss" is Geraldo's, a small museum of memorabilia of early Wanganui assembled by Gerald Weekes, a former information officer (and, of course, named for him). The Schofields also run a lovely champagne cruise and smörgåsbord lunch or dinner, as well as a very good jet-boat river trip (see below) from their wharf across the road from the vineyards.

Admission: Paddlewheeler fare NZ$12 ($7) adults, NZ$8 ($5) children under 16, NZ$50 ($29) family ticket; smörgåsbord lunch (must be booked) NZ$12.50 ($7) per person. Champagne lunch or dinner cruise NZ$35 ($20) for dinner, NZ$30 ($17) for lunch.

Open: Daily 9am–6pm. **Directions:** Take The Wine Trip aboard the paddlewheeler *Otunui* from city marina at the foot of Victoria Ave. or drive out Somme Parade.

BUSHY PARK, 15 miles northwest of Wanganui.

Bushy Park was originally the homestead of James Moore, who came to Wanganui in the mid-1860s. The fine old home was occupied by his descendants until 1962, when house and grounds, plus 211 acres of native forest were bequeathed to the Royal Forest and Bird Protection Society. The large wooden homestead stands in spacious lawns and gardens planted with a large variety of native plants, with a backdrop of some 220 acres of native bush. An Interpretation

Centre houses displays devoted to forest ecology, and visitors are free to walk the forest trails and picnic in the extensive grounds.

There is accommodation for 16 in six bedrooms in the homestead for NZ$40 ($23) single, NZ$45 ($26) double, NZ$10 ($6) per additional adult and/or child age 7 to 15. Guests bring their own food and use a well-equipped electric kitchen. There are two caravan power connections and a new bunkhouse for groups of 12 for NZ$10 ($6) each. Write or call: The Manager, Bushy Park, Kai Iwi, R.D. 8, Wanganui (tel. 06/342-9879).

Admission: NZ$3 ($2) adults, NZ$1 (60¢) children.

Open: Daily 10am–5pm. **Directions:** Turn off Hwy. 3 at Kai Iwi and drive 5 miles to the park.

BASON BOTANICAL RESERVE, Rapanui Rd.

The Botanical Reserve's Homestead Garden is a delightful place for a stroll among more than 100 camellias and a wide assortment of shrubs, vines, annuals, bulbs, and perennials. The ultramodern conservatory holds the interesting display center and tropical plant house.

Admission: Free.

Open: Gardens daily 9:30am–dusk; conservatory Mon–Fri 10am–4pm, Sat–Sun and holidays 2–4pm.

RECREATION

Golfers will find the attractive, centrally located **Gonville Domain Municipal Golf Course** on York Street (tel. 344-5808). **Swimmers** can head for one of two family fun centers, both of which have outdoor pools plus learners and toddlers pools, and there are picnic and barbecue areas. The **Gonville Complex** is on Tawa Street (tel. 345-5990); and **Wanganui East Complex,** which also has an exhilarating water slide, is on Tinirau Street (tel. 343-6650).

RIVER TOURS

Exploring the river by ✪ **jet boat** takes top priority for most visitors to Wanganui, and there are several options for doing it. But let me suggest that before you set out, drop by the information center and purchase the excellent Wanganui River map published by the Department of Lands & Survey (be sure you get No. NZMS 258, Edition 2)—it's an excellent investment, showing the river and its banks in detail, with historical notes on each point of interest. I further suggest that you study the map *before* you book your river trip—while there is certainly no *un*interesting part of the river, there may be some portion you'd particularly like to see, and you'll want to be certain you choose a jet boat that will take you there. The information center can also give you current details on which jet-boat tours are operating, departure and return times, and prices in effect at the time of your visit (I try, but you know what can happen to prices!).

There's a lovely ✪ **2-hour jet-boat tour** from the terminal at Holly Lodge Estate Winery (see above), which takes you out to Hipango Park, with a tea, coffee, or sherry stop before returning. Your guide is not only informative but entertaining as well, with interesting anecdotes about the river and the country through which you are passing.

Another excellent way to explore the river is with **Rivercity Tours** (tel. 06/347-2529; fax 06/345-3355). The company offers 1-day **boat trips** on the river, as well as 1- to 5-day **canoe adventures,** suitable for people of all ages and experience. As either a substitute for or supplement to the jet-boat tours, their ✪ **minibus road tours** are highly recommended. Best of all, friendly Don Adams and his staff will design a tailor-made tour to meet your special interests. Call for schedules and prices.

READERS RECOMMEND: DRIVING

"If you've got the time, the drive from Wanganui up the Wanganui River to Pipiriki over to Raetiki and back down to Wanganui is breathtaking, with deep gorges, interesting Maori villages, oyster shells imbedded in limestone, but about 36 miles of road that was probably the worst we were on." —J. and P. Conrad, San Jose, Calif. [*Author's note:* Bad roads, but fantastic drive!]

READERS RECOMMEND: SHOPPING

"We arranged a private tour of Woolen Mill Ltd. on Kelvin Street, and we bought two 'rally rugs' (like stadium blankets). We also went to the Sovereign Woodware, 79 Tawa St. (tel. 344-2558), where we bought three beautiful inlaid wooden pieces; they were seconds, but the flaws were so slight they didn't detract from their beauty at all. The savings were great." —C. Cluff, Tucson, Ariz.

WHERE TO STAY

That famed Wanganui hospitality extends to virtually every owner or manager of accommodations I have met, and you can be sure of a friendly reception no matter where you end up staying. There are good digs both in town and in the Castlecliff seaside suburb.

Unless otherwise noted, GST is included in the rates listed below.

A LICENSED HOTEL

HURLEY'S GRAND HOTEL, corner of Guyton and St. Hill Sts. (P.O. Box 364), Wanganui. Tel. 06/345-0955. Fax 06/345-0953. 60 rms (all with bath). TV TEL

$ Rates (excluding GST): NZ$50–NZ$150 ($29–$86) per person single or double; add NZ$10 ($6) per person in 2-bedroom suite. AE, DC, MC, V.

You should know right up front that what follows is an unabashedly subjective, totally in-love-with report from yours truly of one of those great old hotels, which has managed to survive with all the spirit and character of the "grand" hotels of yesteryear. Hurley's was owned and operated by Tim Hurley's father for many years before Tim took over; guests still receive all the care and attention of friends who have come for a family visit. Modernization has been limited strictly to facilities and furnishings, with such lovely holdovers from its beginnings as dark-wood paneling and fireplaces in the spacious public rooms, oil paintings in gold-leafed frames, the marvelous old carved-wood staircase, and a bar crammed full of excellent carvings by local Maoris. The furniture is modern (huge, comfortable chairs grouped around low tables in the lounge), yet the decor (upholstering, draperies, etc.) retains a period look in keeping with Hurley's origins.

The guest rooms range in size from those accommodating just one to those sleeping up to five comfortably. Each is individually decorated, a nice departure from the standardized look of most present-day hotel rooms. A two-family suite features two bedrooms, one on each side of the central lounge, and there is one luxurious suite furnished entirely with antiques. In addition to the Strand Bar (a great local favorite), there's a beautiful restaurant.

MOTEL FLATS

ACACIA PARK MOTEL, 140 Anzac Parade, Wanganui East. Tel. 06/343-9093. 12 units (all with bath). TV TEL

$ Rates (excluding GST): NZ$57 ($32) single; NZ$67–NZ$73 ($38–$41) double. AE, DC, MC, V.

One of Wanganui's prettiest motels, the Acacia is set in 2 acres of parkland overlooking the river, with units spread among magnificent old trees. The attractive brown-wood units have radio, electric blanket, and electric heating. Eight are fully self-contained, sleeping four to six, with shower, toilet, fridge, electric range, and full kitchen. Five serviced units sleep up to three and have a fridge, tea and coffee facilities, toaster, and electric fry pan. There's a guest laundry with dryer and drying room, a spa pool, games room with a pool table, children's play area, and a trampoline. The more expensive units have a kitchen. The Acacia is directly across the road from the Wanganui River Jet Boat Tours and paddleboat jetty, 1.5 kilometers (1 mile) from the center of town.

AVRO MOTEL, 36 Alma Rd., Wanganui. Tel. 06/345-5279 or 345-8462. Fax 06/345-2104. 18 units (all with bath). TV TEL
$ Rates: NZ$60 ($34) single; NZ$70 ($40) double; NZ$20 ($11) caravan for two. Weekly rates available in winter. AE, DC, MC, V.
There's much to choose from at the Avro Motel. The gardenlike grounds hold bed-sitters and one-, two-, and three-bedroom units, all with wide windows overlooking the lawns. There's an outdoor swimming pool, two spa pools, a children's play area, and a laundry. Alison and Graham Shaw are the hosts at this nice motel, located about 1 mile from the town center. There's a licensed restaurant just 100 yards from the motel, and a nine-hole golf course nearby.
Incidentally, the Avro has marvelous caravan facilities: 14 hookups, each with a small cabin enclosing a shower, toilet, and dressing room. Caravan guests may also use the laundry.

GATEWAY MOTOR LODGE, corner of Southern Motorway and Heads Rd. (P.O. Box 970), Wanganui. Tel. 06/345-8164. Fax 06/345-4144. 9 units, 2 family units (all with bath). TV TEL
$ Rates (excluding GST): Serviced unit NZ$60 ($34) single, NZ$72 ($41) double; family unit NZ$81 ($46) double. Extra person NZ$12 ($7). Best Western discounts available. AE, DC, MC, V.
This pretty Best Western motel about ½ mile from the center of town, has attractive units with vaulted, beamed ceilings. Serviced units have satellite radio, and tea- and coffee-making facilities. Two-bedroom family units add a full kitchen.

A BED & BREAKFAST

RIVERSIDE INN, 2 Plymouth St. (P.O. Box 4224), Wanganui. Tel. 06/347-2529. 10 rms (1 with shower and toilet), 5 backpacker beds. TV TEL
$ Rates (including continental breakfast): NZ$36 ($21) single; NZ$46 ($28) double; NZ$60 ($34) double with private facilities; NZ$14 ($8) per person bunk. No credit cards.
It is seldom that I run across an inn in the old-fashioned sense of the word, but the Riverside fits that category admirably. Set back from the street in a flower garden, the rambling wooden house, which dates from the early 1900s, has been lovingly brought up-to-date through renovation, with due respect for its age and character. The accommodations are decorated with lace curtains, fringed lampshades, and potted plants. The parlor is furnished in wicker and cane, and there is a TV lounge and breakfast room with tea and coffee facilities. In summer, owners Maree and Don Adams serve tea or barbecues in the garden. Don also runs Rivercity Tours and is a whiz at helping you find just the right activity, be it sightseeing, hiking, or canoeing for 1 to 5 days. Cooked breakfast and dinner are available for an extra charge.

THE Y

YWCA, 232 Wicksteed St., Wanganui. Tel. *064/57-480. 8 rms (none with bath). TV TEL
$ Rates: NZ$12 ($7) per person with own sleeping bag; NZ$15 ($9) per person without sleeping bag. No credit cards.
This big old gracious house right in the center of town parallel to Victoria Avenue serves as Wanganui's YMCA. There are only a few rooms available, with one bed per room in all but one, which sleeps three, and it's necessary to write or call as far in advance as possible. Rooms are simple, but homey and comfortable. Those on the top story have marvelous views. There is a guest kitchen, laundry, and TV lounge. There's no age limit.

CABINS & CAMPING

Four miles east of town, on the city side of the river, the **Aramoho Honday Park** (write c/o Camp Manager), 460 Somme Parade, Wanganui (tel. 06/343-8402), has spacious, shady grounds. There are bunk cabins, each with four bunks; graded cabins that sleep two to six people, with hot and cold running water, small electric stoves, cooking utensils, and heaters; and tourist flats and chalets that sleep up to seven people, with complete kitchen, china, cutlery, pots, toaster, electric jug, and private toilet and shower. One chalet sleeps nine and is equipped for paraplegics. You can rent linen, blankets, and irons. The communal kitchen has gas stoves and fridge, the laundry includes dryers and an ironing board, and toilets and showers are stainless steel and Formica. Very near the river is a family barbecue, and there's a 7-day grocery store just across the road. Tent and caravan sites are also available in tree-shaded spots. Rates run NZ$8 ($5) per person for tent sites, NZ$10 ($6) single for bunks, NZ$30 ($17) double for cabins, and NZ$49 ($28) double for chalets. Rates all include GST.

See also the caravan and camping facilities at the Avro Motel (see "Motel Flats," above).

READERS RECOMMEND

Jill and Gerald Hare, Te Rama, Nukumaru Rd., Waitotara. Tel. 06/342-3837. "We loved staying with Jill and Gerald Hare. They're a charming young couple who seem to enjoy meeting people from other countries, and they made us feel right at home. Their sheep and beef farm is about 30 kilometers (18 miles, about 20 minutes' driving time) from Wanganui, and there's a lovely, casual, family feeling to their place. They can accommodate four adults or two adults and two children (no objection to children here)."—L. Cowley, Surrey, B.C., Canada [Author's note: Guests have their own bathroom and laundry privileges and are made to feel a part of the family, fitting right into whatever is happening on the farm. The rate of NZ$50 ($29) per person includes dinner, bed, and breakfast.]

WHERE TO EAT

Note: There's an excellent deli and bottle store next door to the Garden Bistro, the **Riverside Cellars,** with all sorts of cheeses, cold cuts, salads, frozen meals, and other deli items for eating in your motel flat.

THE BIRD CAGE RESTAURANT, in Hurley's Grand Hotel, Guyton and St. Hill Sts. Tel. 345-0955.

Cuisine: TRADITIONAL. **Reservations:** Recommended, especially on weekends.
$ Prices: Complete dinner NZ$12–NZ$20 ($7–$11). AE, DC, MC, V.
Open: Dinner daily 6–9:30pm.

✪ The in-town Bird Cage Restaurant can only be described as elegant, with lovely old chandeliers, flocked wallpaper, and a beautiful embossed ceiling, which will draw your eyes upward throughout any meal. Breakfast, lunch, and dinner are all served, but it's dinner that deserves special mention. Both the menu and service match the elegance of the room, yet there's not the slightest hint of stuffiness (which so often afflicts elegant restaurants). Dishes such as beef, fish, and a variety of roasts are reasonably priced on the à la carte menu. An excellent wine list complements your choice of entrée. Fully licensed.

CAMERON HOUSE, 281 Wicksteed St. Tel. 345-2690.
   Cuisine: NEW ZEALAND. **Reservations:** Recommended.
$ **Prices:** Lunch NZ$15–NZ$20 ($9–$11); dinner NZ$30–NZ$60 ($17–$34) à la carte, NZ$30 ($17) fixed-price. AE, DC, MC, V.
   Open: Lunch Tues–Fri noon–3pm; dinner Tues–Sat 6:30–10pm.

This lovely, award-winning restaurant is set in a 1911 Victorian villa surrounded by gardens. The house retains its original character, with kauri furniture. Favorites among its specialties are noisette of venison, lamb rump, and filet of salmon. Licensed. Cameron House is located in town.

LIFFITON CASTLE, 26 Liffiton St. Tel. 345-7864.
   Cuisine: SEAFOOD/NEW ZEALAND. **Reservations:** Recommended, especially on weekends.
$ **Prices:** Full dinner NZ$20–NZ$35 ($11–$20). AE, DC, MC, V.
   Open: Dinner Mon–Sat 6–10pm.

✪ I'd list this under the "Worth the Extra Money" heading, except that prices aren't really that astronomical—so let's just call it a "Big Treat." This is a century-old house, located in town, which over the last 5 years has been renovated with loving care spiced up with a generous dollop of humor. You enter over a moat into a bar whose centerpiece is the bar itself, a renovated theater box from the old Majestic Theatre—notice the three jesters behind the bar (no, not the bartenders!), also from the Majestic. There are pressed-tin ceilings from the Wangani Girls College; a dance floor from the Boys Technical College; a handsome, hand-carved 17th-century mantel; arched windows from a local church; an antique English sideboard; and an Armoury Room. All that (plus a good bit more) creates an interesting, warm, inviting—and fun—atmosphere. And there's music for dancing most evenings.

The food? Superb! Steaks are a specialty, all of superior grades and beautifully cooked. Seafood, chicken, venison, and roast beef are also on the menu, and there's a good wine list, reasonably priced. The locals love this place!

SHANGRI-LA, St. John's Hill. Tel. 345-3654.
   Cuisine: DEVONSHIRE TEA/CONTINENTAL/NEW ZEALAND. **Reservations:** Recommended.
$ **Prices:** Devonshire teas NZ$3.50 ($2); sandwiches and light lunches NZ$2–NZ$4 ($1–$2); full lunch appetizers NZ$5 ($3); full lunch main courses NZ$7–NZ$11 ($4–$6). No credit cards.
   Open: Lunch daily 11:30am–2pm; Devonshire teas 9am–5pm.

✪ In a lovely in-town setting—with a window wall overlooking Virginia Lake and the Winter Gardens—the Shangri-La is very much a family-run restaurant. Maurice Vige, the French owner-chef, took his training in Paris, his wife Frances is English-trained, and daughters Annette and Nicole act as hostesses.
⑤ Meals here are home-cooked, very nearly gourmet, and easy on the budget. Maurice is quite meticulous in the preparation of all the food appearing on his tables. As a result, everything from European specialties to basic Kiwi dishes to homemade pies to burgers and fries is culinary perfection. The morning and afternoon Devonshire teas are a real treat. BYO.

THE STRAND, in Hurley's Grand Hotel, Guyton and St. Hill Sts. Tel. 345-0955.
   Cuisine: BISTRO MEALS. **Reservations:** Not required.
$ **Prices:** NZ$6–NZ$15 ($3–$9). AE, DC, MC, V.
   Open: Lunch Mon–Sat 11:30am–2pm; dinner Mon–Sat 5:30–8pm.

Hurley's merits a rave in the food department as well as for its superb accommodations (see "Where to Stay," above). No matter what your price or appetite range, that grand old hotel in the town center comes up with just the right place to eat. For inexpensive hot meals or bar snacks, there's The Strand, a bistro-bar combining the same rich dark woods as other hotel public rooms with a friendly, relaxed pub atmosphere. The same menu is served for lunch and dinner, and features steaks, fish, chicken, and roasts. Fully licensed.

TOP-O-TOWN COFFEE SHOP, 198 Victoria Ave. Tel. 345-7615.
   Cuisine: MORNING & AFTERNOON TEA/LIGHT MEALS. **Reservations:** Not required.
$ **Prices:** NZ$3–NZ$9 ($2–$5). No credit cards.
   Open: Mon–Fri 8am–4pm, Sat 9am–late afternoon, Sun noon–2pm.

My favorite small, inexpensive eatery in the center of Wanganui is a cozy place with friendly people behind the self-service counter. Everything served is fresh and homemade, and the menu includes morning and afternoon teas and light meals. There are savouries, meat pies, bacon and eggs, steak, salad and chips, ham steak, fish, sandwiches, pies, and some of the best homemade cakes and pastries you're likely to find anywhere.

AN EXCURSION FROM WANGANUI

Directly northwest of Wanganui (via Highway 3) lies the province of **Taranaki,** an agricultural and dairy region that has also been called the "energy province" of New Zealand because of its major offshore gas field and those at Kapuni and Stratford, which have spawned a number of petrochemical plants in the region. It is also home to **Egmont National Park.** Although Taranaki is a rather compact area, my recommendation is to plan an overnight in order to appreciate fully its many attractions.

The province has a plethora of scenic splendors and interesting sights to occupy your stay. Mount Egmont is exceptionally accessible, and there are good beaches (famous for surfing), walkways, beautifully kept gardens and parks, interesting artists and craftspeople, farms and industries, rivers and lakes for fishing and water sports, heritage trails, and excellent museums.

The very *first* order of business on your excursion should be a visit to at least one of the three **Visitors Information Centres:** 81 Liardet St., **New Plymouth** (tel. *067/86-086); Miranda Street, **Stratford** (tel. *0663/6708); and High Street, **Hawera** (tel. *062/88-599). Any one of them can furnish brochures and specific Taranaki information, and all will be extremely helpful in planning an itinerary that will make the most of your stay.

The Taranaki landscape is dominated by the conically shaped ✪ **Mount Taranaki/Egmont,** a volcano that has been dormant for over 400 years. This is one of the few mountains you can drive completely around, and there are over 300 kilometers (180 miles) of walking tracks within the national park, ranging from 10 minutes to 5 days, with a selection for both inexperienced and veteran walkers. There are inexpensive **huts** for walkers within the park, maintained by the Department of Conservation (details from the Visitors Information Centres).

New Plymouth is Taranaki's leading city, with numerous near-perfect swimming and surfing **beaches** in close proximity, and well known for its beautiful **parks,** excellent **Govett-Brewster Art Gallery,** and the dazzling array of rhododendrons and azaleas at ✪ **Puketi Rhododendron Trust,** on Carrington Road, a 30-

minute drive south of the city. The Visitors Information Centre can furnish directions
and opening hours for these and many other local attractions. Some 7 kilometers (4
miles) south of New Plymouth, the **Tupare Garden,** 487 Mangorei Rd., has 3.6
hectares (9 acres) of English-style gardens that are some of the finest in the country.
The most spectacular season in the gardens is September to November, and if you
arrive here in late October to early November, a highlight of your visit will be the
annual **Rhododendron Festival.**

In Hawera, the ✪ **Tawhiti Museum,** 47 Ohangai Rd. (tel. *062/86-837), is run
by local potter Nigel Ogle and his wife, Teresa. Housed in an old dairy factory, this
unique museum includes a model of a Maori bush village, a 1/12-scale war canoe, and
many exhibits tracing both Maori and Pakeha histories in this region. Many have
lifelike animated figures illustrating everyday activities over the years.

Well, those are just a few of the highlights—space doesn't permit more details on
this fascinating province. But I reiterate—do plan at least one overnight here if at all
possible.

WHERE TO STAY

Taranaki is loaded with exceptional accommodation possibilities, and I can only offer
you a sampling. ✪ **Mountain House Motor Lodge,** Pembroke Road, R.D. 21,
Stratford (tel. and fax *0663/6100), is just off Highway 3 and only 2 kilometers (1
mile) from the Plateau car park and lookout tower in the national park that is the
highest in Taranaki and starting point of park tramping, skiing, and climbs. The lodge
offers charming and comfortable guest rooms and facilities (including one of
Taranaki's best licensed restaurants) at about NZ$90 ($51) double.

Dawson Falls Tourist Lodge, Manaia Road, R.D. 29, Stratford (tel. *0663/
5457), is a charming, award-winning Swiss alpine lodge that has also won awards for
its excellent restaurant. It's only 45 minutes from New Plymouth and 20 minutes
outside Stratford via a scenic sealed road, and rates start at about NZ$34 ($19) per
person.

✪ ⑤ **Patuha Farm Lodge,** Upper Pitone Road, R.D. 4, New Plymouth (tel.
*067/24469), is run by the Henderson family, who put the emphasis on country
hospitality. Comfortable guest rooms are nicely appointed, and they furnish country-
style breakfasts, lunches, and three-course home-cooked dinners. They are fully
licensed, with good New Zealand wines at moderate prices. Rates are about NZ$66
($38) per person.

Any of the Visitors Information Centres can also furnish local **bed-and-
breakfast, camping,** and **hostel** accommodation details.

EN ROUTE TO WELLINGTON

Following Highway 3 south from Wanganui until it joins Highway 1, you're in for an
easy 3-hour, 122-mile drive along excellent roads: pastoral scenes of grazing sheep and
cultivated fields at first, smashing sea views later, then a four-lane expressway leading
into the beautiful harbor and splendid hills of wonderful, windy Wellington.

READERS RECOMMEND: SIGHTSEEING

*"If you go from Wanganui to Wellington via Palmerston North over Route 2, about 28
kilometers (17 miles) north of Masterton is the Mount Bruce National Wildlife Centre, well
worth a stop. The center is a part of New Zealand's conservation efforts to make certain the
nation's wildlife heritage is passed on to future generations, and there are numerous rare and
endangered species of birds and lizards, many of which can be seen nowhere else in captivity.
It's an enjoyable and educational stop, and you should allow 1 or 2 hours."*—J. Long, Media,
Pa. [*Author's note:* Other readers ditto this. See Section 10, Chapter 7.]

WELLINGTON

"**W**onderful, windy Wellington" it is called—with derision by Kiwis who don't live here, with affection by those who do. Well, there's no denying that it *is* windy: 60-m.p.h. winds sweep through what is the only substantial gap in New Zealand's mountain chain on an average of 40 days each year. Winds notwithstanding, however, Wellington is easily New Zealand's cultural center and one of its most beautiful cities. Indeed, its magnificent harbor rivals any in the world. Your first view of that harbor, with the city curved around its western and southwestern shoreline and surrounding hills abloom with what appear from a distance to be tiny dollhouses spilling down their sides, is likely to make you catch your breath, even if that view should happen to be in the rain (which is a distinct possibility!). On a fine day, there are few city views anywhere to equal it.

This gorgeous place was discovered in A.D. 950 by Kupe, the great Polynesian explorer, and by the time Captain Cook stopped by (but didn't land) in 1773, the harbor was lined with Maori settlements. When New Zealand Company representative Col. William Wakefield's good ship *Tory* arrived on the scene in September 1839, warring between the Maori tribes had become so fierce, and the local tribes were so fearful of their more powerful enemies, that (after a bit of negotiating back and forth, and a few of the usual misunderstandings about land transfers, etc.), they accepted the Pakeha as the lesser of two evils.

By January 1840 settlers began coming in goodly numbers, and after a rather rowdy beginning (when, according to contemporary reports, meetings were held to try to determine how the citizenry could protect themselves from the lawless police force!), the town began a growth that has never really stopped. A tug-of-war with Auckland finally resulted in Wellington's being named the colony's capital on the basis of its central location and the belief that the "middle island" (that's the South Island's claim to being the "mainland," one you'll hear often after crossing Cook Strait) might well pull out and establish a separate colony altogether if it were not afforded better access to the capital than faraway Auckland provided.

Wellington today, while peopled mainly by civil servants, diplomats, and corporate home-office staffs, maintains a conservative—but far from stuffy—air. There is perhaps more sheer diversity here than in any of New Zealand's other cities: Narrow streets and Edwardian buildings nudge modern edifices of concrete and glass; massive office buildings embrace colonial-style restaurants; fashionable boutiques are housed in pseudocolonial-style complexes while craft shops hold sway in avant-garde structures; and the after-dark scene is definitely Kiwiland's liveliest. The last few years, in fact, have seen even more diversity with the legislative requirement that all major buildings must be brought up to earthquake-resistant standards. Those requirements have resulted in massive demolition of older buildings and the erection of even more

WHAT'S SPECIAL ABOUT WELLINGTON

Scenic Splendors

☐ The harbor—one of the world's most sheltered and easily one of the most beautiful.

☐ The gorgeous views from Mount Victoria: the harbor sparkling in daylight, city lights twinkling around its perimeter after dark.

☐ The Botanic Gardens, especially the Norwood Rose Gardens and Begonia House.

Museums

☐ The National Art Gallery and National Museum, with superb collections of international and New Zealand art and South Pacific artifacts.

☐ The Maritime Museum, at Queen's Wharf, to put you in touch with Wellington's long-standing connection with the sea.

Historic Places

☐ Antrim House, on Boulcott Street, with its early–New Zealand interior and exhibits dedicated to the country's historical buildings.

☐ Old Saint Paul's Church, in Mulgrave Street, a lovely old church that provides a peaceful interlude for busy sightseers.

Cultural Events

☐ Performances by the National Symphony Orchestra, National Ballet, and National Opera Company.

---

modern high-rise structures. Indeed, it is estimated that within the next few years as many as half the office and commercial spaces in the city center will be replaced. The times they are truly a-changing in wonderful, windy Wellington!

What is *not* likely to change—and it's important to us as visitors—is the ebb and flow of the city's population as government workers depart on weekends for visits home, then flood back into town on Monday. That means an abundance of accommodations are available over weekends, very few during the week (more about that later under the "Where to Stay" heading, below).

In short, Wellington has from the first been a cosmopolitan city, and it's growing more so all the time. It is also your port of embarkation for the South Island's wonders—but pray don't embark until you've explored this hub around which New Zealand's government revolves. And from a practical point of view, plan your explorations for a weekend when rooms are easier to come by and special rates are offered to fill rooms vacated by that disappearing weekday population.

1. ORIENTATION

ARRIVING By Plane The **Wellington Airport** (tel. 488-9900) is 6 miles south of the city center and is served by the following international airlines: **Air New Zealand** (tel. 488-9900); **Australian Airlines** (tel. 472-5190); **British Airways** (tel. 472-7327); **British Caledonian** (tel. 488-9845); **Lufthansa** (tel. *09/31-529); **Qantas Airways** (tel. 473-8378); **Singapore Airlines** (tel. 473-9749); **United Airlines** (tel. 472-6897); and **UTA French Airlines** (tel. 472-2466). Leading domestic airlines are **Air New Zealand** (tel. 488-9900); **Air Nelson** (tel. 488-2770); **Mount Cook Airlines** (tel. 800/800-737); and several smaller airlines.

The **Wellington Airport Visitors Information Centre** (tel. 488-6451), in the Domestic Terminal, is staffed Monday through Friday from 7:30am to 7pm, Saturday from 8am to 4pm, and on Sunday from 9am to 7pm. There's an **Information Desk** in the International Terminal with the same hours except on Sunday, when it is staffed from 8:30am to 4:30pm.

There's a good, medium-priced **cafeteria** at the airport, serving light meals and snacks, open from 6am to 9pm every day. Also, there are **bars, car-rental desks, bookshops,** and **gift shops** in both terminals, a **duty-free shop** in the International Terminal, and a **nursery** in the Domestic Terminal. The **bank** is open normal hours, as well as 1 hour before any overseas departure and for 1 hour after each overseas arrival. There are ample luggage carts provided at no charge.

Vickers Coachlines (tel. 487-2018) runs a coach service to and from the airport every 20 minutes on weekdays, 30 minutes on weekends, from 6am to 9:20pm. Coaches depart from Bunny Street (close to the railway station), and there are several pickup points in the city. Airport bus stops have white signs with a red, white, and blue "V"; fares are NZ$6 ($3) for adults, NZ$3 ($2) for children. **Taxi** fare between the city center and the airport will run approximately NZ$15 ($9) on weekdays, a little more on weekends.

By Train & Bus   Wellington **Railway Station** is on Waterloo Quay, and **long-distance buses** (except Newmans) depart that station (tel. 472-5409 for long-distance bus and rail information). **Newmans** buses arrive and depart from 260 Taranaki St.

By Car   Wellington is reached via Highways 1 and 2. It's 122 miles from Wanganui; 285 miles from Rotorua; 407 miles from Auckland.

By Ferry   For information on the **Inter-Island Wellington/Picton Ferry,** call 498-3999.

TOURIST INFORMATION   The **Wellington City Information Centre,** Civic Administration Building, Mercer Street (tel. 04/801-4000), is open daily from 9am to 5pm. Ask for the monthly *What's On,* as well as *Wellington Great Time Guide* and other brochures, which are plentiful. The free *Capital Times,* also available from the Visitors Information Centre and leading hotels, is published weekly, with information on current activities. The center also has information on the entire country, not just Wellington.

CITY LAYOUT   The main point of reference in the city is, of course, the harbor, with its exciting waterfront **Lambton Harbour Project. Willis Street** is the main street; for **shopping,** try Lambton Quay, Manners Street, Cuba Street, and Courtenay Place. The best lookout for a panoramic view of the city is 648-foot **Mount Victoria** in the southern end of the city (hop the no. 20 bus for the 15-minute ride); the easiest lookout to reach is **Kelburn,** with its cable car from Lambton Quay.

2. GETTING AROUND

BY BUS & TRAM   There is good city bus service, and the main city bus terminal (tel. 485-9955 for route information) is at the corner of Bunny and Featherston Streets. Eastbourne buses arrive and depart at the railway station (tel. 462-8154 for schedules). Fares are based on distance traveled, and you can purchase 10-trip concession tickets.

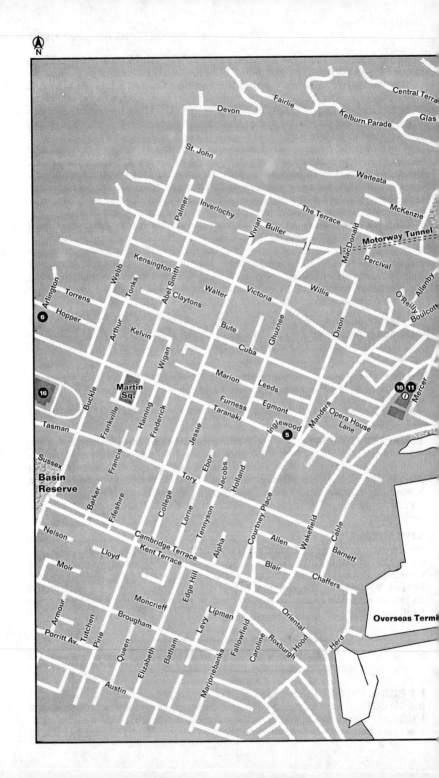

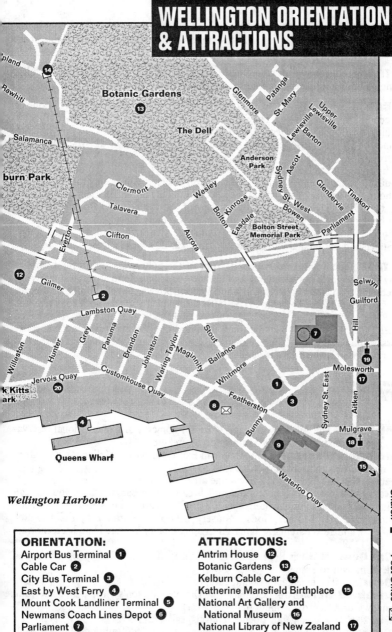

WELLINGTON ORIENTATION & ATTRACTIONS

ORIENTATION:
Airport Bus Terminal ❶
Cable Car ❷
City Bus Terminal ❸
East by West Ferry ❹
Mount Cook Landliner Terminal ❺
Newmans Coach Lines Depot ❻
Parliament ❼
Post Office ❽
Railway Station ❾
Town Hall ❿
Wellington City
  Information Centre ⓫

ATTRACTIONS:
Antrim House ⓬
Botanic Gardens ⓭
Kelburn Cable Car ⓮
Katherine Mansfield Birthplace ⓯
National Museum ⓰
National Library of New Zealand ⓱
Old St. Paul's Church ⓲
Wellington Cathedral ⓳
Wellington Maritime Museum ⓴

Church ✚   Post Office ⊠   Information ❼

The Visitors Information Centre will give you a terrific city map that also shows major bus routes, and timetables for specific routes. Timetables are also available from newsagents.

BY TRAIN InterCity runs commuter trains to suburbs on fairly frequent schedules; phone 472-5399 for timetable information.

BY CAR If you're driving, avoid downtown Wellington traffic by parking in one of the center-city **car parks.** They're on Clifton Terrace, in the Lombard Parking Building on Bond Street near Victoria Street, at James Smith's Council Car Park behind the Opera House (entrance on Wakefield Street), and at the Michael Fowler Centre on Wakefield Street (4-hour maximum stay); prices start at NZ$1 (60¢) for up to 2 hours and go to NZ$10 ($6) for more than 6 hours. Additional off-street parking is available in the Plimmer Building off Boulcott Street, evenings only for NZ$1 (60¢) per hour, free on weekends, and in the Renouf Building on Willis Street on weekends only for NZ$2 ($1) per visit. Ask for a copy of the *Wellington Parking Guide,* with handy maps available at visitor information centers.

For a 24-hour gas (petrol) station, try Central Service Station Ltd. on Jervois Quay, BP Supershop on Taranaki Street, or Multifuels at 221 Wakefield St.

BY TAXI You'll find **taxi ranks** in front of the railway station, in the Lambton Quay shopping area between Grey and Hunter Streets; on Bond Street, just off Willis Street; on Dixon Street between Cuba and Victoria Streets; and on Cambridge Terrace near Courtenay Place. There's a NZ$1 (60¢) surcharge if you telephone for a taxi (tel. 485-9900, 485-9888, or 484-8022), and on weekends and holidays. A so-called "green" (cheaper) fare applies between 6am and 8pm on weekdays; outside those hours, you'll pay the "red" (more expensive) fare—you can check the light on the taxi meter to be sure which fare is in effect.

 WELLINGTON

Airlines The Air New Zealand office for domestic and international reservations and information is at 179 Featherston St. (tel. 488-9900).

American Express The American Express agency in Wellington is Century 21 Travel, 276 Lambton Quay (tel. 04/472-7456).

Area Code Wellington's telephone area code is 04.

Babysitters Most hotels and motels can furnish babysitters, or you can call Wellington Nannies Bureau (tel. 486-3021). Child-care centers that will provide daytime care are: Mother Goose Nursery School, 1 Raroa Rd., Kelburn (tel. 475-7817); and Te Wharemarie Tamariki Crèche, Library Lecture Hall, Mercer Street (tel. 471-1169).

Car Rentals Avis Rent a Car, 25 Dixon St. (tel. 485-0266), is open 7 days a week from 8am to 6pm.

Dentist For emergency dental care, call 472-7-72.

Disabled Services Contact the Disabled Person's Advice Bureau, John Kennedy Good Centre, Wobum (tel. 469-3091).

Doctor For emergency doctor referrals, call 472-2999.

Drugstores There are late-hour pharmacies at 59 Cambridge Terrace, Wellington (tel. 485-8510); corner of Melling Road and High Street, Lower Hutt (tel. 466-1888); and 35 Queen St., Upper Hutt (tel. 428-5858).

Embassies and Consulates The U.S. Consulate is at 29 Fitzherbert Terrace, Thorndon (tel. 472-2068); the Canadian Consulate is at 61 Molesworth St. (tel. 473-9577); the Consulate of Great Britain is at 2 The Terrace (tel. 472-6049).

Emergencies Call 111 for police, fire, and ambulance emergencies.

Hospitals Wellington Hospital is in Riddiford Street, Newtown (tel. 485-5999).

Libraries The National Library, Molesworth Street (tel. 474-3000), is open from 9am to 5pm Monday through Friday. The Wellington Public Library, 8-18 Mercer St. (tel. 472-9529), is open Monday through Thursday from 9:30am to 8:30pm, Friday from 9:30am to 9pm.

Luggage Storage and Lockers There are lockers in the Domestic Terminal at the airport self-claim baggage area and at the railway station's Left Luggage Office.

Newspapers Wellington's morning newspaper is *The Dominion,* and in the evening there's *The Evening Post.* Both are published Monday through Saturday. On Sunday morning, look for *The Dominion Sunday Times.* Overseas newspapers are sometimes available from newsagents and are available in the reading room of the National Library.

Photographic Needs Photo Pharmacy Ltd., 7 Courtenay Place (tel. 484-7391), specializes in photographic services, with hours of 8:30am to 5:30pm Monday through Thursday, until 8:30pm on Friday, and 9:30am to 1:30pm on Saturday.

Police See "Emergencies," above.

Post Office The Central Post Office (CPO) is on Waterloo Quay, open from 8am to 5pm Monday through Friday, with a philatelic bureau on the premises for stamp collectors.

Radio Wellington's leading FM stations are 99 and 100 on the FM dial; Radio Windy Classic Rock in 94.1 and 98.1 on FM.

Telegrams and Fax The General Post Office (see above) has telegram and fax facilities. Many hotels also have fax facilities available for guests.

3. WHERE TO STAY

There are two things that must be said right up front about accommodations in Wellington: You should reserve as far in advance as possible; and, as I pointed out above, you'll stand a much better chance of finding budget accommodations on weekends than during the week. It all has to do with the city's resident population tide—in on Monday, out on Friday evening. It is true that there are a lot of bed-and-breakfast listings, but the majority cater to their permanent guests and few are interested in transients like you and me. That tidal flow does, however, create one unique situation in the capital city: Many superior hotels and motels cut prices drastically over the weekends when they have a surplus of rooms, and that means a little shopping around may well net you a budget price in a "splurge" location. More and more restaurants, shops, and sightseeing attractions are remaining open for the weekend, making it quite possible to take advantage of those special rates without sacrificing your usual holiday activities.

Unless otherwise noted, the rates listed below include GST.

A LICENSED HOTEL

TREKKERS HOTEL, 213 Cuba St., Dunlop Terrace (P.O. Box 27-125), Wellington 1. Tel. 04/485-2153. Fax 04/482-8873. 107 rms (some with bath). TV TEL

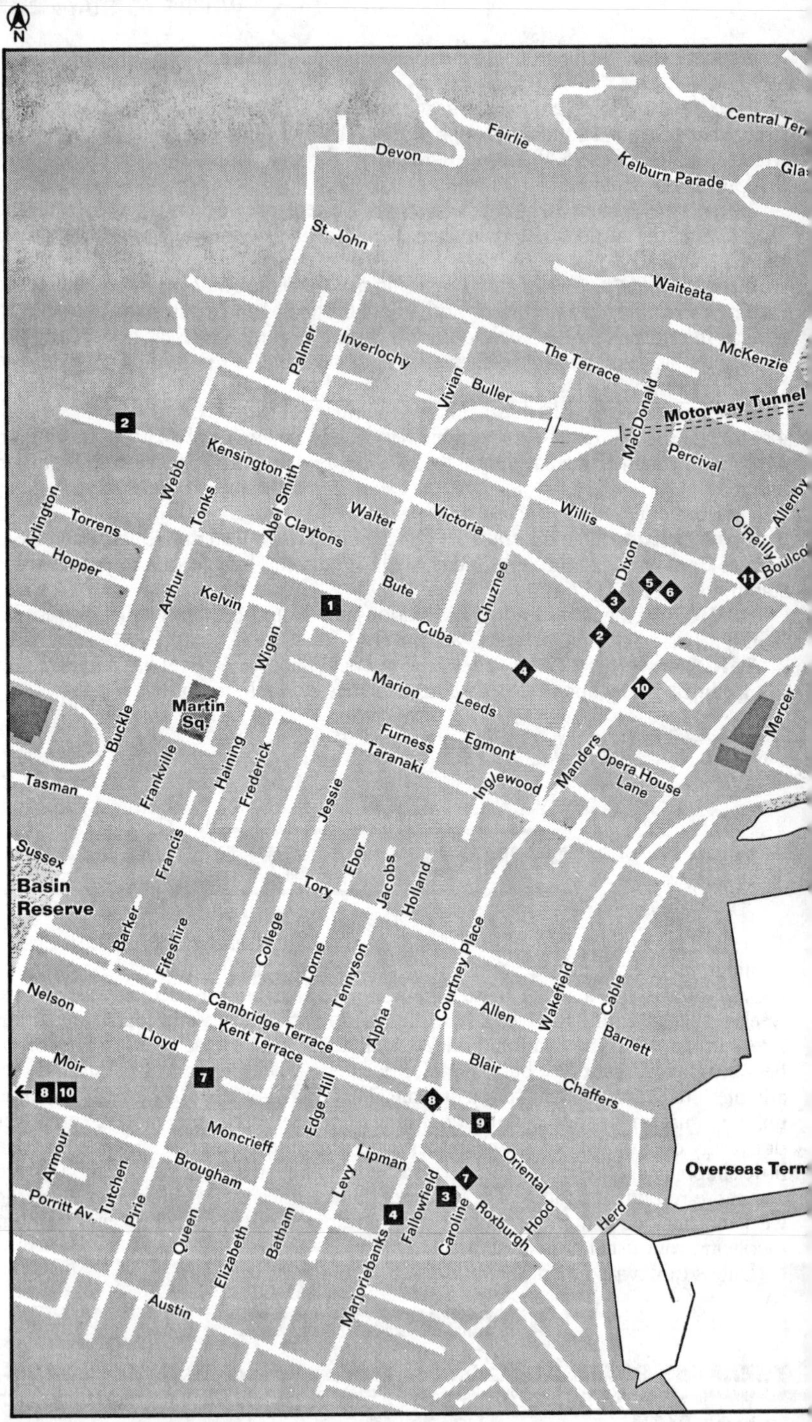
N
Central Ter.
Gla
Fairlie
Devon
Kelburn Parade
St. John
Waiteata
Palmer
Inverlochy
The Terrace
McKenzie
Vivian
Buller
MacDonald
Motorway Tunnel
Kensington
Percival
Webb
Tonks
Abel Smith
Walter
Victoria
Willis
Allenby
Arlington
Torrens
Claytons
O'Reilly
Boulcott
Hopper
Dixon
Arthur
Kelvin
Bute
Ghuznee
Cuba
Wigan
Marion
Leeds
Buckle
Martin Sq.
Furness
Egmont
Mercer
Taranaki
Haining
Frederick
Frankville
Manders
Opera House Lane
Tasman
Jessie
Inglewood
Sussex
Francis
Ebor
Basin Reserve
Tory
Jacobs
Holland
Barker
Fifeshire
College
Courtney Place
Lorne
Tennyson
Wakefield
Cable
Nelson
Cambridge Terrace
Allen
Kent Terrace
Alpha
Barnett
Lloyd
Moir
Blair
Chaffers
8 10
Edge Hill
Moncrieff
Oriental
Overseas Term
Armour
Brougham
Lipman
Tutchen
Levy
Fallowfield
Porritt Av.
Pirie
Queen
Caroline
Roxburgh
Hood
Herd
Elizabeth
Batham
Marjoriebanks
Austin

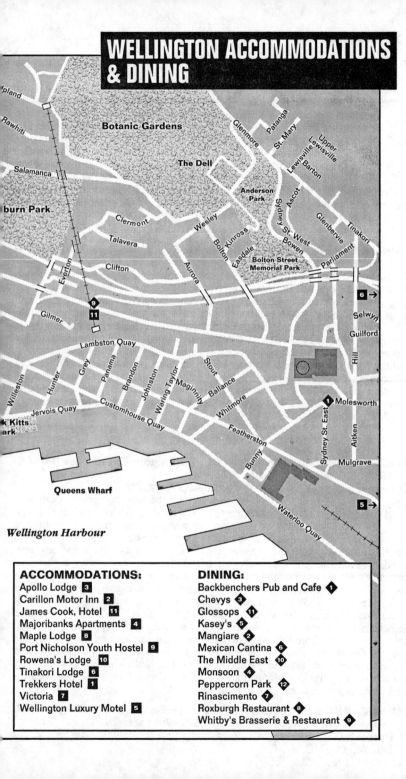

WELLINGTON ACCOMMODATIONS & DINING

Botanic Gardens

The Dell

Anderson Park

Bolton Street Memorial Park

Queens Wharf

Wellington Harbour

ACCOMMODATIONS:
Apollo Lodge **3**
Carillon Motor Inn **2**
James Cook, Hotel **11**
Majoribanks Apartments **4**
Maple Lodge **8**
Port Nicholson Youth Hostel **9**
Rowena's Lodge **10**
Tinakori Lodge **6**
Trekkers Hotel **1**
Victoria **7**
Wellington Luxury Motel **5**

DINING:
Backbenchers Pub and Cafe **1**
Chevys **3**
Glossops **11**
Kasey's **5**
Mangiare **2**
Mexican Cantina **6**
The Middle East **10**
Monsoon **4**
Peppercorn Park **12**
Rinascimento **7**
Roxburgh Restaurant **8**
Whitby's Brasserie & Restaurant **9**

$ **Rates** (excluding GST): NZ$15 ($9) backpacker's bunk; NZ$40 ($23) single without bath, NZ$60 ($34) single with bath; NZ$50 ($29) double without bath, NZ$70 ($40) double with bath; NZ$100 ($57) single or double 1-bedroom motel flat; NZ$120 ($69) single or double 2-bedroom motel flat. AE, DC, MC, V.

This licensed hotel off Vivian Street is very central and offers a variety of accommodations, including small dormitories (two or four bunk beds), singles, and doubles, both with and without private facilities (hot and cold running water in those without), six rooms with facilities for the disabled, and six motel units in a separate block. They vary in style from new and modern to older and recently renovated, and the reception areas and guest lounge all have a bright, modern look. There's a guest laundry, sauna, and spa pool. The attractive restaurant features exceptionally good meals for under NZ$15 ($9). Off-street parking.

A MOTOR INN

CARILLON MOTOR INN, 33 Thompson St., Wellington. Tel. 04/484-8795. Fax 04/485-7036. 26 rms (all with bath). TV TEL
$ **Rates:** NZ$56 ($32) single; NZ$61 ($35) double; NZ$70 ($40) per person in water-bed room. AE, DC, MC, V.

I fell in love with this charming motor inn, although it was a bit hard to find. The rambling, two-story white house sits halfway up one of Wellington's hills, well off the street, and has a magnificent view of the city and harbor. It was formerly a bed-and-breakfast establishment and more economical, but inside, the rooms, most of which are quite spacious, are attractively and comfortably furnished, and the large guest lounge is inviting. All rooms have in-house video, and tea- and coffee-making facilities, and two have water beds. The licensed restaurant is open for breakfast daily and the evening meal Monday through Thursday, with quite modest prices. Off-street parking. The Carillon is located down a driveway between nos. 29 and 35 Thompson Street.

MOTEL FLATS

APOLLO LODGE, 49 Majoribanks St., Wellington. Tel. and fax 04/485-1849. 33 units (all with bath). TV TEL
$ **Rates:** NZ$100 ($58) single or double. AE, DC, MC, V.

This would be a real find even if it weren't the most convenient location in Wellington at anything like budget prices. But the superb location is the icing on the cake—it's so close to city center shopping, entertainment, and sightseeing that you can leave the car and walk (a longish but pleasant stroll) or use the convenient city bus transport, and there are several first-rate restaurants right in the neighborhood. I found the staff here extremely friendly and helpful, always a plus. The attractive units are set in off the street, and eight have separate bedrooms. You have a choice of full kitchen facilities or of serviced units with jug, toaster, and fridge. All are fully carpeted and come with radio, electric blankets, and heaters. Cooked or continental breakfasts are available, and there's a full-service laundry as well as highchairs and a play area for children. If you're traveling with a large party, you might want to book the three-bedroom (sleeps seven) bungalow also on the grounds that goes for the same rate as a motel unit—you'll have to negotiate the price, since it depends on the number of people and length of stay. *Note:* The Apollo is very, very popular with regular Kiwi visitors to Wellington, and your best bet here is weekends (as I seem to keep saying!). Park in front of your door.

MAJORIBANKS APARTMENTS, 38 Majoribanks St., Wellington. Tel. 04/485-7305 or 485-8879. Fax 04/485-1849. 14 apts. TV TEL
$ **Rates:** NZ$100 ($58) single or double. Extra adult NZ$15 ($9); extra child NZ$10 ($6). AE, DC, MC, V.

An American from Washington, D.C., greeted me with an unsolicited recommendation—"This place is fantastic, not only for the facilities and comfort, but for the friendliness of the owner." When I arrived, my encounter with owner John Floratos certainly confirmed the traveler's comments, but in addition, I was much impressed with the bright, nicely decorated apartments in this property just across the street from the Apollo. All have fully equipped kitchen and radio. There are one- and two-bedroom units, and there's good off-street parking. Majoribanks is within walking distance of the city center.

WELLINGTON LUXURY MOTEL, 14 Hobson St., Wellington. Tel. 04/472-6825 or 472-0334. 5 units (all with bath). TV TEL

$ Rates (excluding GST): NZ$81 ($46) single or double. Extra person NZ$10 ($6). AE, DC, MC, V.

About a 5-minute walk from the railway station, this large house was built back in 1912, and has been renovated to create five nice units with such charming extras as bay windows, beamed ceilings, and small leaded windowpanes. Three of the spacious units are bed-sitters, and two have one bedroom and can sleep up to six. All are attractively furnished. There's limited off-street parking. The motel is near Davis Street at the northern edge of the city center.

BED & BREAKFASTS

If you have difficulty booking into a bed-and-breakfast listed here, **Harbour City Home Stays,** P.O. Box 14-345, Wellington (tel. 04/486-2339), has a list of high-standard homes that offer this type of hospitality at quite reasonable rates.

TINAKORI LODGE, 182 Tinakori Rd., Wellington. Tel. 04/447-3478. Fax 04/472-5554. 10 rms (none with bath). TV TEL

$ Rates (including breakfast): NZ$66 ($38) single; NZ$77 ($44) double. Extra person NZ$11 ($6). AE, DC, MC, V.

This charming, century-old home on the northern edge of the city center is presided over by Mel and John Ainsworth. Guest rooms are fresh and bright, comfortably furnished, retain much of the character of the old home, and each has hot and cold running water, electric blankets, and heater. The substantial breakfast is served buffet style, and an attractive feature here is the availability of tea, coffee, hot chocolate, soup, cheese, crackers, and cookies all during the day. The home-cooked dinner is optional. Complimentary morning and evening local newspapers are also available.

VICTORIA, 58 Pirie St., Mount Victoria, Wellington. Tel. 04/485-8512. 4 rms (1 with bath). TV TEL **Directions:** From motorway into Ghuznee St., Taranaki St., Vivian St., across Kent Terrace, and up Pirie St. **Bus:** City bus no. 2 or 5.

$ Rates (including breakfast): NZ$40 ($23) single; NZ$60 ($34) double; NZ$60 ($34) per person in room with private bath. No credit cards.

Elizabeth and Robert McGuigan and their three teenagers live upstairs in this two-story home adorned with lacy cast-iron work. Downstairs, there are three guest rooms and two baths, a TV lounge, and a dining room with tea and coffee makings. The cooked breakfast has won raves from our readers, who also like the location, which is convenient to the city center and to Mount Victoria.

HOSTELS

MAPLE LODGE, 52 Ellice St., Mount Victoria, Wellington. Tel. 04/485-3771. 13 rms (none with bath). TV TEL

$ Rates: NZ$13 ($7) dormitory bed; NZ$18 ($10) single; NZ$30–NZ$32 ($17–$18) double. No credit cards.

Near the center of the city, the Maple Lodge is perched on one of Wellington's picturesque hillsides in a row of small colonial houses. The red-and-white wooden house has been recently renovated, and most rooms are quite spacious. There are singles, twins, and doubles, all with hot and cold running water, and a dormitory. Other facilities include a fully equipped kitchen, dining room, and TV lounge.

PORT NICHOLSON YOUTH HOSTEL, corner of Wakefield St. and Cambridge Terrace (P.O. Box 24-033), Wellington. Tel. 04/801-7280. 27 rms (all with bath). TEL **Directions:** 1 block north of Courtenay Place bus terminal, and 1 block from airport bus stop on corner of Blair St. and Courtenay Place. Shuttle bus service to meet 2:20pm Inter-Island ferry from Picton and 7pm Silver Fern train at railway station.

$ Rates: Dormitory bed NZ$17 ($10) for members, NZ$21 ($12) for nonmembers; double room NZ$19 ($11) for members, NZ$23 ($13) for nonmembers. No credit cards.

The most luxurious and modern youth hostel in New Zealand, this is considered the flagship of New Zealand Youth Hostel Association. There are 22 four-bedded dormitories and 5 double rooms, all with private baths. Mattress cover, duvet (quilt), and clean pillows are supplied free of charge, and there are a limited number of free sleeping sheets (bring your own to be on the safe side). Facilities include a self-catering kitchen, dining room, TV lounge, reading room, and a well-stocked shop for basic food and toiletries. All your travel bookings for ongoing ferry, bus, and train services can be handled right on the premises, and they can also book ahead in other youth hostels around the country.

ROWENA'S LODGE, 115 Brougham St., Mount Victoria, Wellington. Tel. and fax 04/485-7872. 50 rms (none with bath). TV TEL

$ Rates: NZ$13 ($7) dormitory bed; NZ$16 ($9) single; NZ$32 ($18) double. Extra person NZ$10 ($6). No credit cards.

The Rowena has a variety of accommodations: dormitories, singles, doubles, twins, and triples. In addition to the three guest lounges, there's a dining room (cooked or continental breakfasts are available at a small charge), large guest kitchen, barbecue, and picnic area. It's near city center, on four city bus routes, and drivers will appreciate the off-street parking. There's free pickup and dropoff service to trains, buses, and the Inter-Island ferry, and they can book for you on any of these.

CABINS & CAMPING

Since the Lower Hutt City Council a few years ago took over operation of the ✪ ⑤ **Hutt Park Holiday Village** at 95 Hutt Park Rd., Moera, Lower Hutt (tel. 04/468-5913), some 7 miles northeast of the city, great improvements have been made to both grounds and cabins. This is a large camp, abundant with native shade trees. There are 53 cabins, many of which are equipped for wheelchair access. They range from two-berth standard cabins with basic furnishing to fully equipped motel units. All units with kitchens have a full range of cutlery and crockery provided. Bedding and linen is required in most cabins, and is available for hire from the office, along with TV sets. There are two coin-operated laundries, and three facility blocks, each with kitchen, dining area, TV room, showers, and toilets. Motel units, fully equipped, are NZ$63 ($36) single or double; tourist flats with kitchen and toilet are NZ$45 ($26) single or double; tourist cabins with kitchens are NZ$35 ($20); and standard cabins NZ$25 ($14) single or double. Powered caravan sites are NZ$18 ($10) single or double, each additional person NZ$9 ($5); tent sites are NZ$8 ($5) per person. Public transport into Wellington or Lower Hutt is located nearby.

WORTH THE EXTRA MONEY

HARBOUR CITY MOTOR INN, 92-96 Webb St., P.O. Box 16-125, Wellington. Tel. 04/384-9809. Fax 04/384-9806. 9 rms, 16 suites (all with bath). MINIBAR TV TEL

$ Rates (excluding GST): Weekdays NZ$130 ($74) single, NZ$140 ($80) double; weekends NZ$93 ($53) single or double; daily NZ$147 ($84) suite. Best Western discounts available. AE, DC, MC, V.

Harbour City could justify its rates solely on location—it's convenient to all city center attraction, major theaters, shopping, and good restaurants—but its merits certainly don't stop there. Guest rooms are attractively furnished, with comfortable sitting areas and (a feature I always appreciate) excellent lighting. Suites come with kitchens, and there's a covered car park. Other facilities include a guest laundry, dry-cleaning service, videos, and photocopying and fax service for guests. A good, moderately priced, licensed Chinese restaurant is on the premises, and there's a spa pool.

HOTEL JAMES COOK, The Terrace, Wellington. Tel. 04/472-5865. Fax 04/473-1875. 260 rms (all with bath). MINIBAR TV TEL

$ Rates (excluding GST): NZ$240 ($137) single or double. Weekend discounts available. AE, DC, MC, V.

With what has to be the best location in town, this is a "big splurge" well worth considering. It's in the very heart of the city center, and its rooms all come with tea- and coffee-making facilities, fridges, and in-house video. There's same-day laundry and dry-cleaning service (except Sunday), business facilities that include secretarial service and copy machines, a first-class restaurant (see "Where to Eat," below), and an inexpensive coffee shop. It is also just steps away from shopping, sightseeing, dining, and entertainment. The normal rate is lowered dramatically for weekend specials. Highly recommended.

A NEARBY PLACE TO STAY

CONSTELLATION MOTEL, State Hwy. 1, Foxton. Tel. 06/363-8863. 10 units (all with bath). TV TEL **Directions:** 1½-hour drive from Wellington via Hwy. 1.

$ Rates: NZ$57 ($33) single; NZ$69 ($39) double. AE, DC, MC, V.

Some 3 miles from Foxton Beach (and a little over an hour's drive to Wellington), this is a quiet, peaceful base from which to explore Wellington. The motel has 10 kitchen units that are nicely decorated, and there's a spa pool, children's playground, and pool table for guests. Breakfast is available, and there is a good restaurant adjacent to the motel.

4. WHERE TO EAT

You'll find good, inexpensive places to eat along almost any Wellington street. And there's an interesting diversity of cuisine offered in the city's 350 restaurants. Space limitations necessarily mean that my listings will omit many that are worthy of note. Drop me a line if you find that special eatery you think other budgeteers should know about, and I'll include as many as possible in future editions.

If you'd like to have dinner with a Wellington family, **Harbour City Home Stays,** P.O. Box 14-345, Wellington (tel. 04/486-2339), can arrange a home-cooked New Zealand dinner for about NZ$40 ($23) a person, plus GST—but be sure to give them sufficient advance notice. They can also arrange a complete home stay, with bed and breakfast or bed, breakfast, and dinner with a Wellington family.

AS YOU LIKE IT CAFE, 32 Riddiford St., in Newtown. Tel. 489-3983.
    Cuisine: SEAFOOD/STEAK/NEW ZEALAND. **Reservations:** Recommended.
$ Prices: Appetizers NZ$8 ($5); main courses NZ$19 ($11). AE, MC, V.
    Open: Lunch Tues–Fri noon–2pm; dinner Tues–Sun 6–10:30pm.

As you'd expect, the walls of this casual, pleasant suburban eatery are hung with posters of Shakespearean plays. The blackboard menu is surprisingly extensive, with specialties like wild pork roulade with a gin-and-juniper sauce, or spiced chicken breast with a curried lime sauce, or venison pie. All main courses come with vegetables and potatoes or rice, and there's good parking. BYO and fully licensed.

BACKBENCHERS PUB AND CAFE, corner of Molesworth St. and Sydney St. East. Tel. 472-3065.
    Cuisine: SALADS/BURGERS/PASTA/LIGHT MEALS. **Reservations:** Not required.
$ Prices: NZ$8–NZ$12 ($5–$7). AE, DC, MC, V.
    Open: Lunch Mon–Sat 11:30am–2pm; dinner daily 6–10:30pm.

A Wellington friend steered me to this terrific pub and eatery, and I've thanked her ever since. The old building retains the original ceilings from 1917, and its natural brick-and-wood interior creates a sense of history that just can't be reproduced in any more modern edifice. As for the menu, it makes as good reading as the offerings are good eating. Take, for example, "Caygill's Calculation," named for a member of Parliament, and described as "Like his budget deficit, this one got too big!"—and the thickly sliced, medium-rare roast sirloin smothered with homemade tomato relish on salad greens, tomatoes, and chunky rye bread more than lives up to that description. Or you may opt for the lighter "Labour's Lot," and "swim for your life through a fresh hearty minestrone soup and garlic croutons served with slices of a bacon and cheese batard bread." Most other dishes are also named for New Zealand political figures or events, and the ambience in this popular place is lively and convivial. Fully licensed, of course. Backbenchers is located opposite the Beehive (Parliament building) in the city center.

BROOKLYN CAFE & GRILL, 1 Todman St., in Brooklyn. Tel. 485-3592.
    Cuisine: NEW ZEALAND. **Reservations:** Not required.
$ Prices: Appetizers NZ$9 ($5); fixed-price dinner NZ$25 ($14). AE, DC, MC, V.
    Open: Daily 6–11pm.

One of the city's most popular eateries, the Brooklyn Café & Grill occupies a corner in this suburb. Owners Lois Dash (a local food columnist) and Gresort Williams took over several old shops and created a rather spare, but quite comfortable, interior that has won an architectural award. The menu features appetizers that could well serve as a light meal (like the fettuccine with broccoli, smoked salmon, and red-pepper butter), steaks, lamb, fish, chicken and vegetarian dishes such as a tart filled with leeks, capsicums, Gruyère, and sour cream. Vegetables are terrific, and my own favorite is the unique baked cabbage with sour cream and feta. There's limited parking back of the restaurant, and it's BYO.

CHEVYS, 97 Dixon St. Tel. 484-2723.
    Cuisine: AMERICAN LIGHT SNACKS. **Reservations:** Not required.
$ Prices: NZ$10–NZ$20 ($6–$11). AE, DC, MC, V.
    Open: Mon–Thurs 11:30am–11pm, Fri–Sat 11:30am–midnight.

Anyone tempted by the offer of "two meals for the price of one" should head over to

Chevys after 5pm on Monday and Tuesday. You'll see the neon cowboy and his wiggling lasso a few blocks before you arrive at the door. The casual, congenial place has decidedly American fare: BLTs, chicken wings, nachos, barbecued spareribs, Philadelphia steak sandwiches, omelets, seven kinds of burgers, potato skins, and even banana splits. Your final bill will depend entirely on your appetite. Licensed. It's located in the city center.

GLOSSOPS, 149 Willis St. Tel. 484-9091.
Cuisine: NEW ZEALAND. **Reservations:** Not required.
$ Prices: Appetizers NZ$6.25 ($4); main courses NZ$13 ($7). MC, V.
Open: Lunch daily 11:30am–2:30pm; dinner Sun–Thurs 6–9:30pm, Fri–Sat 6–10pm.

This cozy little place in the city center has green-and-white tablecloths and a blackboard menu featuring all home-cooked meals and fresh New Zealand produce. And they are delicious! Salad plates, sandwiches (they're open and hearty-appetite size), seafood, savory croissants, beef, pork, and chicken are featured, and the waist-expanding desserts include homemade ice cream and chocolate-fudge torte. Not licensed, but you're welcome to BYO.

GRETA POINT TAVERN, 467 Evans Bay Parade. Tel. 486-1066.
Cuisine: SEAFOOD. **Reservations:** Not required.
$ Prices: Main courses and vegetables or salad NZ$10–NZ$20 ($6–$11). AE, MC, V.
Open: Lunch Mon–Sat noon–2:30pm, Sun 11:30am–2:30pm; dinner Mon–Sat 5:30–9:30pm, Sun 5:30–9pm.

If you're driving, or happen to find yourself out in the lovely Evans Bay area, 2 miles from the city center, plan on one meal here. Actually, the 2-mile walk from downtown along Oriental Bay, Roseneath, and Evans Bay Parade to the tavern is picturesque and well worth doing. The large black building with rose trim sits right on the waterfront, and has windows the entire length of its south side, looking out to sweeping views of the bay (often filled with sailboats) and a nearby marina with its forest of masts. The large, high-ceilinged room, which once housed a commercial laundry, now has a wooden lifeboat suspended from the overhead pipes. There's a nice upstairs Promenade Deck bar, and downstairs you'll find the Anchorage Lounge Bar, as well as the Galley Restaurant, featuring fresh seafoods. The restaurant is self-service and fully licensed, and the long counter will have you drooling while trying to decide between Bluff oysters, roast baron of beef, marinated mussels, baked leg of lamb, and a host of other tempting dishes on display.

KASEY'S, 8 Edward St. Tel. 485-7043.
Cuisine: INTERNATIONAL. **Reservations:** Recommended.
$ Prices: Appetizers NZ$8–NZ$10 ($5–$6); main courses NZ$16–NZ$25 ($9–$14). AE, DC, MC, V.
Open: Lunch daily noon–3pm; dinner daily 5:30–11pm or midnight.
Sophisticated in menu and decor, Kasey's offers a variety of dishes, including spaghetti in saffron cream with mussels and tomato stew, vegetarian spicy samosa, tandoori spiced chicken, along with fish, lamb, and beef dishes. There is also a large selection of wines by the glass. A jazz band is on hand on Thursday and Saturday. Licensed. It's located in the center of town.

MANGIARE, 35 Dixon St. Tel. 484-4343.
Cuisine: ITALIAN. **Reservations:** Not required.
$ Prices: Average meal NZ$18 ($10). MC, V.
Open: Dinner daily 5:30–11pm.

For good Italian food, excellent service, and just plain fun people-watching, I heartily recommend at least one meal at this upstairs restaurant with draped, striped awnings. There are clusters of wine bottles hanging about on the walls, and a small front room whose windows overlook the busy street below. It's a favorite of locals, a short walk from city center, and at lunch there's the happy buzz of office workers from nearby, while candlelit tables at night are likely to be filled by many of the same who've returned for a more relaxed meal. Specialties are—what else?—spaghetti, cannelloni, pastitsio, ravioli, and calamari, with dessert surprises that include baklava (it used to be a Greek restaurant, and this favorite, as did pastitsio, just stayed on). Service is friendly as well as efficient. BYO and licensed.

MEXICAN CANTINA, 19 Edward St. Tel. 485-9711.
   Cuisine: MEXICAN. **Reservations:** Not accepted.
   $ Prices: Average lunch NZ$10 ($6); average dinner NZ$15 ($9) and under. No credit cards.
   Open: Lunch Mon–Fri noon–2pm; dinner Mon–Fri 6–10pm, Sat–Sun noon–10pm.
This sometimes noisy cantina is set in a former warehouse a short walk from the center of the city, and it's such a favorite with locals that you may find yourself waiting in line at lunch. The atmosphere is casual; the decor is south of the border, complete with a Mexican sombrero on the brick walls; and the menu features all those beans, tacos, and tostados you'd expect. BYO.

THE MIDDLE EAST, Regent Centre, Manners Mall. Tel. 472-4538.
   Cuisine: MIDDLE EASTERN. **Reservations:** Recommended.
   $ Prices: Average lunch NZ$15 ($9); average dinner NZ$30 ($17). AE, MC, V.
   Open: Lunch Mon–Fri noon–2:30pm; dinner daily 6pm–midnight.
This restaurant is exotic in decor as well as cuisine, with lots of brass, tapestries, Israeli lithographs, and Mediterranean-style tables and chairs. It's upstairs in the Regent Centre, a short distance from the city center, and as for the menu, selections include souvlaki, shish kebab, stuffed grapevine leaves, capsicums, and . . . well, there are dishes from Greece, Turkey, Israel, Lebanon, Syria, and Yemen, and you'll dine to the strains of taped music from all those countries. On Thursday and Sunday nights, belly dancers complete the scene. Fully licensed.

MONSOON, 124 Cuba St. Tel. 484-2827.
   Cuisine: BURMESE. **Reservations:** Recommended for dinner.
   $ Prices: Average lunch NZ$15 ($9); average dinner NZ$25 ($14). MC, V.
   Open: Lunch Mon–Sat noon–2pm; dinner Mon–Sat 6–10pm.
This small, cozy place a short walk from the city center specializes in such Burmese and Asian dishes as chicken with ginger and spring onion, Singapore chow mein, beef with green pepper and black-bean sauce, and a host of curries. BYO.

MYKONOS, 23 Coutts St., in Kilbirnie. Tel. 487-7040.
   Cuisine: GREEK. **Reservations:** Recommended.
   $ Prices: Average meal NZ$30 ($17). AE, DC, MC, V.
   Open: Dinner Tues–Sat 6–11pm.
The walls of this lively spot are adorned with pictures of the Greek owner's homeland and wine bottles, with bits of greenery spotted around the room. Menu specialties are lamb, spanakopita, seafoods prepared in the Greek fashion, and that great Greek dessert, baklava. BYO. Mykonos is near the center of the city

PEPPERCORN PARK, 1st floor, Grand Arcade, Willis St. Tel. 472-2255.

Cuisine: BREAKFAST/PASTRIES/SANDWICHES/QUICHE/INTERNATIONAL.
Reservations: Not accepted.
$ Prices: Breakfast NZ$11 ($6); pastries NZ$1–NZ$3 (60¢–$2); sandwiches with salad and fries NZ$8 ($5); quiche NZ$4 ($2); dinner NZ$9–NZ$11 ($5–$6). AE, DC, MC, V.
Open: Mon–Thurs 7am–4pm, Fri 7am–8:30pm, Sat 9am–1:30pm.

This pleasant upstairs self-service restaurant is one of my favorite drop-in eateries in the city center. Their reputation for the best bagels in Wellington certainly gets my endorsement, and the phyllo pastry filled with smoked salmon, chicken, smoked salmon, or some other delicacy just melts in your mouth. For heartier eating, specialties include Indonesian lamb rendang, pork in ginger-and-orange sauce, Mexican beef, lasagne, and on Friday nights, traditional roast meals of pork or beef and vegetables. Licensed.

RINASCIMENTO, 4 Roxburgh St. Tel. 485-8340.
Cuisine: ITALIAN. **Reservations:** Recommended.
$ Prices: Average dinner under NZ$20 ($11).
Open: Dinner Mon–Thurs 6–9pm, Fri–Sat 6–9:30pm.

This casual, rather rustic restaurant serves up really good Italian dishes (pasta, stuffed squid, mussels in white wine sauce, veal in various forms) at really moderate prices from the à la carte menu. BYO. Rinascimento is located a short distance from the center of the city.

WORTH THE EXTRA MONEY

Wellington has several really "big splurge" restaurants that would hold their own anywhere in the world.

ROXBURGH RESTAURANT, 18 Majoribanks St. Tel. 485-7577.
Cuisine: GERMAN. **Reservations:** Required.
$ Prices: Average meal NZ$45 ($26). AE, DC, MC, V.
Open: Dinner daily 6–10pm.

This very pleasant, attractive place is not as expensive as most splurge restaurants. It's in an old, two-story house just off Cambridge Place, a short distance from the city center, and the cuisine here is mostly German, with traditional specialties such as Rheinischer Sauerbraten, venison and other game, and lamb, along with New Zealand seafood. Friendly service, pink linen napkins, fresh flowers at each table, complimentary sherry, and an open fireplace on cool evenings add the pampered feeling that makes your pricey dinner tab seem more than a bargain. No smoking. BYO.

WHITBY'S BRASSERIE & RESTAURANT, in the James Cook Hotel, The Terrace. Tel. 472-5865.
Cuisine: NEW ZEALAND. **Reservations:** Required on weekends; recommended other nights.
$ Prices: Appetizers NZ$8–NZ$10 ($5–$6); main courses NZ$19–NZ$25 ($11–$14). AE, DC, MC, V.
Open: Breakfast buffet daily 7–9am; lunch buffet daily noon–2pm; dinner daily 6–10:30pm.

Terrific breakfast and lunch buffets are served in this elegant room on the second floor of the conveniently located hotel, but it is at dinner that the chef really shines. Chef Albert Hutching, in fact, holds the coveted Lamb Cuisine Award. And if you order his lamb Whitby (a loin of lamb stuffed with white veal liver, served with smoked sweetbreads and a spinach-and-pine-nuts combination in phyllo pastry with a tamarillo sabayon), you'll most certainly want to give him your own personal gourmet award—it's luscious. Other New Zealand specialties, such as smoked venison, quail, pheasant, hare, salmon, Bluff oysters, and filet of beef are on the extensive menu, along with roasts of beef, pork, and lamb. Desserts are fabulous. The room itself is romantic by candlelight, and on Saturday and Sunday nights the Haydn Quartet plays classical music. Wellingtonians favor Whitby's for dining out, especially on the weekends. Licensed. Highly recommended.

READERS RECOMMEND

Carol's, 198 Lambton Quay. Tel. 449-4701. *"We found this great cafeteria-style restaurant with a little of everything. It's located right downtown, and the prices were very reasonable. We liked it so much we came back on our return to the North Island."*—Linda K. Schumm, Mackinaw, Ill.

5. ATTRACTIONS

One of my strongest impressions of Wellington lingers from my very first visit—sore feet and sheer exhaustion from climbing up and down its hilly terrain (I actually managed to kill off trusty walking boots that had seen me through many another tough walking spot!). Of course, I realized later that the blame lay with *me*, not Wellington. This is a city that requires *planned* sightseeing, and to save yourself my own trials and travails, I strongly recommend ("insist" would be a better word) that you head straight for the **Visitors Information Centre** (see "Tourist Information," above) and plot your course before taking one step. A good plan is to concentrate on city-center attractions first, then take the cable car up to Kelburn and Mount Victoria, then *plan* how you're going to reach the outlying places, so that you're not backtracking for something overlooked when you're sightseeing in one direction. There are excellent day-trips by car or even easier organized tours (see below) that can make your life happier and more relaxed as you take in Wellington's splendors. If you prefer a do-it-yourself tour, pick up the *Scenic Drive* booklet and map. Three routes are outlined, and they're color-coordinated with discs on lampposts along each route so you won't go astray. They cover Wellington from top to bottom, traveling southeast on one route, west on another, and north on the third.

You can also do your feet a favor in the city center by taking advantage of the excellent public transport system (as a city walker at home, such a thought never crossed my mind on that first visit). The **Downtowner** bus costs NZ$3.50 ($2) for five rides in the downtown area or on the cable car during off-peak hours (9am to 3pm). The **Daytripper** allows one adult and two children under age 15 to ride all day for NZ$7.50 ($4). This is a fine way to see the city: Jump on any bus, leap off when you see something interesting; go to the beach (take the Lyall Bay, Island Bay, or Seatoun bus from Willis Street) and stay all day or catch the next bus back. Take bus no. 12 or 14 to one of the hill suburbs, have a cup of coffee in a local café, then catch a bus back and enjoy the views all along the way. You can even use the same bus ticket after dinner for after-hours exploring.

While in the city center, do take time to walk down to that magnificent harbor, where the ✪ **Lambton Harbour Development Project** is busily lining its shores with park areas and other amenities for residents and visitors alike that will make it truly the focal point of the city.

Wellington is central to many hiking areas, some that afford prime views of the city and harbor. Ask at the Visitors Information Centre for the *Bus & Walk* brochure, which outlines 16 walks and gives information on getting to them from Wellington and back into town by bus. An easy, educational choice is a visit to the ✪ **Otari Open Air Native Plant Museum** (tel. 475-3245), which offers four hikes of half an hour to an hour, some through 198 acres of native bush and 5 acres of cultivated gardens; take the no. 14 Wilton Route bus to the entrance on Wilton Road. The bus trip takes 20 minutes.

THE TOP ATTRACTIONS

KELBURN CABLE CAR, 286 Wakefield St. Tel. 485-6579.

✪ For the fullest appreciation of Wellington's spectacular setting, take a marvelous 4½-minute ride in a sleek red cable car, which climbs to an elevation of 400 feet up Mount Victoria, leaving from Lambton Quay opposite Grey Street. The beautiful harbor lies at your feet, and it's a great loitering spot to drink in the beauty of that curving shoreline backed by jagged hills.

The **Botanic Gardens** entrance is also at the top of the cable-car ride, open from dawn to dusk, with no admission charge. Stop by the Interpretive Centre for brochures and a full briefing on the gardens. Your downhill stroll through lush greenery can be broken by a stop at the **Begonia House** and its **Tea House** in the **Lady Norwood Rose Gardens** (open from 10am to 4pm) for a look at hundreds of begonias, bush foliage, and ferns. From the foot of the gardens, you can get back to the city on a no. 12 bus.

Fares: NZ$1 (60¢) one-way for adults, NZ$1.70 ($1) round-trip for adults, NZ.50 (30¢) one-way and return for children.

Open: Cable car runs Mon–Fri 7am–10pm, Sat 9:20am–6pm, Sun and public holidays 10:30am–6pm.

ANTRIM HOUSE, 63 Boulcott St. Tel. 472-4341.

Antrim House is headquarters of the New Zealand Historic Places Trust, and its information room has displays of its properties and the organization's work. The turn-of-the-century wooden town house, built in the Italianate style and set in sloping lawns, is a relic of a more gracious era, now dwarfed by high-rise towers on either side. Its interior is noted for the fine hallway with its kauri and totara paneling, embossed ceilings, stained-glass windows, and elaborate fireplaces. This is a good place to get an overview of New Zealand's history as witnessed by surviving buildings and learn about the ongoing efforts to preserve them. In the city center.

Admission: Free.

Open: Mon–Fri noon–3pm.

KATHERINE MANSFIELD BIRTHPLACE, 25 Tinakori Rd., Thorndon, Wellington. Tel. 473-7268.

Katherine Mansfield, New Zealand-born short-story writer, poet, and essayist, first saw the light of day in 1888. One of the country's most prestigious writers—and arguably its most famous worldwide—she inspires such veneration that a nonprofit organization was formed to restore the old house to its decor in the year of her birth. There's a shop with books, cards, posters, and souvenirs, and if you order in advance, you can enjoy a light lunch or morning/afternoon tea on the premises.

Admission: NZ$4 ($2) adults, NZ$2 ($1) senior citizens and students, NZ$1 (60¢) children.

Open: Tues–Sun 10am–4pm.

NATIONAL ART GALLERY and NATIONAL MUSEUM, Buckle St. Tel. 485-9609.

✪ The art gallery emphasizes both New Zealand and international art, and on most Sundays at 2:30pm there's a free music recital, theatrical performance, film, or lecture. Artifacts of South Pacific, New Zealand, and Maori history are featured at the museum.

Admission: Free.
Open: Daily 10am–4:45pm. **Closed:** Christmas Day and Good Friday. **Bus:**
No. 11 stops at Buckle St.; nos. 1 and 3 run to Basin Reserve, about a 5-minute walk.

WELLINGTON MARITIME MUSEUM, Queens Wharf. Tel. 472-8904 or
472-3738.

✪ Those interested in things of the sea will want to visit this museum, where
Wellington's close association with seafarers and their vessels is well docu-
mented, with displays of ship models, paintings, flags, bells, maps, logbooks,
and a reconstructed captain's cabin. The museum is located in the Wellington
Harbour Board Building.
Admission: Free (donations requested).
Open: Mon–Fri 9:30am–4pm, Sat–Sun and public holidays 1–4pm. **Closed:**
Christmas Day and Good Friday.

WELLINGTON ZOO, Newtown. Tel. 489-8130.
This zoo dates back to 1906 and its collection includes kangaroos, wallabies,
monkeys, and flightless birds (there's a nocturnal **Kiwi House** open from 10am to
4pm). In fine weather on weekends and holidays there are miniature railway rides from
noon to 4pm, for minimal charges. You can watch them feed the tigers at 2pm, lions at
3:20pm (except on Monday and Friday).
Admission: NZ$6 ($3) adults, NZ$3 ($2) children; free to those under 5.
Open: Daily 8:30am–5pm. **Bus:** Newtown Park bus (no. 11) from railway
station. Buses to Houghton Bay, View Road, and Melrose also pass the zoo.

MORE ATTRACTIONS

You can tour **Parliament** any weekday free of charge. Just telephone 471-9457 for
tour times. And if by this time you're hooked on New Zealand history and culture,
spend some time at the ✪ **National Library of New Zealand,** which is across
the road from Parliament, at 70 Molesworth St. You can browse in the **National
Library Gallery,** bookshop, and the New Zealand collection of books, all on the
ground floor. The **Alexander Turnbull Library,** in the same building, is the
research wing of the National Library, specializing in New Zealand and the Pacific.
Books, serials, sound recordings, manuscripts, and archives are researched on the first
floor, and newspapers on the ground floor. On the second floor, visitors can peruse
files of photographs, and drawings, paintings, and maps are available for research by
appointment. Hours are 9am to 5pm weekdays (and 9am to 1pm on Saturday for
nonpictorial materials).

To bring this city's history sharply alive, keep an eye out for ✪ **12 shoreline
plaques,** which have been embedded in footpaths to show the sites of early
Wellington: You'll find them at Pipitea Point, on the south side of Davis Street and
Thorndon Quay; at the top of the steps leading to Rutherford House; in Mason's
Lane, on the north side; on Lambton Quay, north of Woodward Street; on the
Lambton Quay footpath near Cable Car Lane; at Steward Dawson's, on the west side
of the Lambton Quay corner; at Chews Lane, on the east side of the Willis Street
footpath; on Mercer Street, outside George Harrison Ltd. on the Willis Street corner;
on Farrish Street, on the southeast side of Farrish and Lombard Streets; on Cuba
Street outside Smith and Smith Ltd., on Taranaki Street outside the Caltex Service
Station; and on Wakefield Street next to the Schaffer Street bus stop.

✪ **Old St. Paul's Church,** on Mulgrave Street, in the suburb of Thorndon (tel.
473-6722), is a marvelous Early English Gothic–style wooden church much beloved
by Wellingtonians. Using the native timbers of totara, matai, rimu, and kauri, the softly
lit church with its dark timbers, soaring wooden arches, and brilliant stained glass
radiates peace and calmness. A relaxing stop in your sightseeing itinerary. There's no

admission (they do welcome donations, though), and it is open to the public from 10:30am to 4:30pm every day except Sunday, when hours are 1 to 4:30pm, Christmas Day and Good Friday.

ORGANIZED TOURS

BUS TOURS The best possible way to get an in-depth look at the city itself and its immediate environs is to take the escorted ✪ **City Scenic Tours bus tour** (tel. 473-9955 to book), which leaves from the Visitors Information Centre on Wakefield Street every day at 10am and 2pm. For the bargain price of NZ$22 ($13) for adults (children ride for half price), you'll be driven some 30 miles, with 2½ hours of informative narrative as you see the financial and commercial center, take a look at government buildings and Parliament's unique Beehive building, visit the lookout on Mount Victoria (with a stop for picture taking), skirt the bays, stop for afternoon tea, then reenter the city via View Road, a scenic drive, which does full justice to Wellington's headlands, hills, bays, and beaches. The Visitors Information Centre can also furnish details on a wide variety of other city and area tours available.

HARBOR CRUISES There's no doubt about it—that spectacular harbor exerts an irresistible pull to see Wellington from the water. The bargain way to accomplish this is via the ✪ **East by West ferry** (tel. 499-1273 for timetable information), which crosses the harbor from Queen's Wharf in Wellington to Days Bay. The 25-minute ride on the *Government Print I* costs NZ$6 ($3) each way, and NZ$3 ($2) for children, or NZ$33 ($19) for a round-trip family excursion ticket that covers two adults and up to four children. The ferry has a full bar and also serves coffee. At Days Bay, you can enjoy the park, have afternoon tea in the pavilion, or take the 3-minute stroll around to Eastbourne for galleries, gift shops, and the new At the Bay Restaurant on the waterfront, recommended if you arrive at meal time.

Other, more costly cruises are offered by **Harbour City Cruises** (tel. 485-2466) and **Bluefin Launches** (tel. 469-8203); both offer day and nighttime cruises, with or without food and beverage.

Incidentally, if the Wellington/Picton **Inter-Island Ferry** (tel. 498-3999) is not on your travel itinerary, ask about their excursion special that lets you pay one-way and return the same day free. It's one of Wellington's very special experiences, so don't miss it. For details, see Section 11, below.

6. SPORTS & RECREATION

Many of the city's **gymnasiums** welcome drop-in guests. An aerobics or stretching class or a weightlifting session costs about NZ$6 or NZ$7 ($3 or $4). The Visitors Information Centre can provide details.

The ✪ **Wellington Regional Aquatic Center,** in the suburb of Kilbirnie (tel. 487-8029), has four heated pools: a lap pool, learners' pool, and adjoining junior and toddlers' pools with an access ramp for the disabled. There are also diving facilities, spa pools, saunas, a sun deck, café, and YMCA fitness center. You can rent swimsuits and towels; goggles are for sale. The no. 2 bus to Miramar takes you to the door.

The **Wellington Renouf Tennis Centre,** on Brooklyn Road at Central Park (tel. 484-6294), has 14 outdoor and 4 indoor courts available for rent at about NZ$28 ($17.50) an hour. It's open from 6am to 11pm Monday through Friday and 8am to 11pm on Saturday and Sunday. Practice or hitting partners can be arranged on short notice, and there's a café on the premises.

Horse racing is a popular sport in Wellington, and it's **Hutt Park Racecourse**

is classified as all-weather. For recorded racing information, call 473-8880 (24-hour service).

7. SAVVY SHOPPING

The prices at the **Robbie Burns Bottle Shop,** at 75 Kent Terrace, are substantially below others in the city; for instance, Mac's beer sells here for several New Zealand dollars less than elsewhere. **John Bull & Co. Ltd.,** 8 Bond St. (near Town Hall), and **Rumble's Wine Cellar,** 32 Waring Taylor St., have good New Zealand wines.

For window-shopping and browsing, stroll the ✪ **Manners and Cuba pedestrian malls,** which are particularly fun on Friday night when the buskers are out. You'll find crafts and secondhand shops on Cuba Street near Ghuznee Street.

The **Wakefield Market** is held on Friday, Saturday, and Sunday, and is filled with clothing, leather goods, and jewelry. Antiques shops are in the suburb of Brooklyn.

Aki, on Victoria Street, is a good souvenir shop. For splurge shopping, head to **Vibrant Handknits** on Kent Terrace. **Leitch Gallery,** in Regent Centre off Manners Mall, sells prints of Wellington that make fine souvenirs.

The **duty-free shop** in central Wellington is at the DFC Centre, on Grey Street, with a branch out at the airport.

One item to look for in Wellington may well become your most treasured souvenir—the whimsical ✪ **Tidy Kiwi poster.** That egg-shaped national bird is shown using its long, pointed bill to pick up papers and put them into a litter bag. It will cost you only NZ$2 ($1.15) and will serve to remind you (and any untidy little birds of your own back home) just how clean and tidy is this very civilized country. You can pick one up at the offices of **Keep New Zealand Beautiful Society, Inc.,** Boulcott House, 47 Boulcott St. (tel. 473-8205). If you can't manage a visit, drop them a line and they'll mail the poster.

8. EVENING ENTERTAINMENT

Check the current issue of the *Capital Times* and the *What's On,* available at tourist information centers, for entertainment.

THE PERFORMING ARTS   The **Downstage Theatre,** in the Hannah Playhouse on Cambridge Terrace (tel. 484-9639), presents first-rate theater in an exciting theater structure that provides for flexibility in staging in the main auditorium and a smaller cabaret in the bar. The Downstage is a year-round enterprise, staging classics and contemporary drama, musicals, and comedies, and works of New Zealand playwrights. Check the newspapers for current showings. Reserve as far in advance as you possibly can, however, for Downstage productions are very popular. Ticket prices are NZ$27 ($15) for the auditorium and NZ$20 ($11) for the gallery. Students, senior citizens, and groups of 10 receive a ticket discount. **Bats Theatre,** on Kent Terrace (tel. 484-9507), presents plays that attract a young audience, as well as folks who are not traditional theatergoers. Tickets are NZ$14 ($8).

Check the newspapers to see what's doing at the new **Michael Fowler Centre,** Wakefield Street (tel. 472-3088), an exciting contemporary structure that has been added to Wellington's old Town Hall to enlarge auditorium space. There are concerts and other events scheduled there throughout the year.

THE CLUB & BAR SCENE   The **James Cook** has a piano bar nightly, classical string quartet on Saturday and Sunday; **Paisley Park,** upstairs at 24 Taranaki St. (tel.

485-7715), is open 7 nights a week from 7pm to 1am for live music (the cover charge varies) or for recorded music, along with Dutch-style food, drinks, and an inviting atmosphere; the ✪ **Greta Point Tavern,** Evans Bay Parade (tel. 486-1066), has live entertainment Friday and Saturday nights; and ✪ **Old Bailey Bar & Café,** at the corner of Lambton Quay and Bailance Street (tel. 471-2021), and sing-along nights from Wednesday to Friday.

9. EASY EXCURSIONS FROM WELLINGTON

THE KAPITI COAST

Within an hour's drive northwest of Wellington, the Kapiti Coast (*kapiti* is the Maori word for "place where the boundaries of Tara and Rangitane divide") is a region of lovely beaches, scenic mountain drives, lakes, and rivers. En route, you'll pass fruit and vegetable stalls selling fresh produce from the region, and you should keep an eye out for the many craft shops along the way. The **Kapiti Information Centre,** Coastlands Shoppingtown car park, Paraparaumu (tel. *058/88-195), can furnish detailed information on the entire region.

Just 5 kilometers (3 miles) offshore at **Paraparaumu Beach** (its Maori name comes from *parapara* [scraps] and *umu* [earth oven], and the name was bestowed by a war party that could find only scraps of food), a regional highlight is ✪ **Kapiti Island,** a bird sanctuary that one of our readers described as "a slice of New Zealand before the Pakeha arrived—primeval bush and tame birds. Most spectacular are the *wekas* (flightless rails) and *kakas* (arboreal cousins of keas), both quite unashamed about sharing your lunch!" Not much I can add to that except to tell you that you must have a permit (NZ$10, U.S. $6, fee) from the Department of Conservation, P.O. Box 5086, Wellington (tel. 472-5821), to visit the sanctuary (if you have difficulty reaching them, ask for assistance from the Wellington Visitors Information Centre). All visitors must wade ashore, so take strong shoes, a pullover, something for your head (it's windy), and your own food and drink. You'll be met by a resident ranger, who will brief you on the island and its wildlife. Around the island, divers, boat people, and fisherpeople have a field day. For transport out to the island, contact **Kapiti Launches,** Paraparaumu Beach (tel. *058/86-085).

Directions: Take Highway 1 north and watch for signposted turnoffs to scenic drives over the **Paekakariki Hill road** and flat roads to **Raumati Beach** and other beaches along this coast, all of which are quite safe for swimming.

WAIRARAPA

Northeast of Wellington, a little less than 2 hours' drive from Wellington, the Wairarapa region is well worth a day-trip from the city—even better, an overnight stay in order to explore all the riches of the region.

En route to Masterton, the region's chief town, plan your first stop in Featherston to visit ✪ **Kahutara Canoes,** R.D. 1, Featherston (tel. *0553/88-453.) Owner John McCosh, also known as "Tuatara Ted" and often called New Zealand's Crocodile Dundee, and his wife Karen have put together a fascinating taxidermy museum. In a spacious Canadian log structure, the museum houses more than 350 mounted animals from around the globe. John is a friendly, colorful character, always happy to show you around and talk about all the specimens. He is also enthusiastic about the small animal park he was just getting started when I visited.

The museum, however, is only a small part of what the McCoshes get up to. They and their staff of expert guides operate a variety of canoe trips on the scenic Ruamahanga River. The canoes range from large, stable Canadian craft down to fast one- and two-man kayaks, and the river trips are designed to appeal to all ages, from toddlers to grandparents. Some are as short as 2 or 3 hours, others for 3 or more hours. You'll have to call ahead for hours, charges, and to book. But no matter if you only plan to visit the museum (NZ$2, U.S. $1; open from 10am to 5pm daily), be sure to allow extra time here—it's *very* hard to pop in and right back out!

In Greytown, look for the **Turkey Red Coffee and Tea Shop,** set in an original homestead of this area. The ✪ **Cobblestone Colonial Settlers Museum** in Greytown also has a tearoom, and hours are 9am to 5pm daily. And all along this route, anytime you're assaulted by a terrible thirst, drop in to almost any bar or tavern, most of which can draw a refreshing pint of local brews. In Carterton, a stop at the ✪ **Paua Shell Factory Shop,** 54 Kent St. (tel. *0593/6777), can yield unique gifts, jewelry, and souvenirs, and there are free factory tours on the hour. Hours are 8am to 4:30pm Monday through Friday, and 10am to 3pm on Saturday and Sunday. Carterton is also a good place to look for New Zealand leather products— **Jeffrey Chandel Leathers,** 69-73 Nelson Crescent (tel. *0593/8927), makes an extensive line of ladies' and men's jackets and coats, as well as a wide range of other leather products, all at competitive prices. They're open from 9am to 5pm Monday through Friday, 9am to 3pm on Saturday, and 10am to 2pm *most* Sundays (call in advance to see if they're open).

The **Tourism Wairarapa Visitor Information Centre,** 5 Dixon St. (tel. *059/87-373; fax *09/80-433), should be your very first stop. The bright modern building houses loads of literature on attractions in the region, the many nature walks, and sporting opportunities. The friendly staff can also furnish information on accommodations (everything from luxury motels to farm stays) and places to eat. With reference to the latter, my own recommendation is[*$] **Le Peht Café,** 8 Bannister St. (tel. *059/85-776), a charming, intimate BYO restaurant where lunch will run about NZ$12 ($7), dinner in the NZ$22 to $24 ($13 to $14) range. They take MasterCard and VISA; hours are 11am to 2:30pm Tuesday through Friday for lunch, 6:30 to 10pm Wednesday through Saturday. This one's so popular you should book as far ahead as you can.

This is one of the best regions in the country in which to explore New Zealand's native bush country. Ask at the visitors center for the *Wairarapa Walks* booklet, which details all manner of walks, trails, and tracks. A great wilderness experience.

Twenty-eight kilometers (17 miles) north of Masterton on State Highway 2, the ✪ **Mount Bruce National Wildlife Centre,** R.D. 1, Masterton (tel. *06505/8004), is one of the most moving wildlife experiences I've run across. Its 15 different aviaries; nocturnal complex inhabited by a large population of kiwi, morepork owls, and weta; and outside paths that wind through native bush are a world apart and one seldom accessible to the likes of you and me. I was especially touched by the work they do with wounded and sick birds, some of which are brought from other parts of the country. I also like the fact that paths have been made wheelchair friendly. In the Visitor Centre at the entrance there's an audiovisual exhibit, a souvenir/craft shop, and tearooms overlooking the natural splendors just beyond wide picture windows. Hours are 9am to 4pm daily except Christmas Day, and there's a NZ$6 ($3) admission fee for adults, NZ$1.50 (90¢) for children, and NZ$12 ($7) for a family ticket. Don't miss this one!

About 13 miles south of Masterton, the little townland of Martinborough is home to Wairarapa's six **wineries.** Most welcome visitors, but few are open at set hours, and it's best to set up a tour of one or more through Martinborough Winemakers Assn., P.O. Box 148, Martinborough, or Mr. Chifney, of Chifney Wines, Huangarua Road, Martinborough (tel. *0553/69-495).

Directions: Take Highway 2 northeast, through the Hutt Valley and across the Tararuas mountain range. Masterton is 62 miles from Wellington.

10. CROSSING BETWEEN THE NORTH & SOUTH ISLANDS

A special tip to those who won't be going on to the South Island (poor souls!): A marvelous ✪ **day-trip** is the round-trip on the ferry. You can take either of the morning departures, enjoy a sea voyage, and have 5 full hours in Picton before returning on the 6:40pm ferry from Picton (see "Harbor Tours," above). I highly recommend it.

From Wellington's Aotea Quay (north of the city center), the Cook Strait ferries depart several times daily for Picton, across on the South Island. Earliest sailing is 8am; the latest, 6:40pm. All tickets must be booked, and sailing times can be affected by weather conditions, so be *sure* to check current sailing times and book by calling 04/498-3999 (or *0800/685-999 from outside Wellington) between 6am and 8pm daily. City buses for the terminal leave from Platform 9 at the railway station 35 minutes before sailing time and meet arriving vessels. Also, since crossings can become quite crowded during summer months and holiday periods, it's a good idea to make your reservations as early as possible (perhaps through InterCity offices at your point of arrival). Fares for the 3⅓-hour, 52-nautical-mile trip are NZ$35 ($20) for adults, NZ$18 ($10) for children, plus GST. Ask about special excursion fares, weekend specials, and seasonal price changes. If you're going on to Christchurch, an express train leaves for Christchurch at 2:10pm (connects with the 10am sailing from Wellington), and for a small charge your luggage can be through-checked at the luggage office at the Wellington Railway Station. Also, buses to and from Blenheim, Nelson, and Christchurch connect with some ferry arrivals and departures.

You'll travel on the Inter-Island Line on either the refurbished *Arahanga,* *Arahura,* or *Aratika,* each of which has a licensed bar, cafeteria, television lounge, information bureau, and shop. The *Arahura* and *Aratika* also have a family lounge with toys to keep young children amused during the voyage, video and movie theaters, a recliner lounge, and a work room. Crossings generally take on a jovial air, with passengers strolling the decks (whatever you do, don't go inside until you've viewed the departure from Wellington's lovely harbor from the rail—a sight you'll long remember) or congregating happily in the lounges, passing the time over friendly conversation and mugs of beer. Warning: Someone once spoke of Cook Strait's "vexed waters," and in truth the swells can be a little unsettling. If you're subject to a queasy stomach at sea, best pick up something from the pharmacy before embarking. Another tip: If you don't want to miss one minute of the magnificent views or the company of friendly schools of dolphins, take along a picnic lunch to eat outside under the sky and the curious glances of seagulls wheeling overhead.

As you approach the Marlborough Sound, its green waters lap shorelines (more than 600 miles in all) of wooded hills, sheer cliffs, sandy beaches in sheltered coves, and tidy little hideaway cottages, some of which may only be approached by water. Most of the islands and native bush reserves are a part of the Marlborough Sound Maritime Park, and there are picnic grounds, lookouts, and forest walks, as well as scenic roads, scattered throughout. The Maoris knew these waters as rich fishing grounds, and today they are still fished for blue cod, snapper, terakihi, grouper, kingfish, and butterfish. Protected sea fish like dolphins (and the occasional seal) romp playfully around the ferries. If you're crossing in the summer, you'll pass scores of pleasure and fishing launches and wave to happy bathers on the beaches.

Picton, your South Island debarkation point, actually lies *north* of Wellington, so you'll be sailing north to reach the South Island. Curious. Situated at the head of Queen Charlotte South, it was named by Captain Cook in 1770 for King George III's wife. He found it "a very safe and convenient cove," and indeed used it as an anchorage for much of his later Pacific exploration. He can also be credited for bringing the first sheep to New Zealand, when he put ashore a ram and a ewe in 1773—prophetic, even though that particular pair survived only a few days, and thus the good captain cannot lay claim to having furnished the fountainhead of today's millions of woolly creatures.

Most travelers scurry from ferry to train, bus, or rental car and are then off to explore an island so different from the one they've just left that there have been times in the past when there was great agitation for its independence as a separate colony. However, if time permits and the Marlborough Sound tempts you beyond resistance, you might consider staying over for some time on the water aboard one of the several launches that offer several-hours-long or day-long cruises. You'll find a cluster of launch operators at the corner of London Quay and Wellington Street near the marina in Picton. The cozy **Seaspray Tearooms Café,** on London Quay, is a good spot to get a quick bite to eat or cup of tea.

WHERE TO STAY IN PICTON

If you're making this crossing south to north and weather should cause a cancellation or delay in your scheduled voyage (as has been known to happen in these fickle waters), you could be looking for a place to spend the night. There are two motels on High Street, just a 5-minute walk from the ferry landing, and others are nearby.

A MOTEL

KOROMIKO PARK, State Hwy. 1 (P.O. Box 86), Picton. Tel. and fax 03/573-7350. 12 units (all with bath). TV TEL

$ Rates (excluding GST): NZ$60 ($34) single; NZ$63 ($36) double. AE, DC, MC, V.

This Best Western motel, hosted by Lyall and Harry Hodgson, has a swimming pool, a spa, trampoline, playground, and a guest laundry with dryer. Golfers will be glad to know there's a course right next door, and the Hodgsons will gladly arrange fishing or yacht charters for watery types. The motel is located 3½ miles from the ferry.

A HOSTEL

PAVLOVA BACKPACKERS, Auckland St., Picton. Tel. *057/36-598. 3 rms, 4 dormitories. TV TEL

$ Rates: NZ$15 ($9) dorm bed; NZ$30 ($17) double. No credit cards.

This inviting white house with wrought-iron trim is an easy walk from the ferry and railway station. In addition to four dormitories and three double rooms, the hostel has a lounge, laundry, kitchen, and large back lawn.

CHAPTER 8
NELSON & THE WEST COAST

Crossing the Cook Strait is something akin to crossing an international boundary, so different are New Zealand's two islands. That's not really surprising, because both geography and history are quite different on the two sides of that stretch of water.

On the South Island the majestic Southern Alps raise their snowy heads along the diagonal Alpine Fault that forms its craggy backbone. Along its West Coast are the lush, mysterious rain forests, while to the east of the Alps the broad Canterbury Plains stretch to the sea. It was on those plains that prehistoric moa-hunters lived in the greatest numbers, roaming the tussocklands in search of giant birds that grazed there. When waves of Maori began arriving, it was to the North Island that they gravitated, since its climate was more suitable for the growing of *kumara* and to their agrarian lifestyle. Thus, there were relatively few Polynesian settlements along the fringes of the South Island. It was the waters of the South Island that first lured sealers and whalers, although whalers found the northern Bay of Islands a more hospitable base for their land operations. Then when Europeans began arriving in great numbers and fierce land wars raged in the more populated North Island, the South Island Maori faced those conflicts only when tribes pushed from their lands in the north crossed the strait to battle southern tribes for territory. Because one tribe after another obliterated those who came before them, little evidence was left of South Island Maori culture, legend, and tradition.

The discovery of gold in Central Otago and on the West Coast finally brought whites pouring into the South Island in vast numbers. They came from Australia, from Europe, and from the goldfields of California to this new "promised land," and the South Island's tranquillity and isolation gave way to a booming economy, which for a time saw it leading the country in terms of both population and prosperity. Inevitably, the goldfields were mined beyond profitability, but then came the advent of refrigeration, which meant that meat could be exported on a large scale, and the South Island's grasslands became gold mines of a different sort. Thus, it is on this side of the strait that you'll see the most of these wooly four-legged nuggets busily eating their way to the butcher. As a tourist, you can give them a tip of the hat as you pass, for it is their need for widespread grazing land that accounts for the fact that today only a little more than one-quarter of New Zealand's population lives on the South Island. This means that you'll find uncrowded roadways, unhurried city lifestyles, and unspoiled scenic grandeur.

---

1. NELSON

68 miles W of Picton, 179 miles NE of Greymouth

GETTING THERE By Plane Service is provided by Air Nelson between Nelson and Auckland and New Plymouth on the North Island, Christchurch

WHAT'S SPECIAL ABOUT NELSON & THE WEST COAST

Scenic Splendors

☐ Abel Tasman National Park, the 54,683-acre park, extending from Separation Point in the north to Marahau Inlet in the south.

☐ Tahunanui Beach, 4 miles south of town, with its golden strand and many tourist conveniences that somehow manage not to commercialize the beach.

Historic Buildings

☐ Christ Church Cathedral, set on a hillside overlooking Trafalgar Street, a magnificent Gothic structure made of local Takaka marble, with its beautiful stained-glass rose window.

☐ Founder's Park Historical and Craft Village, in Atawhai Drive, a charming turn-of-the-century city in miniature that holds such treasures as Old St. Peter's Church, built in 1874.

Crafts

☐ South Street with its artistic population and restored colonial homes that hold all manner of craft workshops and sales rooms.

☐ The Craft Habitat on the Richmond By-Pass, a marvelous of craft workshops and showrooms.

---

and Hokitika on the South Island. **Air New Zealand** flies between Nelson and Auckland, Hastings/Napier, New Plymouth, Rotorua, and Wellington on the North Island; Christchurch and Dunedin on the South Island. **Mount Cook Airlines** have service between Nelson and New Plymouth and Rotorua on the North Island, Invercargill, Mount Cook, and Queenstown on the South Island. The **airport shuttle** van (tel. *82-304) operates regularly and costs only NZ$2.50 ($1.45).

By Train   There is daily rail service between Nelson and Christchurch.

By Bus   There are **Newmans** coaches that meet all daylight ferries in Picton, and they'll have you off to Nelson to begin your South Island odyssey for a fare of NZ$21 ($12). During the 2-hour trip, coaches take a tea break at the tearoom near Pelorus Bridge.

By Car   From Picton, it's a 2-hour drive to Nelson—70 miles along Route 6—filled with clifftop views, seascapes glimpsed from bush-lined stretches of the road, and rolling farmlands: a pleasant, picturesque journey you may want to break with a stop by the giant totara tree in picnic grounds near Pelorus Bridge.

ESSENTIALS   The telephone area code is **03.**

Orientation   Two landmarks will keep you oriented in Nelson: its main street, Trafalgar Street, and Church Hill, crowned by Christ Church Cathedral and surrounded by lush lawns and plantings that are a local gathering point.

Information   You'll find the **Nelson Regional Promotion Office Visitors Centre** on the corner of Trafalgar and Halifax Streets (P.O. Box 194), Nelson (tel. 03/548-2304). Hours are 7:30am to 5pm Monday through Friday, 8am to 5pm on Saturday, and during December and January only, 8am to 5pm on Sunday. *The Tourist Times,* published monthly, and the *Nelson Visitors' Guide* give you an

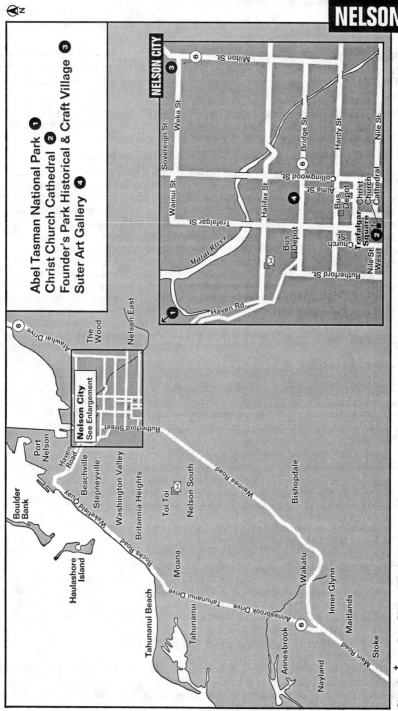

NELSON

NELSON CITY

Abel Tasman National Park ❶
Christ Church Cathedral ❷
Founder's Park Historical & Craft Village ❸
Suter Art Gallery ❹

Church ✝   Post Office ⊠

update on what to see and do; they are available from the visitors center and local hotels and motels.

FAST FACTS The **American Express** company is represented by Cox World Travel, 58 Dalton St. (tel. *03/548-9079). **Taxis** pick up riders outside the Majestic Theatre on Trafalgar Street and on Bridge Street opposite Suburban Bus Company, or you can call **City Taxis** (tel. 548-8225) for 24-hour door-to-door service.

DEPARTING **Newmans Coach Line** (tel. 548-8369) is conveniently housed in the same building as the visitors center, and coaches arrive and depart from here. Check with the visitors center about **rail** schedules and booking.

Nelson sits on the shores of Nelson Haven, sheltered by the unique 7-mile natural wall of Boulder Bank. Its 2,500 hours of annual sunshine, its tranquil waters, and its golden sand beaches make it perhaps the South Island's most popular summer resort. That wonderful climate, combined with the fertile land hereabouts, also makes it an important center of fruit, grapes, hops, and tobacco growing. And maybe all that sunshine has something to do with an easygoing, tolerant outlook that makes it a haven for those of an artistic bent. Potters are here in abundance, drawn by a plentiful supply of fine clay and the minerals needed for glazing; weavers raise sheep and create natural-wool works of art; artists spend hours on end trying to capture on canvas the splendors of a Nelson sunset or the shifting light on sparkling water.

Col. William Wakefield hoisted the New Zealand Company flag on Britannia Heights in December 1841 and placed a 9-pound cannon there as a signal gun (it's there today for you to see), and settlers began arriving on February 1, 1842, a day still celebrated annually in Nelson. They named the new town Nelson to honor that great British seafaring hero, since the company's first New Zealand settlement, Wellington, had been named for Britain's most famous soldier. Lord Nelson's victories, ships, and fellow admirals are commemorated in street names like Trafalgar, Vanguard, and Collingwood. Graves of some of those early settlers lie under the trees at Fairfield Park (at the corner of Trafalgar Street South and Brougham Street), and many of the gabled wooden houses they built still cling to Nelson's hillsides and nestle among more modern structures on midtown streets. Some have become the homes and studios of the artistic community.

Nelson has two distinctions of which it is equally proud: It is known as the "cradle of rugby" in New Zealand, first played here in 1870 (although Christchurch's Football Club is older than Nelson's, it didn't adopt the national sport until some 5 years after its introduction at Nelson's Botanical Reserve); and a native son, Baron Rutherford, has been called the "father of nuclear physics" because it was he who first discovered the secret of splitting the atom, along with other scientific achievements that brought him international renown, and his name is perpetuated in place names like Rutherford Park, Street, and Hotel.

Come harvest time, as many as 3,000 workers—many of them students—come trooping into town to stay until the millions of apples, pears, hops, and tobacco leaves have been brought in from the surrounding fields. With its characteristic openness of spirit, Nelson assimilates them as quickly and easily as it does the hordes of tourists who descend on its beaches year after year. There's a refreshing brand of hospitality afoot in this town, which makes it a fitting introduction to the South Island.

WHAT TO SEE & DO

As always, my strong recommendation is a visit to the visitors center before you even begin wandering around Nelson—they're a friendly bunch, all too eager to arm you with brochures, maps, and helpful advice about seeing the town and its environs.

Walkers will be in their element in Nelson and the immediate vicinity. Good walks abound, both in-city and in the environs, varying from an hour to a full-day's tramp. The visitors center has detailed guide pamphlets from which to select those you'll have time to enjoy. Be sure to ask for *Nelson—The City of Walks,* for which there's a small charge. My personal favorite stroll is along **Shakespeare Walk,** which follows the Maitai River and can be picked up where Collingwood and Halifax Streets intersect at the bridge. You'll see ducks and quaint cottages and cross a pedestrian bridge that will point you back into town.

CHRIST CHURCH CATHEDRAL, Trafalgar St.

There's no way you're going to miss seeing this cathedral, sitting as it does on a splendid elevation at the end of Trafalgar Street in the center of town. And chances are good that you'll find yourself, at some point during your Nelson stay, stopping for a rest in its beautiful grounds—if you follow the lead of the locals, you'll bypass the handy benches to stretch out on the grass. That site, now known as **Church Hill,** has in the past held an early Maori *pa,* the New Zealand Company's depot, a small fort, and a tent church. The present Gothic cathedral is made of local Takaka marble; above its west door are the carved heads of five bishops, one archbishop, and King George V. The most striking aspects of the interior of the cathedral are its stained glass, particularly the rose window, and its unique freestanding organ.

Tours: Guides available between Christmas and Easter.
Open: Daily 7am–4pm (extended hours in summer).

SUTER ART GALLERY, Bridge St. Tel. 548-4699.

Nelson's affection for the arts is exemplified in this excellent museum in the town center. Works by a bevy of important New Zealand painters are on display, and there's an outstanding collection of works by master painter John Gully, who lived here for a time—if they're not on display, they can be seen by appointment. The gallery also has a craft shop selling prints, pottery, and weaving, and a nice restaurant overlooking Queen's Gardens. The gallery has a recently completed multifunctional theater that seats 160 people and an extensive program of film, theater, music, and dance; to find out what's on, check the local newspaper. There's also a restaurant for light lunches and snacks.

Admission: NZ$1 (60¢) per person.
Open: Daily 10:30am–4:30pm.

FOUNDER'S PARK HISTORICAL AND CRAFT VILLAGE, 87 Atawhai Dr. Tel. 548-2649.

This turn-of-the-century city in miniature is a true celebration of Nelson's commercial and industrial development. Old St. Peter's Church, built in 1874, has been moved here. There is a 17-minute audiovisual show and a gift shop with reasonable prices. The unique Visitors Centre, by the way, is a replica of an old mill that used to stand in Nelson where the Visitors Centre is now. Among all the exhibits, my favorites are the Newmans coaches from 1923, 1947, and 1952, which actually saw years of service.

The **Anchor Inn** restaurant, in a building dating from 1853 (entry either from the complex or from the car-park area), is open for meals from 11:30am to 3:30pm and for tea until 4pm. Its award-winning cuisine is based on New Zealand traditional dishes, and they stock a good selection of Nelson wines and ales. The complex is located on the edge of town.

Admission: NZ$4 ($2) adults, NZ$2 ($1) children, NZ$11 ($6) family ticket.
Open: Daily 10am–4:30pm. **Closed:** Christmas Day and Good Friday.

ABEL TASMAN NATIONAL PARK.

⭐ This extremely beautiful and popular park, named for 17th-century Dutch explorer Abel Tasman, covers 54,683 acres, extending from Separation Point, which divides Golden and Tasman Bays in the north, to Marahau Inlet in the south. A popular way to see some of the park is to take an **Abel Tasman National Park Enterprises boat trip** from Kaiteriteri and be dropped off at Bark Bay; then walk the track 2½ hours to Torrent Bay, where you'll have 3 hours to enjoy the area. Other boat trips provide just as much scenery, but less exercise. This area, with its sandy coves, has been called the most beautiful stretch of coastline in New Zealand. Most of the boat trips cost NZ$30 ($17) for adults, half that for children. There's a bus from Nelson to Kaiteriteri, with a round-trip fare of about NZ$10 ($6).

If you feel like splurging (physically, spiritually, and monetarily), link up with one of the **4-day guided walks** through the park offered by Abel Tasman National Park Enterprises. For details of the walks and a host of other services (including a bus and ferry excursion to the park), contact John Wilson, Abel Tasman National Park Enterprises, Green Tree Road, R.D.3, Motueka, Nelson (tel. *0524/87-801).

NEARBY ATTRACTIONS

A map detailing **scenic drives** from Nelson is available at the visitors center, all of which pass points of historical significance as well as natural beauty. There are two **national parks** within driving distance, sheltered **sandy beaches** all along the coast (one of the best is ⭐ **Tahuna Beach,** 3 miles to the south, or if it's too crowded, the beach at **Rabbit Island**), and several wineries open to the public (ask at the visitors center for *A Guide to Nelson's Wineries*). If you don't relish being behind the wheel yourself, several coach tours and scenic flights are available—current details from the visitors center.

One place you should definitely plan to visit is the suburb of **Stoke,** where you'll find the two attractions listed below.

NELSON PROVINCIAL MUSEUM, Isel Park, Stoke.

⭐ Filled with artifacts and displays depicting the area's Maori and European history, the museum also has the largest collection of historical photographs in New Zealand, with more than a million images, as well as a large historical reference library.

The museum sits directly behind an elegant 19th-century stone house with dormer windows and an ornate veranda, which is known as **Isel House,** situated in manicured grounds set back from the Main Road. The house, with its collections of early porcelain, pottery, and furniture, is only open on weekends from November to March from 2 to 4pm, but the park itself is well worth a stroll to relax beneath mature trees, which came to New Zealand from worldwide origins as seeds or mere saplings in the 19th century. The museum is located in town—you can't miss it.

Admission: Free.

Open: Museum Tues–Fri 10am–4pm, Sat–Sun and holidays 2–5pm.

BROADGREEN HOUSE, 276 Nayland Rd. Tel. 03/546-0283.

⭐ This marvelous old cob house (thick walls made of packed earth) was built in 1855 and has been authentically restored and furnished by dedicated volunteers. Their care and attention to detail is evident all through the house, from the drawing room with its slate mantelpiece and original French wallpaper to the upstairs nursery with wicker carriages and antique dolls. All that work has earned the house a New Zealand Tourism Award. Outside, the rose garden holds more than 2,500 plants, with some 250 varieties represented. The house is in town, near Nayland pool.

Admission: NZ$2 ($1) adults, NZ50¢ (30¢) children.
Open: Wed, Sat–Sun, and public holidays 2–4:30pm. Extended hours in Jan–Feb, May, and Aug; check with the visitors center. **Closed:** Christmas Day and Good Friday.

READERS RECOMMEND: TOURING

*"The side trip to **Kaiteriteri beach and Kaka Pa Point,** looking to Abel Tasman, was one of the most magnificent views on the South Island. We also took the road to Totaranui Park in Abel Tasman Park; it was fantastic at the end but the road was awful."*—J. and P. Conrad, San Jose, Calif.

SPORTS & RECREATION

If you've ever cast a line or dropped a hook, the South Island's marvelous fishing waters are bound to be a temptation to tarry long enough to try your luck. The only problem is knowing just where, when, and how to fish all those rivers, lakes, and streams. Well, in Nelson take yourself off to **Sportsgoods (Nelson) Ltd.** on the CML Corner (tel. 548-9899) to see Tony Busch and his staff. Tony knows these waters well and has guided fisherfolk from all over the world who come here just to fish with him. Tony has also written several guidebooks that lead visiting anglers mile by mile to the best fishing spots in New Zealand. His latest book, **A Trout Fishing Guide to New Zealand's South Island,** describes not only fishing areas but the geography, climate, and anglers' techniques used in the South Island. One reader (A. L. Holmes, from Denver, Colo.) wrote in praise of the book: "I have made three trips to New Zealand in the last four years, and without a guide, my fishing has been mediocre at best. I can't afford a guide every day, nor do I want one with me every day. Sometimes I enjoy just the sound of the water and my own thoughts. I have never seen such a thoroughly detailed book, and I firmly believe that anyone with a little talent at all can have a spectacular fishing vacation with Tony's book as his guide." No matter what your time or budget requirements, the anglers at Sportsgoods can put together a fishing expedition to fit, and you may be certain you'll carry home many a "fish story" as a result.

Vern Brabant, of the **Nelson River Guides,** P.O. Box 469, Nelson (tel. 03/548-5095), is highly regarded locally as a guide. He offers excellent trout-fishing forays, with a maximum of two anglers at a time. He'll take you into remote places—using combinations of helicopters and planes—and camping is in tents.

SHOPPING FOR ARTS & CRAFTS

One of the great pleasures of a stop in Nelson is visiting some of its many resident artists and artisans. The visitors center can give you a brochure of names and addresses of those who welcome visitors to their studios and suggested tour itineraries. I can promise in advance that it will be a rewarding experience to talk with painters, weavers, potters, and other craftspeople about the subject dearest to their hearts— rewarding, too, perhaps in that very special memento or gift you may find for sale.

Actually, even without that list, you can spend a marvelous hour or two along ✪ **South Street** with its artistic population. It's lined with small colonial homes, which have been creatively restored, and the street gives you a sense of what early Nelson must have been like. At the corner of Nile and South Streets, visit the **South Street Gallery** in an old, two-story brown house to see some of Nelson's finest pottery. It's open from 10am to 5pm daily.

The **Nelson Community Potters,** 136 Rutherford St., is the hangout of talented amateur potters, and there are regular day schools (just in case you're an aspiring potter yourself). There's usually someone at work there, and many of their finished products are for sale. Drop by **Seven Weavers,** 36 Collingwood St., for prime examples of weaving from natural wools. You'll find crafts happily mingling with art at the **Suter Art Gallery,** on Bridge Street.

Other interesting craft shops are the **Glass Studio,** 276 Hardy St., which also stocks small sculptures, paintings, pottery, and jewelry; and **Jens Hansen,** a cooperative gold- and silversmith workshop and sales room, 320 Trafalgar Sq.

Still farther south, on the Richmond By-Pass (Salisbury Road), Paul Laird runs **Waimea Pottery Ltd.** (tel. 544-7481) as part of the **Craft Habitat** (P.O. Box 3065, Richmond, Nelson), a collection of quality craft workshops and a coffee shop and gallery. His ovenproof stoneware and lusterware are sold in the Richmond showroom and throughout New Zealand, as are the unique hand-printed tiles by Colleen Laird.

WHERE TO STAY

It is true of Nelson, as of most beach resorts, that accommodations are hard to come by in summer (December through January), and many Kiwi families book here from year to year. While it's not impossible to arrive roomless and find a place to lay your head, it is very, very chancy. Book early. Or plan to come in late fall (April and May) or early spring (September or October) when things are not so crowded and the weather is still fine.

As is also true of most resorts, Nelson has a wide variety of accommodations. You'll find them in the city proper and at the beachside suburb of **Tahunanui,** which is 4 miles away, but served by city buses. The visitors center is not set up to handle reservations, but will refer you to the **Nelson District Motel Association,** where members serve on a rotating basis as a central booking agency for all members. They are very accommodating and will do their best to find a vacancy for you in the price range you require. If you come into town when the visitors center is not open, there will be a sign posted in their window giving the name, address, and telephone number of the "on duty" motel.

Unless otherwise noted, the rates quoted below include GST.

MOTEL FLATS

BLUE WATERS MOTEL, 66 Golf Rd., Tahunanui, Nelson. Tel. 03/548-5080. Fax 03/548-6605. 13 units (all with bath). TV TEL
$ Rates (excluding GST): NZ$74 ($43) single; NZ$87 ($50) double. Best Western discounts available. AE, DC, MC, V.
Pat and Duncan Fuller are the congenial hosts at Blue Waters, a very good Best Western, located 4.5 kilometers (3 miles) from the center of town. Units are centered around a pretty landscaped lawn (with a lovely lemon tree) and heated swimming pool. The well-appointed one- and two-bedroom units have TVs with video and electric blankets, and one has a water bed. Amenities include a hot spa, trampoline, and guest laundry, and cooked or continental breakfasts are available.

COURTESY COURT MOTEL, 30 Golf Rd., Tahunanui, Nelson. Tel. and fax 03/548-5114. 15 units, 1 suite (all with bath). TV TEL **Directions:** 4km (2½ miles) from town center, near Tahuna Beach; entrance to Golf Rd. is at Kentucky Fried Chicken in the Tahunanui shopping area.
$ Rates (excluding GST): NZ$73 ($42) single; NZ$85 ($49) double; suite NZ$85 ($49) single, NZ$13 ($7) per extra person. Best Western discounts available. AE, DC, MC, V.

Several factors make this one of my favorite Best Western motels in New Zealand: its proximity to the beach (a short walk); pretty grounds (with well-tended, colorful flowerbeds); and comfortable accommodations. I also like the arrangements of the units around an inner court away from street noises and facing the attractive heated swimming pool. There are bed-sitters, one-bedroom units that sleep as many as four, and two-bedroom units that will sleep six; all have complete kitchen, soft carpets, electric blankets and heaters, radio, a drying rack for hand wash, washcloths, and a complimentary morning paper; one "honeymoon" unit has a water bed and spa bath. A luxury "executive suite" is also available, with space for six. A guest laundry, spa pool, and children's play area are additional conveniences. Owners Deborah and Tony Hocking welcome children and will gladly provide a cot and highchair as well as arrange for babysitters.

MID-CITY MOTOR LODGE, 218 Trafalgar St., Nelson. Tel. 03/546-9063. Fax 03/548-3595. 21 flats (15 with shower). TV TEL
$ Rates: NZ$68 ($39.50) single; NZ$78 ($46) double. NZ$5 ($3) discount to readers who present this book. AE, DC, MC, V.

"Cozy, quiet, and convenient," says Des Puklowski, who with his wife, Sue, runs this motor lodge smack in the center of the city. Well, I have to agree with him, and I must add that you might walk right past it without realizing that it is a motel. You see, this one is located on the first, second, and third floors of a modern five-story office building! Each unit is smartly done up, fully serviced, and has a large shower room and cooking facilities. There's a laundry room and off-street parking. Mr. and Mrs. Puklowski are warm, friendly hosts who are especially fond of American guests. Continental or cooked breakfast is available.

WAIMARIE MOTEL, 45 Collingwood St., Nelson. Tel. 03/548-9418. 5 flats (all with bath). TV TEL
$ Rates: NZ$65 ($37) single; NZ$75 ($43) double. DC, MC, V.
I particularly like this small hotel's setting on the bank of the Maitai River, 1 block from the bus depot and visitors center. There are only a few units, but each has a separate bedroom, fully equipped kitchen, and video. The units are spacious, and there's a garage for parking. From here, you're only a few minutes' walk from downtown. Continental breakfast is available.

MOTEL FLATS/BED & BREAKFAST

TRAFALGAR AUTOLODGE, 46 Trafalgar St., Nelson. Tel. 03/548-3980. 6 flats (all with shower and bath). TV TEL
$ Rates: B&B NZ$35 ($20) single, NZ$55 ($31) double; motel flats NZ$55 ($31) single, NZ$65 ($37) double. DC, MC, V.
In addition to bed-and-breakfast accommodations, the Trafalgar offers motel flats that are bright, clean, and attractively furnished. Each unit sleeps up to four and all have fully equipped kitchens, radio, and electric blankets. Off-street parking and laundry facilities are available. Aida and Bill Verberne are the friendly, helpful owners. It's a short walk to the city center.

BED & BREAKFASTS

CALIFORNIA HOUSE, 29 Collingwood St., Nelson. Tel. 03/548-4173. 4 rms (none with bath). TV TEL
$ Rates (including breakfast): NZ$78 ($45) single; NZ$95–NZ$135 ($54–$77) double. No credit cards.

Near the center of town, this charming yellow house has a flower-trimmed walkway, a wide, wraparound porch, leaded-glass trim, a study complete with Scrabble and Trivial Pursuit, a country kitchen, and delightful rooms. Guest rooms are furnished with antiques, memorabilia, fluffy quilts, and fresh flowers. The home-cooked breakfasts are well known for fresh fruit and berries, juices, and home-baked muffins. Owners Shelly and Neil Johnstone are two Americans who first fell in love with New Zealand as tourists. *Note:* Smoking is restricted to the veranda.

PALM GROVE GUEST HOUSE, 52 Cambria St., Nelson. Tel. 03/548-4645. 6 rms (with shared bath). TV TEL **Transportation:** Courtesy car from bus depot.

$ Rates (including breakfast): NZ$30 ($17) single; NZ$60 ($34) double. No credit cards.

You'll recognize this B&B by the two gigantic palms that tower above the two-story white house. And you'll remember it for the friendly hospitality of Mrs. Devlin, your hostess. The house is bright, cheerful, and sunny throughout, with comfortably furnished rooms, some of which look out to nice mountain views. There's a tea-and-coffee room off the guest lounge, and a light and airy dining room. Only four of the six rooms have hot and cold running water, but all are convenient to baths. There are two singles, two with twin beds, one with three single beds, and one family room with one double bed and one single. No smoking. Highly recommended. The guesthouse is a short walk from the town center.

WILLOW BANK GUESTHOUSE, 71 Golf Rd., Tahunanui, Nelson. Tel. 03/548-5041. 5 rms (none with bath). TV TEL **Transportation:** Courtesy car pickup available.

$ Rates (including breakfast): NZ$47 ($27) single; NZ$66 ($38) double. No credit cards.

This gracious, two-story house is set back from the road on shaded lawns and just a short walk from the beach; it's 4 kilometers (2½ miles) from the center of town. There's a pretty outdoor swimming pool, a spacious TV lounge with pool table, laundry facilities, and off-street parking. Rooms are attractively done up, comfortable, and have hot and cold running water, electric blankets, and thermostatic heaters. You can have a full cooked breakfast or continental breakfast in the spacious dining room.

"FREE" ROOM & BOARD

TODD'S VALLEY FARM, c/o G. R. Roberts, R.D. 1, Nelson. Tel. 03/545-2553.
Well, it isn't exactly "free"—it's room and board in exchange for daily farm and domestic work averaging 4 or more hours a day. For that, you'll be getting three healthy meals, rather basic accommodations, and a rich learning experience in the practice of conservation. If that has an appealing ring, read on.

This is the home, farm, dream, and ecological laboratory of G. R. (Dick) Roberts, a graduate of Cambridge University, teacher of biology and geography, and documentary photographer. After some few years of teaching, Dick decided in 1969 that the time had come to translate ideas into action, and he bought a beautiful, but uneconomical, 250-acre valley farm 6 miles north of Nelson. Only about 15 acres are flat land—the rest rise as high as 1,400 feet above the valley floor. Dick does not claim to be 100% "organic" in his farming methods, but he has nurtured the flourishing vegetable garden with none of the dubious benefits of insecticides. On the slopes, he is working out an integrated approach to biological control by mixing many species of fruit and nut trees according to microclimates. Rough hill pastures are grazed by about 300 sheep.

Dick welcomes visitors who are genuinely interested in conservation, willing to work at it, and ready to take instruction and suggestion. Although the farm is not by any means a commune, he believes that the cooperative efforts of like-minded people contributing toward a constructive alternative way of life provide an important contribution to society as a whole. "Dropouts, unproductive people, and those not willing to accept responsibility," he says, "are not part of that plan." Please do not apply unless you can stay a minimum of 2 weeks (brief visits may be arranged, however, for those with an avid interest in ecological land use). At Todd's Valley, conservation is a way of life: You are expected to recycle all wastes, and to refrain from smoking in the house or using drugs. You are heartily invited, however, to enjoy the warm, sunny valley 2 miles from the sea in all its natural beauty, gorge yourself on the fresh vegetables, and become intimately involved with the land and its problems. When you've contributed what you can and are ready to move on, Dick may be able to put you in touch with others with similar concerns in New Zealand—an entrée into a circle of involved, concerned, vitally interesting people.

If you'd like to stay at Todd's Valley, write or telephone Dick in advance. He can only give beds to a few people at a time, although those who wish to camp are also welcome. *Note:* Occasionally, the farm is closed to visitors.

A HOSTEL

YHA HOSTEL, 42 Weka St., Nelson. Tel. 03/548-8817. 32 beds.
$ Rates (excluding GST): NZ$14 ($8) seniors; NZ$7 ($4) juniors. No credit cards.
This inviting yellow house has a green tin roof and a huge front yard. It has 32 beds in six rooms, hot showers, and a kitchen. All facilities are open all day, and the hostel managers have extensive travel experience, both in the U.S. and New Zealand. It's located a short walk from the center of town.

CABINS & CAMPGROUNDS

The ✪ **Tahuna Beach Holiday Park,** 70 Beach Rd. (Private Bag), Tahunanui, Nelson (tel. 03/548-5159), is one of the largest motor camps in New Zealand, regularly handling as many as 4,500 travelers per night during summer months and even more at Christmas. Spread over 55 acres, the camp is a short 3-minute walk to the beach, and local bus service is at the corner; shuttle service is also available. The well-kept grounds hold a large selection of vacation accommodations as well as tent and trailer sites. If you're not traveling with your own linens, they may be rented for a small charge. Amenities include seven shower-and-toilet blocks, six kitchens and laundries, ironing boards, car wash, TV lounge, children's adventure playgrounds, and miniature golf. A large food shop on the grounds is open every day. This is a beautifully maintained place, with all accommodations kept freshly painted, carpeted, and comfortably furnished. Vacation units are "star graded" for quality and price: top-quality, fully self-contained, four-star units at NZ$64 ($37); self-contained, three-plus-star units at NZ$40 ($23); semiself-contained, three-star units at NZ$35 ($20); two-star and two-plus-star units at NZ$23 ($13) and NZ$28 ($16). Sites are NZ$15 ($9). All rates are for double occupancy, including GST, and American Express, Diners Club, MasterCard, and VISA credit cards are accepted. On all units, there's a surcharge for 1-night stays.

WHERE TO EAT

CHEZ EELCO COFFEE HOUSE, 296 Trafalgar St. Tel. 548-7595.
   Cuisine: SNACKS/LIGHT MEALS. **Reservations:** Not required.
$ Prices: NZ$1.70–NZ$19 ($1–$11). MC, V.

Open: Mon–Sat 7am–11pm, Sun 7am–9pm.

More than just an eating place, Chez Eelco is just about the most popular meeting place in town for students, artists, craftspeople, townspeople, and tourists. In fine weather there are bright umbrella tables on the sidewalk out front. Inside, there are red-and-white café curtains, matching ruffled lamp-shades, and candles in wine bottles after dark. Eelco Boswijk (a Dutchman who came to New Zealand over 30 years ago) has owned the high-ceilinged, cavernous place since 1961, and has always run it much like one of New York City's Greenwich Village coffeehouses. There's the buzz of contented conversation, table-hopping regulars, a back room whose walls are a virtual art gallery, a piano for the occasional pianist, and paper place mats that give names and addresses of local artists. The extensive menu includes toasted sandwiches, hamburgers, scones, omelets, yogurt, salad plates, steaks, chicken, Marlborough mussels, Nelson scallops, native cheeses, and sweets that include fresh cream cakes. In short, it's a place to drop in for coffee or tea and a snack, enjoy a light meal, or order your main meal of the day. Then sit back and dine at your leisure. Incidentally, my own personal favorites are also quite popular with locals—the truly superb mussel chowder and salad bowl with hot roll, each at NZ$5 ($3). The filet steak, at NZ$19 ($11) is the most expensive item on the menu, and most mains are well under NZ$10 ($6). Breakfast is available. Licensed.

CITY LIGHTS, 142 Hardy St. Tel. 548-8999.

Cuisine: NEW ORLEANS. **Reservations:** Recommended.

$ Prices: Appetizers NZ$8.50–NZ$12.50 ($5–$7); main courses NZ$17–NZ$23 ($10–$13). AE, DC, MC, V.

Open: Mon–Sat 5:30pm–late. **Closed:** May–Sept.

Popular with locals and visitors alike, City Lights, with its pink facade and a lively atmosphere, is modeled on popular New Orleans–style restaurants. The chef, who has traveled extensively in the U.S., specializes in Cajun and Creole dishes such as the famous gumbos and jambalayas. Rhythm and blues, along with lazy Southern jazz, create an atmosphere of relaxed conviviality. Utilizing the "hot rocks" cookery method (a block of granite is heated to 300 degrees, put in a heatproof dish, and placed in the center of your table and you actually do the cooking—I knew you'd ask!), your order—fresh crayfish, baby calamari, Nelson scallops, lamb, beef, venison, or other nightly specials—can be cooked exactly as you prefer. Not to worry, however, if you want to leave your cooking at home: There are always meat, fish, seafood, and vegetarian dishes prepared in the kitchen under the supervision of Kiwi owners Frank and Moana Christie. Worth trying is the rack of lamb roasted with a parmesan-and-herb crust. BYO. City Lights is located in the town center.

THE HITCHING POST, 145 Bridge St. Tel. 548-7374.

Cuisine: PIZZA/SALADS/STEAK. **Reservations:** Not required.

$ Prices: NZ$8–NZ$25 ($5–$14). AE, MC, V.

Open: Mon–Fri 8am–9pm, Sat 5–9:30pm, Sun 5–9pm. **Closed:** Sun in winter months; Christmas Day.

One of my favorite Nelson eateries, The Hitching Post sports an old hitching ring on its veranda post and a pot-bellied iron stove inside. Pizzas, salads, and steaks share the menu here, and you'll miss a good thing if you fail to try the large fresh fruit milk shakes for NZ$1.50 (90¢). The dining room is rustic and cozy, but I must confess to a weakness for the courtyard out back. In a setting of Kiwi vines and other native plantings, you dine on white garden-type furniture, and for before- or after-meal entertainment, a giant checkerboard adorns the cement tile floor (even if you don't play, it's fun to watch others while you dine). You can reach the courtyard either through the main dining room or by way of a small wooden door out front, which opens to a narrow pathway leading to the back. The Hitching Post is a friendly, relaxed dropping-in place in the center of town, and really convenient when hunger pangs strike between regular eating hours, since there's food service all through the day.

MANHATTAN COFFEE LOUNGE, 206 Trafalgar St., between Hardy and Bridge Sts. Tel. 548-4475.
   Cuisine: BREAKFAST/PASTRIES/SAVORIES/SANDWICHES. **Reservations:** Not required.
$ Prices: Under NZ$8 ($5). No credit cards.
   Open: Mon–Thurs 7:30am–5pm, Fri 7:30am–9pm, Sat 7:30am–1pm.
   This is one of the best places in Nelson for good, home-cooked light meals in pleasant surroundings. Framed art prints line the walls, owner G. L. Hobbs and the staff behind the self-service counter are friendly and helpful, and all baking is done right on the premises. A full cooked breakfast runs NZ$4.50 ($2.60), and light, inexpensive fare—savories, pies, sandwiches—is served throughout the day.

WORTH THE EXTRA MONEY

JUNIPER'S, 144 Collingwood St. Tel. 548-8832.
   Cuisine: SEAFOOD/GAME/NEW ZEALAND. **Reservations:** Recommended.
$ Prices: Dinner NZ$35–NZ$60 ($20–$34). AE, DC, MC, V.
   Open: Dinner Mon–Sat 6:30pm–1am.
   The house that now is home to Juniper's was built for a vicar, then inhabited by a commune. Today it houses Nelson's top restaurant, which has soft pink walls, black tablecloths, and fresh flowers and candles on all the tables. There's also a small bar with a fireplace for predinner drinks. Entrées include garlic mussels and duck dim sum, and main dishes feature seafood fettuccine, apricot chicken, venison médaillons, quail Chartreuse, and rack of lamb. Need I say more? Hosts Christine and Pradeep Kumar are most welcoming Licensed and BYO. It's located in the town center.

EN ROUTE SOUTH

The choice is up to you: A full day's driving—6½ to 7 hours and an early start—will get you to **Greymouth** or **Hokitika** via Highway 6; or you can proceed at a more leisurely pace and stop off at **Westport,** which is emerging as a center for outdoor-adventure activities and a place that, though fiercely noncommercial, makes a real effort to make visitors feel welcome. You can stop for lunch in **Murchison** (the bus depot tearoom is your best bet—turn left at the Hampton Hotel) or in Westport if you can hold out that long, where there's a wider choice of eateries.

If you're traveling by Newmans Coach, your driver's interesting narrative will fill you in on the history of most of the terrain you'll be covering along a road that is steep and winding at times, drops through heavily wooded mountain gorges at others, touches the sea, then turns south along a dramatic coastline, sometimes seen from high bluffs along which the road passes. If you're driving, look for these key landscape notes:

Between Murchison and Westport, you'll be following the **Buller River** much of the way. Those jagged gaps and high scarped bluffs above the wall of the gorge between Murchison and Lyell are the legacy of a disastrous earthquake in June 1929. Passing through the gold-mining ghost town of **Lyell,** you'll see little left to suggest the thriving, bustling town of gold-rush days. Its last surviving building, the Lyell Hotel, burned in 1963, leaving only a few faint vestiges of those turbulent times. Descending to the lower gorge, you'll be driving through flatlands, then under **Hawkes Crag,** where the road has been hewn from a sheer face of solid rock above the river, and on to a stretch of road between bush-clad walls and rocky ravines.

2. WESTPORT

40 miles N of Greymouth, 140 miles SW of Nelson

GETTING THERE **By Bus** Westport is served daily by **Newmans** coaches via Highway 6 from the northeast, and the coast road from the south.

By Car Westport can be reached via Highway 6 from Nelson or Greymouth.

ESSENTIALS The **Buller Information Centre,** 1 Brougham St. (tel. *0289/6658), opposite the post office, is open from 9am to 5pm Monday through Friday, 10am to 4pm Saturday and Sunday.

Far too many people zip past Westport on their way to Greymouth or Hokitika rather than bothering to turn off Highway 6 onto Buller Gorge Road and drive to the coast. Westport is fast becoming known as the "Adventure Capital" of the West Coast. And no wonder: Its mild climate and magnificent coastal and subtropical mountain scenery provide an ideal setting for outdoor activities as white-water rafting, jet boating, horse trekking, caving, underworld rafting through caves, and rock climbing. The information center can fill you in on just where to go to indulge any of these that suit your fancy. For the not-so-adventurous, this region offers excellent sea and river fishing, gold panning, and a good variety of scenic and historic walkways.

The town of Westport (pop. 5,000) found relative prosperity as a coal-mining center after weathering the gold bust. **Coaltown,** on Queen Street South (tel. *8204), is a mining museum that provides wheelchair access, with a walk-through coal mine and a multiscreen audiovisual presentation. A new wing holds displays on maritime and pioneering history. It's open daily from 9am to 4pm, with admission of NZ$4 ($2) for adults, NZ$2 ($1) for children.

WHERE TO STAY

Westport is a small place, but its accommodations, though limited in number, could well be some of the most pleasant of your trip.

Unless otherwise noted, the rates quoted below include GST.

MOTEL FLATS

BULLER BRIDGE MOTEL, on the Esplanade, Westport. Tel. *0289/7519. Fax *0289/7165. 10 units (all with bath). TV TEL **Directions:** On outskirts of town; take first turn left off the bridge.
$ Rates (excluding GST): NZ$65 ($37) single; NZ$75 ($43) double. AE, MC, V.

This genuine retreat, under the friendly management of Pat and Sylvia Bradley, offers self-contained units in a quiet, spacious garden setting close to all town amenities. Each unit has a complete kitchen and video, and some have water beds. I particularly like the large, grassy courtyard; kids like the play area with trampoline and swings. There is a guest laundry, as well as a luxurious spa pool.

HOSTELS

DALE'S YOUTH HOSTEL, 56 Russell St., Westport. Tel. *0289/8672. 4 rms (none with bath).

$ Rates: NZ$10 ($6) per person. No credit cards.

⭐ ⑤ There are limited accommodations in this small, homey hostel near the town center, but the place is always a hit with those who stay there, mainly because of Dale herself. A mark of her hospitality is the Christmas dinner she serves as a gift for her guests. In the large living room, there's a TV, stereo, piano, and lots of games, books, and magazines.

TRIPINNS, 72 Queen St., Westport. Tel. *0289/7367. Fax *0289/6419. 40 beds in 18 rms (none with bath).
$ Rates: NZ$14.50 ($8) bed; NZ$30 ($17) double. Linen and blanket fee NZ$4.50 ($2.60). AE, MC, V.

⭐ ⑤ This historic old house (100-plus years), set in wooded grounds, opened its doors to travelers in 1989. It can accommodate 40 lodgers in 18 rooms, including two doubles, four twins, and a bunkroom. The inviting lounge has a high ceiling, fireplace, stereo, and TV. There is a games room with a pool table, and the kitchen has a microwave oven. The name of the hostel is a play on manager Maurice Tipping's name (no hallucinogens here). It's located in town, a 5-minute walk from the bus depot.

WHERE TO EAT

Drop by for a drink in the homey **Cosmopolitan Hotel Bar,** on Palmerston Street (tel. *6305). Surely you've been admiring the old hotels along Westport's main street, and this is a good opportunity to go inside one (and one with two fireplaces) and fraternize with the locals. They also serve quite good bar food for less than NZ$10 ($6).

CRISTY'S, 18 Wakefield St. Tel. *7640.
Cuisine: NEW ZEALAND. **Reservations:** Recommended.
$ Prices: Under NZ$35 ($20). AE, MC, V.
Open: Dinner daily 6:30–9pm.

⭐ This is the place to come for an evening out in Westport's town center, and it surely is conducive to lingering. The menu features local dishes of lamb and fish, as well as steak, and there are always blackboard specials. The wine is stored in an old bank vault, and there is coal-mining memorabilia everywhere. The bar is open from 6pm to 1:30am, and at the time of my visit, they were setting up a beer garden, so come by for a drink if not a meal. Licensed.

EN ROUTE TO GREYMOUTH

Turning sharply south at Westport to follow the coastline, you'll pass **Mitchell's Gully Gold Mine** only 12½ miles along your way. It's a fascinating place, not a tourist attraction but a real working mine, open from 9am to 4pm daily except Christmas. It's been in the Mitchell family since 1866, and Ian and Helen McKinnon are the friendly miners. Back on the road, you'll soon pass through Charleston, where gold was discovered in 1866, leading to a population boom, with dance halls, stores, and some 92 hotels—few reminders remain today.

About halfway between Westport and Greymouth, you'll come to one of the West Coast's most unusual natural formations, the ✪ **Punakaiki Pancake Rocks.** (*Note:* Newmans buses stop here so passengers may walk down to see them.) At the top of a steep headland, a simple tearoom, restroom, and shop are on the inland side of the road, along with space for parking to allow you to leave your car and follow the track across the road through native bush to the sea, where limestone structures, which look for all the world like a gigantic stack of pancakes, jut out into the water. When the seas are high and rough, water comes surging into the deep caverns below and is spouted up some 20 to 30 feet into the air, accompanied by a tremendous whoosh of sound. The surrounding area has been kept as a scenic reserve.

From the Punakaiki Rocks, the road is almost continually within sight of the sea until you turn to cross the **Grey River** and drive into Greymouth.

3. GREYMOUTH

247 miles SW of Picton, 179 miles SW of Nelson,
63 miles SW of Westport, 25 miles N of Hokitika

GETTING THERE   By Plane   The nearest air service is nearby Hokitika (see Section 4 of this chapter).

By Train   The **Trans-Alpine Express** train runs daily to and from Christchurch from the Greymouth railroad station on MacKay Street.

By Bus   InterCity coaches reach Greymouth from Christchurch, Dunedin, Fox and Franz Josef Glaciers, Nelson, Timaru, and Westport.

By Car   Greymouth is reached via Highway 6 from the north and south.

ESSENTIALS   The **area code** for Greymouth is 03. The **Information Centre,** in the Regent Theatre Building on the corner of Herbert and Mackay Streets (tel. 03/768-5101), is open daily from 9am to 7pm during summer months. They can furnish detailed information about the area and book accommodations at no charge. They are also the Department of Conservation agency for the region. Movies are shown Thursday through Sunday night at 8pm in the Regent Theatre, with additional showings during school-holiday periods (beware Friday, when the teenage crowd gets frisky and noisy).

At Greymouth, it's decision-making time: whether to stop here or push on another 25 miles to Hokitika. Greymouth offers a wider choice of accommodations; Hokitika has more attractions. Greymouth does have Shantytown, a reconstructed gold-mining town, but there's no local transportation to it, and it's quite possible to double back to see it from a Hokitika base. In the final analysis, your decision may rest chiefly on just how tired and hungry you are when you reach Greymouth, erstwhile "Heart of the Coast."

New Zealand's West Coast is a rugged stretch of country whose incomparable beauty has been molded and shaped by the elements—and its inhabitants are perhaps the most rugged and individualistic of a nation of individuals. Lured by nature's treasures, they have from the beginning seemed to revel in its challenges, and along with a resilient toughness have developed a rollicking sense of fun, a relaxed acceptance of the vicissitudes of West Coast life, and a brand of hospitality that is recognized (and even boasted of) by Kiwis in every other part of the country. "Coasters" are a hardy, good-hearted breed who will welcome you warmly to this unique region.

The coast's beauty and hidden wealth were entirely lost on Captain Cook when he sighted it from the sea, remained offshore, and described it in his journal as "wild and desolate and unworthy of observation." Of course, his sea-based observation could not possibly reveal the presence of nuggets of gold strewn about those "unworthy" beaches. That discovery was left for 1864, when it precipitated an influx of prospectors and miners from as far afield as California (along with a goodly number from Australia), many of whom would remain after the goldfields played out in 1867 to form the basis of a permanent population who take fierce pride in their particular part of New Zealand.

Greymouth, with a population of 12,000, keeps busy these days with coal and timber exports and the import of tourists who come to roam the beaches in search of gemstones and greenstone, fish in the clear streams nearby, and perhaps pan for gold.

WHAT TO SEE & DO

The star attraction at Greymouth is ✪ **Shantytown,** a reconstructed gold-rush mining town. To reach it, drive 5 miles south to Paroa, make a left turn, and drive another 2 miles inland, following a well-signposted route. The colorful town, which has been built with a keen eye to detail, contains several replicas of well-known structures like the Cameron & Co. livery stables from Hokitika in the 1860s and the Beehive store, which has been in business continually in Greymouth since 1865. Then there are true restorations, like the little wooden church with its slender bell tower, which was moved here from No Town, where it was constructed in 1866. There's also a 25-ton steam locomotive, dating from 1897, to ride, bumping along in the wooden passenger cars that were the latest thing back then. And a stagecoach will rattle you over an old bush road.

Shantytown is open every day from 8:30am to 5pm, with an admission (which includes the train and stagecoach rides) of NZ$7 ($4) for adults, NZ$2 ($1) for children. If you have no transport out here, the taxi round-trip runs about NZ$8 ($5).

WHERE TO STAY

Greymouth is blessed with many good accommodations at inexpensive rates. Motel and guesthouse operators are also very cooperative, helping you find a vacancy if your choice is filled.

Unless otherwise noted, the rates below include GST.

MOTEL FLATS

AACHEN PLACE MOTEL, 50 High St., Greymouth. Tel. 03/768-6901. Fax 03/768-6958. 10 flats (all with shower). TV TEL **Directions:** 1 km (½ mile) south of town center on Hwy. 6.
$ Rates: NZ$60 ($34) single; NZ$70 ($40) double. Best Western discounts available. AE, DC, MC, V.
This well-kept Best Western motel offers self-contained bed-sitter units that sleep two or three, all with full kitchen facilities. All have radio, electric blankets, and heating, and full laundry facilities are available. It's handy to a restaurant and supermarket and about a 10-minute walk from the center of town. Cooked and continental breakfasts are available.

SOUTH BEACH MOTEL, 318 Main South Rd., Greymouth. Tel. 03/762-6768. 10 units (all with bath). TV TEL
$ Rates (excluding GST): NZ$55 ($31) single; NZ$67 ($38) double. Best Western discounts available. AE, DC, MC, V.
✪ Just across from the beach, this motel has a quiet location only a 5-kilometer (3-mile) drive from town. Each unit comes with complete kitchen, video, radio, and electric blankets. There's one paraplegic unit, a water-bed unit, and some family units. Amenities include guest laundry, children's playground, barbecue area, and spa. Hosts Maryanne and Allan Fishburn serve complimentary tea and scones in the afternoon.

WILLOWBANK MOTOR LODGE, Hwy. 6 (P.O. Box 260), Greymouth. Tel. 03/768-5339. Fax 03/768-6022. 5 suites (all with bath). TV TEL
$ Rates (excluding GST): NZ$55 ($31) single; NZ$60 ($34) double; NZ$69 ($39) 1-bedroom suite for one or two. Surcharge for 1-night stays. AE, MC, V.
Located just 2 miles north of town on the Greymouth-Westport highway, this motor

lodge offers modern, attractive suites, all nicely furnished right down to potted plants. All units have been given old West Coast hotel names like Welcome Nugget, Diggers Home, and Plough Inn by the gracious hosts, Lois and Ted Gutberlet, one of Greymouth's friendliest couples, who delight in making their guests feel at home. Two-bedroom units are spacious and airy, with slanted roofs and paneled walls. Bed-sitters are more modest in size, but all have full kitchens and electric blankets. There's an outdoor swimming pool and a free private spa pool, as well as a guest laundry with dryer. The one-bedroom suite has a spa bath, full kitchen, hairdryer, lounge, and tea-and-toast breakfast served in your suite. Cooked or continental breakfast available at additional charge.

BED & BREAKFASTS

Unfortunately, most of the B&Bs in Greymouth do not have hot and cold running water in the rooms. They are, however, homey, comfortable, and inexpensive.

GOLDEN COAST GUEST HOUSE, 10 Smith St., Greymouth. Tel. 03/768-7839. 4 rms (none with bath), 1 bed-sitter (with bath). TV TEL
$ Rates (excluding GST): NZ$43 ($25) single with cooked breakfast; NZ$48 ($27) double without breakfast, NZ$60 ($34) double with continental breakfast, NZ$66 ($38) double with cooked breakfast; NZ$55 ($31) double bed-sitter. No credit cards.

Gladys Roche is the hostess at this B&B, just back of the railway station. The red-roofed house is set in a sloping, flower-bordered lawn. The guest rooms are bright and clean, and have heaters and electric blankets. The bed-sitter has its own kitchen and bath. There's a TV lounge with a pretty rock fireplace, where you're welcome to make tea and coffee whenever you wish.

HIGH STREET GUEST HOUSE, 20 High St., Greymouth. Tel. 03/768-7444. 4 rms (none with bath). TV TEL **Transportation:** Courtesy car to public transport.
$ Rates (including cooked breakfast): NZ$47 ($27) single; NZ$68 ($39) double. AE, DC, MC, V.

Set in town in a beautiful older house with dark-wood paneling and ceilings, High Street Guest House is run very much like an English B&B. The bedrooms are bright and cheerful, and there are laundry facilities. The proprietor, Mrs. Jean Thompson, is well known for her sumptuous breakfasts, and one reader wrote of the special attention she gives vegetarians, "We don't eat meat, so she gave us asparagus in cheese sauce." She will also prepare the evening meal (with advance notice) at NZ$18 ($10) per person. There's off-street parking.

HOSTELS

BLACKBALL HILTON, Hart St., Blackball. Tel. 03/732-4705. 18 rms (none with bath).
$ Rates: NZ$13 ($7) backpackers; NZ$17.50 ($10) single; NZ$30 ($17) double. NZ$6.50 ($4) cooked breakfast; NZ$12.50 ($7) cooked 2-course dinner. No credit cards.

David Evans' Blackball Hilton has been described as "ramshackle with character," but it still manages to have a TV room, sauna, a spa pool, pickup service for two or more, and an undeniably wonderful name. The kitchen is freely available for guests, or you can order a cooked meal. The hostel is located 15 miles northeast of Greymouth.

YHA HOSTEL, "Kainga-Ra," Cowper St. (P.O. Box 299), Greymouth. Tel. 03/768-4951. 43 beds, 8 rms (none with bath).

$ Rates (excluding GST): NZ$14 ($8) for members, NZ$18 ($10) for nonmembers. No credit cards.

About a 20-minute walk from the town center, this hostel offers 43 beds in eight rooms with some double and family rooms. It's modern and very well maintained, with a fully equipped kitchen. Book ahead if at all possible.

CABINS & CAMPING

Greymouth Seaside Holiday Park, Chesterfield Street, Greymouth (tel. 03/768-6618), is, as its name implies, situated by the sea. On level, sheltered sites on the beachfront at the southern edge of town there are 50 tent sites, 72 caravan sites, 10 on-site caravans, 28 cabins, 10 tourist cabins, 6 tourist flats, and a backpackers bunkhouse with 20 beds. Chesterfield Street is just off the Main South Road, and the camp is signposted. There's a modern TV lounge, kitchen, washing machines and dryers, hot showers, linen for rent, and a camp store. Grounds and all accommodations are well kept, and a courtesy car is available to and from public transport. Double-occupancy rates are NZ$15 ($9) for tent sites, NZ$17 ($10) for caravan sites, and NZ$32 ($18) for on-site caravans. Rates for double-occupancy cabins run NZ$29 ($17) for cabins, NZ$36 ($21) for tourist cabins, and NZ$54 ($31) for tourist flats; backpackers pay NZ$11 ($6) per person. Children pay half price in each case, and all rates are plus GST.

WHERE TO EAT

BONZAI PIZZERIA & RESTAURANT, 31 Mackay St. Tel. 768-4170.
 Cuisine: PIZZA/STEAK. **Reservations:** Not required.
$ Prices: Under NZ$15 ($9). DC, MC, V.
 Open: Mon–Thurs 11am–midnight, Fri 11am–1am, Sat–Sun 5–midnight.

Recently extended, the Bonzai serves no less than 16 types of pizza, including vegetarian. Besides pizza, you can get soups, sandwiches, omelets, and steaks, all at reasonable prices. The Dutch owner has shellacked European newspapers on the walls as a unique covering. BYO. It's located near the Information Centre.

WORTH THE EXTRA MONEY

CAFE COLLAGE, 115 Mackay St. Tel. 768-5497.
 Cuisine: CONTINENTAL/SEAFOOD. **Reservations:** Recommended.
$ Prices: Average meal NZ$35 ($20). MC, V.
 Open: Dinner daily 6pm–late. **Closed:** Occasionally on Mon.

If you want a bit of dining elegance in Greymouth's town center, best book a table here. Judith Eakin is the chef and her brother, Steve, doubles as maître d' and waiter. The dining room is lovely, with an art deco ceiling and lamps, and main dishes on the constantly changing menu may include such dishes as lamb filet in green ginger wine and rosemary, venison médaillons, and chicken livers in brandy pasta. BYO.

EN ROUTE TO HOKITIKA

The 25-mile drive south follows the coastline closely along mostly flat farmland. But look to your left, and the snowcapped tips of the Southern Alps become clearer and clearer, sharply defined against the sky, as though painted on the horizon, a teasing glimpse of the mountain splendor that awaits in a few days when you turn away from the Tasman Sea.

About 20 miles from Greymouth you'll cross the **Arahura River.** This is where Maori found a great quantity of the greenstone they so highly prized for making weapons, ornaments, and tools. Another 5 miles and you reach Hokitika, where you can see artisans still working that gemstone into a multitude of items, some of which you'll no doubt take along when you depart.

EN ROUTE TO CHRISTCHURCH

If your time in the South Island is limited, you can drive from Greymouth to Christchurch (allow the better part of a day in order to enjoy the drive to its fullest) by way of **Arthur's Pass** and some of New Zealand's most spectacular scenery. Just south of Greymouth, turn left onto Highway 73. Opened in 1866, this road was one of the last in the country to be used by horse-drawn Cobb & Co. coaches. If you come in winter, Mount Temple Basin offers a full range of winter sports; in summer, the wild mountain landscape is a marvel of alpine flowers. Regular coach service is also available from Greymouth to Christchurch.

---

4. HOKITIKA

25 miles S of Greymouth, 91 miles N of Franz Josef

GETTING THERE   By Plane   There is air service via **Air Nelson** between Hokitika and Auckland, New Plymouth, Rotorua, and Wellington in the North Island; Christchurch, Dunedin, Invercargilll, and Nelson on the South Island.

By Train   The nearest rail service is in Greymouth (see Section 3, above).

By Bus   Hokitika is on **InterCity's** Franz Josef/Greymouth route.

By Car   Hokitika can be reached via Highway 6.

DEPARTING   The **airport booking office** is in the House of Travel (a travel agency) on Weld Street (tel. *58-134). **Air Nelson** has an office at Hokitika airport (tel. *58-123). The **InterCity** bus depot is in Tancred Street (tel. *58-557).

ESSENTIALS   At this writing, Hokitika's **area code** is 0288. Remember: The New Zealand Number Update is in the process of changing all telephone numbers to 7 digits. Those numbers in this chapter that have not been changed at press time are marked with an asterisk, and you should call the **Helpline 0155** for the new number. For directory assistance within the country (when you don't know the number), call **018.**

Information   The **Information Centre,** is in the Westlands District Council Building, Sewell Street, Hokitika (tel. *0288/58-322; fax *0288/58-026). Hours are 9am to 5:30pm, Monday through Friday, and 9am to noon on Saturday. The center's friendly staff can furnish detailed information on the area's attractions, adventure bookings, and accommodation bookings.

Mail   The **post office,** on Level Street at Weld Street, is open weekdays from 9am to 5pm. For **taxi** service, ring Gold Band Taxis (tel. *58-437).

As you drive into quiet, peaceful little Hokitika, you'll find it hard to believe that this was once the boisterous, rowdy "Goldfields Capital," where more than 35,000 miners and prospectors kept the dance halls roaring and filled some 102 hotels. And because it was more accessible by sea than overland, ships poured into its harbor, even though the entrance was so hazardous that people would gather on the shore to watch unlucky ships go aground. Even so, there were as many as 80 at one time tied up at Hokitika wharfs, many of them waiting to transport the gold that poured out of the area at the rate of half a million ounces a year. It turned out not to be the endless supply they all dreamed of, and when the gold was gone, Hokitika's fortunes took another turn—this time, decidedly downward.

Today, you'll see only rotting remnants of those once-busy wharfs, and almost no vestiges of all those hotels. Still, Hokitika has more attractions than any other West Coast town, and its present-day prosperity rests on farming, forestry, and tourism— likely to be much more lasting than the glittering gold. The major airport of the West Coast is located here; there's good coach service; and you'll find it an ideal base for exploring this part of the South Island.

WHAT TO SEE & DO

One of the primary reasons for making Hokitika your base on the West Coast is to be there after dark so you can see the **glowworms**—this is the largest outdoor group in the country—in a charming dell at the edge of town, right on the main road. The 40-foot-and-higher wooded banks are filled with sparkling clusters of thousands of glowworms, a truly awe-inspiring sight. And as interesting as are the Waitomo displays, there is something about walking down a dirt path under a natural archway of treetops and standing alone in absolute silence that makes for a mystical personal experience. There's no charge, but there's a donation box at the entrance and all contributions are appreciated by the town, which keeps this wondrous place available for us all. Best bring a flashlight for the first part of the path, but remember to turn it off when you begin to see the glowworms or they'll turn their lights off.

One of the best ways to gain an immediate insight into this fascinating little town is to pick up the ✪ **Hokitika Historic Walk** brochure from the Information Centre or the West Coast Historical Museum. In less than a half hour, you'll have learned about the historical buildings and sites and the part each played in the town's history. As you walk the town's tiny streets, your invisible companions are bound to be the ghosts of those early gold miners, merchants, and sailors who once walked here.

The ✪ **West Coast Historical Museum,** on Tancred Street (tel. *58-322), features reconstructions and artifacts of the 19th-century "Alluvial placer" gold-mining era on the West Coast. Hastily built canvas and slab dwellings display cooking utensils and furnishings, with equipment represented by pit-sawing and a blacksmith's forge for servicing the tools needed to open up cemented wash concealing the golden treasure. In direct contrast to this sort of hardship and poverty, there are church fittings and elaborate furniture from a merchant's home, along with a typical hotel bar. There are horse-drawn vehicles on display, and pictorial records of the rich maritime trade of the river harbor. In addition, a marvelous meccano model gold dredge is operated on request, and there's a 20-minute audiovisual presentation of Westland's goldfields history. Early Maori occupation is represented by authentic artifacts and jade workings. Displays also feature decorative jade craft works. Hours are 9:30am to 4:30pm weekdays, and 10am to 4pm weekends and holidays. Adults pay NZ$2 ($1); children, NZ$1 (60¢); families, NZ$5 ($3).

Hokitika's Rotary Club has provided an excellent orientation base at the ✪ **lookout point** just off the road to the airport. From there you look over valley farmland to the towering peaks of the Southern Alps (each one identified by a revolving bronze pointer, which stands on a stone base) or across the town to the glistening Tasman Sea. It's a spectacular view, within easy walking distance from the center of town.

There are excellent **scenic flights** from Hokitika over the glaciers—not landing on them as some others do, but the flight is longer. The plane flies south from Hokitika to the Main Divide, over the Tasman Glacier, skirts Mount Cook, over Fox and Franz Josef Glaciers, over Okarito Lagoon (nesting place of the white heron) and large stands of New Zealand native timber. It's quite a flight. There's no regular schedule at this writing, but inquire at the information office about times and current prices.

For **canoeing, rafting,** and **heli-rafting** information, contact Scenic Rafting, Kaniere Road, R.M.D. 3 (tel. *0288/57-114).

NEARBY LAKE KANIERE SCENIC RESERVE

This beautiful ✪ **nature reserve,** centered around one of the South Island's largest lakes, is just 18 kilometers (11 miles) from Hokitika—take the main highway south, but drive straight ahead instead of turning right and going over the Hokitika River at Kaniere (just say "Canary") township. If time is too short for a stop, there's a lovely 58-kilometer (35-mile) circular scenic drive past the lake and back through Kikatahi Valley farmlands. Loitering, however, will be rewarded by beautiful, peaceful vistas of the lake ringed by unspoiled forests with a backdrop of distant mountains. You'll find an information kiosk and toilets at The Landing, where the road first comes to the lake's edge, and there are picnic tables, fireplaces, and toilets at Sunny Bight. Pick up advance information on lake and bush walks at the PRO in Hokitika, or contact the Department of Conservation, on the corner of Gibson Quay and Sewell Street, Hokitika (tel. *0288/58-301). Needless to say, this exquisite bit of South Island scenery should be treated with due respect—remember that Tidy Kiwi poster!

SHOPPING

WESTLAND GREENSTONE COMPANY LTD., Tancred St. between Weld and Hamilton Sts. Tel. *58-713.

You really shouldn't miss this place. The piles of rocks you see show their true color (and value) as the diamond-tipped wheels spin, cutting off slices. The workroom is open for you to wander through, watching talented artisans carving tikis and meres, fitting earrings and pins, and shaping a hundred other souvenirs from the gemstone. Then back to the showroom to consider which of their handiwork you will buy (but let me stress that you're under no obligation to make a purchase). There is also an extensive range of lovely paua and pink mussel shell jewelry from which to choose. Open from 8am to 5pm, 365 days a year.

MOUNTAIN JADE, Weld St. Tel. *58-007.

Here you can see some intricately carved pieces from greenstone, real collector's items. Carving is done on the premises. Open daily from 9am to 5pm.

THE GOLD ROOM, Tancred St. Tel. *58-362 or *58-946 after hours.

Rhett and Lix Robinson have put together a marvelous selection of handmade pendants, rings, bracelets, earrings, necklaces, tie tacks, and much more, including some beautifully set opals. Many of the items are fashioned from gold nuggets that came from local gold claims. It's worth a visit even if you don't plan to buy anything. The shop is open daily from 9am to 5pm.

HOKITIKA CRAFT GALLERY, 25 Tancred St. Tel. *58-802.

This cooperative displays and sells the work of 19 top West Coast artists and craftspeople. There are lovely contemporary works in fiber, pottery, wood, art, jade, and bone. Open daily from 9am to 5pm, the gallery will mail worldwide.

GENESIS CREATION, 75 Revell St. Tel. *58-629.

A Dutch couple, Hans and Lida Schouten, display their considerable talents here. Hans works with wood, and specializes in spinning wheels, coffee tables, and stools, all made from local timber; orders taken. A weaver, Lida creates lovely woolens to sell in the small shop. You'll find exceptionally nice hand-knit sweaters of natural wool (I've picked up one on every trip and treasure them all), shawls, leather goods, and pottery. The Schoutens are happy to mail packages overseas to lighten your load. Open from 9am to 5pm weekdays and on

Saturday mornings by request. They live in the back, and you are welcome to ring at the side door should you find the shop closed.

BRENT TROLLE'S STUDIO, 13 Whitcombe Terrace. Tel. *57-250.

✪ Some of the best paintings of the South Island's West Coast are done right here in Hokitika by Brent Trolle, whose work is known throughout the country. You can visit him at his home, which also serves as gallery and studio, by calling for an appointment. I can't think of a nicer way to keep New Zealand memories alive than with one of Brent's paintings. His paintings are also on show at The House of Wood, Tancred Street (tel. *56-061).

READERS RECOMMEND: SHOPPING

"We found a pure gray wool sweater with long-enough sleeves for my tall husband at **Ken Reece and Son,** *27 Weld St. A menswear specialist, Ken was friendly and knowledgeable, cashed a traveler's check, and sold a heavy sweater for less than we saw elsewhere."*
—P. Diehnelt, Ashippun, Wis. [*Author's note:* Ken advises that the sweater in question was actually a 100% pure, nature black, undyed fleece.]

WHERE TO STAY

Granted, accommodations are limited, but I bet you'll be pleased with the ones that are here. Hokitika has no youth hostel, but there is backpacker lodging at the Hokitika Holiday Park (see below); the nearest hostel is in Greymouth.

Unless otherwise noted, the rates shown below include GST.

A LICENSED HOTEL

THE SOUTHLAND HOTEL, 111 Revell St., Hokitika. Tel. *0288/58-344.
Fax *0288/58-258. 15 rms (10 with bath). TV TEL
$ **Rates:** NZ$32 ($18) single or double without bath; NZ$72 ($41) single, NZ$82 ($47) double with bath. AE, DC, MC, V.

✪ This small hotel near the river in the town center has a whole range of accommodations, but all are first class. Rooms are nicely appointed, with attractive decor and comfortable furnishings, and there are units especially ⑤ designed for the handicapped. Facilities include in-house video, a launderette, and spa baths.

MOTEL FLATS

GOLDSBOROUGH MOTEL, 252 Revell St. (P.O. Box 201), Hokitika. Tel. *0288/58-772. 14 units (all with bath). TV TEL
$ **Rates** (excluding GST): NZ$60 ($34) single; NZ$66 ($38) double. Extra adult NZ$12 ($7); extra child NZ$10 ($6). Best Western discounts available. AE, DC, MC, V.

✪ Top billing in Hokitika's motels goes to the Goldsborough, located just across from the Tasman Sea and a short walk from the glowworm dell. Hosts at this Best Western member are Katie and Leo McIntyre. All units, bed-sitters and ⑤ two-bedrooms, have fully equipped kitchens, central heating, and electric heaters. They're all spacious and have parking at the door. There's a guest laundry, a pretty swimming pool, spa pool, and children's playground. A 7-day food store is within walking distance. Continental breakfast costs NZ$5 ($3). The motel is 2 kilometers (1 mile) from the town center.

HOKITIKA MOTEL, 221 Fitzherbert St., Hokitika. Tel. *0288/58-292.
Fax *0288/59-485. 16 units (all with bath). TV TEL **Transportation:** Courtesy car available.

244 • NELSON & THE WEST COAST

$ **Rates** (excluding GST): NZ$55–NZ$57 ($31–$33) single; NZ$62–NZ$68 ($35–$39) double. AE, DC, MC, V.

The Hokitika is just across from the glowworm dell. There are bed-sitters, one-bedroom units, and two-bedroom units with full kitchens, as well as three bed-sitters with only electric jug, toaster, teapot, crockery, and fridge. All units have central and electric heating, electric blanket, and radio. There's a mini-store for essential provisions, car wash, laundry, and a courtesy car to the airport.

A BED & BREAKFAST

CENTRAL GUEST HOUSE, 20 Hamilton St., Hokitika. Tel. *0288/58-232. 9 rms (none with bath). TV TEL

$ **Rates** (including continental breakfast): NZ$39 ($22) single; NZ$59 ($34) double. MC, V.

As its name implies, this guesthouse is centrally located, with banks, restaurants, attractions, and bus station nearby. All bedrooms are heated and have electric blankets, and the lounge has a TV and tea- and coffee-making facilities. Dinner, laundry facilities, and a telephone are also available. Owners Joanna and Brent Williamson can arrange horse treks, canoeing, scenic flights, and white-water rafting. Cooked breakfast may be ordered.

CABINS & CAMPGROUNDS

The ⓢ **Hokitika Holiday Park,** on Stafford Street, Hokitika (tel. *0288/58-172), has accommodation to suit many needs. Tent sites are NZ$6 ($3) per person; caravan sites, NZ$7 ($4) per person (half that for children); bunkhouse accommodation for up to 14 is NZ$8 ($5) per person; backpackers' cabins with double or twin beds, carpet, table and two chairs, but no water, NZ$18 ($10) double, NZ$7 ($4) extra for a heater; economy cabin with two bedrooms, cold-water sink, and breakfast-making facilities, NZ$27 ($15) for two and NZ$8 ($5) per extra person. There are eight tourist cabins with hot and cold running water, kitchen, and toilet for NZ$33 ($19) double; six tourist flats units with kitchen and bathroom are NZ$38 ($22) double.

WHERE TO EAT

GOLD STRIKE SANDWICH BAR, 23 Weld St. No phone.
   Cuisine: SANDWICHES/ICE CREAM. **Reservations:** Not required.
$ **Prices:** NZ$5 ($3). No credit cards.
   Open: Daily 9am–6pm.

Don't miss at least one stop by the Gold Strike. Situated in the Regent Theatre Building, it offers a variety of light meals, made-to-order sandwiches, and luscious ice cream in 16 flavors. With plenty of seating for the sightseeing foot-weary, this eatery (run by West Coaster Ron Hibbs) offers a comfortable rest stop combined with nutritious food and lots of friendly conversation. There's always a brisk business at the ice-cream bar, but take my advice and sample at least one of their unusual and very good sandwiches. All come on hearty, freshly baked bread, and I'm positively addicted to the venison (which, with a bowl of homemade soup, makes a lovely light meal). A local favorite is the honey, walnuts, and raisins combination, with cheese and corn also very popular. Pork, salami, and beef are also available. Sandwiches like these you won't get at home!

PRESTON'S BAKERY & RESTAURANT, 105 Revell St. Tel. *58-412.
   Cuisine: BREAKFAST/SANDWICHES/STEAKS/PASTRIES. **Reservations:** Not required.

$ Prices: Under NZ$10 ($6). No credit cards.
  Open: Mon–Fri 8am–5pm (bakery closes at 6pm), Sat 9am–1pm.
A breakfast tradition in Hokitika is to congregate at this restaurant, which has a perfect small-town decor. Eggs, toast, and bacon or sausage costs NZ$6.50 ($4.05); poached eggs and toast, NZ$3.30 ($2.05); fruit and cereal, NZ$3 ($1.90). Not that breakfast is the only meal; you can get sandwiches, steaks, and sweets, and this is a great place to load up your campervan before driving farther along the West Coast.

**TASMAN VIEW RESTAURANT, in the Southland Hotel, 111 Revell St.
  Tel. *58-344.**
  Cuisine: SEAFOOD. **Reservations:** Recommended.
$ Prices: Average meal NZ$30 ($17). AE, DC, V.
  Open: Dinner daily 6pm–late.
    The Tasman View scores high on its seafood and its view of the Tasman Sea. I am addicted to their lightly sautéed whitebait (only when it's in season, of course), but they also have great dishes you're not likely to encounter elsewhere, such as chili venison balls served with a plum compote or wild pork with port and juniper berries. Crystal and flowers are on the tables and the wood beams are rimu. Licensed.

EN ROUTE TO FRANZ JOSEF & THE GLACIERS

Author's travel tip: There is no pharmacy or bank between Hokitika and Wanaka, although you will find a small country hospital and a doctor in Whataroa. Be sure to stock up on toiletries and cash in advance.
    Nineteen miles south of Hokitika is the little town of **Ross,** well worth a drive over from Hokitika or a stop on your way to Franz Josef Glacier. Look for the **Information Centre** in a restored miner's cabin.
    The **Fur Trading Post Limited** is on Moorhouse Street, the town's main thoroughfare, and it is the creation of Basil Detlaff, a skilled taxidermist, who hopes eventually to have all West Coast wildlife represented. At present there are displays of chamois, keas, and thar, as well as a live opossum, some geckos, and a working beehive. You can buy honey from that hive in the gift shop on the ground floor. Hours are 9am to 5pm daily, and there's a small admission charge.
    Down the street, you'll find **Ross Furs** (tel. *0288/58-108), where Mr. and Mrs. Peter Gray will show you through the workshop in which bush-tailed opossum skins are worked into coats, bedspreads, purses, and a host of other items. Prices in their showroom are often considerably below those in shops. Hours are 9am to 5pm weekdays, and weekends in the summer. They will, however, open other times upon request.
    Next stop is Franz Josef, 73 miles down the road.

5. THE GLACIERS

Glaciers are pretty impressive no matter where in the world you encounter them—tons and tons of snow crystals that have, over thousands and thousands of years, been subjected to such enormous pressures that they fuse into a solid mass of clear ice, which even greater pressures cause to move at an invisible, but inexorable, rate. What makes the Fox and Franz Josef Glaciers so unforgettable (sure to be one of your most memorable New Zealand experiences) is their descent well below 1,000 feet above sea level, framed by valley walls of deep-green bush, until they terminate in luxuriant rain forests. Nowhere in the world outside arctic regions do glaciers reach such low altitudes. Fox is the longer of the two glaciers and has a more gradual slope.

On equal footing with your memories of these giant rivers of ice, however, will be those of the sunsets in these parts. From your motel lawn or window, you'll be treated to a show of great beauty. Julius von Haast, the great explorer who was the first European to explore this region, wrote of the sunsets, "New changes were every moment effected, the shades grew longer and darker, and whilst the lower portion already lay in the deep purple shade, the summits were still shining with an intense rosy hue."

ORIENTATION   The small townships of Franz Josef and Fox Glacier are only 24 kilometers (14½ miles) apart, yet you should allow a full 45 minutes for the drive. InterCity also has frequent **bus service** between the two townships.

The two glaciers are only a small part of the 284,000-acre **Westland National Park,** an impressive reserve of high mountain peaks, glacial lakes, and rushing rivers. It includes a fair bit of the Southern Alps, which cover more territory than the entire country of Switzerland! The park is much used for tramping, mountain climbing, fishing, canoeing, and hunting for red deer, thar, and chamois, as well as for scenic flights offered from several points.

Park rangers run **Visitor Centres** at both glacier townships (tel. *0288/31-796 in Franz Josef; tel. *0288/30-807 in Fox Glacier), and their displays, literature on the park, and visitor activities are essential to a full appreciation of the area.

The only local transportation is by **taxi** (ask locally about telephone number), but for travel between the two townships, InterCity coaches provide dropoff service year round.

WHAT TO SEE & DO

From late December through January, park rangers present a program of nature lectures, slide presentations, and   ✪ **guided walks** for about NZ$4 ($2) per adult, less for children, which makes it possible for budgeteers to enjoy all the park has to offer with a minimal effect on the pocketbook. They also administer the alpine huts and tramping huts available for overnight hikers, and keep track of trampers and mountain climbers (you must check conditions and register your intentions with the rangers before setting out).

Your sightseeing at the glaciers can be as costly or as inexpensive as your budget dictates. There are, it must be said, several sightseeing experiences that can put a large hole in that budget—and they are among the most spectacular travel experiences in the world, worth every cent of their cost. Yet it's quite possible to enjoy Mother Nature's free display and leave with an equally soul-satisfying experience that has cost you nothing. Either Visitor Centre can give you literature outlining self-guided walks, and for just pennies you can buy detailed information sheets on each. For less than a dollar there are booklets that give you a complete rundown on how the glaciers were formed, the movement of the ice, the mountains, the history of the region, and much, much more. If the do-it-yourself approach has no appeal, there are (during certain months) free guided walks conducted by park rangers, as well as free nature lectures and slide shows.

GLACIER TRIPS

Now, about those expensive glacier experiences. You can do three very special things at the glaciers: Take a **skiplane ride,** take a **helicopter ride,** and go for a **glacier walk.**

If this is where you decide to go all out and splurge on one of the finest of all international travel experiences, take the **Mount Cook Line's skiplane** flight from Franz Josef or Fox to the top of the icefields of Fox or Franz Josef Glacier. The six-seater Cessna 185 or Pilatus Porter whisks you over lush forests and glacial moraines, with vistas of sea and ice and spectacular views of Mount Cook and Mount Tasman. You'll actually land on one of the glaciers, put your feet on the soft, deep snow covering, and perhaps have the pilot take your picture before skiing off into the horizon. The views are all the more magnificent as the sun is beginning to set when you return. Admittedly, it is expensive, but it's an experience that will live with you the rest of your days. The hour-long flight is NZ$98 ($60).

There are several shorter flights for less, as well as a wide range of other choices, and the choice may not turn out to be as agonizing as you think—weather can make it for you. It's very unpredictable, and especially if your time is short, my best advice is to take the first one available. Of course, if the weather is fine, it's agonizing time again. But even if weather really closes in and neither is available, not to worry—you'll have another opportunity at Mount Cook.

There are Mount Cook Line **flightseeing centers** at both townships: at Franz Josef, phone *714; at Fox, dial *41-812. You can also book flights through both the THC Franz Josef and the Fox Glacier Hotel, and most motels.

There are a number of ✪ **helicopter flights** to the glaciers every day, including those that make a snow landing, and generally they are shorter and less expensive than the skiplane trips. The trips last 10 to 40 minutes and cost NZ$55 to NZ$160 ($31 to $91). Take my word for it, it's a thrilling way to get close to nature. For details and booking, contact **Alpine Guides** (see below) or **Glacier Helicopters**, Main Road, Franz Josef (tel. *0288/31-745), or Main Road, Fox Glacier (tel. *0288/30-8030).

There is another great way to experience the Franz Josef glacier, which is far less expensive than the flights and which, in my opinion, actually complements them. That is the **glacier walk,** with an expert guiding you along the surface of the ice. If you're in reasonably good shape you'll be able to do the walk, regardless of age. Guides chip steps in the ice, which during warm weather is granular instead of glass-slick. You'll go up into the ice fall, walk among the crevasses, listen to the deep-throated grumble of the moving glacier. Hobnailed boots, waterproof parka, heavy socks, and walking stick are provided, and walks are scheduled at 10am and 2pm in summer, mornings only at other times. And the walk goes regardless of the weather! The cost of the 3-hour trip is NZ$24 ($14); boot rental is extra. Most of the time your guide will be Rangy Tinarau, who's bound to "have you on" with his Maori humor. Rangy came here on holiday 25 years ago and just stayed on.

At Fox, in addition to a glacier walk like the above, there's a half-day ✪ **heli-hike,** when you fly by helicopter to about 1 kilometer (½ mile) up the glacier and walk back down. It's about the same length as the glacier walk (2½ hours), but you're on the ice longer. All equipment is provided. A longer, full-day heli-hike goes all the way to Victoria Falls, and you spend the entire day walking down the glacier (you leave at 9:30am and get back around 4:30pm). You'd want to be reasonably fit for this outing, but if you really want to get to know that river of ice, this is the walk to take. Groups are small, and there's time to really explore things (this is the one the guides themselves like best). The cost, including all gear and an expert guide, is NZ$75 ($43).

For details on all the glacier experiences described above, plus a few more, contact **Alpine Guides (Westland) Ltd.,** P.O. Box 38, Fox Glacier (tel. *0288/30-825; fax *0288/30-825).

If you're reading this book at home and the glaciers have you hooked, or if you were hooked already and are coming to New Zealand primarily to spend time at the glaciers, you might like to know that Alpine Guides also offer several **mountaineering courses,** varying in length from 7 days to 2 weeks. These are the guides who conduct the walks just described (check with them for schedules and prices), and their experience covers mountain and ice climbing from the Himalayas to Antarctica. Write ahead for details on physical requirements, enrollment, and prices.

OTHER ACTIVITIES

If **fishing trips** are a big lure, contact Stan Peterson, Westland Guiding Services, P.O. Box 38, Franz Josef (tel. *30-750). He'll have you out on Lake Mapourika (the name means "Flower of the Dawn") in no time, and you might just come back with a 12- or 15-pound trout or salmon. Stan charges NZ$46 ($26) per hour for up to four people in a boat and a minimum of 1½ hours. He'll also take you on **minibus tours,** including trips to the glaciers; Lake Matheson, with its scenic reflections of Mount Cook and Mount Tasman, and the gold-mining area of Okarito.

Lake Matheson, 3 miles from the Fox Glacier Hotel, shows up on all the postcards, but **Lake Mapourika,** 5½ miles north of Franz Josef and the largest lake in Westland National Park, deserves attention for its own arresting reflections and setting. You can swim in the lake, as well.

In Franz Josef, take a few minutes to visit **St. James Anglican Church,** the Tudor-style church whose east window frames a spectacular alpine view behind the altar. Watch for the sign just south of the Visitor Centre. If you'd like to do an hour-long **hike,** follow the sign opposite St. James Church and you're on your way.

If you managed to miss the **glowworm dells** in Waitomo or Hokitika, you can at least get the idea, on a smaller scale, in Franz Josef. Day or night, follow the sign- and rock-lined path to the heliport pad (it's across the street from the gas station). The path will tunnel through some trees and lead you down 11 steps to where you see the roots of a tree overhanging the path at a height of about 4 feet. Stoop down and take a peak—it's like looking at a starry night in an underground world.

WHERE TO STAY

During peak season, accommodations are woefully short, with a greater choice at Franz Josef than at Fox Glacier. Each township has a licensed hotel; however, both are out of reach of budget travelers (the one in Franz Josef is an excellent THC and books many of the glacier walks and flightseeing trips, and sometimes has off-season special rates). There's no central booking service, but the Visitor Centres can furnish a list of accommodations with current prices. All long-distance telephone calls must be made through the operator.

Unless otherwise noted, all rates listed below include GST.

IN FRANZ JOSEF

Motel Flats

BUSHLAND COURT MOTEL, Cron St. (P.O. Box 41), Franz Josef. Tel. *0288/31-757. 12 units (all with bath). TV TEL

$ Rates (excluding GST): NZ$40 ($23) single; NZ$45–NZ$70 ($25–$40) double. AE, MC, V.

This centrally located hotel has appealing units with high, beamed ceilings incorporating warm rimu wood. Sleeping two to six people, all are immaculate and have central heating, video, radio, and covered carports. Smaller units are available in their Alpine Lodge Wing. There's a laundry, a barbecue area, and a children's playground on the premises. Proprietors Owen and Maggie Morris take great pains to accommodate and will even provide hairdryers and Exercycles on request.

GLACIER GATEWAY MOTOR LODGE, Hwy. 6 (P.O. Box 1), Franz Josef. Tel. *0288/31-776. Fax *0288/31-732. 23 units (all with bath). TV TEL

$ Rates: NZ$70 ($40) single; NZ$85 ($49) double. Extra person NZ$13 ($7). AE, DC, MC, V.

Donna and Kerry Kampjes' attractive motel has studio units as well as doubles, and even some that sleep as many as six. Two have spa baths. Facilities include a spa pool, sauna, guest laundry, and a coffee shop. There's also off-street parking. The property is on the outskirts of the township, just south of the bridge, opposite Glacier Access Road.

**GLACIER VIEW MOTEL, State Hwy. 6 (P.O. Box 22), Franz Josef. Tel.
*0288/31-705.** Fax *0288/31-761. 14 units (all with bath). TV TEL
$ Rates: NZ$75 ($43) single or double. Best Western discounts available. AE, DC, MC, V.
This Best Western member offers attractively decorated serviced units managed by Lee and Peter Nolan. There's a small shop on the premises and a spa pool in a natural setting. The motel is 2 kilometers (1¼ miles) north of the township.

MOTEL FRANZ JOSEF, Hwy. 6 North, Franz Josef, (Private Bag, Hokitika). Tel. *0288/31-742. Fax *0288/31-760. 8 units (all with bath). TV TEL
$ Rates (excluding GST): NZ$70 ($40) single or double. Extra adult NZ$12 ($7). AE, DC, MC, V.
Quiet, trim, and tidy, the Franz Josef has one- and two-bedroom units, all with private patios facing a view of distant low hills, and all with private carports. Rooms are centrally heated and have TVs and radios, and there's a spa pool. Mr. and Mrs. Trevor Gibb, the friendly owners, also have a small canteen with canned and frozen foods. The motel is located 3 miles north of the township.

RATA GROVE, Cron St. (P.O. Box 3), Franz Josef. Tel. and fax *0288/31-741. 10 units (all with bath). TV TEL
$ Rates (excluding GST): NZ$65–NZ$75 ($37–$43) single or double. Best Western discounts available. AE, DC, MC, V.

Just behind the grocery store and souvenir shop, this accommodation is as close to the bus stop and town center as you can get. The units, which vary in size, are quiet and brightly lit, with a kitchen, hot and cold running water, and heaters.

A Hostel

FRANZ JOSEF YHA HOSTEL, 2-4 Cron St. (P.O. Box 12), Franz Josef. Tel. *0288/31-754. 60 beds.
$ Rates: NZ$14 ($8) for members; NZ$18 ($10) for nonmembers. No credit cards.
This modern hostel, with a spacious kitchen, new showers, and 60 beds in 10 rooms, is convenient to shops and the bus stop in the township center. Double and family rooms are available. Facilities include TV and video, a laundry and drying room, a hostel shop, bikes, and a lounge with a piano and small pot-bellied stoves. Ask about half-price nights and other promotions. Breakfast and dinner are available 7 days a week. Advance booking is always advisable, especially during summer months and holiday periods.

Camping

The ✪ **Franz Josef Holiday Park,** on the main road (tel. *0288/31-766), is set in attractive grounds of bush and hills. There are tent sites and eight basic cabins sleeping two to four persons on bunks, all with good, comfortable mattresses. The

24-room Lodge has private bedrooms, hot and cold running water in each, with central heating and internal access to shared bathrooms and kitchen. Bedrooms sleep from two to five people, and there are family rooms. Three cottages sleep two to five people, have hot and cold running water, stoves, refrigerators, crockery, cutlery, cookware, blankets, and heaters. Other facilities include kitchens with microwaves, showers, automatic laundry, TV, recreation room, barbecue, and children's playground. Bedding can be rented, and there's a bus stop near the entrance. Bunks are NZ$8 ($5); cabins NZ$22 ($13) single or double, NZ$8 ($5) each additional person; NZ$14 ($8) per person for Lodge rooms. Tent sites go for NZ$5 ($3) per person.

Worth the Extra Money

FRANZ JOSEF GLACIER HOTEL, Hwy. 6, Franz Josef. Tel. *0288/31-719. 50 rms (all with bath). TV TEL

$ Rates (excluding GST): NZ$130 ($74) single or double. Discounts available May–Sept. AE, DC, MC, V.

The most luxurious accommodations at the glaciers, this modern hotel has superior guest rooms, nicely appointed and furnished, as well as a lounge bar and excellent restaurant. It is frequently the gathering point for glacier walks and other activities. While high-season rates push the Franz Joseph Glacier right out of the question for those of us traveling on a budget, during the off-season they offer drastic reductions that qualify as real bargains. These rates are not highly publicized, so it will pay you to call ahead and inquire about current offerings—if you're lucky, you'll enjoy luxurious accommodations at a budget rate. The hotel is 2 kilometers (1 mile) from the township center.

WESTLAND MOTOR INN, Main St. (P.O. Box 33), Franz Josef. Tel. *0288/31-728 or ***31-729.** 100 rms (all with bath). TV TEL

$ Rates (excluding GST): NZ$120 ($69) single or double. AE, DC, MC, V.

By far the prettiest motel in Franz Josef township, the Westland is centrally located on the main street. It has a licensed restaurant (see "Where to Eat," below) and lounge bar, and a beautiful guest lounge with huge glass windows and one entire wall covered by a native-stone fireplace. Grounds are beautifully planted, and just at the entrance there's an old cobble cart planted with native ferns. The rooms are all serviced and include video, tea and coffee facilities, and central heating. Facilities include two spa pools, a games room, and a guest laundry.

IN FOX GLACIER

Motel Flats

A1 MOTEL, Lake Matheson Rd. (P.O. Box 29), Fox Glacier. Tel. *0288/30-804. Fax *0288/30-706. 10 units (all with bath). TV TEL

$ Rates: NZ$65–NZ$70 ($37–$40) single or double. AE, MC, V.

This motel sits in a valley about a mile from the township down Lake Matheson Road and is managed by Pat and Tony Clapperton and by Brian and Jean Mather. The units are nicely designed, attractively furnished, and sleep two to five people. Other amenities include a laundry, barbecue facilities, a swimming pool, a nine-hole putting green, squash court, spa pool, and children's playground. A continental breakfast is available.

GOLDEN GLACIER MOTOR INN, Hwy. 6 (P.O. Box 32), Fox Glacier. Tel. *0288/30-847. Fax *0288/30-822. 51 units (all with bath). TV TEL

$ Rates: NZ$60–NZ$70 ($34–$40) single; NZ$65–NZ$80 ($37–$46) double. AE, DC, MC, V.

Located in the township center, the Golden Glacier's fully serviced units are enhanced considerably by amenities such as the licensed restaurant, house bar, and open log fire that is a focal point for sociability in the evening. The units are all quite nicely appointed, and there's a laundry and drying room.

A Hostel

FOX GLACIER BACKPACKER HOSTEL AND MOTOR CAMP, at the Golden Glacier Motor Inn, Hwy. 6, Fox Glacier. Tel. *0288/30-847. Fax *0288/30-813. 24 cabins (none with bath). TV TEL

$ Rates (excluding GST): NZ$11 ($6) bunk; NZ$15 ($9) per person tent; NZ$18 ($10) caravan site; NZ$23 ($13) per person cabin. MC, V.

This hostel has heated rooms for up to four people each, with TV, and in-house video. There is also a games room with pool table, table tennis, and darts, a laundry, and a kitchen. There are some double rooms.

Camping

About a quarter mile from Fox Glacier township, you'll find **Fox Glacier Motor Park** (tel. *0288/31-821), with 25 clean, comfortable cabins, some with two bunks, others with four. There are two kitchen blocks with dining rooms, three shower blocks, and a coin-operated laundry. Linen may be rented, and canned and frozen goods are available at the camp store. Double-occupancy rates are NZ$15 ($9) for tent sites, NZ$18 ($10) for caravan sites, NZ$28 ($16) for cabins, NZ$48 ($27) for tourist flats. Lodging in the bunkhouse is NZ$11 ($6) per person. Add GST.

WHERE TO EAT

There are not a great many places to eat in either township, and this may be where you do more home cooking than anywhere else in New Zealand. However, some of the following are quite good.

IN FRANZ JOSEF

CLEMATIS ROOM, in the Westland Motor Inn, at the northern end of the main street. Tel. *729.
Cuisine: NEW ZEALAND. **Reservations:** Recommended in summer.
$ Prices: Average meal NZ$24 ($14). AE, DC, MC, V.
Open: Summer, daily 6–8:30pm; winter, daily 6–7:30pm.

This attractive restaurant, on the northern edge of the township, has slanted-beam ceiling and gaslight-style fixtures overhead, with wide windows that look out to the mountains. The à la carte menu lists many local specialties; it's fully licensed, and has a nice lounge bar for before or after meals, where you're likely to meet a local or two, all glad of a chat. Dinner prices run NZ$15 to NZ$20 ($9.40 to $12.50).

GLACIER STORE AND TEAROOMS, Main Rd. Tel. *31-731.
Cuisine: LIGHT LUNCHES/TEAS. **Reservations:** Not required.
$ Prices: Under NZ$5 ($3). AE, MC, V.
Open: Daily 7:45am–6:30pm (until 9:30pm in summer).

The Glacier Store and Tearooms, in a beautifully designed building in the township center, serve light fare for lunches and teas. It's self-service, and you can lunch well for NZ$5 ($3.15) and under. Select from assorted sandwiches, quiche, filled rolls, soup, croissants, and pastries. The upstairs tearooms offer fantastic views of the snowcapped Southern Alps and the luxuriant west-coast rain forest. Within the same building you can shop for food, hardware, and clothing, and adjacent to the building is the **Fern Grove Souvenir Shop,** which carries a wide range of quality souvenirs, film, and a wide selection of woolen knitwear.

IN FOX GLACIER

The **grocery store** sells foodstuffs, hot meat pies, and sandwiches right along with camping supplies, hardware, boots, heavy jackets, and polyester shirts. The **Tea Rooms** have inexpensive grills and snacks, and **Grandma's Grub Shop,** next door, has inexpensive full meals at budget prices. All are open daily, and hours vary. Meals in the **Golden Glacier Motor Inn's** licensed restaurant are quite good, with moderate prices.

Note: For picnics while you're in the area, pick up supplies at the store. You can get a hearty snack at the bus stop café in Makarora.

EN ROUTE TO QUEENSTOWN VIA HAAST PASS & WANAKA

Author's travel tip: This is a stretch that I have driven only once, and that one experience leads me to make a heartfelt recommendation—do yourself a favor, and let InterCity do the driving from here on to Queenstown, leaving your eyes free to drink in some of the world's most spectacular natural beauty. Tall trees line the road, which twists from one breathtaking view to the next. A final word: If you *are* driving, exercise caution all the way.

This is a day-long drive along a 256-mile route that takes you through some of New Zealand's most striking terrain: cool green ferns; secluded sea coves; deep-walled gorges; high, steep bluffs; alpine lakes; lagoons alive with white herons; and valleys filled with grazing sheep. Before this road was built, the only passage from east to west was an old bridle path, and at the very top of the Haast Pass there's a signpost that will point you to that path, a pretty walk back into the past. The road itself took 40 years to build, and in fact work still goes on in sections as rock slides occur. Some portions are gravel, though most are sealed and a good surface. There are steep climbs and sharp descents, hairpin curves and stretches of one-lane travel. At 1,847 feet above sea level, the Haast Pass is actually the lowest pass through the Southern Alps, very seldom blocked by snow, but peaks on either side rise as high as 10,000 feet.

A picnic lunch is ideal, as there are any number of places to stop and let your senses ramble as you eat. It's a good excuse, too, to loiter at any scenic spot that especially takes your fancy. There are roofed outdoor tables (and restrooms) at a public picnic area about 122 miles into the journey at Pleasant Flat Bridge. Otherwise, the **DB Haast Hotel** (tel. Haast *827) serves a good lunch at reasonable prices (this is where InterCity and most tour coaches break the trip). Incidentally, if you are meandering and would like to see more along the way, the hotel has serviced units that go for NZ$74 to NZ$110 ($42 to $63), plus GST. If you're picnicking, save a bit for a tea break when you reach Lake Wanaka—the view, with 9,975-foot Mount Aspiring in the distance, begs a lingering look.

WANAKA

A popular resort with New Zealanders, Wanaka offers many sports activities, as well as smashing scenery. If you arrive there utterly exhausted, it makes a good overnight stopping place before going on to Queenstown.

Mount Aspiring National Park has its park headquarters in Wanaka, although the park is some 45 kilometers (27 miles) to the northwest. If you plan to spend time here, drop by the **Mount Aspiring National Park Visitor Centre,** on the corner of Ballantyne Road and Highway 89 (tel. 03/443-7660), for information on park activities.

How to get lost and found—and totally bewildered!—in Wanaka? Head for the ✪ **Puzzling Place and Great Maze** on the Main Highway (tel. 03/443-7489). Behind tall fences, there are pathways that lead somewhere and passageways that lead nowhere. The fun comes in finding your way through without becoming hopelessly lost. But there's *much* more to this unique place that has been some 17 years in the making, and far be it from me to spoil your fun by disclosing all. Take my word for it, youngsters (of all ages) will be intrigued and entertained. Admission is NZ$5 ($3) for adults, half that for children.

Where to Stay

BEST WESTERN MANUKA CRESCENT MOTEL, 51 Manuka Crescent, Wanaka. Tel. 03/443-7773. Fax 03/443-9066. 12 units (all with bath). TV TEL
Directions: Off Beacon Rd., about 1 mile from town.
$ Rates (excluding GST): NZ$55 ($31) single; NZ$60 ($34) double. AE, DC, MC, V.

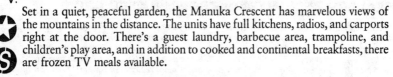

Set in a quiet, peaceful garden, the Manuka Crescent has marvelous views of the mountains in the distance. The units have full kitchens, radios, and carports right at the door. There's a guest laundry, barbecue area, trampoline, and children's play area, and in addition to cooked and continental breakfasts, there are frozen TV meals available.

YHA HOSTEL, 181 Upton St., Wanaka. Tel. 03/443-7405. 42 beds.
$ Rates: NZ$14 ($8) for members; NZ$18 ($10) for nonmembers. No credit cards.
This centrally located hostel offers basic rock-climbing instruction, mountain-bike rental or guided trips, and kayaking outings through its own adventure company, Down to Earth Adventures, and provides discounts for guests for horseback riding, ski rentals, and at Te Karo Wholefood Restaurant. There are 42 beds in six rooms.

Where to Eat

In addition to the restaurants below, **Aspiring Takeaways,** 68 Ardmore St. (tel. 443-7803), has burgers, ice cream, milk shakes, and sandwiches at low prices and is open daily from 8am to 9pm.

RIPPLES, Pembroke Village Mall. Tel. 443-7413.
Cuisine: NEW ZEALAND. **Reservations:** Not required.
$ Prices: Lunch NZ$3–NZ$14 ($2–$8); dinner NZ$30–NZ$40 ($17–$23). AE, DC, MC, V.
Open: Summer, lunch daily noon–2pm, dinner daily 6–10pm; winter, dinner Mon–Sat 6–10pm.

It's hard to say if the setting or the food is more agreeable at this cozy little place in town. In summer, you can dine outside on the veranda with those wonderful views of the mountain in the distance; other times, inside is just as pleasant. The menu offers some truly innovative dishes, and it changes from month to month. A sampling includes pan-fried lamb noisettes dipped in egg and rosemary; wild pork and venison combo; smoked chicken and Camembert triangles wrapped in phyllo pastry; and an avocado, crab, and prawn plate. BYO.

FROM WANAKA TO QUEENSTOWN

You have a choice here, with two routes you could follow to reach Queenstown, one not open to trailers and not recommended to inexpert drivers. That 44-mile stretch of Highway 89 crosses the **Crown Range** and opens up fantastic panoramic views of the entire **Wakatipu Valley,** then descends into the valley in a series of sharp curves until it reaches the aptly named "Foot of Zig Zag," where you make a sharp right turn and level out to drive through farmlands all the way to Lake Wakatipu and

Queenstown. The merits of this drive have been an ongoing source of debate by our readers—see comments below and make your own decision. If you do decide to take Highway 89, I think you should know that the liquor law actually used to state that drivers could have two drinks if going in the direction of Wanaka but only one if headed toward Queenstown!

The other route (the one I strongly recommend unless you're stout of heart and a whale of a driver) is via Highway 6 and is good traveling all the way. You'll drive alongside manmade **Lake Dunstan,** which was formed behind the **Clyde Dam.**

Whichever route you choose, you may want to stop in historic **Arrowtown,** although it's just a short drive back from Queenstown if you're ready to push on to dinner and bed after a long day behind the wheel (and there are good coach tours from Queenstown to Arrowtown, so you won't have to miss it).

READERS RECOMMEND: CROWN RANGE DRIVE

"We took the drive over the Crown Range from Wanaka and were glad we did as the Wakatipu Valley opened before us in the early evening light. It was truly beautiful and well worth the bouncing, although I think it is very wise for you to advise against the road for most drivers"—E. Angeletti, Greenville, S.C.. . . . *"Shame on you! Highway 89 is* the worst road in the world! *It is not only not for the faint of heart, it's not really even for cars! One can rarely exceed 45kphr [27 m.p.h.] (unless one rents a Land Rover or truly hates the poor rental car) and Zig Zag is no less than 25 minutes of 20kphr [12 m.p.h.] in second gear going straight down a 3,500-foot-high cliff!"*—W. Newman, Boston, Mass. [*Author's note:* Well, there you have it—take it if you dare—you're forewarned, and I'll not have the decision on my head! Every update edition seems to bring with it still more comments about the Crown Range drive, each one voicing a very determined viewpoint—herewith, one of the latest.] . . . *"We do not agree that Highway 89 is a difficult road. Its main difficulty is that it is narrow in places, but no more so than many mountain passes in Colorado. It can be easily negotiated by any careful driver and is worth at least one drive. And it is totally misleading for a reader to say that one travels straight down a 3,500-foot cliff—not so!"*—S. Nelson, New Cumberland, Pa. . . . *"The 6½-mile drive to Glendhu Bay is on a paved road and offers a nice view of the mountains. However, those with a little adventure will keep going another 24 miles to the end of the road to the starting point for climbing Mount Aspiring. The mountains and views are great, the road unpaved but good. The only problem is 15 streams to cross (30 round-trip), but our car did just fine."*—J. and P. Conrad, San Jose, Calif.

Where to Eat En Route

CARDRONA RESTAURANT & BAR, R.D. 1 (Hwy. 89), Wanaka. Tel. 03/443-8153.

    Cuisine: SNACKS/NEW ZEALAND/APRES-SKI. **Reservations:** Recommended, but not required. **Directions:** On Hwy. 89, 15 miles from Wanaka, 28 miles from Queenstown.

$ **Prices:** Snacks under NZ$10 ($6); dinner NZ$25–NZ$35 ($14–$20). MC, V. **Open:** Summer, daily 3:30pm–late; winter, daily 10:30am–late. **Closed:** spring and fall.

Sited at the base of two ski fields, this historic old building was born as an inn back in 1865 at the height of the gold-rush era. Now a restaurant and bar, its decor is one of hardwood floors, antique oak tables and chairs, and patchwork cushions on the chairs. It has long been one of the area's most popular après-ski spots, where slopes-weary skiers relax with mulled wine before a blazing log fire. In summer, there's dining in lovely sheltered gardens. The menu features local lamb, game, seafoods, and homemade sourdough bread.

CHAPTER 9

QUEENSTOWN & ENVIRONS

1. QUEENSTOWN
- **WHAT'S SPECIAL ABOUT QUEENSTOWN**

2. TE ANAU

3. MILFORD SOUND

Queenstown is the jewel of South Island resorts—pronounced by gold prospectors to be "fit for any queen," after which they promptly christened it with the present name on a very *un*queenly blacksmith's anvil. The city is nestled at the foot of mountains called the Remarkables, on the northeastern shore of Lake Wakatipu, a 53-mile-long, 1,280-foot-deep beauty encased in a glacial bed. Its shape vaguely resembles that of a reclining figure with its knees drawn up. Maori legend will tell you that's because at the bottom of the lake lies the heart of a great *tipua* (giant) named Matau, who captured a beautiful girl who caught his fancy and took her back to his mountain home. He reckoned without her valiant lover, however, who came to her rescue and set fire to the giant as he lay sleeping on a bed of fern. As the flames flared higher and higher, fed by the fat from his enormous body, he was suffocated by the smoke and sank deep into the earth to form a vast chasm. Only his heart was not reduced to ashes. As the rains fell and mountain snows melted with the heat of the fire, the chasm filled with water to form a lake in the shape of the giant, his knees drawn up in agony. His head, they say, is at Glenorchy, his knees at Queenstown, and his feet at Kingston. His heart beats on from far below, and that, they say, explains the fact that the surface of the lake rises and falls 3 inches every 5 minutes. Of course, scientists have another explanation—they call the phenomenon seiche action. But, then, what do *they* know about giants and beautiful girls and valiant lovers!

Sheepherders were the first settlers in this district, and they endured the onslaught of hundreds of gold miners when the Shotover River, which feeds Lake Wakatipu, was proclaimed "the richest river in the world." The claim was well founded, for as much as £4,000 was dredged by the discoverer of gold in his first 2 months. When the gold played out in fairly short order the sheep men came into their own once more, and today the Wakatipu district is filled with vast high-country sheep stations, a source of less spectacular, but certainly more reliable, riches.

1. QUEENSTOWN

179 miles SW of the glaciers, 105 miles NE of Te Anau,
190 miles SE of Milford Sound

GETTING THERE   By Plane   There is air service via **Mount Cook Airlines** and **Ansett New Zealand** between Queenstown and Auckland, the Bay of Islands, Rotorua, and Wellington in the North Island, Christchurch, Mount Cook, and Nelson on the South Island. The airport shuttle runs to and from the airport regularly and will drop you off or pick you up at your hotel (tel. 442-9803) for about NZ$5 ($3). Taxi fare from the airport to the town center is around NZ$9 ($5).

By Bus   Service is offered by **InterCity** and/or **Mount Cook Lines** between Queenstown and Christchurch, Dunedin, Fox Glacier, Franz Josef, Invercargill,

WHAT'S SPECIAL ABOUT QUEENSTOWN

Scenic Splendors
- [ ] The splendid mountains called the Remarkables, especially at sunrise and sunset, when the play of light is quite spectacular.
- [ ] The legendary Lake Wakatipu, a 53-mile-long, 1,280-foot-deep beauty in the shape of a fatally wounded giant.

Outdoor Activities
- [ ] Skiing at Coronet Peak, Cardrona, Treble Cone, and The Remarkables.

- [ ] The lake cruise aboard the TSS *Earnslaw*.
- [ ] Jet boating on the Shotover River white-water rapids.

Special Events
- [ ] The week-long Winter Festival in July, with its nonstop fun events.

Mount Cook, Milford Sound, Te Anau, and Wanaka. The bus depot is in Beach Street (tel. 442-7420).

By Car Queenstown can be reached via from Dunedin, Highway 1, 8, and 6.

ESSENTIALS Orientation The **lakefront** is the hub of Queenstown, and the street fronting the sheltered, horseshoe bay is **Marine Parade.** On the northern edge, at **Beach Street,** are the jetty, pier, and wharf. To the south are lovely public gardens. **The Mall,** reserved for pedestrians only, runs from Marine Parade for 1 bustling block. It is a busy concentration of activity: shops, information and booking agencies for major attractions, restaurants, the post office, and departure points for most tours. There is no local bus transportation.

Information The **Visitors Information Centre** is in the InterCity Travel office, Clocktower Centre, corner of Shotover and Camp Streets (tel. 442-8238). Hours are 8:30am to 6pm Monday through Friday, and 10am to 6pm Saturday and Sunday. The **Mount Cook Travel Office** is at the corner of Rees and Ballarat Streets (tel. 442-7650). The **Fiordland Travel Centre** is on the Steamer Wharf, Beach Street (tel. 442-7500). The **Department of Conservation Information Centre,** corner of Stanley and Ballarat Streets (tel. 442-7933), is the place to go for information on **walking tracks.**

Fast Facts The **area code** for Queenstown is 03. **Telecom,** Stanley Street (tel. 442-8555), has facilities for international, national, and local telephone calls, as well and fax and telex. The **Thomas Cook Bureau de Change,** in the Mall at Camp Street (tel. 442-8600), is open later than the banks and on weekends. The **post office** is on the corner of Camp and Ballarat Streets. **Fiordland Travel,** Steamer Wharf, Beach Street (tel. 442-7500), provides economical transport for backpackers to and from the hiking tracks, with a flexible **Backpackers Pass** ticketing system with several price and destination options. To call a **taxi,** phone 442-7888. The **American Express** representative in Queenstown is the Visitors Information Centre (tel. 442-8238).

SPECIAL EVENTS Queenstown wears a perpetual festive air, but if you happen to get here during the last full week in July, you can join the annual ✪ **Winter Festival** fun. There's something going on all day and into the night every single day,

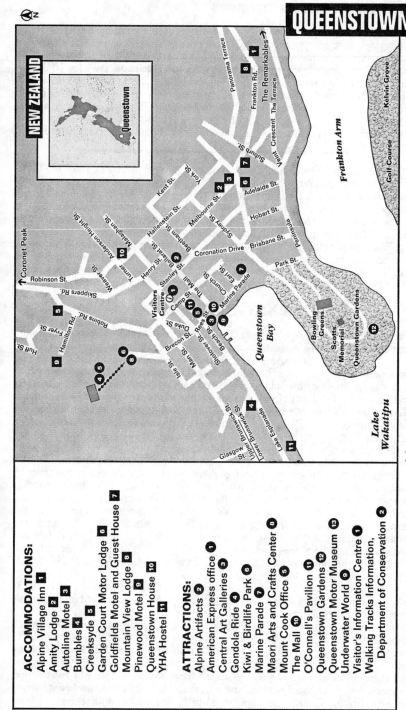

QUEENSTOWN

NEW ZEALAND

Queenstown

N

↑Coronet Peak

Robinson St.

Huff St.

Hamilton Rd.

Fryer St.

Robins Rd.

Skippers Rd.

Weaver St.

Turner

Anderson Heights St.

Malaghan St.

Kent St.

York St.

Hallenstein St.

Beetham St.

Henry St.

Ballara St.

Stanley St.

Visitors Centre

Camp St.

The Mall

Rees St.

Beach St.

Duke St.

Man St.

Shotover St.

Isle St.

Brecon St.

Glasgow St.

Upper Brunswick St.

Lower Brunswick St.

Lake Esplanade

Melbourne St.

Sydney St.

Hobart St.

Coronation Drive

Brisbane St.

Peninsula

Park St.

Earl St.

Church St.

Marine Parade

Adelaide St.

Subub St.

Vein Crescent The Terrace

Panorama Terrace

Frankton Rd.

The Remarkables

Frankton Arm

Queenstown Bay

Bowling Greens

Scotts Memorial

Queenstown Gardens

Golf Course

Kelvin Grove

Lake Wakatipu

Information ℗

ACCOMMODATIONS:

Alpine Village Inn **1**
Amity Lodge **2**
Autoline Motel **3**
Bumbles **4**
Creeksyde **5**
Garden Court Motor Lodge **6**
Goldfields Motel and Guest House **7**
Mountain View Lodge **8**
Pinewood Motel **9**
Queenstown House **10**
YHA Hostel **11**

ATTRACTIONS:

Alpine Artifacts **2**
American Express office **1**
Central Art Galleries **3**
Gondola Ride **4**
Kiwi & Birdlife Park **6**
Marine Parade **7**
Maori Arts and Crafts Center **8**
Mount Cook Office **5**
The Mall **10**
O'Connell's Pavilion **11**
Queenstown Gardens **12**
Queenstown Motor Museum **13**
Underwater World **9**
Visitor's Information Centre **1**
Walking Tracks Information,
  Department of Conservation **2**

and some of the goings-on are downright hilarious. Take, for example, the Dog Derby (when dogs and their masters descend the slopes any way they can except on skis), or the dog barking contest, or . . . well, you can imagine. There are other, really spectacular, events, such as the **Otago Goldfields Heritage Trail** for 10 days in November, the **Arrowtown Autumn Festival** for 10 days in April, and the annual **Volvo Ski Show,** when expert skiing performers display ballet skiing and breathtaking acrobatic feats. There are Ski Bunnies, a Miss Snowbird, visiting celebrities, children's ski events, and fancy-dress competitions, a Mardi Gras night, and all sorts of other activities, some a bit on the madcap side, others real tests of skill.

The lifeblood of Queenstown, with a year-round population of only 11,000, is tourism, and no matter what time of year you come, you'll find visitors from all over the world here to enjoy the lake, the river, and the mountains. From late June through September an international skiing crowd flocks to ski the slopes of Coronet Peak, whose dry, powdery snows are said to be the best in Australasia. Thus this pretty little town, far from being provincial, has a decidedly cosmopolitan air.

Cosmopolitan it certainly is, but mostly, Queenstown is just plain fun. The powers that be have, in fact, adopted as the town's official slogan "Queenstown Just for Fun"—well, I can't top that, only endorse it enthusiastically. For my money, it probably is the Fun Capital of this lovely country!

WHAT TO SEE & DO

There is always so much going on in Queenstown, and so many things to see and do, that your first order of business should be to go by the Visitors Information Centre and pick up their **Queenstown Sightseeing** folder, which lists all current attractions, prices, hours, and booking details. The free booklet **Queenstown A to Z** is a useful directory for public services, accommodations, restaurants, sightseeing, and a host of other details. Look also for the free tourist newspaper **The Mountain Scene,** available from most accommodations and from the Visitors Information Centre. Armed with all that information, your dilemma becomes one of setting priorities.

One thing you won't want to miss, no matter what time of year you come to town, is the ✪ **gondola ride** up to Skyline Point, and don't forget your camera. The view is breathtaking, and if you go at lunch or dinner you can stretch your viewing time by eating at the restaurant or snack bar (see "Where to Eat," below). The gondola operates from 10am, with a round-trip fare of NZ$9 ($5) until the restaurant closes at midnight. If you go up on the half hour, you'll arrive in time to see the thrills-and-spills film **Kiwi Magic,** starring Maori comedian Billy T. James and American actor Ned Beatty, and shown on the hour from 11am to 9pm. To feel as if you're in the middle of the action, be it jet-boating, tobogganing, or flying in a small plane, sit in the middle of the theater toward the front. Admission is NZ$6 ($3) for adults, NZ$3 ($2) for children.

At the base of the gondola ride is the **Kiwi & Birdlife Park** (tel. 442-8059), where, if you're lucky, you can see those illusive kiwi birds feeding and fossicking. It's open from 9am to 5pm.

Queenstown has two top-rated ski areas at its doorstep. **Coronet Peak,** 18 kilometers (10¾ miles) from town, operates five lifts during winter months. In summer, a scenic chair lift, alpine slide, and restaurant are open. **The Remarkables** (named for the colors the peaks turn at sunset), 28 kilometers (17½ miles) from town, has three lifts and a self-service restaurant. Both ski areas offer **ski rental, ski lessons,** and **fast-food restaurants.** Coronet Peak has a **licensed restaurant** as well. Mount Cook Line operates **shuttle buses** to both ski areas from Queenstown. Open year round, except for June.

Another "don't miss" is a ✪ **lake cruise** aboard the TSS *Earnslaw,* a 1912 steamship known affectionately as "The Lady of the Lake," which makes a 1-hour lunch cruise at 12:30pm, for which adults pay a boarding fee of NZ$21 ($12) and lunch is extra, at moderate prices; and a 3-hour cruise at 2pm, with an adult boarding fee of NZ$36 ($21); children pay NZ$10 ($6) on all cruises. It's a leisurely, relaxing way to see the lake and mountains during lunch. The longer cruise explores the lake from Walter Peak to White Point, taking a 40-minute land break at **Mount Nicholas Station,** a working sheep station. There's a 6pm dinner cruise with fares of NZ$50 ($29) with dinner for adults, NZ$25 ($14) without dinner, the same NZ$10 ($6) for children.

Or take the 10-mile, 30-minute **hydrofoil** spin around the lake at 35 m.p.h. on the *Meteor III.* Fares are NZ$22 ($13) and there's no need to reserve—just show up at the Main Town Pier. Check locally for departure times between 10am and 4pm.

In summer, the Shotover River's white-water rapids are the scene of **jet-boat trips** guaranteed to give you a thrill as expert drivers send you flying between huge boulders amid the rushing waters. They'll point out traces of gold mining along the river as you go along. Several jet-boat operators offer a variety of trips and prices. You can drive out to the river (allow a half hour), or there's courtesy-coach service from the Mount Cook World Travel Office. The jet-boat rides range from NZ$38 to NZ$45 ($22 to $26) (children pay half), depending on the length of the trip. Then there's the exciting **Heli-Jet trip,** which takes you by coach out to the airport, where you board a helicopter from the trip to the river, jet-boat through then fly back to the airport. Fare is NZ$80 ($46) per person for the half-day trip.

You won't have been in Queestown for long before finding out about **bungy jumping,** which I'm convinced is more fun to watch than to do. It means taking a 143-foot head-first plunge off the Kawarau Suspension Bridge. There's a superstrong and long bungy cord attached to your ankles so you actually stop just shy of the water (or after you've dunked your head—you can decide). You then swing back and forth about five times. You'll pay about NZ$95 ($54) for this moment of madness that some people consider "fun." Or you can watch the videos for free at the **Danes Shotover Rafts,** at the corner of Shotover and Camp Streets (tel. 442-7318).

If you're a motoring enthusiast, go by the **Queenstown Motor Museum,** on Brecon Street just below the gondola (tel. 442-8775). Opened in 1971, the modern museum houses 50 changing exhibits in two hangarlike wings, and is managed by John and Glenys Taylor, who are happy to chat away about any of the displays, all of which are in perfect road condition and burnished to a smart gleam. There's a 1922 Rolls-Royce Silver Ghost, which once belonged to the lord mayor of London, an 1885 gentlewoman's tricycle, a 12-horsepower 1903 De Dion, and other fascinating reminders of automobile travel as it has evolved over the years. Admission is NZ$5 ($3) for adults, NZ$2 ($1) for children 6 to 14; hours are 9am to 5:30pm daily.

Out on the wharf down at the end of the Mall, ✪ **Underwater World,** Main Town Pier (tel. 442-8437), provides an intimate look at what goes on under the lake's surface. In a viewing lounge lined with panoramic windows, you are brought face to fin with rainbow and brown trout, longfin eels, and scaup duck (who quite often take an underwater dive to feed with the trout). Admission is NZ$5 ($3) for adults, NZ$2 ($1) for children 6 to 14; hours are 9am to 5:30pm daily.

The lake is great for **fishing,** and the Visitors Information Centre can help you get gear and guides together. The same holds true for those hardy souls eager for **backcountry exploring. Golfers** will want to head for the 18-hole Queenstown Golf Club, Kelvin Heights (tel. 442-9169), or the 9-hole Frankton Golf Club (tel. 442-3584).

Right in town—and free for everyone—is the 11-acre ✪ **Queenstown Gardens,** across from the Travelodge. There are tennis courts and lawn bowls to use at no charge, and the park is always open. Also, go by the **Maori Arts and Crafts Center** on Brecon Street to see a Maori carver at work.

Believe it or not, all the above is just a sample of things to do and see in Queenstown! There are scads of tours taking in many of the above and a whole lot more. For example, there's **paraflying** in a twin-seat chair or harness some 250 feet above the lake as a launch tows your parachute; and the **"Grape to Glass"** tour of three regional wineries; and **horse trekking** at Moonlight Stables; and. . . . But best go by the Visitors Information Centre and check over the complete list. They can make any reservations you need, and they'll also assist with onward accommodations and transportation arrangements.

SKIING

Despite the treasure trove of attractions listed above, however, it is skiing that brings Queenstown most alive, when skiers from around the world congregate to take to the slopes of this part of the Southern Alps from late June through most of September. All have good trails for beginners, intermediates, and expert skiers, and there is good public transport to each from town (check with the Visitors Information Centre for current schedules).

The nicest thing about skiing in Queenstown is that you don't have to be an expert to enjoy the sport. In fact, if you fall captive to the town's ski excitement and have arrived sans either equipment or experience, you can rent skis and take advantage of the excellent instruction offered at all four peaks. Treble Cone, in fact, has a **beginner's slope** just waiting for you, and you'll pay about NZ$28 ($16) for class instruction, NZ$55 ($31) for private lessons (children pay much less). Ski rental runs about NZ$26 ($15) for adults, NZ$17 ($10) for children. Lift fees average NZ$45 ($26) per adult, NZ$23 ($13) for children for a full day, less for a half day, and even less for learner lifts. Costs can be cut by taking advantage of ski packages offered by Mount Cook Line. Be sure to check for any specials on offer during your stay.

WALKS

The **Department of Conservation Information Centre,** corner of Stanley and Ballarat Streets (tel. 442-7933), is the place to go for information on all **walking tracks.** They can furnish details and brochures on short walks around Queenstown as well as those farther afield.

There are several excellent walkways through the **Wakatipu Basin,** some well formed and suitable for the average amateur walker, others that require a bit more physical fitness, and still others that should be attempted only by experienced and well-equipped trampers. Before setting out, consult the Department of Conservation and *follow their advice.* Ask, too, for their excellent *Discovering the Wakatipu (On Foot in the Wakatipu Basin).*

Ask, also about the **Hollyford Track,** the popular **Kepler Track** that starts in Te Anau, and the **Otago Goldfields Heritage Trail** that runs throughout Otaga.

The Routeburn Walk Queenstown is the starting point for this famous walk, a 3-day/2-night, 25-mile trek that takes you right into the heart of unspoiled forests, along river valleys, and across mountain passes. It's a soul-stirring experience, and suitable for ages 10 and up (and they won't say how high is "up")—a good level of physical fitness is the only requirement.

The Greenstone Valley Walk This walk also takes you through scenes of natural beauty that will form lifetime memories. It follows an ancient Maori trail used by tribes who passed through the valley en route to rich greenstone lodes near Lake Wakatipu. The trail you'll walk, however, was actually cut by Europeans in the late 1800s as they opened up a route between Lake Wakatipu and Martins Bay on the Fiordland coast. Since the track passes through a valley, it is somewhat less demanding than the Routeburn Walk, but certainly no less beautiful. You'll pass Lake

Howden and Lake McKellar and follow the Greenstone River through deep gorges and open valley land to Lake Wakatipu.

Independent walkers *must* check with the Department of Conservation (see above), which maintains a backcountry-huts system on both routes.

Guided Walks For those less eager to rough it, **guided walks** are a terrific way to enjoy these scenic delights. For **Routeburn Walk** tours, you'll be bussed from Queenstown to The Divide (on the Milford Sound road), then walk to Lake McKenzie, across the Harris Saddle, past the Routeburn Falls, and on to meet the coach that returns you to Queenstown. Along the way, comfortable lodges are provided for overnight stops, and you'll be treated to some of the most spectacular views in New Zealand. Treks run regularly from November through April every year, and the cost in 1992 was NZ$782 ($447) for adults, NZ$675 ($386) for children under 15. Costs include all transport, meals, and accommodation. And you should reserve as far in advance as possible, since this trek is very, very popular with New Zealanders and groups are limited in size.

If the **Greenstone Valley** is your choice, comfortable lodges provide overnight accommodation, and as you relax at night there are books on hand to tell you about many of the plants and wildlife you've seen during the day's walk. Your expert guides can also relate tales of the Maori and how they once lived when they walked this valley. The 3-day/2-night walk costs NZ$670 ($38) for adults, NZ$563 ($322) for ages 10 to 15. The walks operate year round, and you can book through any Visitors Information Centre, travel agent, or **Greenstone Valley Walk,** P.O. Box 568, Queenstown (tel. *0294/29-572).

It is also possible to combine the two walks in a 6-day/5-night excursion called **The Grand Traverse** that follows the Routeburn Track northbound for 3 days and the Greenstone Walk for 3 days. Costs are NZ$999 ($571) for adults, NZ$866 ($495) for children, including GST. This option is only available between November and April each year.

Book all guided walks through travel agents or **Routeburn Walk Ltd.,** P.O. Box 568, Queenstown (tel. 03/442-8200; fax 03/442-6072), or **Track Reservations,** P.O. Box 185, Te Anau (tel. 03/249-7411 in New Zealand, 643/249-7411 outside New Zealand; fax 03/249-7947 in New Zealand, 643/249-7947 outside New Zealand).

NEARBY ATTRACTIONS IN ARROWTOWN

For a marvelous outing, drive 12½ miles northeast to Arrowtown. It was a boom town during the gold-mining days, back in the 1860s, when the Arrow River coughed up a lot of the glittery stuff. Many of the original stone buildings remain, along with a stunning avenue of trees that were planted in 1867. To get a better understanding of the history of the town, go to the fine ✪ **Lake District Centennial Museum** on Buckingham Street (the town's main street) and to the **Reconstructed Chinese Camp** (don't miss Ah Lum's General Store) on Bush Creek at the northern end of town. Other places to explore are the ✪ **Royal Oak Hotel,** the oldest licensed hotel in Central Otago (you can still have a drink there); ✪ **Hamilton's General Store,** which has been in business since 1862; the **Old Gaol;** St. John's **Presbyterian Church,** dating from 1873; and the **post office,** where the staff dresses in period costumes.

Plan to have lunch or Devonshire tea at the **Stone Cottage,** Buckingham Street beside the museum (tel. 442-1860); ✪ **The Stables,** in old stables on Buckingham Street (tel. *21-818), is fully licensed and serves local and ethnic food.

If you're driving from Queenstown, come via Arthur's Point and return via Lake Hayes and Frankton for the maximum in scenery. A red **double-decker bus** that escaped from London makes the round trip from Queenstown twice a day for NZ$25 ($14); it leaves from the top of the Mall and the Earnslaw Wharf at 10am and 2pm.

SHOPPING

Queenstown has perhaps more shops of all sorts—souvenirs, knits, woolens, handcrafts, fashion boutiques, jewelry, etc., than any other one place in the country. There is one, however, that I have found to have one of the widest and most representative stocks of New Zealand goods. ✪ **Alpine Artifacts,** The Mall (tel. and fax 442-8649), has every item ever produced from sheepskin, from rugs to jackets to hats to mittens, etc., plus a fine line of leather jackets, boots, and gloves, woolens of every description, and a nice assortment of paintings by New Zealand artists. They also have silver beech spinning wheels that add a Kiwi decorative touch to Stateside decor even if you've never spun a thread in your life (completely functional, in case you do know how to spin). The staff here is friendly and helpful, they ship overseas with reliable insurance, and prices are competitive.

Barry Wills' ✪ **Central Art Galleries,** Queenstown Bay Centre, Beach Street (tel. 442-7025), has also been a happy hunting ground for me, yielding a painting or two that keep my Queenstown memories alive and well even when I'm half a world away.

Number 10, The Mall (tel. 442-9562), has a good selection of souvenirs, gifts, and woolen sweaters. The popular **T & Ski Shop,** The Mall (tel. 442-9817), is open 7 days and has bright and unusual T-shirts.

You'll find quality shops in **Queenstown Bay Central** and the trilevel **O'Connell's Pavilion,** with an entrance on Beach or Camp Street. *Note:* There's no tax on goods shipped outside the country.

WHERE TO STAY

Queenstown is filled with accommodations, many of them in the budget range, despite the fact that on the whole prices are higher here than in other places, as you would expect in a major resort area. However, it's also filled with visitors vying for these lower-cost lodgings. That means you should try to reserve before you come, be it winter, summer, spring, or fall. Having said that, let me add a bit of consolation if you should arrive without reservations: The Visitors Information Centre is very helpful, and almost every information office keeps a current list of accommodations and prices, and will help you find a place to lay your head if there is one to be had. But I repeat: far better to make your reservations in advance.

Unless otherwise noted, rates quoted below include GST.

A LICENSED HOTEL/MOTOR INN

ALPINE VILLAGE MOTOR INN, Frankton Rd. (P.O. Box 211), Queenstown. Tel. 03/442-7795. Fax 03/442-7738. 50 rms, chalets, and deluxe suites (all with bath). TV TEL **Transportation:** Owners will pick you up at the bus station or the airport.

$ Rates (excluding GST): NZ$72 ($41) single or double room; NZ$85 ($49) single or double chalet; NZ$105 ($60) single or double deluxe suite. Extra person NZ$10 ($6). Rates slightly higher during holidays. Best Western discounts and 2-day holiday specials available. AE, DC, MC, V.

The Alpine Village is 2 miles from the center of Queenstown, but its scenic setting more than makes up for the drive. If you're not driving, there's a courtesy coach to and from town several times a day. Set right on the lake in wooded grounds, Alpine Village offers A-frame chalets with breathtaking views of the lake and mountains on the far shore. They're furnished with tea and coffee makings, and fridge, as well as central heating and electric blankets for those extra-cold nights. In the main building there are standard hotel rooms with the same amenities. Down on the lakefront, there are deluxe suites, certainly the stars of the whole complex. Provided for guests are a laundry and children's playground.

One feature that accounts for the high rate of returnees here is the lakeside cluster of heated spa pools, which are open to the lake but enclosed for privacy on all three land sides. The pools are entered through heated shower rooms, which provide ample dressing space. It's absolutely heavenly to emerge from the warmth of your room into crisp lake air and then sink into the soothing hot water of the pools. The spa pools are very popular with locals, especially on star-studded nights. Equally popular are the lounge bar, where an inviting brick fireplace warms body and spirit, and the licensed restaurant, with its superior menu and lovely lake view. As so many other visitors do, I return again and again to this special New Zealand hostelry, always with pleasant anticipation.

MOTEL FLATS

AMITY LODGE, 7 Melbourne St. (P.O. Box 371), Queenstown. Tel. 03/442-7288. 10 flats (all with bath). TV TEL
$ Rates: NZ$90 ($51) NZ$88 ($55) single or double without kitchen; NZ$101 ($58) single or double with kitchen. AE, DC, MC, V.
Dianne and Peter Smith, young and enthusiastic moteliers, designed and built Amity Lodge, and their attention to comfort and tastefulness shows. Ten units, two with access for the disabled, have the bedroom tucked quietly at the back. Some have a kitchen and water bed; all have tea- and coffee-making facilities, and a VCR. There's a guest laundry, children's play area, and breakfast available. You may not have a stunning view here, but the surroundings and the hosts are equally lovely. The lodge is located in town.

AUTOLINE MOTEL, corner of Frankton Rd. and Dublin St. (P.O. Box 183), Queenstown. Tel. and fax 03/442-8734. 11 flats (all with bath). TV TEL **Transportation:** Courtesy-car service from the bus depot by arrangement.
$ Rates (excluding GST): NZ$75 ($43) single or double. Extra person NZ$13 ($7). AE, DC, MC, V.
This two-story motel with roses out front has exceptionally spacious units (one family size, which accommodates up to six; the others, either bed-sitters or one-bedrooms), all attractively decorated in shades of gold and brown. All have nice views from their sun deck, but the end unit, no. 6, has the best lake view. Kitchens are fully equipped and have complete ranges. There's radio, central heating, and electric blankets in each unit. Additional facilities include an automatic laundry with dryer, hot spa pool, children's play area, car wash, and covered off-street parking. Units are serviced daily. The Autoline is a short walk from shopping and even closer to the gardens.

EARNSLAW LODGE, 53 Frankton Rd., Queenstown. Tel. 03/442-8728. Fax 03/442-7376. 19 flats (all with bath). TV TEL
$ Rates (excluding GST): NZ$75 ($43) single; NZ$85 ($49) double. AE, DC, MC, V.
This is one of the most inviting places you'll happen upon as you drive into town, and the congenial host is Barry Ellis. It's modern, with a skylight in the inviting lobby/bar area. Five of the spacious units have a small kitchen; 14 of them have bay views (for the best views, ask for the upper level). There's also a laundry and dining room, with breakfast available on request, tea and coffee facilities, and a paraplegic unit.

GARDEN COURT MOTOR LODGE, 31 Frankton Rd. (P.O. Box 572), Queenstown. Tel. 03/442-9713. Fax 03/442-6468. 11 units (all with bath). TV TEL
$ Rates (excluding GST): NZ$80–NZ$90 ($46–$51) single or double. Best Western discounts available. AE, DC, MC, V.

⭐ The Garden Court offers eight two-level units, with balconies, two TVs, and an emphasis on alpine views, courtesy of picture windows galore. There are also three studio suites with overstuffed chairs and a kitchenette (Room 49 is a pleasant choice). You can walk into town from here in 5 minutes. Hosts are Pauline Kelly and Ken Chisholm.

**GOLDFIELDS MOTEL AND GUEST HOUSE, 41 Frankton Rd., Queens-
town. Tel. and fax 03/442-7211.** 10 flats (all with bath and shower). TV TEL
Transportation: Courtesy-car service available; airport bus stops at the gate.
$ Rates: NZ$67–NZ$77 ($38–$44) single or double. AE, DC, MC, V.

At Goldfields (see "Bed-and-Breakfasts," below, for a complete description) Diana and Murray Brown round out their budget accommodations with lovely motel flats that sleep two or three. There's a bed-sitting room, full kitchen, and radio. All units are heated, and beds have electric blankets. There's plenty of off-street parking, a guest laundry, and courtesy-car service. Cooked or continental breakfast is available.

MOTEL FLATS & CABINS

**MOUNTAIN VIEW LODGE, Frankton Rd., Queenstown. Tel. 03/442-
8246.** Fax 03/442-7414. 57 units, 10 dormitories (all with bath). TV TEL
$ Rates: NZ$65 ($37) single flat without kitchen; NZ$65 ($37) double flat without kitchen; NZ$75 ($43) single or double flat with kitchen; NZ$36 ($21) bunkroom for two; NZ$44 ($25) bunkroom for three; NZ$52 ($30) bunkroom for four. AE, DC, MC, V.

⭐ In a wooded, hillside setting about a 10-minute walk from town, this lodge offers a wide range of accommodations, all of which overlook stunning lake and mountain views. There are exceptionally nice motel flats, with full kitchens, TV, radio, heater, and electric blankets, which sleep two to four. Other accommodations come with everything except the kitchens (tea and coffee facilities only). Then there's a two-story building farther up the hill, which houses 10 rooms with heaters, but no hot and cold running water, each room with four bunks, carpeting, and a table and four chairs in front of a window with a lovely view. A fully equipped kitchen is shared by all, and there's a TV lounge bar, laundry, and children's playground. You supply bedding, plus cooking and eating utensils.

Mountain View Lodge also has a licensed family-style restaurant on the premises. There are candles at night; windows look out to mountains and lakes, and main-course prices are in the NZ$15 to NZ$25 ($9 to $14) range.

One of Mountain View's structures, the **Bottle House,** built in 1956, is known throughout New Zealand. Constructed entirely of 14,720 glass bottles set in sand and cement mortar, it serves as the motel office. The builder (whose identity is not revealed) says that there's not a single beer bottle included, that he got the bottles from a dealer, and that he emptied not one himself. Cabin 7 also has bottle walls that let in light, but are slightly opaque; it's a little run-down and usually occupied by staff.

BED & BREAKFASTS

**GOLDFIELDS MOTEL AND GUEST HOUSE, 41 Frankton Rd., Queens-
town. Tel. and fax 03/442-7211.** 6 rms, 4 chalet units (none with bath). TV
TEL **Transportation:** Courtesy-car service available, and airport bus stops at the gate.
$ Rates (including breakfast): NZ$40 ($23) single; NZ$62 ($35) double; NZ$68 ($39) chalet for two. Extra person NZ$10 ($6). AE, DC, MC, V.

Ⓢ Diana and Murray Brown's complex of budget accommodations that looks out to terrific views is just a short stroll from the center of town. In addition to heated bedrooms with hot and cold running water and electric blankets in an attractive guesthouse, there are chalet-type units that sleep up to three. All have hot and cold running water, tea and coffee makings, and toaster. A tray breakfast is included in the chalet rates, and a delicious cooked morning meal is served family style around a big wooden table in the homey dining room. At other times that dining room serves as a comfortable TV lounge (with tea/coffee facilities) that's the focal point for congenial evening gatherings. There's a guest laundry and plenty of off-street parking. The complex also includes motel flats with complete kitchen facilities (see "Motel Flats," above).

QUEENSTOWN HOUSE, 69 Hallenstein St., Queenstown. Tel. 03/442-9043. Fax 03/442-7560. 8 rms (none with bath). TV TEL

$ Rates (including continental breakfast): NZ$45 ($26) single; NZ$65 ($37) double. MC, V.

⑤ The big draw here is the lounge with its wicker furniture, plants, and beautiful, old upright piano. Adjacent to it is the dining area where breakfast (fresh fruit, homemade jams, coffee and herbal teas) is served. Dinner (venison, lamb, or salmon, plus dessert and a glass of wine) is served Monday through Friday for only NZ$15 ($9). A few of the rooms have their own sink, and there's also a laundry, showers, and a unique tub you have to climb into. Queenstown House is a short downhill walk into town. A cooked breakfast is available for NZ$5 ($3).

TRELAWN PLACE, P.O. Box 117, Queenstown. Tel. 03/442-9160. 2 rms (both with bath). TV TEL

$ Rates (excluding GST): NZ$50 ($29) per person with breakfast; NZ$75 ($43) per person with breakfast and dinner. No credit cards.

Sitting on a spectacular bluff overlooking the Shotover River on the outskirts of town, this is the private home of Nery Howard. She not only provides double-occupancy rooms, but also a very personal, friendly welcome that has won raves from our readers, as has Nery's cooking. Very popular with guests is the fishing trip and picnic lunch she arranges to what she says is "some of the best trout and salmon fishing in New Zealand."

HOSTELS

BUMBLES, Lake Esplanade at Brunswick St., Queenstown. Tel. 03/442-6298. 70 beds.

$ Rates: NZ$14 ($8) per person; NZ$15 ($9) double or twin room. MC, V.

This lakeside hostel is as welcoming as its bumblebee logo. There's room for 70; women sleep in one dormitory, men in another, and each unit has tea and coffee facilities and a refrigerator. The restaurant draws people like a magnet for roast lamb dinners, burgers, and the like, most priced from NZ$4.50 to NZ$6.50 ($3 to $4). A cottage houses the lounge with a TV and open fire. Kitchen use is from 7am to 9pm. Linens are available for rent. The hostel is located a 1-minute walk from the bus station and town center.

PINEWOOD MOTEL, 48 Hamilton St., Queenstown. Tel. 02/442-8273. Fax 03/442-9470. 80 beds. **Transportation:** Courtesy pickup at bus station.

$ Rates: NZ$13 ($8) per person; NZ$15 ($9) per person in double room. MC, V.

The Pinewood Motel can accommodate 80, and its largest rooms sleep five. There's a store on the premises, cooking facilities, and a TV room with a pool table. Pillow cases are supplied. It's a 10-minute walk from town, and managers Rob and Ros Grey will pick up travelers from the bus station and take them back again if necessary. The hostel is composed of six cheerful red buildings, set against a backdrop of evergreens.

YHA HOSTEL, 80 Esplanade, Queenstown. Tel. 03/442-8413. 100 beds. 4 twin rms, 4 family rms (2 with bath).

$ Rates: NZ$18 ($10) for members; NZ$20 ($11) for nonmembers. No credit cards.

This hostel is in a beautiful location just across the street from the lake, a 10-minute walk from the Mall. The two-story lodge-type building is designed with many windows to take advantage of the view. There are 100 beds in 17 rooms, including four twin rooms and four family rooms, two of which include private bath facilities. The hostel provides good evening meals 7 days a week in summer and winter for about NZ$8 ($5), and there's a large communal kitchen. Other amenities include a laundry, drying room, and TV room. A bonus here is the fact that a large section of the hostel stays open all day.

CABINS & CAMPGROUNDS

Creeksyde, Robins Road (P.O. Box 247), Queenstown (tel. 03/442-9447), definitely the Mercedes of campgrounds, was blessed by the Christchurch wizard when it opened in 1988. In another life it was a plant nursery, so there are plenty of trees around, and room for 36 campervans. The reception area is in a striking 12-sided building; there is complimentary tea and coffee in the lounge in the evenings, a spa bath (great if you've spent the day skiing), bright bathrooms (women get a hairdryer), a bath for the disabled, kitchen, dining area, and complete laundry facilities. This is a family business, run by Toni and Erna Spykerbosch and their children (Anya, Michael, and Uan), and they keep everything immaculate. The rate is NZ$19 ($11) for two, including GST.

The **Queenstown Motor Park,** Main Street (P.O. Box 59), Queenstown (tel. 02/442-7252), is about a half mile from the post office and set on well-kept wooded grounds overlooking the lake. Mountain and lake views greet the eye on every path, and the camp itself sparkles with fresh paint on its bright, airy kitchen, dining, and recreation blocks. There's a TV lounge, a provision shop and take-away bar, a laundry with dryers, and a children's playground. Basic cabins are carpeted and heated, sleep three to four in beds or bunks, and have a table with chairs, at a rate of NZ$27 to NZ$65 ($15 to $37), double or single. Tourist lodges come with hot and cold running water, toilet, shower, and tea- and coffee-making facilities, and cost NZ$42 ($24), double or single. There are also fully equipped motel units (including linens), at NZ$65 ($37) double. The 200 campsites are NZ$8 ($5) per person, and 400 caravan sites go for NZ$8.50 ($5). All rates include GST, and there's a surcharge for 1-night stays in all cabins. *Note:* Rates are reviewed for possible increase on April 1 of each year. Also, be sure to book ahead if you're coming between December 24 and January 10.

WHERE TO STAY IN NEARBY ARROWTOWN

If you're driving, you might consider staying in quaint, historic Arrowtown, 12½ miles from Queenstown.

Motels

LAKE HAYES MOTEL, R.D. 2, Queenstown. Tel. and fax 03/442-1705. 8 units (all with bath). TV TEL

$ Rates (excluding GST): NZ$68 ($39) single or double. AE, DC, MC, V.

Its location—3 miles from Arrowtown, 8 miles from Queenstown—makes this an ideal base for exploring both Arrowtown and Queenstown. On the quiet, peaceful shores of beautiful Lake Hayes, there's a relaxing country air that takes full advantage of its scenic surroundings. The units have full kitchen, radio, and both electric and down blankets. Laundry facilities are available. In the garden there's a children's playground with trampoline and barbecue. The lake is at the bottom of the garden, good for swimming and brown trout fishing, and there's a fishing boat for guests' use without charge. Also convenient is their Travel Desk, which can book sightseeing attractions for you. Parking is in carports.

MACE MOTEL, Oak Ave., Arrowtown. Tel. 03/442-1825. 6 units (all with bath). TV TEL
$ Rates: NZ$66 ($38) single or double. Extra person NZ$13 ($7). AE, DC, MC, V.
Located on Arrowtown's famous Oak Avenue in the town center, this motel is surrounded by lawns planted with pretty shrubs. Units have two or three bedrooms, and with convertible divans in the wood-paneled lounges, they will accommodate up to eight. All have kitchens, videos, electric blankets, central heating, and radios. There's a heated spa pool, children's play area, laundry, and provision store on the premises. It's 15 minutes from Queenstown and from the ski fields.

A Bed & Breakfast

SPEARGRASS LODGE, Speargrass Flat Rd. (R.D. 1), Arrowtown. Tel. 03/442-1411. 3 rms (all with bath). TV TEL
$ Rates (including breakfast): NZ$45 ($26) per person. AE, MC, V.
For country lovers, this bed-and-breakfast farm retreat 2½ miles south of Arrowtown is a real find. It sits on 11 acres that are "as close to Scotland as you can get in the southern hemisphere," according to Denis Jenkins. He and his wife, Jenny, whom he met in catering school in Scotland, own the 6,000-square-foot home, which has three guest rooms; a living room with overstuffed couches and a stone fireplace; and underfloor heating. A bar, pool table, laundry, drying room, and a Jeep are available for guests' use. Dogs, cats, ducks, hens, and sheep rule the farmyard, from which you can see the surrounding ski areas. The Jenkinses show off their culinary skills with a three-course dinner that is available for NZ$25 ($14).

READERS RECOMMEND

Riverview Farm Lodge, P.O. Box 19, Athol, Southland. Tel. 03/248-8866; fax 03/248-8811. "This great place sits against a hill just above the Mataura River in a beautiful pastoral setting about an hour's drive from Queenstown. Sam and Liz Soper, the owners, have two daughters and made us feel right at home. Our Laura Ashley–style bedroom and private bath were lovely, and Liz's cooking is a great experience, especially the homemade jams. From Sam we learned about sheep ranching, politics, and much of the New Zealand way of life. We left New Zealand with regret, but with a better understanding than any hotel could impart, and we have friends there now to return to visit."—J. and K. Niggemyer, Lander, Wyo.
[Author's note: Riverview has undergone extensive upgrading and is now in the "Worth the Extra Money" category, at NZ$144 ($82), plus GST, per person per night, which includes all meals and wine.]

WHERE TO EAT

You won't lack for a place to eat in Queenstown, and in any price range you choose. There are some very good, inexpensive restaurants, many of them in the Mall. Moderate prices for full meals are easy to come by, and I'll tell you about just one of the several places that qualify for a "big splurge."

AVANTI, 20 The Mall. Tel. 442-8503.
   Cuisine: BISTRO/BREAKFAST. **Reservations:** Not required.
$ Prices: NZ$5–NZ$16 ($3–$9). AE, DC, MC, V.
   Open: Daily 7am–11pm.
Fresh pasta is featured daily for lunch and dinner, and there's fresh fish on Wednesday. Any day's a good day for continental breakfast for NZ$3 ($2). The bistro atmosphere is inviting, and in warm weather there's courtyard dining with a view of the gondolas. BYO. Avanti is located in the town center.

CARDRONA CAFE, The Mall. Tel. 442-8542.

Cuisine: PANCAKES/BURGERS/SNACKS/VEGETARIAN. **Reservations:** Not required.

$ Prices: NZ$2–NZ$17 ($1–$10); most items under NZ$8 ($5); children's plates NZ$6 ($3). No credit cards.

Open: 7am–10pm.

The pancakes with maple syrup (among several tasty toppings) make breakfast something special. Omelets, burgers, sandwiches, and other light fare are available, as well as hot meals such as vegetarian lasagne or a nice mixed grill. It's located in the center of town.

THE COW PIZZA AND SPAGHETTI HOUSE, Cow Lane. Tel. 442-8588.

Cuisine: ITALIAN. **Reservations:** Recommended.

$ Prices: Most pizzas and main courses under NZ$10 ($6). Sun and holiday surcharge. AE, DC, MC, V.

Open: Lunch daily noon–2pm; dinner daily 5:30–11pm.

This cozy little stone building is located in the town center at the end of a lane that got its name from the fact that cows were once driven this way each day to be milked. Inside, this place probably hasn't changed a whole lot since those early days—there's a smoke-darkened fireplace, wooden beams, lots of old farm memorabilia around, and wooden benches and tables. It's a friendly gathering spot for locals, many of whom you'll rub elbows with at those long tables. As for the menu, it was *designed* for budget travelers! I counted eight varieties of pizza (including a vegetarian version) and six spaghetti dishes—and the highest price on the menu is NZ$9.95 ($6), unless you go for the extra-large pizza (don't unless you're ordering for two or have an extra-large appetite), which can cost as much as NZ$16.25 ($9). Soup, salad, homemade whole-meal bread and ice-cream desserts are also offered. It's BYO, with a small corkage fee. Take-aways are available, but I strongly recommend that you eat right here—the Cow is a delightful experience, as well as excellent budget eating.

GOURMET EXPRESS, Bay Centre, Shotover St. Tel. 442-9619.

Cuisine: AMERICAN. **Reservations:** Not required.

$ Prices: Appetizers NZ$4.25–NZ$8.75 ($2–$5); main courses NZ$4–NZ$15 ($2–$9). AE, MC, V.

Open: Daily 6:30am–9pm. **Closed:** Christmas Day and Boxing Day.

The Gourmet Express bills itself as an American-style restaurant and coffee shop, and indeed you'll find a very Americanized menu. Hamburgers, cheeseburgers, and baconburgers, club sandwiches, pancakes, hash browns, and omelets are among the lighter fare, with heartier offerings of steak (in several varieties), fish, chicken-in-the-basket, lamb chops, roast lamb, and rack of lamb. In the center of town, it's a large, bright, and cheerful place with blond-wood tables and chairs, and counter as well as table service.

HMS BRITANNIA, The Mall. Tel. 442-9600.

Cuisine: SEAFOOD/STEAK/VEGETARIAN. **Reservations:** Required.

$ Prices: Average meal NZ$35 ($20); fixed-price meal NZ$25 ($14). AE, DC, MC, V.

Open: Dinner daily 6:30–10pm.

This local favorite in the town center is designed like the interior of an 18th-century sailing ship, with nets and ropes hanging from the ceiling, and lanterns and dripping candles giving off a warm glow. There may be more elegant restaurants in Queenstown, but none more pleasant than this. Owner Doug Champion and his staff go overboard to provide painstaking service and a meal prepared to order. The menu features fresh lobster, mussels, fish, steak filet, and vegetarian dishes. As a budget aid, you might take advantage of the fixed-price special that includes soup, a main dish, an ice-cream sundae, and GST. Licensed.

LAKESIDE CAFE, Off Beach St. Tel. 442-7675.

Cuisine: LIGHT MEALS/PASTRIES/SPECIALTY COFFEES. **Reservations:** Not required.

$ Prices: Under NZ$8 ($5). No credit cards.

Open: Daily 8am–5pm.

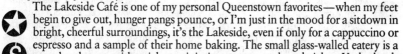

The Lakeside Café is one of my personal Queenstown favorites—when my feet begin to give out, hunger pangs pounce, or I'm just in the mood for a sitdown in bright, cheerful surroundings, it's the Lakeside, even if only for a cappuccino or espresso and a sample of their home baking. The small glass-walled eatery is a great lunch spot, with quiches, mini-pizzas, soup, and sandwiches. Undoubtedly one of its most appealing assets is the friendly service by owner Mark Myles and his staff. The café is set back from the street in a promenade leading to the lakefront.

MILLIE'S RESTAURANT AND BAR, 24 Beach St. Tel. 442-7309.

Cuisine: BREAKFAST/SNACKS/NEW ZEALAND. **Reservations:** Not required.

$ Prices: NZ$8–NZ$35 ($5–$20). AE, DC, MC, V.

Open: Daily 8am–10pm. **Closed:** Christmas Day.

Millie's is one of the friendliest family restaurants in Queenstown, as well as one of the best values for money. High-backed booths allow maximum privacy without isolating you from the general ambience, and in fine weather, there's outdoor dining. Portions are *huge*—most appetizers would be ample for a light meal, and I am especially fond of their cooked breakfasts that range from simple ham, sausage, or hash browns with eggs to pancakes to the pigout Southern Country Breakfast that includes two eggs, hash browns, bacon, sausages, and two pancakes. The extensive menu also includes sandwiches, burgers (including a vegetarian burger), morning and afternoon teas, and New Zealand meats and seafoods. See "Evening Entertainment," below, for comments about the lively bar adjacent to the restaurant. Licensed. Millie's is located in the center of town.

MINAMI JUJISEI RESTAURANT, 3 Rees St. Tel. 442-9854.

Cuisine: JAPANESE. **Reservations:** Recommended.

$ Prices: Appetizers NZ$5–NZ$17 ($3–$10); main courses NZ$19–NZ$50 ($11–$29); fixed-price meals NZ$30–NZ$60 ($17–$34). AE, DC, MC, V.

Open: Lunch daily noon–2pm; dinner daily 6–10pm.

If you've a yen (you should pardon the pun!) for something Japanese, try this marvelous new restaurant in the town center. The upstairs setting is a serene, peaceful room with traditional decor; its kitchen is under the direction of Koji Honda, a chef of distinction, and manager Tony Robertson will be happy to help you with your selection if you're not too sure about the dishes. Specialties include sushi and ise-ebi (crayfish). There's a large selection of Japanese snacks and soups, and a choice of three set meals of six courses and tea (tempura, sashimi, or steak). Licensed.

THE STONEWALL CAFE, Eureka House, The Mall. Tel. 442-6429.

Cuisine: NEW ZEALAND. **Reservations:** Recommended.

$ Prices: Average lunch under NZ$15 ($9); average dinner under NZ$35 ($20). MC, V.

Open: Mon–Sat 7:30am–4pm and 5:30–9:30pm.

This friendly, owner-operated café is set in a historic building that was a bank in the late 19th century, then a house of ill repute. These days, its exposed stone walls and open fireplace provide an inviting setting in the town center for New

Zealand specialties such as char-grilled lamb rumps and venison steaks with gin and green peppercorn sauce.

WESTY'S, The Mall. Tel. 442-8635.
    Cuisine: NEW ZEALAND/VEGETARIAN. **Reservations:** Recommended.
$ Prices: Dinner NZ$16–NZ$35 ($9–$20). MC, V.
    Open: Daily 4–11:30pm.

Vegetarians will always find a special of the day on the menu at this popular restaurant in the center of town. A recent offering was spiced kumera timbal, a lovely baked mousse of creamed kumera and eggs with a cashew-nut butter with avocado fans. While this is not a vegetarian restaurant per se, the emphasis is on wholesomeness, with specialties derived, as they say, from the hoof, the tides, and the wing. I particularly like the lemon chicken with cashews. Seafood is also featured, and the homemade breads and house salads are excellent. Plan a leisurely evening, since there's live entertainment most nights. No children. Licensed.

WORTH THE EXTRA MONEY

SKYLINE CHALET RESTAURANT, Brecon St., Bob's Peak. Tel. 442-7860.
    Cuisine: NEW ZEALAND. **Reservations:** Recommended; required for dinner.
$ Prices: Average lunch under NZ$15 ($9); dinner carvery buffet NZ$39 ($22). AE, DC, MC, V.
    Open: Lunch daily noon–2pm; dinner daily 6–9pm.

Spend at least one of your Queenstown meals at the Skyline Chalet, where the wraparound windows give you a fantastic panoramic view of the town and lake. The restaurant is accessible by Skyline Gondolas. Food service ranges from light snacks to full meals, but the star attraction is the evening carvery buffet, which features lamb, seafood, and other New Zealand specialties. The tariff includes your gondola round-trip, meal, and entertainment (usually a band that plays for dancing). Licensed.

READERS RECOMMEND

Pot-Au-Feu, Camp St. Tel. 442-8333. *"This restaurant was recommended to us the first night we were in Queenstown. It was so wonderful that we returned there the next evening rather than trying other recommendations (highly unusual for us!). Their cuisine is superb, the staff is gracious, and the atmosphere is delightful. A truly special restaurant! Very highly recommended."*—Mari Fagin, Ph.D., Nichols Hills, Okla.

EVENING ENTERTAINMENT

It's worth a trip down to the Steamship Wharf on Beach Street around 10pm, when the ✪**TSS Earnslaw** returns from its evening cruise and becomes a floating piano bar/restaurant.

The three pubs most favored by locals are **Eichardt's,** on the Mall, ✪**Millie's Queenstown Tavern,** on Beach Street (with live entertainment most nights during the ski season), and **"Wicked Willie's,"** the unofficial name for the pub at the Hotel Queenstown.

The **Dolphin Club,** a wine and piano bar at 34 Shotover St. (tel. 442-9692), is another local favorite, with live entertainment every night from 9pm to 3am.

During ski season, private parties go on all over town in almost every hotel and motel, with friendly strangers becoming invited guests at the drop of a smile. As I mentioned in the "Where to Stay" section, an after-dark activity much favored by

Queenstown natives is a starlight loll in those lakeside spa pools out at the **Alpine Village Motor Inn** on Frankton Road (tel. 442-7795), for half an hour or so. After a day on the slopes or trotting around sightseeing, it's hard to imagine anything happier!

EASY EXCURSIONS FROM QUEENSTOWN
MILFORD SOUND

As you'll see from the sections of this chapter that follow, I heartily recommend that you spend at least 1 day in Te Anau and go from there to Milford Sound. If, however, time or pocketbook prevent that, you're not condemned to miss that very special part of New Zealand. **InterCity coaches** and **✪ Fiordland Travel** have excellent day-long (12-hour) trips that include launch trips on the sound. **Fiordland Travel** also has a coach trip to the sound, launch trip, and plane trip back to Queenstown and an exciting **✪ "Fly 'n Sea"** package, using their own fleet of aircraft, that comes with a bonus free ticket for the TSS *Earnslaw* cruise of your choice. **Mount Cook Line** has somewhat pricier (but very thrilling) flight/launch packages from Queenstown.

Taking the coach in and flying out gives you an opportunity to see the scenery from two different perspectives while saving some time as well. Should weather conditions ground the plane at Milford, you can always take the coach back. The cost of this trip is NZ$193 ($110); flying both ways is only a few dollars more.

You can book through the Visitors Information Centre, Fiordland Travel Centre at the Steamer Wharf, or the Mount Cook World Travel Centre in Rees Street. I, personally, am quite fond of the Fiordland trip, mostly because of their superior (luxury-class) coaches and wonderfully informed drivers (count yourself lucky if Doug O'Shea is behind the wheel!). They also furnish commentary tapes in four languages other than English, with a four-channel music system to sooth the return trip. It's a long day, but a memorable one, from a Queenstown base.

All coach excursions to Milford Sound leave Queenstown at 7:15am, returning around 8pm, and fares average NZ$115 ($66) for adults, NZ$65 ($37) for children, inclusive of launch trip. Lunch is available on most launch trips, but you're free to bring your own.

DOUBTFUL SOUND

Captain Cook was doubtful that it *was* a sound when he first saw it, thus the name, **✪ Doubtful Sound.** And the name alone is intriguing enough to make you want to go there. It's not as famous as its neighbor to the north, Milford Sound, but where Milford is majestic, Doubtful is mysterious. Both are undeniably serene. Doubtful Sound is 10 times bigger than Milford, and while it can't boast Mitre Peak, its still waters mirror Commander Peak, which rises 4,000 feet in vertical splendor.

The round-trip overland to Milford is pretty tiring (fly one-way if you can); getting to and from Doubtful is less so. Yet getting to Doubtful Sound does require four modes of transportation: a bus to Te Anau (where you should buy extra food to hold you until lunchtime and a useful booklet called *Manapouri to Doubtful Sound*, which describes everything you will see along the way), a van to Lake Manapouri, a boat across that pristine lake, and another bus to Deep Cove in Doubtful Sound— through lush forest and over Wilmot Pass, 2,208 feet above sea level, stopping along the way at the Manapouri Power Station, spiraling downward 750 eerie feet to view the seven immense underground turbines. It's like delving into the underworld and is absolutely fascinating (those who get claustrophobic don't have to do it).

Deep Cove Village, where you pick up the boat to explore the sound (another mode of transport on this trip), has a population of one—the Fiordland National Park ranger. A highlight of the boat trip through the sound comes at its end when the captain shuts off the engine in Hall Arm and you can hear how incredibly silent it is here. You return to Te Anau and Queenstown the way you came, without the stop at the power station. Another high point is crossing Lake Manapouri again (especially at sunset) and watching as what looks like a wall created by the many islands in the lake magically opens as the boat draws near.

Fiordland Travel is the only operator in Doubtful Sound. The price of the "Triple Trip" described here is NZ$100 ($57), half that for children.

Note: Another difference between Milford and Doubtful Sounds is that at Milford you know civilization is nearby, with the airstrip and the THC hotel right at the boat launch. Doubtful Sound is definitely more remote. If you've never done either trip, I'd recommend Milford Sound for its sheer majesty and save Doubtful Sound as the highlight of your next trip.

EN ROUTE TO TE ANAU

It's a 105-mile drive from Queenstown, on good roads all the way. You'll follow Highway 6 as far as the grass-seed-producing **Lumsden,** then take Highway 94 over the summit of **Gorge Hill,** along the **Mararoa River** and through sheep and cattle country to **Te Anau,** the largest lake in the South Island. Many of the sheep stations that line the road from Lumsden on are being homesteaded by young Kiwi couples who have taken advantage of the government's Land Development Scheme. A lottery drawing determines who will be entitled to purchase at bargain prices large acreages on which the government has built a basic (*very* basic) dwelling, a paddock, and a barn. Those selected then face the difficult task of clearing and developing the land. In its natural state, this is rough, rocky terrain, and the homesteader's life is not an easy one—as you pass scraggly, poorly developed land smack up against hills and pastures that have been brought into near-manicured perfection, give a tip of the hat to those couples who have dug in and applied the backbreaking industry required to carve out a viable family life, in sharp contrast to neighbors who may have simply given in to not much more than a subsistence existence.

2. TE ANAU

105 miles SW of Queenstown, 75 miles S of Milford Sound

GETTING THERE By Bus There is Monday through Friday coach service between Te Anau and Christchurch, Dunedin, and Invercargill via **InterCity** and **Mount Cook Landline;** both lines also have daily service from Te Anau and Milford Sound and Queenstown.

By Car Take Highway 6 to Lumsden, then Highway 90.

ESSENTIALS Information A visit to **The Department of Conservation Visitors Centre,** Te Anau Terrace (P.O. Box 29; tel. 03/249-7921; fax 03/249-7613), is a must for those contemplating any of the celebrated walks, and is highly recommended for anyone headed to Milford Sound.

Orientation Te Anau's main street is actually Highway 94 (called Milford Road within the township). Stretched along each side you'll find the **post office, Wildlife Museum, restaurants, grocery stores,** and most of the township's **shops.** At the lake end of Milford Road sits the **Fiordland Travel** office (tel. 249-7419), where all launch trips may be booked. Across the road and to the left from Fiordland Travel is the **Waterfront Merchants Complex,** with a coffee bar/restaurant, souvenir and gift shop, craft shop, and clothing boutique. Just opposite the lake, on Highway 94 before it turns westward to become Milford Road, is the Te Anau Resort Hotel.

Lake Te Anau spreads its south, middle, and north branches like long fingers poking deep into the mountains that mark the beginning of the rugged and magnificent three-million-acre **Fiordland National Park,** New Zealand's largest and, indeed, one of the largest in the world. Within its boundaries, which enclose the whole of the South Island's southwest corner, lie incredibly steep mountain ranges, lakes, sounds, rivers, magnificent fjords, and huge chunks of mountainous terrain even now unexplored. In fact, one large section has been closed off from exploration after the discovery there in 1948 of one of the world's rarest birds, the wingless takahe. It had not been seen for nearly a century before, seldom even then, and was thought to be extinct. When a colony was found in the Murchison Mountains, the decision was made to protect them from human disturbance. What other wonders remain to be discovered within the vast park, one can only speculate.

Lake Te Anau itself presents a wonder of a sort, with its eastern shoreline (that's where Te Anau—its name means "to arrive by water"—township is located) virtually treeless with about 30 inches annual rainfall, its western banks covered by dense forest nurtured by more than 100 inches of rain each year. To visitors, however, the attractions of this second-largest lake in New Zealand consist of a variety of water sports and its proximity to Milford Sound, 75 miles away. That sound (which is actually a fjord) reaches 14 miles in from the Tasman Sea, flanked by sheer granite peaks traced by playful waterfalls that appear and disappear depending on the amount of rainfall. Its waters and the surrounding land have been kept in as nearly a primeval state as man could possibly manage without leaving it totally untouched. In fine weather or pouring rain, Milford Sound exudes a powerful sense of nature's pristine harmony and beauty—a visit there is balm to my 20th-century soul and is the highlight of every New Zealand trip.

WHAT TO SEE & DO

Lake cruises are the main attraction in Te Anau, and **Fiordland Travel Ltd.,** Lakefront (P.O. Box 1), Te Anau (tel. 03/249-7419; fax 03/249-7022), can give you their latest brochure with current times, rates, and special concessions on launch trips. The most popular is that to **Te Anau Caves,** which runs year round. The tour includes an underground boat ride into the glowworm grotto in the "living" cave, so called because it is still being formed. A crystal-clear river cascades down the cave tiers at the rate of 55,000 gallons per minute, creating frothy white falls. On the second level of the waterbed you'll see the glowworm grotto. In my opinion, the day trip is preferable to the evening, since the scenic 10-mile lake cruise begs to be enjoyed in daylight.

In most cases, the primary reason for coming to Te Anau is to go on to **Milford Sound** and **Doubtful Sound,** and right here I am going to stick my neck out and recommend that even if you're driving you park the car in Te Anau and book a coach-and-launch tour through Fiordland or InterCity, and you'd be well advised to book before leaving Queenstown. My reasons are twofold: First, while the road to Milford is remarkably good for such terrain, after you pass Te Anau Downs you'll need to keep your eyes straight ahead, thus missing a good bit of some of the most splendid scenery to be found this side of heaven; and second, coach drivers provide a wealth of information on the scenery through which you're passing, which adds immeasurably to the pleasure of the 2½-hour drive. Fiordland's half-day trip includes coach and cruise fares. There's no way you can get to Doubtful on your own.

Waterwings Airways Ltd., Lakefront (P.O. Box 222), Te Anau (tel. 03/249-7405; fax 03/442-3050), operates floatplanes flights between Te Anau and Milford Sound. Their 1-hour, 10-minute **scenic flight** is a real delight, at a cost of NZ$232 ($132) per adult, NZ$139 ($79) per child. For NZ$131 ($75) per adult, half that for children, they'll take you on a 35-minute flight to Doubtful Sound. In addition, there's a 20-minute scenic flight around Te Anau, at NZ$66 ($38) and

NZ$40 ($23), and one for 10 minutes that costs NZ$36 ($21) and NZ$22 ($13), respectively. One of their best offerings is the 1-hour combination Fly 'N Boat trip at a cost of NZ$84 ($48) per adult, NZ$51 ($29) per child; they'll take you down the Waiau River to Manapouri via jet boat, then bring you back by floatplane to Te Anau by way of the Hidden Lakes. Highly recommended.

Other activities include Fiordland **helicopter flights, raft trips on the Waiau River, jet-boat rides,** and **fishing** with any one of the experienced guides available. Check with Fiordland Travel Ltd. for these or other activities, and with the Department of Conservation for nature walks and tramping tracks. Then, head for glorious Milford Sound.

THE MILFORD TRACK

Most dedicated trampers consider the world-famous ✪ Milford Track the finest anywhere in the world. Four days are required to walk the 32 miles from Glade Jetty at Lake Te Anau's northern end to Sandfly Point on the western bank of Milford Sound. To walk the pure wilderness is to immerse yourself in the sights, sounds, smells, and feel of nature left to itself—it is utterly impossible to emerge without a greater sense of the earth's rhythms. It's a walk closely regulated by park authorities, both for the safety of hikers and for the preservation of this wilderness area, yet there is no intrusion on individual response to nature once you begin the journey.

You set out from Te Anau Downs, 17 miles north of Te Anau township, where a launch takes you to the head of the lake. You'll sleep in well-equipped lodge/huts with bunk beds, cooking facilities, and toilets, but you must carry your own sleeping bag, food, and cooking utensils. Overnight huts are manned by custodians, should you need any assistance along the way. At Sandfly Point, another launch ferries you across Milford Sound. Upon arrival, you may elect to spend the night at Milford or to return to Te Anau, but reservations are a must, whichever you choose.

You must be over 10 years of age, an experienced tramper, and apply to Reservations, **Milford Track Office,** Te Anau Resort Hotel Resort Hotel, P.O. Box 185, Te Anau (tel. 03/249-7411). Reservations are accepted from early November to mid-April for the following tramping season, which runs from mid-November to early April. No more than 24 people are booked to start the walk on any given day, and applications begin coming in early for specific days.

There are two ways to walk the Milford Track: as a member of an organized group or as one of the ranger-organized "Independent Walkers." THC Milford and Te Anau Resort Hotel offer an excellent ✪ **package plan,** which includes guides, cooked meals at the overnight huts, and accommodations at each end of the trek. Fees run about NZ$950 ($543) plus GST. As an independent, you take care of all these details yourself, with the able assistance of park rangers, at a cost of about NZ$150 ($86).

WHERE TO STAY

Between Christmas and the end of February, accommodations are tightly booked in Te Anau (most are occupied by the week by holidaying Kiwi families), and you should reserve ahead as far as possible or plan to stay outside the township itself (possibly out the Milford Road, at Milford Sound, or at Lake Manapouri, 12 miles to the south). Other times, there are usually ample accommodations available.

MOTEL FLATS

REDWOOD MOTEL, 26 McKerrow St., Te Anau. Tel. 03/249-7746. 6 flats, 1 3-bedroom house (all with bath). TV TEL **Transportation:** Courtesy-car service available.

$ Rates (excluding GST): NZ$48 ($27) single; NZ$62 ($35) double. Extra person NZ$14 ($8). Surcharge for 1-night stay. AE, MC, V.

★ Some of Te Anau's nicest motel units are presided over by friendly hosts Shirley and Allan Bradley. The Redwood is centrally located on a quiet residential street. The units are nicely furnished, sparkling clean, and beautifully equipped. All have central heating, and four even have their own washing machines (guest laundry on the premises for others). Parking is in individual carports. There's also a three-bedroom house on the grounds with full kitchen, bath and shower, and private garden—ideal for families. A children's playground is also on the premises. A continental breakfast is available at a small charge.

AMBER COURT MOTEL, 68 Quintin Dr., Te Anau. Tel. 03/249-7230. Fax 03/249-7486. 9 units (all with bath). TV TEL **Transportation:** Courtesy car available.

$ Rates (excluding GST): NZ$69 ($39) per person single or double. Best Western discounts available. AE, DC, MC, V.

Sue and Jim Duffell are hosts at this Best Western motel. It's in a quiet in-town location, with one- and two-bedroom units that sleep two to eight people. There's a guest laundry and—most unusual—a car wash. The Duffells can arrange sightseeing bookings, and they'll furnish a cooked breakfast at a small extra charge.

BED & BREAKFASTS

MATAI LODGE, 42 Mokonui St., Te Anau. Tel. 03/249-7360. 7 rms (none with bath).

$ Rates (including breakfast): Seasonally, NZ$34–NZ$75 ($19–$43) single; NZ$54–NZ$60 ($31–$34) per person double. Winter rates reduced. AE, DC, MC, V.

⑤ The Matai Lodge is only 1 block from the lakefront, and has seven bed-and-breakfast units in a long block, with toilet and showers at one end. Rooms all have hot and cold running water, are tastefully decorated, and have heaters as well as electric blankets and comforters. The lounge is spacious and airy, with comfortable seating, and there's a separate TV lounge. You're given several choices on the menu for the fully cooked breakfast, and evening meals can be provided on request. Hostess Marilyn Redfern is a "born local" (in her words) who worked in television for over 20 years. She knows the area well and enjoys sharing sightseeing information with guests and booking tours, cruises, or the like. She will also store baggage for trampers, and there is off-street parking for drivers.

SHAKESPEARE HOUSE, 10 Dusky St., Te Anau. Tel. 03/249-7349. Fax 03/249-7629. 6 rms (4 with bath). TV TEL **Transportation:** Will arrange courtesy pickup upon advance request.

$ Rates (including breakfast): NZ$56 ($32) single; NZ$74 ($42) double without bath, NZ$76 ($43) double with bath. Lower off-season rates. AE, MC, V.

★⑤ Shakespeare House is the home of Mike and Rosina Shakespeare (yes, they are descendants of you know who—I knew you'd ask!), who have long welcomed bed-and-breakfast guests to their home. They know the area well and are happy to help you plan sightseeing activities. The warm, cozy rooms are a little on the small side, but each has a shower and hand basin, and four have their own private bathroom. All rooms open onto a large conservatory, which is ideal for relaxing. The TV lounge has lovely mountain views, as does the very pleasant dining room, where an excellent English-style breakfast is served. Ask about off-season rates. It's located a short walk from the center of town.

A HOSTEL

YHA HOSTEL, 220-224 Milford Rd., Te Anau. Tel. 03/249-7847. 52 beds.
$ Rates: NZ$15 ($9) per person; NZ$7.50 ($4) tent sites. MC, V.

This is a real standout, one of the most attractive hostels in the country. It adjoins a sheep meadow in a very central location, and has 40 beds in six pine-paneled rooms with central heating, with plans to add more beds in the near future. There's a nicely equipped kitchen, a lounge (with a pot-bellied stove), dining room, and laundry, and in January, overflow accommodation is available. This is the ideal place to begin and end your Milford Track, Routeburn, Hollyford, Dusky, or Greenstone Track walks. They can also arrange discounted tours and sightseeing fees for YHA members.

CABINS & CAMPGROUNDS

If you want to do some tramping in the Fiordland National Park on a lesser scale than the Milford Track, park rangers will supply a map of trails and overnight hut locations. The park huts are basic shelters that provide a place to bunk down and cook simple fare. For those where fuel (cut wood) is provided, the overnight fee is NZ$10 ($6) per person.

WORTH THE EXTRA MONEY

TE ANAU RESORT HOTEL, 64 Te Anau Terrace (P.O. Box 185), Te Anau. Tel. 03/249-7511. Fax 03/249-7272. 126 rms, 15 villa suites (all with bath). TV TEL

$ Rates: NZ$75–NZ$125 ($43–$71) per person single or double; NZ$150 ($86) villa suite for one or two. Special packages available off-season. AE, DC, MC, V.

This resort hotel is located on the lakefront and is *the* superior accommodation in this area. Guest rooms all have tea and coffee facilities, and hairdryers are available from reception. The villa suites consist of a lounge, bedroom, kitchen, and bath. On-premises amenities include a restaurant, three bars, a swimming pool, spas, saunas, two guest laundries, and a travel office that can book just about any sightseeing activity in the area.

WHERE TO EAT

POP-IN CATERING, Waterfront Merchants Complex, 92 Te Anau Terrace. Tel. 249-7807.
Cuisine: SANDWICHES/LIGHT MEALS. **Reservations:** Not required.
$ Prices: NZ$5–NZ$9 ($3–$5). No credit cards.
Open: Summer, daily 7am–8:30pm; off-season, daily 7:30am–6pm.

Diagonally across from Fiordland Travel, you'll find this window-lined restaurant serving light meals at very moderate prices in a setting that overlooks the lake. A glass-walled conservatory affords 180° views, and I can't think of a nicer place to eat. Everything is home-cooked and baked right on the premises. Sandwiches, meat pies, salad plates, barbecue, Kiwi-style chicken, venison, beef, and baked-on-the-premises pastries can meet just about any size hunger attack. Check this one out first.

BAILEY'S, in the Luxmore Motel, Milford Rd. Tel. 249-7526.
Cuisine: BREAKFAST/LIGHT LUNCHES/STEAK. **Reservations:** Recommended if possible (not always necessary).
$ Prices: NZ$8–NZ$30 ($5–$17). AE, MC, V.
Open: Daily 7:30am–9:30pm.

Right in the center of town, Bailey's offers a range of food, from all-day breakfasts, to morning and afternoon teas, to lunches of sandwiches, pies, and casseroles to full à la carte dinner in the evenings. It's fully licensed.

HENRY'S FAMILY RESTAURANT, in the Te Anau Resort Hotel, 64 Te Anau Terrace. Tel. 249-7411.
Cuisine: NEW ZEALAND. **Reservations:** Not required.
$ Prices: Lunch NZ$8–NZ$15 ($5–$9); dinner NZ$19–NZ$35 ($11–$20). AE, DC, MC, V.
Open: Lunch daily 11:30am–2pm; dinner daily 5–9pm.

The lakefront setting is rustic and the food is inexpensive at Henry's. The atmosphere is much like that of a frontier saloon, with a pot-bellied stove and bare wooden tables. New Zealand specialties include Milford Sound crayfish, Fiordland venison, Stewart Island salmon, and lamb. Fully licensed.

Note: For more elegant (and expensive) dinners, reserve at the THC's **MacKinnon Room,** which specializes in local delicacies, including fresh crayfish. The Te Anau Resort Hotel can pack a very good **picnic lunch** for your Milford Sound day-trip or tramping, if you notify them the night before.

THE MILFORD ROAD

You'll be driving (or riding in a coach) through fascinating geographical, archeological, and historical country, through the **Eglinton and Hollyford Valleys,** the **Homer Tunnel,** and down the majestic **Cleddau Gorge** to Milford Sound. To open your eyes to just what you're seeing, beyond the spectacular mountain scenery, take a tip from this dedicated Milford lover and contact the **Department of Conservation Visitors Centre,** Te Anau Terrace (P.O. Box 29), Te Anau (tel. 03/429-7921; fax 03/249-7613), for information on **Fiordland National Park,** and ask specifically for their pamphlet *The Road to Milford,* which illuminates each mile of the way. It's a good idea, too, to arm yourself with insect repellent against sand flies, which can be murderous at Milford.

Highway 94 from Te Anau to Milford Sound leads north along the lake, with islands and wooded far shores on your left. The drive is, of necessity, a slow one as you wend your way through steep climbs between walls of solid rock and down through leafy glades. Keep an eye out for the keas, sometimes perched along the roadside trying to satisfy their insatiable curiosity about visitors to their domain. **Homer Tunnel,** about 63 miles along, is a major engineering marvel: a three-quarter-mile passageway first proposed in 1889 by William Homer, begun in 1935, and finally opened in 1940. It was, however, the summer of 1954 before a connecting road was completed and the first private automobile drove through. Incidentally, during winter months take those "No Stopping—Avalanche Zone" signs very seriously. No matter how much you may want to stop for a photo, *don't!*—it could cost you your life.

Some 4 miles past the tunnel you'll see **"The Chasm"** signposted on a bridge (the sign is small, so keep a sharp eye out). By all means take the time to stop and walk the short trail back into the forest, where a railed platform lets you view a natural sculpture of smooth and craggy rocks along the riverbed of the **Cleddau River.** As the river rushes through, a sort of natural tiered fountain is formed by its waters pouring through rock apertures. Marvelous! Absolutely unique! Well worth the time and the short walk.

READERS RECOMMEND: LAKE GUNN

"We stopped at **Gunn Lake Park** and walked through the beech forest, where everything was covered with the green velvet of mosses and lichens, to the shores of lovely Gunn Lake. We could have spent much more time here."—A. Schweinsberg, Wilmington, Del. [*Author's note:* Lake Gunn is the only known nesting place of the crested grebe in New Zealand. The birds construct floating nests of mosses and twigs, then weave ropes of grass to anchor them to the shoreline—for that reason, virtually no boats are allowed on the lake, and those few that are must maintain very low speeds.]

WHERE TO STAY EN ROUTE

TE ANAU DOWNS MOTOR BEST WESTERN INN, Milford South Hwy. 94 (P.O. Box 19), Te Anau. Tel. 03/249-7811. 32 B&B units, 22 kitchen units (all with bath). A/C MINIBAR TV TEL

$ Rates (excluding GST): NZ$30 ($17) per person B&B unit; NZ$76–NZ$86 ($43–$49) single or double motel flat. Extra person in motel flat NZ$15 ($9). Best Western discounts available. AE, DC, MC, V.

Dave Moss, president of Best Western NZ, owns and operates this outstanding property on the road between Te Anau and Milford Sound. There are B&B rooms with private facilities and one-bedroom motel flats that are neat and modern, with cooking and eating utensils, fridge, electric rangette, and color TV. There's a laundry available to all guests. Dave also runs a licensed restaurant with a local reputation for serving the largest and best roast dinner in the area at reasonable prices. It's located about 19 miles from Te Anau.

LAKE GUNN MOTOR INN, Milford Hwy., Cascade Creek, Fiordland (Private Bag, Te Anau). Tel. 03/249-7919. Fax 03/249-8151. 29 units, 1 family rm (all with bath). TV TEL

$ Rates (excluding GST): NZ$60 ($34) single; NZ$75 ($43) double; NZ$75 ($43) for two in family room. AE, DC, MC, V.

This peaceful Lake Gunn setting, 48 miles from Te Anau and 1 hour from Milford Sound, is an ideal base from which to explore the Fiordland National Park. It is also very close to the beginning of the Routeburn and Hollyford walks. The luxury units have two-channel video, and piped-in music, as well as coffee and tea facilities. There's an excellent licensed restaurant serving moderately priced meals, and the lounge is a relaxing focal point for guests, who often congregate around the stone fireplace in the evening, with a tiny (but well-stocked!) bar against one wall. Lake Gunn is only about a 10-minute walk down a lovely nature trail, and there's good trout fishing for those with fishing rods in their luggage. Don't, however, just plan to drop in here—reserve at least 48 hours in advance, more if possible.

WHERE TO EAT EN ROUTE

Both the motels listed above operate excellent licensed restaurants, with **Te Anau Downs** serving all meals, and **Lake Gunn Motor Inn** offering morning and afternoon teas, as well as full dinner service. Prices at both are quite reasonable, and you'll be surprised at the superb quality of the cuisine at each.

3. MILFORD SOUND

75 miles N of Te Anau, 179 miles NW of Queenstown

No matter what time of year you arrive or what the weather is like, your memories of Milford Sound are bound to be very special. Its 14 nautical miles leading to the Tasman Sea are lined with mountain peaks that rise sharply to heights of 6,000 and 7,000 feet. Forsters fur seals sport on rocky shelves, dolphins play in waters that reach depths up to 2,000 feet, and its entrance is so concealed when viewed from the sea that Captain Cook sailed right by it without noticing when he was charting these waters some 200 years ago.

It rains a lot in Milford—some 300 inches annually, more than in any other one place in New Zealand. I personally don't mind the rain, for the sound (which is actually a fjord carved out by glacial action) shows yet another side of its nature under dripping skies—the trip out to the Tasman in the rain is as special in its own way as one when the sun is shining. Ah, but on a fine day, when the sky is blue, the water reflects varying shades of green and blue and dark brown, the bush that flourishes even on sheer rock walls glows a deep, shiny green—that day is to be treasured forever.

In summer, coaches pour in at the rate of 30 or more each day for launch cruises. That tide slows in other months, but the launches go out year round, rain or shine. As is the custom at New Zealand's isolated beauty spots, the THC hotel is the center of things, and in the case of THC Milford, that continues a tradition that began in 1891, when Elizabeth Sutherland (wife of the sound's first settler) built a 12-room boardinghouse to accommodate seamen who called into the sound.

WHAT TO SEE & DO

✪ **Milford Sound** must be seen from the deck of one of the launches, with the skipper filling you in on every peak, cove, creature, and plant you pass (the narrative, filled with anecdotes, is so entertaining you won't want to miss a word—I have even taped a cassette to enjoy back home!), to be fully appreciated. Both the THC and Fiordland Travel Ltd. run **cruise excursions.** The half-day cruise for NZ$35 ($20) takes you out into the Tasman where you see the shoreline close and understand how it is that the sound's entrance escaped Captain Cook's keen eye. Even in warm weather, a jacket or sweater will likely feel good out on the water, and if it should be raining, you'll be glad of a raincoat.

Fiordland Travel also runs an inexpensive **fishing trip** on Milford South that runs about NZ$45 ($26). Book through their office in Te Anau or Queenstown.

If you can stay over long enough, there are some marvelous ✪ **walks** from Milford Sound. Some climb into the peaks, others meander along the shore or up close to waterfalls. Ask at Department of Conservation headquarters in Te Anau (see above) or at the reception desk of THC Milford. It's worth the effort to know this timeless place from the land as well as the water.

I find the tiny (2,650-foot-long) ✪ **airstrip** a constant source of fascination on every trip. The air controller here talks in by radio more than 5,000 planes every year, and that without the help of such safety devices as lights or radar. The perfect safety record is accounted for by the fact that pilots must be rated specifically for this airfield, so they know what they're about as they zoom down, dwarfed by those stupendous mountain peaks. I rather suspect, also, that careful monitoring of weather conditions and a watchful eye on all air traffic within radio range have a lot to do with that record. Among the clientele are scenic flights and farmers who drop down in their private planes. The airfield is a short (less than 5 minutes) walk from the THC, and I'll have to warn you that watching those tiny specks against the backdrop of a sheer mountain wall grow into planes that make a perfect landing can become positively addictive.

On the other side of the airstrip, another short walk will bring you to the **fishing facilities** on the Cleddau River, an interesting and colorful sight, since there are nearly always a few of the fishing boats tied up in this safe anchorage.

READERS RECOMMEND

"I found the place so beautiful that I felt compelled to stay at the pricey THC!!! But worth it."—Ian McPherson, Oxford, U.K. [*Author's note:* This reader's comment is listed simply to validate my own admittedly "rave" comments on Milford Sound!!]

WHERE TO STAY

Well, it's either basic budget or bust-out big splurge—no in-between at Milford Sound. Actually, my personal recommendation is to go for the big splurge; on the other hand, basic budget is really quite comfortable, and there's often a nice conviviality among the lodge guests.

MILFORD LODGE, Hwy. 94 (P.O. Box 10), Milford Sound, Fiordland. Tel. and fax 03/249-8071. 23 rms (none with bath).

$ Rates: NZ$16 ($9) per person. No credit cards. **Closed:** Apr 7–Nov 6.

The only accommodations at Milford Sound other than the THC Milford is the Milford Lodge, run by the Park Board. In it, you'll find a simple, dormitory-type lodging in gorgeous surroundings just 1 short, beautiful mile from the sound. Basic rooms mostly hold four beds—nothing more in the way of furnishings—and the toilet-and-shower block is immaculate. There's also a big lounge with a fireplace, cooking facilities, a restaurant, and a free sauna. If you're thinking of walking the Milford Track, this is where many hikers spend the first night back—perhaps to prolong a too-rare close communion with nature in the wooded site.

WORTH THE EXTRA MONEY

THC MILFORD SOUND RESORT HOTEL, Private Bag, Milford Sound, Fiordland. Tel. 03/249-7926. Fax 03/249-8094. 35 rms, 1 suite (all with bath). TV TEL

$ Rates: NZ$130–NZ$180 ($74–$103) single or double; NZ$260 ($149) suite. AE, DC, MC, V.

This is the one "big splurge" I simply would not miss in New Zealand. The hotel sprawls along the waterfront, amid lawns and flowers and shrubs and trees that have grown twisted into stylized, Oriental shapes. To watch the sunset and darkness descend over Mitre Peak from the glass-walled lounge, then gather around its two stone fireplaces for the evening with other guests and off-duty staff members, is to savor this unique environment in the best of all possible accommodations. There's a comfortable patina of the years, just this side of most "luxury" decor, overlaying the lounge, convivial bar, and dining room. Bedrooms are nicely furnished, with tea and coffee makings and satellite TV; video is available each evening in the lounge. Those in front have wall-width windows to take advantage of those striking views, as well as full baths (that means bathtubs!). Periodic specials are real bargains—in 1992 NZ$95 ($54) covered one night's lodging, breakfast, the launch trip, and lunch! Do splurge if you can—it's the icing on Milford Sound's unique cake.

WHERE TO EAT

You can eat very inexpensively in the nearby **Public Bar,** which serves pub grub. Or you can bring a **picnic lunch** with you from Te Anau.

THC MILFORD, waterfront. Tel. 249-7926.

Cuisine: SEAFOOD. **Reservations:** Recommended, if possible.

$ Prices: Average lunch NZ$22 ($13); average dinner NZ$35 ($20). AE, DC, MC, V.

Open: Lunch daily 11:30am–2pm; dinner daily 6–9pm.

Treat yourself to a very special splurge and lunch in the THC Milford, next to a window looking out on the sound and Mitre Peak. The menu features the freshest of seafoods, along with soup, dessert, coffee, and cheese. You might add another bit to the tab for a glass of wine and dine happily in anticipation of the launch cruise ahead. For overnighters, dinners are excellent, often featuring seafoods fresh from local waters.

EN ROUTE TO DUNEDIN

You will, of course, have to return to Queenstown for your onward travel. If time is short, you may want to head straight for Dunedin from Te Anau. If not, don't miss another very special place, Stewart Island, New Zealand's "third island," and almost as far south as you can go in this world before reaching Antarctica (see Chapter 10).

The drive to Dunedin takes about 5½ hours over good roads. Take Highway 94 across Gorge Hill into Lumsden, across the **Waimea Plains** to the milling center of **Gore,** through farmlands to **Clinton,** and across rolling downs to **Balclutha.** From there, it's Highway 1 north along the coast past **Mosgiel** (named after Scottish poet Robbie Burns's farm) to **Lookout Point,** where you'll get your first look at Dunedin. Along the way, you may want to stop in **Mossburn,** where **Wapiti Handcrafts Ltd.** on the main street (P.O. Box 6; tel. 03/248-6087), makes and sells deerskin fashions. They are handsome creations and slightly lower in price here than in shops around the country. They also manufacture a range of smaller items for souvenirs and gifts. As you approach Balclutha, look for ✪ **Peggydale** (P.O. Box 7; tel. 03/418-2345), an ideal stopping point for tea, scones, sandwiches, or salad plates in the lovely Tea Kiosk. Peggydale handles a wide range of handcrafts—leather goods and sheepskin products (some made in their leathercraft shop), pottery, weaving, hand-knits, etc.—even paintings by local artists. They'll send you a mail-order catalog on request.

EN ROUTE TO INVERCARGILL

If Invercargill is your destination, you'll take Highway 94 only as far as **Lumsden** (where **Wapiti Handcrafts Ltd.**—see above—also has an interesting workshop, showroom, and information center in the old railway station) then turn south on Highway 6 to ride through rolling farm and sheep country all the way down to Invercargill, 115 miles from Queenstown.

SOUTHLAND

Invercargill is New Zealand's southernmost city, the "capital" of Southland, a region you entered when you turned south at Lumsden, extending as far northwest as Lake Manapouri and as far east as Balclutha. It is the country's coolest and rainiest region, yet the even spread of its rainfall is the very foundation of its economy, the raising of grass and grass seed, which in turn supports large numbers of sheep stations.

Its coastline saw settlements of Maori (in limited numbers) and whalers, with frequent visits from sealers. From its waters have come those succulent Bluff oysters and crayfish (rock lobsters) you've devoured in your New Zealand travels. In fact they account for about 90% of the value of fish landed in this area.

1. INVERCARGILL

115 miles S of Queenstown, 357 miles SW of Dunedin

GETTING THERE   By Plane   Both **Air New Zealand** and **Ansett** have service between Invercargill and Auckland, Nelson, Rotorua, and Wellington in the North Island; Christchurch, Dunedin, and Hokitika in the South Island.

By Train   The **Southerner** serves Invercargill and Christchurch, Dunedin and Timaru (check with InterCity Rail for days of week). The **railway station** is on Leven Street.

By Bus   Both **Mount Cook Landline** and **InterCity** have coach service between Invercargill and Christchurch, Dunedin, Queenstown, Te Anau, and Timaru. The **bus depot** is also on Leven Street.

By Car   Invercargill can be reached via Highways 1, 6, and 92.

ESSENTIALS   Orientation   Invercargill's streets are laid out in neat grid patterns. Main thoroughfares are **Tay Street** (an extension of Highway 1) and **Dee Street** (an extension of Highway 6). Many of the principal shops and office buildings are centered around their intersection, and the **post office** is on Dee Street. **Queens Park** is a beautiful green oasis (200 acres) right in the center of town and the site of many activities.

Information   You'll find that **Southland Promotions, Inc.,** 82 Dee St. (tel. 03/218-6021), serves as a local tourist office and can furnish a list of local accommodations (although they are not a booking agency), as well as supply sightseeing details.

The first thing you'll notice about Invercargill is its flatness—a bump is likely to take on the dimensions of a "hill" in these parts! Actually, that flatness is due to the fact that a large part of the city was once boggy swampland. In its reclamation, town

WHAT'S SPECIAL ABOUT SOUTHLAND

☐ The Southland Museum and Gallery, this is the only place in the country where you can view tuataras in a natural setting. There's also a fossilized forest from the Jurassic era.

☐ Queens Park, a green retreat for the senses in the heart of the Invercargill. It has a rose garden, rhododendron walk, and a grove of native and exotic trees. Its wildlife sanctuary has wallabies, deer, and an aviary.

☐ The "Glory Walk" in Bluff passes through native bush and trees that form a shady canopy overhead.

☐ The Sterling Point–Ocean Beach Walk follows the coastline around Bluff Hill. Below the surf breaks against rocks.

☐ The Curio Bay Fossil Forest is a sea-washed rock terrace that's 160 million years old. It's the original floor of a subtropical forest from a time before grasses had evolved.

planners have turned what might have made for a dull city into a distinct advantage by creating wide, level thoroughfares and great city parks. Invercargill is a *spacious* city. Many of its broad, pleasant streets bear the names of Scottish rivers, revealing the home country of many of its early settlers.

Among its many attractions, perhaps primary is its proximity to Stewart Island, the legendary anchor of Maui's canoe (which became, of course, the South Island, with the North Island seen as the huge fish he caught). Day-trips to Stewart Island are possible any day by air and several times a week by the ferry that runs from nearby Bluff.

WHAT TO SEE & DO

Allow at least a full hour to visit the ✪ **Southland Museum and Art Gallery** on Gala Street by the main entrance to Queens Park. The collections inside include a multitude of exhibits that will bring alive much of the history and natural resources of this area. In addition, there's a tuatarium, the only place in the country you can view live tuataras in a simulated natural setting. In front of the museum, examine the section of fossilized forest, which dates from the Jurassic era of some 160 million years ago. Hours are 10am to 4:30pm Monday through Friday, 1 to 5pm on Saturday, Sunday, and public holidays.

✪ **Queens Park,** right in the heart of the city, is just one (the largest) of Invercargill's parklands (a total of 2,975 acres) and might well keep you occupied for the better part of a day. Within its 200 acres there's a **rhododendron walk; iris garden; sunken rose garden; grove of native and exotic trees; wildlife sanctuary with wallabies, deer, and an aviary; duck pond; a winter garden; an 18-hole golf course; tennis courts,** and—perhaps most of all—a cool, green retreat for the senses. A very special thing to look for is the beguiling children's fountain encircled by large bronze animal statues. Over the years this beautiful botanical reserve has seen duty as grazing land, a racecourse, and a sporting ground. The entrance is from Queens Drive at Gala Street. There's a delightful **Tea Kiosk** for light refreshments.

Drive out to **Bluff,** Invercargill's port some 27 kilometers (16½ miles) to the south. This is home port for the Stewart Island ferry, and site (on the other side of the harbor at Tiwai Point) of the mammoth Tiwai Aluminum Smelter (the only one in the country) whose annual production is 259,000 tons. If you'd like to tour the complex (a fascinating experience), contact **Tiwai Smelter Tours,** NZ Aluminum Smelters Ltd., Private Bag, Invercargill (tel. 03/218-5999). You must be at least 12 years of age and wear long trousers or slacks, heavy footwear, and clothing that covers your arms. There's no charge, but usually tours are limited to one each day, so it pays to reserve well in advance.

There are two great ✪ **walks** in Bluff (ask the Southland Promotions office in Invercargill for the Foveaux Walk, Bluff pamphlet). The **"Glory Walk"** (named for a sailing vessel, *England's Glory,* which was wrecked at Bluff) is 1½ kilometers (about a mile) long and passes through native bush and trees, which form a shady canopy overhead. Ferns and mosses add to the lush greenery. The **Sterling Point—Ocean Beach Walk** begins where Highway 1 ends at Foveaux Strait. It's almost 7 kilometers (4¼ miles) long, following the coastline around Bluff Hill, with marvelous views of beaches, offshore islands, and surf breaking against coastal rocks. Parking facilities are provided at both ends of the walk, and you are asked to follow the signposts and to leave no litter in your footsteps.

READERS RECOMMEND: BLUFF

"At Bluff, we visited a lookout high on a hill where you can gaze south over Foveaux Strait to Stewart Island and imagine Antarctica. A young man there advised us to eat at a small take-out place called Johnsons on the Wharf. Usually they have oysters, but not this time, so we had paua patties and mussel rolls, both absolutely delicious. Both had been minced, mixed with seasonings, rolled in crumbs and batter, and fried. The paua was almost navy blue and very strange looking. It was the only place we ate it, and we loved it. Then we drove on down the coast road to the very tip of the South Island, where there is one of those signposts pointing in all directions. It was a lovely drive, and we passed an interesting house that an older couple have decorated inside and out with paua shells over the years. It was funny and quaint, but they were so pleased with it that we enjoyed the visit." —A. Schweinsberg, Wilmington, Del.

WHERE TO STAY

You should have no trouble finding a place to lay your weary head in Invercargill. There are good budget accommodations in ample quantity, as well as more upmarket motels and hotels.

Unless otherwise noted, rates listed below include GST.

LICENSED HOTELS

Invercargill's leading hotels are administered by **Invercargill Trust Hotels.** At the top of the line, the ✪ **Ascott Park Hotel,** corner of Racecourse Road and Tay Street (tel. 03/217-6195), is a modern luxurious complex set in landscaped grounds 4 kilometers (2½ miles) from the city center, with both hotel rooms (NZ$130 to NZ$135, U.S. $74 to $77) and motel flats (NZ$80 to NZ$85, U.S. $46 to $49). The **Kelvin Hotel,** corner of Kelvin and Esk Streets (tel. 03/218-2829), is a center-city high-rise hotel with luxury guest rooms at rates of NZ$96 to NZ$100 ($55 to $57).

For the more budget-minded, there's the graciously restored ✪ **Grand Hotel,** Dee Street (tel. 03/218-8059), and **Don Lodge,** 77 Don St. (tel. 03/218-6125), both in the city center, with exceptionally attractive rooms and rates ranging from NZ$45 to NZ$80 ($26 to $46). Add GST to all rates; all four hotels accept American Express, Diners Club, MasterCard, and VISA credit cards.

For more details and booking, contact: The Marketing and Sales Manager, Invercargill Trust Hotels, P.O. Box 208, Invercargill (tel. 03/218-7146; fax 03/217-7002).

MOTEL FLATS

COLONIAL MOTOR INN, 335-339 Tay St., Invercargill. Tel. 03/217-6058. Fax 03/217-6118. 10 flats (all with bath). TV TEL
$ Rates: NZ$70 ($40) single; NZ$78 ($45) double. AE, DC, MC, V.
There are one- and two-bedroom units with fully equipped kitchens, and a dining area at the Colonial, located 5 minutes from the city center. Other facilities include a guest laundry, room service, and off-street parking. Continental breakfast is available on request.

TAYESTA MOTEL, 343 Tay St., Invercargill. Tel. 03/217-6074. Fax 03/217-7075. 12 flats (all with bath). TV TEL
$ Rates (excluding GST): NZ$68 ($39) single; NZ$75 ($43) double. Best Western discounts available. AE, DC, MC, V.
This attractive one-story blue-and-white motel has one- and two-bedroom units, each with large picture windows in the lounge, fully equipped kitchen, central heating, video, and radio. There's a laundry, play area with swings and sandpit, and at-door parking. Lola Staite is the friendly Best Western hostess. Continental or cooked breakfasts are available for a small charge. The Tayesta is located 2 kilometers (1 mile) from the city center.

A BED & BREAKFAST

GERRARDS RAILWAY HOTEL, 1 Leven St., Invercargill. Tel. 03/218-3406. Fax 03/214-4567. 20 rms (8 with bath). TV TEL
$ Rates (including breakfast): NZ$47 ($27) single without bath, NZ$55 ($31) single with bath; NZ$64 ($37) double without bath, NZ$68 ($39) double with bath. Children under 9 stay free in parents' room. AE, MC, V.
This interesting old B&B hotel is just across from the rail and bus stations. Built in 1896 of rosy-pink brick with white trim, its facade has had a face cleaning and rooms have been redone, thanks to owners Keith and Margaret Gerrard. These are not fancy accommodations, but they are comfortable, clean, and very centrally located at the corner of Esk and Leven Streets. Rooms with or without private facilities are available, and showers and toilets are conveniently located for those that share. There's a guest TV lounge, cocktail bar, and moderately priced restaurant. Interesting place, good value for money.

A HOSTEL

YHA HOSTEL, 122 North Rd., Waikiwi, Invercargill. Tel. 03/215-9344. 44 beds.
$ Rates (excluding GST): NZ$14 ($8) per person. No credit cards.
The 44 beds here are in six rooms, and other facilities include showers and a kitchen. There's a barbecue and picnic area available for use during the day, and the resident manager can arrange reduced fares to Stewart Island on a standby basis. He can also advise about hostel-type accommodations on the island (there are tentative plans for a YHA hostel, but no timetable as yet). The hostel is located on an extension of Dee Street, before it becomes Highway 6.

CABINS & CAMPGROUNDS

The **Invercargill Caravan Park,** at the Showgrounds on Victoria Avenue, Invercargill (tel. 03/218-8787), has one bunkroom, five cabins that sleep up to four, and six that sleep up to six. On the premises is a kitchen, showers and toilets, a laundry, store, car wash, and play area. There are facilities for the disabled, plus 50 campsites and 60 caravan sites. Rates for bunks are NZ$9 ($5) per person; cabins are NZ$24 ($14) for two; caravan sites, NZ$15 ($9) for two; tent sites, NZ$6 ($3) per adult—including GST.

WHERE TO EAT

Invercargill has numerous coffee shops offering good value. The coffee lounge in the **D.I.C. Department Store** has good morning and afternoon teas as well as light lunches, all inexpensive.

GERRARDS RAILWAY HOTEL, Esk and Leven Sts. Tel. 218-3406.

Cuisine: NEW ZEALAND/CONTINENTAL. **Reservations:** Recommended.

$ Prices: Average lunch NZ$12 ($7); average dinner under NZ$35 ($20). AE, MC, V.

Open: Lunch Mon–Fri noon–2pm; dinner daily 6:30–9pm.

There's a bright, café air about this restaurant, which is a great favorite with locals. The menu is a mixture of native New Zealand and continental dishes and includes specialties like coquilles St-Jacques and escalopes de porc with mushroom and brandy-cream sauce, local Bluff oysters, and fresh blue cod in a lemon-and-wine sauce. Service is friendly, and it's fully licensed. Gerrards is located in the city center, opposite the rail and bus stations.

THE GRAND HOTEL, 76 Dee St. Tel. 218-8059.

Cuisine: NEW ZEALAND. **Reservations:** Recommended.

$ Prices: Average lunch NZ$15 ($9); average dinner NZ$35 ($20). AE, MC, V.

Open: Lunch daily noon–2pm; dinner daily 6–9:30pm.

This beautiful and elegant hotel in the city center is a joy to go into, even if you don't eat. The lovely formal dining room serves seasonal dishes of mostly local ingredients, using many traditional recipes. If oysters are on the menu in any form, let that be your order—they'll be from Bluff, and superior to any you've tasted before. Fully licensed.

JOY'S GOURMET KITCHEN, 122 Dee St. Tel. 218-3985.

Cuisine: LIGHT MEALS/SNACKS. **Reservations:** Not required.

$ Prices: Average lunch under NZ$8 ($5); less for snacks.

Open: Sat–Thurs 7:30am–6pm, Fri 9am–9pm.

This is the place for quiche, baked potatoes with a variety of fillings, 26 different salads, nutritious hot meals, light lunches, carrot cake, muesli munch, soups, and cakes—all made daily on the premises and all very good. Try one of their traditional Kiwi roast meals. They also have take-aways. Incidentally, owner Peter Breayten and his staff are only too pleased to give advice on sightseeing in the city. It's located in the city center.

A CARVERY TREAT

Friday night in Invercargill means a carvery treat at the ✪ ⑤ **Ascot Park Hotel**—to residents as well as visitors—so reservations are a very good idea (in fact, I heard about this feast way up in the North Island when I mentioned coming to Invercargill). The Ascot Park, on the corner of Racecourse Road and Tay Street (tel. 217-6195), is a luxury hotel of the first order, and the carvery is spread in an enormous room with different levels for tables. The spread is just about as enormous as the room, with every kind of seafood currently available, endless fresh salads, great roasts for nonseafood lovers, and luscious desserts. You'll see parties of locals chatting away with visitors, and there's a party atmosphere all through the place. The price is NZ$28 ($16), for which you get full value, indeed. Highly recommended.

EN ROUTE TO DUNEDIN
VIA THE COAST ROAD

You can drive from Invercargill to Dunedin in a little over 3 hours by way of Highway 1, through Gore, past farmlands and mile after mile of grazing sheep. It's a pleasant drive, and one you'll enjoy.

However, if you have a day to spend on the road, let me urge you to follow the Southern Scenic Route along Highway 92 and allow a full day to loiter along the way, rejoining Highway 1 at Balclutha. If you make this drive, the leaflet **Drive New Zealand's Southern Scenic Route** from the Southland Promotions office, 82 Dee St., in Invercargill, is quite helpful as it details the reserves through which you will pass.

The **Southern Scenic Route,** as it is known, takes you through a region of truly unique character. There are great folds in the land covered with such a diversity of native forests that from Chaslands on you'll be in one national forest reserve after the other. Short detours will take you to the coast and golden sand beaches, prominent headlands, and fine bays.

Highway 92, let me hasten to add, is not paved its entire length—however, even unpaved portions are in good driving condition, albeit at a slower speed than the faster Highway 1. Picnic spots abound, so you can take along a packed lunch from Invercargill, or plan to stop in the country pub in Owaka's only hotel for lunch (stop for refreshments even if you lunch elsewhere—it's an experience you wouldn't want to miss). One very special detour you might consider follows.

Just beyond Fortrose, follow the Fortrose-Otara road to the right, and when you pass the Otara School, look for the turnoff to **Waipapa Point.** The point is the entrance to Foveaux Strait, a treacherous waterway that has scuttled many a sailing vessel and is now marked by a light, which was first used in 1884. Follow the Otara-Haldane road to Porpoise Bay, then turn right and drive a little over 1 kilometer (about ½ mile) to the ✪ **Curio Bay Fossil Forest,** which is signposted. This sea-washed rock terrace dates back 160 *million* years and is the original floor of a Jurassic subtropical forest of kauri trees, conifers, and other trees that were growing at a time when grasses had not even evolved. At low tide, you can make out low stumps and fallen logs that have been petrified after being buried in volcanic ash, then raised when the sea level changed. You can then retrace your way around Porpoise Bay and follow the signs to Waikawa and continue north to rejoin Highway 92 and travel on to Chaslands.

There are a few simple rules you must follow when stopping in the scenic reserves. If you picnic, you may light fires only in the fireplaces provided in picnic areas, and be sure to extinguish them thoroughly (only dead wood is permitted as fuel); dogs and cats may not be brought into the reserve except with permission from the reserve's ranger; it is an offense to pick or damage any of the trees, shrubs, or plants in the reserves; and (need I add?) you are expected to leave your picnic area clean and tidy.

If you'd like more information about this lovely part of a lovely country, contact the **Department of Conservation,** Otago Conservancy, P.O. Box 5244, Dunedin (tel. 03/477-0677; fax 03/477-8626).

---

2. STEWART ISLAND

30km (18 miles) SW of Invercargill, across Foveaux Strait

GETTING THERE By Plane The major transport to Stewart Island is via **Southern Air,** P.O. Box 860, Invercargill (tel. 03/218-9129), and during the 20-minute flight, the nine-seater Britten-Norman Islander gives you breathtaking views of the coastline, changing colors of the waters below (which mark the passage of an oceanic stream flowing through the strait), bush-clad islands, and Stewart Island itself, where you land on a sealed runway and are minibused into Oban. Southern Air flies 7 days a week, almost every hour in the summer; there is a minimum of four flights a day, and extra ones are added upon demand. The airline schedules even allow for a day visit if you're pressed for time. These flights are extremely popular and you should either book ahead by telephone or through travel agents or airline offices (Mount Cook Line and Air New Zealand can both make reservations) before you arrive in Invercargill. The airline can arrange accommodation or fishing trips on Stewart Island. Adult fare is NZ$67.50 ($39) one-way, NZ$135 ($77) round-trip; children pay half. Two adults traveling together get a break with the NZ$118 ($67) **"Twosome"** round-trip fare; the **Golden Age fare** for those over 60 is NZ$104 ($59) round-trip; and **students** can go standby for NZ$67.50 ($39) round-trip. *Note:* Southern Air can also help you plan and book your entire Stewart Island holiday. They know the island well and are happy to arrange accommodations, meals, etc. to suit your preferences.

By Boat   You can go aboard the good vessel *Acheron,* maintained by Stewart Island Charter Service. It sails at 9am from Bluff on Monday, Wednesday, and Friday; the fare is NZ$40 ($23) per person, plus GST, each way. The glorious, 2-hour voyage crosses waters that are comparatively shallow, but they can be exceedingly turbulent.

ESSENTIALS   The town of **Oban** centers on Halfmoon Bay and holds a general store, post office, travel office, craft shop, hotel, forestry office, small museum, and the pier at which the ferry docks.

Seen on the map, Stewart Island is not much more than a speck. But seen from the deck of the *Acheron* or from the air, its magnitude will surprise you. There are actually 1,600 kilometers (975 miles) of coastline enclosing 1,680 square kilometers (625 square miles) of thick bush (most of it left in its natural state), bird sanctuary, and rugged mountains. Only a tiny stretch of that long coastline has been settled, and it's the little fishing town of **Oban** that will be your landfall. There are about 20 kilometers (12 miles) of paved road on the island, which are easily covered by the minibus tour, and many of the houses you see are the holiday "batch" or "crib" of Kiwis from the South Island who view Stewart Island as the perfect spot to escape the pressures of civilization.

The pace here is quite unhurried—few cars, friendly islanders more attuned to the tides and the running of cod and crayfish than to commerce—and the setting is a botanist's dream. The Maori called the island Rakiura, "heavenly glow," a name you'll find especially fitting if you are lucky enough to see the southern lights brighten its skies or to be here for one of its spectacular sunsets.

While its beauty and serenity can be glimpsed in the few hours of a day-trip, I heartily recommend at least one overnight to explore its beaches, bush, and people so as to savor this very special place to the fullest. Incidentally, should you hear yourself or other visitors referred to as "loopies" by the islanders, not to worry—it'll be said with affection.

WHAT TO SEE & DO

Either for previsit briefing or as a memento of your Stewart Island visit, the Des Rillstone video *Beyond the Mainland* is a good investment. It's available from Des's video shop at 287 Hubert St. in Invercargill.

On the island, the only thing you really must not miss is the hour-long ✪ **minibus tour** given by Lloyd Wilcox at Stewart Island Travel (tel. 03/219-1269). Lloyd will not only cover every one of those 20 kilometers (12 miles) of paved road, he'll give you a comprehensive history of Stewart Island—the whalers who settled here, the sealers who called in (it was, in fact, the mate of a sealer who gave his name to the island), the sawmill and mineral industries that came and went, and the development of the fishing industry—and will point out traces they left behind scattered around your route. He also knows the flora of the island (you'll learn, for instance, that there are 17 varieties of orchids on the island) and its animal population (no wild pigs or goats). You'll see many of the 18 good swimming beaches and hear details of the paua diving, which has proved so profitable for islanders (much of the colorful shell that went into those souvenirs you've seen around New Zealand came from Stewart Island). From **Observation Point** right to the road's end at **Thule Bay,** Lloyd gives you an insider's view of his home. And questions or comments are very much in order—it's an informal, happy hour of exchange: a perfect way to begin a stay of several days, an absolute essential if the day-trip is all you will have. Check when booking for schedule and fare.

The **Rakiura Museum** in Halfmoon Bay features photos and exhibits that follow Stewart Island's history through its sailing, whaling, tin-mining, sawmilling, and fishing days. It also has shell and Maori artifact exhibits. Hours are 11am to 2pm on Monday, Wednesday, and Friday (daily during the summer holidays). Admission is NZ$2 ($2) for adults, NZ$1 (60¢) for children.

Visit the small ✪ **deer park** just across from Stewart Island Travel. Small red deer are right at home in the enclosure and seem delighted to have visitors.

Just next to the deer park is the office of the ✪ **Department of Conservation,** P.O. Box 3, Stewart Island (tel. 03/219-1130), which has an interesting display of island wildlife in a small exhibition room. More important, the rangers there can supply details on many beautiful **walks** around Oban and farther afield. If you're interested in spending a few days on the island tramping, I suggest that you write ahead for their informative booklets on just what you'll need to bring and what you may expect. There are recently upgraded tramping huts conveniently spaced along the tracks (ranging in size from 6 to 30 bunks), but they are heavily used and must be booked with the rangers (no charge). A 2-night stay is the maximum at any one hut. *Note:* The office is usually open daily from 9am to 5pm, but if you find it closed, just ask locally—the ranger may well have just popped out for a short spell.

Popular **short walks** around Oban are those to Golden Bay, Lonneckers, Lee Bay, Thule, Observation Point, and the lighthouse at Acker's Point. Ringarina Beach is a mecca for shell hounds (I have New Zealand friends who serve entrées in paua shells they've picked up on the beach here!), but your finds will depend on whether the tides are right during your visit. *Important:* If you're here on a day-trip, check locally to be sure you can make it back from any walk you plan in time for the ferry or air return.

You can engage local boats for **fishing** or visiting nearby uninhabited islands at prices that are surprisingly low. Contact Phillip Smith, master of the *Maturgi,* or check with Stewart Island Travel.

WHERE TO STAY

There is no reservations agency as such on Stewart Island, but **Stewart Island Travel,** P.O. Box 26, Halfmoon Bay, Stewart Island (tel. 03/219-1269; fax 03/219-1293), can send you a complete list of accommodations and prices, and will do all they can to help you book. If you write from the U.S., be sure to enclose $3 U.S. to cover postage. Accommodations are extremely limited, and in summer they're booked months in advance, so if your plans include a visit here, write or call just as soon as you have firm dates for your visit. It is sometimes possible to rent one of the holiday homes or apartments not currently in use, and Beryl is the one to contact. *Note:* Where a P.O. Box is not listed below, the address is simply Stewart Island, New Zealand.

A LICENSED HOTEL

SOUTH SEA HOTEL, P.O. Box 52, Halfmoon Bay, Stewart Island. Tel. 03/219-1059. Fax 03/219-1120. 18 rms (none with bath). TV TEL

$ **Rates** (excluding GST): NZ$25 ($14) single, NZ$20 ($11) per person double room with no sea view; NZ$50 ($29) single, NZ$75 ($43) double room with sea view. Half price for children 2–10. MC, V.

Stewart Island's only hotel is run by Bruce and Sue Ford, and sits right in the curve of Halfmoon Bay, in the village center across the street from the water. Its public bar, bar lounge (whose windows overlook the bay), and licensed restaurant are the center of much island activity, and even if you lodge elsewhere, you're likely to find yourself in and out of the South Sea many times during your stay. Rooms all share the bath and toilet facilities down the hall, and there are exactly six singles, eight twins, two doubles, and two triples. This is the kind of charming, old-fashioned inn that seems exactly right for this island—the guest lounge, for example, has an open fire glowing on cool days, and the staff takes a personal interest in all guests (and in casual visitors, for that matter). Breakfast is extra at NZ$9 ($5).

MOTEL FLATS

The **Shearwater Inn** complex (see "A-Hostel," below) has single, double, and family rooms in addition to its backpacker accommodations, as well as a bar and licensed restaurant.

RAKIURA MOTELS, P.O. Box 96, Stewart Island. Tel. 03/219-1096. 5 flats (all with bath). TEL

$ **Rates:** NZ$40 ($23) single; NZ$60 ($34) double. Extra adult NZ$15 ($9); extra child under 12 NZ$10 ($6). MC, V.

Elaine Hamilton offers self-contained motel units located about 1 mile from Oban. Units sleep up to six, are heated, and have kitchens and private baths.

A HOSTEL

SHEARWATER INN, Ayre St. (P.O. Box 25), Halfmoon Bay Oban, Stewart Island. Tel. 021/391-114. Fax 021/44-681. 80 beds, 10 private rms.

$ **Rates:** NZ$20 ($11) per bed; NZ$28 ($16) single room; NZ$26 ($15) per person double or family room; NZ$10 ($6) per child. MC, V.

When the Shearwater Inn complex opened in conjunction with Southern Air in 1989, it was the first major new accommodation on the island in 50 years. Situated right in the heart of Oban, near the post office, shops, and beach, it's an associate YHA hostel, and also has single, double, and family rooms. The 80 beds are in two to four-bed rooms; there's a communal lounge with an open fireplace and TV; kitchen (all utensils furnished); a licensed restaurant for moderately priced à la carte meals; and a courtyard used for barbecues. The inn provides wheelchair facilities.

WHERE TO EAT

In addition to the listings below, the **Shearwater Inn** (see "Where to Stay," above) has a good à la carte restaurant serving breakfast from 8 to 9am, and dinner from 6pm to 9pm daily at reasonable prices. The South Sea Hotel can pack a **picnic lunch** if notified in ample time, and there's a **general store** where you can pick up picnic makings for a day in the bush. For light lunches, morning and afternoon teas, or take-aways, it's the **Travel Inn Tearooms,** adjacent to Stewart Island Travel in the village center.

ANNIE HANSEN'S DINING ROOM, in the South Sea Hotel, Oban, Halfmoon Bay. Tel. 219-1059.

Cuisine: SEAFOOD/NEW ZEALAND.

$ Prices: Average lunch NZ$15 ($9); average dinner NZ$25 ($14). MC, V.

Open: Lunch daily noon–1pm; dinner daily 6–7pm.

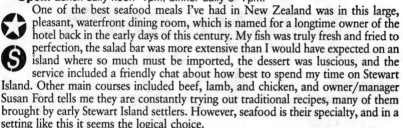 One of the best seafood meals I've had in New Zealand was in this large, pleasant, waterfront dining room, which is named for a longtime owner of the hotel back in the early days of this century. My fish was truly fresh and fried to perfection, the salad bar was more extensive than I would have expected on an island where so much must be imported, the dessert was luscious, and the service included a friendly chat about how best to spend my time on Stewart Island. Other main courses included beef, lamb, and chicken, and owner/manager Susan Ford tells me they are constantly trying out traditional recipes, many of them brought by early Stewart Island settlers. However, seafood is their specialty, and in a setting like this it seems the logical choice.

CHAPTER 11

DUNEDIN & MOUNT COOK

1. DUNEDIN
- **WHAT'S SPECIAL ABOUT DUNEDIN & MOUNT COOK**
2. MOUNT COOK

You won't find pipers in the streets of Dunedin—and the citizens of "New Edinburgh on the Antipodes" are quick to tell you they're *Kiwis*, not Scots. Still, one look at the sturdy stone Victorian architectural face of the city with its crown of upreaching spires will tell you that the 344 settlers who arrived at this beautiful Upper Harbour in March 1848 could only have come from Scotland. And when you learn that Dunedin is the old Gaelic name for Edinburgh, that the city produces New Zealand's only domestic whisky, has the only kilt store in the country, and that the strains of a pipe band are common here, there's no mistaking its Scottish nature!

A reader once wrote that "very few people are lukewarm about their feelings when it comes to bagpipes—either they are very enthusiastic or they're anti-bagpipes." I think she's right and you might as well know up front that I am one of those enthusiasts who will drop everything at the skirl of a bagpipe and travel miles to listen to its curious music. This fact may account in large part for the place Dunedin holds in my affections. That affection, however, is mightily reinforced by the city's serendipitous character—lighthearted chatter in pubs hiding behind somber facades, instant friendliness that belies the much-touted "dour" Scottish nature, and the spirit of fun unexpectedly encountered in almost any Dunedin gathering. Nor is that twinkle exclusively Scottish—there's a decidedly *Irish* flavor to the fact that Science Department professors in the august University of Otago regularly choose St. Patrick's Day to conduct chemical experiments that will turn the waters of the Waters of Leith, which flow through the campus, green for most of that day!

1. DUNEDIN

357 miles NE of Invercargill, 185 miles SE of Queenstown,
206 miles S of Mount Cook, 223 miles SW of Christchurch

GETTING THERE **By Plane** Both **Air New Zealand** and **Ansett** provide air service between Dunedin and Auckland, Hokitika, Napier/Hastings, New Plymouth, Rotorua, and Wellington in the North Island; Christchurch, Invercargill, and Nelson in the South Island.

Airport coaches drop you off at the visitors center on the Octagon for fares of NZ$8 ($5) for adults, NZ$4 ($2) for children. The minibus airport shuttle (tel. 03/479-2481) provides 24-hour service, with hotel pickup and delivery, for a NZ$10 ($6) fare. The airport is a full 30 minutes from the city, which makes a taxi prohibitive at fares of about NZ$45 ($26).

By Train/Bus The **Southerner** train runs between Dunedin and Christchurch and Invercargill. The **railway station** (a sightseeing attraction; see below) is at the foot of Stuart Street. **InterCity, Mount Cook Lines,** and **Newmans** all provide

WHAT'S SPECIAL ABOUT DUNEDIN & MOUNT COOK

Wildlife

☐ The Albatross Colony at Taiaroa Head, the world's only known mainland nesting ground of the magnificent royal albatross.

☐ Penguin Place, a fascinating colony of the rare and dignified yellow-eyed penguin.

Historic Buildings

☐ Dunedin's railway station, a splendid Flemish Renaissance-style edifice, built of Kokonga basalt, with Oamaru limestone facings, a large square clock tower, red Marseilles tiles on the roof, and a colorful mosaic floor.

☐ Olveston, one of the country's best-known stately homes, Jacobean in style, built in 1904–06.

☐ Larnach Castle, a magnificent Neo-Gothic Victorian mansion begun in 1871, whose shell took 200 workmen 3 years to build, and a host of European master craftsmen another 12 years to complete the interior.

Museums

☐ Otago Early Settlers Museum, a fascinating collection of exhibits and displays that depict the daily lives of Dunedin's first European citizens and the city's development up to the present.

Gardens

☐ The Botanic Gardens, established in 1869, and noted for their masses of rhododendrons and azaleas.

☐ Glenfalloch Gardens, a 30-acre estate whose grounds hold native bush, ancient English oaks, rhododendrons, and azaleas.

Scenic Splendors

☐ Skiplane scenic flights at majestic Mount Cook.

---

service between Dunedin and Christchurch, Invercargill, Picton, Queenstown, Te Anau, and Timaru. The **bus terminal** is several blocks away at 200 Cumberland St. For **train and/or bus information,** call 477-2620.

By Car   Dunedin can be reached via Highways 1 and 58.

DEPARTING   There is an **Air New Zealand** (tel. 477-5769) ticket office at the corner of the Octagon and Princes Street. For bus schedules and booking, call **InterCity** (tel. 477-2620) or **Mount Cook Landline** (tel. 474-0674).

ESSENTIALS   Orientation   Most cities have a public square, but Dunedin has its eight-sided Octagon, a green, leafy park right at the hub of the city center that was totally remodeled in 1989. Around its edges you'll find **St. Paul's Anglican Cathedral** and the **Town Hall.** Within its confines, there's a statue of Scotland's beloved poet Robert Burns (whose nephew was Dunedin's first pastor), shady pathways, and park benches for foot-weary shoppers or brown-bagging lunchers. The Octagon divides the main street into **Princes Street** to the south, **George Street** to the north.

The city center, at the head of Otago Harbour, is encircled by a 500-acre strip of land, the **Green Belt,** that has been, by edict of the founders, left in its natural state, never to be developed regardless of the city's growth. Thus it is that when driving to

DUNEDIN ACCOMMODATIONS, DINING & ATTRACTIONS

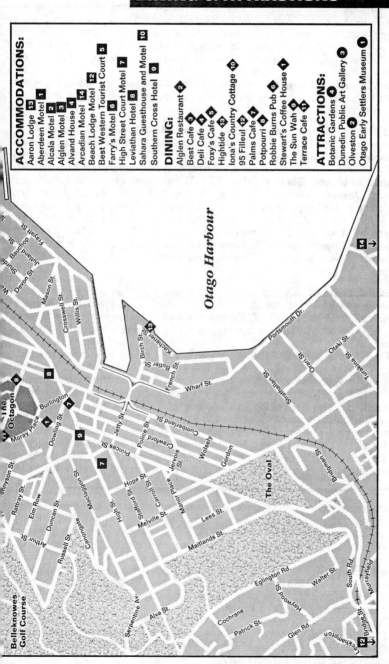

ACCOMMODATIONS:

Aaron Lodge **13**
Aberdeen Motel **1**
Alcala Motel **2**
Alglen Motel **3**
Alvand House **4**
Arcadian Motel **14**
Beach Lodge Motel **12**
Best Western Tourist Court **5**
Farry's Motel **6**
High Street Court Motel **7**
Leviathan Hotel **8**
Sahara Guesthouse and Motel **10**
Southern Cross Hotel **9**

DINING:

Alglen Restaurant **2**
Best Cafe **3**
Deli Cafe **4**
Foxy's Cafe **5**
Hightide **13**
Iona's Country Cottage **10**
95 Filleul **12**
Palms Cafe **7**
Potpourri **8**
Robbie Burns Pub **6**
Stewart's Coffee House **1**
The Sun Wah **9**
Terrace Cafe **11**

ATTRACTIONS:

Botanic Gardens **4**
Dunedin Public Art Gallery **3**
Olveston **2**
Otago Early Settlers Museum **1**

Otago Harbour

any of Dunedin's suburbs, you pass through verdant forestland from which there are glimpses of the harbor.

Information   You'll find the **Dunedin Visitor Centre,** The Octagon (tel. 03/474-3300), just off George Street under the Town Hall clock, open from 8:30am to 5pm weekdays, 9am to 5pm weekends, with extended hours in summer. The staff here is surely one of the friendliest and most helpful in the entire country, and they will cheerfully help you plan your sightseeing, point you to eateries, and answer just about any query you could dream up.

The **InterCity Travel Centre,** 200 Cumberland St. (tel. 03/479-3263), is just opposite Queens Gardens. They can make bookings for all airlines, rail, and coach services throughout New Zealand.

Fast Facts   Dunedin's **area code** is 03. **American Express** is represented by Brooker Travel, 369 George St. (P.O. Box 6309; tel. 03/477-3383). The **Automobile Association (Otago)** is at 450 Moray Place (tel. 477-5945), open from 8:30am to 5pm weekdays. For after-hours **medical and dental emergencies,** contact **St. John Ambulance Service** (tel. 477-7111) for names of on-call doctors and dentists. **Camera House,** 115 George St. (tel. 479-2200), provides 1-hour film developing and other photographic needs. **Citizens Advice,** P.O. Box 5263 (tel. 477-1111), can put you in touch with such agencies as the Women's Resource Centre, Women's Collective, and Gayline/Lesbian Line. Dial 111 for **police, fire,** and **ambulance emergencies.** The **Chief Post Office** (CPO) is at 283 Princes St., at the corner of Water Street (tel. 477-0999), open Monday through Friday from 8:30am to 5pm.

SPECIAL EVENTS   Dunedin, as I said, is fun to visit anytime of the year, but you'll be doubly blessed if you arrive during one of its special events. Probably the highlight of them all is the late March ✪ **Scottish Week,** when the city breaks out with kilts, bagpipes, Scottish country dancing, and a host of other activities that reflect its heritage.

There's its annual ✪ **Festival Week** in early February, with art and craft displays, a vintage-car rally, a family fun run, and street carnival, and—the highlight—a Festival Procession that features gaily decorated floats, clowns, bands, and marching girls. Then in early March, there's the 1-day **Food and Wine Festival,** first celebrated in 1990, held outdoors in the Woodhaugh Gardens. A large variety of Dunedin restaurants set up stalls and sell a selection of dishes from their menus; there's live music and entertainment; and cooking demonstrations. And the third week of October each year, **Rhododendron Week** celebrates the city's most famous floral asset by decking out just about every public space with the lovely blooms and hosting tours of private and public gardens in and around town.

The city's foundations were planted on the solid bedrock of a "Free Church," but its fortunes changed drastically with the goldfield discoveries in Otago, which brought thousands pouring in to bring, along with the gold speculators, the bustle of industry and commerce. From 1861 to 1865 its population erupted from 2,000 to over 10,000, and since that time it has never lost its position of prominence among New Zealand's cities. Amazingly, it has held onto its priorities of education (the first New Zealand university was founded here), conservation of its natural beauties (witness the town Green Belt, which encircles the city), and humanitarian concerns (the Plunket Society for good infant care originated here).

Dunedin, with a population of 100,000 today, is likely to be one of your most fondly remembered New Zealand cities—and you really shouldn't go away without exploring the 12-mile-long Otago Peninsula (it's pronounced "O-*tah*-go") that curves around one side of that beautiful harbor.

GETTING AROUND Most **city buses** leave from the intersection of High and Princes Streets, just off the Octagon. There's frequent bus service during the week, a little spotty on weekends. Fares are zoned and range from NZ$1 to NZ$1.60 (60¢ to $1), half that for children. If you buy a packet of 12 tickets, you essentially get two rides free. The **InterCity Special,** for stops along the route from the bus terminal to Frederick Street, costs NZ50¢ (30¢) a ride, or 12 rides for NZ$5 ($3). A 1-day tourist ticket for families costs NZ$10 ($6) and allows unlimited travel on all timetable services.

A smooth-working **one-way street system** makes driving easier than in most cities; all central streets have metered parking; and there's a municipal parking building near City Hall. The **Automobile Association** office is at 450438 Moray Place (tel. 477-5945). Central 24-hour **gas (petrol) stations** are: Kai Valley Service Station, 433 Stuart St. (tel. 477-8391); Downtown Motors Ltd., at the corner of Gardner and Granford Streets (tel. 477-1256); and Everedi Service Station, opposite the Oval, which also sells groceries (tel. 477-5566).

Taxi ranks may be found at the Octagon, all terminals, and near the CPO (tel. 477-7777 or 477-1771).

WHAT TO SEE & DO

First of all, if you find yourself in the vicinity of Water and Princes Streets, diagonally across from the CPO, you'll be standing on what was the waterfront back when the first settlers arrived in Dunedin and what had been a Maori landing spot for many years. Look for the **bronze plaque** that reads: "On this spot the pioneer settlers landed from a boat off the *John Wickliffe* on the 23rd day of March, 1848, to found the city and province." It's a good jumping-off point for your exploration of the city as it is today.

Now, for all my fellow ✪ **bagpipe** fanatics, let me suggest that you try to arrange to hear the lovely instruments while you're in this little bit of transported Scotland. You may be in town for a scheduled event at which they're featured, but if not, just take yourself to the **Visitor Centre,** 58 The Octagon, or call 474-3300. They'll do their best to get you to a pipe-band rehearsal, if nothing else (which could turn out to be more fun than a formal performance!). Also ask about attending an **evensong choral service** at St. Paul's Cathedral or a **welcoming haggis ceremony.** Now that that's out of the way, it's on to regular sightseeing activities.

Your first order of business should be a stop by the **Visitor Centre;** consider watching their half-hour color video *Southern Adventure* for NZ$3 ($2); it will give you a good overview of the region and of Dunedin's attractions, culture, and that whimsical city personality I mentioned above. Also, pick up their inexpensive sightseeing map and look for their ✪ *Dunedin City Centre Walk* (it's No. 1 of the "Know the City" series) brochure to guide you around city streets.

There are terrific **scenic drives** around the city and out the peninsula, so stop by the Visitor Centre and request their brochures: Dunedin's ✪ *Golden Arrow Scenic Drive* and *The Otago Peninsula.* Both provide maps and clear directions, and the first is keyed to golden arrows along the route, which give you a good 1-hour view of the city and its immediate environs. The *Green Belt* drive is closer to the city, with marked trails leading off through the bush.

There are three very good lookout points from which to view the city and its environs: ✪ **Mount Cargill Lookout,** 8 kilometers (4¾ miles) from the city center (turn left at the end of George Street, then left on Pine Hill Road to its end, then right onto Cowan Street, which climbs to the summit); **Centennial Lookout,** or Signal Hill (turn into Signal Hill Road from Opoho Road and drive 3 kilometers or 1¾ miles, to the end of Signal Hill Road); and **Bracken's Lookout** (at the top of the Botanic Gardens).

According to the *Guinness Book of Records,* Dunedin has the ✪ **steepest**

street in the world, beating out San Francisco and alpine Switzerland. Just minutes from the city center, the little street begins gently, then rears skyward dramatically to come to a dead end on the hillside. It's quite an experience to walk up, and for the hale and hearty, there's a footpath with a railing on one side of the street, while on the opposite side, no less than 270 steps take you to the top. Steps or footpath, walking is your best way up—residents on the street groan when they see (or more likely, hear) a car attempting to climb the hill. Cars stall when you try to change gears; braking power is so much less when the car rolls backward that cars often careen backward down the hill, completely out of control; and gas tanks leak if a car is parked with fuel tanks pointed downward. So, as you *walk* up, remember that the view from the top of the city and harbor goes beyond spectacular. Just where will you find this hilly highlight? Its name is Baldwin Street, and you get there by taking the Normandy bus to North Road, and Baldin is the 10th street past the Botanic Gardens.

TOURS, CRUISES & TRAIN RIDES

Dunedin is blessed with excellent tour operators, who provide easy and enjoyable ways to do sightseeing the easy way. One word of advice, however: If possible, telephone or fax ahead to book, since—especially during summer—the tours are very popular, and if your time in town is limited, you may miss out on the one you most want.

Coach Tours

Newtons Coach Tours, P.O. Box 2034, Dunedin (tel. 03/477-5577), conducts excellent tours of varying durations, all with knowledgeable guides providing valuable insight into the city's sightseeing highlights, along with the occasional human-interest anecdote to liven things up. All tours may be booked directly with Newtons or with the Visitor Centre—*be sure to check exact departure times,* since they can vary from time to time. If requested, they will pick up and drop off at your hotel, motel, motor camp, or hostel.

If you book for both tours 1 and 2, there's a 10% **discount,** and if you opt for all three, Tour 1 is free.

Tour 1, with a morning departure, leaves from the Visitor Centre for a guided tour of Olveston House, Queens Drive Scenic Reserve, the city's historic buildings, Otago University campus, and other city sights. Fare (including all admissions) is NZ$18 ($10) for adults; children pay NZ$8 ($5).

Tour 2 departs the Visitor Centre shortly after noon for the Travel Summit Road, Otago Peninsula, guided tour of Larnach Castle, and a visit to Glenfalloch Woodland Gardens. Fares, including all admissions, are NZ$24 ($14) for adults, NZ$13 ($7) for children.

☼ **Tour 3,** an early afternoon tour, takes you from the Visitor Centre departure point along a 75-kilometer (45-mile) coastal drive of unsurpassed scenic beauty, a tour of the Royal Albatross Colony, Fort Taiaroa, the yellow-eyed penguin colony, and the seal colony. Adults pay NZ$36 ($21), children NZ$19 ($11).

Wild South, P.O. Box 963, Dunedin (tel. 03/474-3300; fax 03/474-3111), runs the popular **Castle Bus** morning tour to Larnach Castle on the Otago Peninsula (see below) and city beaches. The bus runs daily (call for departure time and booking), and the fare is NZ$19 ($11) per person.

The **Architectural History Tour** conducted by Wild South is limited to 12 persons per tour, so my best advice is to book even before you arrive in Dunedin. Although changes in the tour's format are planned, at this writing you're given a historical introduction to the city, a guided tour of Olveston, morning tea in a private house, and a look at industrial, residential, and public buildings, with a knowledgeable commentary about each. The cost at the time of writing is NZ$30 ($17).

Wild South's unique ☼ **Twilight Wildlife Conservation Experience,** with a maximum of 12 persons, is an 8-hour day-trip that includes an introduction to Dunedin's history, and visits to the Otago Peninsula Ornithological Section, peninsula beaches, and albatross, seal, and penguin colonies. You'll have to call for exact departure time and for booking, and the fare at time of writing is NZ$46 ($26) per person.

Tours for a Terrible Thirst

Wilsons Distillery Whisky Tours takes you behind the scenes in New Zealand's only whisky distillery (incidentally, while all other such spirits are "whiskey," in the case of Scotch, it's always "whisky"). The tour begins with a short video describing the history of whisky making in Dunedin, with a detailed description of the distilling process from the original grains right through to the bottled product. You're then taken through the distillery to see that process in action, after which you're treated with a tasting in the distillery's Visitor Centre, which has a number of whisky products, including crystal decanter sets and cherries in whisky, for sale. Each tour takes about 1½ hours and costs NZ$5 ($3). All bookings must be made through the Visitor Centre, 58 The Octagon (tel. 474-3300), which can also provide more detail and tour times.

Tours of **Speights Brewery,** 200 Rattray St. (tel. 477-9480; Mr. Brian Milner), run only in the morning, usually at 10:30am, for the very good reason that the brewing process only occurs in the morning, and an afternoon tour would be far less interesting. You're taken through the entire brewing process of Speights beer, "The Pride of the South," then presented with a sample of the end product. Tours run Monday through Friday, take about 1½ hours, and cost NZ$4 ($2). Book directly with the brewery.

Sweet-Tooth Tours

Cadbury Confectionery Ltd.'s factory in Dunedin is among the very few in the world in which the complete chocolate-making process is performed under one roof. The tour begins with a 10-minute video on the company's history, which dates back to the early 1800s. As you're taken through the factory, you'll see the manufacturing process of several different chocolate products, with samples of each. Unfortunately, if one or more of those samples sparks off an appetite for more, you'll have to buy them through retail outlets, since the factory has no showroom or shop. The tours run Monday through Thursday at 1:30pm and 2:30pm. There's no charge, and because of their immense popularity and a limit of 24 people per tour, early booking is essential. To book, contact Joy Schultruss, Cadbury Confectionery Ltd., 280 Cumberland St. (tel. 474-1126).

Cruises

To see Dunedin and the Otago Peninsula from the water, check with **Otago Harbour Cruises Ltd.** (tel. 03/477-4276), or go by their waterfront office at the corner of Wharf and Fryatt Streets to see what they have on offer while you're there. They run a variety of interesting cruises, including the **Wildlife Cruise, Heritage Cruise,** and ✪ **Cruise 'n Coach.** They also book late spring/early autumn **salmon fishing charters.** The season runs from October through April; fares range from NZ$35 to NZ$60 ($20 to $34); there are discounts for senior citizens, students, and YHA members; and they accept American Express, MasterCard, and VISA. For more detail and booking, contact them directly, or inquire at the Visitor Centre.

A Train Excursion

The small excursion train to the **Taieri Gorge** is a terrific way to spend an afternoon. It runs through the spectacular Taieri Gorge, with scenery easily on a par with the famed Silverton-Durango train in Colorado. There are stops for picture taking, and a fine commentary is provided all along the way. Afternoon tea and snacks are available in the snack-bar car, as well as beer, wine, and spirits. Departure for the 4-hour trip is from Dunedin railway station, with varying days-of-the-week and departure-time schedules throughout the year. Fare for adults is NZ$40 ($23), and up to two school-age children ride free with each adult. Students get a 20% discount. Buy tickets at railway station or the Visitor Centre.

CITY SIGHTS

Dunedin's ✪ **railway station** is a marvelous old Flemish Renaissance–style edifice, designed by George A. Troup. He won the Institution of British Architects Award for his efforts and was later knighted, but never climbed to any position lofty enough to leave behind his affectionate local nickname, "Gingerbread George." Built of Kokonga basalt, with Oamaru limestone facings, the station's most prominent feature is its large square clock tower, but equally impressive are the Aberdeen granite pillars supporting arches of the colonnade across the front, the red Marseilles tiles on the roof, and the colorful mosaic floor in the massive foyer depicting a "puffing billy" engine and other bits of railroad life (more than 725,000 Royal Doulton porcelain squares!). Look for a replica of Dunedin's coat-of-arms, stained-glass windows above the balcony (the engines on both look as if they're coming straight at you, no matter where you stand), and the plaque honoring New Zealand railway men who died in the 1914–18 war. The lovely illuminated **Star Fountain,** the centerpiece of the Octagon until it was moved in 1989, now puts on its colorful musical show in front of the railway station.

Dunedin's lovely ✪ **Botanic Gardens** are at the northern end of George Street. Established in 1869, they are noted for their masses of rhododendrons and azaleas (at their best from October to December). The rock garden, winter garden, and native kohai and rata trees are also noteworthy. Morning and afternoon teas, as well as hot snacks and smörgåsbord lunches, are available in the kiosk restaurant on the grounds. No matter how rushed your schedule, you owe yourself a stroll through this lovely, peaceful spot.

OTAGO EARLY SETTLERS MUSEUM, 220 Cumberland St. Tel. 477-5052.

✪ This museum is a fascinating look back into the daily lives of Dunedin's first European citizens and follows the development of the city and province right up to the present. It's just down from the railway station in the city center. Look for the sole surviving gas streetlamp outside, one of many used on the city's major streets circa 1863. Inside, there's a reconstructed blacksmith's shop; three period rooms; *Josephine,* a double Fairlie steam engine, which pulled the first Dunedin–Port Chalmers express; a Penny Farthing Cycle you can actually ride (although you won't go anywhere since it's held by a frame and mounted on rollers—still fun, though); and all sorts of other relics of life in these parts many years ago. There are other hands-on exhibits, such as toys and mechanical musical instruments, and life in the 20th century is also vividly portrayed. In the Furniture Room, faded sepia photographs of early settlers peer down with stern visages at visitors—one has to wonder what they think of their progeny who wander through. The Archives and Research Department holds records of thousands of Otago families, and is open weekdays except Thursday for a charge of NZ$10 ($6), which includes admission to the museum.

Admission: NZ$4 ($2) adults, NZ$3 ($1) senior citizens, free for accompanied schoolchildren.

Open: Mon–Fri 8:30am–4:30pm, Sat and public holidays 10:30am–4:30pm, Sun 1:30–4:30pm.

OLVESTON, 42 Royal Terrace. Tel. 477-3320.

Olveston is a "must see" of any Dunedin visit (the Golden Arrow Drive will take you right past it). It's one of the country's best-known stately homes, fully furnished, open to the public—and it's magnificent. The double brick house is Jacobean in style, faced with Oamaru stone and Moeraki gravel, surrounded by an acre of tree-shaded grounds. A much-traveled and very prosperous couple, the Theomins, built the 35-room home in 1904–06 as a 25th-anniversary gift for each other, and it's as much a work of art as the multitude of art works within its walls. The house was bequeathed to Dunedin in 1966, and has been carefully maintained in virtually its original state. There are more than 250 pictures in a variety of media in Olveston, including those of some 37 New Zealand artists. The dining room's Regency table and Chippendale chairs are graced by a range of table settings allowing the variety of glass, porcelain, and silver, also seen in the butler's pantry, to be enjoyed by visitors. At every turn there is evidence of the comfort and convenience, as well as visual beauty, built into this home. Although reservations are not essential, they are given preference, and you can only view the house with a guided tour.

Admission: NZ$8 ($5) adults, NZ$2 ($1) children.
Guided tours: Mon–Sat 9:30 and 10:45am, and 1:30, 2:45, and 4pm; Sun 1:30, 2:45, and 4pm.

DUNEDIN PUBLIC ART GALLERY, in Logan Park. Tel. 477-8770.

Don't miss a visit to this art gallery, which holds a special collection of more than 40 works by Frances Hodgkins, Dunedin born and considered to be the finest painter ever produced by New Zealand. In addition, there's a fine collection of old masters, which includes Gheeraerdts, Landini, Lorrain, and Monet, that was given to the gallery by the de Beer family, who have a long connection with Dunedin. It's located at the end of Anzac Avenue.

Admission: Free (donations encouraged).
Open: Mon–Fri 10am–4:30pm, Sat–Sun and holidays 2–5pm.

THE OTAGO PENINSULA

To explore the peninsula's 40 square miles, take one of the excellent tours mentioned above, or head out **Portobello Road,** which runs along the harbor.

In my book, the Otago Peninsula star is the ✪ **Albatross Colony** at Taiaroa Head. The magnificent royal albatross, perhaps with an instinctive distrust of the habitations of mankind, chooses remote, uninhabited islands as nesting grounds. With the single known exception, that is, of this mainland colony. The first egg was found here in 1920, and a sanctuary was promptly established. Today the colony consists of up to 20 breeding pairs, as well as several nonbreeding juvenile birds, each year. You *must* make arrangements to view the birds (at a respectful distance) through the Visitor Centre with a NZ$12 ($7) donation per adult, NZ$6 ($3) per child, required to help with the sanctuary's maintenance.

Near the albatross colony is **Penguin Place,** where the dignified yellow-eyed penguin can be seen emerging from the surf and climbing to nests on the rocky little islet they share with a frolicking southern fur seal colony about 10 yards offshore. Binoculars are available on request. Admission is NZ$4 ($2) for adults, free for children. Book through the Visitor Centre; late afternoon is a good time to go, or if you're staying overnight on the Otago Peninsula, you can get the key and view the penguins on their early-morning march to the water. (Turn off where you see the Penguin Place sign to pick up the key.)

In addition to the listings below, other places you'll want to visit on the peninsula include a **Maori church at Otakou** and an excellent **aquarium** at the Portobello Marine Laboratory operated by the University of Otago near Quarantine Point. Details from the Visitor Centre.

GLENFALLOCH GARDENS, Portobello Rd. Tel. 476-1006.

⭐ A good morning or afternoon tea stop on your Otago Peninsula excursion, Glenfalloch provides a microclimate within its grounds that allows plants to grow even in winter. At the 30-acre estate, allow time to wander through native bush, under English oaks (some as old as 200 to 300 years), and among magnificent and unusual rhododendrons and azaleas not to be found anywhere else in the country, fuchsias, and primroses. Full lunches and dinners, as well as teas, are available in the fully licensed Chalet Restaurant (open daily from 9:30am to 10pm—booking is recommended for dinner), with strolling peacocks occasionally fanning their glorious plumage just outside.

Admission: Donation only at this writing. Check with Visitor Centre for any change in this policy.

Open: All day, every day, with no restriction on hours.

LARNACH CASTLE, Highcliff Rd. Tel. 476-1302.

⭐ This Neo-Gothic Victorian mansion is right out of one of those old English movies, but much more grand than anything you've ever seen on film. William Larnach came from Australia in the late 1860s to found the first Bank of Otago. He began building the grandiose home (which he called "The Camp") in 1871 for his French heiress wife. It took 200 workmen 3 years to build the shell and a host of European master craftsmen another 12 years to complete the interior. Total cost: £125,000. Larnach's concept was to incorporate the very best from every period of architecture, with the result that the hanging Georgian staircase lives happily with Italian marble fireplaces, English tiles, and colonial-style verandas. One of the most magnificent examples of master craftsmanship is the exquisite foyer ceiling, which took three craftsmen 6½ years to complete.

William Larnach died by suicide—after rising to the post of M.P. but suffering a series of personal misfortunes—committed in his typically dramatic fashion in a committee room in the Parliament Buildings in Wellington. (Larnach's first two wives died, and his younger third wife dealt him a fatal emotional blow by dallying with his son.) After his death, the farm around the castle was sold off and the Crown used the castle as a mental hospital. It is now the private home of Mr. and Mrs. Barry Barker, who found it in a thoroughly dilapidated condition in 1967 and have spent the intervening years lovingly restoring it to its original glory. Pick up a printed guide at the reception area and wander as you choose, climbing the spiral staircase to battlements that look out onto panoramic views, and strolling through gardens and outbuildings. The stables now house hostel-type accommodations, and there are also excellent accommodations in the lodge. Lunch is available.

Admission: NZ$9 ($6) adults, NZ$4 ($2) children.

Open: Daily 9am–5pm. **Closed:** Christmas Day. **Directions:** Take Portobello Rd. 2 miles north of Glenfalloch Gardens and follow the signs inland.

TWO DRIVES NORTH OF THE CITY

⭐ **MOERAKI** About an hour's drive north of Dunedin (49 miles), there's a unique natural phenomenon that is definitely worth the drive. On the beaches around the picturesque fishing village of Moeraki (just south of Hampden), huge rounded boulders are scattered around as though some prehistoric giant had used them for a game of handball. The curious rocks were, according to scientists, formed by the gradual accumulation of lime about 60 million years ago, but the Maori have a different story. According to legend, one of the great migration canoes capsized nearby, and large gourds and kumara seeds scattered on the beach and were turned to stone; they are known as *te kai-hinaki*, "the food baskets." Now, maybe rocks don't sound like a sightseeing attraction to you, but just take my word for it and go by to have a look. Incidentally, if you travel from Dunedin to Christchurch by rail or bus, you'll get a good view. If you happen to arrive shortly after noon, you may be able to buy fish straight from the fishing boats coming in about that time—a real dinnertime treat.

You may well be tempted to linger in this entrancing setting, and it can easily be arranged by contacting **Walter and Theresa Kiener,** R.D. 2, Palmerston (tel. 03/439-4759), who can provide a variety of accommodation, including flats, cabins, and caravan or sheltered tent sites, all at modest rates.

✪ **PORT CHALMERS** Half an hour's drive from the city on the northern shore of Otago Harbour lies historic Port Chalmers. It was from here in 1884 that a ship sailed for England with the country's first shipment of frozen meat, creating an important new industry for New Zealand. A bit of an artists' colony today, Port Chalmers has a visitor center and a small seafaring museum. This area is popular for salmon and trout fishing from October to April. Drive over by taking Oxford Road out of Dunedin through the rolling hills to Port Chalmers and return via the harbor road for completely different scenery. While you're in the town, drop into **Carey's Bay Pub,** where all the fisherpeople go.

RECREATION

When the time comes for a break in all that sightseeing, the **Moana Pool,** at the corner of Littlebourne Road and Stuart Street (tel. 474-3513 for pool information, 477-7792 for water slides, 477-6592 for café), can provide a refreshing hour or two. There's a 50-meter, 8-lane swimming pool, a diving pool, learner's pool, and water slides. Those slides are fully enclosed tubes, and you can choose a leisurely ride in the slow tube or a more adventurous one in the fast tube. Other watery options are scuba instruction, aqua fitness classes, underwater hockey, and water polo. On the less wet side, you can take advantage of the poolside circuit gym, sunbeds, and sauna. Plan lunch at the café, or in summer bring a picnic on the sun terrace, where there are barbecues, trampolines, and a children's play area. There's also Flippers Poolside Crèche (day-care center) for children under 5, which is open daily to give parents a bit of time off to enjoy all the above. Hours vary, so call ahead, and fees depend on the activities you choose.

SHOPPING

Dunedin offers excellent shopping: Shops stay open to 9pm on Thursday instead of Friday nights in South Dunedin and Port Chalmers; few shops open on Sunday; and parcels may be checked during shopping hours for a nominal fee at the Women's Public Rest Rooms in the Lower Octagon.

The **Golden Centre,** 251 George St., between St. Andrew and Hanover Streets, is a glass-enclosed concentration of shops specializing in everything from leather to woolens to women's fashions to cosmetics to gifts to books to . . . well, whatever you want, you'll probably find it here, including the **Golden Food Centre Court,** with a variety of eateries. The **Carnegie Centre Marnegie Market,** 110 Moray Place, was built in 1908 as the city's public library, and the impressive building now houses a myriad of shops, where you'll find crafts, jewelry, hand-knits, folk art, curio shops, sheepskin products, and stained glass, among other shopping categories.

Some of the cheapest spirits on sale anywhere in New Zealand can be purchased at the **bottle shop** at the **Robbie Burns Hotel,** 374 George St. The markup is also slight on New Zealand wines. Open Monday through Thursday from 11am to 10pm, on Friday and Saturday until 11pm.

Dunedin has more than its fair share of **gift shops,** but one I can highly recommend is the ✪ **New Zealand Shop,** 132 Lower Stuart St., at Bath Street (tel. 477-3379)—tentative plans are to relocate in the future, so look for them if they're not in residence here—with a fine collection of quality wool sweaters and other items, along with a large selection of T-shirts; it's open weekdays and Saturday mornings, and will open just for you if you give them a call. For leather and lambskin items, **Glendermid Limited,** 192 Castle St. (tel. 477-3655), are leading specialists, with a wide selection of both.

Moray Gallery, 32 Moray Place (tel. 477-8060), has an excellent selection of paintings by New Zealand artists.

GP Books Ltd., 123 Princes St., has all sorts of publications on New Zealand, travel books, maps, and general books (open from 8:30am to 5pm Monday to Friday). ✪ **Whitcoull's Ltd.,** 143 George St. (tel. 477-4120), has one of the city's largest selections of publications, with hours of 9am to 5:30pm Monday through Thursday, 9am to 9pm Friday, and 9:30am to 12:30pm Saturday. ✪ **Hyndman's Ltd.,** 17 George St., in the Civic Centre (tel. 477-0174), was established back in 1906 and today stocks specialty books not readily found elsewhere, as well as a wide range of general-interest books. Hours are 9am to 5:30pm Monday to Friday, and 10am to 1:30pm Saturday.

✪ **Daniels Jewellers Ltd.,** 72 Princes St. (tel. 477-1923), has a wide variety of quality gifts, crystal, silverware, wooden items, leather items, pottery, Marlestone, diamond rings, gold, and silver, with hours of 9:30am to 5pm Monday to Friday.

WHERE TO STAY

Dunedin has many fine accommodations in all price ranges. It also has, however, a large student population (with lots of visitors!) and a great deal of through traffic en route to the Southern Alps and Southland. All of which adds up to *reserve in advance.* This especially holds true during summer months.

Unless otherwise noted, rates quoted below include GST.

A LICENSED HOTEL

LEVIATHAN HOTEL, 65-69 Lower High St., Dunedin. Tel. 03/477-3160.
Fax 03/477-2385. 77 rms, 6 suites (all with bath). A/C MINIBAR TV TEL

$ Rates (excluding GST): NZ$45–NZ$50 ($26–$29) single; NZ$50–NZ$60 ($29–$34) double; NZ$103 ($59) suite. AE, DC, MC, V. **Parking:** Free (garage).

This three-story triangular hotel is a Dunedin landmark dating back to 1898. It's on a corner directly across from the Early Settlers Museum, 1 block from the railway station and bus depot. The old building is in excellent condition and offers a high standard of central, budget accommodation plus fully equipped suites, which are much favored by visiting M.P.s. Rooms are attractively decorated and furnished with built-in wardrobe, chest of drawers, and overbed lights. All have electric heater. Two family units sleep five. There's a games room with a pool table and two TV lounges. The elegant dining room serves meals in the moderate range. There's an elevator, hall telephones for guests, and a garage in the building.

MOTEL FLATS

AARON LODGE MOTEL AND HOLIDAY PARK, 162 Kaikorai Valley Rd., Dunedin. Tel. 03/476-4725. 7 flats (all with bath). TV TEL

$ Rates: NZ$27 ($15) per person. Extra adult NZ$10 ($6); extra child NZ$5 ($3). MC, V.

Near Brockville Road, the Aaron Lodge offers one-bedroom units with electric heaters, radios, and electric blankets. All are nicely carpeted and well maintained. See "Cabins and Campgrounds," below, for a complete description.

ABERDEEN MOTEL, 46 Bank St., Dunedin. Tel. 03/474-0133. Fax 03/
473-0130. 18 units (all with bath). TV TEL
$ Rates (excluding GST): NZ$65 ($37) single; NZ$75 ($43) double. Best Western
discounts available. AE, DC, MC, V.

Margaret and Colin Brosnahan are the thoughtful Aberdeen hosts who provide
such little extras for guests as a complimentary morning newspaper, a video on
Dunedin attractions plus an entertainment video free of charge in the evening,
and a collection of Dunedin restaurant menus. The attractive chalet-type units
have one or two bedrooms, and in some the bedrooms are upstairs. You can
order continental or cooked breakfasts to be delivered to your unit, and if you
choose to cook your own, you can buy the fixings at the supermarket just a short walk
away. Frequent bus service gets you into the city center and back home again. The
motel is located 2 kilometers (1 mile) from the city center, across from the Botanical
Gardens.

**ALCALA MOTEL, corner of George and St. David Sts., Dunedin. Tel.
03/477-9073.** 23 units (all with bath). TV TEL
$ Rates (excluding GST): NZ$72 ($41) single; NZ$78 ($45) double. MC, V.

This large, attractive Spanish-style complex is near the university and medical
school, just a 20-minute walk from the Octagon. Each unit has a full kitchen,
video, radio, and thermo-mattresses, and other facilities include a laundry, spa
pool, and off-street parking. A cooked or continental breakfast is available at a small
fee, and there's a licensed restaurant, shops, hairdresser, and service station close by.

ALGLEN MOTOR HOTEL, 137 St. Andrew, Dunedin. Tel. 03/477-0572.
Fax 03/477-0293. 38 units (all with bath or shower). A/C TV TEL
$ Rates (excluding GST): NZ$90 ($51) single or double. AE, DC, MC, V.

The spacious units at the Alglen Motor Hotel all come with private bath
(bathtub or shower), and three units are wheelchair-accessible. There's a guest
laundry, and an excellent restaurant for all three meals, as well as snacks during
the day at modest prices (see "Where to Eat," below). It's located 2 blocks from the
Octagon, at Cumberland Street.

**ARCADIAN MOTEL, 85-89 Musselburgh Rise, Dunedin. Tel. 03/455-
0992.** 11 units (all with bath). TV TEL
$ Rates: NZ$44 ($25) single; NZ$50 ($29) bed-sitter; NZ$54 ($31) 1-bedroom unit
for two. Extra adult NZ$10 ($6); child under 12 NZ$8 ($5). MC, V.

This modest motel is run by Isabelle Gerken and her winsome cousin, Wilf Radford,
both in their 60s. Units include one-, two- and three-bedroom accommodations and a
bed-sitter (in the old house on the property). All have full kitchens, comfortable
furnishings, and get morning and afternoon sun. Guests have access to a full laundry,
and markets, butchers, greengrocers, and a fish-and-chips shop are nearby. The
Arcadian is within walking distance of St. Kilda Beach, and there's bus transportation
nearby.

**BEACH LODGE MOTEL, 38 Victoria Rd., St. Kilda, Dunedin. Tel. 03/455-
5063.** 18 units (all with bath). TV TEL
$ Rates (excluding GST): NZ$65 ($37) single; NZ$70 ($40) double. Extra person
NZ$12 ($7). Best Western discounts available. AE, DC, MC, V.

Adjacent to beautiful St. Kilda Beach and a good children's playground, the
Beach Lodge is run by Judy and Graeme Duthie, who go out of their way to
make this a "home away from home." The units range in size from bed-sitters
to three bedrooms (which sleep up to 10). All are on the ground floor, of a nice size
and contain a kitchen (continental breakfast may also be ordered), video, radio, and

thermo-mattress or electric blanket. There's a spa pool, guest laundry with dryer, a car wash, and off-street parking. For a peaceful retreat after strenuous sightseeing or a quick swim to start the day off, you couldn't have a better location than the Beach Lodge—the safe beach (with a lifesaving-club station) is a 300-yard walk across a golf course and sand dunes, and there's a view of hills in the distance. The drive into the city is direct and takes about 5 minutes. Dunedin Stadium and Forbury Park Raceway are nearby.

BEST WESTERN TOURIST COURT, 838-842 George St., Dunedin. Tel. 03/477-4270. Fax 03/477-4272. 9 units (all with bath). TV TEL
$ Rates (excluding GST): NZ$56 ($32) single; NZ$66 ($38) double. Extra person NZ$12 ($7). Best Western discounts available. AE, DC, MC, V.

Each of the spacious units here can sleep three to five people, and has a full kitchen, radio, central heat, and electric blanket. There's a guest laundry, and a continental breakfast may be ordered for a small fee. Units are exceptionally well appointed, and each has an iron and ironing board. It's on a main bus line, but within easy walking distance of the Octagon.

FARRY'S MOTEL, 575 George St., Dunedin. Tel. 03/477-9333. Fax 03/477-9038. 15 units (all with bath). TV TEL
$ Rates: NZ$75 ($43) single; NZ$83 ($47) double. Extra person NZ$16 ($9). AE, MC, V.

The units are tastefully furnished, with large picture windows in all lounges. Each is centrally heated and has a fully equipped kitchen, in-house video, and radio. Standard units will sleep up to five, and special executive suites have private spa baths, water beds, and videocassette movies. There is a guest laundry, a children's play area with swings and trampolines, and off-street parking. A continental breakfast is available for a small charge. The motel is near city bus transportation, the university, and shopping.

HIGH STREET COURT MOTEL, 193 High St., Dunedin. Tel. 03/477-9315. 8 units (all with bath). TV TEL
$ Rates: NZ$75 ($43) single; NZ$83 ($47) double. Extra person NZ$16 ($9). AE, MC, V.

With the same ownership and management as Farry's (see above), this pretty place has a facade of white stucco and black wrought-iron trim. Units are tastefully furnished, with large picture windows in all lounges. Each is centrally heated and has a fully equipped kitchen, in-house video, and radio. Standard units will sleep up to five, and special executive suites have private spa baths, water beds, and videocassette movies. There is a guest laundry, a children's play area with swings and trampolines, and off-street parking. A continental breakfast is available for a small charge. If you're on foot, it's an uphill hike from the city center. There's city bus transportation nearby.

BED & BREAKFASTS

ALVAND HOUSE, 3 Union St., Dunedin. Tel. 03/477-7379. 3 rms (none with bath). TV TEL
$ Rates (including breakfast): NZ$40 ($23) single; NZ$55 ($31) double. Extra person NZ$15 ($9). MC, V.

One of my favorite finds is this B&B perched at the top of a hill, with tidy, white shingles and red trim and a carnation- and rose-trimmed walkway leading to the red front door and lace-curtained windows. There are only three bedrooms, with high ceilings, carpeted floors, tall windows with stained-glass touches, electric blankets, and coffee- and tea-making facilities. Guests have the use of a washing machine and clothesline, and they often linger on the sunny porch reading the newspaper that the gracious hostess, Farah Jamali, leaves out. She will prepare a meal by arrangement for NZ$15 ($9), including wine. Alvand House is located near the university and Botanic Gardens; there's city bus service nearby.

MAGNOLIA HOUSE, 18 Grendon St., Dunedin. Tel. 03/467-5999. 3 rms (none with bath). TV TEL
$ Rates (including breakfast): NZ$35 ($20) single; NZ$60 ($34) double. No credit cards.

⭐ The suburban home of George and Joan Sutherland, Magnolia House is set on a half acre of sloping lawns and gardens, surrounded by native bush. The Victorian house is framed by a white picket fence at the lawn's edge. The house itself is quite spacious and graciously decorated, with a warm, welcoming sitting room and a drawing room that holds a piano and opens onto a sun balcony. There's central heating throughout, and bedrooms have fireplaces and antique furnishings. There are also two cats in residence and a no-smoking rule. The Sutherlands, who have lived in Dunedin for the past 25 years, are gracious hosts who enjoy helping guests plan their time in the city for the utmost enjoyment and provide a courtesy car upon request. There's city bus transportation nearby.

SAHARA GUESTHOUSE AND MOTEL, 619 George St., Dunedin. Tel. 03/477-6662. 12 rms (none with bath), 10 motel units (all with bath). TV TEL
$ Rates (including breakfast): B&B NZ$43 ($25) single room; NZ$65 ($37) double room; motel unit NZ$55 ($31) single, NZ$65 ($37) double. AE, DC, MC, V.

Ⓢ This gabled brick guesthouse sports elaborate iron grillwork, is just a 5-minute walk from the Octagon, and is on major bus routes. Built as a substantial family home back in 1863, it now holds nice-size rooms with hot and cold running water, with one to three twin beds, all immaculate and cheerful. Room 12 is especially bright, with a stained-glass window. Behind the house, there's a block of motel units, four of which sleep up to five, all with kitchens, baths, telephones, color TVs, and use of laundry facilities. The home-style breakfast is a hearty one, and there's a health-food restaurant just next door for other meals.

HOSTELS

LARNACH CASTLE, P.O. Box 1350, Dunedin. Tel. 03/476-1302. Fax 03/476-1574. 40 beds, 10 rms (none with bath). TV TEL **Directions:** Take Portobello Rd. 2 miles north of Glenfalloch Gardens and follow the signs inland.
$ Rates (excluding GST): NZ$20 ($11) single without linens; NZ$30 ($17) double without linen. Linen and quilts NZ$7 ($4) extra per person. AE, DC, MC, V.
There are hostel-type accommodations out on scenic Otago Peninsula at this historic mansion. The four-bunk rooms, plus showers and toilets, are upstairs in what was the hayloft of the 116-year-old stables. A kitchen is in the old groom's room downstairs, and the tables and chairs are from an old priory in Dunedin. An open fire and coal range (with radiators running from it) furnish the heating. Otherwise, the stables have been restored to their original state. A cooked or continental breakfast is available (extra charge) in the castle dining room, and the tearoom in the ballroom serves the meal of the day.

YHA HOSTEL, Stafford Gables, 71 Stafford St. Dunedin. Tel. 03/474-1919. 60 beds, 20 rms (none with bath).
$ Rates: NZ$15 ($9) for members; NZ$20 ($11) for nonmembers. No credit cards.

Ⓢ Dunedin's YHA hostel is housed in a grand old early-1900s mansion located right in the city center, near the Chief Post Office. It is also near food stores and a large supermarket. There are 60 beds in 20 rooms with high ceilings, carpeting, and attractive wallpaper, and ranging in size from twins, doubles, and four- to six-bed dormitories. Four common rooms include a pool room, smoking room, and TV room, and there are kitchens, a dining room, and a coin-operated laundry. An in-house café offers a blackboard menu and vegetarian and meat dishes, and is open from 6:30 to 8:30pm. There is 24-hour access to the hostel for guests, and there are no duties or linen charges.

CABINS & CAMPGROUNDS

The **Aaron Lodge Motel and Holiday Park,** 162 Kaikorai Valley Rd. (near Brockville Road), Dunedin (tel. 024/476-4725), is a whole complex of cabins, cabin blocks, and motel units on a main artery with a grassy hill out back. Seven motel units are in front (see "Motel Flats," above), and there are 15 family rooms in two large red-and-gray cement cabin blocks. Four- or five-berthed, all are spacious, and have carpets, large wardrobes, a table and chairs, and electric heater. Beds can be curtained off for privacy. There are two modern kitchens with TVs, showers, and a laundry with dryer. Across a grassy lawn and up the hill are eight two-berth cabins with built-in beds, a shelf, and a chest of drawers; a kitchen (crockery and cutlery provided), toilets, and showers are adjacent. There's a children's playground on the premises, and a supermarket adjacent. Rates for all cabins are from NZ$27 ($15) per adult couple, NZ$5 ($3) per child, NZ$10 ($6) per extra adult. Tent and caravan sites are also available. The Aaron Lodge is owned and managed by Margaret and Lindsay McLeod and may be reached via the Bradford or Brockville bus from the Octagon. GST is included in all rates.

READERS RECOMMEND

Farmlands Camper Caravan Park, Waitati Valley Rd., Waitati, Otago. Tel. 03/482-2730. "About 15 minutes north of Dunedin, we found this marvelous campground. It's right off State Highway 1, and we found it to be one of the best on the South Island, run by one of the nicest families we met in New Zealand. Jan and John Leslie are the very essence of Kiwi charm and hospitality. The park has all the amenities you'd expect, and a few you wouldn't, such as donkey rides. Nearby there are bush walks, mountain tracks, and beaches. While enjoying the peace and quiet, it was nice to know the city was close by for evening enjoyment. Ask Jan or John how to get to Murdering Bay—you're in for a treat!"—S. McGinn and C. Frodigh.

Worth the Extra Money

SOUTHERN CROSS HOTEL, 118 High St., Dunedin. Tel. 03/477-0732.
Fax 03/477-5776. 102 rms, 7 suites (all with bath). A/C MINIBAR TV TEL
$ Rates: NZ$135 ($77) single or double room; NZ$220 ($126) single or double suite. AE, DC, MC, V.

A favorite of visiting government officials, the Southern Cross has a perfect city-center location, off Princes Street, and the appeal of a place that's been around in one incarnation or another for more than 100 years. Guest rooms are spacious and they come with a satellite TV (with U.S. channels), minibar, a small table and two chairs, and a bath with a tub, shampoo, and foaming gel. The lobby restaurant is quiet and elegant, adorned with flowers, candles, and crystal; the Deli Café is more casual and very reasonably priced. If your stay falls on a Friday or Saturday night, pick a room above the second floor so disco sounds won't disturb you.

WHERE TO EAT

Dunedin is literally broken out with good places to eat—name your price range, and you're sure to find half a dozen or more that fill the bill. You can even eat quite well for a pittance without lifting a finger in the kitchen: ✪ **Smorgy's Dial-a-Meal** (tel. 477-3323) takes telephone orders and offer appetizers like marinated mussels, shrimp cocktail, and barbecue spareribs for under NZ$5 ($3); pizzas that will serve three for NZ$15 to NZ$17 ($9 to $10); and main courses that include a roast of the day, seafood catch of the day, ham steak, lamb kebabs with curry sauce, and peppered ribeye steak, for NZ$10 to NZ$14 ($6 to $8). There's a NZ$17 ($10) minimum-order requirement, and delivery time runs 30 minutes or more.

A LOCAL INSTITUTION

STEWART'S COFFEE HOUSE, 12 Lower Octagon. Tel. 477-6687.
Cuisine: SPECIALTY COFFEES/SANDWICHES/PASTRIES. **Reservations:** Not required.
$ **Prices:** Under NZ$10 ($6). AE, MC, V.
Open: Mon–Thurs 9am–5pm, Fri 9am–6:30pm.

Dunedin residents have long treasured this coffeehouse for its fresh-roasted coffee, espresso, and cappuccino, (you'll love the smell!); its cozy basement location—also very central—and sandwiches, which far surpass those in most such places, both in quality and selection. For example, the plain old egg sandwich becomes a curried egg sandwich at Stewart's. There's soup and a nice array of cakes and other sweets. You can, of course, get tea, but it's the coffee that's a standout, and you can buy it by the pound to enhance meals back in your motel kitchen (and I must confess 1 pound traveled back to the U.S. in my luggage).

RESTAURANTS

ALGLEN MOTOR HOTEL RESTAURANT, 137 St. Andrew. Tel. 477-0572.
Cuisine: BREAKFAST/SEAFOOD/INTERNATIONAL/SNACKS.
$ **Prices:** Breakfast NZ$6–NZ$8 ($3–$5); snacks under NZ$10 ($6); appetizers NZ$8–NZ$13 ($5–$7); main courses NZ$13–NZ$18 ($7–$10). AE, DC, MC, V.
Open: Daily 8am–9pm (breakfast served until noon).

This inexpensive motel restaurant (see "Where to Stay," above) offers probably the best value for money in the city. Nothing fancy, but the atmosphere is pleasant, the staff is friendly, and the food is quite good. It's a nice place for breakfast out, and their "Anytime Snack" menu lists all kinds of burgers, croissants, American-style pancakes, and toasted sandwiches. The extensive main-course menu includes seafood, Italian-style garlic shrimp, grilled schnitzel, and pork Diane. It's located 2 blocks from the Octagon, at Cumberland Street.

THE BEST CAFE, 30 Stuart St. Tel. 477-8059.
Cuisine: SEAFOOD/STEAK. **Reservations:** Not required.
$ **Prices:** Main courses NZ$12–NZ$15 ($7–$9). MC, V.
Open: Mon–Fri 11:30am–7pm.

This friendly, family-run café in the city center specializes in seafood served in down-home surroundings, complete with plastic tablecloths and a linoleum floor. Steaks and grills are also on the menu, and it has been welcoming families with children since 1937.

DELI CAFE, in the Southern Cross Hotel, 118 High St. Tel. 477-0752.
Cuisine: DELI/ROASTS. **Reservations:** Not required.
$ **Prices:** Appetizers NZ$2–NZ$3 ($1–$2); main courses NZ$6.50–NZ$9 ($4–$5). 20% surcharge on anything served midnight–5am. AE, DC, MC, V.
Open: Mon–Fri 10am–11pm, Sat–Sun 24 hours.

This luxury hotel (see "Where to Stay," above) has a very good budget eatery at street level—it's bright and casual, and open round the clock on weekends. It has the feel of a late-night diner, even in the afternoon. Food is served cafeteria style and there's a smoking room upstairs. You can get a snack for under NZ$5 ($3), as well as roasts and other hot dishes. It's in the center of the city.

FOXY'S CAFE, in the Robbie Burns Hotel, 370 George St. Tel. 477-8100.
Cuisine: INTERNATIONAL. **Reservations:** Recommended.

$ Prices: Appetizers NZ$5–NZ$6 ($3–$4); main courses NZ$14–NZ$16 ($8–$9). AE, DC, MC, V.
Open: Dinner Mon–Wed 6–10pm, Thurs–Sat 6pm–late.

Foxy's rambles through four rooms that look just about as they might have 125 years ago when the city-center hotel was built. There are two operating fireplaces, and fittings throughout are reminiscent of days long gone. Starters include tacos and enchiladas, as well as mussels provençal; grills feature steaks in a variety of sizes and styles; and other main courses include a seafood basket, chili con carne, tandoori chicken, Italian pasta, and Mexican pancake. All grills are served with potato and side salad. Fully licensed.

HEFFE'S, 244 King Edward St. Tel. 455-1017.
Cuisine: ROASTS. **Reservations:** Not required.
$ Prices: Under NZ$15 ($9). MC, V.
Open: Mon–Thurs 11am–10pm, Fri–Sat 11am–11pm.

One of the best food buys in Dunedin is to be found at this atmospheric old pub, with collections of spoons and mugs on display. There are also, at last count, about 500 whisky jugs and Jim Beam Bourbon bottles, and the picturesque setting is often the focus of "photo ops" for video-camera-toting Americans. Dunedin residents love it for the convivial atmosphere, and also for the tremendous portions of roasts plus five to seven vegetables. Licensed, of course. It's located in the city center.

HIGH TIDE, 25 Kitchene St. Tel. 477-9784.
Cuisine: NEW ZEALAND. **Reservations:** Recommended.
$ Prices: Appetizers NZ$7 ($4); main courses NZ$17 ($10). DC, MC, V.
Open: Lunch Tues–Sat noon–2pm; dinner Tues–Sat 6–9pm.

If you have a penchant for sitting by the water and gazing out to sea, you'll feel right at home here. This L-shaped restaurant is in a former heliport building with a dozen large windows looking onto the harbor. Ceiling fans gently stir the air in this peaceful spot, where the blackboard menu tempts with chicken, sirloin steak, lamb, pasta, fish, and seafood. BYO. High Tide is a short drive from the city center.

IONA'S COUNTRY COTTAGE, 412 George St. Tel. 477-7769.
Cuisine: LIGHT MEALS/SNACKS. **Reservations:** Not required.
$ Prices: Under NZ$10 ($6). No credit cards.
Open: Mon–Fri 8am–4pm.

Teas and light meals are served at moderate to budget prices at this cozy cottage across from Knox Church in the city center. All the food, which includes muffins, quiche, and soup, is homemade.

PALMS CAFE, 84 High St. Tel. 477-6534.
Cuisine: NEW ZEALAND. **Reservations:** Recommended.
$ Prices: Appetizers NZ$5 ($3); main courses NZ$16 ($9). No credit cards.
Open: Lunch Tues–Fri noon–2pm; dinner Tues–Sat 6–9pm.

This has got to be one of Dunedin's prettiest eateries, at Dowling Street. Its window walls, ornate ceiling, and two intimate dining rooms make it romantic, as well. The blackboard menu usually lists an excellent chowder, and main dishes might include lamb satay, vegetable quiche, or pan-baked flounder. It's strictly no-smoking and BYO.

POTPOURRI, 97 Stuart St. Tel. 477-9983.
Cuisine: VEGETARIAN/SALADS. **Reservations:** Not required.
$ Prices: Under NZ$10 ($6). No credit cards.
Open: Mon–Fri 9am–8pm, Sat 10am–2pm. **Closed:** 3 weeks at Christmas.

Make Potpourri (locals pronounce it "Pot-*pour*-ee") one of your first choices for a meal because you'll probably want to return again and again. If you've been neglecting your vegetables, this is your chance to make up for it. Check the blackboard for the quiche and main dish of the day, or choose salads (you can order half portions), open-face sandwiches that come with three small salads, fresh scones and muffins, spanakopita with a half salad, and tacos. Good news for frozen yogurt lovers—it's available here. It's located in the center of the city.

ROBBIE BURNS PUB, in the Robbie Burns Hotel, 370 George St. Tel. 477-8100.

Cuisine: MEXICAN/SEAFOOD/ROASTS. **Reservations:** Not required.
$ Prices: Under NZ$10 ($6). AE, MC, V.
Open: Lunch Mon–Fri noon–2pm.

The downstairs bar in the Robbie Burns Hotel, in the city center, features a good array of Mexican dishes, plus roast beef and seafood. There are frequent menu changes, depending on what fresh meats are available locally. Lunch only is served, with prices under NZ$10 ($6). This place is extremely popular with locals, and your best bet to avoid the crowds is to get there exactly at noon or close to 2pm. Fully licensed.

THE SUN WAH, 218 George St. Tel. 477-0162.

Cuisine: CHINESE. **Reservations:** Recommended.
$ Prices: Appetizers NZ$6–NZ$9 ($3–$5); main courses NZ$14–NZ$24 ($8–$14). AE, DC, MC, V.

My cardinal rule for finding really good Chinese restaurants is to go where the Chinese go—and the large Chinese clientele at the Sun Wah attests to its excellence in ambience, food, and service. It's a pleasant, rather plain upstairs room done in muted reds and greens, with an attractive lounge and bar, cane furniture, and soft Chinese music in the background. That Connie and Dong Lung and their partner, Toni Gin, keep a close eye on the kitchen is evident when such marvels as lychee meatballs and deep-fried chicken wings just melt in your mouth. And among their other specialties are beef and ginger, crispy-skin chicken cooked in bean curd, and prawns in black-bean sauce. It's an extensive menu, and I would venture to say there's not a bummer on the list! Sun Wah is in Harvey's Arcade in the city center.

TERRACE CAFE, 118 Moray Place. Tel. 474-0686.

Cuisine: SEAFOOD/MEDITERRANEAN/ETHNIC. **Reservations:** Required.
$ Prices: Average meal NZ$35 ($20). MC, V.
Open: Dinner Tues–Sat 6pm–late.

This little place is a real gem! By that, I don't mean this is a spit-and-polish, take-yourself-seriously little gem—on the contrary, it's a down-to-earth, as-casual-or-as-dressy-as-you-feel sort of place that looks like a Victorian parlor. With only 10 tables and seats for just 27, the Terrace comes up with a coziness that often prompts patrons to take a turn at the old upright piano over to one side. On cool nights, the fireplace glows with yet another inducement to relax as you enjoy a menu composed of great homemade soups (if they have pumpkin, you're in luck), main courses that might include deviled kidneys with bacon and mushrooms, fish curry, veal, chicken cooked in any one of a number of inventive ways, at least one vegetarian dish, Mediterranean and ethnic cuisine, crisp salads, and homemade desserts like carrot cake or chocolate gâteau. Everything is fresh and the service is friendly (as are your fellow diners—this has long been a Dunedin favorite). It's across from the Fortune Theatre.

WORTH THE EXTRA MONEY

95 FILLEUL, 95 Filleul St. Tel. 477-7233.

Cuisine: NEW ZEALAND/INTERNATIONAL. **Reservations:** Required.
$ Prices: Main courses NZ$35–NZ$80 ($20–$46). AE, DC, MC, V.
Open: Dinner daily 6:30pm–late.

This pink two-story house with the same name as its address holds one of the best restaurants in New Zealand, with several prestigious awards to prove it. The restaurant, on a small back street in the city center, is the creation of husband-and-wife team Ken and Jane Greenhill. He concocts fine, inventive dishes such as grilled lamb prepared with fresh thyme and black peppercorns, spicy blackened fish, poached filet of beef with bacon-and-herb dumplings and fresh shiitake mushrooms. Be sure to order the bread basket filled with rolls and loaves made daily (walnut loaf is the house specialty). Jane Greenhill makes the desserts; top billing goes to the ginger-lemon pie, surely a first cousin to key lime pie. All the dishes are elegantly displayed on oversize black china. Dessert wines are available by the glass. BYO.

ON THE PENINSULA

HARBOUR LIGHTS, 494 Portobello Rd. Tel. 476-1604.

Cuisine: SEAFOOD/GAME. **Reservations:** Required.
$ Prices: Appetizers NZ$7–NZ$9 ($4–$5); main courses NZ$15–NZ$24 ($9–$14); set Sun lunch NZ$16 ($9). MC, V.
Open: Lunch Sun noon–3pm; dinner daily 6pm–midnight.

Book as far in advance as possible for dinner or Sunday lunch at Harbour Lights—the popular eatery is chockablock with Dunedin residents virtually every night of the week. And no wonder, for it is surely one of the city's most pleasant places to eat, with fine views across the harbor to the city, a bar for predinner drinks, a balcony for fine-weather dining, and a two-level main dining room. Among the excellent dishes on the menu are fresh fish in phyllo, mussels, salmon, and New Zealand venison and other game. Fully licensed. Harbour Lights, at Macandrew Bay, is a 10-minute drive from the Andersons Bay causeway.

EVENING ENTERTAINMENT

THE REGENT THEATRE, on the Lower Octagon. Tel. 477-8597.

The Regent often has international artists such as Cleo Laine, Charlie Pride, Kris Kristofferson, Glen Campbell, Johnny Cash, and Rita Coolidge in performance. Check local newspapers or call the theater for current appearances.

Tickets: NZ$10–NZ$45 ($6–$26), depending on the show.

THE FORTUNE THEATRE, corner of Stuart St. and Moray Place. Tel. 477-8323.

The Fortune presents theatrical performances in a century-old leithstone building, which was once the Trinity Methodist Church. The southernmost theater in the world, it mounts productions of works by internationally known playwrights throughout the year in its Mainstage and Studio auditoriums.

Tickets: NZ$20 ($11) adults, NZ$16 ($9) students with ID.

TAM O'SHANTER LOUNGE BAR, in the Robbie Burns Hotel, 370 George St. Tel. 477-8100.

This is a favorite gathering spot for the younger set, where you'll find university students and the 9-to-5-ers making merry almost any night of the week. The ○ **Plough Bar** at the same address, has a quieter ambience, and the emphasis is on good conversation, which, while lively, is almost never loud. Take your pick, but don't miss dropping in at the Robbie Burns if you're a pub person.

CLUB 118, in the Southern Cross Hotel, 118 High St. Tel. 477-0752.

This long and narrow club features disco music on Thursday and Saturday from

9pm to 3am; drinks are served, but no food. The club is in the old part of the hotel and retains the original ceiling.

CLARENDON HOTEL, 28 Maclaggan St. Tel. 477-9095.

Do as the locals do and drop into the Clarendon for a drink at the end of the day. The building, which has been beautifully and lovingly restored, is no longer a hotel, only a bar and restaurant.

FROM DUNEDIN TO CHRISTCHURCH

If you're driving the 223 miles from Dunedin to Christchurch, be sure to stop in **Oamaru** for half a day or an overnight. With its streets lined with two-story buildings and covered walkways, it looks like a frontier town, and indeed in the 1870s it claimed eight hotels, 30 grog shops, and 14 brothels. But the importance of Oamaru today is its **architecture.** Rightfully nicknamed the "White Stone City," it is filled with impressive buildings made of gleaming-white limestone quarried in Weston, 4 miles away (you can visit the **quarry** weekdays from 9am to 5pm, well worth the mini-excursion). Once you've walked along the main street and admired the architecture of the courthouse, bank, post office, and the fine Forrester Art Gallery, walk a little farther to the Harbour–Tyne Street **historic district** that the preservation-minded citizens of Oamaru have fought to save.

The **Oamaru Information Centre** is open from 9am to 5pm Monday through Friday; the helpful staff can provide a map and show you how to get to the **basilica** and the **Waitaki Boys' School** to see more incredible examples of how the local limestone has been put to good use; **Dooley's Stone Carving Studios,** which range from large garden statues to small souvenirs and ornaments, all carved from Oamaru limestone; and the local **Museum and Art Gallery,** which often features displays by local artists of the beautiful North Otago scenery. Ask at the information center about **architectural walks,** which can sometimes be organized for parties of two or more upon request. They can also tell you about **Moeraki Nature Tours** from Oamaru to those famous Moeraki boulders (see above for full description) just 25 miles south of town. Save some time during your visit to Oamaru to stroll through the **Public Gardens,** especially Wonderland. For a quick bite, drop by one of the many coffee shops along the main street.

EN ROUTE TO MOUNT COOK

The 5-hour, 206-mile drive is on good roads, leaving Dunedin on Highway 1 and driving north through hills and along the coastline. Some 57 miles from Dunedin, you might want to stop at the **Mill House,** in Waianakrua (tel. 03/439-5515), a handsome three-story stone building, which was once a flour mill, but is now a handsome restaurant and motel complex. The colonial-style dining room is beamed and attractively furnished, and meals are reasonably priced. There's a wine license, and it's open Wednesday through Monday.

At **Pukeuri,** turn inland onto Highway 83, where the road rises slowly to reach Highway 8 at **Omarama,** where you begin to see the Southern Alps glistening in the distance. At Lake Pukaki township, you turn sharply left and take Highway 80 along the lake and Tasman River to the glacial beauty of Mount Cook.

---

2. MOUNT COOK

206 miles N of Dunedin, 199 miles SW of Christchurch

GETTING THERE   By Plane   With regularly scheduled service, **Mount Cook Airlines** has flights between Mount Cook and Auckland, Kerikeri, Rotorua, and

Wellington in the North Island; Christchurch, Nelson, and Queenstown in the South Island.

By Bus   There is daily bus service via **Mount Cook Landline** and **InterCity** between Mount Cook and Christchurch, Queenstown, and Timaru.

By Car   Mount Cook can be reached via Highway 83.

ESSENTIALS   Orientation   A T-intersection at the end of the highway marks the entrance to **Mount Cook Village.** Turn left and you pass the THC's **Glencoe Lodge,** a modern, moderately priced motor hotel, then the lower-priced **Mount Cook Motel,** the youth hostel, post office, grocery shop, **Alpine Guides Mountain Shop,** and finally the **National Park Visitor Centre.** Turn right at the intersection and you pass **Mount Cook Chalets** before reaching the elegant, peak-roofed, internationally famous **Hermitage.**

Information   At the **National Park Visitor Centre** (opposite the post office, open daily from 8am to 5pm), rangers can give you the latest information on weather and road conditions, and it's a strict requirement that trampers into the wild check in with them. They can also fill you in on high-altitude huts, picnic grounds, and recommended walks in the area. During summer months and school holidays, they conduct guided walks and present excellent slide shows. **Alpine Guides** (tel. 03/435-1834) opposite park headquarters and between the post office and the Public Bar, can also provide a wealth of information on alpine activities, schedules, and fees.

Tiny Mount Cook Village is known the world over for its splendid alpine beauty and its remoteness. It sits within the 173,000 acres of **Mount Cook National Park,** some 2,510 feet above sea level and surrounded by 140 peaks over 7,000 feet high, 22 of which are over 10,000 feet. Most famous of all the Southern Alps is **Mount Cook,** which soars 12,349 feet into the sky. A full third of the park is permanent snow and ice, and the famed **Tasman Glacier** is the longest known outside of arctic regions—18 miles long and 2 miles wide. More difficult to get onto than either Fox or Franz Josef, it is still accessible for guided strolls or for one exhilarating downhill swoop on skis.

The park's most noted plant is the mountain buttercup known as the Mount Cook lily, a pure-white blossom with thickly clustered petals and as many as 30 blooms to a stalk. There are, however, more than 300 species of native plants growing within park boundaries. Many have been marked by park rangers so you may identify them as you walk. Bird sounds fill the air, most notably that of the mischievous kea, that curious little native parrot, which has clearly earned the nickname "Clown of the Snowline," and I strongly advise you to heed the "Do Not Feed" advice from park rangers. Most animal life has been introduced—Himalayan thar, chamois, and red deer. Hunting permits are issued by park rangers.

WHAT TO SEE & DO

No need to tell you what to see—it's all around you! And if you missed the ✪ **skiplane scenic flights** at Fox and Franz Josef, you'll have another chance here. The planes lift off some 2,000 feet above sea level to begin an hour-long flight, which includes glimpses of Fox and Franz Josef and a 5-minute snow walk; the less expensive 40-minute flight surveys the Tasman Glacier only; and there are other options, as well, with fares ranging from NZ$120 to NZ$238 ($69 to $136) for adults, NZ$89 to NZ$179 ($51 to $102) for children. Book through **Mount Cook Airlines** (tel. 03/435-1849 locally, or toll free *0800/800-737 nationwide).

Alpine Guides (Mount Cook) Ltd. (tel. 03/435-1834) conducts 2-hour **coach excursions** to the Tasman Glacier for about NZ$35 ($20) per person.

Skiers will undoubtedly head for the Tasman during the June-to-October ski season, but you should know in advance that skiing is neither inexpensive nor for those whose expertise leaves anything to be desired! Skiing on the glacier involves two runs of about 7 miles each, with skiplanes returning you to the top after the first run and flying you out at the end of the day. Before you embark on the great adventure, you'll have to convince the Alpine Guides or Mount Cook Airlines (both of which offer ski packages) that you're reasonably good on skis. The price for this glorious day to add to your ski tales will run about NZ$450 ($257). That's if *the weather is right*—it could run considerably higher if you have to wait for the weather to break, which could be a few days, and that means additional lodging, eating, and drinking expenses. Book through **Mount Cook Airlines** (tel. 03/435-1849 locally, or toll free *0800/800-737 nationwide) or **Alpine Guides (Mount Cook) Ltd.** (tel. 03/435-1834).

All those high-priced activities (and in my opinion, they're worth every penny if you have the pennies) do *not* mean there are no budget activities at Mount Cook. First of all, the sheer grandeur of the place costs nothing and is there for all. Park rangers will furnish a map of **easy walks,** which take anywhere from half an hour to half a day—no charge, and you'll commune with Mother Nature all the way. Individual booklets are available to explain about the flora you'll be seeing.

Alpine Guides, opposite park headquarters and between the post office and the Public Bar, rents ski and climbing equipment and can furnish guides to take you **mountain climbing.** There's a 4-day hike, which leaves you at Fox Glacier via a transalpine crossing; a range of climbing experiences for those from novice to expert level; and special guided expeditions to the top of Mount Cook itself. These are *not,* however, budget activities. Alpine Guides, P.O. Box 20, Mount Cook (tel. 03/435-1834), can give you full details and make bookings.

WHERE TO STAY

Most accommodations—at any price level—are owned by the THC (though at this writing they are up for sale), and the pickings are poor in the budget range. One alternative, if you're driving, is to stay at nearby locations: Twizel, Fairlie, Tekapo, Ohau, Omarama, Otematata, and Kurow are all under a 2-hour drive, and all have motels aplenty, with well-equipped motor camps at Fairlie, Tekapo, Omarama, Otematata, and Kurow. Needless to say, with such a scarcity of rooms, advance reservations are an absolute necessity!

Unless otherwise noted, rates listed below include GST.

CHALETS

MOUNT COOK CHALETS, Mount Cook Village. Tel. 03/435-1809. 20 chalets (all with bath). TV TEL
$ Rates (excluding GST): NZ$95 ($54) single or double. AE, DC, MC, V.

These THC-owned chalets are A-frame prefab structures, but are attractive, comfortable, and convenient, with foldout couches and several bright chairs in the felt-floored living area. There's a hotplate, fry pan, small fridge, bathroom facilities, and electric heaters. Two curtained-off sections hold two small bunks in each, and linen is provided. It's an efficient use of space, which manages to be pleasing to the eye as well. The complex, located in the village, includes parking space and a laundry with washers, dryers, and irons.

A BED & BREAKFAST LODGE

GLENCOE SKI LODGE, Mount Cook National Park. Tel. 03/435-1809. 57 rms (all with bath). TV TEL

$ Rates (including breakfast, excluding GST): NZ$180 ($103) single; NZ$195 ($111) double. AE, MC, V.

The Glencoe Ski Lodge is an attractive block of 57 deluxe private rooms with nice decor. There's a restaurant and a convivial house bar that serves as a magnet for après-ski or après-sightseeing/flightseeing gatherings. One reader even ranks the Glencoe above The Hermitage. It's located in the village.

A HOSTEL

YHA HOSTEL, Corner of Bowen and Kitchener Drives (P.O. Box 26), Mount Cook 8770. Tel. 03/435-1820. 59 beds.

$ Rates: NZ$18 ($10) for members; NZ$20 ($11) for nonmembers. MC, V.

There are 59 bunks in 10 rooms at this pretty alpine-style hostel in the village. Cooking facilities are good, and there is a large common room. Best of all, the large peaked window wall frames a fair share of that gorgeous snowcapped mountain scene. Booking is essential during summer months.

CAMPING

Camping and caravaning are permitted free in the park, but only at designated sites (*not* in the bush), which have water and toilets. If you use these facilities, remember that the lighting of fires is prohibited within park boundaries. Check with the park visitor information center for locations and conditions. Hikers and mountaineers have the use of 12 huts in the park, all of which have stoves, cooking and eating utensils, fuel, blankets, and radios with emergency lines. Only two of these are within reach of the casual tramper—the others are at high altitudes and you would need to be an experienced, expert climber to reach them. Fees for overnight use of the huts are about NZ$12 ($7) per person, and arrangements and payment must be made at the park visitors information center.

WORTH THE EXTRA MONEY

HERMITAGE, Mount Cook. Tel. 03/435-1809. Fax 03/435-1879. 80 rms (all with bath). TV TEL

$ Rates (excluding GST): NZ$230 ($131) single or double. AE, DC, MC, V.

Rooms at the world-famous Hermitage can only be classified as a "Big Splurge," but in this isolated wonderland, this may be the place to do it. The rooms qualify in every sense as "premium," views are magnificent, and there are good restaurants and bars. The hotel is located in the village.

NEARBY PLACES TO STAY

Because of the scarcity of accommodations at Mount Cook, Twizel (less than an hour's drive away) makes a good base.

BASIL LODGE TWIZEL, P.O. Box 30, Twizel. Tel. 03/627-0671. 60 rms, 4 family rms (all with bath). TV TEL

$ Rates (excluding GST): NZ$12 ($7) hostel bed; NZ$19 ($11) per person in single, double, or family room. MC, V.

The Basil Lodge is set amid lawns and shade trees just minutes away from shops, a skating rink, tennis courts, squash courts, a golf course, and swimming pools. Nearby Lake Ruataniwha offers boating, jet skiing, windsurfing, and picnic areas. Incidentally, this area has some of the best fishing in the country, as well as excellent mounting tramping. The lodge holds single, double, and family rooms, all serviced daily. The comfortable backpacker beds are in rooms with hot and cold running water, with centrally located bathroom facilities and a self-catering kitchen. There is a licensed restaurant/café open all day, and a TV lounge.

MACKENZIE COUNTRY INN, Ostler Rd., Twizel. Tel. 03/627-0869. Fax
03/627-0857. 80 rms and motel flats (all with bath). MINIBAR TV TEL
$ Rates (excluding GST): NZ$89 ($51) single, double, or triple room. AE, DC, MC,
V.

This attractive member of Pacific Park Hotels offers serviced rooms and motel flats
with tea and coffee facilities and a communal kitchen. On the premises, there's a
licensed restaurant, a bistro, bars, games room, and a guest laundry. It's located in
town.

WHERE TO EAT   Budgeteers will gravitate to the **Alpine Guides Shop,** which
stocks grocery items and is open daily from 9am to 6pm.

At **The Hermitage,** you can take your pick of price levels; inexpensive light
meals, sandwiches, and snacks in the coffee shop; the Alpine Room serves a
sumptuous **✪ smörgåsbord lunch,** beautifully presented, for NZ$25 ($14), as
well as terrific à la carte dinners featuring seafood and game at about NZ$60 ($34).

EVENING ENTERTAINMENT   The liveliest spot after dark is the **Tavern** at The
Hermitage, as campers and hostelers come crowding in after a day on the slopes in all
that mountain air. Open only to THC residents (which includes the lodge and
chalets), the **Snowline Bar** is more elegant and features more mountain views. The
house bar at the Glencoe is the **Chamois Bar and Lounge.** That's most of Mount
Cook Village's nightlife—and after a day amid so many of Mother Nature's wonders,
it's likely to be enough!

EN ROUTE TO CHRISTCHURCH   Christchurch is about a 5-hour drive. Follow
Highways 80 and 8 to **Fairlie,** about 93 miles. At **Lake Tekapo,** take a minute to
visit the **chapel,** whose altar is made from a large block of Oamaru stone and
features a carved shepherd. The chapel was built of rock, wood, and stone from the
area, and is dedicated to early settlers. Highway 79 takes you through Geraldine back
to Highway 1, through the Canterbury Plains filled with grazing sheep. And across the
level terrain, you'll see the spires of Canterbury's capital, Christchurch, long before
you arrive.

CHRISTCHURCH

Christchurch is as English as Dunedin is Scottish—in fact, it's even more so. Gothic buildings built of solid stone are everywhere, modern glass-and-concrete buildings scattered among them like afterthoughts. London's red buses are emulated here. English trees, brought out by settlers as a bit of home, flourish along the banks of the Avon River. A primary preoccupation of its citizenry is with private gardens of the English variety. And cricket, that most English of all sports, is played by all little Christchurch boys. One of its most prized appellations is that of the "Most English City Outside England."

It is also a prosperous city—New Zealand's third largest after Auckland and Wellington, with a population of 300,000—staunchly conservative, with much to be proud of. An equitable climate (2,120 hours of sunshine annually), an airport considered to be the finest in the country, civic centers and sports arenas that outshine all those in other New Zealand cities—all are factors in Christchurch's 20th-century image.

For the visitor, Christchurch offers a variety of restaurants and entertainment, as well as excellent accommodations and more sightseeing attractions than you'll ever find time for. Seattle and Christchurch are sister cities, by the way, so if you hail from Seattle, be sure to sign the Sister City Visitors Book at the information center.

1. ORIENTATION

Christchurch is 223 miles northeast of Dunedin and 199 miles northeast of Mount Cook

ARRIVING By Plane Christchurch has frequent air service via **Air New Zealand, Mount Cook Airlines, Air Nelson,** and **Ansett.** In the North Island, there's service to and from Auckland, Hokitika, Kerikeri (Bay of Islands), Napier/Hastings, New Plymouth, Rotorua, and Wellington; in the South Island, Dunedin, Invercargill, Mount Cook, Nelson, and Queenstown.

Christchurch International Airport is the busiest in the country, and is located 6 miles from Cathedral Square, out Memorial Avenue. The **Info-service Centre,** in the domestic terminal, will book accommodations and transportation at no charge. There's a cafeteria and fully licensed (expensive) restaurant; car-rental desks; a bank with money-changing desks; a bookshop; gift and souvenir shops; a flower shop; hairdressers for both men and women; showers; and a large duty-free shop.

WHAT'S SPECIAL ABOUT CHRISTCHURCH

Gardens
☐ The Botanic Gardens in Hagley Park, with its tropical plants, ferns, mosses, cacti, and succulents.
☐ Private gardens in Royds Street, and at the Sanitarium Health Food Company in Papanui.

Public Spaces
☐ Cathedral Square in the city center, with its collection of "eccentrics and nutters" such as the colorful Wizard of Christchurch.

Walks
☐ The romantic Riverside Scenic Walk along the banks of the Avon River that runs through the heart of the city.
☐ The 2-hour guided city walk from the information center that explores the city center and provides an in-depth commentary on its history.

Cathedrals
☐ The magnificent Cathedral of the Blessed Sacrament, on Barbados Street, with its Classic Revival architecture.

☐ Christchurch Cathedral, in Cathedral Square, with its 120-foot tower that affords such splendid panoramic views.

Museums
☐ The Canterbury Museum, a one-stop look at Antarctica memorabilia, New Zealand birds, Oriental art, Maori culture, and a re-creation of a 19th-century Christchurch street.
☐ The fascinating International Antarctic Centre Visitors Centre that re-creates the current life, landscape, and scientific activity on that icy continent.
☐ The Air Force Museum, in nearby Wigram, that features exhibits detailing New Zealand's aviation history.

Crafts
☐ The Arts Centre, in Worcester Street, a workplace and showcase for some of New Zealand's best craftspeople.

The **airport coach** to Worcester Street (opposite Noah's Hotel) costs NZ$4 ($2); the **express bus** to the airport from hotels, motels, and backpacker lodging costs NZ$7 ($4). The **airport shuttle bus** runs regularly and picks up travelers from hotels, motels, and backpacker lodging, with a NZ$5 ($3) fare. Call 366-9660 anytime.

By Train/Bus   There's train service to and from Christchurch via **The South-erner** (Dunedin), **The Trans-Alpine Express** (Greymouth), **The Coastal Pacif-ic** (Picton). The **railway station** is on Moorhouse Avenue, south of the city center.

Bus lines with service between Christchurch and Dunedin, Fox and Franz Josef Glaciers, Greymouth, Invercargill, Mount Cook, Nelson, Picton, Queenstown, Te Anau, Timaru, and Wanaka are: **InterCity, Mount Cook Landline,** and **Newmans.** InterCity and buses arrive and depart from the railway station on Moorhouse Avenue; Mount Cook Landline's terminal is at 40 Lichfield St. (tel. 379-0690); and Newmans coaches leave from 347 Moorhouse Ave. (tel. 379-5641).

For **bus or train information,** call 379-9020.

TOURIST INFORMATION   The **Canterbury Information Centre,** 75 Worcester St. (tel. 03/379-9629), occupies a lovely old (1886) red-brick building that was the first home of Christchurch City Council, and hours are 8:30am to 5pm

N

ACCOMMODATIONS:

Alexandra Court Motel **1**
Camelot Court Motor Lodge **2**
  (off map)
City Court Motel **3**
Cora Wilding YHA Hostel **4**
Diplomat Motel **5**
Eliza's Manor House **6**
Foley Towers **7**
Holiday Lodge Motel **8**
Mrs. Roberta Conway **9**
  (off map)
Russley Park Motor Camp **10**
Turret House **11**
Windsor Private Hotel **12**
Wolseley Lodge **13**

DINING:

Aldersgate Cafeteria **1**
Coachman Inn Restaurant **2**
Dux de Lux **3**
Italia Caffè **4**
Grimsby's **5**
The Mythai **6**
Oxford Victualling Co. **7**
Pedro's **8**
Strawberry Fare **9**
Tiffany's **10**

ATTRACTIONS:

Air Force Museum **5**
The Arts Centre **4**
Canterbury Museum
  and Botanic Gardens **3**
Cathedral of the
  Blessed Sacrament **6**
Cathedral Square **1**
Christchurch Cathedral **2**
Court Theatre **7**
Thomas Edmonds
  Bank Rotunda **8**

← **5** **13**

Bealey A
↖Highway N

Carlton Mill Rd.

Dublin St.

Park Terrace

Dorse

Harper Ave.

North Hagley Park

Victoria Lake

Canterbury Museum 3

Botanic Gardens

3

3

Rolleston Ave.

Avon River

↖
10
5

Riccarton Ave.

South Hagley Park

St. Asaph St.

Antigua St.

Hagley Ave.

Purdie

Balfour St.

Horatio St.

↙ Banks Peninsula

Moorhouse Ave.

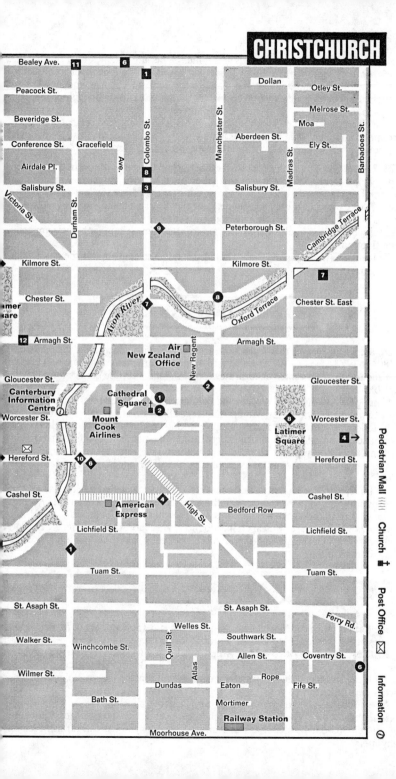

weekdays and 9am to 4pm weekends and holidays. Be sure and pick up a copy of the *Christchurch and Canterbury Visitors' Guide,* a gold mine of information that is published bimonthly by the Canterbury Tourism Council and distributed through hotels and the information center. It not only gives up-to-date information on goings-on in the city, but also includes the surrounding area.

The information center can also provide sightseeing advice, and arrange transport, accommodation, and sightseeing bookings. There's a well-stocked gift shop that may be just the place to pick up craft items, maps, postcards, etc.

CITY LAYOUT   The center of things is **Cathedral Square,** the point from which to get your bearings. Above it rise the spires of the Gothic Anglican Christchurch Cathedral, from whose tower you can look out over the flat, neatly laid-out city. The **Avon River** runs lazily through the heart of the city, spanned by no fewer than 37 bridges as it wends its 15-mile course from Ilam (west of Christchurch) to the sea. The graceful willows that line its banks are said to have come from Napoléon's gravesite on St. Helena.

Colombo Street bisects Cathedral Square north to south and is the city's main thoroughfare.

2. GETTING AROUND

There are **local buses** that leave from the square, with zoned fares ranging from NZ80¢ to NZ$4 (45¢ to $2). From 9am to 4pm, fares are reduced by one-half (check with the information center or local newspapers), and a 10-ride concession ticket is available.

Getting behind the wheel of a car and **driving** can be difficult until you master the city's complex one-way street system. And since all on-street parking is metered, one of the following centrally located municipal parking buildings is your best bet: Oxford Terrace near Worcester; Manchester Street near Gloucester; and Lichfield Street near Durham. Check locally for the locations of others.

You'll find **taxi ranks** at Cathedral Square and all terminals. To call a cab, phone 379-9799.

As for seeing the city **on foot,** that's the only way to go as long as you're concentrating on the city center near the square. To ramble through other, more far-flung sections, best take a public bus and then hoof it.

Bikers will find the city ideal cycling country, since most of the terrain is dead flat. Traffic may frighten the life out of you in the city center, but move out a bit, and the bike will do just fine.

FAST FACTS: CHRISTCHURCH

Airlines   The Air New Zealand ticket office is at 156 Armagh St.; Mount Cook Airlines at 91 Worcester St.; and Ansett at 78 Worcester St.

American Express   The American Express agency in Christchurch is Guthreys Travel Centre, 126 Cashel St. (tel. 03/379-3560). They accept mail for cardholders, issue and change traveler's checks, and replace lost or stolen traveler's checks and American Express cards.

Area Code   The telephone prefix for Christchurch is 03.

Babysitters   There's a crèche (child-care center) at Plaza Corner, Cathedral Square (tel. 365-6364), with hours of 9am to 5pm. Many hotels can furnish evening babysitters.

Currency Exchange All leading banks, American Express, and most large city hotels can cash traveler's checks and change currencies.

Disabled Services Call Disabilities Information Service, 314 Worcester St. (tel. 366-6189).

Doctors For emergency referrals, contact After Hours Surgery, 931 Colombo St., on the corner of Bealey Avenue (tel. 365-7777).

Emergencies For police, fire, and/or ambulance emergency service, dial 111.

Hospitals Christchurch Hospital is on the corner of Oxford Terrace and Riccarton Avenue (tel. 364-0640); ask for Accident and Emergency Department.

Libraries The public library is on the corner of Gloucester and Oxford Terrace (tel. 379-6914), with weekday hours of 10am to 9pm, weekend and holiday hours of 10am to 4pm.

Post Office There's a large, centrally located post office in Cathedral Square.

Safety In Christchurch, as in any unfamiliar city, stay alert. Be aware of your immediate surroundings. Wear a moneybelt and don't sling your camera or purse over your shoulder. This will minimize the possibility of your becoming a victim of crime. Every society has its criminals. It's your responsibility to be aware and alert even in the most heavily touristed areas.

Telephone, Telegram, and Fax Remember, the New Zealand Number Update is in the process of *changing all telephone numbers to 7 digits*. Those numbers in this chapter that have not been changed at press time are marked with an asterisk, and you should call the Helpline 0155 for the new number. The telephone area code in New Zealand is known as the STD (subscriber toll dialing); if a given number has no STD, you must go through the operator. For operator assistance within New Zealand, dial 018. For an international operator, call 0170; if you need directory assistance for an international call, dial 0172.

All telegrams are sent through the post office, either by telephone or in person. The cheapest rate is "Letter Rate," which takes about 24 hours for delivery; rates for telegrams sent after regular post office hours can be as much as double.

Fax facilities are offered at many hotels and motels, and there's a commercial fax service at 148 Manchester St. (tel. 365-3111; after hours 351-7708), with hours of 9am to 4:30pm weekdays.

3. WHERE TO STAY

Christchurch has an abundance of good accommodations in all price ranges. Most are convenient to public transportation, a boon to those not driving, who will be able to consider motels because of the ease of transport.

Unless otherwise noted, rates quoted below include GST.

MOTEL FLATS

ALEXANDRA COURT MOTEL, 960 Colombo St., Christchurch. Tel. 03/366-1855. Fax 03/379-8796. 9 flats (all with bath). MINIBAR TV TEL **Bus:** No. 4.

$ Rates (excluding GST): NZ$72 ($41) single; NZ$78 ($45) double. Best Western discounts available. AE, DC, MC, V.

⭐ Units at Alexandra Court are spacious and nicely decorated, have outside patios, and all bathrooms come with both bathtub and shower (important to me, since a long soak can work wonders at the end of a long day of travel). Bonus facilities here are in-room video and a fax service. There's an electric fireplace (complete with mantel) in each unit, which makes for a homey atmosphere, and equipment includes an iron, ironing board, and radio. The guest laundry also holds a dryer. One-bedroom units can sleep up to four; those with two bedrooms will sleep six; and all have complete kitchens. There's at-your-own-door parking, with covered carports, at all except four units (with covered parking space for those across the courtyard). Nearby, there's a swimming pool and golf course.

CITY COURT MOTEL, 850 Colombo St., Christchurch. Tel. 03/366-9099
or 379-4728. 6 flats (all with bath). TV TEL

$ Rates: NZ$50 ($29) single or double, NZ$5 ($3) surcharge for 1-night stay. AE, MC, V.

The City Court Motel welcomes families with children. There's a one-bedroom unit and five with two bedrooms (two large enough to sleep eight). A bonus here is the washing machine in every unit. The immaculate and spacious units all have large kitchens, separate lounge, electric heater and blanket, and bathtub, as well as shower. There's a children's play area on the premises, and a 7-day food store just across the street. Babysitters can be arranged. The motel, on the corner of Salisbury Street, is 6 blocks from Cathedral Square.

DIPLOMAT MOTEL, 127 Papanui Rd., Christchurch. Tel. 03/355-6009.
Fax 03/355-6007. 16 units (all with bath). TV TEL

$ Rates (excluding GST): NZ$87 ($50) single or double studio; NZ$100 single or double 2-bedroom flat. Low-season and Best Western discounts available. AE, DC, MC, V.

⭐ Melanie and Ken Anderson are the friendly and helpful hosts at the Diplomat, one of my personal Christchurch favorites. The attractive units have cathedral ceilings with timbered rafters and are surrounded by landscaped grounds. Ⓢ Artwork in each unit is outstanding, most by New Zealand artists and representing a wide range of art styles. They are also some of the most spacious flats I've encountered, with complete kitchens, queen-size beds, and a personal safe for your valuables. There's a nice spa, also in a landscaped garden setting, as well as a guest laundry. Both cooked and continental breakfasts are available. Located 2 kilometers (1 mile) from city center on a city bus route, the Diplomat is a 3-minute walk from Merivale Mall.

HOLIDAY LODGE MOTEL, 862 Colombo St., Christchurch. Tel. 03/366-6584. Fax 03/366-6822. 15 flats (all with bath). TV TEL

$ Rates (excluding GST): NZ$50 ($29) single; NZ$55 ($31) double. AE, MC, V.

Ⓢ The spacious and immaculate two-bedroom units at Holiday Lodge are housed in two blocks on either side of a parking lot. Those in a yellow stucco building are all duplexes with bedrooms and a glassed-in sun porch upstairs. All units have radio, electric blanket, electric heater, and bath with tub and shower. There's daily maid service, a sauna, laundry, and children's play area; a bus stop is nearby.

BED & BREAKFASTS

MRS. ROBERTA CONWAY, 11 Clissold St., Christchurch. Tel. 03/355-4806. 1 rm (with bath). TV TEL

$ Rates (including breakfast): NZ$40 ($23) per person double. No credit cards.
Mrs. Roberta Conway is a charming woman who welcomes bed-and-breakfast guests

in her private home on a quiet, residential street. Guests are made to feel part of the family, with a good deal of personal attention (lots of help on what to see and do). Mrs. Conway can also arrange farm stays. There's a bus stop nearby.

ELIZA'S MANOR HOUSE, 82 Bealey Ave., Christchurch. Tel. 03/366-8584 or 366-4946. 10 rms (6 with bath). TV TEL
$ Rates (including breakfast; excluding GST): NZ$60–NZ$75 ($35–$43) per person. AE, DC, MC, V.

When a reader wrote me to say that she considered this "the ultimate in accommodations," I must confess I was a little skeptical—until I walked up the curving drive and saw for myself the splendid old two-story mansion that has been lovingly restored. The carved kauri staircase is magnificent. There's lots of carved woodwork, and colored lead-lite windows, stained glass, antique pieces, and bits of Victoriana scattered about all add to the charming interior of this 1860s house. All of the rooms are beautifully furnished. One wing of the house holds a moderately priced restaurant (see "Where to Eat," below). Buses stop nearby.

TURRET HOUSE, 435 Durham St. North, Christchurch. Tel. 03/365-3900. Fax 03/365-5601. 10 rms (all with bath). TV TEL
$ Rates (including continental breakfast): NZ$56 ($32) single; NZ$75–NZ$90 ($43–$51) double. AE, DC, MC, V.

Turret House, built in 1885, has been renovated to the same style as Eliza's Manor House, which is next door. The two buildings shared the same owners until 1989, although this one feels newer than Eliza's. The rooms all have private facilities, and there's a nice guest lounge. Owners Gayle and Robin Chambers can provide fax service, laundry service, and babysitting. There's a nearby bus stop.

WINDSOR PRIVATE HOTEL, 52 Armagh St., Christchurch. Tel. 03/366-1503. Fax 03/366-9796. 40 rms (none with bath). TV TEL
$ Rates (including breakfast; excluding GST): NZ$49 ($28) single; NZ$72 ($41) double. Discount for groups of three or four. Children pay half. AE, DC, MC, V.

Don Evans, the charming—and caring—host at Windsor Private Hotel has built a devoted following over the years, primarily because of his personal interest in all his guests. The carefully renovated, rambling old brick home has nicely decorated rooms (some with hot and cold running water). Hallways are heated for the trip to conveniently placed bathrooms. The TV lounge holds lots of chairs and stacks of magazines, and there are tea facilities as well as a laundry. The outstanding breakfast often includes omelets or some other special item. Parking off the street is available. The hotel, off Cranmer Square, is located near a bus stop.

WOLSELEY LODGE, 107 Papanui Rd., Christchurch. Tel. 03/355-6202. 14 rms (none with bath). TV TEL
$ Rates (excluding GST): NZ$25 ($14) single with continental breakfast, NZ$30 ($17) single with full cooked breakfast; NZ$50–NZ$60 ($29–$34) double. Discount for children. AE, MC, V.

This lovely old red-and-white home is set in a flower-filled, tree-shaded lawn. Guest rooms in the two-story house all come with hot and cold running water and nice furniture, and all have electric blankets, reading lamps, and tea- and coffee-making facilities. The lounge has overstuffed chairs and TV, and the dining room overlooks the garden. There's a guest kitchen for making tea, and a laundry with washer, dryer, and ironing board. A large parking lot is in the rear. A hot breakfast and dinner are optional, and babysitting services and economical rental cars are available. Frank and Lilly Mills are the helpful hosts in this place that feels like grandma's house. It's near Bealey Avenue and bus service.

HOSTELS

CORA WILDING YHA HOSTEL, 9 Evelyn Couzins Ave., Avebury Park, Richmond, Christchurch. Tel. 03/389-9199. 40 beds. **Bus:** No. 10.

$ Rates: NZ$14 ($8) for members; NZ$18 ($10) for nonmembers. No credit cards.

This lovely old white mansion is on a tree-shaded residential street about 1½ miles from Cathedral Square. It has stained-glass panels in the front door and is crowned by turrets and cupolas. There are seven rooms sleeping 40, all bright and cheerful, and a comfortable lounge. To one side is a large parking area, and in the rear, a children's playground across the park. The laundry has coin-operated washers and dryers.

FOLEY TOWERS, 208 Kilmore St., Christchurch. Tel. 03/366-9720. 28 beds (some with bath). TEL

$ Rates: NZ$10–NZ$14 ($6–$8) dormitory bed; NZ$12 ($7) double without bath, NZ$16 ($9) double with bath. No credit cards.

Formerly the Avon View Guest House, this comfortable two-story house is just a short walk from Cathedral Square in the city center. There are 28 beds, the more expensive have private facilities, less expensive in 11 rooms (double and share), a lounge, laundry, and kitchen, plus off-the-street parking at this privately owned hostel. It's strictly no-smoking and no children.

CABINS & CAMPGROUNDS

Russley Park Motor Camp, 372 Yardhurst Rd. (on State Highway 73), Christchurch (tel. 03/342-7021), is only 2 miles from the airport, close to Riccarton Racecourse, and about 6 miles west of Cathedral Square. Ten chalets in a green, grassy setting are all individual dark-timber structures with slanted roofs and natural light-wood interiors. All have foam mattresses, floor mats, jugs, toasters, cooker, dishes and cutlery, cooking utensils, and electric heaters. Small chalets sleep three in two single beds and one upper bunk. The large ones will sleep five in two singles, one double, and one upper bunk, and have dividing curtains for privacy, as well as a small front porch. Also available are three deluxe chalets (same as the large, but with hot and cold running water and fridge). Three tourist chalets sleep five, with two separate rooms plus kitchen, lounge, shower, toilet, two-ring rangette, electric fry pan, and blankets (linen is for rent). Amenities include a kitchen, TV lounge and leisure room, spa pool, children's play area, and a laundry with automatic washing machines and dryer. There's a food shop close by. Caravan and campsites are also available. Rates for chalets range from NZ$29 to NZ$38 ($17 to $22). The tourist chalet is NZ$46 ($26). Camp and caravan sites are NZ$17 ($10). All include GST. Sheets and blankets can be rented. Take the Yardhurst Road bus from the city.

WORTH THE EXTRA MONEY

CAMELOT COURT MOTOR LODGE, 28-30 Papanui Rd., Christchurch. Tel. 03/355-9124. Fax 03/355-8698. 40 units (all with bath). A/C MINIBAR TV TEL

$ Rates: NZ$98 ($56) single or double studio; NZ$120 ($69) single or double suite. Extra person NZ$12.50 ($7). Best Western discounts available. AE, DC, MC, V.

This is one of the prettiest motels I've come across anywhere, and on my research trip for this update, they were busily renovating to make it even prettier. The Camelot theme is carried out in a series of cottagelike apartments that are luxury personified. They're so spacious (they can sleep up to six) and furnishings are so posh that you may be tempted to just settle in and not leave. Some have water beds, and there's a lovely honeymoon suite available. In a two-story block behind these "executive suites," standard studio flats are also quite nice, with kitchen and private bath facilities. There's a cozy lounge bar on the premises, as well as an elegant licensed restaurant that serves gourmet meals. It's a short distance from the city center, near a bus stop.

4. WHERE TO EAT

ALDERSGATE CAFETERIA, 309 Durham St. Tel. 366-6745.
Cuisine: SNACKS/SAVORIES/PASTRIES. **Reservations:** Not required.
$ Prices: Under NZ$7 ($4). No credit cards.
Open: Mon–Fri 8am–2:30pm for light snacks and take-aways (hot dishes served 11:45am–1:45pm).

The Aldersgate started out in the 1950s as a soup kitchen, and today it is still operated by the Methodist Central Mission, serving up some of the best—and certainly the most inexpensive—home-cooked meals in Central Christchurch. The blackboard menu changes every day, but you can always count on good, well-prepared food (the managers call it "unpretentious gourmet"), a salad bar, sandwiches, savories, and home-baked cakes, rolls, and croissants.

COACHMAN INN RESTAURANT, 144 Gloucester St. Tel. 379-3476.
Cuisine: STEAK/NEW ZEALAND. **Reservations:** Recommended.
$ Prices: Main courses NZ$10–NZ$17 ($6–$10). AE, DC, MC, V.
Open: Daily 7am–11pm.

Meals here are an excellent value. The attractive dining room has a rustic interior, lots of natural brick, heavy dark-stained timber beams, and lighting by old-fashioned lanterns. The Coachman specializes in steaks, and has won the New Zealand Restaurant Association Award of Excellence for such dishes as peppered porterhouse, T-bone, garlic sirloin, lamb chops, and pork chops.
Tender, juicy steak sandwiches are also on the menu, and there's a nice variety of entrées and desserts, as well as a very good salad bar. It's fully licensed, and the adjoining Black Velvet Irish bar has live entertainment Monday through Saturday. It's located in the center of town near Cathedral Square.

DUX DE LUX, corner of Montreal and Hereford Sts. Tel. 366-6919.
Cuisine: VEGETARIAN/SEAFOOD/SALADS. **Reservations:** Not required.
$ Prices: Appetizers NZ$4–NZ$5 ($2–$3); lunch main courses NZ$10 ($6); dinner main courses NZ$15 ($9). AE, DC, MC, V.
Open: Daily 11:30am–11pm.

Dux de Lux is a favorite eating and meeting spot among Christchurch locals. It calls itself a gourmet vegetarian restaurant and serves such creative dishes as phyllo pastry stuffed with mushrooms, asparagus, and corn, and corn-and-coconut soup. For nonvegetarians, there's also a seafood bar and a brew bar, where they serve their own home-brewed beer. Portions are generous. Hot main dishes come with a choice of salads and cold vegetables. There are two congenial dining rooms and a tree-filled courtyard with picnic tables. Service is cafeteria style, and if there's a line, it's worth the short wait. There's music Thursday through Saturday nights. It's located in the city center, near the Arts Centre.

ITALIA CAFFE, Guthrie Centre Cashel Mall. Tel. 365-5349.
Cuisine: ITALIAN. **Reservations:** Not required.
$ Prices: NZ$10–NZ$12 ($6–$7). AE, DC, MC, V.

Open: Mon–Thurs 8am–7pm, Fri 8am–10:30pm, Sat 8am–4pm.
This pleasant little café in one of Christchurch's best city-center shopping malls is fully licensed and serves quite nice wines (as well as mixed drinks, of course) to go with their terrific Italian dishes. I was especially taken with the antipasto, which at NZ$12 ($7) was the most expensive item on the blackboard menu. The heaping portions of meats, cheeses, and salads was so delicious that I went back to sample the pasta. Freshly made, it came with a selection of napoletana (tomato, basil, and garlic), bolognese (spicy beef and tomato), or carbonara (bacon, onion, cream, egg, and parmesan cheese) sauce. To top it all off, there was one of the best cups of coffee of my entire trip. Cappuccino, espresso, and other specialty coffees are also available. This one's a real delight for a lunch break or dinner at the end of a shopping or sightseeing foray in the city center. Everything on the menu is available as a take-away if you want to head back to your Christchurch home.

THE MYTHAI, 84 Hereford St. Tel. 365-1295.

Cuisine: THAI. **Reservations:** Required for dinner Fri–Sat.
$ Prices: Appetizers NZ$5–NZ$7 ($3–$4); main courses NZ$10–NZ$13 ($6–$7). MC, V.
Open: Mon–Fri noon–9pm, Sat–Sun 4–9pm.
You could walk right past this unpretentious little place in the city center, but that would be a real mistake if you like authentic Thai food. There's an extensive menu of chicken dishes (try the *pad gai benjarong,* chicken with vegetables in peanut sauce), pork, beef, lamb, seafood, and vegetarian choices. The spicy fish cakes with cucumber and sweet chili sauce are outstanding among appetizers, as is the traditional dessert of *mythai gluay ghium* (banana with coconut sauce). The Mythai is very popular with office workers at lunch, but don't be put off if the place is crowded—there's a larger back dining room, and you seldom have to wait very long. It's a different story, however, for dinner on Friday and Saturday, when you could well be disappointed if you don't book ahead. It's BYO, and everything on the menu is available as a take-away.

OXFORD VICTUALLING CO., 794 Colombo St. Tel. 379-7148.

Cuisine: BISTRO/NEW ZEALAND. **Reservations:** Not required.
$ Prices: Average meal under NZ$17 ($10). AE, MC, V.
Open: Sun–Thurs 11am–9pm, Fri–Sat 11am–10pm.
This fully licensed restaurant is in a 125-year-old building that for many years was a hotel and tavern. Nowadays it houses a complex of bars and a large restaurant that serves fish, roasts, grills, and salads at prices that make it truly one of Christchurch's best buys. Recent renovations have given birth to a tasteful garden bar built out onto the banks of the Avon—a terrific place to while away a sunny afternoon at the umbrella tables.
In the upstairs bar, bistro food is served from noon to 3pm and 6 to 9pm, and in the adjacent **Conservatory** you can enjoy a buffet or light fare such as soup and bread or a choice of salads for under NZ$5 ($3). With the installation of a "karaoké" laser system, this upstairs bar has become one of the city's most popular evening spots. A bottle shop is conveniently located on the premises. It's located near the city center, at Oxford Terrace.

PEDRO'S, 143 Worcester St. Tel. 379-7668.

Cuisine: SPANISH. **Reservations:** Recommended.
$ Prices: Average dinner NZ$38 ($22). AE, MC, V.
Open: Tues–Sat 6–11pm.
Pedro's has been called the country's best Spanish restaurant, and one meal there may convince you that it is also one of the most upmarket. No bullfighting-poster-studded walls in this attractive city-center eatery—instead, its tasteful decor is accented by an old Spanish sideboard and the crockery imported from Spain. Specialties include the

traditional paella (outstanding!), grilled king prawns (*langostinos a la plancha* on the menu), and pork médaillons in tomato and red-bean sauce (*cerdo a la Navarra*).

STRAWBERRY FARE, 114 Peterborough St. Tel. 365-4897.
 Cuisine: DESSERTS/SAVORIES. **Reservations:** Not required.
 $ Prices: Desserts NZ$10–NZ$14 ($6–$8); savory meals NZ$10–NZ$14 ($6–$8). No credit cards.
 Open: Mon–Fri 10am–midnight, Sat–Sun noon–midnight.
For a dip into decadence, rush to Strawberry Fare and order a luscious dessert or a light meal. Desserts are their specialty, of course, but they also have an interesting selection of savoury meals. Assuage that sweet tooth with such temptations as Death by Chocolate, Chocolate Mud Pie, or Devil's Dream Cake—or settle for a savory such as salmon in phyllo or Brie-and-avocado quiche. It's just off Colombo Street, set back from the street.

WORTH THE EXTRA MONEY

GRIMSBY'S, Cranmer Courts, corner of Kilmore and Montreal Sts. Tel. 379-9040.
 Cuisine: ENGLISH/FRENCH. **Reservations:** Required.
 $ Prices: Appetizers NZ$10–NZ$15 ($6–$9); main courses NZ$30–NZ$55 ($17–$31). AE, DC, MC, V.
 Open: Dinner Mon–Sat 7–10:30pm.
You'll be dining in magnificent Gothic splendor at Grimsby's. It is a marvelous old stone building opened in 1876 as Christchurch Normal School, which operated until 1954, when it became the Post Primary Department of Christchurch Teacher's College until 1970. After that it lay vacant and was severely vandalized until developers took it in hand in 1980 to create co-op apartments in one wing and this elegant restaurant on the ground floor. You enter through heavy wooden doors into a medieval hall, thence into a high-ceilinged dining room beautifully furnished, with tables resplendent in crisp white linen, exquisite china, crystal, and silverware. Classical music plays softly in the background. Service is as elegant as the surroundings, and the food is worth every effort involved in managing a splurge meal. The menu features beef steak and oyster pudding, beef Wellington, roast venison, scallops parisienne, and rack of Canterbury lamb. Licensed. Highly recommended—you'll have had a "big splurge" of true elegance after a meal at Grimsby's! It's located in the city center.

TIFFANY'S, corner of Oxford Terrace and Durham St. Tel. 379-1350.
 Cuisine: NEW ZEALAND. **Reservations:** Required.
 $ Prices: Appetizers NZ$14–NZ$17 ($8–$10); main courses NZ$25–NZ$40 ($14–$23). AE, DC, MC, V.
 Open: Dinner Tues–Sat 7pm–late.
Perched alongside the Avon River in the city center, this award-winning restaurant is as pretty as its picture window. It was named after the oldest daughter of the building's owner, and the house dates from 1908. It has a sophisticated, unhurried atmosphere conducive to lingering. The very best of New Zealand cuisine is featured on the menu—lamb, venison, seafood, beef, and chicken—and the service is both polished and friendly. Enter from the river side along the brick walkway.

5. ATTRACTIONS

Your first stop should be the **Canterbury Information Centre,** 75 Worcester St. (tel. 03/379-9629), opposite Noah's Hotel, and open from 8:30am to 5pm weekdays and 9am to 4pm weekends and holidays. They have an exhaustive supply of information brochures on Christchurch and all of Canterbury. Be sure to pick up both **City Walk** brochures and the ✪ **Riverside Scenic Walk.** The information center can also book you on a 2-hour ✪ **guided city walk** that leaves from the information center at 9:45am and 1:45pm daily (from October through April), and 15 minutes later from the kiosk in Cathedral Square. From May through September, the tours are held by prior booking only at 1:30pm, leaving from the information center.

THE TOP ATTRACTIONS

✪ **Cathedral Square** is the hub of the city center—it will almost certainly be your orientation point, and it's great people-watching territory. If you happen to be in that area around 1pm, look for the Wizard of Christchurch, a colorful character (and actually a very learned individual) with very definite ideas about almost everything in the universe. If the Wizard's in town, you're in for some unusual entertainment, for which you won't be charged a cent. Christchurch treasures its "eccentrics and nutters," as the plaque outside the post office on the square attests. It's in memory of another local character, the Bird Man.

More imposing architecturally than Christchurch Cathedral, described below, is the magnificent **Cathedral of the Blessed Sacrament,** also called the basilica, on Barbados Street, about a 15-minute walk from Cathedral Square (or take no. 3J or 3K bus). It Classic Revival architecture features colonnades, galleries, and an Italian mosaic floor, embellished with tapestries and bronzes.

One of the loveliest spots for photographing in Christchurch is the **Thomas Edmonds Bank Rotunda,** near Cambridge Terrace and Manchester Street. Now filled with diners rather than musicians, it's a graceful, octagonal Italianate building on the banks of the Avon. Punts on the river dock right at the landing here, to make your photos even better.

CHRISTCHURCH CATHEDRAL, Cathedral Sq. Tel. 366-0046.

Begun in 1864, just 14 years after the first settlers arrived, it was completed in 1904. The cathedral choir sings a half-hour choral evensong at 5:15pm on Tuesday and Wednesday and the service is sung by the Boy Choristers on Friday at 4:30pm (except during school holidays). The cathedral is open for prayer weekdays, and holy communion is also celebrated daily. Climb the 133 steps in the 120-foot tower for a splendid panoramic view of the city and its environs.

Admission: NZ$1.50 (90¢) adults, NZ$1 (60¢) children, NZ$4 ($2) families.
Open: Cathedral guided tours Mon–Fri 8am–5pm; Sat 8:30am–5pm, Sun 7:30am–8:30pm; tower Mon–Sat 9am–4pm, Sun 1–4:30pm.

CANTERBURY MUSEUM AND BOTANIC GARDENS, Rolleston Ave. Tel. 366-8379.

✪ The Canterbury Museum has an excellent permanent Antarctica exhibit, along with The Hall of New Zealand birds, Oriental art, Maori culture, and a re-creation of a 19th-century Christchurch street. Look for the Victorian exhibit, and check to see if the "Unearthing New Zealand" exhibition on 1,000 years of human settlement in New Zealand is still in residence.

The museum is at the entrance to the 75-acre Botanic Gardens, where show houses display tropical plants, ferns, mosses, and a comprehensive collection of cacti and succulents. More than one reader agrees with me that these lovely gardens should not be missed. They are particularly impressive in the spring, when there are hosts of daffodils. Keep an eye out for the huge Albert Edward oak, the first tree planted in the gardens (July 7, 1863).

Within the gardens, you'll find the **McDougall Art Gallery,** which holds an impressive collection of Australasian and European art, with constantly changing exhibits. Located in Hagley Park, it's a short walk from Cathedral Square.

Admission: Free; donations accepted.
Open: Museum daily 10am–4:30pm; gardens daily 7am–sundown, show houses daily 10am–4pm; MacDougall Art Gallery daily 10am–4:30pm. Call for extended summer hours. Free guided museum tours daily at 10:15 and 11:30am and 1:15 and 2:30pm.

THE ARTS CENTRE, 2 Worcester St. Tel. 366-0989.

The Arts Centre, a popular gathering spot for locals and visitors alike, is filled with a variety of craft workshops (visit the Wool Studio), galleries (the Carpet Gallery is a unique must), restaurants, coffeehouses (Le Café is open daily from 7am to midnight, and also has an Express Take-away Bar), theaters, a concert hall, and artists' studios. On weekends year round there is a lively **Arts and Crafts Market** held here, complete with musicians, booths filled with clothes and jewelry, a sampling of international cuisines in the exotic Food Fair (10am to 4pm), and a lively, inviting atmosphere. Festivals and other events are scheduled regularly. The center is located off Rolleston, opposite the Canterbury Museum and Botanic Gardens.
Admission: Free.
Open: Daily 7am–late.

FERRYMEAD HISTORIC PARK, 269 Bridle Path Rd., Heathcote. Tel. 384-1970.

The 100-acre, 15,000-square-foot Ferrymead Historic Park holds a fascinating collection of things from the past, including Moorhouse Township (an Edwardian township complete with a church, schoolhouse, jail, operating bakery, print shop, cooperage, and livery stables), Hall of Fame, Hall of Wheels, working exhibits, and lots more. There's a 1.5-kilometer (1-mile) tramway link between the two main areas of the park, with restored electric trams from Dunedin and Christchurch, an 1881 Kitson steam tram, and a horse-drawn tram.
Admission: NZ$7 ($4) adults, NZ$3.50 ($2) children; NZ$19 ($11) families; children under 5, free.
Open: Summer, daily 10am–7:30pm; winter, weekends and holidays only 10am–4:30pm. **Closed:** Christmas. **Transportation/Directions:** Bus no. 3 from Cathedral Sq.; if driving, take Ferry Rd. south and make the first right turn after Heathcote Bridge.

WILLOWBANK WILDLIFE RESERVE, 60 Hussey Rd. Tel. 359-6226.

This delightful natural park includes a zoo of exotic animals, a farmyard of endangered breeds, and the New Zealand Experience, featuring native birds, including the kiwi (floodlights help you see this and other nocturnal creatures). A fully licensed restaurant serves morning and afternoon teas, lunch, and dinner.
Admission: NZ$7 ($4) adults, NZ$3 ($2) children.
Open: Daily 10am–11pm. **Directions:** It's a 15-minute drive from the city; take Harewood Rd., turn right onto Gardiners Rd. and right again into Hussey Rd.

MORE ATTRACTIONS

Christchurch **gardens** are known throughout the country, and there is fierce competition every year between neighborhoods. To view some of these glorious gardening achievements, visit **Royds Street,** opposite Boys' High, which has won the competition for many years running. In the business community, it's the exquisite garden at **Sanitarium Health Food Company,** 54 Harewood Rd., Papanui, which comes out on top time and time again. However, just about any street you stroll will display garden patches of exceptional beauty, and if you express your delight in seeing them, the nearest gardener will have you deep in conversation in no time flat! In February there are bus tours of the award-winning gardens.

Christchurch has been the gateway to Antarctica since Scott's first expedition arrived in 1901. Since the 1950s, it has also been the American supply base and communication center for **Operation Deep Freeze,** the U.S. Antarctic Program, a scientific study program some 2,000 miles to the south. In September of 1992, the ☼ **International Antarctic Centre Visitors Centre** opened, re-creating current life, landscape, and scientific activity on the ice, with hands-on exhibits and sophisticated sound, film, and light presentations that bring you a firsthand glimpse of the unforgettable grandeur of that icy continent. It's on Orchard Road, about a 5-minute walk from the Christchurch International Airport terminal, and it's open every day except Christmas Day from 9am to 5pm (no admission fee at this writing).

Farther afield, the **Air Force Museum,** Main South Road, Wigram, Christchurch (tel. 343-9532), is a must for aviation buffs. It's located in Wigram Aerodrome, a short drive south of the city via Riccarton Road or Blenheim Road (both of which merge into Main South Road), where New Zealand's Air Force was established in 1923. The fascinating aviation history of the country is depicted in dramatic re-creations, videos, and comprehensive displays of planes, exhibits such as the Bomber Command and Battle of Britain exhibits, and memorabilia. There's also a cafeteria overlooking the busy airfield, still in use by the air force. Hours are 10am to 4pm Monday through Saturday, 1 to 4pm on Sunday, and you'll probably want to spend an hour or even two. No admission at this writing.

A breathtaking way to spend a day is to take the scenic ☼ **Trans-Alpine Express** train trip to Arthur's Pass or Greymouth. You can make the journey round-trip by train, or come back by bus for completely different views.

ORGANIZED TOURS

There are many good **coach tours** for seeing the city and its surroundings, all of which may be booked through the visitors center, your motel, or directly with the tour operators. One of the best and least expensive is that given by the **Christchurch Transport Coachlines,** (tel. 379-4268), which leaves Cathedral Square daily. The 10am tour takes you through the garden suburbs and past impressive city buildings for fares of NZ$16 ($9) for adults, half that for children.

The ☼ **Christchurch Roundabout and Highlights Tour,** run by Gray Line Tours (tel. 379-0690), covers city highlights, then takes the spectacular Summit Road to Lyttelton Harbour, with panoramas of snowcapped Alps, plains, and sea, and makes a stop at the baronial Sign of the Takahe for tea on the way back. Adult fare is NZ$22 ($13); children pay half. Highly recommended.

Gray Line Tours (tel. 379-0690) also has **day tours** to ☼ **Kaikoura** (adults pay NZ$42, U.S. $24; children NZ$30, U.S. $17) and **Mount Cook** (adults NZ$78, U.S. $45; and children NZ$56, U.S. $32). The Mount Cook tour runs from November through April only.

A DAY-TRIP TO NEARBY KAIKOURA

If you follow Highway 1 north along the coast for the 3-hour drive to **Kaikoura**— almost midway between Christchurch and Picton—you will have arrived at a place whose name means "crayfish food," and which is the only place on New Zealand's east coast where the mountains (the Kaikoura Range) meet the Pacific. It is also fast gaining an international reputation for the animal and marine life that calls it home: seals, dolphins, whales, and numerous seabirds, including albatross, terns, penguins, and petrels. Sperm whales are most often seen between April and August; dolphins, between August and April. Seals and birds are always on hand. **Kaikoura Tours Limited,** in the Kaikoura Railway Station (tel. 03/319-5045), organizes daily 3-hour ☼ **whale-watching cruises**—they must surely be the highlight of any Kaikoura visit, and to avoid disappointment, you should book as far ahead as possible. The fare runs about NZ$75 ($43); check schedules when booking; and remember that you'll see the most whales between April and August. If you plan to wander on your own, just follow the **Shoreline Walk** along the coast to the tip of the peninsula and you should see seals and a variety of birds; the walk is almost 3 miles long and takes 1½ hours. Or you could opt for the ✪ **Cliff-Top Walk,** which affords panoramic views; it's 3 miles long and takes an hour.

Daily **coach tours** to Kaikoura from Christchurch are also available from **Mount Cook Landlines** (tel. 03/379-0690) and **Newmans Coachlines** (tel. 03/379-5641). There is also a **rail excursion;** book at the railway station on Moorhouse Avenue in Christchurch (tel. 03/379-9020).

6. SPORTS & RECREATION

Bicycling Christchurch's flat terrain invites cycling, and bike lanes are marked off in several parts of the city, including parks. Parking lots even include bike racks. Join the bikers by renting from **Rent-a-Bike,** 139 Gloucester St. (tel. 366-4409), opposite the Coachman Inn Restaurant; the price is NZ$3 ($2) an hour or NZ$8 ($5) a day. There are numerous other bike rentals, and the information center can supply a list of names and addresses, as well as brochures on cycling in Christchurch and its environs.

Boating You won't be in Christchurch long before you notice the ✪ **punts,** maneuvered by young men in straw hats, on the Avon River. The way to get from the bank into one of those boats is to reserve a ride through the information center, then link up with a boat at one of four landings: at the information center, at the Town Hall restaurant, at the Thomas Edmonds Rotunda, or at Mona Vale gardens, about a mile from downtown. The punts depart on demand from 10am to 6pm October to March, until 5pm in April and September, and until 4pm May to August. A 45-minute ride costs NZ$12 ($7) per person or NZ$32 ($10) per family, half that for 20 minutes.

You can also take matters in hand and paddle your own canoe down the lovely Avon River, which is landscaped its entire length. Canoes are for rent at about NZ$9 ($5) per hour from **Antigua Boatsheds,** 2 Cambridge Terrace (tel. 366-5885), as they have been from this same company for over a century. Prices for canoes and paddleboats are NZ$4 ($2) per person per hour; open daily from 9:30am to 4pm.

Walking If you prefer walking, you're in the perfect place to do it; the information center can supply pamphlets mapping out scenic strolls, or simply follow the river or wander through the Botanic Gardens.

Skiing/Outdoor Sports About 57 miles southwest of Christchurch and 21 miles north of the agricultural center of Ashburton, Methven lures those afflicted with downhill fever. It is the gateway to the **Mount Hutt** ski field, which is blessed with a long season, often from late May through early December. Other outdoor activities in the region include **mountaineering, fishing, boating, trekking,** and **golf.**

7. SAVVY SHOPPING

There's good shopping in Christchurch, and I find prices here among the most reasonable in the country. For some of the best buys in New Zealand woolens and crafts, go by the **Arts Centre,** 2 Worcester St., where The Galleria houses most of the permanent craft shops under one roof. You'll find a concentration of 20 shops at the **Canterbury Centre,** at the corner of Cashel and High Streets, City Mall, with everything from jewelry, fashions, cameras, wools, a bookstore, and several eateries. The **Hide Shop,** at the corner of Gloucester and Colombo Streets (tel. 366-7141), is the place to look for all sorts of leather goods, sheepskin, and woolens. Wayne and Marlene Wright are the knowledgeable owners of **Garden City Antiques,** 192 Papanui Rd. (tel. 355-4226). Aside from marvelous old furniture you couldn't possibly fit into your luggage (but which they'll be glad to ship back home for you), they have a nice assortment of porcelain, silver, art, and jewelry—just the place to look for that special memento of your New Zealand visit. Another concentration of New Zealand products is to be found at **The Tannery,** 89 Worcester St. (tel. 366-5406)—a great collection of goods, and one of the most helpful staffs in town. There's a **duty-free shop** at Cathedral Square.

8. EVENING ENTERTAINMENT

For current after-dark happenings, check the *Tourist Times* or the *Christchurch and Canterbury Visitors' Guide.* Even if you're not a discogoer, consider dropping by the **Palladium,** on the upper level in Chancery Lane (tel. 379-0572), definitely New Zealand's top nightspot. The style is sparkling pseudodeco; the light-and-laser show is electric; and the videos and music exhilarating; and there's a live band Wednesday through Saturday. You'll find it much less crowded if you show up early, at about 8pm (you can always stay until 3am). On weekends, expect to share the space with 500 people, more or less. The cover charge is NZ$5 ($3) Friday and Saturday, NZ$10 ($6) after 10pm, with Wednesday free and other nights sometimes free before 10pm.

A gathering place of a different kind, ✪ **Rumpole's Bar,** in the Park Royal hotel at Victoria Square, features honky-tonk piano music on Monday and Tuesday from 5:30 to 7pm; the bar is fun, even when there's no music. **Dux de Lux** vegetarian restaurant has live music Thursday through Saturday nights. And the ✪ **Coachman Inn's Cocktails and Dreams** cocktail lounge, at 144 Gloucester St., has live entertainment Monday through Saturday from 8pm to 12:30am.

The **Court Theatre,** at 20 Worcester St. (tel. 666-992), mounts plays throughout the year; past productions have included *Steel Magnolias* and *A Streetcar Named Desire.*

9. THE BANKS PENINSULA

I went to ✪ **Akaroa** and the Banks Peninsula at the urging of my home-stay host in Christchurch, and I will always be indebted to her. This area has a beauty and charm all its own and I urge you to experience it for yourself. You can drive or take a bus 52 miles from Christchurch to Akaroa (sit on the right-hand side for the best views), or for more of a tour, change to the mail-run bus at Duvauchelle and experience the beauty of the Eastern Bays (the bus departs Akaroa at 9:30am and returns at 2:30pm); be assured that the driver will point out places of interest, in between delivering mail, milk, and passengers. En route you'll pass **Lake Ellsmere,** 111 square miles but only 6½ feet deep at its deepest part, and home to the Australian black swan, and **Lake Forsyth,** New Zealand's dramatic easternmost lake (you'll find an information center and restrooms here). Stop at the **Hilltop Tavern** for a view of Akaroa across the harbor. The town, with a population of a scant 800, is the southernmost French settlement in the world, and New Zealand's only French inroad. In 1840 the French tried to establish a colony here, but England had just laid claim to the country in the Treaty of Waitangi. The original 63 French settlers loved the area so much, however, that they stayed on at the north end of town; French was spoken in that area until 1890. The English colonists who arrived in 1850 lived in the southern end, and to this day the street names reveal the dichotomy.

The Maori word "Akaroa" means "long harbor," and the water is very much a constant reality here. And if you spend any time at all, seduced by the delicate play of light and shadow on water and land alike, you may be overcome by an irresistible urge to try your hand at watercolors. At the very least, you'll feel as if you've wandered into one. No wonder so many artists gravitate here!

Akaroa is known for its walnuts—it was the French who first brought the trees here. You can get a sense of much of Akaroa's character by wandering along **rue Lavaud** and **rue Balgueri.** Admire the winsome wooden buildings and houses dating from the 19th century, and by no means miss the cottages at the junction of Bruce Terrace and Aubrey Street (behind the Village Inn motel). The old **French cemetery** is just off rue Pompallier.

WHAT TO SEE & DO

Experience Akaroa Harbour firsthand on the ✪ **Canterbury Cat,** which departs daily at 1:30pm year round from the main wharf (tel. 03/304-7641). From November through March, there's also an 11am cruise. During the 2-hour cruise you'll spot penguins and dolphins (they're in residence November to April) and visit a salmon farm. Fares are NZ$19 ($11) for adults, NZ$9 ($5) for children, NZ$47 ($27) for the family ticket.

Akaroa's land-side attractions include its fine **museum,** the best place to start your visit, especially since it doubles as the town's **information center** and can provide a good map; the **Langlois-Eteveneaux House,** part of the museum and probably the oldest in Canterbury; the ✪ **lighthouse,** which was in service from 1880 to 1980; and the **herb farm,** about half a mile up rue Grehan, open from July through April, where on the first Saturday of each month local craftspeople gather to sell their wares from 11am to 2pm.

If you want to buy a book on the area or perhaps a woolen souvenir, go to **Pot Pourri,** at rue Balgueri and rue Lavaud, open from 10am to 5pm daily.

WHERE TO STAY

For a little place, Akaroa has an impressive array of accommodations, including some of New Zealand's finest offerings of bed-and-breakfast and backpacker accommodation. No matter where you stay, you'll want to linger. Rates quoted below include GST.

A HOTEL

GRAND HOTEL, 6 rue Lavaud, Akaroa. Tel. 03/304-7011. Fax 03/304-7304. 8 rms (all with bath). MINIBAR TV TEL
$ Rates: NZ$23 ($13) per person per night. AE, MC, V.

If the truth be known, a few Germans were mixed in with those French immigrants, and one of them, Jacob Waeckerle, built the Grand Hotel in 1860 at the entrance to Akaroa. Ironically, back then it was called the French Hotel; it burned in 1882 but was rebuilt and renamed. Among the vestiges of the past that remain are the staircase, the coal ranges, and the foot scrapers at the entrance. The hotel has something of a split personality right now, since the downstairs has been renovated—beautifully—while the upstairs is waiting its turn. Guests get to choose from eight rooms; Room 3 is nice and looks out onto the street below. There's a bistro/bar and restaurant on the premises, a lounge with TV and coffee and tea facilities, and a beer garden.

MOTEL FLATS

DRIFTWOOD MOTEL, 56 rue Jolie, Akaroa. Tel. 03/304-7484. 12 units (all with bath). TV TEL

$ Rates: NZ$68–NZ$75 ($39) single or double. Extra adult NZ$12 ($7); NZ$9 ($5) extra child under 12. MC, V.

The one-bedroom units in this waterfront motel all have private balconies and sleep up to four adults. Each comes with a fully equipped kitchen, but continental breakfast delivered to your unit is available at a small charge. Facilities include a private spa pool, children's playground, guest laundry, courtesy coach, boat ramp, and dinghies for hire. There's good off-the-street parking, and babysitting can be arranged.

A BED & BREAKFAST

GLENCARRIG, 7 Percy St., Akaroa. Tel. 03/304-7008. 3 rms (all with bath). TV TEL

$ Rates (including breakfast): NZ$45 ($26) per person. No credit cards.

Picturesque Glencarrig was built in 1853 by the first Anglican vicar in Akaroa for his wife and six children. You'll love the large farmhouse kitchen with its drying rack and Rayburn wood-burning stove that also runs the central heating, and the original timberwork. The lovely single room and two doubles all sport country decor, and two sitting rooms come with open fireplaces. The property, which sits prettily on 1½ acres a short drive from the town center, even has a stream and mill wheel on it, as well as a pool. Friendly hosts Kaye and Mike Stokes have an impressive art collection on display throughout the house. Look for Glencarrig's red roof peeking out from behind the hedgerow when you go up the hill.

A HOSTEL

MOUNT VERNON LODGE, at the end of rue Balgueri, Akarao. Tel. 03/304-7180. 6 rms (all with bath). TV TEL

$ Rates: NZ$13 ($7) bungalow bed; NZ$40 ($23) double. NZ$50 ($29) chalet for two. Extra person NZ$8 ($5); NZ$3 ($2) per person surcharge for 1-night stay. Linen fee NZ$3 ($2). NZ$3 ($2) per-person surcharge for 1-night stay in chalet. No credit cards.

Put on your hiking shoes. Mount Vernon Lodge has the premier site overlooking Akaroa Harbour, and it's no mean feat to get to it if you're on foot. The reward is a beautiful farmyard setting with well-maintained bungalows. Each room has two levels with two beds in each level. There is a kitchen, lounge, barbecue area, and swimming pool. The lodge also has double rooms, as well as a marvelous A-frame chalet perfect for a couple who want to retreat from the world or for a family. It has a double bed looking out at the hills, three more beds upstairs, a tub and washing machine, a kitchen, and a TV. Horseback riding is available, and hiking is a given.

WHERE TO EAT

A popular place to sit and have breakfast or a "cuppa" is the **Akaroa Bakery,** on Beach Road. For lunch, choose either the **Harbour View Tearoom** or the **Montarsha Tearoom,** depending on which has the better specials posted for the day; both are on Beach Road.

LA RUE RESTAURANT, 6 rue Balgueri. Tel. 304-7658.
  Cuisine: SEAFOOD/NEW ZEALAND. **Reservations:** Required.

$ Prices: Appetizers NZ$9–NZ$12 ($5–$7); lunch main courses NZ$11–NZ$18 ($6–$10); dinner main courses NZ$20–NZ$30 ($11–$17). AE, DC, MC, V.
Open: Lunch Wed–Sun noon–2:30pm; dinner Wed–Sun 6:30–9:30pm.
Closed: 3 weeks in July, Christmas.

Overlooking Akaroa harbor, La Rue is undoubtedly the best restaurant in town, and it's been a Taste New Zealand Award winner for 4 years running. The menu changes seasonally, always of course featuring seafood, with crayfish and Bluff oysters appearing in season. Lamb, venison, and pork dishes are also on the menu.

METRIC MEASURES/MILEAGE CHARTS

LENGTH

1 millimeter	=	0.04 inches (or less than ⅙ in)
1 centimeter	=	0.39 inches (or just under ½ in)
1 meter	=	1.09 inches (or about 39 inches)
1 kilometer	=	0.62 miles (or about ⅔ of a mile)

To convert kilometers to miles, take the number of kilometers and multiply by **.62** (for example, 25km × .62 = 15.5 mi).

To convert miles to kilometers, take the number of miles and multiply by **1.61** (for example, 50 mi × 1.61 = 80.5 km).

CAPACITY

1 liter = 33.92 fluid ounces or 1.06 quarts or 0.26 gallons

To convert liters to gallons, take the number of liters and multiply by **.26** (for example, 50 liters × .26 = 13 gallons).

To convert gallons to liters, take the number of gallons and multiply by **3.79** (for example, 10 gal × 3.79 = 37.9 liters).

WEIGHT

1 gram	=	0.04 ounces (or about a paperclip's weight)
1 kilogram	=	2.2 pounds

To convert kilograms to pounds, take the number of kilos and multiply by **2.2** (for example, 75kg × 2.2 = 165 pounds).

To convert pounds to kilograms, take the number of pounds and multiply by **.45** (for example, 90 lb × .45 = 40.5kg).

TEMPERATURE

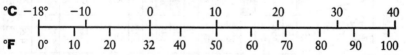

To convert degrees C to degrees F, multiply degrees C by 9, divide by 5, then add 32 (for example, 9/5 × 20°C + 32 = 68°F).

To convert degrees F to degrees C, subtract 32 from degrees F, then multiply by 5, and divide by 9 (for example, 85°F − 32 × 5/9 = 29°C).

DISTANCES BETWEEN MAJOR CITIES: SOUTH ISLAND
(In Kilometers)

	Blenheim	Christchurch	Dunedin	Franz Josef	Greymouth	Invercargill	Milford Sound	Mount Cook	Nelson	Oamaru	Picton	Queenstown	Te Anau	Timaru	Westport
Alexandra	767	455	190	373	552	202	370	242	876	223	795	93	249	307	653
Arthurs Pass	440	150	451	241	98	668	922	412	388	336	468	645	801	252	199
Blenheim		312	674	503	324	891	1,085	643	116	559	28	798	964	475	260
Christchurch	312		362	427	248	579	773	331	428	247	340	486	652	163	333
Dunedin	674	362		563	742	217	411	331	790	115	702	283	290	199	695
Franz Josef	503	427	563		179	575	769	498	469	596	579	404	560	493	280
Gore	825	513	151	509	688	66	260	378	941	266	853	169	139	350	789
Greymouth	324	248	742	179		754	860	510	290	434	352	583	739	350	101
Haast	645	738	421	142	321	433	539	356	611	376	673	262	418	418	422
Hanmer Springs	262	135	497	395	216	714	908	466	306	382	290	621	787	298	218
Invercargill	891	579	217	575	754		278	444	1,007	332	919	187	157	416	855
Milford Sound	1,085	773	411	769	860	278		550	1,150	526	1,113	291	121	610	961
Mount Cook	643	331	331	498	510	444	550		759	216	671	328	484	211	664
Nelson	116	428	790	469	290	1,007	1,150	759		675	110	873	1,029	591	226
Oamaru	559	247	115	596	434	332	526	216	675		587	316	472	84	580
Picton	28	340	702	579	352	919	1,113	671	110	587		826	992	503	288
Queenstown	798	486	283	404	583	187	291	328	873	316	826		170	335	684
Te Anau	964	652	290	560	739	157	121	484	1,029	472	992	170		489	840
Timaru	475	163	199	493	350	416	610	211	591	84	503	335	489		497
Wanaka	736	424	276	287	466	278	394	211	756	231	764	117	273	273	567
Westport	260	333	695	280	101	855	961	664	226	580	288	684	840	497	

DISTANCES BETWEEN MAJOR CITIES: NORTH ISLAND
(In Kilometers)

	Auckland	Gisborne	Hamilton	Hicks Bay	Kaitaia	Masterton	Napier	New Plymouth	Palmerston North	Rotorua	Tauranga	Wanganui	Wellington	Whakatane	Whangarei
Auckland		504	127	508	325	638	423	369	528	234	206	454	660	302	170
Bulls	509	424	382	604	834	139	208	204	30	311	397	44	151	396	679
Gisborne	504		394	180	829	449	216	599	394	287	298	468	550	202	674
Hamilton	127	394		398	452	511	296	242	401	107	107	327	533	192	297
Hicks Bay	508	180	398		833	629	396	603	574	291	302	596	730	206	678
Kaitaia	325	829	452	833		963	748	694	853	561	531	779	983	627	155
Masterton	638	449	511	629	963		233	343	109	440	526	183	101	543	808
Napier	423	216	296	396	748	233		412	178	225	311	252	334	310	593
National Park	330	432	203	474	655	305	244	222	196	183	269	122	317	268	500
New Plymouth	369	599	242	603	694	343	412		234	312	398	160	355	397	539
Paihia	241	745	368	749	108	879	664	610	769	475	447	695	901	543	71
Palmerston North	528	394	401	574	853	109	178	234		331	417	74	145	416	698
Rotorua	234	287	107	291	561	440	225	312	331		86	305	462	85	404
Taihape	422	492	295	515	747	217	285	274	108	224	310	114	238	309	592
Taupo	280	350	153	373	605	358	143	296	249	82	168	223	380	167	450
Tauranga	206	298	107	302	531	526	311	398	417	86		391	548	96	376
Waitomo Caves	202	437	75	441	527	451	307	183	342	150	151	268	463	235	372
Wanganui	454	468	327	596	779	183	252	160	74	305	391		195	390	624
Wellington	660	550	533	730	983	101	334	355	145	462	548	195		547	819
Whakatane	302	202	192	206	627	543	310	397	416	85	96	390	547		472
Whangarei	170	674	297	678	155	808	593	539	698	404	376	624	819	472	

INDEX

GENERAL INDEX

DESTINATIONS

Key to abbreviations: Hs = Hostel; CG = Campground; B&B = Bed & Breakfast; W = Worth the extra bucks; $ = Super-value choice; * = Author's favorite

Now Save Money On All Your Travels by Joining
FROMMER'S ™ TRAVEL BOOK CLUB
The World's Best Travel Guides at Membership Prices

FROMMER'S TRAVEL BOOK CLUB is your ticket to successful travel! Open up a world of travel information and simplify your travel planning when you join ranks with thousands of value-conscious travelers who are members of the FROMMER'S TRAVEL BOOK CLUB. Join today and you'll be entitled to all the privileges that come from belonging to the club that offers you travel guides for less to more than 100 destinations worldwide. Annual membership is only $25 (U.S.) $35 (Canada and all foreign).

The Advantages of Membership

1. Your choice of three free FROMMER'S TRAVEL GUIDES (you can pick two from our FROMMER'S COUNTRY and REGIONAL GUIDES and one from our FROMMER'S CITY GUIDES).
2. Your own subscription to **TRIPS AND TRAVEL** quarterly newsletter.
3. You're entitled to a **30% discount** on your order of any additional books offered by FROMMER'S TRAVEL BOOK CLUB.
4. You're offered (at a small additional fee) our **Domestic Trip Routing Kits.**

Our quarterly newsletter **TRIPS AND TRAVEL** offers practical information on the best buys in travel, the "hottest" vacation spots, the latest travel trends, world class events and much, much more.

Our **Domestic Trip Routing Kits** are available for any North American destination. We'll send you a detailed map highlighting the best route to take to your destination—you can request direct or scenic routes.

Here's all you have to do to join:
Send in your membership fee of $25 ($35 Canada and foreign) with your name and address on the form below along with your selections as part of your membership package to **FROMMER'S TRAVEL BOOK CLUB, P.O. Box 473, Mt. Morris, IL 61054-0473**. Remember to select 2 FROMMER'S COUNTRY and REGIONAL GUIDES and 1 FROMMER'S CITY GUIDE on the pages following.

If you would like to order additional books, please select the books you would like and send a check for the total amount (please add sales tax in the states noted below), plus $2 per book for shipping and handling ($3 per book for all foreign orders) to:

FROMMER'S TRAVEL BOOK CLUB
P.O. Box 473
Mt. Morris, IL 61054-0473
1-815-734-1104

[ ] **YES**. I want to take advantage of this opportunity to join FROMMER'S TRAVEL BOOK CLUB.
[ ] **My check is enclosed**. Dollar amount enclosed_____*

Name_____

Address_____

City_____ State_____ Zip_____

To ensure that all orders are processed efficiently, please apply sales tax in the following areas: CA, CT, FL, IL, NJ, NY, TN, WA and CAN.

*With membership, shipping and handling will be paid by FROMMER'S TRAVEL BOOK CLUB for the three free books you select as part of your membership. Please add $2 per book for shipping and handling for any additional books purchased ($3 per book for all foreign orders).

Allow 4-6 weeks for delivery. Prices of books, membership fee, and publication dates are subject to change without notice.

FROMMER GUIDES

	Retail Price	Code		Retail Price	Code
Alaska 1990–91	$14.95	C001	Jamaica/Barbados 1993–94	$15.00	C105
Arizona 1993–94	$18.00	C101	Japan 1992–93	$19.00	C020
Australia 1992–93	$18.00	C002	Morocco 1992–93	$18.00	C021
Austria/Hungary 1991–92	$14.95	C003	Nepal 1992–93	$18.00	C038
Belgium/Holland/			New England 1992	$17.00	C023
Luxembourg 1993–94	$18.00	C106	New Mexico 1991–92	$13.95	C024
Bermuda/Bahamas 1992–93	$17.00	C005	New York State 1992–93	$19.00	C025
Brazil 1991–92	$14.95	C006	Northwest 1991–92	$16.95	C026
California 1992	$18.00	C007	Portugal 1992–93	$16.00	C027
Canada 1992–93	$18.00	C009	Puerto Rico 1993–94	$15.00	C103
Caribbean 1993	$18.00	C102	Puerto Vallarta/ Manzanillo/		
The Carolinas/Georgia 1992–93	$17.00	C034	Guadalajara 1992–93	$14.00	C028
Colorado 1993–94	$16.00	C100	Scandinavia 1991–92	$18.95	C029
Cruises 1993–94	$19.00	C107	Scotland 1992–93	$16.00	C040
DE/MD/PA & NJ Shore 1992–93	$19.00	C012	Skiing Europe 1989–90	$14.95	C030
Egypt 1990–91	$14.95	C013	South Pacific 1992–93	$20.00	C031
England 1993	$18.00	C109	Switzerland/Liechtenstein 1992–93	$19.00	C032
Florida 1993	$18.00	C104	Thailand 1992–93	$20.00	C033
France 1992–93	$20.00	C017	USA 1991–92	$16.95	C035
Germany 1993	$19.00	C108	Virgin Islands 1992–93	$13.00	C036
Italy 1992	$19.00	C019	Virginia 1992–93	$14.00	C037
			Yucatán 1992–93	$18.00	C110

FROMMER $-A-DAY GUIDES

	Retail Price	Code		Retail Price	Code
Australia on $45 a Day 1993–94	$18.00	D102	Israel on $45 a Day 1993–94	$18.00	D101
Costa Rica/Guatemala/ Belize on $35 a Day 1991–92	$15.95	D004	Mexico on $50 a Day 1993	$19.00	D105
Eastern Europe on $25 a Day 1991–92	$16.95	D005	New York on $70 a Day 1992–93	$16.00	D016
England on $60 a Day 1993	$18.00	D107	New Zealand on $45 a Day 1993–94	$18.00	D103
Europe on $45 a Day 1993	$19.00	D106	Scotland/Wales on $50 a Day 1992–93	$18.00	D019
Greece on $45 a Day 1993–94	$19.00	D100	South America on $40 a Day 1991–92	$15.95	D020
Hawaii on $75 a Day 1993	$19.00	D104	Spain on $50 a Day 1991–92	$15.95	D021
India on $40 a Day 1992–93	$20.00	D010	Turkey on $40 a Day 1992	$22.00	D023
Ireland on $40 a Day 1992–93	$17.00	D011	Washington, D.C. on $40 a Day 1992	$17.00	D024

FROMMER CITY $-A-DAY GUIDES

	Retail Price	Code		Retail Price	Code
Berlin on $40 a Day 1992–93	$12.00	D002	Madrid on $50 a Day 1992–93	$13.00	D014
Copenhagen on $50 a Day 1992–93	$12.00	D003	Paris on $45 a Day 1992–93	$12.00	D018
London on $45 a Day 1992–93	$12.00	D013	Stockholm on $50 a Day 1992–93	$13.00	D022

FROMMER TOURING GUIDES

Amsterdam	$10.95	T001	New York	$10.95	T008
Australia	$10.95	T002	Paris	$ 8.95	T009
Barcelona	$14.00	T015	Rome	$10.95	T010
Brazil	$10.95	T003	Scotland	$ 9.95	T011
Egypt	$ 8.95	T004	Sicily	$14.95	T017
Florence	$ 8.95	T005	Thailand	$12.95	T012
Hong Kong/Singapore/ Macau	$10.95	T006	Tokyo	$15.00	T016
Kenya	$13.95	T018	Turkey	$10.95	T013
London	$12.95	T007	Venice	$ 8.95	T014

FROMMER'S FAMILY GUIDES

California with Kids	$16.95	F001	San Francisco with Kids	$17.00	F004
Los Angeles with Kids	$17.00	F002	Washington, D.C. with Kids	$17.00	F005
New York City with Kids	$18.00	F003			

FROMMER CITY GUIDES

Amsterdam/Holland 1991–92	$ 8.95	S001	Miami 1991–92	$ 8.95	S021
Athens 1991–92	$ 8.95	S002	Minneapolis/St. Paul 1991–92	$ 8.95	S022
Atlanta 1991–92	$ 8.95	S003	Montréal/Québec City 1991–92	$ 8.95	S023
Atlantic City/Cape May 1991–92	$ 8.95	S004	New Orleans 1993–94	$13.00	S103
Bangkok 1992–93	$13.00	S005	New York 1992	$12.00	S025
Barcelona/Majorca/ Minorca/Ibiza 1992	$12.00	S006	Orlando 1993	$13.00	S101
Belgium 1989–90	$ 5.95	S007	Paris 1993–94	$13.00	S109
Berlin 1991–92	$10.00	S008	Philadelphia 1991–92	$ 8.95	S028
Boston 1991–92	$ 8.95	S009	Rio 1991–92	$ 8.95	S029
Cancún/Cozumel/ Yucatán 1991–92	$ 8.95	S010	Rome 1991–92	$ 8.95	S030
Chicago 1991–92	$ 9.95	S011	Salt Lake City 1991–92	$ 8.95	S031
Denver/Boulder/ Colorado Springs 1990–91	$ 7.95	S012	San Diego 1993–94	$13.00	S107
Dublin/Ireland 1991–92	$ 8.95	S013	San Francisco 1993	$13.00	S104
Hawaii 1992	$12.00	S014	Santa Fe/Taos/ Albuquerque 1993–94	$13.00	S108
Hong Kong 1992–93	$12.00	S015	Seattle/Portland 1992–93	$12.00	S035
Honolulu/Oahu 1993	$13.00	S106	St. Louis/Kansas City 1991–92	$ 9.95	S036
Las Vegas 1991–92	$ 8.95	S016	Sydney 1991–92	$ 8.95	S037
Lisbon/Madrid/Costa del Sol 1991–92	$ 8.95	S017	Tampa/St. Petersburg 1993–94	$13.00	S105
London 1993	$13.00	S100	Tokyo 1992–93	$13.00	S039
Los Angeles 1991–92	$ 8.95	S019	Toronto 1991–92	$ 8.95	S040
Mexico City/Acapulco 1991–92	$ 8.95	S020	Vancouver/Victoria 1990–91	$ 7.95	S041
			Washington, D.C. 1993	$13.00	S102

Other Titles Available at Membership Prices—
SPECIAL EDITIONS

	Retail Price	Code		Retail Price	Code
Bed & Breakfast North America	$14.95	P002	Marilyn Wood's Wonderful Weekends (within 250-mile radius of New York City)	$11.95	P017
Caribbean Hideaways	$16.00	P005			
Honeymoon Destinations	$14.95	P006	New World of Travel 1991 by Arthur Frommer	$16.95	P018
			Where to Stay USA	$13.95	P015

GAULT MILLAU'S "BEST OF" GUIDES

Chicago	$15.95	G002	New England	$15.95	G010
Florida	$17.00	G003	New Orleans	$16.95	G011
France	$16.95	G004	New York	$16.95	G012
Germany	$18.00	G018	Paris	$16.95	G013
Hawaii	$16.95	G006	San Francisco	$16.95	G014
Hong Kong	$16.95	G007	Thailand	$17.95	G019
London	$16.95	G009	Toronto	$17.00	G020
Los Angeles	$16.95	G005	Washington, D.C.	$16.95	G017

THE REAL GUIDES

Amsterdam	$13.00	R100	Morocco	$14.00	R111
Barcelona	$13.00	R101	Nepal	$14.00	R018
Berlin	$11.95	R002	New York	$13.00	R019
Brazil	$13.95	R003	Able to Travel (avail April '93)	$20.00	R112
California & the West Coast	$17.00	R102	Paris	$13.00	R020
Canada	$15.00	R103	Peru	$12.95	R021
Czechoslovakia	$14.00	R104	Poland	$13.95	R022
Egypt	$19.00	R105	Portugal	$15.00	R023
Florida	$14.00	R006	Prague	$15.00	R113
France	$18.00	R106	San Francisco & the Bay Area	$11.95	R024
Germany	$18.00	R107	Scandinavia	$14.95	R025
Greece	$18.00	R108	Spain	$16.00	R026
Guatemala/Belize	$14.00	R109	Thailand	$17.00	R114
Holland/Belgium/ Luxembourg	$16.00	R031	Tunisia	$17.00	R115
Hong Kong/Macau	$11.95	R011	Turkey	$13.95	R116
Hungary	$12.95	R012	U.S.A.	$18.00	R117
Ireland	$17.00	R110	Venice	$11.95	R028
Italy	$13.95	R014	Women Travel	$12.95	R029
Kenya	$12.95	R015	Yugoslavia	$12.95	R030
Mexico	$11.95	R016			